SAUDI ARABIA and the GULF WAR

Dr. Nasser Ibrahim Rashid
Chairman, Rashid Engineering
Riyadh, Kingdom of Saudi Arabia (KSA)

Dr. Esber Ibrahim Shaheen
President, International Institute
of Technology, Inc., Joplin, Mo.
United States of America (USA)

International Institute of Technology, Inc.
IITI Building, 830 Wall St.
Joplin, Missouri 64801 U.S.A.

Library of Congress Cataloging-in-Publication Data

Rashid, Nasser Ibrahim.
    Saudi Arabia and the Gulf War / Nasser Ibrahim Rashid,
Esber Ibrahim Shaheen.
       p.   cm.
    Includes bibliographical references and index.
    ISBN 0-940485-01-X
    1. Persian Gulf War, 1991–Saudi Arabia. 2. Saudi Arabia–
History. I. Shaheen, Esber I. II. Title.
DS79.724.S33R37   1992
956.704'3–dc20   92-9853
                                                   CIP

Table of Contents

Preface

The blitzkrieg invasion of Kuwait sent shockwaves across the four corners of the world. Despite Saddam Hussein's numerous promises that he would not attack Kuwait, his attack came at exactly 2:00 o'clock in the morning on Thursday, August 2, 1990. The brutal occupation of the State of Kuwait changed the course of history in the Middle East and left an everlasting impact on the *New World Order*.

The United Nations was energized and played a historic role in repelling the Iraqi aggression against the small, peaceful state of Kuwait. World leaders moved vigorously to the side of justice against tyranny. Courageous and historic decisions were made. King Fahd of Saudi Arabia and President George Bush of the United States of America were indeed key players in the shaping of events which eventually led to the liberation of Kuwait from the grip of Saddam Hussein and his forces.

The occupation of Kuwait and the atrocities committed by Saddam Hussein and his forces against innocent Kuwaiti citizens, refugees and hostages from the international community, all played a major role in heightening awareness and compassion for those suffering from the grip of a ruthless dictator. Out of a deep sense of justice and goodwill, events in the Arabian Gulf impressed us and moved us very deeply. During and after the war, massive research was conducted, covering top sources from all across the globe and in several languages. Then, *"Saudi Arabia and the Gulf War"* was written as a unique book of interest to everyone, especially students of history. It is a *historical document of current events*, reflecting the truth, in a narrative lyrical style, rich with documentation, valuable information and presented in an interesting, logical approach.

Since the Kingdom of Saudi Arabia was the focal point in the Theater of Operations and because of the great central role it has played in the liberation of Kuwait, it is essential to start with some background information on the Kingdom. The First Chapter covers the *"Brief History of the Kingdom of Saudi Arabia."* This includes a description of the Arabs and the rise of Islam. It also covers Saudi beginnings, coupling of Islamic Puritanism with Saudi leadership and the rise of Abdulaziz, founder of the Kingdom of Saudi Arabia. His long arduous struggle for unity is a fascinating story. Although the chapter is brief, it gives a vivid description and an interesting account of a rising Kingdom under the banner of justice and the rule of law.

While Saddam Hussein of Iraq has spent his country's fortunes warring with Iran for eight years and armed his forces to the teeth, in contrast, the Kingdom of Saudi Arabia, a peaceful nation of moderate policies, embarked on a massive program of modernization. Thus, Chapter Two covers "Phenomenal Progress at Home and Spreading Goodwill Abroad." The Kingdom had no military ambitions against its neighbors or anyone, so it concentrated on building its impressive infrastructure, improving the quality of life for its people and spreading goodwill and good deeds around the globe. In the meantime, the Saudis strengthened and modernized their military forces. The chapter briefly covers the five year development plans, the new constitutional reforms, the tremendous progress in education including the seven different universities of higher learning, the development boom, strengthened by funds and credits, covering all sectors, including transportation and communication, industrial development, building construction and development of Hajj facilities, health, social justice and youth welfare. The great care for the Hajj facilities, printing of the Holy Qoran and the massive expansion projects of Al-Haramein, all make the Kingdom of Saudi Arabia, a nation worthy of being the Guardian of Islam. The spectacular achievements realized by the Kingdom are truly mind-boggling. The reader cannot help but be fascinated by the great progress that has been realized in a record time. Saudi Arabia floats on a sea of oil, with proven reserves in excess of 255 billion barrels. A massive income from this great resource was wisely used and invested, bringing with it modern technology to the Kingdom and truly making the desert bloom. From the time of his predecessors to his golden era, King Fahd has been the man at center stage who dedicated his abundant energies, total support and farsighted thoughts into making the dream of modernization come true. The Custodian of the Two Holy Mosques, King Fahd, was truly the pioneer and the heartbeat of this gigantic modernization process. What has been achieved is unmatched, certainly in this century and for that matter, in the history of man. A national policy of peace and tranquility, intertwined with impressive achievements in modernizing the Kingdom, is central to the basic thought and plans of the leadership. Saudi Arabia is blessed with a wise leadership dedicated to prosperity at home and peace in the world. This fact coupled with its phenomenal oil reserves and oil exports that are the largest in the world, earned the Kingdom a distinguished position of leadership and moderation in the Arab world, the Moslem world, as well as the international community. The role of the Kingdom in *spreading goodwill and compassion* toward mankind is described, along with the Saudi assistance to developing nations and the needy everywhere.

This brief description about Saudi historical background and progress brings the reader to Chapter Three covering *"Historical Perspective on Iraq and the Gulf."* Early Mesopotamia to present day Iraq and beginnings of Kuwait are described as well. This brief background on Iraq, the State of Kuwait and the Gulf paves the way to describing some other topics relevant to the Gulf War. The conflicts after the fall of the Monarchy in 1958 and the rise of Saddam Hussein to power in Iraq, along with the Iran-Iraq war, gives the reader the necessary prelude leading to the heart of the crisis and then the invasion of the state of Kuwait by Iraq.

Chapter Four covers *"The Invasion of Kuwait."* An elaborate description is given for the events prior to the invasion. Several attempts were made to stop any possible hostilities. All led to nowhere! Narration of events as they developed was given by King Fahd describing the meeting in Jeddah prior to the invasion of Kuwait, then the coming of Coalition Forces to defend Saudi Arabia and pave the way for liberating Kuwait. The blitzkrieg is described in detail and the decisiveness and courage from President Bush and King Fahd are highlighted in the chapter. U.N. Resolutions and statements by the Council of Senior Ulama are presented, due to their serious impact on events in the Arabian Gulf. The mounting pressure from the world community and especially the United Nations, did not phase Saddam Hussein. Instead, he continued his threats, his acts of aggression and atrocities not only against the people of Kuwait but also against the innocent people who were working in Iraq and Kuwait, trying to make a living to support themselves and their families around the world. He defiantly aggravated the situation by holding thousands and thousands of innocent foreign people as hostages.

Chapter Five, covering *"Occupation of Kuwait and Atrocities of an Aggressor,"* describes the agony of the hostages and refugees. It covers the atrocities committed in Kuwait and the suffering of the Kuwaiti refugees. It also gives a moving narration of the human suffering in Kuwait. This brutal occupation brought with it devastation, agony, destruction and sometimes death to thousands of Kuwaitis and millions of people from all over the world. This moving chapter makes one wonder if Saddam Hussein borrowed several pages from the horror chambers and practices of Hitler, Stalin and Ceausescu. His evil acts did not deter the Kuwaitis nor did they shake the powerful forces of the world which were energized to a mighty strata gathering a formidable storm, which in due time will sweep away Saddam and his barbaric forces.

Chapter Six deals with *"Countdown to War in the Gulf."* The world community was resolved to do whatever necessary to force the ruler of Iraq and his troops out of Kuwait and bring justice to the Kuwaitis. The United Nations embargo had some good effect; the Coalition Forces were vast in number and at a high pitch of preparedness. Various scenarios are described along with some cost estimates of *Desert Shield*. An account of the many troops pouring into the Theater of Operations is given. The frenzy of diplomatic action and worldwide condemnation of Iraqi aggression is described. Saddam Hussein's continued stalling for time is followed in detail. The resolutions and recommendations of the International Islamic Conference regarding the situation in the Gulf are presented. The reader will find involvement of extremist Moslem Fundamentalists described. Note is made that despite the flood of reporters and reports emanating from Amman, Jordan, the true center of power and moderation came from Saudi Arabia. Appeasement did not work in the case of Hitler nor will it work in the case of Saddam Hussein. Decisive action by the United Nations through *Resolution 678 of November 29, 1990, giving the January 15, 1991 deadline* is presented because of its historic importance. The *raging debate* in America and the world is described along with some clarification about the War Powers Resolution and the careful monitoring of Soviet moves. The chapter is concluded with a speech by King Fahd answering an open letter from Saddam Hussein, and a statement by the Secretary General of the United Nations to the press on January 15, 1991, just prior to Desert Storm.

In the Seventh Chapter, *"The Air War Begins."* The liberation of Kuwait had begun "on January 16, 1991, around 6:40 P.M. U.S. Eastern Standard Time (EST) which corresponded to January 17, 1991, around 2:40 A.M. Iraqi time. Armed with strong support from Riyadh and other Allies, the United States of America, with a clear mandate from the United Nations, began massive air strikes against Iraqi targets. In this endeavor, it was supported by the Royal Saudi Air Force, the British Air Force and others, who joined shortly after the initial blitz. This chapter, rich with information and documentation, covers the initial air attacks and the great role played by high tech in Desert Storm. Terrorists' options are described and the military activities for the various weeks of the air war are presented, based on authoritative sources. The Scud missiles began to shower Riyadh and the Eastern Region of Saudi Arabia along with some other areas. The use of Scud missiles against Israel caused the world, especially the Allies, to be very concerned about the possibility of Israel entering the war. The double kill in the sky is vividly described, where an alert Saudi pilot shot down two Iraqi planes. An account of massive *environmental terrorism* in the Arabian Gulf is given. Important quotations and presidential statements are used to strengthen a thesis, a theory or a topic. The *battle of Khafji* is described in accurate detail. The air attacks continued and a Baghdad bunker was hit. The reader will follow Saddam's fruitless political exploitations, in spite of which, the hour of decision continued ticking. He will fail in his obstinacy and wicked designs. The moment of truth had come! The final blow to his occupation of Kuwait was nearing by the second. An *ultimatum* was again given for the Iraqi ruler to get out of Kuwait or else! This paved the way for the ground war.

Chapter Eight is a vivid, documented account of *"The One Hundred-Hour Ground War,"* covering the rejection of President Bush's ultimatum and the will of the United Nations and Coalition Forces by which Saddam Hussein sealed his fate in Kuwait! An ejection order was given to drive the dictator and his forces out of Kuwait. The land war had begun, in parallel with the ongoing air war against the Iraqi forces. The reader will follow with interest Desert Storm yielding to the Ground War, the coordination of air and land power which rained disaster and decimation to Saddam's forces in Kuwait and Southern Iraq. The meticulous account of Coalition Forces' ingenuity and daring courage at the front which forced Saddam Hussein to begin his retreat from Kuwait within a short time, unparalleled in the history of warfare, keeps the reader spellbound. *Kuwait was liberated!* Accounts of the miraculously low casualties and the decimating tank battle with the Republican Guard, on the last day of the Ground War, take the reader rapidly along as Saddam is soundly defeated. Soon after the temporary cease-fire, rebellion erupted in the south and moved up until it reached Baghdad and way into the northern reaches of Iraq, where the Kurdish rebellion began, again. Another chapter on the atrocities of Saddam Hussein had already begun, almost before another tragic chapter had begun to fold!!! The landmark U.N. Security Council Resolution 687 defined the terms for a permanent cease-fire.

The reader will not be surprised to find that while Saddam's propaganda machine was busy declaring victory to the Iraqi people, thousands upon thousands of defeated soldiers, demoralized, hungry, and wounded, were streaming into the southern cities of Iraq and then way beyond to reach the four corners of the Iraqi nation. They brought with them stories of a horrifying defeat and abandonment by their leadership. The Ninth Chapter dealing with, *"The Never Ending Atrocities of a Tyrant,"* covers the Shi'ite rebellion in the south, presents a brief history of the Kurds and describes the Kurdish rebellion in the north. As one reads this chapter, he will see how, the collapse of both rebellions, led to the tragedy of the Kurdish refugees, which attracted world attention and caused Shi'ite refugees to flee to Iran and some to the border with Kuwait. While the rope was getting shorter, the Iraqi leader remained evasive and tried to avoid implementing U.N. resolutions, but to no avail! His weapons of mass destruction were being systematically destroyed by teams of the United Nations. The reader will find that Saddam, his accomplices and inner circle met all the conditions and requirements of *international law and Islamic law (Shari'a) for trial as war criminals!* Sooner or later, all men who preach terror and hate will eventually meet their fate.

The book is very rich with *Appendices* which include a very interesting detailed chronology of world events relating to the Arabian Gulf War. It also includes, all United Nations Security Council Resolutions relating to the situation between Iraq and Kuwait because of their historical importance. Interesting, informative descriptions of some key Arab countries are included. An extensive list of *References* completes this book. These are very valuable to the reader and to any student of history.

Dr. Nasser Ibrahim Rashid,
Riyadh, KSA
Dr. Esber Ibrahim Shaheen,
Joplin, MO., USA
June, 1992

Acknowledgments

H.R.H. Prince Mohammed Bin Fahd Bin Abdulaziz, Governor of the Eastern Region—focal point of Desert Storm—was certainly helpful in our research.

Special gratitude and deep appreciation are due Mrs. Shirley King for her dedicated effort in typing several drafts of this book. She was always eager and enthused about this work. Professor G. E. Ray was very loyal and delighted to offer good advice while proofing our work. Similarly, both of them were very helpful during the writing and publishing of our book entitled "King Fahd and Saudi Arabia's Great Evolution."

The authors extend their sincere thanks to the Royal Embassy of Saudi Arabia in Washington, D.C., for some of the documentation used in our research. Al-Youm newspaper of Dammam made available to us a number of photos.

Appreciation is expressed to the United Nations in New York for the efficient help in responding to our queries and for supplying us with all U.N. Resolutions regarding the Iraq-Kuwait situation.

The Executive Office of the President, Office of Administration in Washington, D.C., was very helpful in making available several of the President's speeches. Also, the U.S. Department of Defense sent us military briefings, speeches and some data. All this is very much appreciated.

We express our thanks to others throughout the world who were helpful in our work.

**In the name of God
The Compassionate
The Merciful**

Chapter 1
Brief History of the Kingdom of Saudi Arabia

Introduction

Early civilizations flourished between the regions extending from Egypt to Mesopotamia. Arabia, the heartbeat of this region, was called "the Cradle of Civilization." The Southern portion of Arabia was known to the Romans as "Arabia Felix," meaning "Happy Arabia;" a prospering land and a major source for frankincense and myrrh. Trade through the Indian ocean was brought to Arabia. Ships unloaded at Aden. From there, transportation was mainly by land to markets in the Western Mediterranean, Egypt and Mesopotamia.

The Arabs

Some of the Semitic tribes who inhabited the Arabian Peninsula were known as the Arabs. Two different groups of Arabs lived in this Peninsula. One was mainly nomadic, roving the huge deserts that extended between the Euphrates River and the center of the Peninsula. The other group were the inhabitants of the southern portion, namely, Yemen. Largely the nomadic group were referred to as the Arabs.

Prior to the birth of Islam, and during the epoch of Jahiliyya (meaning ignorance), the Arabs were the nomads of Jazeerat al-Arab, meaning the "island of the Arabs," a great portion of which is nowadays Saudi Arabia. Many of these people moved northward into the Fertile Crescent which included countries such as Syria, Jordan, Palestine, Lebanon and Iraq. The migrants mingled with the old civilizations of the Babylonians.

There were Arab Jews and Christians before the rise of Islam. They still form a minority in the Arab land. With the spread of Islam and the great Arab conquests, the Arab Empire became a melting pot in which was formulated what may be called the Arabic character. An Arab may be short or tall, white or black, blond or brown, dark or blue-eyed. He may be of Assyrian, Berber or Phoenician origin. The Arabic language and the Moslem religion are both strong unifying factors. In modern times, an Arab is defined as any person whose native language is Arabic.

The Arab world stretches from the Atlantic ocean to the Arabian Gulf. It is endowed with fabulous wealth, and it is the cradle of old civilizations. It is here where three great religions of the world were born: Judaism, Christianity and Islam.

Although the Arabs have been mentioned as far back as the Eighth Century B.C., they were propelled to prominence with the birth of Islam.

Islam

With the rise of Islam, the Arabs built a large empire and a fascinating culture as well. They were the heirs to an ancient civilization that flourished on the banks of the Tigris and the Euphrates Rivers and along the land of the Nile at the Eastern shore of the Mediterranean Sea. The Arabs excelled by using and improving on the Greek and Roman cultures.

They in turn played a dynamic role in transferring to the European nations the newly-born civilization, which had benefitted from all the ancient ones preceding it. This transfer ultimately led to the awakening of the Western world by setting a steady pace toward Renaissance.

During the Dark Ages of Europe, the Arabs contributed to the progress of humanity more than any other people of the time. However, the distinct entity of the Arabs did not clearly manifest itself and assert its prominent position until the birth of Islam.

Around the year 570 A.D., the Prophet Mohammed was born in Mecca. He was a humble member of an Arabian tribe called Qoureish. To nearly a billion Moslems around the world today, Mohammed is the last of all prophets of God, that included Abraham, Moses and Jesus. By the year 610 A.D., the first verses of the Holy Qoran (also written as Koran) were revealed to the Prophet Mohammed in Mecca. These revelations continued until the year 632 A.D. The words that descended from God were gathered into various chapters called Suras. They constituted what is known as the Holy Qoran, which in Arabic means recitation (from the verb qara'a meaning to read or recite). The Qoran is the cornerstone of the Moslem faith. It is the Moslem Holy Book, which in time became the greatest pillar of the Arabic language and Arabic literature. Beyond any doubt, the Qoran contains the finest and truly most beautiful prose of any literature in any time. Basic in the Moslem faith is the call to worship of one God, namely: "there is no God but God and Mohammed is His Prophet." The Arabic equivalent is: La Ileha Illa Allah! Mohammed Rasoul Allah.

The birth of Islam and the lightening speed with which it spread, brought about great Arab conquests. The Arabian Peninsula became of great importance for the Arab world as well as all Moslems everywhere.

The Arab Empire reached its climax during the reign of Horoun Al-Rashid (786–809 A.D.). However, the fall of this Empire led to a dark period in Arab history. It suffered under a cloud of Ottoman rule of oppression that lasted until the early part of the Twentieth Century.

Saudi Beginnings

With the fall of the Arab Empire, Moslems lost the drive and enthusiasm for practicing the faith of their ancestors. Erroneous practices and behaviors veered away from the religious simplicity originally preached by the Prophet Mohammed.

While Islam was still strong in the Hijaz, it became weak and diluted in other parts of Arabia. Certain settlements of Najd were practicing and teaching Islam. Also at Uyaynah, which was not far from the main Saudi settlement of *Diriya*, people were practicing Islam.

Present Saudi ancestors came from the Qatif region and settled in the historical community of Diriya in the middle of Wadi Hanifa in the northwest corner of Riyadh. Saud Ibn Mohammed Ibn Moqrin ruled Diriya from 1720 until his death in 1725. Then, *Mohammed Ibn Saud* became the ruler for nearly forty years, extending from 1725 until his death in 1765. During this period the title of Imam was adopted for Al-Saud.

Puritanism and Saudi Leadership

The rule of Mohammed Ibn Saud coincided with the rise of a religious cleansing under the leadership of *Sheikh Mohammed Ibn Abdulwahhab*. He was born in 1703 (1115 A.H.) in Uyaynah and was from the Banou Sinan tribe. His family was deep-rooted in the knowledge of Islamic Shari'a (law).

He studied law under his father and the Imam Ahmad Ibn Hanbal. He traveled to Hijaz seeking knowledge and also to Basra where he studied the Hadith and read many books on the art of language. Aside from reading in Basra, he also preached the Unitarian faith. "To Allah alone is worship. We walk in the light of a Wali, imitating his example; but we pray only to Allah." His earnest preachings started after he moved with his father from Uyaynah to Huraimala. He preached against the false worship and the idolatrous practices by many. Then he wrote his first book entitled: "The Book of Unitarianism."

He enthusiastically advocated the return to the simple message of the Qoran and the great teachings of the Prophet Mohammed. His call gave moral basis for unifying the Arabian Peninsula under the House of Al-Saud. The words Wahhabi and Wahhabism were sometimes applied to the followers of this religious leader. His call to the faithful (Da'wa in Arabic) should never be viewed as a separate sect. Therefore, the words Wahhabis, Wahhabist or Wahhabism are unacceptable.

Initially, these preachings were not well received at home and, in 1744, Ibn Abdulwahhab was forced to leave his hometown. He had to move southeast about twenty miles to a community called Diriya. The Amir's wife, a wise woman, and his brothers, along with an ardent disciple named Ibn Swailem, all appealed to the Amir for protection and alliance with Mohammed Ibn Abdulwahhab.

The Amir of Diriya, Mohammed Ibn Saud, went along and formed an alliance to spread the faith and unitarianism across the land. The founding of Saudi Arabia was a culmination of the coupling and fusion of Sheikh Ibn Abdulwahhab's call with Saudi family leadership, which remained a dedicated champion of this religious correction. This relationship flourished and was cemented through intermarriages. They became strong allies in a mission of true Jihad seeking Purity in Islam and unity of the nation.

This alliance has endured nearly two and a half centuries since it was contracted in the year 1744 A.D. (1157 A.H.). At that time Mohammed Ibn Abdulwahhab was about forty-two years of age. With the great Saudi support, his mission, or Da'wa, spread like wildfire, covering every part of Arabia from Yemen and Asir up to Jabal Shammar and across to Hasa on down to Oman.

Sheikh Mohammed Ibn Abdulwahhab died in 1792. By then, his call reached as far south as the *Rab'a al-Khali* (*Empty Quarter*). While the south and east of Arabia accepted this effort, the Hasa region, especially the oasis of Qatif and Houfouf, were defeated in battle.

By now the Saudi State had extended its domain to cover most of the Arabian Peninsula, including Oman, Hijaz, and some portions of Yemen.

Expansion of this puritan Islamic call became worrisome to the Ottoman Empire in Constantinople. The Pasha of Baghdad appealed to the Ottoman authorities for help in crushing it. His requests were initially ignored since its strong influence was underestimated. However, the loss of the Holy cities, which meant a loss in prestige and income, made the Ottoman government more decisive in undermining its progress. The viceroy in Cairo, Mohammed Ali, was asked to take the necessary action. He did, and the first expedition was led by the viceroy's son around 1811. Modern weaponry was of no practical use against the special tactics of the desert tribesmen. Although Mecca and Medina had fallen, the stiff resistance displayed by the people of Arabia forced Mohammed Ali himself to come and lead the military campaign. Reinforcements came under Ibrahim Pasha, another son of Mohammed Ali.

The defenders were strong and formidable but were finally shaken with the death of their leader Saud in 1814. However, by 1814–1818, his successor Abdullah retreated to Diriya. Ibrahim Pasha, the Egyptian leader reached Najd in 1818. He bombarded and ravaged Diriya until it was turned to ruins. The town fell in that year after an arduous struggle and siege. Abdullah, the Saudi chief, was taken to Constantinople and executed.

Despite this debacle and defeat, the Saudi House regained political power over central Arabia and Islamic fervor gained new momentum. Abdullah's uncle, Turki, organized his troops and vowed to oust the Egyptians from Najd. He established his rule in Riyadh because Diriya had been destroyed. He moved on to reconquer Najd and the Eastern Province. The Egyptian garrison was harassed and attacked until it was forced to transfer to Hijaz.

Turki warned against political oppression of the people, but internal tension and squabbling led to his assassination in 1834, by a family rival. His son Faisal took up the reigns of the government and ruled for the years 1834–38 and 1843–65. Although Faisal suffered some early defeats from the Egyptians, he later re-established Saudi rule in Najd and the Eastern Region of Arabia. His strong supporters in these military feats were led by Abdullah Ibn Rashid of Jabal Shammar in the Northern Region of Arabia.

Mohammed Ali decided to bring Arabia into his own sphere of influence around 1834. He supported a rival claimant to Saudi leadership: Khaled Ibn Saud (1840–41), a cousin to Faisal who had been imprisoned in Egypt since Abdullah's capture some twenty years earlier. Faisal was a token prisoner for the Egyptian forces, who then occupied Najd & Hijaz and directed the functions carried out by Khaled. However, they overextended themselves in a number of areas and Mohammed Ali had to withdraw in 1840.

Faisal escaped from Egypt in 1843 and regained his position of leadership. Like his father Turki, he did his best to bring law and order to the land. He died in 1865 and the rivalry between his sons brought on a civil war that lasted for many years. All the stability and cohesion built during Faisal's era were in shambles and ruins due to this civil war that erupted between his sons: Abdullah (1865–71, 1875–89) and Saud (1871–75). This provided a window of opportunity for the Turks to occupy the Eastern Region in 1871.

When the rule of Saud, son of Faisal, was established, anarchy was dominant in the region. After his death in 1875, Abdul Rahman (1875, 1889–91), the younger brother of Saud and Abdullah announced his succession. Abdullah regained power after one year and then ruled until he died in 1889, when Abdul Rahman became the ruler again. Disputes between sons and brothers caused serious damage and distractions that led to challenges from the growing power of the Rashids, who had been placed into power by Al-Saud in the Hail area, governing the Northern Province of Arabia named Jabal Shammar. By the time

Faisal's youngest son, Abdul Rahman, was finally forced out of Riyadh, much of Najd was under the control of Mohammed Ibn Rashid. In 1891 the house of Rashid appointed a governor and established a garrison in Riyadh. Leaving the city of his ancestors, Abdul Rahman and his family were exiled in Kuwait.

A bright young man of the family was an eleven-year-old son named *Abdulaziz*, who, in the years to come, would become the founder of the Kingdom of Saudi Arabia. The Rashid successor was a man of minor administrative talent. He governed harshly and succeeded in alienating the tribes under his rule, thus paving the way for the eventual recapture of the region by its just rulers Al-Saud. This was achieved through the sheer courage, superb genius and daring leadership of Abdulaziz, known in the West as Ibn Saud.

The Rise of Abdulaziz

He was born at the Amir's Palace in Riyadh on December 2, 1880. His mother was Sarah Al-Sudeiri. She had a proud heart and a strong physique. She died in Riyadh in 1910. Among his ancestors were pious men and many Kings across many generations of courageous fighters. Great ancestry was credited to his name. Beyond that, destiny did not grant him any material wealth or any established rule.

When Abdulaziz was barely eight years of age he learned to use the sword and the rifle along with jumping on a horse while moving. He was taught to cope with difficulties and especially the severe conditions normally encountered in the desert. He was taught patience and was trained to exercise self-control. Abdulaziz grew to be tall and handsome. He was seldom in a state of rest, always bustling with energy and enthusiasm.

In the year 1890, when Ibn Rashid conquered the city of Riyadh, Abdul Rahman was permitted to live in one wing of the castle. A man named Salem was appointed to rule Riyadh. Once there was a meeting between Salem and Abdul Rahman, Salem devised a plot requesting that all the family of Abdul Rahman be present, having in mind a sinister plan to slay them all at one time. However, Abdul Rahman took his sword along with his men as a precaution. Before Salem could execute his murderous plan, he himself was slaughtered. The young man present at the time was Abdulaziz who learned a lesson about intrigue and bravery. He was sitting in the lap of a big man who protected him from becoming a victim. Abdulaziz was to say later in life: "I learned here that I should be the first to hit when I am exposed to danger."

Preferring not to fall as a prisoner or become a victim, Abdul Rahman gathered about twenty of his supporters and his family along with some food supplies and left Riyadh in the darkness of night. The party moved on southward looking for shelter in the desert. After a short time, they divided into two groups: one made of his wife and some servants went to Bahrain, while the other group remained with the father and headed south.

For a brief period, the family was in Bahrain and then Qatar. Finally, permission came for the Saudi family to have their refuge in Kuwait, where they would be in the hospitality of Al-Sabbah for nearly ten years.

When Abdulaziz reached twenty years of age, it became clear that he was gifted with qualities of greatness which destiny rested upon his shoulders. He was over six feet tall, a giant of a man!

Toward the end of the year 1922, the noted author Ameen Rihani met for the first time with, then Sultan Ibn Saud. He was fascinated and deeply moved by the sheer greatness of this man. In his tent, by candle light, he described his spontaneous impressions:

"I have now met all the Kings of Arabia and I find no one among them bigger than this man. He is big in word, gesture and smile, as well as in purpose and self-confidence. His personality is complex . . . The shake of his hand and the way he strikes the ground with his stick proclaim the contrary traits of the man . . . He gives you the report about yourself and then pats you on the back telling you that he knows better. He gives you at the first meeting a bit of his mind and his heart, without fear, without reserve . . . He knows himself as well as he knows his people. Hinna 'l-Arab (we are the Arabs)! The man in him is certainly bigger than the Sultan, for he dominates his people with his personality, not with his title . . . strange, indeed! I came to Ibn Saud with an unburdened heart, bearing him neither hatred nor love, accepting neither the English view of him nor that of the Sherifs of Al-Hijaz. I came to him in fact with a hard heart and a critical mind, and I can say that he *captured my heart at the first meeting.*"

Mr. Leopold Weiss wrote in the Atlantic Monthly of August, 1929: "Ibn Saud is very tall and possesses superb virile beauty. He has a high, thoughtful forehead, a slightly bent nose, a small mouth with thick lips. Anyone who meets him is at once impressed by his smile— a charming, understanding, and inexpressibly sweet smile and one cannot but love him."

Newsweek issue of May 12, 1934 said about Abdulaziz:

"A broad-shouldered, enormously powerful man of 54, the King towers over most of his subjects. But he stands before them bare-legged and unshod, wrapped in a plain brown and white Arab robe with intricate gold work on the collar. His jet-black eyes, sometimes spectacled, size up the caller shrewdly. But Abdulaziz likes men who talk up to him, and seldom takes offense."

On March 5, 1945, Time magazine reported about the King after his famous meeting with the American president Franklin D. Roosevelt:

"At 65, he is justly called Servant of the Almighty, strong as a lion, straight as a scepter. He is, beyond cavil, the greatest of living Arab rulers."

His deep affection for his family was one of his most lovable and admirable traits. His love and admiration for his sister Noura were something to be treasured. She was a very capable woman who helped in managing the palace in Riyadh. "She even undertook many of the duties of regent when her brother was engaged in war or raiding." Her influence over Abdulaziz was powerful. Charging with his men, his battle-cry was: "Ana akhou Noura"–"I am the brother of Noura." In more ways than one, his love, compassion and respect for women was unique!

While in Kuwait, his character was developing and his resolve was hardening. Not having all the luxuries of life added more to his resiliency, which gave him more strength and patience. In due time, all these virtues helped him greatly in grasping the opportune moment to reclaim the kingdom of his ancestors.

In the latter part of 1901, Abdulaziz left for Riyadh with forty men from the Al-Saud family and their supporters, along with twenty more followers. He led his weary and tired men to the northern fringes of the Empty Quarter, where he spent several months hoping to recruit more support from the local tribes. Support was not forthcoming and he grew impatient in his wait, especially since life was difficult for his men under the harsh conditions of this barren expanse of sand dunes. Being true and dedicated to his religion, he fasted with his men during Ramadan. On the twentieth of Ramadan, Abdulaziz moved with his party of sixty men; his destination-Riyadh. On the third of Shawwal, the following month, he continued his trip to the outskirts of Riyadh. He and his men were moving at night hiding behind rocks and sand dunes by day. They were finally within an hour and a half walking distance from Riyadh. They hid between the trees until the fall of dusk. That night Abdulaziz told his companions that he was determined to enter the city and conquer it. Whoever wanted to go with him was welcome, and whoever was reluctant should stay. He moved on, with seven of his men. He told the rest around nine o'clock at night, that "by dawn if you do not receive a word, you should run for your lives, because we would have all been killed; and if God grants us success, whoever wants to join us, God be with him."

Abdulaziz moved with the company of his seven men toward the heart of Riyadh with the purpose of taking Fort Musmak–residence of the appointed governor, Ajlan. However, the city had a defense wall surrounding it. Abdulaziz and his men cut a palm tree and used it as a ladder to climb the surrounding wall. Later, Abdulaziz sent word to his brother Mohammed, who was stationed in the palm groves to bring the thirty-three men for support. A brief battle ensued and Abdulaziz was the victor.

The capture of Riyadh paved the way for a holy struggle that eventually led to the founding of the Kingdom of Saudi Arabia.

The Long Arduous Struggle for Unity

After the capture of Riyadh on January 15, 1902, the struggle for unification began. At this time, Abdulaziz Ibn Mit'ab Ibn Rashid was preoccupied by warfare against Kuwait. Thus, he delayed his military response until late in the fall.

Abdulaziz rebuilt the defenses of Riyadh and the city was fortified and prepared to withstand adverse conditions of attack or blockade. His father came back from Kuwait and was placed in charge of the city, while he moved on to unify the nation.

For years Abdulaziz dwelled in tents, moving from place to place, often as a fugitive, and frequently with a price on his head, sometimes eating, but more often going hungry. He moved across the desert, sometimes hunting, sometimes hunted. Abdulaziz did not come by a single square foot of Arabian territory without fighting for it. Every war he fought, he made a religious war, a war for a principle.

By the time Ibn Rashid decided to move on south, he did not attack Riyadh directly, but made a move on Al-Kharj. However, Abdulaziz was waiting for him in an ambush and when his army advanced, a fierce battle raged. Ibn Rashid retreated to Hail. Winning this battle was a great moral victory, uplifting the spirit of Abdulaziz and his men. His rule was established in the city of Riyadh southward on to Rab'a al-Khali (Empty Quarter). Being very proud of these achievements, his father, the Imam, acknowledged his son's heroism and effective leadership. He abdicated the title of Amir, and bestowed upon Abdulaziz the authority over the Emirate.

Toward the end of May, 1904, Ibn Rashid organized an army strongly supported by Turkish troops and their heavy armaments. The Turks were concerned about the expansion of Abdulaziz; because he was a friend to Moubarak, the ruler of Kuwait who, in turn, was a friend of

Fort Musmak–Gateway to the modern history of Saudi Arabia.

the British. Moving from the town of Buraidah in al-Qasim, Abdulaziz led his force to meet the advancing forces of his enemy. In a very heated battle the Turks and Ibn Rashid were defeated. Many of them fled for their lives!

The controversies continued and hostilities led to another showdown which took place near Buraidah on April 14, 1906 (18 Safar 1324 A.H.). This was the decisive historical *battle of Rawdhat Muhanna.* The two forces of Ibn Saud and Ibn Rashid were locked in fierce fighting; there was no apparent gain in the afternoon and by sunset each returned to his camp. Ibn Rashid did not sleep much that night! He moved from one section of the camp to another, rallying his troops and making preparations for the next round of battle. Before dawn, in the pitch of darkness, his senses betrayed him when he thought he was still in a corner of his camp; unlucky for him! He was in the camp of Abdulaziz Ibn Saud. He was urging the people to battle, thinking they were his men, but these were the men of Abdulaziz who recognized his voice and slaughtered him with a hail of bullets. He was killed instantly! (His successor was Mit'ab Ibn Abdulaziz Ibn Rashid). Violent death was almost a way of life for the rulers of the House of Rashid not only prior to this battle, but afterward for some time to come. Brothers, cousins, and other relatives were engaged in a mayhem of murder, revenge, and bloodthirsty campaigns. This conquest was the beginning of the end for the contest between Abdulaziz Al-Saud and the Rashids.

The struggle for unifying the land was steady, coupled with dedication, determination, wisdom, and sheer courage. The successors of his opponent were in disarray and confined to the northern portion of Najd, while the central and south of Najd were under the solid control of Abdulaziz. Problems cropped up frequently. Whenever one was settled, another or many more popped up. By 1908, Sherif Hussein was appointed by the Turks as the Amir of Hijaz. A brother of Abdulaziz, named Sa'ad, was captured by him. He held the brother as a hostage until Abdulaziz was pressured to acknowledge the Ottoman Sovereignty along with recognizing the hegemony over Qasim. However, as soon as his brother was released, the Ottoman control was eliminated.

Settling the Bedouins

Abdulaziz devised a genius plan to settle the nomad tribes. By doing so, he reasoned, a great service would be rendered to the people and a stronger union would result. Once the bedouins were settled, some differences which developed between warring factions would be minimized or eliminated. Abdulaziz devised the *Hijra Plan* for settling the bedouins. This became the focal point of his long-range planning.

Hijra meant an agricultural oasis settlement. Here, the bedouin settled to a peaceful and fruitful life. Mud houses replaced tents. The bedouin was better able to protect himself from the seering heat in the summer and from severe cold in the winter. The inhabitants of the Hijra were taught basic methods of agriculture and were given seeds. *Artawia*, the first farming settlement of the Ikhwan, was established in 1912. Many other agricultural settlements were established all over the realm of the Arabian Peninsula. Their number totaling 122 during the life of King Abdulaziz.

Basic Islamic teachings were stressed. Religious teachers were sent to teach the tribesman and preach the new approach. This effort met with tremendous success. Learned religious leaders were delegated to lead the Hijra settlements. The settled bedouins were known as *Ikhwan*, which means brethren.

A powerful force was ready and available to carry its Holy mission of unifying the nation. By 1912, this force of Ikhwan reached eleven thousand. By 1916 all the bedouin tribes were ordered to become part of the Ikhwan and also to pay Zakat as all Moslems should. With the religious fervor of the Ikhwan, the genius and great courage of Abdulaziz, the wars of unification became truly Holy Wars that would with time overcome the enemies and their selfish desires in keeping the country divided and torn in a state of anarchy and lawlessness. The beliefs were strong in austerity, purity of Islamic concepts and the founding of an Islamic society that practices decency and justice. However, some of their concepts were primitive and their zeal sometimes bordered on fanatic extremism. Abdulaziz, with his genius and vast experience, was able to cope with the situation and make successful use of their enthusiasm and religious zeal. When asked about how he kept the bedouins under control, he answered,

"We raise them not above us, nor do we place ourselves above them. We give to them when we can. We satisfy them with an excuse when we cannot. When they go beyond their bounds we make them taste the sweetness of our discipline."

However, the Ulama were a power that held the Sultan and his people together. They were a medium of control. They seldom meddled in politics. Their main concern was to uphold the five pillars of Islam, namely: five prayers a day, the Zakat, the hajj, fast of Ramadan and the Shahadah (there is no God but Allah-Mohammed is his prophet).

End of The Contest With Al-Rashid

When Saud Ibn Abdulaziz Ibn Rashid was the Amir of Hail, a powerful woman named Fatimah Sibhan was a power behind the throne. All her servants were loyal and protective. She was able to direct the rule for many years, overcoming the powerful storms emanating from the Ikhwan of Abdulaziz Ibn Saud. Thus, for nearly fifteen years, Fatimah Sibhan was the veiled power in Hail, which earned her hatred and bitter enmity of Ibn Saud's fighters. After many years, this Rashid was to join the fate of his other three brothers and was killed by a claimant to the throne named Abdullah Ibn Talal who did not survive since the protective and loyal servants of the Amir also slaughtered Ibn Talal in the melee.

Abdullah Ibn Mit'ab, grandson of Abdulaziz Ibn Rashid, became the ruler. It did not take him long to surrender, and become the honored guest of Abdulaziz Ibn Saud in Riyadh. However, the Ikhwan continued the siege of Hail which refused to surrender! The last Amir of Hail was Mohammed Ibn Talal, who was a brother to the murderer and murdered Abdullah. He thought he would be able to consolidate the House of Rashid and bring back old glory. He held on for three months, but the overwhelming power of the Ikhwan was devastating. The last chapter of Hail was closed and sealed with a disastrous siege where only famine, fire, and bloodshed were rampant.

Abdulaziz conquered the Rashid headquarters of Hail on November 2, 1921 (29 Safar, 1340 A.H.), thus ending a long dispute and competition. After three months of blockade, the city of Hail gave up the rebellious fight. This long rivalry between the two Houses was finally put to rest. The domain was extended north and west of Hail. This consolidation of territory took place in 1923.

Abdulaziz was always generous in victory. After the fall of Hail, he prevented the troops from any looting. The hungry people were fed from his army's supplies. Surviving members of the Rashids were taken to the capital city of Riyadh. They lived at his expense as his personal guests.

Some captains of the Rashid army were taken into Abdulaziz's army. Two captains at the gates of Hail who refused to be bribed during the siege of the city were promoted rather quickly relative to the one who accepted the bribe. The man who held the fortress at the final stand, became the honored father-in-law of Abdulaziz, who also married the widow of Saud Ibn Rashid. He adopted her children and made peace with her relatives. Thus, the powerful institution of marriage helped to foster the peace and cement a relationship of loyalty and understanding.

The last ruler of Hail was taken to Riyadh. Not long after that, he was given his freedom; prior to his coming to the Majlis where his freedom was to be granted, he was well dressed in new clothing, befitting an Amir. When he came into the big hall of the Majlis, he looked every bit an Amir. He was about twenty-five years old, tall with firm features and bright eyes. He sat right next to Sultan Abdulaziz Ibn Saud, who went on to say:

"You of the House of Rashids, all of you, are as dear to me as my own children. You live here as I live, neither better nor worse. Your clothes are like mine, your food is like mine, your horses are even better than mine. No. Wallah (by God)! There is nothing in the palace that you may not have. Will any one of you say if he has ever desired anything that is under my hand and did not get it? And you, Mohammed Ibn Talal, it was your own stupid actions that forced me to treat you as a prisoner. Wallah, Billah (by God)! All the time you were held, I was in grief for you–in grief, Wallah! as if for my own son. Be loyal as I am friendly and any ill that befalls you will stir my heart before my tongue to your help. You are now one of my own house. All the resources of defense, which in time of danger I use to protect my Harem, my children, and my people will be put in force to protect you–to protect all of you of the House of Rashid."

His speech was truthful, effective, and sincere. When he spoke like this, some of the people wept!

With such goodness and generosity, Abdulaziz won the hearts of the Rashids who remained loyal to him through the last days of his life. This loyalty carries on to his family. It is reflected in the cohesive unity of the nation.

Hijaz

Sherif Hussein who was appointed by the Turks as a ruler of the Hijaz (Western region) and guardian of the Holy cities of Mecca and

King Abdulaziz, a man with legendary courage–He is the founder of the Kingdom of Saudi Abrabia.
Courtesy, N. I. Rashid collection for Abdulaziz paintings by H. Wood.

Madina, was essentially a tool for their policies. When he turned against them in World War I, he was able to throw the Turks out of Mecca and Jeddah. However, he was lacking in leadership, dynamism, and wisdom. The British agent T. E. Lawrence, also known as Lawrence of Arabia, moved to fill in the void and provide the leadership. To achieve this, he used his mind, the two sons of the Sherif, Abdullah and Faisal, along with British sterlings and the British political stamina gained through many centuries. The revolt gained strength but it was never an expression of Arab aspirations. It was indeed a reflection of British might and Lawrence's desire. The fallacy of such a policy which did not respond to Arab aspirations contained the ingredients for its

own defeat. With time, the Sherif had bigger ambitions of becoming a King of all Arabia and his demands of the British to achieve that end were becoming a nuisance. British promises were made without taking into account the mighty rising star of Ibn Saud.

At the Uqair Conference, the treaty between Ibn Saud and the British helped to control the tribes on the borders with Iraq and Trans-Jordan. The British also asked that Ibn Saud keep out of the coastal territories of Qatar Kuwait, and Oman. The treaty stipulated that in return Ibn Saud would receive an annual stipend of sixty thousand sterling. The British stopped their payments in 1923. Thus, in their unique British way they did not clearly specify their purpose. However, it was obvious, with the treaty essentially void, Ibn Saud could have attacked Qatar, Kuwait, and Oman. Instead he poised his guns and his fierce fighters to liberate Taif, Mecca, Madina and Jeddah; then soon after to bring the downfall of Sherif Hussein in Hijaz.

Mustafa Kamal, the ruler of Turkey, decided that the time was ripe to end the Caliphate. At the same time the Ottoman Sultanate vanished. Sherif Hussein took advantage of this opportunity to proclaim himself, on March, 1924, as the Caliph and thus became the King of the Arabs and Caliph of all Moslems. Big titles but empty indeed! Such action provided another conflict with Abdulaziz. The end result was disastrous.

The passionate desire of Abdulaziz and the Ikhwan to capture Hijaz was formidable, especially since they were not allowed to make the pilgrimage while the Holy Shrines were under the control of Sherif Hussein. In less than six months after the breakdown of the Kuwait Conference, the massacre in Taif took place on September 3, 1924. The score was ready to be settled with the King and Caliph of Hijaz. Abdulaziz was not on the scene in Taif, but Sultan Bin Bijad terrorized the inhabitants. By the time Abdulaziz arrived, all acts of brutality ceased and order prevailed. Efforts to halt the Ikhwan between Taif and Mecca were in vain. Mecca was taken October 18, 1924. Hussein was defeated and escaped to Jeddah, where he was forced to abdicate in favor of his son Ali. A siege followed, until Madina capitulated on the fifth of December, 1925. On the nineteenth of December, Ali abdicated, and four days later Abdulaziz entered the city of Jeddah. Following the conquest of Mecca, Abdulaziz spoke to the pilgrims at Arafat mountain saying:

"We should rise to the good faith God has instilled in us; we should not be divided or have hate because this will be among the reasons for our destruction. They are wrong, those who think that some of the western politicians are the ones that have worked to cause our division! By God, no! We tore ourselves as we obeyed the malicious ones among us. But who could tear a nation unified in the word of God and in its deep closeness which is indivisible?"

In Madina he addressed the people by saying:

"I consider your elders as my father, your middle aged as a brother and your young as my son. So be one hand with warmth in your hearts to help me perform the important task which God has rested on my shoulders. In this Arab Islamic land, I am a servant to the religion and a servant to my people. The rule is for God alone."

Asir which was previously independent, was added in 1926 to the conquered territories. Finally, in 1927, Abdulaziz was crowned

King of Hijaz, Najd and its dependencies. In the same year a British treaty was signed in Jeddah, recognizing the territories conquered by Abdulaziz extending from the Arabian Gulf to the Red Sea.

After the great conquest of Hijaz, the Ikhwan leaders, who were very helpful and instrumental in this undertaking, grew more zealous and attacked an Iraqi border fort. The attack was carried out against the clear orders of Abdulaziz. This challenge to his authority was a serious breach, but he used his wisdom in every way possible to avoid a conflict with the Ikhwan. However, they grew more overbearing and refused to curb their raids across Iraq and the Jordanian frontiers. The raids were in direct conflict with an agreement that was concluded with the British at Uqair in 1922. The insubordination and rebellion could not be tolerated. In the fall of 1928, Abdulaziz called a congress of the chieftains and Ulama to Riyadh to solve these differences. Tribal leaders came with the exception of Sultan Bin Bijad and Ad-Dawish, who were behaving as outlaws. They were strong in opposition, and they were derogatory and rebellious against Abdulaziz. They declared him a "heretic" because he made treaties with the infidels and brought to the land instruments of the devil such as the telephone, telegraph, airplane and the automobile. The Ulama at this conference declared that these instruments were permissible by law and indeed most desirable from a religious point of view. They increased the strength and knowledge of Moslems. Also, by authority of the Prophet of Islam, treaties with non-Moslem nations were very desirable, especially if they brought peace and freedom to the Moslem world.

The patience of the King was wearing thin. Finally, after a number of skirmishes between rebels and loyal tribes, the decisive battle of Artawia was fought in the spring of 1929. Abdulaziz crushed the rebellion after eighteen months of intermittent warfare that led to the open revolt in 1928. Bin Bijad surrendered and was taken to Riyadh. Ad-Dawish was wounded severely and was thought to be dying. Abdulaziz, gracious as ever, sent his personal doctor to care for him. Abdulaziz defeated all the rebel leaders and finally dismantled the power of the rebellious settlement of the Ikhwan. Northeastern security was established. Then Abdulaziz became the undisputed leader of Arabia. On September 23, 1932, the united land became the Kingdom of Saudi Arabia. Abdulaziz was proclaimed the King.

No sooner than Abdulaziz thought all his conquests were over, trouble erupted in the Southern Province. Imam Yahya of Yemen captured Najran. He was helping and encouraging liberal tribes to carry on mischief and revolt. The two sons of Abdulaziz, Saud and Faisal, led an expedition into the mountains and captured the port of Hodeida in Yemen. The dispute was settled and a peace treaty was signed in May, 1934, at Taif.

Now that his headaches were over and the scars of war had healed, Abdulaziz focused his attention on resources and development. His luck and ingenuity would strike again! Not only the water wells he sought . . . but also a desert underbelly of "black gold."

Oil Exploration

His dire need and desperation for new financial resources prompted him to grant the first oil exploration rights to a British firm in 1923. The concession was not used and the contract was not renewed in 1933. Prior to that period, Americans who visited Arabia in the 1920s and early 1930s made a very positive impression on King Abdulaziz. Thus, he later chose an American company to prospect for oil. This proved to be one of his most important decisions. In 1933, exploration rights were granted to the Standard Oil Company of California (SOCAL).

Tests from the Dammam Dome were not very encouraging, but the hope and determination were alive for continuing drilling and exploration. Drilling was continued to a depth exceeding thirty-two hundred feet. A total of eight additional wells were drilled, but again results were not very encouraging.

By the spring of 1937 and upon completion of the Dhahran residential camp, American wives and children joined their men in the field. By July, 1937, there were 53 American employees exploring for oil in the Kingdom of Saudi Arabia.

The drilling of well Number 7 which started in 1936 was halted. But why despair? Marco Polo who traveled the Fertile Crescent on his journey to China in the Thirteenth Century A.D. noted something that is of great focus and attention in the world today. He wrote: ". . . a fountain from which oil springs in great abundance. This oil is not good to use with food but is good to burn." Drilling was resumed in the fall of 1937. This proved to be a great decision and the turning point in the history of Saudi Arabia and the Company's good fortune.

When this well was drilled to a depth of 4,727 feet, large quantities of oil began gushing out and a new era in history was beginning to unfold for the Kingdom and the World. This well was completed in March, 1938, many years after the drilling of Dammam Number 1. After five years of arduous effort, oil was discovered in large quantities in 1938. The Arabian American Oil Company (Aramco) was founded. In the early 80's it became Saudi Aramco.

Treasures of the Earth

A beautiful and touching story about Abdulaziz comes to mind! It is compassionately related by his son King Fahd. The essence of the story follows: "One of his habits in the last ten days of Ramadan, in the days when the Riyal was worth a lot more–when his income from Zakat or other collections was meager, he himself moved around at night seeking the families who would not ask and would not wish to ask for anything even at times when days would go on and they could not eat anything. Through darkness he went (no electricity to light the way) and distributed what God allowed him, like a Riyal or two or three . . . Of course the Riyal had a big effect. King Abdulaziz told the story:

"There was one woman. I knew her. She was old and had children. I furnished what she needed and gave her three Riyals. She held my hand in the dark and said:

"Who are you?" I was quiet and did not say anything because I did not want her to know me. She said:

"You are Abdulaziz!"

I said: "Yes, Mam!"

She faced Mecca opened her pocket and said: "Say, Amen! Amen! may God open the treasures of the earth to you!" Abdulaziz repeated the words of an old woman . . .

The treasures of the earth at that time meant that God will give rain so that the earth would be covered with a green pasture and those that had palm trees and farms will benefit from the rain and could plant grains and eat from them and that camels would increase along with sheep, yogurt, butter, and dates. This was the thought of King Abdulaziz at that time, who went on to say:

"After the discovery of oil in our country I knew that this was the treasure of the earth." It is our good luck that oil was not discovered until after the independence of the nations around us; if it was discovered at that time colonialists would have come.

Why the colonialists stayed away from our nation in particular? Because they could not subdue it and because the nations, which they had occupied around us, have rivers and resources . . .

I knew that oil would be discovered some day, and it did! It was in 1938 when production began!

I knew that the discovery of oil was the reality of the expression: "may God open the treasures of the earth to you."

King Fahd continued: "Oil was sold with hard currency which enabled us to import what brought benefits to the nation. Despite my young age at that time, I was able to realize that the national treasury was at the end of the castle or where Abdulaziz resided. There was a person named, Shalhoub who was designated by King Abdulaziz to distribute to the people their monthly stipend, no more, no less. One could barely make ends meet, until God opened the treasures of the earth."

Today, the Kingdom ranks among the top in its contributions and foreign aid around the world. It certainly meets its share of responsibilities, and much more for the well-being of the human race.

The goodwill of Saudi Arabia and its generous contributions cross many borders around the globe. Its compassion, generosity and help stretches from the earthquake victims of Yemen and Mexico, volcano and flood victims of Columbia, the devastated Moslems and Christians of war-torn Lebanon, to the famine-stricken nations of Africa, Southeast Asia and other peoples in need everywhere.

With this great gift from God, oil revenues increased and exceeded all other revenues. Abdulaziz's great love and devotion for the nation and the people, along with his deep religious beliefs, were the driving force in the initiation of many programs and services which led, some years later, to the development of major projects and great achievements. He was able to use these funds for initiating the building of roads, telecommunications, schools, health and welfare, industrial developments and other needed infrastructure befitting a nation of the Twentieth Century.

The proven oil reserves in Saudi Arabia now stand over 255 billion barrels; this is more than twenty five percent of the world's crude oil reserves, giving the country the distinct capability of being the largest exporting oil producer in the world.

Oil discovery and production by 1938 added to the strategic and spiritual importance of this land, birthplace of the Prophet, and guardian to the Holy Moslem Shrines. Saudi Arabia is the heartbeat of the Arab world, the spiritual leader for all Moslems of the globe, and the energy giant with undisputable worldwide moderating force and influence.

In his article entitled: "*Saudi Arabia: the Overnight Superpower,*" published in the Readers' Digest issue of June 1978, Smith Hempstone wrote:

"In the politics of power, few of the world's 150-odd nations matter. The oil-rich desert Kingdom of Saudi Arabia, a family fiefdom with one foot planted firmly in the 13th century and the other in the 20th, is one that matters very much.

For Saudi Arabia has the United States, and the rest of the industrial world, over a barrel of oil. Whether life will be good or bad for Americans in the 1980s, whether communist governments will rule in Italy and

France, whether Japan remains in business–all depend largely on how much oil the Saudis are willing to pump and at what price, decisions made by men whose principle preoccupations but a few years ago were tribal warfare, falconry and camel racing."

However, throughout the world and, especially, in the organization of Petroleum Exporting Countries (OPEC), the Saudi voice has been a vibrant voice for moderation and stability. On May 6, 1991, Hisham Nazer, Minister of Petroleum and Mineral Resources said: "Our oil policy should not be viewed apart from the overall conceptual framework of planning. As owners of at least a quarter of the world's oil reserves, we have to take the long term view, for Saudi Arabia will be producing oil when many other fields would have gone dry. Short term aberrations in the oil market will spring forth every now and then. One has to be flexible and efficient enough to meet them head on. Saudi Arabia is not deflected by them to lose sight of the long term goal of market stability and a comprehensive integration of the oil industry . . . our joint venture with Texaco, in the United States, and other upcoming joint ventures around the world will give us the downstream linkages which will contribute to the stability of the market. Our control of our own tanker fleet will add further to the integration process.

The establishment of the Saudi Arabian Marketing and Refining Company (SAMAREC) . . . is another major pillar of our reorganization . . . Samarec's efficiency and flexibility was recently acknowledged by the allies during the Gulf crisis when it kept the allied war machine fully oiled. Let me quote just one example from a letter I received from General Schwarzkopf about Samarec: "The skill and speed with which you were able to react to this crisis attest to your efficiency and organizational skills. We at United States Central Command are very proud of your success in meeting the enormous challenges we faced."

Saudi-American mutual interests were strengthened at the core from a special friendship between King Ibn Saud and the American President Roosevelt. This eventually grew into a special Saudi-American relationship which proved to be very precious and valuable indeed, during the recent Gulf War. King Fahd and President George Bush have been good friends for several years. They both share basic beliefs of justice, compassion for mankind and free enterprise. Their genuine personal friendship and understanding are at the core of this *special relationship* between the Kingdom of Saudi Arabia and the United States of America–a relationship founded on solid principles of mutual interest, tracing back in modern history for over half a century.

King Ibn Saud And President Roosevelt

Two great men were destined to become friends and share philosophies of common interest. King Abdulaziz had just concluded his successful struggle for uniting his country; which, by 1932, became the Kingdom of Saudi Arabia. Franklin D. Roosevelt became President of the United States of America in March, 1933. Both were dedicated men in the service of their respective countries. Both sacrificed remarkably in contributing their share for peace and justice in a turbulent world ravaged by war and division. While the Kingdom chose to be neutral at the beginning of World War II, so did the United States of America for some time, until it was pushed against the wall by the Japanese. Both men were of similar age. They espoused philosophies that had many viewpoints in common. They were farmers in the depth of their heart and they both had some physical injuries. The President was forced to use a wheelchair; the King was able to move with difficulty; he was not able to climb the stairs because of wounds in his legs.

Roosevelt was the President of a rich, powerful, and productive country–a self-governing democracy with dynamic, just, and freedom–loving people. These were qualities admired by Abdulaziz. Thus, President Roosevelt was a symbol of hope and friendship.

The first political moves of the United States in the Middle East took place during the Versailles Conference for Peace, held in 1919 after World War I, coming on the heels of President Wilson's declaration on human rights and freedom. The rights, along with self-determination, were declared in Congress on January 8, 1918.

Great Britain was the dominant force at the time. *King Abdulaziz Al-Saud, known in the west as Ibn Saud,* used his political genius to gain the necessary help in liberating those parts of Arabia under Turkish rule and foreign influence.

While Great Britain and France were determined to limit the Arabs to self-rule, the United States of America declared its support for self-determination. Good relations were established with the U.S. and careful diplomacy was used to avoid antagonism with the British.

Abdulaziz was lending a good ear to these developments and to the awakening of a new American giant coming on the horizon. British power and influence on Arab affairs was waning.

American ingenuity coupled with the massive oil potential of the Kingdom, along with the sharp minds of two great leaders, helped create an atmosphere of rapport between two charismatic personalities.

As the Palestine problem was getting more acute by 1936, King

Abdulaziz extended his hand of cooperation to the Arab countries. He concentrated his efforts on Britain, under which Palestine was a protectorate. His efforts were also geared toward the United States, which was emerging as a world leader.

With the country's fabulous wealth just lying beneath the surface, American oil interests were developing momentum. This prompted President Roosevelt to declare in 1943 that defending Saudi Arabia was a vital interest to the United States of America. This way, the Kingdom became eligible for a lend-lease assistance program. However, this assistance was to be delivered through the British, since they still were the power in the region. This courting and coziness were looked upon disapprovingly and suspiciously by the British.

President Roosevelt invited King Abdulaziz to visit him aboard an American destroyer in the Suez Canal upon his return from the Yalta Conference. Preparation for this meeting was conducted with the utmost of secrecy, especially because of the prevalent dangers at that stage of the war. The King left Jeddah at 4:30 P.M. February 12, 1945, aboard the destroyer Murphy, for a historic meeting with President Roosevelt which took place on February 10, 1945.

The Saudi people were bewildered and astonished. Malicious rumors were spread about the King leaving the country, running from his people like Sherif Hussein. Others said he had been kidnapped by the Americans. Of course none of that was true. Ibn Saud was on a mission of peace, honor and justice aboard an American warship anchored in Great Bitter Lake in the Suez Canal, near Cairo. The visit took place as President Roosevelt was heading homeward after the Yalta Conference.

In a speech, President Franklin D. Roosevelt said: "Our conversations had to do with matters of common interest. They will be of great mutual advantage because they gave us an opportunity of meeting and talking face to face, and of exchanging views in personal conversation instead of formal correspondence. For instance, from Ibn Saud of Arabia I learned more of the whole problem of the Moslems and the Jewish problem in five minutes than I could have learned by the exchange of a dozen letters."

Shortly before his death, President Roosevelt sent in April, 1945 a note to King Ibn Saud saying:

"Your Majesty will recall that on previous occasions I communicated about the attitude of the American government toward Palestine and made clear our desire that no decision be taken with respect to the basic situation in that country without full consultation with both Arabs and Jews. Your Majesty will also doubtless recall that during our recent conversation I assured you that I would take no action, in my capacity as Chief of the Executive Branch of this government, which might prove hostile to the Arab people."

Destiny had other plans for the fate of Palestine! President Roosevelt died two months after this successful meeting and the promises about Palestine were nullified by the rise to power of Harry S. Truman as the next President of the United States.

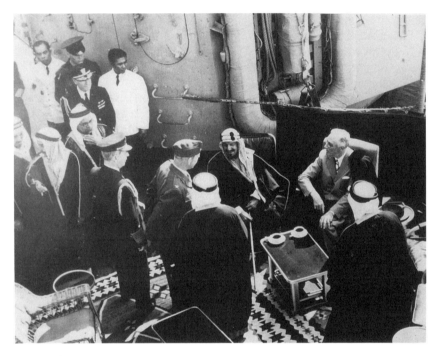

King Ibn Saud (Abdulaziz) meeting with President Franklin D. Roosevelt on February 10, 1945–Saudi American relations were built on mutual interests, and respect. They were cemented and nourished through the decades.

Anti-Arab influence was massive. Despite strong appeals for justice and respect for mutual interest and human rights, the road was paved for establishing Israel in Palestine. Truman, under formidable Zionist pressures, summoned his ambassadors from the Arab World to Washington. He declared, "I'm sorry, gentlemen, but I have to answer to hundreds of thousands of people who are anxious for the success of Zionism. I do not have hundreds of thousands of Arabs among my constituents." Communist Russia was equally eager to recognize the state of Israel.

King Fahd with his wise leadership and political valor devised an ingenious peace plan guaranteeing the rights of all concerned in the Arab-Israeli conflict. This inventive solution coupled with serious *American peace initiatives*, should have cleared the way toward an acceptable compromise for ending this devastating tragedy.

However, much destruction had taken place in the span of a few years. The Middle East had been wrecked by bickering differences, wars, and the creation of nearly four million Palestinian refugees. This resulted in a great burden that settled upon and choked many nations of the region.

One nation that suffered the most in recent times from the aftermath of creating these refugees, is the once fascinating and beautiful country of Lebanon, best known as "the land of milk and honey" and the "Switzerland of the Middle East." It was a beauty crowned with majestic nature where the air smelled of goodness and delight, and ancient land that was a shining example of tolerance among many religions and nationalities.

Unfortunately international intrigue, hatred and division in the Arab world brought an ugly civil war that tore the country apart. The result has been the transformation of Beirut, formerly known as the Paris of the Middle East, into the world capital for tragedy and terror.

It is imperative that the United States should exercise its unique position of leadership by helping this region in gaining peace and tranquility. In carrying such an honorable mission, America can count heavily on the special American-Saudi relationship and true friendship as defined by the Custodian of the Two Holy Mosques, King Fahd Bin Abdulaziz:

"Since the earliest days of the Kingdom, the United States and Saudi Arabia–our governments and our peoples–have been friends. Our friendship has flourished because it is rooted in mutual respect and mutual interests."

Such a policy, vigorously carried by the U.S., will be beneficial to all parties concerned. It will frustrate designs of communists and brutal dictators and will shatter their dreams of dominating this strategic and vital part of the world.

Although modern Arabs remain divided into many independent nations, they are eager to reach a just solution to the Palestinian problem. They also yearn for Arab unity and a single Arab nation from the Atlantic Ocean to the Arabian Gulf; but this remains largely a dream.

With the fires of nationalism have come faint communist "Eastern" winds that are basically alien to the Arab tradition and to the Moslem religion of the Arabs. These winds shall fade away, for the Arabs are

God-fearing people, who have a deep respect for Western technology, and great pride in their heritage.

Prior to concluding this chapter, one major institution initiated by Abdulaziz, must be described here. It is the famous Saudi Majlis.

The Majlis Where Citizens Meet Their Leaders

A formidable tradition, the Majlis, is deeply honored and treasured by the descendents of Abdulaziz. To a visitor at a Majlis, King Fahd Bin Abdulaziz, who was then a Crown Prince, said; "you notice that no one here has much room for protocol, I am only Fahd to these men. My brothers are Khaled, Abdullah, Sultan, etc. We are all equal under God, and such men bow to no one."

After sipping Arabian coffee and tea, it was time to "share our culture and have dinner." All those present, from the highest dignitaries to the most humble of men, all would follow Fahd to a large dining room capable of seating over 200 people. Fahd would say to his guest; "Look about you! The room is full of ministers, princes, servants, drivers, clerks, businessmen. Whoever is in the Palace at meal time joins us—without exception. It is a tradition that King Abdulaziz started and that we continue."

At another Majlis, Fahd said: "It is not that the people lack food. Some of them eat better at home than they do here. But they come to discuss their personal problems, and they stay for dinner. Anyone in the Kingdom is welcome to this table, no matter what his status. If they were all bankers or army generals, it would be assumed they were invited because of their position. But these are simple people. Anyone, anyone can come here, and that gives them confidence in their government. It is very important psychologically that they know they may look to us for help."

Prince Mohammed Bin Fahd Bin Abdulaziz, a symbol of the second generation of the Saudi Royal family and Governor of the Eastern Region, made great strides in bringing progress to this vital part of the Kingdom. It is a miraculous and fascinating transformation. Under the wise guidance and leadership of King Fahd and during the Gulf War, Prince Mohammed contributed his share in steering this strategic gateway of Desert Storm to a safe path commanding world attention and respectability befitting the Kingdom of Saudi Arabia.

Prince Mohammed Bin Fahd holds, regularly, a private Majlis with officials of the government in the Eastern Region. The majestic gathering nourishes an exchange of ideas and helps in cementing a relationship of loyalty and cooperation between the governor and the team enacting his policies. One cannot help but be deeply moved in the private Majlis

Prince Mohammed Bin Fahd Bin Abdulaziz, Governor of the Eastern Province–Gateway to Desert Storm–meets the people at his Majlis. One watches with admiration and emotion how carefully and compassionately the Amir listens to every petitioner.

which reflected harmony, loyalty and deep respect between the Governor and those who carry his policies for the good of the people.

The public Majlis, held the day after, was very touching as well. One watches with admiration and emotion how carefully and compassionately the Amir listened to every petitioner. One senses how reassuring and comforting Prince Mohammed's words have been to everyone . . . The ultimate in genuine care and compassion.

The Prince has mastered this great Saudi tradition, following the footsteps of his legendary grandfather King Abdulaziz, founder of the Kingdom, and harnessing the wisdom and teachings of his father King Fahd, the education pioneer, the father of modernization in the Kingdom of Saudi Arabia and the Great Liberator!

The Kingdom of Saudi Arabia shall stay in caring, steady and safe hands, today, tomorrow and far into the future. It is men like Prince Mohammed Bin Fahd who will continue the mission and tradition of goodness, compassion and progress.

The Era After Abdulaziz

By mid October, 1953, while in Taif, Abdulaziz suffered a heart attack. Despite his weakened condition and limited activity he insisted on holding his treasured Majlis. By the end of October, he became seriously ill and was finally confined to his room. In the early morning of November 9, 1953, King Ibn Saud, the great statesman, desert warrior, father and founder of the Kingdom of Saudi Arabia, was dead. The same day he was moved and buried next to his father in Riyadh. A tribute to his greatness is that his spirit and his mission live on.

After this great leader's death, his sons followed in his footsteps of dedication and love for their country and world peace.

On November 9, 1953, the successor to the throne was King Saud the son of Abdulaziz. In his twenties, he led many campaigns in the battles of unification. Attempts were made at building some roads, hospitals, schools and improvement of Hajj facilities, but the financial situation deteriorated with time, so did his health. Finally, he abdicated from the throne and Faisal was proclaimed King in 1964.

Faisal was born in Riyadh on April 9, 1906, less than four years after the capture of Riyadh. His birth coincided with the day Abdulaziz won a decisive battle in his struggle to unify the country. The battle was Rawdhat Muhanna.

Since youth, Faisal received traditional education and was interested in racing horses and camels. He learned the Qoran, and enjoyed poetry. However, his best education according to him came from his father "Abdulaziz who was the best teacher from whom Faisal learned his lessons and experience." At the age of thirteen he accompanied his father in battle. His talent in the battlefield impressed Abdulaziz very much. A born-commander, Faisal was a great asset in the long struggle for unification.

In 1919, he visited Britain, France and Belgium. His travels to Europe broadened his horizons. Upon returning to the Kingdom, his father, obviously pleased with his son's performance, smiled and said" "We were right to name you after your grandfather, Faisal Bin Turki." After the conquest of Hijaz, Faisal was appointed Viceroy with his headquarters in Mecca. This position was very important throughout the Moslem world, especially since the Holy cities were under Faisal's domain.

Abdulaziz recognized Faisal's talent and experience by appointing him the first Foreign Minister for the Kingdom in 1930. Matters of international nature fell under his realm. He always listened to the voice of wisdom and received proper guidance from his father. In 1945, he headed the delegation representing Saudi Arabia at the founding of the League of nations in San Francisco, U.S.A.

The many visits of Faisal to Europe, Britain, France, Germany, Poland, the former Soviet Union, Turkey, Iran, Italy, Iraq and Kuwait, among other nations took several months and lead to good results that strengthened relations with the Kingdom of Saudi Arabia. In 1953, upon the establishment of the Council of Ministers, Faisal was appointed Deputy Prime Minister. A few weeks later, Abdulaziz died and Faisal became the Crown Prince. His ascension to the throne on the 27th of Joumada thani 1384 A.H. (1964), paved the way for the basic steps in modernizing the Kingdom. Two years prior to that, Faisal declared the ten principles that became historically associated with his program in governing. Briefly, these principles are:

1. Rules are to be enacted according to the Holy Book and the Sunna of the Prophet.
2. Organizing local administration in various regions of the Kingdom in order to help in the administrative, political and social progress of the nation.
3. Establishing a Ministry of Justice, a Supreme Council for Jurists and an independent judiciary.
4. Proclaim a Council for "Fatwa" from the Ulama to look into Moslem matters and to give the proper Fatwas when needed.
5. Work to spread the mission of Islam, strengthen its foundation, and defend it by words and deeds.
6. Good morality to be practiced in line with the high Moslem objectives.
7. Improve living standards of the nation by offering free medical care, education and by subsidizing basic foods so that the citizen will be able to have them at reasonable prices. Establishing social insurance to give the proper care for the elderly and the workers.
8. Organizing economic and social progress.
9. Executing programs for building roads, dams, exploration for water, building manufacturing plants both for heavy and light industries, and establishing a general Petroleum and Minerals Organization (Petromin).
10. Completely abolishing slavery and granting freedom to all.

On top of this, and for the first time in the Kingdom's history, he opened new doors for Saudi women so that women will receive education along the same footing as their male counterpart, going from kindergarten to the university level. Faisal worked strongly toward laying the foundation for modernizing the Kingdom. He made great effort toward improving Arab unity and toward better relations with the Moslem world. His work for world peace was reflected in his genuine peaceful relations with all nations of the world. His experience, sharp mind and dedication led to laying the foundation for the first Five-Year Development Plan. His keen intelligence, pious traits and wisdom steered the country into proper foreign policy and successful domestic policy as well. However, King Faisal did not live long enough to see the fruits of his labor. He was assassinated on the 25th of March, 1975, by his nephew Faisal Ibn Musa'ad Ibn Abdulaziz.

His successor was King Khaled who was born in Riyadh in 1913. Since youth, Khaled enjoyed the desert life and treasured Arabian traditions. He felt at ease and at home in the desert. He was very much trusted by the various tribes of the Kingdom. He helped his father on a number of missions during the struggle for unification. Khaled became the Governor of Hijaz in 1932 and a Minister of the Interior in 1934. He was involved in agricultural work. His brother Faisal took him to the United States of America and also to a number of European countries. When Faisal became King, Khaled was made a Crown Prince; he then became the King in 1975. After the death of Faisal, a smooth transfer of power took place, and King Khaled appointed Fahd as the Crown Prince and First Deputy Prime Minister. He also made Prince Abdullah the Second Deputy Prime Minister and Head of the National Guard.

The second Development Plan ended during his time in May, 1980. This plan centered on diversification of the economic base so that the government will not be dependent only on petroleum for its income. In cooperation with his trusted men, Khaled held the historic Summit Conference of Moslems which included thirty eight nations that were represented in Taif and Mecca in 1981. In this same year, he initiated the founding of the Six-nation Gulf Cooperation Council (GCC). During his time and in the span of a decade, the standard of living was substantially raised, at least threefold. The per capita income increased to nearly thirteen thousand dollars by 1980. Noticeable progress covered all sectors of the economy and all social, educational and human services.

King Khaled continued the mission of his predecessors in promoting peace and goodwill among the Arab and Moslem nations as well as the world community. During this time the Kingdom occupied its position of prominence in world affairs, on both the political as well as the economic fronts. When King Khaled acceded to the Throne in 1975, his righthand man was chosen to be Crown Prince Fahd. The two made a very successful team. Extensive administrative duties for running the Kingdom were delegated to Crown Prince Fahd. The second Five-Year Plan was successfully finished with great accomplishments. The third Five-Year Plan was begun in 1980. The industrial and educational evolution was well underway when King Khaled died in June, 1982.

On June 13, 1982 Crown Prince Fahd Ibn Abdulaziz became the new King of Saudi Arabia. He is a man of great wisdom and decades of experience in top government positions. His policies and foresight, coupled with the contributions of his predecessors, brought to the Kingdom of Saudi Arabia great progress and development, the likes of which are unparalleled in the history of mankind.

While Abdulaziz was the father of the nation, Fahd, on the footsteps of his father and predecessors, became the pioneer and founder of the Modern Kingdom of Saudi Arabia.

Chapter 2

Phenomenal Progress at Home and Spreading Goodwill Abroad

The founder of the Kingdom of Saudi Arabia, Abdulaziz Ibn Saud, laid solid foundations for security and stability. He made impressive strides toward progress, considering the meager resources he had at the time. Since the mid-1970s, development has accelerated at a rapid pace. In fact, the years between 1975 and 1985 could truly be called the golden decade of the Kingdom of Saudi Arabia. The spectacular achievements realized by the Kingdom are truly amazing, especially, in such a short time. One cannot help but be fascinated by the great progress that has been realized. Saudi Arabia floats on a sea of oil with proven reserves in excess of 255 billion barrels. The massive income from this great resource was wisely used and invested, bringing with it modern technology to the Kingdom and truly making the desert bloom.

From the time of his predecessors to his golden era, King Fahd has been the man at center stage who dedicated his abundant energies, total support and farsighted thoughts into making the dream of modernization come true. The Custodian of the Two Holy Mosques, King Fahd was truly the pioneer and the heartbeat of this gigantic modernization process. He once said: "Our goal shall always be—God willing—to maintain the equitable distribution of wealth among all the citizens and to promote the welfare of each Saudi Arabian, no matter how remote his village or how far his city is from the center of construction and industrial activity." A wise decision was made to produce oil in large quantities which helped ease any shortages and in the process generated the financial resources to fuel the massive progress desired. Although, at the time, some voiced the view that oil was more valuable kept underground. These voices were not heeded and a historic opportunity became a reality because of the foresight of King Fahd. The income from oil was wisely spent, benefiting everyone across the entire Saudi spectrum.

Custodian of the two Holy Mosques, King Fahd reviewing expansion plans of the "HARAM" in Mecca (Above).

Entering the "HARAM" in Medina (Below).

Five-Year Development Plans

Rapid modernization in the Kingdom of Saudi Arabia was the result of several Five-year Development Plans which were scientifically and administratively designed with specific objectives in order to meet particular requirements of the economy and society. In 1970, under the leadership of King Faisal, the First Five-Year Development Plan started. Under the guidance of the Ministry of Planning and with the support of other Ministries and sectors of the economy, these plans played a pivotal and critical role in developing the country. In implementing the various five-year plans, the long term goals of developing the country centered around these basic principles:

1. Keeping religious values of Islam by receiving spiritual guidance from Shari'a.
2. Maintaining internal security, social stability and defending Islam.
3. Balancing economic growth by developing the country's resources. Increasing income from oil and conserving non-renewable resources.
4. Diversifying the economy and reducing dependence on crude oil as a primary source of the nation's income.
5. Developing human resources through education, training and increasing the standards for health.
6. Completing the infrastructure that is basically necessary in reaching the ultimate goals.

Hisham M. Nazer, Minister of Petroleum and Mineral Resources and formerly Acting Minister of Planning said: "We must define what we view to be the goals of development. In brief we can say that this goal is the happiness of man. Such happiness is two-sided, the spiritual and the material . . . these two aspects of man's happiness complement each other. They are mutually reinforcing and are stressed accordingly in the development philosophy of the Kingdom." In a lecture delivered at Harvard Business School on May 6, 1991, he also said, "underlying the entire process of economic growth there is a spiritual content issuing from our faith and culture. This aspect is not always realized by many outside observers. Apart from the "technological determinism" generated by the industrial civilization, there is also a "moral determinism" which has upset many societies on the path to modernization. No doubt we have developed in the world of concrete, steel, and microchips. But we have not lost our identity nor our cultural existence."

The first Plan, initiated in 1970 stressed two major principles:

1. Developing the needed human resources through education and training.

2.   Building a comprehensive economic infrastructure. Develop-
     ment projects were designated as a top priority in this plan.
  Thus, human resources development, along with infrastructure,
economic resources and social resources received 58.2% of the total
money allocated in this plan; while defense, loans, aids, subsidies
and administration received 41.8%. The total amount of money available for this plan was 11.5 billion dollars.
  The second Five-Year Development Plan between 1975 and 1980
received a tremendous boost from an oil income that surpassed all
expectations. This good fortune was a great shot in the arm for the
terrific boom in construction, infrastructure development and human
resources as well. Sixty-four percent of the total money available for
this plan was geared toward development of the infrastructure as well
as human, economic and social resources. While the balance of 36%
was spent on defense, loans, subsidies, aids and administration. The
total amount allotted for this plan skyrocketed to 139 billion dollars.
  Achievements were numerous, covering ports, airports and highways that connected the country's far corners. As well as a building
boom that was manifested in many parts of the nation. Services were
strengthened and improved along with development of natural resources. Bridges, communications, telephone and telegraph along with
developing human resources, natural resources, industry and agriculture, all were given special attention.
  Diversification of the economy began in earnest during the Third
Plan which brought the conclusion of infrastructure developments.
Again development received 62% of the total money allotted in this
plan, while other sectors received 38%. The total sum of money allotted
for this Plan also skyrocketed to a new record of 315 billion dollars.
While the planned expenditures for these Plans were respectively 41;
498 and 1,133 billions of Saudi Riyals, the actual expenditures were
respectively, 190%, 138% and 103%. For these years, revenues were
respectively 176, 719 and 1,379 billions of Saudi Riyals. After the
infrastructure was well under way, the third development plan of 1980–
1985 incorporated an increase of investment in development of human
resources and in the training of manpower needed to optimize the
benefits from expanding the industrial sector.
  The following goals were stressed in this plan:
1.   Diversifying the economy.
2.   Building light industries.
3.   Increasing joint ventures with foreign companies and thus en-
     couraging technology transfer.
4.   Maximizing effectiveness of training, manpower, industrial de-
     velopment and housing efforts.

5. Eliminating imbalance between the various regions of the Kingdom, as far as per capita income and investment.

6. Completing infrastructure activity and especially the massive
industrial complexes at Jubail and Yanbu. Petrochemical industries began to take their share in the world market on a competi-
tive basis.

All these plans, along with the ones to follow, encouraged the
free market and *free enterprise* system.

The third plan for development, 1980–1985, continued the job
started in the previous plan so that infrastructure projects would be
completed. Some of these were massive and needed more time than
allotted in the second five-year plan.

Despite the problems and conflicts that continued to plague the
region, especially the Iran–Iraq War of 1980–1988, the fourth Development Plan of 1985–1990 moved on in an atmosphere of security and
tranquility. This plan differed from the previous three in the fact that
it concentrated on the productive and private sectors more than infrastructure.

This plan defined eight strategic goals:

1. Improving the economic standard for services and benefits that
are offered directly by the government to the citizen such as
education and security services, or indirectly such as electricity,
transport and basic foodstuffs.

2. Encouraging the private sector to be involved in many of the
economic functions of the government. Economic activities that
can be accomplished by the private sector will cease to be
handled by the government.

3. Giving opportunities to the private sector to manage, maintain
and delete some sectors that are presently run by the government
on a condition that this will result in a true benefit to the
citizen by decreasing cost and giving better services for the
people. Also giving investment opportunities so that the citizens
could own and direct the basic industries through the public
offering of stocks for companies such as Sabic and Petromin,
providing opportunities for the private sector to participate
and manage these organizations at a proper time.

4. Improve and be selective in the subsidies and aids offered by
the government, be it direct or indirect. Governmental departments who direct public services will practice economic feasi-
bility and cut waste.

5. Review education and training. Also continue development
of human resources. Stress the need for quality training and
concentrate on technical development for middle and higher

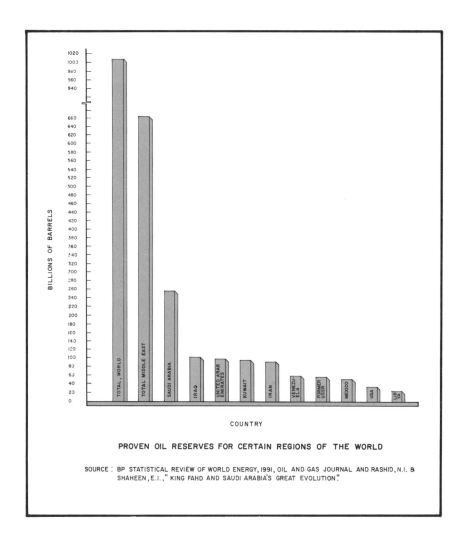

PROVEN OIL RESERVES FOR CERTAIN REGIONS OF THE WORLD

SOURCE : BP STATISTICAL REVIEW OF WORLD ENERGY, 1991, OIL AND GAS JOURNAL AND RASHID, N.I. &
SHAHEEN, E.I., " KING FAHD AND SAUDI ARABIA'S GREAT EVOLUTION".

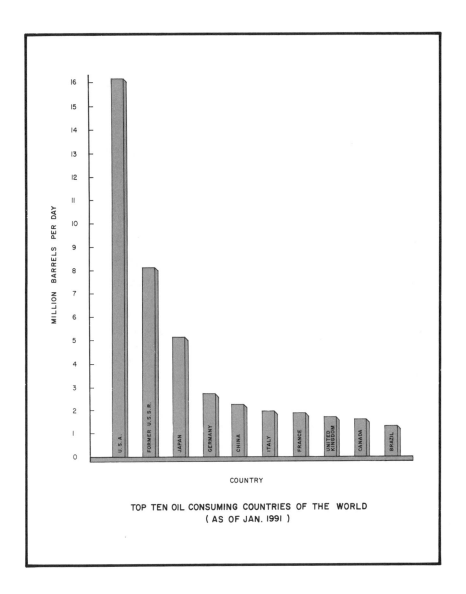

TOP TEN OIL CONSUMING COUNTRIES OF THE WORLD
(AS OF JAN. 1991)

levels. Concentration on training for management with special emphasis on the library, so that students may develop the habit of reading and researching.

6. Developing Saudi society and making available proper social and health care to Saudi citizens. Stress the importance of work as a religious and social value so that the individual in society will develop and change, in some ways, his outlook toward trades and technician jobs which do not receive the proper acceptance from a number of citizens. Also, spreading education by encouraging publishing, increasing public libraries, establishing museums and safeguarding old places of historical value. Build a national library that will contain a book depository for every Saudi author. Introduce national programs to help the handicapped. Continue the programs for environmental protection and development. Continue to increase programs for the youth.

7. Prepare a defense and security plan to guarantee protection of the nation.

8. Balancing revenues and expenditures.

As these plans were implemented, foreign expertise was used whenever and wherever needed. "However, the realization of the Kingdom's targets and policies originate from the Kingdom's own will and it does not come from any foreign companies." Saudization was one of the major objectives of the fourth Plan. By the end of this plan, over 600,000 foreign workers who were not among the experts category left for their respective countries. In the meantime, the economy absorbed over 375,000 Saudis in the work force. For Saudization to succeed, the Saudis should accept jobs in various parts of the economy that are normally occupied by expatriates.

The fifth development plan (1990–1995), costing 200.8 billion dollars, was designed to continue with previous goals of the recent past. However, this plan was to emphasize economic diversification. Oil resources, while they would still play a very vital role, would no longer be the sole export commodity. Other products along with oil will make a sizeable contribution to the overall health of the economy. Participation of the private sector in a number of areas would be encouraged such as: transportation, services and utilities. Human resources would continue to be a top priority of the fifth development plan. It will be allotted the sum of 37.6 billion dollars. Education, training, research and development as well as employment opportunities would receive great emphasis.

The infrastructure, involving transportation, telecommunication and post, along with housing, environmental protection and regional affairs will be allotted the sum of 31 billion dollars. Greater efficiency will be sought wherever feasible and possible. Cooperation between ministries will be increased and standardization will be practiced so that efficiency in municipal services will improve. All projects undertaken by the government will be subject to environmental impact assessment. The goal being to minimize any ill effects to the ecosystem. The sum of nearly 18 billion dollars will be spent for the well being of the Saudi society through health care, social and youth services, religious and judicial services as well as cultural and information services. The major expansion work undertaken in Mecca and Madina will be on its way to completion. Diversification and strengthening of the manufacturing sector is to receive special attention in the strategy of the fifth development plan. In this regard, about 95 billion dollars were allocated, so that the private sector will play the role desired. Credit funds will provide an additional ten billion dollars. Since energy, mineral resources and water are of great importance to the Kingdom of Saudi Arabia, their sector will receive about 19.5 billion dollars.

Gigantic projects have been accomplished. The boom placed a heavy demand on services and brought a distinct awareness for improving them. Maintenance and service companies are counted on to deliver their share.

New Constitutional Reforms

These development plans have proved to be very successful. The practice of applying them will continue in the future bringing progress and prosperity to everyone in the Kingdom of Saudi Arabia. Moreover, achievements will thrive under a new umbrella of justice, consultation (Shoura) and security–all inspired from the Holy Qoran. On the 29th of February, 1992 (26 Sha'aban, 1412 A.H.) the Custodian of the Two Holy Mosques, King Fahd Bin Abdulaziz made a historic move by announcing basic reforms incorporating:

   a. 83 articles for the *Basic System of Government* with guarantees for the sanctity of home and personal freedoms.
   b. 30 articles Governing the *Consultative Council (Majlis Al-Shoura)* which will consist of 60 members and a Speaker.
   c. 39 articles specifying the Rules for the *Provincial System* governing the various Regions of the Kingdom.

The first article defines the foundation of the Nation, specifying that the Kingdom of Saudi Arabia is a sovereign Arab Islamic state whose religion is Islam and whose constitution is the Holy Qoran and the Sunna of the Prophet. These milestone articles codify governmental protections for personal freedoms and human rights. They may be looked upon as an extended modern constitution of the Modern Kingdom of Saudi Arabia. Their impact is far-reaching and certainly befitting and complementing the great progress in the Kingdom.

The *Basic System of Government* includes important articles relating to general principles and the Monarchy where the rule will be confined to the sons of the Kingdom's founder Abdulaziz Bin Abdul Rahman Al-Faisal Al-Saud and grandsons. The most suitable among them will be enthroned to rule under the guidance of the Holy Qoran and the Prophet's Sunna. Also, for the first time, the Basic System of Government spells out that the King is the one who will appoint the Crown Prince and will have the authority to relieve him from his duty by a Royal Order. Basics of Saudi society, economic principles, rights and duties, governmental authorities regarding the judiciary, executive and regulatory branches, monetary affairs, control and general rules are also covered.

The rules governing the *Consultative Council* will replace the system of the Shoura Council of 1347 A.H. All regulations, instructions and resolutions valid until the implementation of this system would continue until they are accordingly amended. This system will be implemented within a period of six months. Selected members will be of good reputation, well educated, well qualified Saudi nationals by origin and birth. All the rules are spelled out in detail, similar to other parliamentary bodies in the world, but reflecting a true Saudi spirit.

The first article of the *Provincial System* governing the Provinces of various Regions of the Kingdom specify the goal to raise the standard for administrative work and development of all parts of the Kingdom. It calls for safeguarding law and order and for the protection of citizens' rights and their freedoms within Islamic Shari'a. Here, the articles cover: rules for the Provinces and Emirates, districts and centers, governors (Amirs) of Regions (who report to the Minister of the Interior), oath, responsibilities of the Amir, yearly meeting of the Minister of the Interior with the Amirs (Governors), meetings of the Amirs with the directors, district managers and their appointments, the formation of Provincial Councils in every region or Emirate and various rules and regulations governing these councils. The Provincial System will be put into effect within one year.

Work will continue by all ongoing regulations, instructions and resolutions when this system is implemented until amendents take place.

This new evolution will prove to be another inspiring and courageous move by King Fahd–the Education Pioneer.

The educational and industrial evolutions that have taken place are indeed mind-boggling. . . . They are truly unparalleled in the history of mankind! The cornerstone for such progress has been education. Thus, we begin here by describing the progress in the realm of education and then moving on to detailing the miraculous progress in all other areas of the Saudi society.

Education

The first Minister of *Education* appointed in 1953 was Fahd Bin Abdulaziz, the present King of Saudi Arabia. He pioneered a major role in establishing the educational system of the country. He had the foresight, determination and deep dedication to develop education in the Kingdom, knowing that without education the dream of progress would not be achieved. King Fahd once said: "The human being plays the basic role in the development of his society–for wealth comes and goes, leaving the effort and sweat of man to develop a society."

He reminisced about the status of education at the time, saying, "I remember when I became Minister of Education there was only one secondary school in the Kingdom, in Mecca. The total number of students attending schools in Saudi Arabia at the time was only 35,000." Today, the Kingdom prides itself on a fine system of education, covering the whole spectrum from primary, intermediate and secondary, to technical and vocational schools, colleges and universities.

Not long ago there was not even one university in the Kingdom. In the span of a few years, seven major universities have been built.

There was a time when a new primary or secondary school was being opened every two weeks all year 'round. By 1992, school enrollment exceeded three million boys and girls. A great leap forward from 1951 total of merely 30,000 students.

The educational system in the Kingdom of Saudi Arabia is very modern. This system begins with kindergarten, when the child is four or five years of age. Here, he spends a year or two preparing for the elementary school. Children reaching six years of age enter the general education level, which includes the elementary school. Here they study for six years.

The intermediate level requires three years of further study. At the end of this period, students take a general examination. If successful, they will earn a general intermediate certificate allowing them to enter into the secondary school system.

Students with practical and applied inclination are guided toward the intermediate stage with vocational technology in mind.

Boys and girls have similar opportunities, but each attend separate schools.

Educating the future leaders of the Kingdom.

Students holding the general intermediate education certificate will be admitted to schools of secondary education. The duration of study for this level is three years. There are secondary schools in the evening and others during the day. Those in the evening will accept adult students. Successful completion of this program will lead to awarding the students the general secondary education certificate, with two branches: one in science, the other in arts. Branching off takes place after the first year.

In 1975 a comprehensive secondary school was started. This school uses the credit system. The school year is divided into two semesters, each of fifteen weeks duration. In addition there is an optional summer session of ten weeks. Depending on the aptitude and drive of the student, these schools require about six semesters or the equivalent of three years.

Only male students are admitted to technical institutes, secondary vocational or commercial schools and to the agricultural institutes. The duration of study here is three years after the general intermediate education certificate or the modern intermediate education certificate.

There are also secondary commercial schools and higher institutes for financial and commercial sciences. The study in the secondary commercial schools requires three years. The fields covered are: accounting and finance, administration, secretarial work, banking, purchasing and sales, collection and cash matters. The period of study at the higher institutes is two years after the commercial secondary education certificate. Day classes are held for regular students and evening classes for working people. Upon successful completion of this program, students are awarded a diploma in Commercial and Financial Sciences.

There is also training in the technical area of agricultural education. Such training takes place, for example, at the model Technical Agricultural Institute in Buraidah, that was established in 1977.

The necessary manpower for different trades is trained at various institutes, such as the Health Institutes where the level of training is between the elementary and secondary stages. These institutes train such assistants as: statisticians, nurses, technicians, x-ray technicians, surgical operations assistants, health supervisors, laboratory technicians, assistant pharmacists and nutrition assistants.

Nursing schools, like the Health Institutes, are for both males and females. The required minimum for admission is an elementary education certificate or its equivalent. The period of study is three years.

The Ministry of Municipal and Rural Affairs directs some Technical Assistant Institutes. These include: surveying, foremanships of construction, water and roads, architectural drawing and health supervising. These institutes admit boys holding the intermediate education certificate. The duration of study is two years. Graduating students work in municipalities or in technical and engineering offices.

There are also Tailoring Centers, Postal and Telecommunication Institutes and Arabic Language sections at Islamic University.

The Institute of Public Administration is an autonomous government agency mainly for training civil servants. Programs include:

1.   Short seminars for top executives.
2.   Some training programs in accounting, personnel administration, computer and secretarial work.
3.   Training programs of about two years duration in various fields such as computers, financial controls, typing, hospital administration and legal studies.
4.   Special programs to meet designated needs of certain agencies.
5.   English programs for civil servants who are sent abroad for training, or for those who need the English language in their daily work.

The Vocational and Pre-vocational Training Centers prepare the necessary skilled and semi-skilled manpower needed in industry. The program of study takes from one year to one and a half years. Evening courses last about five months. Vocational specialties include: auto-mechanics, auto-body repair, refrigeration, air conditioning, plumbing, painting, electricity, radio-TV, welding, construction, carpentry, metal works, etc.

The Instructors' Institute was established in 1980 to train qualified instructors for the vocational training centers including various governmental departments and agencies offering certain specialty training.

Training of teachers is directed by the Ministry of Education or the Presidency of Girls' Education. Normally, the period of study in these schools is three years after the intermediate education certificate. Graduates are normally qualified to teach in elementary and intermediate schools.

Science and mathematics centers for men-teachers were established in 1974 to meet the chronic shortage of qualified Saudi teachers to teach in these areas. Students holding the secondary education certificate (the scientific branch) are admitted. Those holding the arts certificate or the diploma of the Teacher Training Institute also may be admitted if they successfully complete the courses during the preparatory year. The first stage is finished in two years and then a diploma is awarded. After the second stage, the teaching proficiency degree for teaching math and sciences is awarded. This requires the successful completion of courses in an additional year of study.

The first two Junior colleges for men-teachers were established in 1976 in Riyadh and Mecca. Five more colleges were built the following year in Dammam, Madina, Abha, Russ and Taif. Students holding the general secondary education certificate or its equivalent may be admitted to this program. Teachers working in elementary schools may be admitted to improve their status and knowledge.

Junior colleges for women-teachers were established in 1979 along similar lines as the junior colleges for men teachers.

Special Education Programs for the physically or mentally handicapped include: Al-Nour Institute for the Blind, Al-Amal Institutes for the Deaf, Institutes for the Mentally Retarded and Adult Education for Eliminating Illiteracy.

In the span of a decade, the numbers of students, schools, and those working in them have doubled many times. For example, the number of elementary schools in the academic year 1975–76 was 2,414; in the year 1984–85 it increased to 4,413 schools. The number of intermediate schools for the year 1984–85 was 1,323. The increase during the ten years was more than 800 schools. Secondary education schools have increased by 359 since 1975–76. The number reached 462 in the year 1984–85. The total number of schools reached 16,584 in 1988–1989.

Between 1970 and 1983 (1390 A.H.–1403 A.H.) the number of students at various levels of education increased from nearly 400,000 to 1.8 million. The enrollment of girls increased from less than 200,000 to 700,000 in that period. The total number of schools increased from 3,282 to 14,256.

The Kingdom had 226 schools and 30,000 students in 1951. In 1992, "the number of male and female students in different stages of education exceeded three million." Nearly 500 new schools opened their doors in 1989, bringing the total number of schools and educational facilities at all levels from nearly 3,300 in 1970 to over 17,000 in 1990. Females are claiming their educational share. The academic year of 1988–89 had 1.16 million student females, out of a total student population of 2.65 million.

Gigantic steps are being taken to eradicate illiteracy through educational programs for the elderly.

Literacy educational programs are conducted in various corners of the Kingdom in schools, camp scouts, institutes, libraries and sports arenas. Total expenditures for these programs exceeded two billion dollars.

It is noteworthy to learn that student-faculty ratio, around fifteen to one, is among the best in the world. The goal was good quality education. This was coupled with improvements in curricula, the quality of instruction and the upgrading of the teaching and administrative staff. Decentralization and delegation of authority are practiced wherever feasible to improve efficiency.

The educational policy placed special emphasis on safeguarding religious and moral values along Islamic lines. This has been the core of educational development from a humble beginning in 1949 when the Shari'a College was established, to the great achievements in education crowned by good universities in the four corners of the Kingdom.

The Holy Qoran urges followers to "seek knowledge from the cradle to the grave." The Saudi Arabian society is based on the teachings of Islam, which decrees a high value for education to develop human potential. A very good, close relationship between home life and school environment contributes to the family structure, which is at the heart of Saudi life.

Attention to girls' education has progressively expanded since 1960. In the year 1983–84, the budget of the General Presidency for Girls' Education was about 1.7 billion dollars. This constituted over 21% of the total budget of eight billion dollars for education and human resources. In the span of a very few years, education for women became available in over 800 communities, covering every village and city in the Kingdom of Saudi Arabia.

The Saudi Islamic Academy was established in Alexandria, Virginia, U.S.A., in 1984 under the auspices of the Ministry of Education. Saudi children in the U.S. and others may attend. Students receive their instruction in line with cultural heritage and religious teachings of Islam. They learn the Arabic language along with math, science, history and english. Students attend this Academy up to the eleventh grade. Over 700 students from twenty-six different nations attend the academy. There are plans for a high school system to be implemented along with a two-year junior college.

Since Saudi Arabia has the commitment for building a future based on industry and a good level of technology, nearly 70% of all foreign workers eventually will be replaced by Saudi citizens that have been well educated and prepared for their jobs. Of course, this requires not only the levels of education just described but an active program of higher education as well.

Higher Education

The Ministry of Higher Education oversees policies in about 82 colleges and institutes of higher learning in Saudi Arabia. This ministry was allocated 31% of the budget for the 1980–85 plan for education

(2.5 billion dollars). Another 120 million dollars was shared by The Saudi Arabian National Center for Science and Technology (known today as King Abdulaziz Center for Science and Technology) and The Institute of Public Administration. The first has activities in research grants and scholarships; (KACST) designs the Saudi policy in science and technology. It renders its assistance to the private sector and carries applied research independently and jointly with other international organizations. It also grants awards for research and study. One of its added functions is coordination of the activities for government agencies research centers and scientific organizations. The latter trains current and possible government employees. It also provides consultation to various departments of the government.

The Presidency for Girls' Education encompasses the Undersecretariat for Girls' Colleges. It supervises and manages institutes of higher learning such as the College of Education for Girls in Riyadh which was established in 1970, the College of Education for Girls established in Jeddah in 1974, Mecca 1975, and the Higher Institute for Social Work in Riyadh, 1975, the College of Arts in Riyadh, 1979, also the College of Arts and Sciences in Dammam, 1979. Three Colleges of Education for Girls were opened in 1981 in Madina, Buraidah and Abha. In 1982 another College for Education was opened in Tabouk.

About half of the colleges and institutes in Saudi Arabia carry scientific studies and have a total Saudi teaching staff exceeding 12,000. The number of students registered at the University level increased from 8,000 in the year 1970–71 to 85,000 in 1983–84 and 122,100 in 1989–90. In the academic year 1990–91, the number of students at Saudi universities was approaching 125,000. By the year 1984, the total number of male and female students graduating from these institutions of higher learning exceeded 50,000. While in the academic year 1990–91 alone the number of graduates is around 12,000. Some students go abroad for higher education, most of them head for the U.S.A.

There are seven major universities spreading over sixteen campuses and covering the entire Kingdom. Three of these place emphasis on Arts and Sciences, three others are of a specialized type. The Ministry of Higher Education supervises six of these universities while the seventh, the Islamic University, is supervised by the Council of Ministers. These universities are as follows:

King Saud University (KSU)

KSU was established in Riyadh in 1957. It has a beautiful new campus built in the nearby community of Diriya, located on the outskirts of the nation's capital, Riyadh.

The new campus now accommodates more than 25,000 students. KSU is an example to the great faith in education espoused by the country's leaders, especially King Fahd. The basic mission of the university is to disseminate knowledge and build men of the future for the Kingdom. Traditions and religious heritage are intertwined in this process of dissemination.

The educational atmosphere is very inspiring and supported with good faculty from many parts of the world. It has a good, modern library. The students receive free textbooks, food and lodging, along with a monthly stipend. The semester and credit hour system have been modified to be more practical and suitable. There are many services that are offered by the university. For example, various faculty with a particular expertise are, available for consulting to the ministries and agencies of the government and make a valuable contribution to the development plans. Impressive numbers of seminars and conferences are held by the university. Scientists, medical doctors, engineers and men of learning interact with the student body and the faculty. Various sports, cultural and social activities are also practiced.

In 1961 fifteen students graduated from the university. By 1981 the total number of graduating males and females was over 5,000. By the academic year 1990–91 the total number of students graduating was over 25,000.

King Saud University (KSU) in Riyadh.

When King Saud University opened its doors, it had twenty-one students and nine professors. Within twenty-five years of expansion, culminating with a majestic piece of architecture costing over two billion dollars, the campus today accommodates nearly 30,000 students.

Now, the University prides itself with many colleges. These are: Literature, Science, Administrative Sciences, Pharmacy, Agriculture, Engineering, Education (in Riyadh and Abha) Medicine, Dentistry, Medical Assistance Technology, Medicine (in Abha), Agriculture (in Kasim), Commerce and Administration (in Kasim), and the college of Arabic Language. The Bachelor's degree is granted to graduates from these colleges: Agriculture, Education, Engineering and Pharmacy. The campus also includes a teaching hospital for medical students; it is King Khaled University Hospital, which has a capacity of 870 beds and cost more than 360 million dollars. Lodging for faculty and personnel can accommodate a population of nearly 45,000.

Islamic University at Madina

This International Institution for Islamic studies was established in 1960. It has five colleges with eleven different branches. These include: the college of Shari'a, colleges relating to the Qoran and religious studies and the college of the Arabic language. The student body comes from all over the world. Over eighty countries are represented.

The university hospital cares for the health needs of the university community. Studies continue year 'round and the programs require four academic years of nine months each. Postgraduate schools offer the master's and doctor's degrees.

King Fahd University of Petroleum and Minerals (KFUPM)

This was known previously as the College of Petroleum and Minerals (CPM) and was established in 1963. Classes began in 1964 with 67 students and a total faculty of fourteen. Programs were progressively developed to cover a number of disciplines both in the areas of Applied Engineering and Engineering Science. The first graduation ceremonies were held in June, 1972, in Dhahran, home of the University. The college became the University of Petroleum and Minerals (UPM) in 1975 and on December 25, 1986, the University was renamed King Fahd University of Petroleum and Minerals (KFUPM). The University has several colleges including: Engineering Science, Applied Engineering, Sciences, Business Administration and Environmental Design.

King Fahd University of Petroleum and Minerals (KFUPM) in Dhahran–
Higher education is thriving in the Kingdom.

The number of students at KFUPM was 3,047 in 1980–81. By 1984–85 the student body numbered 3,810; 397 of these graduated with a B.S. degree and 77 with M.S. degree. During the academic year 1985–86, the total number of graduates from the University were 508. They were distributed as follows: one doctorate in electrical engineering (the first granted to a Saudi at KFUPM), 81 M.S. and 426 B.S. degrees. In 1988–89 the total number of students was 4,533 and by the academic year 1990–91, this number was nearly 5,000.

This prestigious university desires to be judged in comparison with other elite universities in the Western World, especially American universities. To rank well in this comparison, the university has recruited top faculties from around the world and incorporated in its programs innovative techniques in education, research and public service. KFUPM was able to attract eminent engineers and outstanding technical personnel.

In its quest for excellence, KFUPM is also assisted and advised by a consortium of distinguished American universities. Massachusetts Institute of Technology (MIT), Princeton University, University of Michigan, California Institute of Technology, Mississippi State University, Texas A & M University, Colorado School of Mines, University of Rochester and Milwaukee School of Engineering. Each university selects its representative to the consortium committee, which acts in an advising capacity. The representatives cover a spectrum of technical know-how that is relevant and helpful to the university's goals and mission. The consortium committee meets at least twice a year, both in Dhahran and in the U.S. It acts as a visiting-type accreditation committee which evaluates achievement and academic performance; it gives specific recommendations covering curriculum, research and laboratory work. Standards of the Accreditation Board of Engineering and Technology (ABET) are strictly observed.

The Bachelor of Science, the Master of Science and Doctor of Philosophy degrees are offered in a number of disciplines.

Supporting services include an excellent library with access to the latest in science and technology through its association with other international libraries. Other support services include: Data Processing Center, Central Research Workshop, English Language center, Physical Education and the Co-op Study Program.

In many ways the students are very fortunate. They are attending a college of higher learning with excellent educational facilities. Their education is totally free. The typical student is paid a monthly salary. Books are free and so are room and board.

A major branch of King Fahd University of Petroleum and Minerals is the *Research Institute*. Research is done for industry, the general public and the government. It covers various fields from petroleum and gas technology to energy resources, geology and minerals, environment and water resources, along with economics and industrial development, meteorology, standards and materials. By the start of 1992 the Research Institute had already conducted hundreds of research projects. The first Arab Astronaut, Payload Specialist, Prince Sultan Bin Salman aboard the American space mission Discovery, conducted a series of six different experiments specifically designed by a team of engineers and scientists at KFUPM.

King Fahd University of Petroleum and Minerals, with its fine mission of excellence and good achievements in education, technology transfer and human resources, has earned its place among all universities of the world, especially those in the Middle East. Fortune Magazine called it: "A Jewel of a University on Arabian Sands."

King Abdulaziz University (KAU)

Saudi businessmen, acknowledging the basic role of education in modernizing Saudi Arabia, founded this university in 1967. The rapid development of the university prompted its founders in 1971 to petition the government so that operations would be under its realm.

The College of Economics and Administration was the first college at the University and began instruction with 60 males and 30 females in 1967.

On August 8, 1971, the university became a public institution under the wing of the Kingdom. The colleges of education, Shari'a and higher studies at Mecca, established in 1949, became part of King Abdulaziz University. As of 1981 (1/7/1401 A.H.), the branch in Mecca became an independent institution under the name of Omm Al-Qora University.

The university campus covers an area of 400 acres in the northeast portion of Jeddah and has over nine colleges granting degrees up to the Ph.D. level. These include: the Colleges of Economics and Administration, Arts and Humanities, Education (in Madina), Physical Education, Engineering and Applied Science, Environmental Design, Medicine and Medical Sciences (supported by various departments and especially the university hospital with over 800 beds), Earth Sciences, Institute of Applied Geology, Institute of Meteorology & Arid Lands Studies and Institute of Oceanography.

Separate and equally well-equipped facilities have been established for women. Parallel courses are taught for men and women.

The first budget in 1967–1968 for the university was less than one million dollars. With seventeen years of progress, the budget jumped in 1983–84 to 373 million dollars. The total number of students for the same year was 14,403. Among them were 10,243 males and 4,150 females. Of these 3,255 students were non-Saudis and the balance of 11,148 students were Saudis. By 1989–1990 academic year the number of students enrolled at KAU were 22,474 and those graduating were 1,465.

KAU is enriched with a university hospital and many specialized centers such as computer, media educational technology, english language and a good library.

Like many other university campuses, residential quarters are made available for students, staff, faculties and their families. The future capacity for the whole campus should run as high as 40,000.

Imam Mohammed Bin Saud Islamic University, Riyadh

This university was founded in 1974 and the Council of Ministers defined its basic purposes. It became an annex to the Riyadh Ilmi Institute (scientific institute), which was built in 1950. The various faculties which were progressively added include: College of Shari'a, Arabic Language, Higher Judicial Institute, Faculty of the Basics of Religion, Institute for Islamic Call, Faculty of Social Sciences, the College of Shari'a and Basics of Religion in Abha, (and Qasim in 1976). Also, a College for Arabic Language and a College for Social Studies were added in Abha and Qasim, an Institute for Islamic Call in Madina and a College for Shari'a and Islamic Studies in Hasa. It has a branch for teaching Arabic to foreigners and also a branch for teaching English to students at the university.

Four academic years are needed for graduation with a Bachelor's degree. Two academic years are required for the Master's program and the Doctorate degree may be earned in two to four years after registration of the dissertation topic.

The university has three branches outside the Kingdom; at Ras Al-Kheima, Mauritania and Djibouti. Two branches for teaching the Arabic language are located outside the Kingdom, one in Indonesia and one in Japan. The number of students totaled 16,134 in 1983–84. Those pursuing graduate studies numbered 2,725. For the five-year plan ending in 1982–83, 6,232 students graduated from the university and a cumulative total of 14,970 for the academic year 1989–1990.

King Faisal University (KFU)

This university was founded in 1975. Instruction began with 170 students that same year, in four of the basic colleges: the College of

Agriculture, Veterinary Medicine (in Hasa), Construction and Planning and the College of Medicine and Medical Sciences in Dammam. A branch for girls' education and a college of Business administration were later established.

Academic activities in the various colleges are complemented by applied scientific centers that strengthen the educational process at the university. These include: centers for agriculture, animal science, research facilities, libraries and University King Fahd Hospital in Khobar with nearly 400 beds.

KAU has agreements with various American universities, including Harvard, Cornell, Rice, Texas A & M and others to help in the progress and development of academic programs.

Umm Al-Qora University, Mecca (UQU)

Founded in 1981, the university includes the Faculty of Shari'a and Islamic Studies which has existed since 1969 and the Faculty of education in Mecca that began in 1952. For a period, both were under the Ministry of Education (1971–1972), then became a part of King Abdulaziz University prior to becoming part of Umm Al-Qora University.

Since 1981, the university expanded on many fronts including: College of Shari'a and Islamic Studies, Education, Applied Science and Engineering, Arabic Language, Education in Taif, College of Da'wa and Basics of Religion (Da'wa and Osoul Al-Deen).

Since 1983 two other colleges have been added: the College of Social Sciences and College of Agricultural Sciences. Many centers for research and related endeavors are very active at the university, including a center for computer science and television education.

Universities in the Kingdom seek excellence in education in their respective missions and endeavors. All have made great progress. Indeed, an era of renaissance is taking place reflecting giant steps forward in reviving Arab contributions to science, technology and society.

Education and training are the foundation for developing human resources–the dynamo for superb achievements in the Kingdom. This panorama of progress is vividly described in the following pages.

The Development Boom

Progress in the Kingdom has covered all sectors of the economy. On previous pages, achievements in education and the oil sector were described. Here, other aspects of this miraculous progress are presented.

Funds and Credits

Funds which have played an important role in the various development plans include: the Public Investment Fund, the Saudi Agricultural Fund and the Real Estate Development Fund for both projects and power plants. Long term interest-free loans, and assistance to private citizens as well as public and semi-public institutions, were extended through these funds.

Citizens with industrial licences are eligible to receive long term loans (up to 15 years duration) equivalent to 50% of the total cost of a project.

The Saudi Industrial Development Fund (SIDF) that was established in 1974 was designed to support and promote the development of private industry in the Kingdom. The fund contributed extensively by providing medium term loans and the necessary advisory services to many local manufacturers.

Loans from the Real Estate Development Fund (REDF) increased from nearly one billion Saudi Riyals in 1974–75 to about nine billion Saudi Riyals in 1983–84. For the Saudi Industrial Development Fund (SIDF), the loans increased substantially to 5.2 billion Saudi Riyals in the same period. The Public Investment Fund (PIF) gives credit to the public or semi-public corporate sector of the economy. It extended nearly six billion Saudi Riyals in 1977–78 and the loans increased to nearly 11 billion in 1981–82 moving to 8.1 billion in 1983–84. The credit dispersed by the various public financial institutes showed a very steep growth from a miniscule sum of 16 million Saudi Riyals in 1969–70 to the staggering figure of about 26 billion Saudi Riyals in the year 1983–84. Cumulative credit given by all financial institutions until the middle of 1984 totaled nearly 184 billion Saudi Riyals. These disbursements were gradually lowered since credit needs were reduced. After their peak years, they reached a level of 5.3 billion Saudi Riyals in 1988–89.

Transportation

The building of modern highways, paved and unpaved roads, airports, seaports, railroads, bus transport, telephone, telegraph and post services, were all very essential in providing the basic foundation for development.

Today a *road network* connects the four corners of the Kingdom with modern expressways complete with various types of interchanges reminiscent of the most modern highways that you will encounter in Western Europe or most of America. In 1970, the total road network was about 17,000 kilometers. In 1990, the Kingdom had 116,511 kilometers of roads both paved and unpaved.

While all this was under construction, great care was taken to protect the environment and animals of the desert, be it sheep, goat, camel or others, so crossing paths were provided at various intervals on major highways. The transportation infrastructure received special attention because of the major role it plays in the further development of the economy and the society. Today cities and villages of the country are easily reached by modern roads. These modern roads became very useful to the pilgrims and to the Saudi citizen and his family. Along many roads, they find special places for rest along with modern facilities. There are gardens planted and manicured in various parts of this network of highways. Traffic jams around major cities were solved via bridging or bypassing through city belts. Also there are modern roads connecting the Kingdom with its neighbors, such as the road to Yemen and the road connecting the Kingdom with Kuwait. Two roads connect with Jordan. One road connects with Qatar; it extends to the United Arab Emirates and the Sultanate of Oman.

King Fahd causeway, or bridge, connects the Kingdom with Bahrain. On November 11, 1982, the cornerstone of the bridge was jointly placed by King Fahd and the ruler of Bahrain, Sheikh Issa Bin Salman Al-Khalifa. This highway is, essentially, a four-lane highway; two lanes in each direction with one lane for emergency in both directions. It is 25 meters in width and about 25 kilometers in length (15.5 miles). At one time 2,000 workers, specialists and engineers worked on it. The cost of 1.2 billion dollars was paid by the Saudi Arabian government in line with its policy of increased cooperation and welfare among the Gulf Cooperation Council (GCC). The bridge was technically finished on April 26, 1986, after nearly five years of work.

An ultra modern *rail system* is the only one in the Arabian Peninsula. A major railroad connects Riyadh and Dammam. This system is being expanded and made more efficient through the Saudi Government Railroad Organization. A new dual line connecting the Eastern Region with Riyadh has been built. It reduces travel time from seven hours previously, to three and a half hours, with stops in Dammam, Abqaiq, Hofuf, Ain Aradh, Al-Kharj and Riyadh. Still the number of those traveling by railroads is modest, increasing from 117,000 in 1970 to 225,500 in 1990. The railroad freight in ton-kilometers increased from 34 million in 1970 to nearly 1,100 million in 1984. This represented an average annual growth of about 26%. In 1990, the railway system used 47 locomotives, 2,165 freight cars and 58 air conditioned passenger cars.

The Saudi Public Transport Company, founded in 1979, manages urban and cross-country public transport. It carried 146 million passengers in 1982–83. This is compared to 119 million passengers in the previous year. A fleet of nearly nine hundred buses gives a needed service to the commuter and helps in reducing traffic jams and congestion in major cities. It provides efficient transport facilities, comfort and safety for the pilgrims performing the Hajj each year, at the Holy places in Saudi Arabia.

Twenty-three *airports* connect the four corners of the Kingdom and give easy access to most countries in the world. Three of these airports are international in nature, competing in size, modern services and quality with the best airports in the world. These are: King Khaled International Airport on the outskirts of Riyadh, King Abdulaziz International Airport near Jeddah, and The International Airport in Dhahran in the Eastern region. The first phase of King Fahd International Airport located between Dhahran and Jubail, is on its way to completion. When completed, it will be able to handle 16 million passengers and 176,000 tons of freight per year.

Seaports also play an important role in opening the gates to the outside world through import and export. They are a basic necessity, in order to respond to the vast needs of the various development plans. Twenty-one seaports rank among the most modern in the world. Leading among these are: the Jeddah Islamic Port, King Abdulaziz Port in Dammam, Jubail Commercial Port, King Fahd Industrial Port in Jubail, Yanbu Port and Jizan Port. These ports have a total of 133 piers. The largest two being the Jeddah port and the port in Dammam, having respectively 45 and 39 piers. The expansion of seaports was extensive, having the capability of handling 135 ships at one time. It is possible to unload over 65 million tons of cargo per year.

Communication

The Kingdom has also made great achievements in the area of modern communications. *Telephone* services have received tremendous improvements in quality and reliability. You can call anywhere in the Kingdom and 185 countries around the world. The service is ultra modern. In many instances it far surpasses the best telephone systems anywhere in the industrialized world. The expansion of telephone lines in Saudi Arabia has truly been phenomenal.

The local network is supplemented with an advanced international network of communication including four earth stations for communication via satellites. Television programs are also broadcast by the

Kingdom to the outside world, especially to the Islamic countries on special religious occasions. The Kingdom is connected to brotherly nations with a network of cables and microwaves. An earth station can receive and transmit from the Arab satellite (ARABSAT) which was put into orbit on June 17, 1985. The same year, it was used to transmit the Hajj procession to the Islamic world, live on the air. King Fahd Telecommunications City was inaugurated in 1987. This seventh earth station for reception and transmission is considered to be the largest in the world.

Telex and Fax services have also expanded and a large network is now in operation giving instant access to the four corners of the globe.

The expansion rate and modernization of the telecommunication system in Saudi Arabia is truly unmatched anywhere in the world. Local and international services are indeed first rate.

The *Postal service* also improved both in quality and reliability since the early 70's. A giant leap forward was realized by introducing the most modern methods and equipment, especially automatic handling and separation of mail, including the zip code and express mail for a number of Saudi cities.

In the field of *information* (television, radio and press), impressive strides have been made. The television studios in Riyadh are among the most modern in the world. The television tower graces the majestic and huge marble building of the Ministry of Information. Two major television stations, one in Arabic and another in English are run by the government. News is televised in Arabic, English and French. The Eastern Region of the Kingdom is capable of receiving several stations from the neighboring Gulf countries, including stations from as far away as Iraq and Iran. The Kingdom also has 37 radio transmission stations.

At least three major daily newspapers are published in English as well as over a dozen in Arabic. Some of these have a wide circulation on the international scene, especially Europe and the Arab World.

The Kingdom of Saudi Arabia was in the forefront of exhibitors at the World's Fair for communications and transport, Expo 86 held in Vancouver, Canada. The Kingdom's pavilion was a reflection of its fine achievements in this sector. Visitors to the Fair were very much impressed with the spectacular progress. Among the visitors were Prince Charles and Lady Diana of England, who inaugurated the opening of the International Fair.

Around the same time, the Kingdom was well represented at the International Fair in Paris, France. The Saudi pavilion was a great success. Among its first visitors was Jacques Chirac, the former French

Prime Minister, who inaugurated its opening. He expressed his admiration for what he saw as testimonials to formidable progress.

The Kingdom takes pride in sharing the story of its modernization and culture with the rest of the world community. In this spirit, the Exhibit of "Saudi Arabia Yesterday and Today" was successfully shown in a number of countries. It was well received in 1989–1990 especially in a number of American cities, including, Washington D.C., Atlanta, Georgia, New York City, Dallas, Texas and Los Angeles, California.

Water and Agriculture

Saudi Arabia,–a desert country–placed prime importance on water availability without which agricultural and industrial progress could not be made. The government worked diligently to make drinking water available to all the population. The Kingdom is a world leader in water desalination. Currently it has over 27 desalination plants on the shores of the Arabian Gulf and the Red Sea, producing over 560 million gallons of drinking water per day, in comparison to only 5 million gallons per day produced in 1970.

Scientific studies show that nearly two-thirds of the Kingdom's surface is of sedimentary rock-beds that contain a number of acquifers. These acquifers complement other sources of water and are harnessed by digging deep wells which now exceed 4,800 in number.

The Kingdom has built over 183 dams. There were only sixteen dams in 1975. One of these is the biggest in the Middle East, built in the region of Bisha in the southern part of the Kingdom, and will hold 86 billion gallons of water. These dams collect water from the occasional rainfalls and have a storage capacity in excess of 450 million cubic meters.

Water reclamation and recycling is also gaining momentum. Water is the life line for agriculture. It has made the desert bloom!

The special attention given to agriculture is in line with the policy of diversifying the economic base. About half the Kingdom's population lives in rural areas. Many of them work in agriculture. It is strategically important to increase good production for the increasing numbers in the population.

The government encourages farmers by granting them agricultural land and giving interest-free loans. The Agricultural Bank has contributed extensively in this regard. Generous support by the government for the agricultural sector materialized as follows:

Payment up to 50% of expenses for fertilizer; payment up to 50% of the animal feed; supporting potato production by allowing the farmer to have five tons free and after that paying 1,000 Riyals for every ton with a maximum of 15 tons; equipment for poultry and dairy, absorbing up to 30% of the cost; transport of animals by airplanes, absorbing 100% of the cost.

The Agricultural Bank, the Saudi Credit Bank and the Agricultural Development Fund were responsible for providing finances to the farmers. For the period 1975–1985 the small and medium term loans to the farmer exceeded 42 billion dollars. In the Five-Year Plan 1980–1985, the government allotted twenty-one billion dollars to agriculture.

Between 1975 and 1985, the land under cultivation increased by over 1,300%. In this period wheat production increased by 400 times. One of the shining achievement in the development plans is the production of wheat. It reached two million tons in 1986 and over three and a half million tons in 1991. This is more than twice the amount needed for local consumption. Saudi Arabia, basically a desert land, became an exporter of wheat.

Poultry and meat production increased threefold. Egg and dairy production doubled. Thus, the Kingdom became self-sufficient in meat, poultry, eggs, dairy products and began to export to the international market: wheat, dates, certain vegetables and fruits.

By 1989, land under cultivation had increased to three million hectares (7.41 million acres).

The generosity of the Kingdom extends far beyond its borders. It has granted several million dollars to the International Fund for Agricultural Development (IFAD) to finance projects in nearly 80 developing countries. Millions of dollars were donated to the international food program, along with large quantities of dates and thousands of tons of wheat were given to other nations in need. In the summer of 1986, Egypt was the grateful recipient of 200,000 tons of wheat surplus from its sister country, Saudi Arabia.

On November 9, 1984 the Food and Agricultural Organization in Rome, Italy, acknowledged these achievements in agriculture by giving an award to the Kingdom's Ministry of Agriculture and Water.

Industrial Development

Basic to an industrialization boom are the availability of reliable sources of energy, especially *electrical energy*. The Saudi government generously supported this sector of the economy. Its goal was to acquire and provide an abundant supply of electrical energy for industry as well as all Saudi citizens.

The Saudi Industrial Development Fund was very generous in its loans to the various electrical companies. This provided the impetus for building the necessary power stations. Availability of abundant sources of cheap oil and gas also were a great incentive.

General electric power increased seventeen fold from about 1.8 billion kilowatt-hours to 31 billion kilowatt-hours in a decade. The number of electrical subscribers increased from nearly 400,000 in 1976 to over one and a half million in 1984. The phenomenal growth of installed electric capacity increased by an average of 32% per year from 418 megawatts (MW) in 1970 to nearly 14,600 megawatts in 1984. Between 1985–1988, domestic consumption of electricity increased by 23%.

King Fahd gave special personal attention to development projects, especially electrical power generation because electricity is a service of great importance touching the lives of citizens everywhere. His directives were to make electricity available in the cities, villages and far away settlements. As early as March, 1986, King Fahd inaugurated the eighth electrical power station in the capital, Riyadh. It is considered among the biggest electrical generating stations in the world with a production capacity of 800 megawatts, which will increase to 1,000 megawatts. The station covers an area of nearly 600,000 square meters and cost nearly one and a half billion Saudi Riyals.

The Kingdom's electrical generating capacity reached over 20,000 megawatts in 1990, serving nearly two and a half million subscribers.

With abundant energy from oil and electricity along with large income from oil, *manufacturing plants* are being built at an average rate of 45 a year. The government played a key role in developing the basic hydrocarbon industries and the private sector has done its share in building other industrial projects. The number of licensed factories was 207 in 1970. It increased to 3,252 in 1984. In the same period, operating plants rose from 207 to over 1,600 at an average of 92 per year for this period. In 1992 the number is in excess of 2,200 operating plants.

The Saudi Basic Industries Corporation (Sabic) expanded its global distribution network to improve its marketing strategy and wide reach in service to customers around the world. It plays an important role in the Kingdom's drive for industrialization and diversification of the economy.

Sabic was created as a basic umbrella having joint ventures with various companies on a 50–50 basis. Possible partners were recruited based on established expertise. Many American firms such as Mobil, Shell, Exxon, Cales, and Texas Eastern were all recruited along with a consortium of Japanese firms led by Mitsubishi.

Sabic brought into reality eleven basic industries since it was first formed in 1976. These industries include massive projects in the metal sector, fertilizer and petrochemicals. Sabic competes on equal footing with major chemical companies of the world. Its main purpose is providing excellent service to customers while selling top quality products. Its wide international distribution network is the result of hard labor that began in 1980. A number of joint-ventures with American and Japanese companies enable Sabic to efficiently present its products to world markets.

The Saudi Industrial Development Fund, also played a major role by financing more than one thousand projects at a cost exceeding fifteen billion dollars. Industrial centers were built near a number of Saudi cities such as Riyadh, Jeddah, Qasim, Dammam, Hofuf and Hasa.

In the industrial cities of *Jubail and Yanbu*, Sabic ventures were built from ground zero.

The Royal Commission for Jubail and Yanbu was established September 21, 1975 and was responsible for the development of the two cities. The commission operates as an independent agency directly under the chairmanship of King Fahd.

These two industrial cities encompass some of the most important industrial complexes in the world today. Jubail is a city on the Arabian Gulf with an area of 900 square kilometers and a population of 30,000. It was designed to accommodate 350,000 people. Yanbu, on the Red Sea, has an area of 150 square kilometers, and a population of 18,000. It is designed to accommodate a population of 150,000. About twenty primary industries and four secondary industries are in operation in these cities; others are in the building stage. Petrochemicals, fertilizers, methanol, industrial gases, plastics, iron, steel and many more are produced.

The two cities are indeed shining examples of the tremendous industrial progress achieved by the Kingdom of Saudi Arabia. "Undertaken during the last decade, the projects of Jubail and Yanbu stand as landmarks to Saudi Arabia's transition into the industrial age and toward international competition. They were constructed on what was essentially waste land, using the most advanced concepts in urban planning and employing the most efficient production technologies."

Industrialization in Jubail and Yanbu turned the previously wasted gas that had accompanied oil production operations into a very useful source, instead of allowing it to be wasted and burned just to dispose of it and to be an environmental health hazard. Gas fuels the industry and is the major source of feedstock for petrochemicals.

At one time, the mammoth project of the twin industrial cities was employing a skilled labor force in excess of 100,000 people. By any standards, a Herculean task and a gigantic accomplishment!

When the Jubail industrial project was inaugurated in 1977 it heralded a new era in the modern and industrial history of the Kingdom of Saudi Arabia. But vision, dreams and ambitions become truths as the Kingdom reaches and approaches its goal of industrialization and diversified economic base.

Applied and scientific research is conducted at various Saudi Universities and much support is received from King Abdulaziz Center for Science and Technology (KACST). It has the responsibility of directing and formulating Saudi Arabia's national science policy to promote scientific research. The Kingdom's technological and scientific needs are supported by scientific research developed by these research centers. Joint projects also are carried on with other international scientific centers in the world. Great cooperation is being achieved between KACST and American scientific organizations. An example of this is the Saudi-U.S. program for cooperation on solar energy. Over thirty separate projects have been undertaken since 1979, for conducting solar energy experiments in the U.S. and the Kingdom.

A major Research Institute (RI), which is an independent center affiliated with King Fahd University of Petroleum and Minerals (KFUPM), has conducted solar research since 1977. This Research Institute, described under educational progress, carried on a variety of other research projects responding to the needs and long range goals of the Kingdom. This impressive institute has the most modern scientific equipment and latest in computer technology. It has about one hundred laboratories. Since the late 60's, KFUPM scientists have been investigating water desalination, hydrogen production, solar cooling and environmental research.

An agreement was signed in 1983 between the National Aeronautics and Space Administration (NASA) and KACST for cooperation in space-related research. This cooperation helped in mapping programs, ground water exploration and sand drift monitoring. The General electric company was granted a contract to supply and install a remote sensing facility station for the reception, processing and analysis of space photos sent by satellite. New joint research agreements are continually being made. Notable among these is the one with the Canadian National Research Council.

Building Construction and Developments of Hajj Facilities

A central goal of the Saudi government was to provide proper care for all Saudi citizens. Large sums of money have been invested in the construction of homes for low income groups. Also, long term interest free loans are granted to citizens so that they can build their own homes. Apartment buildings have been built by investors. Loans are interest-free and for a long number of years. From 1975 until 1984,

403,000 units were built; out of which 287,000 were built by the private sector, with loans from the Real Estate Development Fund. The availability of housing had reached 65 units per 1,000 people in 1989 as compared to only 5 units per 1,000 people in 1980. During the Fourth Development Plan of 1985–90, 285,000 housing units were built. The Ministry of Public Works and Housing along with the Royal Commission for Jubail and Yanbu, both have built a large number of units. Housing projects specifically built for employees were carried by other government institutions, leading among these are: the National Guard, various universities, Ministry of Defense, Ministry of Interior, and some other ministries.

Many public buildings possess a unique architecture blending Arab traditions and making ample use of marble.

The Ministry of *Municipal and Rural Affairs,* along with supporting agencies, made large investments in the public utilities sector. Water and electrical networks along with sewage and rainwater drainage systems have been built. Municipal services, construction of beautiful public parks, market centers and streets were completed.

Saudi cities rank among the most modern in the world. If one had the chance of visiting these cities in the early seventies, chances are, he would not recognize them today.

One witnesses progress everywhere: going from Hail in the north, to Jizan in the south, or from Jeddah on the Red Sea to Riyadh, in central Najd and on to Dhahran, Khobar and Dammam in the east!

Maintaining the *Haramein,* or the Holy sites in Mecca and Madina, is considered as an honor and a duty. Thus, in this spirit of custodianship, the official title preferred by King Fahd became: Custodian of the two Holy Mosques. Since Saudi Arabia is the focal point for all Moslems of the world, special attention has been given to large and comprehensive expansions of the Holy places. To make the pilgrims' journey to Arabia a safe, spiritual experience, mammoth projects have been achieved. The number of pilgrims has increased at an average annual rate of 6.3 percent, reaching over two and a half million today. Hajj is considered the largest single human gathering in the whole world.

Twenty tunnels have been dug into the mountains, nineteen bridges and fly-overs for pedestrians were built, along with the construction of one hundred kilometers of multi-lane road network to ease traffic in the Hajj area. Large reservoirs were built to store the water needed by the pilgrims. More than forty pilgrim cities were built in various parts of the Kingdom to help accommodate the guests.

Further expansion of the two holy Mosques was begun in 1986. These expansions eventually increased the capacity of the Prophet's Mosque in Madina from 28,000 to over quarter of a million worshippers and the great Mosque in Mecca was enlarged to accommodate nearly one million worshippers.

Madina is also the site of state-of-the-art facilities where the Holy Qoran is printed in millions and distributed to various Islamic centers throughout the world; in most cases as a gift from the Custodian of the two Holy Mosques. Printing is done by safe hands guaranteeing that the Holy Qoran will be safeguarded from revisions by any enemies of Islam. Al -Aqsa Mosque, third holiest shrine of Islam, is being rejuvenated and extensively maintained by the good deeds and generosity offered by King Fahd. This makes the Custodian of the two Holy Mosques, the first moslem leader in history to carry the gigantic steps of expansion and maintenance in Mecca, Madina and Jerusalem. This project, together with the construction of the tunnels, fly-overs and other necessary services to bring comfort, peace and smooth transportation to millions of pilgrims, along with the expansion of the two Holy Mosques, will perhaps be considered in history among the most important achievements of King Fahd and his predecessors. These gigantic steps are befitting the Kingdom's position as an honorable guardian of the Holy Places, and a leader of the Moslem World. History will undoubtedly engrave in golden letters these good deeds of King Abdulaziz and his sons.

Health, Social Justice and Youth Welfare

An advanced and comprehensive **health care** system has been developed. Specialized hospitals have been built and equipped with the latest equipment. Some of the specialty treatments are for the eye, heart disorders, kidney, burns, tuberculosis, cancer and more.

For example, King Khaled Eye Specialist Hospital in Riyadh is considered as one of the best equipped and largest hospitals for eyes in the world. Resident physicians are pioneers in the eye treatment area. Patients come to this hospital from many corners of the world including Spain, Egypt, England and the United States of America.

King Faisal Specialist Hospital and Research Center is considered among the most competent and best in the world. With a commitment to provide the best medical care for the citizens, the Ministry of Health arranged a surgery exchange program between the well known Baylor College of Medicine in Houston and the hospital in Riyadh.

Many Saudi students come to the United States for training in medical care. Also a number of medical schools exist in the Kingdom. The universities having medical degrees include: King Saud University in Riyadh, King Abdulaziz University in Jeddah and King Faisal University in Dammam. The Abha district also will have a medical college. King Khaled University Hospital with a capacity of 870 beds, is a teaching hospital within King Saud University Medical School.

King Fahd Medical City in Riyadh built at a cost of 533 million dollars, is a massive medical complex that includes four major hospitals for Pediatrics, Maternity, Psychiatry and General care. An estimated staff of 3,000 is housed in a specially built complex. Also included are a burn treatment center and a kidney transplant center.

Another unique feature of the Saudi Arabian health system is the Flying Medical Corps. In this manner health care is made available to people in remote areas of the Kingdom.

A number of government agencies and ministries provide medical services for their dependents and also for other citizens. These are: the National Guard, Ministry of Interior, Ministry of Defense and some other agencies that run modern hospitals and health centers for their own personnel.

The Saudi Red Crescent Society complements the Ministry of Health in first aid, accidents and other emergencies. During the Hajj period, health facilities are made available in cooperation with the Red Crescent. About 12,000 doctors, nurses and other medical personnel are ready to treat the pilgrims.

In the fourth Five-Year Plan, the private sector played a larger role in the medical field. Twenty more hospitals were built, along with 1,000 health centers and 100 diagnostic and obstetric centers. The number of professionals and technical personnel increased to 63,452. Stimulated by generous government loans, the private sector now plays a significant role in the health sector. A special emphasis in the nineties is being placed on the quality of medical care now that major facilities have already been built. The Kingdom had 145 hospitals, 26,410 beds, 2,041 primary care health centers and a medical staff of 49,641 in 1984–85. The number of physicians was 14,267. The number of hospitals operated by the Ministry of Health was 93. The medical staff increased from 6,174 in 1970 to more than 56,000 in the various categories that include doctors, pharmacists and technicians. There were 74 hospitals in 1970 with 11,000 beds, 600 clinics, 3,300 nurses and 1,200 doctors. In early 1990, there were more than 254 hospitals with 50,000 beds, 2,000 clinics, 38,000 nurses and 18,000 doctors.

A unique charity hospital will be opened on the outskirts of Riyadh. It is designed for treatment and research of leukemia and lymphomas in children. It is known as King Fahd Children's Medical Center and Research Hospital (KFCMC). The cost is over eighty million dollars. The hospital will have an intensive care unit of forty beds and will be equipped with the best and latest specialized medical technology. The most modern laboratories, support facilities, staff housing and engineering support will be provided.

Children will be admitted to KFCMC without regard to ability to pay. KFCMC will guarantee payment of the cost of treatment for any child without other means of support.

Much of the plan for this hospital was modeled after the well known St. Jude Children's Research Hospital in Memphis, Tennessee, USA. The hospital is designed so that most clinical services are centered around an Outpatient Treatment Center. This charity Research Hospital was founded by Dr. Nasser I. Rashid, co-author of this book, entirely at his own expense after one of his sons was stricken with leukemia and was saved.

Not only good health care is provided but also the *welfare* of the Saudi citizen is utmost on the minds of Saudi leaders. The purpose is to bring comfort, peace of mind and happiness to the Saudi citizen.

Employees are protected through a social insurance or employment insurance. The number of those insured in 1973 was 145,000. It jumped to over three and a half million in 1985. The total number of establishments that were covered by this employment insurance was only 1,064 in 1973. It jumped to 12,594 in 1984.

Social services budget in the fourth plan (1985–90) was about four billion dollars, not including social insurance or housing construction. This amounted to four times more than the amount allotted in the first development plan of 1970–75.

The government guarantees a proper income in case of disability or retirement. In case of death a proper income should be given to the employees' dependents.

Disabled people and others stricken by disasters are afforded a decent standard of living by the government. Pensions are disbursed to these people. In 1962, the upper limit of these benefits was 410 dollars per family. In early 1991 these benefits are 3,000 dollars. While aid for this sector was 3.7 million Saudi Riyals in 1979–80, it became 137.4 million Saudi Riyals in 1989–1990. Rehabilitation programs for the physically and mentally handicapped are offered along with various other social services.

The social security system fills a basic social need. The total amount given to recipients increased by 33.7% on an annual average, from 41.7 million Saudi Riyals in 1969–1970 to one and a half billion Saudi Riyals in 1983–1984.

Youth Welfare comes under the General Presidency of Youth Welfare whose president is Prince Faisal Bin Fahd. Strong efforts have been made to meet the needs and aspirations of the youth.

King Fahd is President of the Higher Council for Youth. His deep interest in their guidance and upbringing is a natural extension of

Saudi Arabia, yesterday and today!

his love as a father and educator. Programs have been designed to strengthen the minds, morals and spirits of the young. Basic principles of good behavior, adherence to traditions and respect for fellowman are inherent in many youth activities.

Modern recreational and sports facilities were built in Jeddah, Dammam, Abha, Hail, Qasim, Riyadh, Al-Khobar, Tabouk and other Saudi cities. Swimming pools, cultural libraries, literary clubs, dormitories, science centers, game centers, arts and crafts also received special attention. The King Fahd Stadium built in Riyadh is an ultra modern sports facility having a capacity for 100,000 spectators. Sports are popular, especially soccer and basketball. In 1985, the national soccer team reached a high point by gaining a victory in the Asian Cup. In June of 1989, another victory was won by the Saudi team which was the World Under-16's Championship in Britain.

The General Presidency of Youth Welfare orients young people and supports their interest. This program provides an overall global policy to cope with and gainfully use the free time of the youth so that they will be able to take advantage of their talents and potential. Strengthening the bodies and imparting in their souls the profound teachings of Islam along with Arab traditions, are given priority attention.

In the second five-year plan the amount of money allotted to the General Presidency for Youth Welfare increased dramatically from 22.3 million Saudi Riyals in 1973–1974 to 142.9 million Saudi Riyals in 1974–1975. In 1976–1977, the numbers jumped to 1,500 million Saudi Riyals. By 1981–1982 the numbers again skyrocketed to nearly two billion Riyals and by 1990 these were over three billion dollars (11.53 billion Riyals). Recreation and education of the youth are very much strengthened through 192 social and cultural athletic clubs.

The Gulf Cooperation Council has Deputy Ministers for Youth and Sports who meet on a regular basis to discuss ways and means of cooperation and competition. Prince Faisal is very active in this regard both nationally and internationally. From time to time he makes special visits to get better acquainted with what other youths are doing on the international scene. The latest practices are sought, studied, sometimes adapted and adopted. Faisal Bin Fahd responded to an invitation by the chairman of the Nobel Peace Prize to visit Norway and the city of Stockholm. He met with top leaders of the country and visited sports and recreational facilities along with other youth centers. He closely observed the various programs and sports centers, always seeking ways to improve, innovate, implement and bring new ideas for Saudi youth who are the Kingdom's treasure and its bright hope for the future.

Miraculous Progress

What has been achieved is unmatched, certainly in this century, and for that matter, in the history of man. The speed with which it has been achieved and the high standards that have been applied gave fantastic results that one would normally see in dreams, not reality. In the 1990 issue of Economy and Oil Magazine, the Canadian Ambassador to Saudi Arabia A. N. Lever described the great progress in the Kingdom as the "miracle of the twentieth century."

The Kingdom continues to seek the best talent in the world. It actively seeks joint ventures with a number of experienced and proven companies, be it from Japan, West Germany, Europe or the United States of America.

Dignitaries, journalists, politicians, members of parliaments, planners, scientists and engineers all around the globe are astounded by this massive modernization.

A national policy of peace and tranquility, intertwined with impressive achievements in modernizing the Kingdom, is central to the basic thought and plans of the leadership. What has been achieved in slightly over a decade far surpasses what other nations would seek to achieve in hundreds of years. The pace at which development has taken place is the envy of many across the globe. This great enthusiasm and devotion to the welfare of the citizens bring the leadership very close to the heart of the people. This commitment of personal service is a key factor in the mutual trust and admiration between the government and the governed.

Goodwill and Compassion Toward Mankind

Saudi Arabia is blessed with a wise leadership dedicated to prosperity at home and peace in the world. This fact coupled with its phenomenal oil reserves and oil exports that are the largest in the world, earned the Kingdom a distinguished position of leadership and moderation in the Arab world, the Moslem world, as well as the international community. Not only is King Fahd the man of achievement on the national and regional scene, he also is the man of moderation, wisdom and peace among the family of nations.

A cornerstone of the Kingdom's policy is to encourage and support peace and goodwill in the world community, especially in the Arab and Moslem world. Brotherhood and solidarity are supreme. They are both preached and certainly practiced by the Saudi leadership. Arab differences are considered a family affair and the Kingdom spares no effort or cost toward bringing understanding, peace and harmony among the fraternal nations of the Arab world.

The Kingdom is a dynamic member of the Gulf Cooperation Council (GCC); It is also a prominent member of the Arab League and the Organization of Islamic Conference (OIC).

Anywhere you go, wherever you move across the Arab world, you sense and observe the peaceful efforts, the great moderating and economic might of the Kingdom. Saudi Arabia's contributions toward economic, political, cultural and military activities whose goal is to boost Arab solidarity, are all truly enormous! A dialogue is sought and a hand-of-peace is extended to all, no matter how difficult the circumstances may be and how deep the wounds may have become! In its search for peace and goodwill toward mankind, especially Arab brothers, Saudi Arabia pursues its efforts with zest and determination, even when the odds against harmony and peace are very high.

Saudi Arabia is an active member of the *United Nations*. The Saudis are especially proud of being a founding member of the United Nations charter which was signed on June 26, 1945. Among the fifty founding nations, the Kingdom takes deep interest in strengthening the organization and offering substantial help to many projects carried by it toward the welfare of other nations of the world.

Upon his ascension to the throne in June, 1982, King Fahd asserted to the nation that Saudi Arabia is active "within the framework of the United Nations, its agencies, and committees. We are committed to its charter. We reinforce its endeavors."

The Foreign Minister of Saudi Arabia Prince Saud Al-Faisal, described the UN as "a safety valve trusted and respected for the preservation of international peace and security." Saudi Arabia, he declared, "Stands up against any action that attempts to weaken it or replace the authority of international law with the instruments of force and the means of terror." The Kingdom actively participates in various organizations and functions of the United Nations. Its generous financial contributions speak well for the Kingdom's dedication to the UN's success and welfare. The Kingdom ranks fifteenth in its contributions among the one hundred and sixty-nine member nations. It ranks tenth in terms of per capita contributions.

The goodwill of Saudi Arabia and its generous contributions cross many borders around the globe. Its compassion, generosity and help stretches from the earthquake victims of Yemen and Mexico, volcano and flood victims of Columbia, to the famine-stricken nations of Africa and other peoples in need everywhere. The Kingdom strongly supports self-determination and economic development for the family of nations. The World Organization, the United Nations Educational, Scientific and Cultural Organization (UNESCO), the UN's International Children's Educational Fund (UNICEF), among other organizations, are all strongly and enthusiastically supported by the Kingdom. It certainly meets its share of responsibilities and much more for the well-being of the human race.

Saudi Assistance to Developing Nations

Assistance* offered by the Kingdom of Saudi Arabia to developing nations in the period 1973–1989 in the form of grants and easy development loans through bilateral, regional and international channels amounted to $59.47 billion, representing 5.45% of the Kingdom's GNP. Out of that total, $34.38 billion was given as grants, representing 58% of the total amount of assistance.

Seventy developing nations have benefited from this assistance; 38 in Africa, 25 in Asia, and seven in other regions of the world.

The percentage of official assistance the Kingdom offered through 1973 to 1981 reached 7.7% of the country's GNP. The average assistance offered in the period from 1981 to 1989 represented 3.2% of the Kingdom's GNP.

As for the absolute size of assistance, the Kingdom occupies the second place of donor nations after the United States. In the period from 1982 to 1986, the Kingdom ranked fourth among the donor nations in the world. In terms of the percentage of donations to the GNP, the *Kingdom ranks first.* In 1988, that percentage was 2.8%. That is more than seven times the 0.36% for the industrial nations that are members of the DAC.

Among the OPEC members, the Kingdom occupied first place, with Saudi assistance representing 79% of the total OPEC aid package in the period from 1980 to 1987. In 1989, that percentage rose to approximately 90%.

The percentage of grants, monetary and development loans offered by the Kingdom ranged from 55% to 60%. These included several interest-free long-term loans that might reach up to 25 years with a 10 year grace period. The overall average percentage of grants to the total size of the unredeemable aid package amounts to 82%.

The less developed nations, which numbered 42 according to the United Nations classification, have been awarded special attention by the Kingdom in view of the harsh economic conditions they faced. The Kingdom meant from the beginning to make most of the aid package to these nations in the form of grants. The development loans included

---

* Source: Royal Embassy of Saudi Arabia, Washington, D.C.

in these packages carried very easy conditions with terms reaching 25 years and a grace period up to 10 years.

The volume of direct loans amounted to approximately $5 billion, benefitting 26 developing nations. Since most of the beneficiary countries are classified as less developed nations suffering from chronic economic problems, the Kingdom–in response to requests from some of these nations–agreed to postpone payments due on these loans. Accordingly, loans totaling $1.61 billion were rescheduled in the period 1981–1989, benefiting 10 nations.

Loans made by the Saudi Development Fund amounted to $7.34 billion from 1976 to February 1989 benefiting 60 nations and financing development projects for social, health and human services such as roads, water, railways, education, culture, and other infrastructure projects. The percentage of grants in the total package of the Saudi Development Fund was 55% with a repayment period of 25 years and average interest ranging from 2.5% to 3%.

The Role of the Kingdom in International Cooperation for Development

A report by the United Nations Conference on Trade and Development released in 1984 stated that the average of official aid offered by the Kingdom in the period from 1973 to 1981 represented 7.7% of the Kingdom's GNP, and for the period from 1981 to 1987, the percentage was 3.16% of the GNP. This percentage exceeds by far the 0.07% officially set by the United Nations as percentage of development aid to GNP of donor nations. In addition to its prominent role on the bilateral level, the Kingdom is a principal contributor to the resources of a large number of regional and international development organizations, contributing no less than 20% of the capital of 12 of these organizations, notably the OPEC International Development Fund, the Islamic Bank for Development, the Arab Bank for Economic Development in Africa, the African Development Bank, the African Development Fund, the Arab Fund for Economic and Social Development, and the International Fund for Agricultural Development. Furthermore, the Kingdom undertakes an active role in supporting international financial institutions. In addition to its growing contribution to the group of the World Bank and the IMF, the Kingdom provided huge loans in the last few years to the two institutions adding to their ability to respond to the growing needs of the developing nations and helping them to expand their different programs.

In this respect, the Kingdom made it possible for many developing nations to acquire assistance to implement programs of economic reform and adjustment. In addition, the Kingdom has recently decided to participate in financing the programs of structural reform undertaken by the IMF, thus contributing $200 million to provide additional financing to the impoverished nations targeted to benefit from such programs in view of their acute financial problems, deterioration of their balance of payments and the increasing burden of their foreign debts.

On the international level, the Kingdom contributed to the programs and organizations of the United Nations, enabling them to carry out their various human, social and development programs. In addition to its direct contributions to the resources of these organizations, the Kingdom provides about 47% of the funding for the Arab Gulf Program of aid to the United Nations development agencies.

With regard to the African nations in particular, the Kingdom's assistance totaled more than $17.4 billion in the period 1973–1989, of which $10.114 billion were grants representing 59% of the total aid to these nations. The rest, $7.3 billion, was offered in the form of very easy loans with no conditions attached. African nations below the Sahara enjoyed a considerable share of the Kingdom's attention in recent years in view of the dire need that required immediate consideration. The Kingdom was at the top of the list of nations that rushed to confront the drought problem that has plagued Africa since 1981. The Kingdom contributed a total of $430 million as non-refundable grants to be used for drilling wells and in rural development in the Sahel countries. These grants were also meant to alleviate the impact of the drought through increasing water and food supply in other affected areas, and helping find solutions to the problems of the refugees. The Kingdom is committed to contribute $100 million to the World Bank Program in the countries of Africa below the Sahara.

Honorable Role

In their joint 1991 message to the Pilgrims, King Fahd and Crown Prince Abdullah said,
". . . There were also those who called for the redistribution of wealth with a view to securing equality between the rich and the poor and who would insinuate, whenever they referred to Saudi Arabia explicitly or implicitly, that the Kingdom had failed to do what it should–in their opinion–have done in this respect. We wish that these critics had given as freely and generously to the cause they claimed to espouse as the Kingdom has since it received Allah's Bounty in plenty.

The Kingdom of Saudi Arabia has spent thousands of billions of its income on charity. It has given a great deal to developing and sisterly countries in a spirit of genuine and brotherly cooperation, keeping all the time a low profile and never trying to play up its role in this connection. So many are those by whom the Kingdom stood in joy and adversity, in private and in public.

The Kingdom has often taken the initiative to give relief aid to victims of natural disasters in various countries. It has been doing all that as part of its duty under the umbrella of Islamic brotherhood and in compliance with a saying by the Prophet–peace be upon him– which states that Moslems are like a structure in which the various parts reinforce one another . . .

It follows therefore that if they mean by their call the need for the implementation of the laws of Islamic Shari'a, it must be clear by now that the Kingdom has satisfied the requirements specified by the rules of Islam many times over. Likewise, if what they mean is to promote the concept of mutual support, do justice to the underprivileged and come to the aid of the helpless, it should prove easy to establish that the Kingdom has fully satisfied this need. But if some other motive is behind their call, then it is only fair that we should not honor it with a comment. For our part it is enough to have the satisfaction that all the things we do are done with clear conscience . . .

What else remained to be said, brothers? Justice has emerged triumphant, falsehood has fizzled out and the clouds of distress have cleared away. Kuwait is now liberated and Saddam Hussein stands haunted by his own crimes. Those who backed him up in the past are no longer sure that they did the right thing and are now busy reconsidering their previous policies, but remorse at this point is of little value.''

Chapter 3

Historical Perspective on Iraq and the Gulf

A brief background history on Iraq, the State of Kuwait and the Gulf will pave the way to describing some other topics which will prove to be relevant to the Gulf War. The conflicts after 1958 and the rise of Saddam Hussein to power in Iraq, along with the Iran-Iraq War, will give us the necessary prelude leading to the heart of the crisis and then the invasion of the State of Kuwait by Iraq.

Mesopotamia To Present Day Iraq

The history of today's Iraq reaches far back into ancient times. The fertile valley between the Tigris and the Euphrates rivers witnessed the founding of earliest kingdoms and civilizations. This land has been known since ancient times as Mesopotamia. The name Mesopotamia comes from "mesoe," meaning middle and "potomas," meaning river. Thus, "the land between the rivers." This region between the Euphrates and Tigris rivers extends all the way from the mountains of Armenia south to the Arabian Gulf and from the Syrian desert east to the Iranian Plateau region. The two famous rivers have their sources from the mountains of Asia Minor and flow in a southeasterly direction toward the Arabian Gulf. Despite the vast expanse of desert, from 4,000 to 3,000 B.C., a stretch of fertile land called the Fertile Crescent extended from the Arabian Gulf around the northern parts of the Arabian peninsula to Palestine on the west. The valley of the two rivers, being part of this Crescent, was fertile because of silt deposits. Although average rainfall over Mesopotamia was small, about three inches per year, the abundance of water from the two rivers was a lifeline for men and agriculture in ancient times and in present day as well. Various canals and dikes were built and the earliest of civilizations were formed before 3,000 B.C. The Sumerians, appearing on the scene around 3,500 B.C., established a civilized community. Discoveries unearthed by archaeologists compelled historians and scholars to realize that this is where old civilization had begun!

Shortly after the Third Millenium B.C., the Sumerians began a steady decline. The cities which were built by them, namely Ur, Lagsh, Kish and Uruk were forced into an Empire under the domain of a Semitic people called the Akkadians. The Akkadians, under the leadership of Sargon built their Empire around the year 2,350 B.C. They built the city of Akkad in the northern part of central Mesopotamia. The Sumero-Akkadian culture was finally superseded by the Semitic people known as the Babylonians. This took place around the year 2,000 B.C.

The height of the ancient Kingdom of Babylonia was reached around the reign of Hammurabi, who was the sixth King of the Babylonians. He was famous for the legal code which was a collection of laws inscribed on a large stone containing 282 articles with a prologue in which Hammurabi recognized the existence of seventeen gods and goddesses. At the foundation of the legal code was the dictum "an eye for an eye and a tooth for a tooth." Under this code, commerce, industry and agriculture were carefully controlled by the government. People who failed to keep their canals and dikes in good condition or those who did not cultivate their fields were punished.

With the dawn of the twelfth century B.C., Babylon was declining rapidly. The Assyrians took this opportunity to rise. These semitic people had built their state called Assur (Ashur) around the year 3,000 B.C. in the northeastern part of Mesopotamia. This city-state was built on the banks of the Tigris river. The Assyrians established a kingdom which grew very powerful and became an empire after conquering Babylonia, Syria and Egypt. The Assyrian Empire reached its zenith under Sargon the Second between 722–705 B.C. However, a swift decline had begun during the second half of the seventh century B.C. Finally, their capital, Nineveh, had fallen in the year 612 B.C. and a total collapse of their Assyrian state took place in the year 606 B.C. The downfall of the Assyrians happened at the hands of the Chaldeans, inhabitants of ancient Babylonia, in cooperation with the Medes and the Persians. The Medes had built a state around the year 1,000 B.C., on the eastern side of Mesopotamia. The Babylonians established their independence in 625 B.C. under their own King and during the years 604–561 B.C., his son, the legendary Nebuchadnezzar, became the ruler. By 587 B.C., his strong army reached the gates of Jerusalem. After a siege of eight months, the city was captured and thousands of Jews were exiled to Babylonia. Upon the death of this famous King, rapid decline befell Babylonia which was captured by the Persians in 538 B.C.

During the sixth century B.C., Babylon was the largest and most prosperous city known to the world. The Chaldeans, resident of Babylonia, were well known for astrology, a science which affected the Romans and the West hundreds of years later.

Around 550 B.C. the Persians, who were the original inhabitants of the Plateau named Iran, had a famous ruler named Cyrus the Great. The Persians were allied with, but were dominated by, the Medes. Cyrus the Great overthrew the Medes government and became their master. He then attacked Babylon and all of Mesopotamia fell to him in the year 538 B.C. The Persians ruled the land until 330 B.C., when Alexander the Great overtook the Persian Empire. He died in Babylon in the year 323 B.C. His successors were the Seleucids. Their rule covered Syria, Mesopotamia and Persia. They built their capital, Seleucia, on the Tigris river not far from Baghdad. The Parthians conquered the Seleucids in the year 138 B.C. From that time on, a continued struggle persisted and Mesopotamia became a battleground, initially, between the Parthians and the Romans, then between the Sassanids and Byzantines.

This incessant warring and division between the various factions persisted until the seventh century, thus opening the doors to Arab Moslem conquerors appearing on the horizon. The struggle for supremacy raging between these powers made Mesopotamia again a battleground for the various rival contenders seeking the Arab Caliphate. In the year 637 A.D. present-day Iraq was conquered by the Arabs. For nearly a century, the Umayyad Caliphs ruled Iraq as a part of the Islamic and Arab World Empire. However, between the years 750 to 1258 A.D., Baghdad became the capital of the Abbasid Caliphate. It became the center for the Moslem world and the main focus of Arab power. The zenith of the Arab Empire was reached in the year 787 to 809, during the time of the Caliph Haroun Al-Rashid. Under his rule and also the rule of his enlightened son, the Caliph Al-Ma'moun, the capital city of the Abbasid dynasty, Baghdad, became a great center of civilization and cultural interaction. In fact, it represented the brightest period in Arab history for science, literature, astronomy and the arts. But this glory was not to last forever! The Mongol invasion took place in the early part of the 13th century. It destroyed a flourishing economy, devastated a budding culture and in the year 1258 Genghis Khan's grandson Hulagu Khan sacked Baghdad, bringing devastation and total destruction to the city and whatever progress it represented. Over eight hundred thousand people were killed and libraries were burned.

Many translations of scientific work took place during the apogee of the Arab Empire. Impressive works in literature, astronomy, philosophy, algebra, geometry and medicine were accomplished. Progress in science, technology and arts were transferred to the west when the west was in the darks of civilization. The famous "Arabian Nights" stories also contributed to making Haroun Al-Rashid a legend for all times.

The attack of the Mongols was the dawn of a very dark period in Arab history, where civilization declined and population decreased markedly. Canals and other means of civilized progress were destroyed.

By the year 1410 A.D. the Turkomans coming from Anatolia gained control of Mesopotamia, where incompetent administrations and dynastic strifes gave rise to a disastrous situation. Tamerlane conquered Baghdad in the year 1393. While in the year 1508 Safawid Ismail who was a Persian, occupied Baghdad and was able to hold control over Mesopotamia. His rule did not last beyond the year 1534, when the region came under the nominal control of the Ottoman Turks. In the year 1534 it was Suleiman the Magnificent who conquered and ruled Baghdad except for a brief period between 1621 and 1638 when the Safawid Persians reoccupied Baghdad for a short duration. From the year 1534 onward Baghdad the former Abbasid capital, and for that matter the Arab world, was under the control of the Ottoman Empire. This grip over Arab territory, sometimes strong, at other times nominal, was exercised in the name of Islam and unfortunately represented the darkest period in Arab history. It continued until the dawn of World War I in 1914 which brought about the defeat of Turkey along with the Axis powers at the conclusion of the War in 1918.

British Role

Great Britain, being a major world power in the nineteenth and twentieth centuries and having the control over India, had much interest in securing the safe routes for trade to its colonies. The Ottoman railroad concession to Germany in 1899 alarmed the British. Between 1912 and 1914, the section of the Berlin-Baghdad railway connecting Baghdad and Samarra was finished. Mesopotamia became important to Great Britain and later on to the rising power of Germany which allied itself with Turkey during the war. Great Britain, along with the Allies, raced to defend their interests and secure free routes for the survival of their trade. They had to stop any encroachments or threat to their interests. With the outbreak of World War I, Great Britain occupied the lower part of Mesopotamia and Baghdad was captured in 1917. Mosul was also captured in 1918. The League of Nations gave Great Britain a mandate over most of what had been known in ancient history as Mesopotamia, and the land became the Kingdom of Iraq in August, 1921. Faisal, son of Sherif Hussein of the Hijaz, was awarded the throne for Iraq as a reward for his fight against the Turks, and his brother Abdullah also became the ruler of Trans-Jordan for the same reason. The Arabs were disappointed with the outcome of World War I because they were promised independence upon the liberation from the Turks. However, the Allies divided their spheres of influence in the region and allotted whatever minimal rewards they desired at the time. Arab hopes were raised because of the promises made by the Allies and by the fourteen points declared, in support of self-determination, by President Wilson of the United States of America. However, many of these hopes were dashed away by the proceedings at the Peace Conference. The mandate system implied international control and recognized provisional independence of the countries under a mandate. But it also stipulated that a country under a mandate would be guided by the mandatory power until such a time when it could muster its own energies and experience to rule itself. The San Remo Conference of April, 1925 giving Britain the mandate power over Iraq, stirred nationalistic feelings in the Iraqis.

A parliament was established and met for the first time in 1925. By 1932, Iraq was admitted to the League of Nations and its independence was formally recognized. Older treaties with Britain were replaced by a 1930 treaty which allowed Great Britain to have two air bases in Iraq. King Faisal died on September 7, 1933. He was replaced by his twenty-two year old son Ghazi I, who was born in 1912. He was educated in England at Harrow and at the Military college in Baghdad. He was married in 1934 to his cousin the Amira Alia who was the daughter of King Ali, brother of Faisal I. After ruling for six years, he was killed in an automobile accident in April, 1939. Faisal II, born on May 2, 1935, the son of Ghazi, was an infant. He was proclaimed successor to the throne, but under the Regency of his maternal uncle Abdul Ilah, who was appointed Regent and heir to the throne by an act of parliament. He had a British education at Victoria college in Alexandria, Egypt. The young King received an elite, British education. On Saturday, May 2, 1953, upon reaching maturity, Faisal II was proclaimed King of Iraq. The young King was well liked by his people who held high hopes for bringing progress ànd modernization to Iraq.

However, problems were brewing for the independent state of Iraq. In 1933 troubles developed from the Assyrians and some tribes revolted between 1935 and 1936. The fires of nationalism energized emotions against Great Britain who was sponsoring Zionism and establishing homes for the Jews in Palestine, as proclaimed in the Balfour declaration of 1917. Fuel was added to the fire by Nazi propagandists who had their own design on the region. By this time, around 1935, three major political alignments were taking place in Iraq, one was the predominantly national and partly liberal group, the second faction was the tribes, and the third was the growing power of the army. The latter gained popularity by enforcing order and by smashing uprisings, especially in 1935. The opposition was suppressed by the government. In due time, a coalition between the Ahli group and the Army led to

the Bakr Sidqi Coup d'Etat of October, 1936. All the officers professed nationalism, while the Ahli group advocated socialism. The balance tipped in favor of the Army and the cabinets became essentially subservient to the prevailing force of the Army. Its leader Bakr Sidqi was assassinated. The Army continued to be the main deciding force behind the rise and fall of almost all cabinets between the years 1937 and 1941. This created a fertile ground for overthrow of governments and recurrence of Coup d'Etat's by the military. Thus, the political life in modern Iraq was not a healthy one. Administrative instability was predominant. With the outbreak of World War II, Britain was alarmed by the strong German influence on Iraqi affairs. It demanded that the Treaty of 1932 be applied. Iraq remained nonbelligerent until January, 1943. Ill-feelings about British influence, division among politicians and strong Nazi propaganda, led to another military Coup d'Etat in 1941. Sporadic violence and varied degrees of sabotage took place against the British, especially under the government of Prime Minister

Rashid Ali Kaylani. The coup was supported by Nazi Germany but the expected help for the coup leaders did not arrive in the quantities needed and thus, the coup failed. British forces put down the uprising without much difficulty. After this failed coup, Iraq observed the terms of the Anglo-Iraqi Treaty and by 1943 declared war on the Axis. Iraq became a member of the Arab League, which was formed on March 22, 1945, and also in 1945 it became a charter member of the United Nations organization. During the Regency of Abdul Ilah the most influential political figure was Nuri Al-Sa'id. By 1954, he became Prime Minister of Iraq for the twelfth time.

During this period, strong nationalist forces were emerging in Egypt. With the overthrow of King Farouk of Egypt, the road was paved for a new personality that was to become international in stature and influence, namely Gamal Abdul Nasser. Under the Premiership of Nuri, Iraq was strongly pro-western. In fact, by February, 1955, Iraq claimed an alliance, called the Baghdad Pact, which included Iraq, Turkey, Pakistan, Iran and great Britain. Although the United States was not a member of the Alliance, it was nevertheless a member of a number of committees and supportive of the Pact.

Nuri Al-Sa'id was the first Chief of Staff of the Iraqi Army. In this capacity, and because of his Premiership along with his strong preference for the West and Turkish alliance, he was a good target for liberal forces in Iraq and the Arab world. In fact, he encumbered much hate from these forces. The sentiment was fanned by nationalistic fevers, various political moves, and a powerful propaganda machine emanating from the voice of the Arabs in Cairo, Egypt. All this made Nuri Al-Sa'id a symbol of hate among the Arab masses. The invasion of the Suez Canal by the British, French and Israelis in 1956 did not make life any easier for the government in Iraq. They remained pro-Western, although they professed allegiance to the common Arab cause. However, nationalist aspirations were better espoused, diffused and extensively used by President Nasser of Egypt. This avalanche of nationalist feelings energized by Nasser led to the union between Egypt and Syria on February 21, 1958 under the name of United Arab Republic (UAR). This in turn led to a hasty union between the Hashemite Kingdom of Jordan and the Kingdom of Iraq on May 12 of the same year. The former union was not to last but a short three years and the latter only a matter of a couple of months.

During these difficult times, when turbulent undercurrents were developing and jolting the basic foundation of Iraq and for that matter the entire Middle East, Iraqi politicians and military officers were keeping an eye on a wealthy neighbor to the south, namely, the State of Kuwait.

Beginnings of Kuwait

Archaeological discoveries on Failaka Island in the Arabian Gulf, date as far back as the year 525 B.C. Findings seem to indicate that this region of the Gulf was an important supply route for nations trading with the large Indian Continent. There is evidence that some seafaring inhabitants also had early migrations to the Eastern shores of Africa.

More recent history of Kuwait begins in the early part of the eighteenth century. Around the year 1716 A.D., several people of the Utaiba tribe migrated from the Uneiza region in Saudi Arabia. These tribesmen emigrated from Najd in Central Arabia in search of water and livelihood and settled on the shores of the Arabian Gulf in present-day Kuwait City; building a fort in the area and thus the name of Kuwait or little fort is mentioned. Kuwait is the diminutive for "kut" which means "fort." These migrants made their living from searching for pearls, fishing and trading. Also they built small sailing vessels known as Dhows.

With the dawn of the year 1756, the settled tribesmen chose a leader from the Sabbah family. He was Sheikh Sabbah Abu Abdullah and thus the present Sabbah ruling dynasty was founded. The settlers in Kuwait enjoyed the waters of the Gulf and left their nomadic ways behind. They became merchants and sailors. They built mud houses, used ports, and rapidly became seafaring traders in pearls and other merchandise. Despite the wealth derived from waters of the Gulf, the Kuwaitis remained relatively poor.

Although the Turks had occupied the Arab land for many years, their control over Kuwait was minimal. In fact, Kuwait has never been under the Ottoman rule or ruled by them in any substantial manner; it has always discharged its authority relatively independently of the Turkish government and certainly wasn't accustomed to receiving any orders or directives from any country under Turkish occupation, such as the state of Iraq. While the Turks appointed rulers in a number of other Arab countries be it Iraq, Syria, or others, they did not have to appoint a ruler for Kuwait.

Prior to World War I, the Sabbah dynasty ruling Kuwait carried out a shrewd policy to secure their independence and freedom of movement, despite the various winds of influence which came from the major powers of the time, be it the Turks, the Germans or later on the British. Kuwait was relatively independent from Ottoman rulers. This fact is substantiated by a number of facts including:

- The Islamic history of Kuwait territory makes it a part of the region which extended from Mount Sanan and the northern border of the Empty Quarters in the south of Arabia, and included the Eastern Region of the Arabian peninsula. The tribes inhabiting the region had no allegiance of any kind to the rulers of Iraq. Their land was never a part of any Iraqi domain. "Kuwait has never been within Iraqi boundaries."

- The Turkish Sultan did not appoint the ruler of Kuwait.
- There is no proof of a payment of taxes for government employees managed by the Ottoman rulers.
- Ottoman castles and other influences on populations are not found in Kuwait, when they are abundantly found in a number of other Arab countries.
- The Kuwaiti ruler never asked assistance from the Sultan of Turkey.
- Kuwait was not under the dominance of Basra, nor the nineteenth province of present day Iraq. In fact, many a time those opposing the power and authority of the Turkish rulers sought refuge in Kuwait. For example, the British historian Bridges, who was an employee of the East India Company, fled to Kuwait in the year 1794 because of a dispute which materialized between the Turkish rulers in Basra and the company. The historian was well received by the ruler of Kuwait. Certainly, if Kuwait was a part of Basra which is a city in southern Iraq, the ruler of Kuwait would not be at liberty to accept someone who objected to Ottoman authority in Basra, especially if Kuwait was under the grip of the Ottoman authorities. Again, this British historian stated that Moustafa Agha or Moustafa Al-Kurdi fled with a friend whose name was Al-Sa'doun who was the ruler of Al-Mountafiq, since both of them had some dispute with Souleiman Pasha who was the Turkish ruler of Baghdad. This took place in 1789; these two political refugees were welcomed in Kuwait. Certainly, Kuwait could not have been a part of the Basra province which was under the grip of the Turks. If they were, they would not dare accept political refugees fleeing from the Turkish authorities.
- In any event, the Turks did not show much interest in Kuwait which was at the time a barren desert with meager resources, if any! Thus, they left it relatively independent, just as they did with the Najd realm of Saudi Arabia where they satisfied themselves with having a minor influence on the Hasa region of the Eastern Province. However, as mentioned in the first Chapter, on the eve of World War I in 1913, Ibn Saud, with his daring attack on the Turks in this region, was able to dislodge them and remove any remaining influence they might have had on that part of Arabia.

- The Al-Saud family sought refuge in 1890 and were certainly welcomed by the ruling family of Sabbah in Kuwait. It is a known fact that the Ottoman Empire was supporting Ibn Rashid who was their ally and who was in fact ruling the Saudi realm of Najd by appointing his own governor in Riyadh. Thus, if the Kuwaitis did not have the relative independence from the Ottoman grip, knowing the fact that Ibn Rashid was an ally of the Turks, they would not have dared to have the Al-Sauds come in as refugees, when the competition was supreme and severe between the Al-Rashids and the Al-Sauds. Ibn Rashid was certainly financed and militarily supported by them. It is a historical fact that Al-Sauds were guests of Moubarak Al-Sabbah, ruler of Kuwait at the time. They remained in his hospitality for over a decade, until the young Ibn Saud returned to Riyadh in January, 1902 and liberated the city. From there, he carried on his struggle to unite the people of Saudi Arabia, until in 1932 his land became the independent and unified Kingdom of Saudi Arabia. It is quite a historical coincidence, a fate of destiny, that nearly a hundred years have elapsed and we come to witness the rise of Saddam Hussein and his false claims against Kuwaitis, through invading it, occupying it and making refugees out of an entire population. And where did the Kuwaitis go to receive comfort, compassion and care? They went to none other than Saudi Arabia and were the guests of the Al-Saud family and the people of the Kingdom of Saudi Arabia.
- Going back again prior to World War I, at a time when Sheikh Moubarak Al-Sabbah ruled between 1896 and 1915, he feared that his nation might be annexed either by the Ottomans or other major powers. He was very concerned and had some rapprochement with the British. He had every reason to be concerned since the Russians were seeking to set a Coaling station in his country and also the Germans and Turks were planning to make Kuwait City a terminus for the famous Berlin-Baghdad Railroad. Special attention was being given to Kuwait by the European powers and in order to fend off the growing influence of Germany and Turkey in Kuwait, the ruler of this small nation, Sheikh Moubarak appealed to Great Britain for protection. In the year 1899, an alliance was forged and a treaty was signed between Moubarak representing the State of Kuwait and the representatives of the British Government, in which the ruler of Kuwait agreed not to let his territory be subject to the influence

of any foreign power nor receive any such foreign representatives without the agreement of the British. The British in return would pay yearly financial aid to Kuwait in the sum of 50,000 Rupees, the currency used in India which was also under British rule. The agreement was also binding not only to the ruler but also to his heirs. Again, the British government would guarantee the protection and defense of Kuwait, who was in need for a strong protector and this was achieved through this agreement with the British.

● The following is a copy of this agreement signed in 1899.

Agreement of January 23, 1899
Between Great Britain and the Sheikh of Kuwait
(In the name of God Almighty)

The object of writing this lawful and honorable pact is, that it is hereby stipulated and agreed, between Lieutenant-Colonel Malcolm John Meade, I.S.C., His British Majesty's Political Resident, on behalf of the British Government, on the one part, and Sheikh Moubarak-bin-Sheikh Sabbah, Sheikh of Kuwait, on the other part, that the said Sheikh Moubarak-bin-Sheikh Sabbah, of his own free will and desire, does hereby pledge and bind himself, his heirs and successors, not to receive the agent or representative of any power or government at Kuwait, or at any other place within the limits of his territory, without the prior approval of the British Government; and he further binds himself, his heirs and successors, not to cede, sell, lease, mortgage, or give for occupation or for any other purpose, any portion of his territory to the government or subjects of any other power without the previous consent of His Majesty's Government for these purposes. This agreement also extends to any portion of the territory of the said Sheikh Moubarak which may now be in possession of the subjects of any other Government.

In token of the conclusion of this lawful and honorable pact Lieutenant-Colonel Malcolm John Meade, I.S.C., His British Majesty's Political Resident in the Persian Gulf, and Sheikh Moubarak-bin-Sheikh Sabbah, the former on behalf of the British Government, and the latter on behalf of himself, his heirs and successors, do each, in the presence of witnesses affix their signatures, on this the 10th day of Ramadan, 1316, A.H. corresponding to the 23rd day of January, 1899.

(L.S.) M. J. MEADE, Political Resident in the Persian Gulf
(L.S.) MOUBARAK-AL-SABBAH

Witnesses:

(L.S.) E. Wickham Hore, Captain, I.M.S.

(L.S.) J. Calcott Gaskin

(L.S.) Mohammed Rahim-Bin-Abdul Nebi Saffer

- The iron clad agreement demanded loyalty from both sides and served the interests of both nations. While it may have sounded very restrictive, in reality the Kuwaiti ruler was given a free hand to conduct his internal policy. When it came to foreign policy, sincere and serious consultations were always conducted and the wishes of the Amir were always respected. The Amir also remained loyal to the British who protected the independence of the Emirate.

- On the eve of World War I, in July, 1913, the war fever was brewing in Europe. The Turks and the British concluded the Anglo-Turkish agreement recognizing the State of Kuwait as an autonomous district of the Ottoman Empire. Also, the frontiers were formally established. However soon after that, the Turks allied themselves with Germany and ratifying the Accord was delayed. To bolster their interests in the Gulf region, the British recognized Kuwait as an independent entity from the Turks, right on the eve of World War I. This led to full cooperation from the Kuwaiti ruler who helped the British in their campaign against the Turks in Iraq.

- With the dismantling of the Ottoman Empire, the victorious allies which included, Great Britain, France and Russia, divided the former Ottoman territories into various new nations and new spheres of influence. Many border disputes ensued. Many attempts were made to solve them. In 1922, the British High Commissioner Sir Percy Cox held a Conference in Uqair. The Conference included, Saudi Arabia, Kuwait and Iraq. Some territorial adjustments were made at the Conference and a Neutral Zone was created, where tribes from neighboring countries could use it without bringing about conflicts and thus endangering relations among each neighboring country. In order to dissipate any misunderstanding about the borders between Iraq and Kuwait, it became necessary to exchange letters of understanding between the British Ministry of Foreign Affairs and the Prime Minister of Iraq at the time, Nuri Al-Sai'd. The letters were dated April 17, 1924. These considered Kuwait as an independent nation and an international political entity. One of the Foreign Office reports dated February 6, 1929, certifies this fact about the independence of the State of Kuwait and that the Sheikh of Kuwait had contractual treaty relations with the government of his Majesty and that the

Sheikh was recognized as an independent ruler of the State of Kuwait.

The Uqair Conference settled the borders for a long time to come. Although Iraq was left with a coastline on the Gulf of about 26 miles long, its passage to the Arabian Gulf was through the Shatt Al-Arab Waterway which is at the end of the convolution of the Tigris and Euphratis. With Kuwait possessing about 120 miles of shoreline on the Gulf, a great natural harbor, in fact, the largest in the region, Iraq kept a sharp eye toward its neighbor, Kuwait despite the fact that it had its own outlet on the Gulf. These borders were confirmed again after Iraqi independence was declared in 1932. It was not long after that, Iraq began to press and agitate for the right to lease some of the Kuwaiti Islands located off the Gulf Coast, claiming that these were essentially, the property of Iraq. Relations began to worsen after the death of King Faisal I in 1933. Iraqi meddling and agitation against Kuwait and the Sabbah family began to gain momentum.

The Sheikh of Kuwait granted an oil concession in 1934 to the Kuwait Oil Company which was owned by the Anglo-Persian Oil Company and American Gulf Exploration Company. In 1938 oil was discovered in the Burgin Oil field about 80 miles from the Saudi border. Due to the outbreak of World War II, production and further exploration did not occur until in 1946 when oil was produced in commercial quantities. The history of Kuwait was never to be the same!

When exploration began around 1934 it brought with it special attention and increased importance for Kuwait. It also brought special worries and sinister designs on the small state, which had the potential of becoming very rich. Around that time, growing tension was developing between the Sabbahs and other merchant families seeking to limit the power of the ruling family and criticizing the lack of development plans. Some people had their eyesight on the possibility of great wealth from oil. Also the rise in Arab nationalism brought more stress and strain into the Kuwaiti political fabric.

In 1938, King Ghazi of Iraq kept an eye and an attentive ear on the possible bright future of Kuwait, due to oil exploration and the possible discovery in large amounts. He had his designs on absorbing the State of Kuwait. In fact, it is reported that he had a radio station in his own place broadcasting through it strong attacks and diatribes against the small peaceful state of Kuwait. He portrayed himself as an Arab nationalist also attacking the French rule in Syria and Zionist designs on Palestine along with attacks on the British influence in the Gulf region. His intention to annex the State of Kuwait was the first time such a definite claim was made. King Ghazi was dreaming of extending his Monarchy to encompass the territories of the Fertile

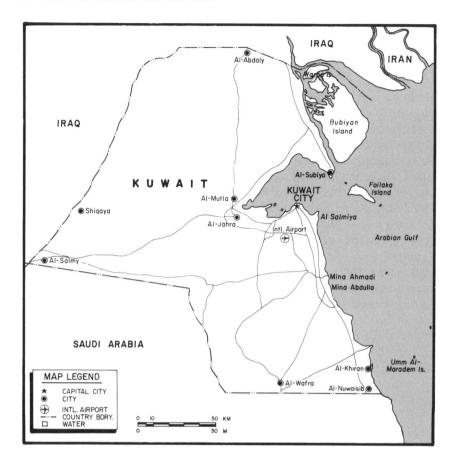

Crescent: a fertile region extending from Syria to the Arabian Gulf and including Syria, Iraq, Jordan, Palestine and Lebanon. He attempted to incite the Kuwaiti population against their rulers, but his attempts failed. When he sent a force to invade the small country, his expansionist moves crumbled, then backfired. The British were always there to support the Kuwaitis and honor their treaty obligations with them. Also, fate came to the aid of the small nation, because King Ghazi died in an automobile accident in April, 1939.

Relative calm existed on the borders of Kuwait from that time until the late fifties. The dawn of 1958 brought more difficult and ominous signs to the safety and security of the State of Kuwait.

Fall of the Monarchy in Iraq in 1958

Political stability was not in the cards for the Iraqi government nor the Iraqi people. The fires of nationalism and sometimes extremism swept the country and the region. Another attempt was made at controlling Kuwait during the Hashemite Union between Iraq and Jordan toward the end of February, 1958. The agreement was to acknowledge the independence of Kuwait on a condition that the government of the union would be responsible for foreign policy, the military and custom matters of the state of Kuwait, along with a number of other control practices and consultations with the Amir of Kuwait would be the practice on matters of foreign and defense prior to final decisions. However, this attempt at luring Kuwait into the Union did not succeed and was short-lived, because of a fateful turn of events which took place immediately thereafter . . .

Accumulation of contempt and hatred gathered through the years against the rule of Abdul Ilah and the Prime Minister Nuri Al-Sai'd of Iraq. Other reasons as well, taking their lead and inspiration from the recent history of the Iraqi army and a series of coup d'Etats in the recent decades led to some sinister plans and designs to overthrow the Iraqi Monarchy, although the young King, Faisal II, was well liked by the populace. The power then was invested in Faisal's uncle, Abdul Ilah and his Prime Minister Nuri Al-Sa'id.

A number of military officers began secret designs for overthrowing the government and Monarchy. A group led by General Abdul Karim Qassem developed their successful plan. On the dawn of July 14, around 4:00 A.M. this General, his officers and supporting army executed a Coup d' Etat taking over Baghdad in progressive steps. By 6:00 A.M. an army detachment surrounded the Rihab Palace in order to subdue the Royal family. Bullets were pouring on the castle. One of the Royal Guard officers informed the Royal Family that the twentieth regiment of the army engineered the revolution and now controlled Baghdad. The Royal Guard exchanged fire with the Revolutionary Army until support came from the Military School for Light Equipment which was near the Royal Palace. Finally, the upper floor of the castle was on fire. The Royal Family tried to avoid the searing flames to no avail. The revolutionary officers demanded that the Royal Guard inform the Royal Family to give up and surrender to the Revolution. A short while later, the Commander of the Royal Guard ceased to resist and decided to cooperate with the Revolution by ordering the Royal Guard to leave their weapons and stop shooting immediately. At this moment Abdul Ilah and the Royal Family decided that the situation was hopeless and came out to surrender. They all came out to the garden of the castle holding a white banner. They were surrounded by the revolutionary military men and their officers. Despite their surrender, mercy was not in the hearts of the revolutionaries nor their chief. They poured on their bullets which tore the Royal Family apart and brought death to the young King, his uncle Abdul Ilah and to Queen Nafisa, mother of Prince Abdul Ilah and also the Princess Abdiyah.

Many atrocities were committed after the brutal death of the young King and his Royal Family. The car that was carrying the bodies of the Royal victims was stopped by wild mobs of people. The body of Abdul Ilah was pulled out of the car which was on its way to the Ministry of Defense. His body was torn to pieces and whatever was left was hung in front of the Ministry of Defense. Some of the mad people in the mob took gruesome souvenirs such as a finger, an ear or an organ from the body of Abdul Ilah. However, the thirst of the masses for revenge, death and destruction was not quenched by this alone. The attention of the Revolution and the masses poured toward Nuri Al-Sai'd, the Prime Minister. A group of army soldiers and officers raced to his offices but he was alerted in time and fled for his life in his night clothes. He jumped from a house opening overlooking the Tigris river, took a small boat, and sought refuge trying to avoid imminent death. In the morning of July 15, the Prime Minister was on the move again, this time wearing women's clothing, but the masses were then on the lookout for him. Someone, finally, discovered him because his pajamas were peaking from under the long dress. A shop owner recognized him and shouted, "Nuri Al-Sa'id, catch him!" Within an instant, the masses held him to the ground. He was killed instantly and his companion, the wife of a friend was also killed. His body was torn to pieces by the masses.

An accomplice of Qassem's was Colonel Abdul Salam Aref, who read a statement proclaiming the Monarchy in Iraq was dead. Immediately, a huge mob went through the streets calling for revenge and destruction. They attacked the British Embassy, killed a number of Jordanian Ministers and extracted revenge from the Royal Family and their supporters. The revolutionaries promised a new government by the people–a people's republic. However, this was not but a momentary dream, because in no time Qassem became the "Sole Leader." He established an authoritarian regime that brought nothing but instability and turmoil to his land.

One of the ironies of his time was the formation of the people's court under a close relative named Al-Mahdawi. This court became, essentially, a mockery to justice and a kangaroo court.

The proceedings of the Mahdawi court were broadcast on nationwide television for everybody to watch and be entertained. It was certainly a circus! Upon opening sessions of the court, the presiding Mahdawi entered along with the other members of the court and officials. The spectators explode into a spontaneous demonstration with applause and slogans reverberating through the "Hall of Justice." At times, this went on for a quarter of an hour or more, followed by popular poetry and other speeches interrupted only by cheers and more deafening applause. When a frenzy had been reached, it became time for the presiding judge Mahdawi to rise and give his commentary on political life and the great virtues of the revolution under Qassem. Here he attacked the enemies of the republic, the so-called traitors and the errors of the Monarchy, always ending with the luscious praise of the great virtues and achievements of the "Sole Leader," Qassem. In this atmosphere of excitement and expectation to punish the enemies of the revolution, Mahdawi sat in his chair and presided over the court. Such proceedings went on and on for several months. (Proudly displayed in the court was the Lenin Prize of Justice granted to Mahdawi.) Many sentences were short but some received the death penalty. By September, 1959 the Mahdawi court had condemned to death and executed fourteen people.

The Arab Nationalists were agitating for unity with President Nasser of Egypt, who by now had already formed a union between Egypt and Syria in February, 1958. Although President Nasser was very happy to see his rival Nuri Al-Sa'id out of power, he urged his followers in Iraq to press for union with the United Arab Republic. However, Qassem was not much impressed by the idea of union with Egypt and Syria. In no time conflicts began to develop between Qassem of Iraq and the nationalists who supported Nasser of Egypt. In order to stem the tide of the nationalists, Qassem sought support from other quarters. This time, he invited the leader of the Kurds, Moustafa Barazani, to come back to Iraq after he was exiled in Moscow. This way he thought he could bring about a balance with the forces opposing him. The Kurdish leader, initially, received good treatment but Barazani quickly realized that Qassem would not meet basic autonomy demands for the Kurds in Iraq. There was always a fear that such autonomy would lead to independence for the Kurdish people, and thus Iraq would lose a good bit of its oil-rich northern territory. Good relations with the Kurds were not meant to last. They reached a low ebb in September, 1961 when a civil war between the Iraqi army and the Kurds exploded into open warfare.

Prior to September, 1961 another major event for the region was developing. The small, but very rich, state of Kuwait was declared independent by the British on June 19, 1961. Not more than six days later, on June 25, 1961 the Iraqi government, under the leadership of the "Sole Leader" Qassem declared Kuwait an integral part of Iraq. Their argument was that Kuwait as well as Iraq were ruled by the Turks and that Kuwait was under the same province as Basra. Thus, their logic concluded that Kuwait was a part of Iraq. The Iraqi ruler

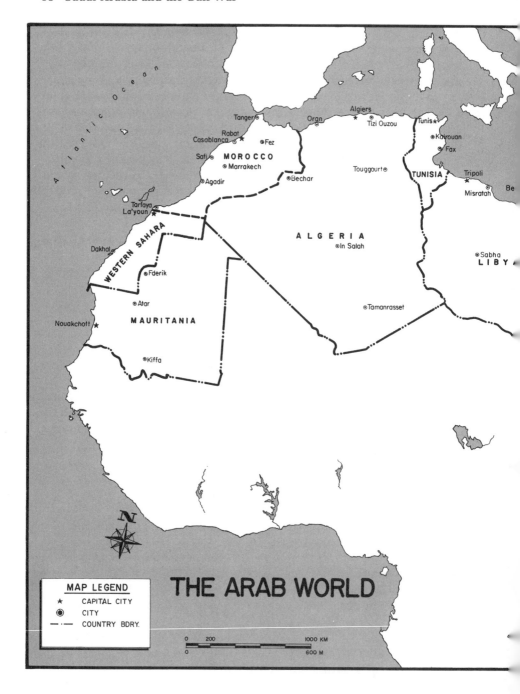

THE ARAB WORLD

MAP LEGEND
★   CAPITAL CITY
◎   CITY
—·—   COUNTRY BDRY.

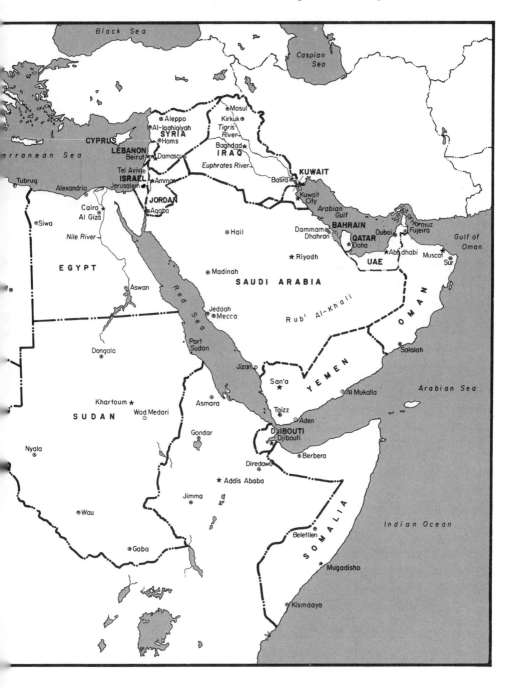

stated that socially and ethnically, Iraq and Kuwait were the same. This kind of talk was deeply disturbing to the Kuwaitis and their friends, especially the British and the Saudis. The Iraqi regime amassed a large number of troops along the Kuwaiti border and threatened to occupy the newly independent state of Kuwait. The ruler of this small nation, Abdullah Al-Sabbah, immediately appealed to the British and the Saudis for help. With the imminent danger to the existence of this small but rich nation, Great Britain and Saudi Arabia quickly responded to Kuwait's call for help and sent military assistance. The Speed of action and resolve deterred the Iraqis from occupying Kuwait and a tragedy was averted or postponed. By July 20, the Arab League which was formed in 1945, admitted the State of Kuwait as a full-fledged member. This was a direct answer to any Iraqi claims that Kuwait was an integral part of Iraq. Qassem and his Iraqi troops were forced to withdraw from the border. Kuwait also became a member of the United Nations. Being a member of these two prestigious organizations, Kuwait sought the protective umbrella and the peace motives inherently associated with these two world organizations. More than six thousand British and Saudi troops moved into Kuwait. By August, 1962 through some peaceful diplomatic moves, the Arab League replaced the forces in Kuwait with Arab forces from Jordan, Sudan and the United Arab Republic.

With the Kurds engaged in a civil war against Qassem and his army in September, 1961, and the nationalists stirred by fervor and calls of unity from Nasser of Egypt, not many political entities remained on the side of Qassem. Only the Communist Party remained for a while on his side and essentially, became an important pillar of his regime. The Communist Party had most of its membership from the Kurds, Shi'ites and a number of other minorities. It gained a foothold among the populace and finally formed the "Popular Resistance Force." This militia of the people had many excesses and began to frighten the populace. Of course, this led to deep rivalry with the forces of Arab unity supported by Nasser. Because the excesses were getting somewhat out of hand, Qassem felt compelled to limit their chaotic behavior. By doing so, he alienated the only organized group which remained supportive of his regime. In effect, on March, 1959 while the communists were holding a political rally in Mosul, the Arab nationalist officers in the city's garrison revolted but were immediately defeated and the Communists went on a wild rampage killing Arab nationalists and causing destruction and havoc. Several hundred people died. The Qassem regime embarked on a campaign of arresting and purging members of the Ba'ath Party and other nationalists. On October 7, 1959 a Ba'athist attempt on Qassem's life failed, but he was not as lucky the next time around. On February, 1963 another Ba'athist coup took place and the Qassem regime was overthrown. The coup was organized by the Ba'athists and their supporters from the Arab National-ist Officers Corps. It was led by Abdul Salam Aref. Qassem pleaded for his life to no avail! He was killed by a firing squad at the State television studio. In order to prove to the populace that Qassem was indeed shot and killed, the new revolutionaries exhibited his body in a gruesome manner dangling his head back and forth for a further proof that he was killed beyond any doubt. Battles raged in the streets of Baghdad for several days. Settling of scores was prevalent and over a thousand people were killed. Prisons were filled! Interrogation and torture became the norm. Not long after this period, on November 18, 1963, the radical Ba'athists became excessive and the Aref regime sup-ported by the moderates in the Ba'ath Party and moderate Ba'athist officers were able to crush the Ba'ath militia. Of course, the army as usual was the instrument of executing the plan. The new president appointed Ahmed Hasan Al-Bakr, a Ba'athist and previously one of the free officers that helped topple the Monarchy, as Vice President of Iraq. The new military machine was supportive of Arab nationalist movements for Arab unity, whose outspoken leader was Nasser of Egypt.

The overthrow of the Qassem regime brought a change in the mental-ity of the Iraqi military rulers, as far as the status of their neighbor in Kuwait was concerned. It was a breathing spell and a welcome happen-ing for the Kuwaitis. Not long before that date they had been shaken to the core because their beloved country was threatened to be deleted. Now the previous agreements that were reached were being honored, so was the Charter of the Arab League which respects the independence, sovereignty and integrity of all members of the League. Furthermore, a new agreement for understanding, cooperation and friendly relations was achieved. In fact, this agreement became a cornerstone for the settling of any border disputes between Iraq and Kuwait. This agreement was officially presented to the United Nations and it became an official document that was published among the Treaties that are supported and blessed by the United Nations. This move gave the agreement the international blessing and flavor deeply desired by the Kuwaiti rulers.

This legal document is presented here to show specifically, clearly and unequivocally that a binding agreement of substance and clarity existed between Iraq and Kuwait, where Iraq acknowledges the indepen-dence, political entity and integrity of the State of Kuwait and its borders.

United Nations–Treaty Series
1964
[Translation¹–Traduction²]

No. 7063. Agreed Minutes³ Between The State Of Kuwait And the Republic of Iraq Regarding The Restoration Of Friendly Relations, Recognition And Related Matters. Signed At Baghdad, On October 4, 1963

In response to the desire felt by both parties to eliminate all that blemishes the relations between both countries, the official Kuwaiti Delegation visiting the Republic of Iraq on an invitation from the Iraqi Prime Minister, held a meeting with the Iraqi Delegation in Baghdad on October 4, 1963.

The Kuwaiti Delegation was constituted as follows:

H.H. Shaikh Sabah Al-Salim Al-Sabah, Heir Apparent and Prime Minister;

H.E. Shaikh Saad Al-Abdullah Al-Salim Al-Sabah, Minister of the Interior and Acting Minister of Foreign Affairs;

H.E. Khalifa Khalid Al-Ghunaim, Minister of Commerce;

H.E. Ambassador Abdulrahman Ateeqi, Under-Secretary of the Ministry of Foreign Affairs.

The Iraqi Delegation was constituted as follows;

Major-General Ahmad Hassan Al-Bakre, Prime Minister;

First General Saleh Mahdi Ammash, Minister of Defense and Acting Minister of Foreign Affairs;

Dr. Mahmoud Mohammad Al-Homsi, Minister of Commerce;

Mr. Mohammad Kayyara, Acting Under-Secretary of Foreign Affairs.

The talks between the two delegations were conducted in an atmosphere rich in fraternal amity, tenacity to the Arab bond and consciousness of the close ties of neighbourliness and mutual interests.

Both sides affirming their deep-rooted desire in reinforcing their relations for the welfare of both countries, inspired by the high Arab aims; and

Believing in the need to rectify all that blemished the Iraqi-Kuwaiti relations as a result of the attitude of the past Kassim regime towards Kuwait before the dawn of the blessed revolution of the 14th of Ramadhan;

Source: United Nations in New York and Embassy of the State of Kuwait in Washington D.C., U.S.A.

¹ Translation provided by the Government of Kuwait.
² Traduction transmise par le Gouvernement de Koweit.
³ Came into force on October 4, 1963 by signature.

Convinced with the national duty dictating the inauguration of a new page consistent with the bonds and relations between the two Arab countries which are free from the artificial gap created by the past regime in Iraq;

Spurred by the belief of the two Governments in the entity of the Arab Nation and the inevitability of its Unity;

And after the Iraqi side having seen the statement delivered by the Government of Kuwait at the Kuwaiti National Assembly on the 9th of April, 1963, embodying the desire of Kuwait to work for the termination, in due time, of the Agreement concluded with the United Kingdom;

The two delegations have agreed to the following:

1. The Republic of Iraq recognized the independence and complete sovereignty of the State of Kuwait with its boundaries as specified in the letter of the Prime Minister of Iraq dated 21.7.1932 and which was accepted by the ruler of Kuwait in his letter dated 10.8.1932;

2. The two Governments shall work towards reinforcing the fraternal relations subsisting between the two sister countries, inspired by their national duty, common interest and aspiration to a complete Arab Unity;

3. The two Governments shall work towards establishing cultural, commercial and economical co-operation between the two countries and the exchange of technical information.

In order to realize all the foregoing objectives, they shall immediately establish diplomatic relations between them at the level of ambassadors.

IN WITNESS WHEREOF the heads of the two delegations have appended their signatures unto these minutes.

Sabah Al-Salim AL-SABAH   Ahmad Hassan AL-BAKRE
Head of Kuwaiti Delegation   Head of Iraqi Delegation

While the Kuwaitis, the Arab world and the World community were indeed happy to see such an agreement materialize, the future was holding dark secrets, indeed! The star of a man named Saddam Hussein was beginning to rise! In time it showered the region and especially the Kuwaitis with disaster and doom!

The Rise of Saddam Hussein

Saddam Hussein was born on April 28, 1937 in the town of Al-Auja near Tikrit. It is located about one hundred miles Northwest of Baghdad, the capital city of Iraq. This town, on the banks of the Tigris river, was to gain some fame in the years to come. When Saddam became the ruler of Iraq, he made his birthday a national holiday. He was born into a modest family of peasants. His father, Hussein Al-Majid died prior to Saddam's birth. His mother, Subha, met another man and married him. In general, his childhood, because of its harshness and cruelty, was not well known nor did Saddam Hussein want it to be known that much either. It is reported that his stepfather, Ibrahim Hassan, was a tough and uneducated farmer who did not much like or care for his stepson, Saddam. Fighting with his stepfather was a frequent occurrence; there was essentially no love lost between the two. His relatives decided that all Saddam was good for was to be a farmer where he could take the sheep and run other farm errands.

It was not until 1947 at ten years of age that Saddam Hussein started his schooling. At the time, he was living in a town named Shawish. One night, when his family was sleeping, Saddam left home! He walked in the dark until he reached some other relatives who were surprised by his arrival. It was reported that these relatives encouraged him in his desire to attend school in Tikrit. He was given a pistol, then placed in a taxi heading for Tikrit. His maternal cousin, Adnan Khairallah was studying there and was happy to have Saddam join him at school. He spent one year there and moved on to Baghdad where he stayed with his Uncle on his mother's side, Khairallah Tulfah, who was a school teacher in Baghdad. Tulfah was the father of Adnan, who later became Minister of Defense for Iraq. Saddam's uncle had been removed from the Iraqi army because he participated in a pro Nazi Coup d'Etat in 1941. As mentioned previously, the British crushed the uprising and this must have left in him an everlasting deep hatred and dislike for the British, in particular, and imperialists in general. The uncle later became the Mayor of Baghdad and was certainly an influential man who left a strong impression on his young nephew. Saddam finished his intermediary school around the age of sixteen. Since his uncle was an officer in the army in the early forties, Saddam also wanted to be an officer in the army. However, the elite Baghdad Military Academy would not accept him, despite the influence of his uncle, because Saddam had a poor record in school. The army, since Iraqi independence, had become a mighty institution in its own right and officers of the military had a special status in society. Saddam wanted very much to be an officer but he did not succeed in this regard, although he was always in love with the gun, starting at an early age. In later years, his career made up for what he missed by not being accepted at the Military Academy.

He lived with his uncle on the western shore of the Tigris river, in an area called Al-Karkh with an abundance of people from Tikrit. He entered the secondary stage of his schooling and by 1957, when he was twenty years of age, he joined the Ba'ath Party known officially as the Arab Ba'ath Socialist Party (ABSP); it is also known briefly as the Ba'ath which in Arabic means Renaissance. This party professes the union of the Arab nations under progressive socialist renaissance. A brief history of this party will be described in the following section. Saddam was impressed by the principles of the party which adhere to Arab nationalism. The nationalization of the Suez Canal in 1956, led by President Gamal Abdul Nasser of Egypt, and the wave of nationalism engulfing the Arab land, coincided perfectly well with Saddam's views. In the years to come, the Ba'ath became a cornerstone in his political career. His star rose rapidly in the party and his gun-toting talents served the goals of the Ba'ath. Time proved that he lived up to his reputation and name which means "the confronting one!" Not long after the overthrow of the Monarchy by Qassem in 1958, Saddam Hussein began to prove his worth and use of the gun. It was reported, at the age 14, he murdered a communist, his own brother-in-law, who supported Qassem in his hometown of Tikrit. The Ba'ath party and the communists were arch-rivals for a long time. His uncle Adnan Khayrallah urged him to do his deed. Saddam and his Uncle were arrested and spent a short time in jail. It was there that Saddam met a number of his Ba'ath party comrades.

The chaos and confusion which followed the revolution led to many crimes being committed without any punishment being meted out. When Saddam was released from prison, the message came that the Ba'ath party needed his talent in the capital city, Baghdad. He left Tikrit and hurried to the capital where he mastered the use of various guns and automatic weapons. The urgent question from his comrades in the party was "Would you be willing and interested in participating in a plot to kill Qassem?" His mettle had already been proven and Saddam was only too anxious and delighted to be on the team of assassins! This was a great honor for him, indeed! Among the conspirators was another party member named Izzat Ibrahim, who later became Vice President of Iraq under Saddam Hussein.

On October 7, 1959, Qassem was on his way to attend a ceremony to celebrate the national day for East Germany. The Ba'ath party had various observation posts to track the movements of Qassem along various routes that led to the Ministry of Defense. As soon as he left, an accomplice inside the Ministry, named Saleh Mahdi Ammash informed his cohorts. Around six o'clock in the evening, the conspirators came down to the Rashid street with their hidden weapons. As soon as Qassem's car approached, it received a hail of bullets from many directions. The driver was killed instantly and others were injured. Qassem received several injuries especially in his left arm. He was taken to Salam Hospital, while one of his attackers was killed in the melee. Two others were injured, Saddam Hussein was among them. They were able to reach Republic street, which was across from Rashid street, where cars were waiting to take them away from the scene.

The identity of the one killed from the group led to identifying those who had taken part in the assassination attempt. Qassem, injured in his left shoulder and left arm, stayed in the hospital until January, 1959. Most of the attackers were apprehended. Their trial began on December 26, 1959 in the Mahdawi Court. Five of the attackers escaped and fled via Syria to Cairo, Egypt, but 57 of the group were tried. Seventeen of them were condemned to death. Others received lighter sentences. However, on March 30, 1961, Qassem commuted all sentences. Saddam Hussein had been hit in the left leg. His injury was minor. When he realized that the attempt on Qassem's life did not succeed, he made his move and ran for his life. He spent the night in a hideout in Baghdad. The next morning he put on a long Arabic dress and moved in a hurry away from the capital and headed for Tikrit. He somehow acquired a horse and moved on along the Tigris river. He had obtained some money from the Party for his expenses. He was supposedly stopped on the way a few times but was able to outwit security officers and continued his travel toward his hometown. Glamorous stories abound to glorify the attack on Qassem and the journey taken by Saddam afterward—all in heroic style. He allegedly swam across the Tigris river reaching the other bank at night—cold and wet! He was seeking refuge and food. When he knocked on a door, a woman came out screaming, "Thief! Kill him!" Again Saddam was able to convince them that he was not a thief saying, "Just look at me. Do I look like a thief?" How little did they know? (Years later, tragic events showed that he was not a thief on any small scale; he only wanted to absorb the entire state of Kuwait and its wealth of 100 billion barrels of oil along with the tens of billions of dollars he owed to neighboring Arab countries and other nations around the world . . .) After reaching his brother Adham at a village called Oweinat, they both went on to another area, Ouja. There, the Ba'ath party had already arranged for his departure along with some other party comrades, setting their journey on to Syria. They traveled by night and hid by day. They went by jeep and then by donkey. Their valuable guide knew the terrain and safe passages to neighboring Syria. They finally reached Aboukamal in Deir Al-Zour, then continued their journey to the capital city Damascus where Saddam was to stay for about five months.

Saddam Hussein set his sights high and moved on to Cairo, Egypt, where President Nasser was at his political apogee. Saddam reached his destination around February 21, 1960. For the rest of the academic year 1960–1961 he attended Kasr Al-Nil private school to finish his secondary education. He had not finished his secondary education while in Baghdad due to his deep interest in serving the party and being on one of the teams that attempted to assassinate Qassem. He finally finished his high school at the age of 24, then enrolled at Cairo University's Law School in 1961. He did not graduate from the university but at a later date he received an honorary law degree in 1970 in Baghdad, after he became the second man in command of the nation. While in Cairo, he was very active in the Ba'ath Party and especially in its command. His activities led to his arrest twice, but he was subsequently released. Both arrests were due to a certain degree of violence, one for threatening to kill an Iraqi, another for chasing a Ba'athist colleague through the streets of Cairo with a knife drawn in his hand. He married his uncle's daughter, Sajida while he was still in Egypt in 1963. This is the daughter of Khairallah Tulfah.

Immediately upon the assassination and overthrow of the Qassem regime on February 8, 1963, Saddam returned to Iraq to claim his position in the revolution. As mentioned previously, this Ba'ath coup was not to last more than nine months when President Abdul Salam Aref took over in Iraq. Members of the party were then eased out. Some were hunted down, including Saddam Hussein himself. During the Ba'ath brief reign, Saddam became an interrogator at "the Palace of the End," known in Arabic as Kasr Al-Nihaia. That is where young King Faisal II and his family were murdered during the revolution of July, 1958. This became a center for torture and various forms of interrogations under the short-lived Ba'ath regime. When Aref had full command, Saddam, the young enthusiastic Ba'athist thought that the party should be substantially strengthened in order to stand for the regime and bring about another Ba'athist revolution. In 1963, he traveled to Syria to attend the Seventh National Conference of the Ba'ath Party, held in Damascus. He had special guidance and inspiration from the leader of the party, Michel Aflaq. During the Party split of 1963, Saddam was a strong supporter of the faction headed by Michel Aflaq who was a co-founder of the party. This gave Saddam a good boost and his star began rising in the party rapidly, especially when Michel Aflaq returned the favors and promoted Saddam in 1964 to become the Regional Commander of the Ba'ath Party of Iraq.

When he returned to Iraq he supervised the military organization of the party. His goal was to develop full control of the Ba'ath. He started by improving the financial situation of the party and by gathering an arsenal of weapons for future use. He plotted to enter the palace where officials of the new government were meeting in September,

1964 and planned to rain a hail of bullets over these military and civilian leaders. His attempt never materialized because the authorities were alerted to it. Many arrests were made and Saddam was wanted again, dead or alive! He was arrested and jailed between 1964 and 1966. He spent some time in jail and tried unsuccessfully to escape once. He later tried again with some of his Ba'athist comrades and made it.

Saddam and his party cohorts prepared extensively for an overthrow of the Aref regime. Finally, on July 17, 1968, Saddam and his Ba'athist comrades staged a Coup d'Etat. Saddam donned his military uniform and along with his comrades headed a tank assault on the Presidential Palace which fell to the attackers, bringing an end to the Aref regime. All controls were then in the hands of the Ba'ath Party. Saddam had very strong feelings against Abdul Razzak Naif who became the new Prime Minister. Saddam, with his revolver drawn, ordered Naif to raise his hands and submit to his wishes. He told him that any false move would result in him being killed instantly. After appeals from Naif for the sake of his children, Saddam Hussein told him the only way he would survive would be for him to leave Iraq immediately. The man had no choice! A plane was waiting for him at the Rashid camp. Saddam accompanied Naif in a car to where the plane was waiting. He gave him instructions not to make any wrong moves or leave any questionable impressions of any kind which might reveal the gravity of the situation. Thus, at the point of a gun, at which Saddam Hussein became a master, he became a master of the new revolution once Naif was out of the country heading for Morocco.

Ahmad Hassan Al-Bakr became the President and Secretary of the Revolutionary Command Council (RCC) and also Prime Minister and Commander in Chief. Saddam Hussein was chosen to be Deputy Chairman of the Revolutionary Command Council and the Vice President of Iraq. Saddam would remain Deputy and the real power in Iraq for the next ten years. He was in charge of internal security which proved to be a position of great power and influence. It paved the way to the total control of the government and populace of Iraq. Following his escape from prison Saddam Hussein concentrated his efforts on rebuilding and strengthening the party. The internal security was substantially fortified and the "instrument of yearning," or Jihaz Haneen, became notorious for efficiency, torture and summary execution of the enemies of the party! Saddam's iron hand methods evolved into a small legend.

In his new position in Security he helped prepare and train many recruits who were very loyal to him and the party. His brothers and cousins were to receive his prime attention in training for key positions which were sensitive. This was to guarantee total control of the regime and the Iraqi population. Among these was his cousin, Ali Hassan Al-Majid, who was to later become the commander that conducted poison gas attacks against the Kurds during the Iran-Iraq War in March, of 1988. Al-Majid gained other notoriety in the recent invasion and terrorizing of the State of Kuwait on August 2, 1990. The list of cousins and family fiefdoms is endless, many of them from the region of Tikrit. These people have their last names followed by the adjective "from Tikrit," in Arabic "Al-Tikrity"; thus, Saddam Hussein Al-Tikriti and so on and so on, for the many that came from that region of Iraq. When Saddam Hussein became Mr. Deputy at the age of thirty-one, he was young enough to have many years to gain the vast experience in internal security, especially, terrorist and terrorizing activities. On October 9, 1968, very shortly after the Coup, the regime announced a ring of spies which were supposed to be Zionists. On January 15, 1969, seventeen of these went on trial, fourteen of them were hung. Liberation Square in Baghdad was the sight where their bodies dangled for many days. The gruesome site was reminiscent of the many brutal acts which had taken place before, especially during the overthrow of the Monarchy in 1958.

The effervescence in the pot of revolution and change was well nourished through the philosophy of an Arab nationalist party known as the Ba'ath.

What Is the Ba'ath Party?

The word Ba'ath in Arabic means renaissance. The official name of the party is the Arab Ba'ath Socialist Party, "ABSP." One of its basic principles is unification of the Arab land from the Arabian Gulf to the Atlantic ocean. Such a goal has wide appeal among Arab masses, especially after being energized through nationalist feelings and independence movements in the forties and fifties. This political movement had its origin in Syria and was founded in 1944 by two high school teachers in Damascus, Michel Aflaq and Salah Bitar. Both of them studied at the Sorbonne University in Paris, France between the years 1928 and 1932. Aflaq was a Christian of the Greek Orthodox faith and Bitar was a Sunni Moslem. While they were studying in Paris it was reported that they admired Hitler of Nazi Germany and his brand of politics, a mix between socialism and nationalism. The short-lived coup which took place in Iraq in 1941 was pro Nazi; it received their admiration and they supposedly formed a "society to help Iraq." This society formed a nucleus for the Ba'ath party of Iraq in later years.

The major slogan of the Ba'ath party is "One Arab nation with an eternal mission." Their basic slogan is "Wahda, Hurriah, Ishtirakiyya," meaning "Unity, Freedom, Socialism." The Ba'ath developed into a national liberation movement opposing colonialism and the French mandate over Syria, Lebanon and other parts of the Arab land. (Zakki Al-Arsuzi, an Alawite was one of the co-founders but his name was dropped at a later date.) Michel Aflaq was the thinker and founding ideologue of the party. Other parties in Syria were the Communists, the Syrian National Party, which aimed at a secular union of Greater Syria and one other influential group was the Moslem Brotherhood. The Ba'ath were well known for their views on Pan-Arabism–a union of all the Arabs across Arab lands.

The two founders ran for parliament several times and finally Aflaq gave up, but Bitar was elected in 1954 as a Deputy for Damascus. He became an organizer and a tactician for the party. Aflaq remained the party philosopher and ideologue. He is a mild mannered man who talked at a slow pace in a rather monotone way but quietly on the hypnotic side. By 1952 the Ba'ath party merged with the Arab Socialist Party of Akram Hourani. At that time, Party leaders were in exile in Lebanon trying to devise a way to topple the regime of Adib Shishakli, a military officer who was President of Syria.

With the wave of nationalist feelings calling for Arab unity, the Ba'ath party which gained a number of parliamentary seats in 1956, agreed to dissolve itself in 1958 so a union could take place between Egypt and Syria, under the new name–the United Arab Republic. Of course, the dissolution of the party did not please many members; some of them were extremely disappointed and disturbed by the decision taken by Aflaq and Bitar. The union between Egypt and Syria did not last for long. In March, 1963, a group of disgruntled Ba'ath party members succeeded in staging a Coup d'Etat which toppled the union, and the United Arab Republic remained in name only. Other Ba'ath coups followed, one in 1966 and another in 1970. The latter brought to power General Hafez Al-Assad, current president of Syria. During the coup of 1966, the Ba'ath regime in Syria decided to put aside the old guard of Aflaq and Bitar. An irrevocable split took place between the two wings of the Ba'ath party. The Syrian wing followed one path and the Iraqi wing followed a diametrically opposing political path. Aflaq, the party thinker, moved on to Baghdad, Iraq. He stayed there until his death in 1989. He was revered, highly regarded, respected and admired by Saddam Hussein who was by then well entrenched in Iraqi political intrigue.

The Ba'ath party began to gain some footing in Iraq after 1949; Syrian teachers working in Iraq brought with them the ideas of the Ba'ath and spread the teachings of the Party. By 1951, a Shi'a engineer named Fouad Al-Rikabi from Nasiriyya took control of the Ba'ath party which numbered about fifty at that time. By 1955 the number of members was less than 300. Since Rikabi was a Shi'ite, a number of the people belonging to the party were from the same religious sect. Usually, family and religion played a strong role in political affiliations, much of the time ideology is superseded by these two factors. In 1957 a national front was organized. It consisted of the Ba'ath, the Communists and the National Democratic party along with the Istiqlal party (independence). When the Monarchy was overthrown in 1958, this front was very elated and supportive of the military regime. Within a short time the Ba'ath party became divided and reorganization took place with guidance from its supreme ideologue, Michel Aflaq and later Saddam Hussein. The Ba'ath party came to power in Iraq in a coup in 1963, but their rule did not last more than nine months. Again in 1968, after the Aref regime was toppled, the Ba'ath Party came to power and remained at the helm until this very day.

The Strong Man of Baghdad

July 16, 1979 President Bakr resigned, urged by Khayrallah Tolfah and other members of the Tikriti clan. However, it was reported that, Bakr resigned because of health reasons. On that day Saddam Hussein became the President of Iraq, Secretary General of the Ba'ath Party and Commander In Chief of the Armed Forces. He also was the Chairman of the powerful Revolutionary Command Council (RCC). The era of terror had already begun some years ago and now that he was at the helm, all power became completely, totally invested in his person.

In order to commemorate his ascendency to total power in Iraq, on July 22, he held a top level party meeting where more than a thousand comrades met. Drama, intrigue and terror reached a climax at this meeting. A Shi'ite who had been Secretary of the Revolutionary Command Council (RCC), Hussein Al-Mashhadi, a party member for over twenty years, stood up and read a "confession" essentially fabricated, which gave details to the participation in a conspiracy supposedly engineered by the Syrian government and backed by it. He hoped that through this cooperation his life might be saved. This confession was followed by a tirade from Saddam Hussein about traitors and their fate and how important party loyalty must be. He read a list of those condemned for their conspiracy and treacherous acts. The audience responded in a frenzy, calling, "to the gallows! To the gallows, they must go!" Saddam then declared, "We do not need Stalinist methods to deal with traitors here. We need Ba'athist methods." A few days later, Saddam was joined by senior party members and ministers to witness the execution of their comrades. Many more were tortured then killed and their bodies mutilated. Hundreds of people were savagely executed. This is in line with Saddam's declaration in 1971, "With party methods, there is no chance for anyone who disagrees with us to jump on a couple of tanks and overthrow the government." This indeed, reflects the obstinacy with which he clings to power until this very day, despite all the odds and the vast debacle that befell him and his people . . . Making his colleagues participate in the executions and crimes renders them as collaborators and accomplices to the crimes. As such, they acquire a personal stake in defending and preserving a regime which is hell-bent on torture and death. They realize that the fate of Saddam becomes their own fate as well.

East Germany played a key role in training the secret forces and in supplying them with high technology for bugging and torture. When Nicolae Ceausescu was toppled from government in Rumania, despite his Securitate and his vast machine of terror, Saddam ordered his men to study the political developments there and to review a film on the uprising so he could learn from such a historic revolt against an arch dictator, and thus be able to preserve his regime when the time came for his masses to rise against him.

Terrorism was practiced not only internally, but on an international scale. The party and the state became synonymous. It was mandated that all teachers belong to the party; if they did not, they could not teach any longer; to enter elite military schools, you must belong to the party; to have a job of any significance you must belong to the Ba'ath party. Thus, the control of Saddam Hussein and the Ba'ath party became total. Middle East Watch wrote in its report of 1990 on human rights in the State of Iraq: "Iraq under the Ba'ath party has become a nation of informers. Party members are said to be required to inform on family, friends and acquaintances including other party members." In summary, executions became the norm and people could receive the death penalty for very minor infractions. In fact, any insult to President Saddam Hussein or top leaders of the state or the party is punishable by death or in some cases imprisonment for life. It is reported that in Iraq twenty-four offenses carried the death penalty. When Saddam was not able to get hold of an offender, he punished his family nevertheless. When the Kurds sought autonomy, the Saddam regime used brutal military force against them. Up until the end of 1974 the Kurds were supported by the Shah of Iran, but finally a meeting of the minds took place in Algiers, between Saddam Hussein and the Shah. Algeria brokered the peace between Iraq and Iran on the disputed land of Shatt Al-Arab. Signing of the 1975 agreement led to the collapse of the Kurdish rebellion. Saddam Hussein and his army slaughtered thousands of Kurds and moved them by the hundreds of thousands from their enclaves in the North to be spread in various parts of the country; whole series of villages were raised to the ground . . .

The success of the extremist Islamic Fundamentalist Revolution in Iran brought tensions that were never far below the surface. These tensions led to an open war between Iraq and Iran. On the pretext of an imminent threat from Iran, Saddam Hussein started the war with his neighbor. This will be briefly described at the end of this chapter.

Saddam Hussein trusts no one. In fact, many of his closest friends and allies have disappeared from the scene. In December, of 1988 and March of the following year, hundreds of officers were arrested and several were killed. Maher Abdul Rashid, who was a General of the Army and whose daughter was married to the son of Saddam Hussein, disappeared from the public domain altogether. Saddam himself, summarily, executed many people in his military. When an officer lost his courage in a wave of assaults by Iranian youth, Saddam Hussein took his ever-present revolver, shot him and killed him. During the Iran-Iraq war, when Saddam was visiting the injured, a mother whose son was in the hospital with blown off limbs, appealed to Saddam to stop this war. Saddam drew his revolver–shot her dead and continued his visit to the injured troops at the hospital.

His oldest son, Uday, murdered his father's valet, Kamal Hanna Gegeo in October, 1988. Because of a slight dispute, he bludgeoned the innocent man to death with a heavy club. Of course, Saddam was initially infuriated, bowing to popular pressure, his son was forgiven and he is free and thriving until this day. His closest friend from childhood days, his cousin Adnan Khayrallah who was his school companion, confided in 1989, after a feud with Saddam Hussein, to a visiting Kuwaiti that his life was in danger. Adnan was a brother to Saddam's wife. When ordered to punish, terminate or eliminate someone, he took his time hoping Saddam would change his mind! Although Adnan Khayrallah was very popular and performed well as the Minister of Defense, it wasn't but two months later that he died in a helicopter accident.

As a psychological reaction to this humble beginnings, Saddam compensates by granting himself the title of General and all the other titles of government that he acquired. He dresses neatly, sometimes in western clothes, sometimes in Arab dress and at others in shapes and forms reflecting the great leaders of the past and especially the one he admired most: Babylonian leader Nabuchadnezzar who occupied and destroyed Jerusalem in the sixth century B.C. (around 587 B.C.). In fact, the family tree he portrays to the Iraqis traces his roots to the Prophet Mohammed.

Saddam Hussein has five children from his wife Sajida. They are two sons, Uday and Qusay and also three daughters named Raghd, Rana and Hala. His wife was a head mistress in a school.

One son was about sixteen years of age when he was asked about his academic interests. He expressed interest in physics and chemistry but wanted to specialize in nuclear physics at the university. Saying that, "Iraq would need scientists in this field, once it had entered the nuclear club." This son took some military training and has been a member of the Ba'ath party since the age of twelve. He said that his father, Saddam, "brought us up to tell the truth and be honest."

Saddam Hussein likes hunting. He used to smoke but quit. However, when introduced to Cuban cigars he started smoking the cigar. When asked about his employment when he was serving time in prison, his answer was: "I am a revolutionary in the Arab Socialist Ba'ath Party." He has been characterized as paranoid and a megalomaniac. Saddam places special emphasis on equal opportunity. He once said: "We want the citizens to feel that they are living in a country where justice reigns, not connections." However, the whims of wind went differently in the state of Iraq; for decades it has been ruled by family members and close associates from the town of Tikrit.

A senior British diplomat who dealt with Saddam Hussein for some time said: "He is an extremely shrewd, cold blooded, clever thug. He is the type of man that is willing to do anything and everything to reach his goals. Human life means nothing to him." A Time correspondent, Dan Goodgame says about Saddam, "On meeting him, a visitor is first struck by his eyes crackling with alertness and at the same time cold and remorseless as snake eyes on the sides of dice. They are the eyes of a killer." When free discussion took place between students at Cairo University, Saddam's advice was simple, he said, "Why argue? Why don't you just take out a gun and shoot him?"

Saddam does not like a challenge to his authority. When a senior general in the Iraqi army informed Saddam that a certain attack during the Iran-Iraq war would lead to heavy causalities, he was taken to the next room and simply shot and killed by Saddam. The stories go on and on . . .

The Iran-Iraq War

Conflicts between Iran and Iraq trace their origins into antiquity, during the time of Persia and Mesopotamia. There were periods of relative peace and guarded relations between the two countries; in modern history the conflicts were controlled but they were there. Mohammad Reza Pahlavi, the Shah of Iran strove to bring modernization to this country and extensively strengthened his army until it became the major military power in the region and probably the fifth largest army in the world. He was a strong ally of the United States of America and the West as a whole. On the international scene, the Shah exercised policies of restraint and good neighborly relations according to the spirit of the U.N. Charter. However, on the domestic front, his security organization, namely the Savak practiced suppression of the populace. Despite his serious efforts in modernization and improving the standard of living for his people, deep hatreds developed among the religious groups of the country who were essentially left aside. Leading among these was a spiritual leader named *Ayatollah Khomeini*. His opposition to the Shah's regime led to his dismissal from Iran and departure to neighboring Iraq where he sought political asylum.

He remained in the hospitality of Iraq mainly in the Holy Shi'ite cities of Najaf and Karbala for about fourteen years until, in October, 1978, he was ordered out of the country after some rapprochement had taken place between Iraq and Iran. He moved on to Paris where he spent a few months using the democracy and freedom of the French Republic as a platform for conducting his extensive and enthusiastic religious campaign against the Shah and his government. His fiery speeches, pronouncements and messages were picked up by the world media. They were transmitted to Iran and then moved like a seering fire via cassette tapes blaring from balconies and parks across the four corners of the land. His followers in Iran were Islamic extremist fundamentalists who responded to his appeal with great zeal and fanaticism. By February 1, 1979, the Iranian revolution was in full swing and Khomeini was back in Iran, as a hero on his way to becoming the undisputed leader of Iran. His spiritual leadership gradually gave him the overwhelming support of the entire nation. His words became the law! All leaders and officials of the government, from the President to the Speaker of the Parliament, all other major positions and functions of the Islamic Republic of Iran, were under his unequivocal control. However, initially anarchy prevailed and the settling of scores was rampant in the land. Trials for former Savak personnel, former government leaders and Army officers took place. Many people were executed. These trials and executions caused serious setbacks to Iran's military capabilities. Several top officers who were educated and trained in top military schools in America and the West were deleted and with them disappeared a large pool of knowhow and vast experiences which were the backbone of Iran's army under the Shah.

Khomeini was viciously attacking America and the West. The East as well did not escape his wrath. However, America was declared as the great Satan and the number one enemy. The masses of extremist Islamic fundamentalists heeded his call with fervor. In November, of

1979, so-called Iranian students occupied the American Embassy in Tehran and held sixty-two American hostages. They allowed ten of them, women and black men to leave in a few days, but they held fifty-two hostages for an agonizing period of four hundred and forty-four days. The holding of American hostages was a devastating blow to the American foreign policy and the normal conduct of business by the American administration. This became a central issue in U.S. foreign policy. World opinion was very much against holding innocent people as hostages. The exception to this were the cheers of extremist Islamic Fundamentalists in Iran and elsewhere.

In this electrified atmosphere of revolutionary Iran, coupled with trials of army officers and vicious attacks on America and American interests, along with relentless attacks on the Kingdom of Saudi Arabia, the Gulf countries and Iraq, there came to the forefront in July, 1979, Saddam Hussein, the new President of Iraq. He had been well groomed and entrenched in power for many years before ascending to the Presidency of the Iraqi Republic. He was watching very carefully and with great interest the developments in Iran, his neighbor to the East and his enemy from way back in history! Saddam Hussein was also holding his personal grudges against Iran from the time of the Shah. In the early seventies, Iraq continued to have difficult problems with its Kurdish population. By 1974, the Kurdish Guerilla War was in full swing. Their main support came from the Shah of Iran. Some political moves were shaping up and Algeria succeeded in brokering a peaceful settlement between Iran and Iraq. In 1975, Saddam Hussein, representing Iraq at a Conference in Algiers, Algeria, signed a treaty with the Shah of Iran whereby Iraq gave up its claim to the total ownership of the Shatt Al-Arab Waterway. In return, the Shah withdrew his support for the Kurdish rebellion in the northern part of Iraq. Prior to this, Saddam Hussein and Iraq laid claim to the entire outlet of the Tigris and Euphrates rivers including the banks on the Iranian side, claiming their need for a good and proper outlet to the Arabian Gulf. At the time this treaty was signed in Algiers, the Shah was in a strong position and his army was the strongest in the Middle East. Saddam Hussein and the Iraqis were fighting a losing guerilla war with the Kurds in the north. Saddam swallowed a bitter pill and accepted this treaty so the Kurdish Guerilla War could be put to rest. Indeed, this rebellion was stopped immediately after the signing of this treaty. Relations between Iraq and Iran became civil and proper until the departure of the Shah.

Saddam Hussein was waiting for the opportune moment to renege on the treaty and claim again the full control of Shatt Al-Arab Waterway. Sensing the turmoil and convulsions of the Iranian revolution under

Khomeini and the alienation that Khomeini was harnessing for Iran through his strong attacks on the major powers of the world and especially, the United States of America, he thought that an ideal situation was now presenting itself for Iraq and the Iraqi people. The onslaught of Islamic Fundamentalism against the Iranian Army and the Governmental apparatus of the Shah–decimating their top military echelons–coupled with the strong attacks by Khomeini against his former host Iraq and the Iraqi leadership, also, last but not least, Khomeini's call to the Iraqis and especially the Shi'ites in Iraq to rise up in arms and topple their government under the secular Ba'athist leadership of Saddam Hussein, paved the way toward a major confrontation between Iraq and Iran. Border skirmishes and dangerous clashes became a daily occurrence.

An assassination attempt was made on the life of Tariq Aziz, the Deputy Prime Minister and Foreign Minister of Iraq, in April, 1980. It was thought that the Da'wa party–a Revolutionary Islamic Shi'ite group–was behind the plot. During the funeral procession for those who died in this terrorist attack, another attempt was launched by the Da'wa group. Since membership in this party was punishable by death, the response by Saddam Hussein was very swift. A campaign of arrests and harassment was in full swing against the Shi'ite activists. Some of the Shi'ite clerics were arrested after disturbances took place in the southern part of Iraq during the 70's. Leading among these was Mohammed Baqer Al-Sadr who was arrested several times and in June, 1979, was arrested again on his way to visit a former colleague, Ayatollah Khomeini. His sister Amina Bint Al-Houda was also arrested. This led to bloody demonstrations in Karbala and Najaf. Finally, this religious leader and his sister were placed under house arrest and then executed. Thousands of Iranian sympathizers and Iraqis of Iranian extraction were expelled from Iraq. As the battle heated for gaining the souls of Iraqis, Saddam Hussein warned that he would cut off the hand of anyone trying to interfere in Iraq . . . "Iraq is prepared to enter into any kind of battle to defend its honor and sovereignty." With imminent threat to the security of his own regime, Saddam Hussein nurtured the idea and thought of himself as the savior and champion of Arab causes, "the sword of the Arab Nation." He edged closer and closer to war with Iran.

He called for total control of the Shatt Al-Arab Waterway, although the Algiers agreement stated that sovereignty is only over half of the channel. On top of this, he added other territorial claims so that Iran would relinquish its authority over the islands of Abou Mousa, Greater Tumb and Lesser Tumb. These strategic islands, near the Strait of Hormuz, were occupied by the Shah in 1971. Furthermore, Saddam also demanded that Iran must provide self-rule for the Arab population in Khuzistan/Arabistan and also for the Kurdish and Baluch minorities. This latter demand was essentially rhetorical and did not carry much practicality, since Saddam Hussein himself did not give the necessary self-rule for his own countrymen, the Kurds.

On September 17, 1980, Saddam Hussein convened his National Assembly, abrogating the treaty of Algiers and declaring it "null and void." The Iran-Iraq War was imminent. The Iranians made no special secret of their strong desires for exporting their brand of Islamic extremism not only to Iraq and Saudi Arabia but to all the Arabian Gulf countries and beyond. This was not a small threat in any stretch of the imagination. Iran was in turmoil! Their army was in total disarray, counter-balanced by the Revolutionary Guard Militia which was an ill-trained, deeply disorganized force. Saddam was ready for the attack . . . On September 22, 1980, he gave his fateful orders to his mighty military force and carried out a blitzkrieg attack on Iran, realizing gains in rapid succession. The attack was carried at four different points along a long border stretching 760 miles to the east of Iraq. Ten airfields and targets in several cities were bombarded. Air attacks were mounted against Khorramshahr, Abadan, Bushire, Kharg Island terminals and Shiraz in the south up into Isfahan and the capital city, Tehran, in the northeast, to Qasr-e-Shirin in the west and way up to Tabriz in the north and close to the former Soviet Union who has a border with Iran of 1,250 miles. Mainly, oil installations and strategic facilities were initially attacked. It was a matter of a few hours before Iran counterattacked with its Air Force hitting oil facilities and major installations in Basra in the south and in Baghdad, the capital city in the heart of Iraq, then moving on further north to Mosul and Kirkuk.

On September 27, 1980, the British Broadcasting Corporation (BBC) reported a statement by General Adnan Khairallah, who is a cousin to Saddam Hussein and Minister of Defense and Deputy Commander in Chief of the Iraqi Armed Forces, explaining the Iraqi reasons for such an attack, he said: "We decided to lay our hands on points vital to Iran's interests inside Iranian territory to deter Iran from striking our national sovereignty and to make it recognize our full sovereignty over Shatt Al-Arab."

Along with the massive air attacks, Iraqi armored units carried on a heavy thrust across the Shatt Al-Arab with the goal to overtake the vital port of Khorramshahr and make inroads into Abadan with its huge oil refinery having a capacity of 587,000 barrels per day. Ahwaz and Dezful received heavy bombardments causing the destruction of a strategic oil pumping station on the pipeline linking oil facilities in

Abadan and the south with Tehran, the capital city of Iran. Within a week, Iranian resistance stiffened with an influx of militia. Despite this, Khorramshahr fell to the Iraqis on October 24, 1980.

The Iraqis hoped for the regime's collapse because of the state of chaos it had reached, but the Iraqi attack generated nationalism and consolidation of the revolution around Khomeini. The Iraqi army penetrated Iranian territory for a distance of about 45 miles, then began to dig in but continued heavy attacks on the oil city of Abadan. Five Iranian towns were occupied and the city of Abadan was besieged. The province of Khuzistan/Arabistan, with its Arab population, did not rise up in arms to welcome the army of Saddam Hussein, but instead the area was evacuated. The targets in the neighboring city of Basra received heavy bombardment from the Iranian air force. However their airplanes were not going to function efficiently for very long especially because of their desperate need for spare parts which were made in America. Relations between Iran and the U.S. being at their lowest ebb, made these parts unavailable from America. Since Israel hated Iraq more than Iran's Ayatollah, it had in turn supplied some of these spare parts at hefty prices. This air force, supported by Iranian navy attacks on Basra, prevented Iraq from further shipping of oil across the Arabian Gulf. The damage from these air raids was not very significant and Iraq retaliated on a number of Iranian targets, especially the oil complex on Kharg Island, where fourteen tankers at a time could load crude oil for shipping abroad. This remained a major target throughout the entire war, with constant air raids from Iraq.

At the time of the war, the population of Iran was about 42 million and that of Iraq was about 13.5 million, Iran being several times larger than Iraq with a common border of 800 miles (1,300 kilometers). Iraq covered an area of 169,000 square miles (437,600 square kilometers), while Iran had an area of 636,300 square miles (1,648,000 square kilometers). For all practical purposes Saddam Hussein was taking on a very risky situation and a zealous enemy. Who would pick a fight with such imbalance in demography and geography? Despite the fact that the Iranian army was in total disarray, this adventure by Saddam Hussein proved to be one of history's greatest follies.

However the Iraqis continued to have the upper hand for the first few months of the war, until March, 1981. At that time, the Iranians rallied around their spiritual leader with tremendous zeal. No sooner than Saddam thought he was the master of the Gulf, hordes of extremist fundamentalist Iranians, young and old, responded and rallied behind Khomeini who fired their zeal with his pronouncements and declarations of a Holy war: Jihad. He urged a fight to the death until the "government of heathens in Iraq is toppled." He dismissed the "godless" rulers of Iraq as "stooges of the great Satan" and Saddam Hussein as an "infidel guilty of blasphemy."

The Iranian forces drove the Iraqis away from Abadan in September, 1981 and when Saddam called for a one month cease-fire during Ramadan, it was quickly rejected by the Iranians. With a major offensive in March, 1982 and Iranian Jihad forces promised to be in heaven upon martyrdom, they drove the Iraqis from Khorramshahr. The tide of the war had begun to change. Now the outcry was for Saddam's removal as the Satan of Satans and any appeal by Iraq for a cease-fire went unheeded, always hinging on Saddam's removal from power as a precondition for any negotiations or any peaceful possibilities with Iraq.

On September 28, 1980 the United Nations called for a cease-fire in a Security Council Resolution number 479. Saddam Hussein was quick to accept the U.N. call for stopping the hostilities, but the leadership in Iran rejected this resolution outright.

The war moved into a stalemate and progressively the war of cities and tanker wars went on unabated. The capital city of Baghdad and other major cities, along with Tehran the capital city of Iran, and other Iranian cities were hit by missiles. Many innocent people were killed or maimed. The tanker war threatened the oil tanker fleets of many nations and posed a direct threat to the free movement and flow of oil to other regions of the world and especially, the Western world. The United States along with other Western navies and the former Soviet Union pushed for the free passage of ships in the Gulf. The Iranian forces launched high speed boat attacks and placed a large number of floating mines in the Gulf. Kuwaiti and Saudi shipping were especially threatened. The Kuwaiti government was then forced to seek protection by signing its tanker fleet under American flags. (Kuwait inquired about reregistering under the American flag on December 10, 1986. Kuwait applied for reflagging on March 2, of the same year and on March 10, 1987 the U.S. administration informed Congress of the offer for reflagging and protecting Kuwaiti ships. Finally, Kuwait accepted the offer on April 2, 1987.) While this helped in protecting their oil tankers, it did not completely deter attacks from Iran. Iranian oil tankers and other ships of various nationalities, transporting oil from Kharg Island or carrying merchandise and equipment to Iran, were attacked by the Iraqis. The Gulf was not very safe for shipping! Because of these attacks from both sides, several people were killed and many ships were destroyed. Shipping insurance rates by the Lloyds of London skyrocketed. Khomeini and the extremist Islamic fundamentalists continued their zealous attacks on American interests, not only in the Gulf, but through terrorist activities around the four corners of the globe, while continuing to hold American hostages in the U.S. Embassy in Tehran, until the day President Reagan took over his office on January 20, 1981. The Khomeini regime succeeded enormously in harnessing to his regime the dislike of the international community. With the tide of the war turning in March of 1982, Iraq sought the help of various powerful countries around the world, especially the former Soviet Union, the United States of America, France, Britain and several other countries. To serve his immediate goal, Saddam Hussein used his propaganda machine and the softening of his anti-western positions which had been established through the years. Since the U.S., the western world, and for that matter the international community were faced with the extremist and fanatic deeds of Khomeini and his followers, their decision in choosing sides in the war was simple to make. Thus, they somewhat threw their lot on the side of Saddam Hussein. Saudi Arabia, Kuwait and the Arabian Gulf countries, along with Egypt and several other Arab countries supported Iraq with money and war material. Only Syria and Libya were on the side of Khomeini, giving him some moral support, without actually committing any military forces on his side. With the strong and vicious campaign of threats against Kuwait, Saudi Arabia and the Arabian Gulf coming from Khomeini, and his calling for the overthrow of their governments in order to establish his brand of revolutionary Islamic fundamentalism, these countries found it imperative to support the Iraqi people in their struggle against Iran to avert defeat and prevent an ominous victory by Iran. In fact, Kuwait suffered extensively during this war from various acts of hostilities committed by Iran and also through terrorist activities which were carried on especially against the interests of Saudi Arabia and Kuwait.

Saudi Arabia helped Iraq when it was in dire need during the war, to the tune of nearly 27 billion dollars. It also allowed Iraq to transport its oil through a pipeline going from the Eastern region to the shores of Yanbu on the Red Sea. Iraq was able to transport two million barrels of oil per day through this pipeline–courtesy of the Saudi Arabian government. The pipeline which used to transport oil for Iraq through Syria was shut down in 1982.

Despite the intensive Iraqi bombing, by January, 1985, Iran's oil exports decreased only to a level of 1.4 million barrels per day. To circumvent Iraqi attacks on their oil facilities, Iranians responded by shuttling oil from Kharg Island which is in the heated battle zone to Sirri Island, a loading point further south in the Arabian Gulf. Thus, commercial tankers would not be exposed to Iraqi bombardment in the Northern Gulf war zone. By January, 1987, Iraq carried out around

130 attacks on ships in the Gulf since the beginning of the tanker war, damaging over 40 tankers. Iran attacked around 70 ships and damaged more than ten. Soviet ships carrying arms for Iraq were escorted by their missile frigates. These ships carried arms to Kuwait and from Kuwait by land to Iraq. The U.S. had a number of warships in the Gulf to protect shipping lanes and also to protect the Kuwaiti oil tanker fleet.

For many years, America's policy was to guarantee freedom of navigation in the Gulf. Under the Reagan Administration, America was more determined than ever to follow such a policy and vowed to keep the narrow Strait of Hormuz and the Gulf open for free shipping. By 1987, about 42 U.S. warships and nearly 25,000 troops, including special forces, were in the Gulf. Other warships from Britain, France, Netherlands, Belgium and Italy were also in the Gulf to help in securing freedom of navigation and in keeping the strategic flow of oil unhindered by the conflict raging between Iran and Iraq. U.S. Naval escorts of U.S.-flagged Kuwaiti cargo ships began on July 21, 1987. On April 18, 1988, a direct confrontation between Iran and the United States took place. Iran lost four frigates, a missile-equipped patrol boat and three fast patrol boats, along with two oil platforms and more than 200 men.

Supplies and war machines needed by Iraq were coming mainly through Saudi Arabia and the ports of Kuwait, then transported by land to their destination in Iraq. Kuwait and Saudi Arabia found it necessary to furnish this critical aid for the protection of the Iraqi people and to prevent spilling of the conflict to their own borders. It was feared by America and its Arab allies that a victory by Iran would mean the destruction of Iraq and the establishment of an Islamic Fundamentalist government which would be as extreme as the Khomeini regime in Iran. Thus, all indicators and basic interests were pointing in one direction: to do whatever necessary to defend Iraq and prevent the extremists from taking over, because such an event would bring extreme dire consequences to the entire region.

So the world community was tilting and leaning more heavily with time on the side of Iraq which received state of the art equipment from the French. They also received equipment and supplies from Germany, Britain, the U.S. and a number of other countries around the world. All this aid pouring into Iraq was given with the blessing of the United States of America and for many good reasons. The world community took this stand simply because the leadership in Iran was spreading hate, terrorism and fanaticism and continued to define the two main capabilities which favor Iran in this war as being: Martyrdom along with the innovation and creativity in the terrorizing tactics used in the war against the whole world.

Egypt and Jordan came to the extensive aid and rescue of Iraq. Thousands of Egyptians who were working in Iraq volunteered or were drafted into the army. By 1982 there were over 20,000 Egyptians fighting on the side of their Iraqi Brethren. By 1987, this number reached nearly 50,000. Many critical supplies and military equipment were shipped to Iraq from Jordan which became strongly allied with and economically dependent on Iraq.

A victory for Iran was not in the cards nor was it going to be achieved for many reasons, leading among them, the fact that mullahs or religious authorities in Iran never trusted the Army nor did they give it the support it needed. The extremist demands of the Iranian government did not help in ending the war, nor did the fact that the entire world community was appalled and turned off by the extremism which was emanating from Iran and spreading ill will and terrorism around the globe!

Iran-Contra Affair

With the massive Iranian offensive in late 1986 and early 1987, Saddam Hussein was forced to use more concentrated air power in attacking waves of large Iranian ground forces and thus exposed his Air Force to higher risks. In fact during these battles many airplanes were lost, nearly ten percent of his entire Air Force. Around this time the Iran-Contra Affair was exposed to the world where the U.S. was in essence trading arms with Iran for American hostages held in Lebanon by extremist Shi'ites sympathetic to and controlled by Iran.

A secret arrangement was made to ship a limited supply of spare parts and missiles. Iran was to pay for it in hard currency and was to exercise its influence and control to secure the release of some American hostages held in Lebanon. The money from the deal was supposed to be siphoned off for use in Latin America to help the Contra rebels who were engaged in a guerrilla war trying to overthrow the leftist Sandinistas in Nicaragua. Although the U.S. public opinion and President Ronald Reagan were against the Sandinistas and supportive of the Contras, Congress passed a law forbidding military aid to the Contras. When the Iran-Contra affair was uncovered, it mushroomed into a scandal involving international intrigue and threatening the integrity and credibility of the Reagan presidency. By mid-November, 1986, President Reagan acknowledged that "for eighteen months now, we have had underway a secret diplomatic initiative to Iran . . . to open a dialogue. . . . During the course of our secret negotiations, I authorized the transfer of small amounts of defensive weapons and spare parts for defensive systems to Iran." The President continued to say, "The U.S. has not swapped boat loads or plane loads of American weapons for the return of American hostages." However, U.S. negotiators urged Iran to use its influence in freeing the hostages. He emphasized that the shipments of arms were not a ransom but rather a signal to Iran indicating the U.S. interest in a dialogue for bringing a thaw to American-Iranian relations.

The scandal hinged around the money that went to the Contras and whether or not the President knew of such a transfer, which would have been contrary to the law passed by Congress. President Reagan was absolved; he denied any knowledge of such aid and his Presidency was saved.

This delicate and potentially disastrous, but intriguing, operation had the state of Israel at center stage. It is believed that back in the Fall of 1985, Iran was making payments to Israel through some Swiss bank accounts. Prices were highly inflated. Some of the money went to a secret account for the Contras. Some U.S. TOW missiles and Hawk ground-to-air missiles were supplied from Israeli stockpiles, and the U.S. replaced the arms sold to Iran. For this purpose, between February and October of 1986, nearly seven plane loads of TOW antitank missiles, other missiles and spare parts weighing over 25 tons were flown to Israel. While arms shipments cost the U.S. Government 12 million dollars, Israel charged the Iranians about 50 million dollars. Iran deposited this sum into the Swiss bank account. Middlemen took about 15 million dollars commission; twelve million dollars went to the U.S. Department of Defense to cover the original cost and the balance of 23 million dollars had been channelled to an account for the Contras, but much of it disappeared in the maze. As for the hostages in Lebanon suffering in captivity, the freedom score was as follows: Benjamin Weir was released on September 14, 1985 after two plane loads of arms were delivered to Iran by Israel; Lawrence Jenco was released on July 26, 1986 and the last to be released was David Jacobsen on November 2, 1986; just prior to his freedom, a Lebanese magazine called Shira'a broke a story that exploded into public uproar; it stated that former National Security Advisor Robert McFarlane flew to Tehran on May 28, 1986 for a four-day meeting with Iranian officials. In no time, America was in an uproar and the world was astonished and mystified!

The Iran-Contra affair brought to the surface some serious doubts about America's intentions in the Gulf. In fact, when Saddam Hussein was decorating his airmen for their air raid performance in battle, he said that the antiaircraft activity coming from the Iranians was much more intense than before and this heavy toll on his Air Force was due to the "Zionists and the Americans who supplied the Iranians with these weapons in order to inflict harm on Iraq and the Iraqi armed forces." The shipments of American arms, especially antiaircraft missiles were well publicized in Iraq and the Arab world. It was not long after such revelations, an Exocet missile was launched in May, 1987, by an Iraqi pilot on the American frigate, U.S.S. Stark. This tragic incident caused the death of 37 Americans and the injury of dozens. The Iraqi government said it was an accident. They apologized for it and paid 27 million dollars compensation to the families of the deceased and injured. Questions remain as to the authenticity of their claim and their apology, especially coming on the heels of Saddam Hussein's recent verbal attack on Americans. With the massive waves of Iranian attacks, the Iraqis were using their Air Force more frequently, aiming at crippling the Iranian economy and keeping the international community at a higher state of anxiety about their interests in the region. This was the dual purpose of pushing Iran to a negotiated settlement and a cease-fire.

UN Resolution

Finally on July 20, 1987, the U.N. Security Council adopted *Resolution number 598* to enforce Iran's compliance for a ceasefire. In fact since 1982 the major goal of the military operations of Saddam Hussein were to convince the other side to come to the negotiating table.

Here is the official text of the resolution:

The Security Council, Reaffirming its *Resolution 582* (1986),

Deeply concerned that, despite its calls for a ceasefire, the conflict between Iran and Iraq continues unabated, with further heavy loss of human life and material destruction,

Deploring the initiation and continuation of the conflict,

Deploring also the bombing of purely civilian population centres, attacks on neutral shipping or civilian aircraft, the violation of international humanitarian law and other laws of armed conflict, and, in particular, the use of chemical weapons contrary to obligations under the 1925 Geneva Protocol,

Deeply concerned that further escalation and widening of the conflict may take place,

Determined to bring to an end all military actions between Iran and Iraq,

Convinced that a comprehensive, just, honourable and durable settlement should be achieved between Iran and Iraq,

Recalling the provisions of the United Nations Charter and in particular the obligation of all member states to settle their international disputes by peaceful means in such a manner that international peace and security and justice are not endangered,

Determining that there exists a breach of the peace as regards the conflict between Iran and Iraq,

Acting under Articles 39 and 40 of the Charter of the United Nations,

1. Demands that, as a first step towards a negotiated settlement, Iran and Iraq observe an immediate ceasefire, discontinue all military actions on land, at sea and in the air, and withdraw all forces to the internationally recognized boundaries without delay.

2. Requests the Secretary-General to despatch a team of United Nations observers to verify, confirm and supervise the ceasefire and withdrawal and further requests the Secretary-General to make the necessary arrangements in consultation with the parties and to submit a report thereon to the Security Council.

3. Urges that prisoners of war be released and repatriated without delay after the cessation of active hostilities in accordance with the Third Geneva Convention of August 12, 1949.

4. Calls upon Iran and Iraq to co-operate with the Secretary-General in implementing this resolution and in mediation efforts to achieve a comprehensive, just and honourable settlement, acceptable to both sides, of all outstanding issues, in accordance with the principles contained in the Charter of the United Nations.

5. Calls upon all other states to exercise the utmost restraint and to refrain from any act which may lead to further escalation and widening of conflict, and thus to facilitate the implementation of the present resolution.

6. Requests the Secretary-General to explore, in consultation with Iran and Iraq, the question of entrusting an impartial body with inquiring into responsibility for the conflict and to report to the Security Council as soon as possible.

7. Recognized the magnitude of the damage inflicted during the conflict and the need for reconstruction efforts, with appropriate international assistance, once the conflict is ended and, in this regard, requests the Secretary-General to assign a team of experts to study the question of reconstruction and to report to the Security Council.

8. Further requests the Secretary-General to examine in consultation with Iran and Iraq and with other states of the region, measures to enhance the security and stability of the region.

9. Requests the Secretary-General to keep the Security Council informed on the implementation of this resolution.

10. Decides to meet again as necessary to consider further steps to ensure compliance with this resolution.

Last Stages of the Iran-Iraq War

The battle for Iran was supposed to be Qadisyat Saddam–a grandiose reminiscence referring to the ancient battle of Qadisya between the Arabs and the Persians, and alluding to Saddam as being "the Savior-Knight and Shining Armor of the Arabs." By 1987 the Arab League categorized Kuwait, Saudi Arabia and Iraq as being the beleaguered victims of the Iranian aggression. This prompted Saddam Hussein to declare on August 27, 1987 that his armed forces and his goals are unselfish and that they are not only for the defense of Iraq but also Kuwait, Saudi Arabia and the Gulf: "Iraq's policy always considers Iraqi national security to be an indivisible part of Pan Arab Security . . . Arab Gulf States are currently being exposed to certain circumstances and threats. In the light of this threat, Iraq considers its national security an integral part of the security of the brothers in Saudi Arabia and Kuwait. What threatens or harms them also threatens and harms Iraq." When Iran launched a surface-to-air missile attack against Kuwait in September, 1987, Iraq countered by attacking a number of economic targets in Iran as a reprisal for the attack on Kuwait and stated: "A day of revenge to underscore the bonds of blood, religion, history and destiny between Iraq and Kuwait and as a salute from Iraq."

If it wasn't for Kuwait and Saudi Arabia's support for Iraq, Saddam Hussein could not have avoided an economic or military collapse. On November 11, 1987 during the Arab Summit Conference held in Amman, Jordan, Saddam declared: "We should first of all eliminate the problem from which the Arabs have suffered–namely, the bane of interference of others based on claims and illusions such as populations, geographical areas that tempt some to impose trusteeship on others and interfere in their affairs. Without eliminating this problem, the Arab situation will never be rectified." With these "sincere" pronouncements and the imminent danger from the extremists in Iran, the Gulf countries and other countries around the world did not have much choice but to support or tilt toward Saddam Hussein, despite the numerous reservations they had about him at that time. The alternative could be disastrous. Defeat in the battle with Iran would be very alarming indeed!

Although the U.N. passed a resolution against attacks on civilian targets, the restraint from doing so did not last beyond March, 1985. In fact, by 1986, Iraq attacked Iranian cities and economic facilities.

Around September 13, 1986, Iraq hit a power plant and antiaircraft systems in Tehran. Iran kept its artillery attacks on Basra and Skud missile attacks on Baghdad and Basra. Iraq continued to have a massive advantage in the air despite heavy losses of aircraft and personnel. The war of the cities stopped for a short time and then resumed again in February, 1988 when Iraq launched an air attack on Iran's oil refinery. Iran also struck back with missiles. In 1988, the Iraqis recaptured the Fao Peninsula which was occupied by Iran in February, 1986. It has been reported that Iraq used poison gas in liberating the Fao Peninsula.

Chemical warfare was practiced between Iran and Iraq. The United Nations confirmed this fact in a report published in March, 1986 which concluded that Iraqi forces used chemical weapons in violation of the 1925 Geneva Protocol and that the use of chemical weapons in 1986 appears to be more extensive than in 1984; they were also used again in April, 1987. Both sides used chemical warfare. By March, 1988, Saddam Hussein used poison gas against his own people, the Kurds, in the town of Halabja located in Northern Iraq. This Kurdish city was viciously attacked with poison gas. More than 5,000 people were killed and more than 10,000 were wounded.

The chemical attacks, on Halabja and on the Iranians at other occasions, demoralized the nation and directly affected the spirit of those volunteering for the Revolutionary Guard (the Pasdaran).

Halabja was occupied by the Iranians in March of 1988. This prompted Saddam Hussein to attack the city with poison gas killing thousands of his own people.

On July 2, 1988, an Iranian airbus with 290 people aboard was downed by a missile attack from the USS Vincennes. The airplane was attacked by mistake and all people aboard perished in the tragic accident. This attack took place after America announced a policy of naval engagement which would allow it to protect neutral as well as merchant ships with a U.S. flag in the Arabian Gulf region. Soon after this tragedy, the Iranian government accepted U.N. Resolution 598 which called for immediate cessation of hostilities. Prior to this cease-fire, Iraq engaged in extensive attacks and occupied some Iranian territory. In August, the cease-fire between the warring factions took effect and Khomeini declared that "making this decision was more deadly than drinking poison." Nevertheless, he adhered to the cease-fire. Saddam Hussein declared himself the victor. The political stalemate between Iraq and Iran continued. The war lasted for eight years devastating the economies of both countries and causing one million casualties. Nearly a quarter of a million Iraqis and three quarter million Iranians were killed in this war. Many more were injured . . . In hindsight one Iranian said that the Iran-Iraq war was a direct "outcome of the

Islamic Revolution both in terms of the threat it posed to Iraq and the opportunity it presented."

Terrorism

Added to all these tragic losses is the terrifying endless list of a wave of terrorism which was inspired and, directly or indirectly, supervised by the extremist regime in Iran. Leading among the terrorist activities have been, as mentioned previously, the occupation of the U.S. Embassy in Tehran on November 4, 1979 and holding 52 Americans as hostages for 444 days. A devastating car bombing of the U.S. Embassy in Beirut, Lebanon killed 63 people on April 18, 1983. The truck bombing attack on U.S. Marine barracks, also in Beirut, Lebanon, took place on October 23, 1983 and killed 241 Americans and 58 French soldiers. On top of this, a series of bombings, kidnappings and murders took place in several parts of the world. Some of the people kidnapped during this period of time, around 1984 and 1985, were still hostages in 1991, suffering at the hands of their captors in Lebanon (they were finally released toward the end of 1991). Again on September 20, 1984, the U.S. Embassy annex in Beirut, Lebanon was demolished by using a truck-bomb and 14 people were killed. On December 12, 1983, attacks against the U.S. and French Embassies in Kuwait were carried out by car-bombing; seven people were killed and 17 of the terrorists were jailed until freed in August, 1990 by Saddam's army of occupation in Kuwait; Kuwaiti Airline flight 221 was hijacked and taken to Tehran on December 3, 1984. Two Americans from the State Department were tortured and murdered. TWA flight 847 was hijacked on June 14, 1985 and a U.S. Navy diver was killed on the tarmac in Beirut, Lebanon. In September, 1986, several bombs exploded at various busy locations in Paris, France where nine people were killed and 163 wounded. On February 17, 1988, the Marine Lieutenant Colonel Richard Higgins, an American with a U.N. observer team in Southern Lebanon was kidnapped and later executed. The Kuwaiti airline flight 422 was hijacked on April 4, 1988 and two people were murdered. The tragedy of the Pan Am flight 103 which exploded in mid-air in December, 1988 over Lockerbie, Scotland, killed 270 people (Libya was implicated).

During the Hajj season of 1988, Iranian pilgrims carrying 94 suitcases with explosives were stopped at Customs, but Saudi authorities chose not to publicize this fact in order to avoid inflaming the situation. On July 31, 1987, Iranian pilgrims in the Holy city of Mecca demonstrated and committed acts of violence in one of the holiest places of Islam. The wave of Iranians inspired and guided by Khomeini hurled rocks and other instruments at worshippers. Some of them had clubs and knives. Cars were overturned and burned. Many innocent people were killed and by the time order was established, the demonstrators had trampled over hundreds of people; 402 people died, among them 275 Iranians, and nearly 750 people were injured. When the Sacred Mosque in Mecca was seized in 1979 by a fanatic terrorist group, disinformation reports were circulated and encouraged by the Khomeini regime saying that Americans were the responsible party for the seizure of the Holy Mosque. Crowds in a number of Islamic countries were disturbed by such reports and in fact a mob took over the American Embassy in Karachi, Pakistan in November of 1979. Before the crowd dispersed, the Embassy was in flames, one army warrant officer and one American Marine were killed, along with two Pakistani clerks and two from the crowd. Inflammation of such passions and fanaticism was inspired by statements from Khomeini and his propaganda machine such as, "We will close the spy nest; it is a struggle between Islam and the infidels; America–the mother of corruption; the U.S. is number one enemy of humanity; death to Carter! Khomeini struggles, Carter trembles; Khomeini "knows that (Carter) is beating an empty drum. Carter does not have the guts to engage in a military operation." Long after the cease-fire took effect, Khomeini continued to be defiant and threatening. In March of 1989 he said, "as long as I am alive I will never stop cutting off the hands of agents of the U.S. and the Soviet Union." President Bush was quick in his response and said: "Such threats are deeply offensive to the norms of civilized behavior and Tehran will be held accountable."

The long arm of terrorism reached a number of cities in America, although on a much smaller scale than it was in other countries around the world. In fact, terrorism reached the family of Captain Will Rogers III who was the skipper on the guided missile cruiser, the USS Vincennes, which sent by mistake a cruise missile that destroyed the Iranian airbus which killed 290 on board. While his wife was driving to work to Lajolla Country Day School north of San Diego, California, U.S.A., she heard two popping sounds coming from the back of her white Toyota van. She jumped out of the car and the van exploded seconds later. Soon after that, the family changed their living quarters and identity in order to avoid the onslaught of terrorism from Iran.

Imagine, the naive and blind beliefs that allow one nation alone like Iran to stand against the entire world! Did Saddam Hussein learn his lesson? We shall see when he attacks Kuwait and stands against all odds. He too thought he could stand against the entire world . . . Throughout history dictators never learn!

Khomeini's inflammatory remarks energized some of the extremist terrorist forces around the world and helped in unifying the world against him and siding to some degree with Saddam Hussein, not out of love for Saddam's tyranny and terror, but essentially choosing "the lesser of two evils." Right after the disturbances at the Holy Mosque in Mecca by the Iranian pilgrims, Iranian mobs took over the Saudi Embassy and killed one Saudi official. Other terrorist activities inspired by Khomeini were carried against the interests of the Kingdom throughout 1987 and 1988 reaching from the burning of the Saudi Educational Mission in Beirut to the cold-blooded murder of Saudi Embassy officials elsewhere.

Saddam Hussein was carefully observing all these tragic terrorist activities, sometimes practicing his own brand and at other times watching, exploiting, learning, improving and waiting for the opportune time to strike against his friend and foe alike. Thinking he was a victor in the war and the sheer cease-fire in itself was a small victory—Saddam with his eighty billion dollars debt and his one million men army—seasoned in war—did not waste any time in preparing for his next moves of threats, occupation and terrorism.

Chapter 4

The Invasion of Kuwait

With the end of the Iran-Iraq war, Saddam Hussein brought economic destruction not only to Iran but also to his country, Iraq. He accumulated over 80 billion dollars in debt while prior to the war he had reserves of 30 billion dollars. In the meantime, he was the master of a well-armed, well-seasoned army of one million men, with over 500 fighter planes and 5,500 tanks. It was the fourth largest army in the world and certainly the most powerful in the Arab world, if not the entire Middle East.

In contrast, the Kingdom of Saudi Arabia, a peaceful nation of moderate policies, embarked on a massive program of modernization. The Kingdom had no military ambitions against its neighbors or anyone, so it concentrated on building its impressive infrastructure, improving the quality of life for its people and spreading goodwill and good deeds around the globe. In the meantime, the Saudis strengthened and modernized their defensive military forces. Although some lobbyists in the U.S. opposed selling them arms, the British were very willing and happy to do so. Luckily, friends around the world came to the Kingdom's defense in her hour of need!

In the Aftermath of the Iran-Iraq War

All along, Saudi Arabia was hoping that Saddam Hussein would come to his senses! Also, with a firm cease-fire with Iran sponsored by the United Nations, the world was hoping that he would concentrate on rebuilding his shattered economy and country. Instead of dismantling his mighty war-machine, he kept the one million men under arms and was accelerating his efforts to acquire more advanced weaponry and certainly moved at a fast pace acquiring more chemical and biological weapons and worked frantically to develop nuclear weapons. No sooner had the cease-fire taken effect between Iran and Iraq than Saddam Hussein was on his way to extract revenge from his arch enemy, President Hafez Assad, of Syria. Toward this endeavor, he supplied weapons to certain factions who were fighting against Syrian influence in Lebanon and against the peace proposals backed by them. Since Syria had leaned toward Iran during the war with Iraq, without sending any troops, Saddam Hussein wanted to punish Syria for this position. Shipping arms to fuel the civil war was done with fervor, barring no limits or barriers even the ancient enmities between Iraq and Israel. It has been reported that cooperation and collaboration with Israel were sought and received in this regard, so that Israel, with its dominance over the shores of Lebanon would not interfere with these shipments of arms. This meddling in the Lebanese quagmire did not help in resolving the civil war, nor did it lessen the stubbon and adamant attitude of some who were "liberating" Lebanon from Syrian domination. In fact, the entire duration of this so called "war of liberation" which lasted nearly two years did not lead to liberating any Lebanese territory. Instead, it led to more destruction, devastation and death of innocent people. Fresh support from Saddam Hussein, strengthened the resolve of those opposing the Taif Agreement which was destined to become the cornerstone for bringing peace to war-torn Lebanon.

In any event, President Hafez Assad proved to be a shrewd and intelligent man who sensed dynamic changes in the world and was able to adapt to the "new world order". With support from Syria, the Lebanese Government crushed Aoun and his followers. Aoun sought asylum at the French Embassy (later, he was moved to France). Saddam was not able to save him, let alone save himself from the onslaught which later developed against him by the world community.

Saddam Hussein's ambitions led him to initiate the founding of a small common market, called the Arab Cooperation Council (ACC), which included: Iraq, Egypt, Jordan and North Yemen (which became the Yemen Arab Republic). This Arab gathering was merely for commercial and economic reasons and supposedly did not constitute any threat to any other country. But down deep, Saddam intended this force to be not only a counter-measure to the Gulf Cooperation Council which included the oil rich Arab countries of the Gulf, but he wished to harness some political and military mileage from it. Cozy relations, be it on the economic or political scale, developed between Saddam's Iraq, King Hussein of Jordan and Yasser Arafat of the Palestine Liberation Organization as well as some improvement of relations with Yemen and Sudan. Egypt was cordial but always leery of Saddam's designs.

With former President Gorbachev's Glasnost and Perestroika dominating the headlines and essentially becoming contagious in Eastern Europe, where a wave of freedom and democracy swept the continent, Saddam sought to ease the minds of his creditors and would-be contractors who would help in rebuilding Iraq, by announcing in April, 1989 his intentions about having elections and a multi-party system. His announcements did not result in any freedom or democratization and his parliament remained a rubber-stamp institution. Creditors remained leery and wary of Saddam's intentions and his blood-thirsty reputation and repressions. As a camouflage to his inner intents and ambitions, he dispatched his diplomats around the world to preach the good word about Baghdad and its leadership and to emphasize Iraq's desire to be closer with the moderate Middle East forces. He declared that the National Assembly or Parliament would officially have non-Ba'athists as members, and any candidates who are considered "dangerous to Iraq" would not be permitted to have a seat.

His mighty force was worrisome and had to be reckoned with. His meddling and sinister designs brought many question marks, but he was a neighbor to be dealt with, with extreme caution. Any wrong moves could trigger his madness and onslaught!

Attacks on America and the West

Saddam Hussein had already started attacking the West, especially after he concluded that Russia's dominance as a mighty power was dwindling and communism in Eastern Europe had met its demise. He thought that the West was carrying a campaign against him because of Zionist influence on American and Western policies. When the Arab Cooperation Council met in Amman, Jordan on its first anniversary on February 24, 1990, he was on the attack. He railed against America and the presence of American Naval forces in the Arabian Gulf, although, such forces have been there for nearly half a century.

U.S. Assistant Secretary of State John Kelly visited Baghdad, Iraq on February 12, 1990. He met with Saddam Hussein to discuss relations between Iraq and the United States. The U.S. was still hoping to patch difficulties with the Iraqi leader in the hope that he and his government would moderate their views and seek good relations with America, the West, and moderate Arab leaders. With Saddam's credentials in terrorism, tyranny and the large arsenal of weapons and trained men under arms, it seemed this was the proper course of action to take in the remote hope that one could reason with him so that he would not veer too far off in the direction of terrorism and possibly war. In fact, Saddam was praised as a force for moderation in the region and the U.S. expressed its wish to broaden relations with Iraq. However, Saddam Hussein had other plans for Iraqi-U.S. relations and sinister plans for the Arabian Gulf, especially Kuwait, the United Arab Emirates and Saudi Arabia.

On February 15, 1990, the voice of America broadcast a program beamed to the Arab world in which criticism was voiced about dictators around the world. Saddam Hussein was among those attacked as being one of the worst tyrants. When the Iraqi President heard of the broadcast he was very infuriated because of the mixed signals he sensed. In order to soothe his feelings and appease him, an apology was sent stating that views on the Voice of America do not necessarily reflect the policy of the United States. It was hard for Saddam to accept this explanation, but he was promised that editorials and commentaries regarding Iraq would be submitted to the U.S. government for prior approval. In any event, on February 21, 1990, the U.S. State Department published a report on human rights violations around the world. It included violations by Israel and some other nations, including a twelve-page section on the State of Iraq. The authorities in Iraq were described as the "worst violators of human rights". Certainly, this did not set well with Saddam and his Ba'athist colleagues.

On February 23, 1990, Saddam Hussein arrived in Amman, Jordan for the first anniversary meeting of the Arab Cooperation Council. His message to the gathering was broadcast on Jordanian television. The main diatribe was aimed at the United States of America. He warned his fellow Arab countrymen of the declining power of the former Soviet Union and thus the rise in power of the United States of America. Such a shift in the geopolitical equation favoring America spelled the dominance of the U.S. over the Arab world. He went on to say that the country exerting the greatest influence on the region, on the Gulf and its oil, will consolidate its superiority as an unrivaled superpower. Thus, if the Gulf population and the Arab world for that matter are not alert enough, the area will be ruled according to the wishes of America. Saddam's message was clear; he, as a master of the Gulf, would far better safeguard the interests of the Gulf countries and the Arabs than America or anyone else. This subtle message was very clearly understood especially, by the President of Egypt, Hosni Moubarak who did not like what he heard, nor was he impressed by the designs of Saddam Hussein; so he walked out of the meeting and the Conference ended a day earlier than planned, although King Hussein of Jordan tried to patch differences by arranging a meeting between all three.

He stressed to his audience that America is beatable, saying, "We saw the U.S. as a superpower departing Lebanon immediately when some Marines were killed; these men who are considered to be the most prominent symbol of America's arrogance!" Then shifting to the brief attack on Panama, he declared that if the American forces had been continually engaged by the Panamanian armed resistance, the U.S. would have also been defeated. He went on to state that the U.S. had been defeated in a number of other areas around the world. "The U.S. had entered a fatigue, decaying and frustrating process coupled with hesitation when committing aggression on other peoples' rights and displaying motives of arrogance and hegemony." He also attacked America for helping Soviet Jews in their immigration to Israel. By this broad attack, he covered his bases with the Palestinians and some of the Arab masses supporting him, and thus tried to acquire a wider appeal to the Arab populace. Furthermore, in stating: "The country having greatest influence in the region, through the Arab Gulf and its oil, will maintain its edge as a superpower without an equal competitor," he implied that if the Gulf people, along with all Arabs, were not careful, the area would be governed by American wishes . . . Oil prices would be fixed in line with a special perspective benefitting American interests and ignoring the interests of others.

Saddam Hussein urged the Arab people in governments with investments in the West to pull their money and invest them in Eastern Europe and the former Soviet Union. He went further by using derogatory comments, such as, "There is no place among good Arabs, for cowards who claim that a superpower, namely the United States of America, should decide everything and that everyone else should submit." His unveiled remarks were aimed at President Hosni Moubarak whose courageous, wise and moderate leadership and friendship with America was being attacked in addition to side swipes against other moderate forces like Saudi Arabia and the Gulf countries who would not fall in line with his policy. The moderated radical Saddam Hussein was no more! Statesmen around the world continued to think it was still possible to do business with him and that he was simply uneasy about the future of his government and his country!

John Kelly continued to think that there was "Still a potentiality for positive alterations in Iraqi behavior." At the same time, a number of politicians and statesmen around the world were facing the reality and dangers of Saddam Hussein. While some people thought him still a man that one could do business with and avoid his tyranny and evil, others in the Arab world continued to think of him as the "knight in shining armor of the Arab nation." Many intellectuals and people that suffered from his dictatorial rule called him "a blood-thirsty tyrant and the Butcher of Baghdad." His ironfist policy was gaining momentum to punish his former friends and allies as well as his countrymen at home.

During the ACC Conference in Amman, Jordan, he passed on a message to King Hussein and President Moubarak that he expected the Arab Gulf countries, especially Kuwait and Saudi Arabia, to forgive him his war debt to the tune of over 42 billion dollars and that he expected on top of this another 30 billion dollars in cash. If the Gulf countries did not respond to his demands, he said, "I shall take steps to retaliate. Let the Gulf regimes know that if they do not give this money to me, I know how to get it." President Hosni Moubarak countered by saying, "Your demands do not make any sense. You are going to cause a lot of trouble." This was not the last of his continual fiery statements or the end of his bellicose pronouncements.

The case of Farzad Bazoft brought world outcry. He was a journalist, Iranian by birth, but a British citizen, working for the London Weekly, the Observer. He was arrested in September, 1989 while investigating a mysterious explosion at a military complex which was supposed to be a secret one, not far from the capital city of Baghdad. In March of 1990, he was put on trial and charged for espionage. He was executed a short time later despite many appeals for mercy. His execution brought a wave of protestation throughout the world.

On the second of April, 1990, more veiled threats and fiery statements were made. He announced to the world that Iraqi scientists have developed state of the art chemical weapons. They had an ample supply of them and certainly would not hesitate to use them against Iraq's enemies. He then made his promise: "I swear to God, we will make the fire eat half of Israel, if it tries to do anything against Iraq . . . Whoever threatens us with atomic weapons will be exterminated with chemical weapons." His Scud missiles moved to Western Iraqi territory, closer to the Jordanian border, posing a threat to the safety and security of Israel. Although the threat was not known at the time, but it was intended to be used against the innocent populations in Dhahran and Riyadh of the Kingdom of Saudi Arabia. The U.S. State Department branded his speeches and moves as being "inflammatory, irresponsible and outrageous." Ten days after his bellicose statements and boasts, a team of U.S. Senators visited him in Iraq. The mission was to smooth matters and to assure him that those legislators threatening to impose sanctions against Iraq would not succeed. Again, in the faint hope that soothing relations with Iraq and strengthening the approach of establishing friendly relations between Iraq, Egypt, Jordan and Saudi Arabia would help in drawing Iraq "into a web of friendly relationships" and thus Saddam's action could be kept within bounds. All this proved to be nothing but wishful thinking, as events uncovered his intentions in a few months to come. Even the Democratic Senator, Howard Metzenbaum of Ohio, who has been well known for his strong sympathies with Israel, praised Saddam Hussein in Mosul, Iraq on April 12, 1990 saying, "I am now aware that you are a strong and intelligent man, and that you want peace." By August 8, the switch was very swift and the Senator declared in Washington D.C., "I support the president's leadership . . . it is in the interest of the United States and the entire world to turn back Saddam Hussein." Many mixed signals were beamed to Saddam. His assessment was that the United

States would do anything to keep the peace with Iraq and avoid a confrontation with him. This was his first major miscalculation . . .

Supergun and Weapons of Mass Destruction

Saddam Hussein spent billions and billions of dollars on armaments—over 50 billion in the span of a decade. He ranked as the top man in the world in the purchase of biological, chemical and nuclear materials for his ever growing arsenal. He was very active in developing the supergun—a sixteen inch barrel which is a modified version of the 172 feet long gun developed by Gerald Bull (a Canadian who was a naturalized American artillery specialist). Bull did not live long enough to enjoy the monetary rewards he was receiving from Saddam Hussein. He was shot and killed in Brussels, Belgium, on March 22, 1990. A version of this cannon in Yuma, Arizona had set a world record. This was 120 feet long and was able to shoot a projectile about 112 miles straight up. A sixteen inch bore, 120 foot gun named Baby Babylon was assembled and tested in Iraq. It failed! Replacement parts for it were intercepted by the British customs and this thwarted the development of a second version called Big Babylon. This was supposed to be a monstrous gun, 512 feet long and with a diameter of 30 inches. Fifty-two pieces of pipe were to be used in building it. While 44 of these pieces had been sent to Iraq, the remainder were intercepted by British customs. These could form the muzzle of the enormous gun which had the potential capability of raining targets with biological, chemical or nuclear shells and reaching far into the distant horizons. The pipe manufacturer, Sheffield Forge Masters, and Saddam Hussein himself denied that the pipes were destined to be the major component parts of the supergun; it was stated that instead they were to be used for petrochemical and industrial activities. This huge gun was a dream-come-true for the designer and for the designs of Saddam Hussein. At a 45 degree angle, this gun could send projectiles very far into neighboring territories. The designer estimated that a three stage rocket shot out of a sixteen inch gun could fly way over 1000 miles. Huge projectiles could be lobbed at the enemies and friends of Iraq with much less expense than sending ballistic missiles to cause terror and destruction in neighboring areas. In any event, such a gun would be highly inaccurate, and could send terror and destruction aimlessly at broad targets chosen by Saddam Hussein. Also, it could have been used for launching satellites.

Around April 2, 1990, agents of Saddam Hussein were caught in an undercover operation jointly run by the United States and the British. The investigators found electronic capacitors from a manufacturer in

California. The manufacturer had immediately informed U.S. authorities. Saddam denied that he was building an Atom Bomb and Iraqi authorities insisted that the capacitors were for peaceful uses and not as detonators for making a nuclear bomb. Earlier the Israelis had attacked the Iraqi nuclear plant, Osirak, but the Iraqis had been able to salvage 27 pounds of enriched uranium. This is a quantity sufficient to produce an atom bomb after it is properly processed. Iraq had signed a non-proliferation treaty and such an amount should have been under the supervision and inspection of the International Atomic Energy Agency. Thus, Iraq embarked on a separate nuclear weapons program which would bypass this agency and would allow them to acquire uranium from various parts of the world and seek the necessary centrifuge equipment which would refine and produce the needed enriched uranium for making an atom bomb. Leading on Saddam's shopping list was the acquisition of electronic devices which would be the key units to trigger the uranium core of a nuclear bomb. An indictment by U.S. authorities states that in September, 1988, the American CSI technologies in San Marcos, California which is located North of San Diego, was contacted for such purchases. The Iraqis intended to buy capacitors, units that would store electricity and deliver it in a single jolt. The Iraqis needed high voltage, coaxial, low-inductance capacitors capable of withstanding vibration in altitude. Although capacitors can be used in a number of other devices such as explosives, mechanisms for separating rocket stages and as lasers, but the Iraqis were asking for the type of capacitors used for triggering a nuclear bomb. A responsible party of the company immediately informed the U.S. Customs Service which worked on the case. The Iraqis also wanted to buy krytrons, high-speed switches that detonate explosions through the release of the electricity stored in capacitors. These devices were to be obtained from another company. A shipment of forty capacitors which could be used to detonate nuclear warheads was delivered via Heathrow Airport in London and another forty-five capacitors were also sent which could be used for other military purposes. Arrival of the shipment in London triggered the authorities into action. They replaced the nuclear capable capacitors with defective types. When the Iraqi agent was about to board an Iraqi airline flight, he was arrested along with four other accomplices and the capacitors were seized.

The making of a nuclear weapon consists mainly of the uranium core surrounded by explosives and a web of detonators. The firing circuit surrounds the detonators. A special capacitor with high stored energy along with a trigger called krytron are used to start and activate the firing circuit. When ignition takes place, conventional explosives are activated and the explosion compresses the enriched uranium core until the critical mass is exceeded and triggers its explosion reaction and thus one has at hand a nuclear bomb with devastating effect.

Developing such nuclear capability would add to the might of Saddam Hussein and would transfer him from a regional superpower to a world nuclear power having an abundant supply of weapons for mass destruction. Using such a scenario, he went on to dream in his private thoughts to control the oil riches of the Arabian Gulf and thus becoming the major world power as well.

More Threats at the Arab Summit and the Arab League

During the Arab Summit Conference on May 28, 1990, held in the capital city of Iraq, Baghdad, Saddam Hussein took the opportunity to unleash his diatribe against the hands that fed him and defended him in the Iran-Iraq war. In a private session, he denounced his fellow Arabs. He stated that the Gulf States were keeping the price of oil too low and this in his opinion, was an economic war against Iraq.

In this closed session of the Arab Summit, the host of the Conference, Saddam Hussein, gave a speech behind closed doors in which he attacked those states that he felt were undermining the economic well-being of Iraq. Although the conference was supposed to deal with the immigration of Soviet Jews to Israel, his speech concentrated on his Gulf Arab neighbors. His tone was threatening and belligerent! His accusations were harsh and to the point. He accused those who were overproducing oil beyond their quota of, essentially, declaring an economic warfare against Iraq. Thus, he stated that continued violation of these quotas amounted to a "declaration of war on Iraq." He said, "war is fought with soldiers and much harm is done with explosions, killing and coup attempts; but it is also done by economic means. Therefore, we ask our brothers who do not mean to wage war against Iraq: is this in fact a kind of war against Iraq? . . . I believe that all our brothers are fully aware of our situation . . . We have reached a point where we can no longer withstand pressure." He explained to Arab heads of state that the drop in the price of a barrel of oil by one dollar, amounted to a loss to the Iraqi treasury equivalent to one billion dollars a year. His threats and attacks were mainly directed against Kuwait and the United Arab Emirates along with a veiled threat to other Gulf states.

The tone of his speech, the gravity of his accusations and his vehement threats were an ominous sign for a dangerous scenario in the making. King Fahd of Saudi Arabia, President Hosni Moubarak of Egypt, the ruler of Kuwait, Sheikh Jabir Ahamad Al-Sabbah, as well as a number of other moderate Arab leaders were amazed and dismayed by the tone of the speech and the gravity of the situation. They counseled patience and moderation! Toward the end of June, Iraq dispatched its Deputy Prime Minister, Sa'adoun Hammadi (a graduate of an American University) on a tour of the Arabian Gulf states. Saddam Hussein's emissary was seeking a contribution of ten billion dollars and a decrease in oil production from the Gulf states, so that the price of oil would jump from about 18 dollars a barrel to 25 dollars a barrel. This would be a great infusion to the treasury of Iraq. Oil production continued at levels unacceptable to the Iraqis. However, on the tenth of July, after a coordination meeting of the Gulf Oil Ministers in Jeddah, Kuwait and the United Arab Emirates (UAE) were convinced to agree and abide by the oil quotas allotted by OPEC.

Since Saddam Hussein did not receive his 10 billion dollars nor an acceptable reduction in oil production, especially, from Kuwait and the United Arab Emirates, he unleashed his Foreign Minister Tariq Aziz who arrived in Tunis to attend a meeting of the Arab League on July 16, 1990. This meeting was called in order to get support of the Arab nations for the Palestine Liberation Organization. However, a number of Arab countries did not attend. On July 16, Tariq Aziz came to the office of the Secretary General of the Arab League, Chadli Klibi and handed him a memorandum. It was a very shocking one, indeed! A letter written by him, dated July 15, 1990 (22 Thoul Hijja, 1410 A.H.) was delivered and then distributed on July 17 to members of the Arab League. In this letter, accusations were very strong and severe. The pressure on Kuwait especially, and the United Arab Emirates as well, was very excessive and very threatening. First, the letter addressed border disputes between Iraq and Kuwait mentioning the contacts that took place in the 1960's–1970's and stating that these did not succeed in settling the dispute. He went on to accuse Kuwait of putting "a plan into operation, a carefully and premeditated plan to eat away at Iraqi territory. Kuwait began to build military installations, and oil producing infrastructures and farms on Iraqi soil." He then reiterated Iraqi accusations that Kuwait and the United Arab Emirates, both had conspired to undermine Iraq and its economy. He said, "Kuwait with the complicity of the U.A.E., has hatched a plot to inundate the oil market with a surplus far in excess of the quota allocated by OPEC." Thus, he put the blame for any dangerous collapse in the price of oil squarely on these two small nations. The Foreign Minister of Iraq explained that between 1981 and 1990, and because of the depressed oil prices, the Arab countries lost the sum of 500 billion dollars since

Arab oil production was, according to him, 14 million barrels per day. Of this large loss, he alleged that Iraq sustained the total loss of 89 billion dollars, again due to depressed oil prices during that period. He continued to say, since prices this year have dropped several dollars below the 18 dollar fixed by OPEC, Iraq had suffered according to him, a loss of earnings of several billion dollars, at a time when her economy was in difficulty due to the military expenses incurred in the "legitimate defense of her territory, her security and her Holy places, as well as the territories of the other Arabs, their security and their Holy places, for eight long years." Then he dropped another bomb shell accusation: "The Kuwaiti government has not been content with these attacks. It has launched others more specifically against Iraq. It has installed an oil producing infrastructure in the Southern part of the Iraqi field at Roumailah and has begun to extract oil from it." He stated emphatically that the value of the oil extracted by Kuwait from this field was estimated to be approximately 2.4 billion dollars. This, according to him, inflicted intentional damage against Iraq twice. Once by weakening its economy and again by stealing its wealth.

He accused the two small nations of carrying a policy which was directly and openly being executed as part of an imperialist, Zionist plan against Iraq and the Arab nation. His threats got more severe when he said, "We condemn the action of the governments of Kuwait and the Emirates, considering it a direct act of aggression against Iraq, and clearly, against the whole Arab nation." His bellicose attitude and extremely dangerous threats were carried a notch higher when speaking of Kuwait: "The government of Kuwait has indeed, committed a double aggression against Iraq: first by seizing part of her land and her oil fields and then by stealing our national wealth. A behavior such as this is equivalent to military aggression. From another angle, the government of Kuwait deliberately tried to achieve the decline and destruction of Iraqi economy while Iraq is subject to ruthless, imperialist–zionist threats. Such acts of aggression are no less serious than a military aggression." As for the aid received from these two countries, during the Iran-Iraq war, he mentioned some interest free loans which were suspended after 1982. Such statements are simply contrary to the truth. Since the war lasted much longer than they expected, costing them the equivalent of 100 billion dollars in military purchases for defending their homeland with a long border of over 740 miles (1200 kilometers) with Iran, he complained about the aid and loans being registered as debt against Iraq despite the appeals to eliminate this debt. There was no positive response to such an appeal, although it went on for nearly a year since the Arab Summit Conference in Baghdad.

Iraq was producing 2.6 million barrels of oil per day prior to the Iran-Iraq war and since this production was slashed down and finally stopped around 1982; between September 1980 and September, 1985 when the 700 mile-pipeline crossing Saudi Arabia was used, Iraq had lost, due to the war and the decrease in its exports of oil, close to 106 billion dollars. This sum went into the coffers of the other oil producing countries in the region and according to him, the debts from Kuwait and the Emirates constitute a fraction of this profit.

President Saddam Hussein reiterated these points when he made a strong threatening speech on July 17, 1990, during Revolution Day celebrations. This was the 22nd anniversary of the revolution carried on by the Ba'ath party. He vehemently attacked Kuwait and accused it and the U.A.E. of conspiring with zionism and world imperialism to "cut off the livelihood of the Arab nation." Then he said, "that imperialists would not dare to attack Iraq which is the true defender of all the Arabs," especially since it has such a formidable military force. He implied that Kuwait and the United Arab Emirates were tools of imperialists and that the real agents of imperialism were the Gulf rulers who kept the price of oil down and "thrust a poisoned dagger into the back of Iraq." He threatened that Iraq would not be patient for too long and because "one would be better off dead than having his own livelihood cut off." He called on Kuwait and the United Arab Emirates to come to their senses, but if they don't he stated, "if words fail to afford us protection, then we will have no choice but to resort to effective action to put things right and insure the restitution of our rights." These demands had been made on a number of occasions and more recently formalized through presentation at the conference held by the Arab League in Tunis. They had been restated over and again, indicating that the Iraqis fully believed in their position. This wasn't merely Saddam's rhetoric. This was a repetition of his previous threats that became more ominous with the tick of time. However, Saddam's demands were taken as a bargaining position and not interpreted as an ultimatum for possible attack.

The Foreign Minister of Kuwait, Sheikh Sabbah Al-Ahamad Al-Jabir Al-Sabbah, answered the Iraqi accusations on July 18, 1990 (26 Thoul Hijja, 1410 A.H.). He refuted them all and condemned the ominous threats voiced against Kuwait. Within twenty-four hours of Saddam's speech, an answer was dispatched to the Secretary General of the Arab League refuting all Iraqi accusations. Kuwait stated that it had always been at the forefront of the Arab national struggle and it expressed dismay that a sister Arab nation like Kuwait would be treated as such by another Arab country, namely, Iraq. Kuwait offered aid to many countries around the world and especially the Arab brotherly countries, who received the lion's share. Kuwait had sacrificed much for its defense and support of Iraq during its war with Iran. The whole world knows how much Kuwait had suffered and sacrificed from such a position! It had been exposed to attacks, direct attacks which exacted a heavy toll on its citizens' establishments, petroleum facilities, and its fleet of oil tankers. All of this for the sake of Iraq and defending Iraq. It is a sad commentary, indeed when wicked aims prevail to hide the truth! What is really surprising in this regard is that these accusations against Kuwait came at a time when the echoes of praise for the courageous Kuwaiti position were, not long ago, reverberating from Iraq.

As for the accusations of Iraq concerning Kuwaiti oil production from the Southern Roumaila field, it should be certified here that this part of the field was inside Kuwaiti territory and Kuwait had produced oil from wells that are inside Kuwaiti territory South of the line specified by the Arab League and at a good distance from the international borders and according to international standards.

The Foreign Minister of Iraq responded to the Kuwaiti letter on July 21, 1990 where he reiterated his accusations that were stated previously and restated again the accusations of Saddam Hussein in his bellicose speech of July 17, 1990. He raised his accusation one big notch saying that when Iraq was busy with its war with Iran, the Kuwaiti government was very busy in devising a gradual movement on Iraqi land, building security zones, farms, military establishments and petroleum facilities, while Iraq did not pay attention to this because it was involved in a battle of destiny for itself and for all the Arabs. He then accused the Kuwaiti government of following the desires of U.S. policy. Then he declared to the Kuwaiti government that he who plots against the Arab nation and threatens its basic interests in the heart, the foreigner will not be able to protect him. This was signed by Tariq Aziz and dated Baghdad, July 21, 1990 (29 Thoul Hijja 1410 A.H.)

The threats that were stated in the Iraqi letter of July 15, 1990 were explained and made available to the United Nations.

Ominous Situation

By July 24, 1990, events were moving at a rapid pace. The U.S. State Department sent a confidential cable advising a number of American Ambassadors to inform their host governments that the United States of America was worried about the threats enunciated by the Iraqi President, because of their gravity and what they could entail. It warned that military force might be used by Saddam against his neighbors in the Gulf. In fact, on this very day, the Iraqi army began moving

Southward toward Kuwait, posing a direct threat to the existence of the neighboring Gulf countries and especially Kuwait. On the 25th of July, over 30,000 Iraqi troops were deployed to the border with Kuwait, in close proximity with the border of the Kingdom of Saudi Arabia. These were alarming moves to the Saudis, the Gulf countries and other moderate Arab leaders. American warships were put on a state of alert! Egyptian President Hosni Moubarak made a sudden visit to Iraq, Kuwait and Saudi Arabia for the purpose of mediating a peaceful resolution to the conflict hoping to defuse the situation and solve the problems between Iraq and its Gulf neighbors especially, Kuwait and the U.A.E. Iraq remained very obstinate and vehement in its demands that oil prices rise to 25 dollars per barrel. It also demanded reparation of 2.4 billion dollars as a compensation from Kuwait for the allegedly "stolen" oil from Roumeila field despite the fact that a portion of this field lies inside the international borders of the State of Kuwait. President Moubarak succeeded in convincing Saddam Hussein to send a delegation for a meeting in Jeddah, where the Kingdom of Saudi Arabia would mediate between Iraq and Kuwait in order to resolve their dispute which was moving to a critical state having the potential of exploding any moment. Saddam Hussein assured the Egyptian leader that he would not attack Kuwait. In fact, most world leaders thought that the movement of the Iraqi troops to the Kuwaiti border along with the excessive threats and bellicose statements that emanated from the Iraqi leader were in the rhetoric realm and essentially constituted a bargaining position, so that Iraq could extract from Kuwait more favorable terms in a possible deal, namely, leasing or acquiring the two strategic islands of Boubiyan and Warba. This would give them a better outlet on the Gulf and according to Iraq would ease their oil shipping problems. They also wanted all debts against them which had been accumulated from the Iran-Iraq war to be forgiven, simply because they thought they had been defending the Gulf countries and they deserved these billions of dollars to be forgotten. On top of all this, they demanded without any apologies or civil diplomacy, but through the use of a language of threats of attacking if their demands were not met. They demanded the immediate payment of 10 billion dollars from the state of Kuwait. While all these moves were concentrating on Kuwait and in a secondary manner on the United Arab Emirates, the message was very clear and the gravity of the situation was not lost on other nations in the Gulf, especially the Kingdom of Saudi Arabia which is a major force in the Gulf area, a major economic power and focal point for one billion Moslems around the globe. While Saddam Hussein's threats were directed against the two small nations, his threatening rhetoric always implied, under a thin veil, that the major economic power, namely, Saudi Arabia, should follow the line he had established for the region and must in one way or another understand who is the master of the Gulf. By implication, he was essentially saying indirectly, through his threats to Kuwait and the United Arab Emirates that Saudi Arabia should also take the lead in forgiving the 27 billion dollar debt to its brotherly Arab state. He stated that Iraq had defended the Gulf, not only for the sake of Iraq, but also for the sake of the Gulf countries, especially Saudi Arabia and Kuwait, when they fought their vicious war for eight long years with Khomeini. On top of this, since Saddam was asking Kuwait to give him outright another 10 billion dollars on top of forgiving whatever debt they have against him, then by implication he was expecting more than forgiveness of debt from the Kingdom of Saudi Arabia and the other Gulf countries. The demands were very rigid, severe and carried with them the threat of the mighty military force of the one million man army under the thumb and direct control of a tyrant who never shied away from using his force or his personal gun, whether against his own people or people from other lands.

In the midst of these dangerous developments and facts, well known to leaders around the world, especially those in the Arab world and the Gulf, about Saddam Hussein, his true character and ruthlessness, King Fahd of Saudi Arabia and President Hosni Moubarak of Egypt led strong efforts toward peace. They did everything humanely possible to prevent these serious developments from exploding and thus bringing tragedy not only to Kuwait and possibly other Gulf countries, especially Saudi Arabia, but also to prevent the imminent disaster that would eventually befall the state of Iraq and its people.

Glaspie Meets Saddam

As the situation heightened in gravity, Saddam Hussein summoned the U.S. Ambassador in Iraq, Ms. April Glaspie who had been there for about two years, but had never had a meeting with the president since her arrival there. The Iraqis released a tape recording of the meeting which took place between the two. At a later date Glaspie appeared before Congress for an inquiry concerning the discussion which had taken place between her and the Iraqi leader. As implied, the U.S. attitude was essentially conciliatory and it assured Saddam Hussein of the good intentions of the United States for good relations between the U.S. and Iraq. The signals which transpired from this meeting were mixed. They added to the confusing situation that was ominously developing in the region. Saddam Hussein made another tragic and serious miscalculation! Saddam with bravado "mocked"

American hesitance to get involved in wars abroad, he said, "Yours is a society that cannot afford 10,000 dead in one battle (we can)." He went on to say, "but when planned and deliberate forces push the price of oil down without good commercial reasons, then that means another war is being waged against Iraq. Military war kills people by bleeding them and economic war kills their humanity by depriving them of their chance to have a good standard of living. Kuwait and the U.A.E. were at the front of a policy aimed at weakening Iraq's position and depriving its people of higher economic standards; and you know that our relations with the Emirates and Kuwait were good. On top of all that, while we were busy at war, the State of Kuwait began to expand at the expense of our territory." U.S. Ambassador Glaspie reassured the Iraqi leader that she had direct instructions from the President to seek better relations with Iraq. In fact she expressed apologies for the media campaign which was portraying Saddam Hussein for what he was. Ambassador Glaspie went on to say, "Mr. President, not only do I want to say that President Bush wants better and deeper relations with Iraq, but he also wants an Iraqi contribution to peace and prosperity in the Middle East. Frankly, we can only see that you have deployed massive troops in the south. Normally, that would be none of our business; but when this happens in the context of what you said on your National Day, then when we read the details in the two letters of your Foreign Minister, and when we see the Iraqi point of view that the measures taken by the U.A.E. and Kuwait are, in the final analysis, parallel to military aggression against Iraq, then it would be reasonable for me to be concerned; for this reason, I received an instruction to ask you, in the spirit of friendship–not in the spirit of confrontation–regarding your intentions! I simply describe the concern of my Government; and I do not mean that the situation is simple; but our concern is a simple one."

Saddam Hussein answered: "It is natural for you as a superpower to be concerned; but what we ask is not to express your concern in a way that would make an aggressor believe that he is getting support for his aggression."

In an assessment of the effort made by his Arab brothers, Saddam said: "On this subject, we agree with President Moubarak that the Prime Minister of Kuwait should meet with the Deputy Chairman of the Revolutionary Command Council in Saudi Arabia, because the Saudis, aided by President Moubarak's efforts, initiated contact with us. He just phoned me a short time ago to say the Kuwaitis have agreed to that suggestion. A protocol meeting will be held in Saudi Arabia. Then the meeting will be transferred to Baghdad for deeper discussions directly between Kuwait and Iraq. We hope we will reach some result. We hope that the long range outlook and real interests will overcome Kuwaiti greed."

Then, Glaspie asked: "May I ask you when you expect Sheikh Sa'ad to come to Baghdad?" Hussein answered: "I told brother Moubarak that the agreement should be in Baghdad Saturday, (August 4, 1990) or Sunday. You know that brother Moubarak's visits have always been a good omen. Brother President Moubarak told me they were scared. They said troops were only 12 miles (20 kilometers) north of the Arab League (border) line. I said to him that regardless of what is there, whether they are police, border guards or army—regardless of how many are there, and what they are doing—assure the Kuwaitis and give them our word that we are not going to do anything until we meet with them. When we meet and when we see that there is hope, then nothing will happen. But if we are unable to find a solution, then it will be natural that Iraq will not accept death, even though wisdom is above everything else. There you have the good news!" In reassuring Saddam about the U.S. wish for better relations, Glaspie also said: "We have no opinion on the Arab-Arab conflict, like your border disagreement with Kuwait. All we hope for is that you solve those matters quickly." This statement of far-reaching consequences was interpreted by him as a green light to do what he intended to do in the Gulf. After all, he thought he was the master of the Gulf, anyway! In reality, the faint hope was still that Saddam Hussein would modify his behavior if the U.S. sought friendship with him. President George Bush acknowledged at a later date, "there was some reason to believe that perhaps improved relations with the west would modify his behavior." When congressional hearings were held at a later date, Ambassador, Glaspie was asked if she told Saddam Hussein that the U.S. would meet him with force if he attacked Kuwait? Her answer was very clear, "No, I did not!"

Invasion Is Imminent

On July 31, 1990 the Central Intelligence Agency and the Defense Intelligence Agency both agreed that some type of Iraqi military attack against the State of Kuwait was imminent. The Assistant Secretary of State For Near Eastern and South Asian Affairs, John Kelly, was before the House Foreign Affairs sub-Committee. In response to a question from its chairman, Representative Lee Hamilton, relating to any defense policy regarding the State of Kuwait, Kelly said, "we have no defense treaty relationship with any Gulf country. That is clear . . . We have historically avoided taking a position on border disputes." After the testimony, Hamilton said that Kelly "left the impression that it was the policy of the United States not to come to the defense of Kuwait." Such drastic statements added to the miscalculations of Saddam Hussein and his theory of gaining a green light for a dastardly attack on the State of Kuwait.

On July 26, the OPEC Ministers met in Geneva, Switzerland and agreed to limit the over-production of oil and thus gave a boost to oil prices. Kuwait pledged to abide by this agreement. On July 28, satellite photos taken by the United States detected Iraqi preparations for a possible imminent offensive against the small State of Kuwait. The Pentagon and the Central Intelligence Agency of the United States both estimated that an attack was highly likely. However, diplomats throughout the world believed that Saddam Hussein was, at this juncture, still only trying to frighten Kuwait into territorial concessions and a ransom of large sums of money, without resorting to an outright invasion. President George Bush sent a message to the Iraqi President stating that the U.S. wanted better relations with Iraq, but was deeply concerned about Saddam's threats to use force against his neighbors.

On July 29, King Hussein of Jordan visited Saddam Hussein in Iraq and said, "The Iraqis are bitter . . . Kuwait would not write off Iraq's debt, or end the border dispute, or stop stealing oil."

On July 31, 1990, the Kuwaiti Crown Prince and his delegation met with Iraqi Vice President Izzat Ibrahim and his delegation in Jeddah, Saudi Arabia, in order to discuss their differences. About this time, the Kuwaiti army of 20,000 troops were faced with the possible and imminent onslaught of 100,000 Iraqi troops massed on the border with the small State of Kuwait. The good offices of Saudi Arabia were being extensively used to bring about some peaceful settlement to this dangerously developing crisis. However, despite the miraculous efforts exercised in Jeddah, the talks between Iraq and Kuwait did not succeed, but a further meeting was planned for Saturday (August 4, 1990) which was to be held in Baghdad, Iraq. This meeting never took place. Iraqi tanks and troops crossed the border with Kuwait and a blitzkrieg attack against the small state began around 2:00 in the morning, local time. The small state of Kuwait was occupied within eight hours and the Kuwaiti ruler Sheikh Jabir Al-Ahmad Al-Sabbah, along with his government, fled for their safety to the Kingdom of Saudi Arabia and the protection and hospitality of King Fahd and the Saudi people.

King Fahd followed the rapid unfolding of these tragic events and he later narrated actually what took place during the critical negotiations in Jeddah and afterward. Now we will take the reader, to the Salam Palace in Jeddah, Saudi Arabia, where *King Fahd responded to an important question from one of his citizens*. During a dinner with representatives of the Saudi populace, on Tuesday November 27, 1990 (10 Jumada the first, 1411 A.H.) **King Fahd** of Saudi Arabia gave a detailed **narrative account** of the steps taken prior to Iraqi occupation of Kuwait. This gathering took place in Jeddah at the Salam Palace. The Custodian of the Two Holy Mosques said:

"The relationship amongst us in this nation of ours is built on a basic foundation. Most important in it is the Islamic base which we are very proud of. We hope, God willing, we will serve our Islamic belief with all the understanding and meaning of the book of God and the Sunna of his Prophet, peace be upon him.

I believe that everyone shares the opinion that in this land there is nothing that we are more proud of, and it does not exist anywhere else except here, and that is Mecca, Madina and the House of God and Mosque of the Prophet, peace be upon him. For this reason the people in this land have many duties in all directions. We speak of duties which are in practice the largest and greatest duties that people could bare.

It is a source of pride and happiness from God Almighty who dedicated us to the service of Islam and the Moslems. May we strive to accomplish what we must for all that God has bestowed upon us, having placed us in these Holy places.

Concerning the world events which we are facing, there are given situations which may lead to many concerns that we may predict, but predictions are one thing and facts are something else.

Unparalleled Historical Event

Of the important events in my view personally, and I believe that we all share this point of view, is a tragic event which is unparalleled in history. That event is, one Arab country neighboring another Arab country with whom it is supposedly in agreement and with whom it has a treaty of recognition, moves after midnight and occupies the neighboring country at the point of a gun. This affects our Arab position. Maybe others will ask why the Arab nation is not able to unite in a frame strengthened with love and understanding.

I have previously mentioned that the first one who was surprised with what happened to Kuwait by Iraq was me. I know these problems and I lived with them for years; especially in the latter days since we all know about this matter coming to the forefront.

There was a dispute relating to the production of petroleum–I mean at the beginning of the problem. A while after that, problems started again between Iraq and Kuwait in relation to the borders and also to an oil field named "Roumeila Field." A discussion began about this problem. This was not new and it was possible that the Kingdom of

Saudi Arabia with its good relations with Kuwait and Iraq might come up with good results in solving this matter.

This problem was discussed with the two parties and we got some results from Kuwait. It was possible that we could discuss matters with a friendly approach and then it was possible to reach what is beneficial and constructive.

Futile Attempts
We contacted Iraq and they had the same response but with some arrogance.

I tried myself as much as possible to do something, but events were moving faster than a human being could follow them with ease. It was determined that the speed of events was for a specific purpose. This purpose we did not know at the time, nor did we know to expect what has happened.

It appears to me that the situation was prepared prior to the latest Arab Conference in Baghdad and maybe even before that.

Matters began to take shape in an aggressive way which did not indicate that the situation could be corrected in a useful and constructive manner. Despite this, I tried to contact the Iraqi president since we have supported Iraq in an open way (during the Iraq-Iran War). We have supported Iraq because it is a neighboring Arab country–a part of the Arab nation and we are part of this nation.

What position could Iraq or President Saddam Hussein identify and say that the Kingdom of Saudi Arabia hurt him? He is not able to identify such a position! And I believe we all heard the Iraqi President Saddam Hussein on many occasions when he said that the Kingdom of Saudi Arabia did not shrink once from doing what it could to live up to its duties toward Iraq, whether in the supply of materials, military equipment or the use of its ports for whatever Iraq needed.

After these good deeds in supporting Iraq, how could one ever think that one day Iraq could come after midnight and occupy Kuwait? I believe that no one thought this kind of action possible, no matter how observant we might have been about some straining in relations. However, such straining did not have to lead to what has happened between Iraq and Kuwait. When we knew there was some tension, I sent his Royal Highness Prince Saud Al-Faisal to Saddam Hussein and said:

"We observe preparations and maneuvers in the region of Fao! We do not understand the reason for such activities. With respect to Iran, the problems have ended and an agreement has been reached between you and the Iranians!"

The answer came that the Iraqis were thinking of nothing except that their military forces needed some training from time to time to guarantee that no problems would arise between them and Iran. Also, if acceptance of the Security Council Resolutions (for Iran-Iraq) was to falter, then something undesirable could happen.

We were supposed to believe this talk? We observed something unnatural! Such action did not attract attention to the degree that would make an individual believe that there would be no escape from the fight taking place.

As I mentioned previously, we were in contact with President Hosni Moubarak (of Egypt) and discussed this affair. We were observing these matters! I told President Moubarak that his R. H. Prince Al-Faisal, our foreign minister, went to Iraq and Saddam convinced him and we believed that these training and military movements could not be interpreted as being directed against Kuwait and that this thought should not even cross the imagination ever. Yes! These are his words, himself:

"There is a problem of frontiers between us and we hope that it will be solved by peaceful means."

I was personally very close to both of these two countries—Iraq and Kuwait—and I felt the Kingdom of Saudi Arabia was capable of doing something so that matters would not reach the point that they did.

Here is what happened! There was a discussion between me and President Hosni Moubarak concerning the results reached through the visit of Prince Saud. We were convinced naturally, that there was no way but to believe Saddam Hussein, because there was no problem between us and Iraq, only good relations existed. This is exactly what we have known, as it appeared! President Moubarak said he must also go to Iraq and Kuwait and we agreed this was a good idea. We were trying to push away the phantom of any problems that may exist in the mind. We felt there was no danger of war.

Political Activities and Meeting in Jeddah

President Moubarak went to Iraq and Kuwait and was assured as was I. After that, he contacted me and said:

"I have reminded the Iraqis that we have observed that discussions have ceased—discussions that were supposed to continue between Kuwait and Iraq." President Saddam mentioned this thought and said: "It is possible to resume discussions concerning the border problem. That is what the Iraqi President mentioned. He said: "Fine, but I will not accept that we will go back to where we were when we stopped and we should have our meeting in the Kingdom of Saudi Arabia."

President Hosni Moubarak contacted me and it was natural that I concurred on this and welcomed the two countries. Iraq and Kuwait agreed. It was agreed upon that two delegations would come, one from Kuwait and one from Iraq. The Kuwaiti delegation was under the leadership of the Crown Prince and Prime Minister of Kuwait and the Iraqi delegation was headed by the Vice President Izzat Ibrahim and other officials accompanying him.

They arrived about ten o'clock in the morning to the Jeddah airport and were welcomed by his R. H. Prince Abdullah Bin Abdulaziz. First to arrive was the Crown Prince of Kuwait. Prince Abdullah accompanied him until they arrived here to the Diwan. Then, Prince Abdullah returned to accompany the Vice President of Iraq.

What is important is that we all met in the reception area and a conversation took place between the heads of the two delegations. We were happy with this because we considered it an undertaking toward goodwill. After they stayed for awhile, I told them that there were places ready for their comfort and for their meeting whenever they desired.

The two parties welcomed this suggestion. Prince Abdullah Bin Abdulaziz took them to the quarters specified for them. Following the initial meeting, the two delegations met alone. The Kingdom of Saudi Arabia did not have any interference or mediation between the two countries, because they were two neighbors and they are supposed to have an understanding among themselves and did not need a mediator. The item which caused the discussions to stop previously was solved with the meeting, so they continued the discussion among themselves. In the first instance the two met together alone, and later representatives from the Kuwaiti and Iraqi delegations joined in the discussion.

Their discussion ended. Each went to their allotted quarters, then later came to a dinner prepared for them at 9:30 P.M. The chief of the Iraqi delegation, the Vice President of Iraq, requested from the Chief of Protocol to prepare one car which would take the Vice President of Iraq and the Crown Prince of Kuwait and that the car would have two flags, the flag of Iraq and the flag of Kuwait. When the Chief of Protocol told me this, I was happy because this meant that an agreement had been reached . . . it meant that a principle had been established! The two arrived together in one car and after a short duration, dinner was ready, so we went to the place for dinner. Initially, I did not talk to either party. We considered the subject to be among two neighboring countries.

It is certainly natural when people are next to each other, in a place for eating, that a discussion among them takes place. I asked the Crown Prince and Prime Minister of Kuwait about the meeting; I said "God willing things are taking a natural course!" He said, "I was aware of the previous talk and what it led to. When the discussion stopped between us and Iraq, I mentioned to the head of the Iraqi delegation Izzat Ibrahim that I am ready to discuss with him any items he desired, or review what happened regarding recent or old matters."

A Meeting In Baghdad

We all know that the subject of the borders between Kuwait and Iraq had been a problem since Abdul Karim Qassem. Many disturbances had taken place but were finally settled.

His Royal Highness Sheikh Sa'ad told me that the head of the Iraqi delegation, Izzat Ibrahim talked to him some, but in the end, the head of the Iraqi delegation wished that the discussion be continued in Baghdad. As I was told by the Crown Prince of Kuwait, they agreed that their meeting here was to bring a thaw in relations between the two countries. They agreed that they would meet in Baghdad on Saturday.

Certainly, I blessed this thing and I was happy that matters were clearing. They left from here around eleven o'clock at night. Shortly after that time, the head of the Iraqi delegation left for Iraq and the head of the Kuwaiti delegation left for Kuwait, on a condition that they would meet again on Saturday.

I believed that everyone would be happy concerning the clearing of matters and improvement between the two Arab countries and that the situation was now a matter of dialogue.

Attack On Kuwait

I was surprised early in the morning on Thursday, when the concerned authorities told me that Kuwait was being attacked. Truly, at first hand, it was difficult for someone to absorb a matter like this. Attacked from which direction? They said, from Iraq! I needed to verify the information so I called our Embassy in Kuwait. I asked, "What is the truth about what I heard, exactly?" Officials in the Embassy said the Iraqi army had begun occupying Kuwait. After this, I believed one could not say anything except that what has happened would not have happy results. Anyone would be surprised by such an event, especially us, since we are neighbors and were in agreement with one another. It did not occur to us that such a thing would happen despite existing problems. We felt these problems could be solved.

Attempt to Stop Hostilities

I tried to contact President Saddam immediately but was not able to. Those who answered the phone said that President Saddam was far away and he could not be reached so I understood what that meant! He did not wish to take my call. After that he did call at 8:00 in the morning.

When I tried contacting him, I wished to see if it was at least possible to stop the fighting and then see what are the possibilities. When he contacted me in the morning he said he would send his Vice President, so I welcomed him–hoping! The Vice President arrived. We found the answer to be clear and frank and that was, "the situation is not anything strange nor should it be a cause for any problems . . . part of Iraq has been returned to Iraq." Naturally, this may be said to someone else, but I know that this is not true and that Kuwait is an independent nation since old time. History about it is long, if we wish to go back hundreds of years.

Add to this the fact that an agreement has been signed between Iraq and Kuwait and such a treaty constitutes recognition (of Kuwait by Iraq) during the era of President Hasan Al-Bakr. During that time, I believe the Vice President was Saddam Hussein. The agreement was published and I believe those present have seen it before. The agreement compels the two parties to respect one another. Who are those respecting one another? They are Arabs . . .

What Happened Is Unacceptable
Of course, I told this to the Iraqi Vice President and I said I do not need to answer you but you could answer yourself. If Kuwait is part of Iraq it was not necessary for you to sign an agreement with Kuwait. We do not accept what has happened under any circumstances. It is rejected and this will bring about many matters which were not necessary. Another thing, is Iraq now in need of petroleum? I believe the answer is, no! Is Iraq in need of land? No! Is Iraq poor? No! It has rivers. It has agricultural land. Iraq has been known and famous for its agriculture prior to the discovery of oil. It is a rich country with petroleum, a rich country with minerals and a country with enough people! Then there is no reason for Iraq to commit an aggression against Kuwait, except for a specific purpose. The attack which took place before dawn was a vicious attack; on Thursday morning, we were surprised by it and by the preparations which were in place. Facing the Kingdom of Saudi Arabia were more than 3,500 tanks, about 150,000 soldiers, armored vehicles and airplanes–big preparations.

Our brothers probably noticed our silence on Thursday and Friday. But silence was for a reason–to study a new strange situation! And what is after Kuwait?

During these two days we were able to conclude that what is after Kuwait is with certainty the Eastern Region of the Kingdom of Saudi Arabia. If not, why this great force? Why this surprise?

I believe what your government, my fellow countrymen, has done and initiated is what the Kingdom of Saudi Arabia should do.

The World Comes To Our Aid

We prepared the army of the Kingdom of Saudi Arabia to join Arab armies in case anyone wanted to commit aggression against us. This was the goal! This is the orderly manner. These agreements with the Summit meetings dictate this and we abide by it. This is the Charter of the Arab League which defines these matters. To have any thought that an Arab nation would commit aggression against another Arab nation, this did not occur at all!

I believe that logic and clear thinking permit us to say, and in my capacity as a responsible in front of God and in front of the people of the Kingdom of Saudi Arabia, that the only decision was to declare our support officially, beginning with the Arab nations, the Islamic nations and the friendly nations who wished to support the forces of the Kingdom of Saudi Arabia; because it was certain that the Iraqi army, which has been dispatched in the desert between us and between Kuwait and the desert between us and Iraq and is confronting the Kingdom of Saudi Arabia–did not come in vain.

Are we to allow the second plan for occupying a part of the Kingdom of Saudi Arabia to take effect? I believe with certainty that no one would accept this. When one is entirely responsible, the situation will not allow for any hesitation; one must act. Myself or someone else, we have to accept the responsibility. We should accept it in such a way as to carry its burden.

I believe that there is no citizen of the Kingdom of Saudi Arabia who does not consider this course of action to be logical and right. One of God's gifts to us is the fact that the great nations, representing the *biggest countries of the world* with respect to military power, responded to the Kingdom of Saudi Arabia in the speediest manner possible. This is the power of God and it is not our power, the power of God Almighty who made these countries respond to the call for help by the Kingdom of Saudi Arabia.

Yes! We have a strong military! But it is not of the level of an army which fought eight years with billions of dollars spent on it as aid from the Kingdom of Saudi Arabia and Kuwait! The fact that Arab countries, Islamic countries and friendly countries come to the aid of Saudi forces, I believe as I mentioned before, that this is the will of God Almighty and it is not the power of anyone else at all.

The Whole World Rallies

This has happened for the first time in history. It has happened from God Almighty and because of the respect of the world as a whole for the Kingdom of Saudi Arabia. It is well known that the Kingdom of Saudi Arabia is a nation which respects itself. Those who respect themselves are respected by others. The truth is that international relations and policies of the Kingdom of Saudi Arabia were built on solid foundations for several decades. Not one day, the Kingdom of Saudi Arabia tried to create a problem for anyone. On the contrary, it distances itself from creating any problem for any country, let alone Arabic nations who have responsibilities toward us and we have responsibilities toward them. Logically speaking, it is not possible in any way whatsoever that we cause harm to a neighboring Arab country or a distant one. I do not believe that anyone would cause the Kingdom of Saudi Arabia harm except out of greed and injustice. It is the right of the Kingdom of Saudi Arabia to defend itself. The situation as we see it now, has begun to become more critical and has taken international dimensions.

The Kingdom of Saudi Arabia cannot say to the countries of the world, "Do not stand on the side of justice!" There is a principle. I believe everyone knows it and that is the principle of the Kingdom of Saudi Arabia and there is no other solution but it. That is, Iraq must withdraw from Kuwait without any preconditions. It should return to Iraqi territory and the Kuwaiti people should return to their homeland under the leadership of the government of Kuwait and the leadership of his Highness Prince Jabir, just as Kuwait was previously.

The Only Acceptable Solution
This is the only solution which can possibly be acceptable. Anything else is finally unacceptable. I do not believe that anyone who is knowledgeable and knows their far-reaching consequences, is to accept anything else; but is it for the interest of Iraq to stand in front of the entire world and say, "No?" In the end, we see the world issuing declarations and organizing commitments among the largest nations of the world. Finally and without doubt, these agreements will possibly bring tragedy for Iraq. We do not wish a tragedy on Iraq! I am still calling from this platform, as I have appealed before, that President Saddam Hussein must use reason; it is not strange for him to declare tomorrow that he will in fact, withdraw from Kuwait totally–withdraw to Iraqi territory and leave Kuwait to those responsible in the Kuwaiti government, the people of Kuwait and the leadership of Kuwait. I do not believe this will constitute a drawback on him but on the contrary! However, will he respond to this? He has the answer and I do not have it.

This is the position of the Kingdom of Saudi Arabia. No other position will be accepted ever. We will not accept any position except that Kuwait returns as it was previously with the help of God. When the Iran-Iraq war ended, we were happy. Concerning Kuwait, I tell you the facts and the truth and that is we will not relinquish our position and negotiations will not be accepted at all. Negotiations for what? Giving a reward for someone who occupied a nation! (Aggressors will not be rewarded.) I don't believe that this will cross anyone's mind and I don't believe that anyone would accept this for himself by any means whatever. As for the future, no one will be able to predict it or predict what will happen.

Coalition Forces Will Not Stay
My fellow citizens, rest assured that the armies, which came to support the army of the Kingdom of Saudi Arabia based on the request of the Kingdom of Saudi Arabia, came and are now present. These forces will return to their respective countries when we request them to do so. We hope that these matters will end in a just way. After that, every army will return to its nation.

As far as we are concerned, we did not have an agreement with any party stating that any army would stay in the Kingdom of Saudi Arabia at all. But at this moment, I extend my sincere thanks to those who came to our aid in the most difficult days and nights without any preconditions. If this is an indication of anything, it speaks of the respectable position enjoyed by the Kingdom of Saudi Arabia around the world.

The World Stood On The Side Of Justice
For example, if we took a poll to know who among the countries of the world, stood on the side of the Kingdom of Saudi Arabia, from *East to West, South to North*. I believe that it would be all countries of the world: Islamic countries in Asia—more than 450 million—and in Africa the same number and in the Middle East, the European countries, North and South America. What is important is—why did all nations of the world stand with the Kingdom of Saudi Arabia and Kuwait? They stood with us because we are right.

Add to this that the will of God made the entire world stand with Kuwait whose capabilities have been pillaged and its integrity had been desecrated. You all have witnessed the situation. We don't just say it lightly. But we have seen it on television, we heard it from people. Never in history has an Arab nation invaded another Arab nation. As for whoever is seeking a solution, he should ask the question to President Saddam Hussein . . ."

Blitzkrieg Attack on Kuwait
Saddam Hussein made numerous promises that he would not attack Kuwait–promises made to many world leaders, leading among them

King Fahd of Saudi Arabia, President Hosni Moubarak of Egypt, President George Bush of the U.S. and President Mikhail Gorbachev of the former Soviet Union. Nevertheless, the attack came at exactly 2:00 o'clock in the morning on Thursday, August 2, 1990 in a moon-lit night, 100,000 Iraqi soldiers armed to the teeth moved with might and speed on a journey of only 40 miles toward Kuwait City which they reached within five hours. Also, two additional commando units moved on by air and from the Gulf as well.

The Amir of Kuwait, Sheikh Jabir Al-Ahmad Al-Jabir Al-Sabbah defined Kuwait's peaceful and fraternal mission. He said, "Kuwait lives under the protection of Islam as its religion, Arabism as its homeland, co-operation as it strategic path, tolerance as its motto, fraternity as its guidance, consultation as it modus operandi, justice as its rule, progress as its responsibility and peace as its goal." A nation with such peaceful mission does not deserve the brutality and mutilation dished out of Baghdad.

This dastardly and brutal occupation of a peaceful and friendly neighbor brings to mind a true story about Saddam Hussein and his mastery of deceit and deception. Once, shortly before the war, the ruler of Kuwait, Prince Jabir Al-Sabbah came to visit him in Iraq. Saddam turned to the Amir, in the company of their families and said, "We revolutionaries do not know or cannot even predict longevity of our existence. Today we are here, tomorrow we are gone! If anything happens to me, Jabir (the Amir) will be your father."

On another occasion, the ruler of Kuwait, Jabir was moved by such expression of faith and told Saddam: "My people in Kuwait would love to see you come and visit our country. We extend to you our official invitation. We would certainly like to show you our hospitality and love for you and the Iraqi people." Saddam Hussein was quick to say, "I will be coming to visit Kuwait; you yourself will not even know when I will be coming. I will surprise you!" And what a surprise it has been! What a tragedy! What a betrayal!

In a speech to Arab lawyers delivered on November 28, 1988 in Baghdad, Saddam Hussein said: "An Arab country does not have the right to occupy another Arab country . . . God forbid, if Iraq should deviate from the right path, we would want the Arabs to send their armies to make things right. If Iraq should become intoxicated by its power and move to overwhelm another Arab state, the Arabs would have the right to deploy their armies to keep it in check. How will it be possible for us to live together and trust each other, if the minimum mutual trust is lacking? . . . Walking with your brother and your gun at the ready is like keeping the company of Chicago gangsters." How disarming and deceitful such statements have been, not only for the people in the Gulf, but for leaders around the world as well!

When Saddam Hussein wanted to sign a non-aggression pact with Saudi Arabia, the government was surprised for such a move! King Fahd told him, "This is not needed between friends!" Saddam answered, "Such friendship and non-aggression treaty will put to rest designs of enemies who practice their play in murky waters." When King Fahd visited Iraq on an official visit and to sign this pact, he was received by the Iraqis as a great hero of the Arabs, because of all the sacrifices and extensive aid he offered Iraq in its time of need during its lengthy ordeal and war with Iran. However, the change of heart and the true color of Saddam Hussein finally came to the surface. His indirect plots against the Gulf countries were picking up speed and soon enough he directly attacked the Royal family, and especially King Fahd of Saudi Arabia, in a scathing manner laying aside and forgetting all the great sacrifices and help that came from the Kingdom and the Arab Gulf countries.

When the news of the Iraqi buildup along the border with Kuwait reached the Kingdom of Saudi Arabia, King Fahd immediately dispatched his Foreign Minister, Prince Saud Al-Faisal, to Iraq for clarifications. Saddam Hussein was very reassuring in informing the Foreign Minister that he should not worry about the buildup of troops along the Kuwaiti border. His response was, "These are just a few regiments from the Republican Guard who are just practicing and making military exercises in the south of the country. There is definitely no motive of any aggression." Of course, these same assurances were given to many world leaders around the globe. In fact, most observers and leaders initially thought that these maneuvers were essentially saber-rattling in order to extract maximum concessions from the Kuwaitis and to tilt any negotiations and peaceful moves toward the demands and desires of Saddam Hussein, namely, extracting more billions of dollars from the Kuwaitis and possible border adjustments. That is why, when the attack came, no one in the area had the slightest idea that Saddam would go through, all the way to Kuwait City, and occupy the entire little country.

Saddam breached his promises to world leaders and Arab leaders who had helped him in his tragic war with Iran, including King Fahd of Saudi Arabia with whom he signed a friendship and non-aggression treaty and President Hosni Moubarak with whom he founded the Arab Cooperation Council (ACC). He breached his promise to the United States of America, the British, the French, the former Soviet Union and other major powers around the world.

In the early morning hours of August 2, 1990, a day which will go down in history as a "day of infamy", Saddam Hussein committed one of the biggest follies a dictator could commit in the history of mankind. He unleashed his military might against the peaceful small state of Kuwait. His well trained army and modern war machine was on the move for vicious action against the innocent population of Kuwait. Saddam Hussein, his military and his party were shooting for the big prize and were not going to just occupy the islands of Boubiyan and Warba on the Arabian Gulf, instead the thrust was southward to the oil riches of Kuwait and beyond. This plan must have been in the minds of Saddam and his Revolutionary Command Council for some time. It had been brewing and finally, it was executed in defiance of the whole world. He chose the month of August for a number of reasons, leading among them was the fact that during this month the seering temperature in the region can reach as high as 130 degrees Fahrenheit in the shade, and because of such severity in the weather many Kuwaitis go outside to other countries for their summer vacation. In fact, over a third of the population was out of the country at that time. Of course, this lessened any expected resistance. He did not expect much of a resistance since the balance of power was very much lopsided, favoring Iraq many times over. The morning thrust was a perfect timing for the Iraqi army since the cool desert air is very comfortable at this time of night. If he were to attack during the day the seering heat would lessen the drive of his troops and the impact of his thrust would also expose him to possible attacks from the air by nations that would come to the aid of Kuwait. He applied a blitzkrieg speedy attack so that the Kuwaitis and any would-be supporters would not have the time or chance to rally their forces and counter-attack the invading Iraqi army. About four hundred Iraqi tanks rolled across the border, rumbling down with their commanders along a super modern six-lane highway. This superhighway was built by Kuwait as a symbol of friendship and good neighborly relations with its brotherly Arab neighbor to the north, Iraq.

Spearheading the attack was the eighth brigade, known as the Republican Guard. These troops are well known for their loyalty to Saddam Hussein and for their extensive training. The invading forces were under the general command of Najm Al-Din Abdullah. The Iraqi Chief of Staff was Major General Abdul Karim Al-Khazragi (He was executed with a number of senior officers, two months after the invasion).

As for the balance of power between Iraq and Kuwait, there was hardly any match! The difference is staggering from every angle. Iraq is a large country of about 170,000 square miles, while Kuwait is about 7,000 square miles. Iraq has a population of seventeen and a half million while the Kuwaitis themselves are barely one million. The Iraqi army is a very well trained, well seasoned army of one million men, having about 5,500 tanks, over 500 combat aircraft and 51 ships. Kuwait has an army of about 20,000, less than 300 tanks; their combat aircraft is around 36 and ships around 46. Also, during the attack, Kuwaiti army was not in a state of alert, fearing that such an action might excite Iraq into aggression. So there was essentially no match, especially since Kuwait had to depend on the goodwill of its neighbor knowing that it had suffered terribly during the Iran-Iraq war, just because it was supporting the Iraqis and pouring billions of dollars into their coffers. Kuwait also depended on the goodwill of the world community, on treaties and international law, especially, the protection and prestige of the United Nations, the Arab League, the Moslem World Organization and many more. All these were disregarded altogether by the decision of Saddam Hussein to attack and occupy Kuwait. In fact, the path of the invading forces was a clear one without any delaying tactics or defenses which would interfere with any speedy action of any invading force. Simply, Kuwait was not prepared to defend itself against an attack by its brotherly Arab neighbor to the north.

The attack was on two fronts: the first one moved from Safwan and then Abdali in the direction of Jahra. The second wave started from Umm Qasr, just north of the Kuwaiti border to Sibla to reach the bridge of Boubiyan Island and Bahra. On these islands, the invading forces did not encounter any resistance, although any resistance would have been decimated by the overpowering might of the Iraqis. The major invading force found some resistance north of Jahra. However, this was overtaken decisively in a very short time. After that encounter, any resistance was dealt with very swiftly; nothing really stood between the invading forces and the heart of the state of Kuwait. In less than five hours the crack combat troops of Saddam Hussein, with their latest Soviet T-72 tanks and armored personnel carriers, reached Kuwait City. Iraqi landing craft and escorting ships trying to secure the takeover of Kuwaiti oil rigs met with resistance. A tough battle developed when the Iraqis were attempting to secure the oil rigs off Kuwait's shores. A good bit of action took place here and the Kuwaiti defending forces and their missile boats succeeded in sinking and scorching a good number of Iraqi landing craft along with their escorting ships. About that time, MIG jet fighters were dominating the skies over the capital city of Kuwait. While dominating the skies, on land, Saddam's troops were securing Kuwait City street by street. Small pockets of resistance were smashed and soon thereafter the tough forces of Saddam were claiming various Ministries and government establishments.

There was total panic! People were fleeing for their lives! People felt total shock and disarray! Brutality was rampant and the battered Kuwaitis were fleeing south toward the safety of Saudi Arabia. The Iraqi invaders brutalized and abused people everywhere, even those

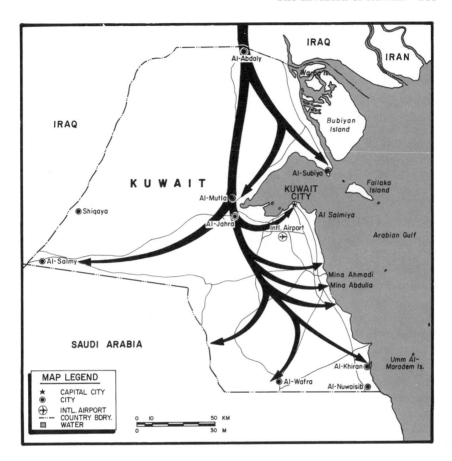

**IRAQI BLITZKRIEG ATTACK
ON KUWAIT, AUGUST 2, 1990**

fleeing for their life. They stole their belongings and cars with telephones were attacked. The Iraqi military encircled Kuwait City from its beltway and moved inward. A furious battle raged around the Amir's Dasman Palace. This was defended by an elite group of the Kuwaiti army. The ruler's younger brother Fahd, who was in charge of olympics and sports activities in Kuwait, was at Kazmiah in Kuwait. He received a call informing him that the Iraqis were invading the Palace. He came and took charge of the out-gunned and out-numbered defensive forces. He courageously fought his attackers. He machine-gunned and killed many of them; but in the heat of the battle, he was killed by the Iraqi invaders. His friends pulled his body and took him to the hospital.

He was left there for a month before he was buried. His son Khaled was arrested and imprisoned by the Iraqis. Saddam's brother, Siblawi, told him: "Out of respect for the relationship between me and your father, your life will be spared, otherwise we would cut you to pieces."

The Royal Palace was just near the U.S. Embassy. The Amir, Sheikh Jabir Al-Ahmad Al-Sabbah, and his family along with the Crown Prince and his family and other officials of the Kuwaiti government were able to leave and flee the ravaged city prior to the arrival of the invading forces. The Amir's family left and a number of the government Ministers were able to flee to the South which still remained relatively safe. The border with Saudi Arabia was just a short 30 miles distance away.

Ferocious fighting developed around the Palace and the defending forces put on a courageous fight against all odds. Iraqi parachutists, who swarmed on top of the Palace, faced very tough resistance. However, the invaders, with their overwhelmingly superior force and after a stiff resistance for nearly two hours, finally were able to take over the Palace.

The gallant Kuwaiti defenders were overwhelmed by the battle-hardened forces of Saddam Hussein. But the Iraqis paid a heavy price; several of them were killed and many helicopters were damaged. The invading forces received strong support from the air force and also naval support from torpedo boats and other gun boats loaded with missiles which showered the city. These ships were waiting for the zero hour of attack. They unleashed their hail of missiles and bullets against the innocent Kuwaitis. One Canadian eyewitness said, "It is chaos, military jets are flying over all the time, we can still hear artillery fire, but we don't know where it is coming from." Other witnesses said the bombardment was ferocious and vicious. Even the British Embassy was hit by shells. Kuwaiti television and radio stations were quickly overtaken by the occupiers, but a hidden transmitter was able to continue broadcasting appeals for help against the raiding Iraqi army. Desperate pleas were aired: "Oh Arab brothers, Kuwait's blood and honor are being violated. Rush to our rescue!"

Another desperate appeal went on, "the children, women and old men of Kuwait are calling on you!"

In the early afternoon, prior to the fall of dusk, all resistance to the Iraqi army subsided leaving them in full control of Kuwait. Several hundred Kuwaitis were killed in this assault. The Iraqis moved southward securing the rest of Kuwait and eastward along the Arabian Gulf shore, and simultaneously westward to the corner of Kuwait where it meets Iraq and Saudi Arabia. It was not long before the mighty army of Iraq was poised in a threatening and possible attack disposition against the Kingdom of Saudi Arabia. Now begins another tragic story of propaganda, lies, intimidation and deceit! Now begins a campaign of theft, larceny, terrorism, death, destruction and agony. All rampant everywhere in Kuwait!

These atrocities gained a special momentum, especially since the marauding forces of Saddam Hussein failed in their attempt of arresting and holding as captives the ruler of Kuwait, his Crown Prince and their ministers. This was a great disappointment to the ruler of Iraq and his Revolutionary Command Council. In fact, many of the officers in charge of the operation upon their failure to secure the arrest of the ruler of Kuwait met their death by none other than the gun of Saddam Hussein.

The Kuwaiti Air Force moved on to the safety of Saudi Arabia, and whatever could be salvaged and saved from the army moved along to the Kingdom as well to start preparation for the war of liberation.

The Amir of Kuwait and his government were established shortly thereafter in Taif–a resort town in the west of Saudi Arabia. The Kuwaiti government-in-exile was headquartered at Al-Hada Sheraton Hotel where it strove to function with full and total support from King Fahd of Saudi Arabia and unequivocal legitimate recognition from the World community.

Decisiveness and Courage From President Bush and King Fahd

The world had been shocked and dismayed at this naked aggression committed against the peaceful nation of Kuwait.

Shock waves went throughout the world. The global community was dismayed and deeply disturbed for what has taken place.

Saddam explained that the Iraqi army came to assist the revolutionaries who have taken over in Kuwait. He said, "these revolutionaries have staged a Coup!" But in reality nothing like this has ever happened in Kuwait. In fact, Saddam Hussein announced the formation of a government in Kuwait but such a government never lasted more than a few days. He was not able to recruit the services of one single Kuwaiti to be a member in this government.

When Saddam Hussein sent a delegation to Jeddah, to explain to King Fahd the situation, they were quick to state: "The matter is over! Kuwait is now a part of Iraq." Of course, King Fahd and his government were astonished, disappointed and dismayed. However, in a very wise move, King Fahd of Saudi Arabia gave his directive to all organs of his government to observe a strict atmosphere of silence regarding the blatant aggression against the brotherly people of Kuwait. While the world was wondering about such a silence and not many expressions

of outrage coming from the Gulf Cooperation Council (GCC), such a
policy proved to be a wise one indeed! While on one hand silence
was a virtue, on the other, action on many fronts was being taken at
a rapid pace. King Fahd contacted world leaders around the globe.
He discussed the critical situation and thought deeply about his options.
If the Saudi news media, and Saudi government officials were to de-
nounce the outrageous occupation of the State of Kuwait, it was feared
that Saddam Hussein would be antagonized enough to move on with
his putsch and bring havoc and destruction to the Eastern Region of
the Kingdom of Saudi Arabia which floats on a sea of oil. The great,
miraculous achievements of the Kingdom, which were made in a record
time of slightly over a decade, would all have been in shambles. The
great industrial complex in Jubail, the world-class refinery at Ras
Tanura, the tremendous oil facilities of Aramco and the entire Eastern
Region of Saudi Arabia would all have been aflame and would have
received massive destruction from the potent war machine and hordes
of Saddam Hussein. Saudi silence set the stage for avoiding any excitement of Saddam, and leaving him to think that the peace treaty, previously signed with Saudi Arabia, would lead the Saudis to swallow
the bitter pill and accept the fait accompli of a permanent loss of the
State of Kuwait to Iraq.

In fact, early in the blitzkrieg attack, it became apparent to the
Saudis, especially to King Fahd and major world leaders, that Saddam
Hussein was amassing troops against the border of Saudi Arabia, posing
a direct threat for an imminent attack on the Eastern Region of the
Kingdom. With Saddam consolidating his position in Kuwait, the apparent theory seemed to imply a *sinister plan* where, after a few short
days of consolidation, Saddam and his troops would move in a vicious
blitzkrieg attack on the Eastern Region of Saudi Arabia and from there
on could move without anybody being able to stop them, until they
reached the Gulf of Oman. Foremost on his mind was the Eastern
Region of the Kingdom. With this scenario and at the same time, the
military rulers of Sudan would send their missiles and airplanes, which
had already been installed by Saddam Hussein, across the Red Sea
into Jeddah and the Western region of Saudi Arabia, the Hijaz. King
Hussein* of Jordan was a party to this plan. His troops were to come
down south toward the Holy places of Mecca and Madina, claiming
his ancestral attachment where Sherif Hussein was, once upon a time,

---

* The aid granted by the Kingdom of Saudi Arabia to Jordan was made public; it amounted
to a staggering figure of approximately 6.7 billion dollars. This generous aid to a small
nation helped prop King Hussein's Government and financed many vital projects in
Jordan (see Appendix D for an example of the type of foreign aid given by Saudi Arabia).

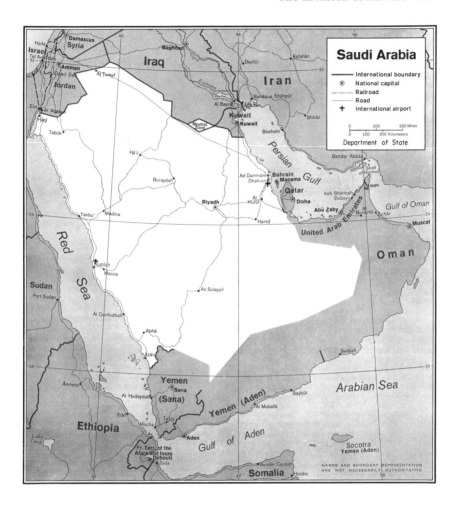

the King of the Hijaz. It seems that King Hussein forgot the special relationship he had with Saudi Arabia, and the extensive sums of money and aid poured into his Kingdom by the Saudis. So did, for that matter, all the conspirators who were actively involved in this plan.

From the South of the Kingdom of Saudi Arabia would have come the troops of Yemen who had their own claims on southern portions of Saudi Arabia. Thus, activation of this plan and its execution would have ultimately and certainly led to the dismantling of the unified Kingdom of Saudi Arabia as we know it. All the progress and miraculous achievements would have been in ruins because of such a wicked, vicious plan!

These adventures were discussed and plots were made in Baghdad. Supporting Saddam Hussein in his sinister plan brought division to the Arab world and fed the flames of fire during the Gulf War. When Qassem of Iraq threatened to occupy Kuwait on June 25, 1961, he failed without recourse to war because the Arabs were united in their support for Kuwait.

It certainly was a great move that King Fahd ordered silence across the realm of his Kingdom, so Saddam would not be antagonized for the immediate and terrifying few days after his occupation of Kuwait! King Fahd kept his lines of communication open, hoping that Saddam may realize his grave mistake and withdraw from Kuwait.

Through the tireless efforts of King Fahd, the Amir of Kuwait, President Bush, Prime Minister Margaret Thatcher of England, France, the former Soviet Union, China and a host of other leaders around the world, the United Nations was energized to immediate action. In an early morning session of the U.N. Security Council, a United Nations Resolution was passed by 5:00 o'clock in the morning of August 2, 1990. The United Nations Security Council condemned Iraq's occupation of Kuwait in Resolution 660 and demanded its unconditional and immediate withdrawal. The vote was 14 in favor and zero against. Only one member, namely Yemen* did not participate in the vote. The following is a copy of this resolution:

U.N. Resolution 660, August 2, 1990**
The Security Council,

Alarmed by the invasion of Kuwait on August 2, 1990 by the military forces of Iraq,

Determining that there exists a breach of international peace and security as regards the Iraqi invasion of Kuwait,

Acting under Articles 39 and 40 of the Charter of the United Nations,
1. *Condemns* the Iraqi invasion of Kuwait;
2. *Demands* that Iraq withdraw immediately and unconditionally all its forces to the positions in which they were located on August 1, 1990;
3. *Call upon* Iraq and Kuwait to begin immediately intensive negotiations for the resolution of their differences and supports all efforts in this regard, and especially those of the League of Arab States;

---

* Despite the fact that Yemen was the greatest beneficiary of Kuwaiti aid (Kuwait helped them build dozens of schools, a university, hospitals, clinics and residential areas. Also Jordan, The PLO and Sudan had received extensive Kuwaiti aid.)

** Source: United Nations, New York.

4. *Decides* to meet again as necessary to consider further steps to ensure compliance with the present resolution.

Condemnation and Historic Moves

President Bush and King Fahd exchanged urgent telephone conversations. They discussed the gravity of the situation and the brutal aggression against Kuwait. Shortly after these discussions, thirty B-52 bombers were ordered to the Indian Ocean Island of Diego Garcia. In the meantime, President Bush and the Prime Minister of Great Britain, Margaret Thatcher, met in Aspen, Colorado and pressed for collective action by members of the United Nations to rally to the help of Kuwait and for ejecting Saddam Hussein from the beleaguered nation. At 8:05 in the morning, Washington time, on August 2, 1990, President Bush made very clear statements concerning this aggression. He said: "The United States strongly condemns the Iraqi military invasion of Kuwait. We call for the immediate and unconditional withdrawal of all the Iraqi forces. There is no place for this sort of naked aggression in today's world . . .

Last night I instructed our Ambassador at the United Nations, Tom Pickering, to work with Kuwait in convening an emergency meeting of the Security Council. It was convened, and I am grateful for that quick, overwhelming vote condemning the Iraqi action and calling for immediate unconditional withdrawal . . .

Second, consistent with my authority under the International emergency Economic Powers Act, I have signed an executive order, early this morning, freezing Iraqi assets in this country and prohibiting transactions with Iraq. I have also signed an executive order freezing Kuwaiti assets. That's to ensure that those assets are not interfered with by the illegitimate authority that is now occupying Kuwait. We call upon other governments to take similar action.

Third, the Department of State has been in contact with governments around the world urging that they, too, condemn the Iraqi aggression and consult to determine what measure should be taken to bring an end to this totally unjustified act. It is important that the international community act together to ensure that Iraqi forces depart Kuwait immediately.

Needless to say, we view the situation with the utmost gravity. We remain committed to take whatever steps are necessary to defend our long standing vital interests in the Gulf; and I am meeting this morning with my senior advisors here to consider all possible options available to us."

Another reason for the initial Saudi silence were the ceaseless efforts of King Fahd who energized top diplomacy across the globe and touched on all ramifications of the tragic aggression. He consulted his advisors and thought of possible alternatives in case his strong desire and peaceful moves were to fail. Coupled with this thrust of the Saudi leadership and the courageous expressions of condemnation emanating from the White House, the world community rose to the occasion and echoed the sentiments expressed by Bush and the Saudi leadership still working behind the scenes and hoping against all odds for quiet diplomacy to work and bring Saddam Hussein to his senses!

In the meantime, Iraq's propaganda machine was churning far-fetched stories about sending their troops at the request of revolutionaries who staged a Coup d'Etat in Kuwait. The Revolutionary Command Council, with President Saddam Hussein at the helm, issued a statement saying that, "Iraq is supporting the Provisional Government of Free Kuwait." They also stated that the government was made of "Revolutionary Youths."

Saddam Hussein was quick to warn all foreign governments against any possible aid they may render toward the freeing of Kuwait. To stem the tide of a frenzy of diplomatic activities against him, he blared his ominous message on radio Baghdad, saying, "We swear to God that we will make the Gulf a graveyard for those who think of launching any aggression (against us), starting with these cowardly American Navies."

These extreme threats are nothing new to the lexicon of Saddam Hussein. He had used brutal expressions on numerous occasions such as: "We will chop the hand that will rise against us; We will chop the heads of our enemies; We will cut the shoulders of any aggressors; We will make the Americans and our enemies swim in their blood; cutting necks is better than cutting means of living. Oh God Almighty, be witness that we have warned them;" the language of threats, and terrorism goes on and on . . .

These tactics were never to succeed in deterring the will power of the world community which was rallying and rushing to the rescue of Kuwait. The Amir of Kuwait and his emissaries around the world were desperately seeking help to save their nation and their people who had been transformed into refugees overnight! A distinguished Kuwaiti and an eloquent speaker, emotionally and passionately appealed to the world for help. He represented the sentiment of all Kuwaitis—leaders and populace alike. This was the Kuwaiti Ambassador in Washington, Sheikh Saud Nasser Al-Sabbah. He stated the case for Kuwait in heart-touching expressions. He said: "The Iraqis have occupied all of Kuwait! . . . We are desperate for any help we can get."

He then said, "We don't stand a chance, if we don't get any aid from our friends. U.S. intervention at this stage is of paramount importance!"

The Republican leadership was in tune with the statements of condemnation expressed by President Bush. A number of other senators and congressmen expressed similar feelings. The senator from Oklahoma, David Boren who is Chairman of the Senate Intelligence Committee said, "I think it would be a direct threat to the security of this country if Iraq headed to occupy oil fields in Saudi Arabia." Another senator said, "Saudi Arabia might be next and then Saddam Hussein would have a strangle-hold on the Western oil supply." A member of the House of Representatives expressed the view of many by saying, "The attack (by Iraq) is a financial attack on America and on the rest of the world that is dependent on Middle Eastern oil." In line with these sentiments, the House of Representatives of the United States of America voted in a very speedy manner, in a totality of 416 against zero, approving a pending bill of economic sanctions against Iraq. However, there were a few members who expressed extreme caution and some doubt. For example, Senator Sam Nunn, a Democrat of Georgia and chairman of the powerful Senate Armed Services Committee said, "We do not have aircraft within striking distance (of Iraq and Kuwait) unless we fly land-based, long-range bombers into that region. And I do not think the time is now for us to talk about military force. We would not want to get into a ground war in that area."

Voices of excessive caution, doubt and doom picked up momentum with time and the Senator from Georgia was leading the chorus, until echoes were reverberating across America with orchestrated slogans such as, "No blood for oil," were repeated over and over again across the land. This became a strong media campaign and was aimed to blur the true picture of what was actually taking place in the Gulf. It was encouraged and fed by the propaganda machine of Saddam Hussein for several months to come. In the final analysis, the voice of truth and world courage prevailed. But the information blitz and war of words went on unabated. This will be discussed in more detail in the next chapter.

A flurry of activities was taking place across the globe. The aircraft carrier USS Independence and six escorts were sent to the Gulf area, steaming from the Indian Ocean. However, they would be many days before they could be within a "striking distance" position outside the Arabian Gulf. Margaret Thatcher advised the President to follow a tough course in dealing with Saddam Hussein, known as "the iron lady", the Prime Minister of England, was characteristically to the point and told Bush, "Saddam Hussein is not going to stop with Kuwait." Frantic diplomatic activities abounded, Prince Bandar Bin Sultan, Ambassador of the Kingdom of Saudi Arabia to the United States of America, came for a breakfast meeting with President Bush on Friday, August 3, 1990 at 7:00 A.M. The topic was obviously the Gulf Crisis. The President ordered the Central Intelligence Agency to give a detailed briefing to Prince Bandar, including satellite pictures of the Iraqi military moves in Kuwait and their threatening deployment on the border with Saudi Arabia. The President reiterated his pledge which he had already made to King Fahd of Saudi Arabia, to come to the help of the Kingdom and to do all that America could do toward the defense and preservation of the Kingdom of Saudi Arabia. The President and King Fahd agreed that the U.S. Secretary of Defense Dick Cheney should leave immediately for the Kingdom.

The former Soviet Union joined in the condemnation of the invasion and suspended all arms shipments to Iraq. All major and friendly countries of the world condemned the invasion.

On Saturday, August 4, 1990, Prince Bandar Bin Sultan flew to Saudi Arabia so that he could provide the Saudi leadership with necessary briefings prior to Dick Cheney's arrival. The Secretary of State for the United States, James Baker flew to Moscow and joined his counterpart, the Foreign Minister of the former Soviet Union, Edward Sheverdnadze. They both issued a joint statement condemning the Iraqi aggression and the invasion of Kuwait, urging world leaders to rise to the occasion and halt all arms shipments destined for the State of Iraq. The next day, Sunday, August 5, President Bush of the United States dispatched his Secretary of Defense to Saudi Arabia to discuss possible responses necessitated by the explosion of the Gulf Crisis. Momentous and historic decisions had essentially been made. These were the outcome of the serious discussions conducted by phone between King Fahd of Saudi Arabia and President Bush of the United States. The historic decisions taken were also based on serious consultations with other world leaders such as the Prime Minister of England, Margaret Thatcher, the President of the French Republic, François Mitterrand, the Chancellor of Germany, Helmut Kohl, the Prime Minister of Japan, President of the former Soviet Union, Mikhail Gorbachev, the Prime Minister of China, along with many other world leaders as well as certain Arab leaders, leading among them, President Hosni Moubarak of Egypt, King Hassan II of Morroco, including President Hafez Assad of Syria. Also the twelve members of the European Community were all in tune with the policies enunciated, including stopping any arms shipments to Iraq or accepting any oil shipped from Iraq or Kuwait.

While the mission of Cheney and his top aids to Saudi Arabia was to have secured Saudi Arabia's agreement for U.S. military aid, essentially, this was done during the conversations of President Bush and King Fahd. In the meantime, Saddam Hussein met with a U.S. Embassy official in Iraq and told him, "The invasion (by Iraq) was a done deal! Kuwait now belongs to Iraq!" Feeling the mounting world pressure, the Iraqi ruler announced that Iraq was pulling its forces from Kuwait, beginning Sunday, August 5. In fact, they showed on television what was identified as "withdrawal operations" of their forces. This proved to be nothing but a ploy which was used by Saddam Hussein and his propaganda machine in order to lull the mounting opposition against him, and to stop the deluge of protests and condemnation. Statements of this nature were made off and on again; but it was very evident for the world that Saddam Hussein was stalling for time and using demagoguery.

On the very same day, Saddam Hussein warned against any attack against his forces in Iraq or Kuwait saying that such an attack would be "confronted by decisiveness which would sever the arm of the attackers from their shoulders."

On Monday, August 6, when the U.S. Secretary of Defense, Dick Cheney, was leaving the Kingdom of Saudi Arabia, the final ramifications of the historic decision had been accomplished. The Secretary of Defense carried with him the approval of King Fahd for seeking military support from the United States in defending the integrity and security of the Kingdom of Saudi Arabia. On another front, extensive efforts were being made to secure support from friendly Arab nations for dispatching forces to the defense of Saudi Arabia. In the meantime, Yasser Arafat*, chairman of the Palestine Liberation Organization, after discussing the crisis with Saddam Hussein, met with Egyptian President, Hosni Moubarak in Alexandria in order to gain his support for the Iraqi-backed plan which he carried with him. Then he went to Saudi Arabia for the same purpose. This was referred to as the PLO-Libyan Plan which involved a large sum of money to be paid by Kuwait to Iraq; it also called for holding elections in Kuwait so that a new government would be installed to replace the government of the Amir. The control of the two strategic islands, Boubiyan and Warba would also be under Iraqi dominion. Arafat threw his solid support behind Saddam Hussein and lobbied enthusiastically for such a plan which was doomed to fail, and it did.

---

* Saudi Arabia and Kuwait have always been loyal supporters of the Palestinian cause. They donated hundreds of millions of dollars to the PLO, and remained true defenders of Palestinian rights through the decades. As for Yasser Arafat, he had lived in Kuwait for several years.

The United Nations Security Council was very active in developing and sponsoring resolutions that carried weight and power with it. For the first time in the history of the United Nations, such unanimity was exhibited. All the permanent members of the Security Council, along with the vast majority, voted in favor of Resolution 661. The actual vote was 13 in favor, zero against and two abstentions (Cuba and Yemen abstained from voting). This resolution was sponsored by: the United States of America, the United Kingdom, France, Canada, Colombia, Côte D'Ivoire, Ethiopia, Finland and Malaysia. The resolution called for a trade and economic embargo on Iraq and also the occupied state of Kuwait, since it was at that time entirely controlled by Iraqi forces. A special sanctions committee was established in order to oversee the complete implementation of this resolution. It also called on all United Nations members to protect assets of the State of Kuwait.

This milestone resolution laid the ground work for further pressures against Iraq. It, essentially, paved the way toward the liberation of Kuwait which was to come a few months later. Because of its importance, this resolution is presented here in its entirety:

U.N. Resolution 661, August 6, 1990*

The Security Council, Reaffirming its resolution 660 (1990) of August 2, 1990,

Deeply concerned that the resolution has not been implemented and that the invasion by Iraq of Kuwait continues with further loss of human life and material destruction,

Determined to bring the invasion and occupation of Kuwait by Iraq to an end and to restore the sovereignty, independence and territorial integrity of Kuwait,

Noting that the legitimate Government of Kuwait has expressed its readiness to comply with resolution 660 (1990),

Mindful of its responsibilities under the Charter of the United Nations for the maintenance of international peace and security,

Affirming the inherent right of individual or collective self-defense, in response to the armed attack by Iraq against Kuwait, in accordance with Article 51 of the Charter,

Acting under Chapter VII of the Charter of the United Nations,
   1. *Determines* that Iraq so far has failed to comply with paragraph 2 of resolution 660 (1990) and has usurped the authority of the legitimate Government of Kuwait;
   2. *Decides*, as a consequence, to take the following measures to secure compliance of Iraq with paragraph 2 of resolution

---

* Source: United Nations, New York, U.S.A.

660 (1990) and to restore the authority of the legitimate Government of Kuwait;

3. *Decides* that all States shall prevent;

   a) The import into their territories of all commodities and products originating in Iraq or Kuwait exported therefrom after the date of the present resolution;

   b) Any activities by their nationals or in their territories which would promote or are calculated to promote the export or trans-shipment of any commodities or products from Iraq or Kuwait; and any dealings by their nationals or their flag vessels or in their territories in any commodities or products originating in Iraq or Kuwait and exported therefrom after the date of the present resolution, including in particular any transfer of funds to Iraq or Kuwait for the purposes of such activities or dealings;

   c) The sale or supply by their nationals or from their territories or using their flag vessels of any commodities or products including weapons or any other military equipment, whether or not originating in their territories but not including supplies intended strictly for medical purposes, and, in humanitarian circumstances, foodstuffs, to any person or body in Iraq or Kuwait or to any person or body for the purposes of any business carried on in or operated from Iraq or Kuwait, and any activities by their nationals or in their territories which promote or are calculated to promote such sale or supply of such commodities or products;

4. *Decides* that all States shall not make available to the Government of Iraq or to any commercial, industrial or public utility undertaking in Iraq or Kuwait, any funds or any other financial or economic resources and shall prevent their nationals and any persons within their territories or otherwise making available to that Government or to any such undertaking any such funds or resources and from remitting any other funds to persons or bodies within Iraq or Kuwait, except payments exclusively for strictly medical or humanitarian purposes and, in humanitarian circumstances, foodstuffs;

5. *Calls upon* all States, including States non-members of the United Nations, to act strictly in accordance with the provisions of the present resolution notwithstanding any contract entered into or licence granted before the date of the present resolution;

6. *Decides* to establish, in accordance with rule 28 of the provi-

sional rules of procedure of the Security Council, a Committee of the Security Council consisting of all the members of the Council, to undertake the following tasks and to report on its work to the Council with its observations and recommendations:

a) To examine the reports on the progress of the implementation of the present resolution which will be submitted by the Secretary-General;

b) To seek from all States further information regarding the action taken by them concerning the effective implementation of the provisions laid down in the present resolution;

7. *Calls upon* all States to co-operate fully with the Committee in the fulfillment of its task, including supplying such information as may be sought by the Committee in pursuance of the present resolution;

8. *Requests* the Secretary-General to provide all necessary assistance to the Committee and to make the necessary arrangements in the Secretariat for the purpose;

9. *Decides* that, notwithstanding paragraphs 4 through 8 above, nothing in the present resolution shall prohibit assistance to the legitimate Government of Kuwait, and calls upon all States:

a) To take appropriate measures to protect assets of the legitimate Government of Kuwait and its agencies;

b) Not to recognize any regime set up by the occupying Power;

10. *Requests* the Secretary-General to report to the Council on the progress of the implementation of the present resolution, the first report to be submitted within thirty days;

11. *Decides* to keep this item on its agenda and to continue its efforts to put an early end to the invasion by Iraq.

On his way back to the United States of America, the Secretary of Defense, Dick Cheney stopped in Egypt to confer with President Hosni Moubarak and also in Morocco to secure support from King Hassan II. Both leaders are very moderate and good friends of both America and the Kingdom of Saudi Arabia. He urged them to send Arab forces for the defense of the Kingdom. On August 7, the official announcement was made stating that the Saudi Government invited American troops to come to the defense of the Kingdom. This historic, courageous decision, coupled with the decision of President Bush for rising to the occasion to defend America's interests and America's friends in the Gulf, will no doubt be recorded in the annals of history with golden letters.

President Bush Addresses the Nation

President George Bush addressed his nation on August 8, declaring the dispatching of American troops to Saudi Arabia, which have already been pouring in, and stating that this is essentially a defensive mission, "a line has been drawn in the sand . . . they (U.S. troops) will not initiate hostilities but they will defend themselves and the Kingdom of Saudi Arabia and other friends in the Persian Gulf." Portions of his *historic speech,** which was delivered at 9:00 A.M. Eastern daylight time from the Oval Office of the White House, will be included here. The President said:

"In the life of a nation, we're called upon to define who we are and what we believe. Sometimes these choices are not easy. But today as President, I ask for your support in a decision I've made to stand up for what's right and condemn what's wrong–all in the cause of peace.

At my direction, elements of the 82nd Airborne Division, as well as key units of the United States Air Force are arriving today to take up defensive positions in Saudi Arabia. I took this action to assist the Saudi Arabian government in the defense of its homeland.

No one commits America's Armed Forces to a dangerous mission lightly. But after perhaps unparalleled international consultation and exhausting every alternative, it became necessary to take this action. Let me tell you why.

Less than a week ago, in the early morning hours of August 2nd, Iraqi armed forces, without provocation or warning, invaded a peaceful Kuwait. Facing negligible resistance from its much smaller neighbor, Iraq's tanks stormed in blitzkrieg fashion through Kuwait in a few short hours. With more than 100,000 troops, along with tanks, artillery and surface-to-surface missiles, Iraq now occupies Kuwait.

This aggression came just hours after Saddam Hussein specifically assured numerous countries in the area that there would be no invasion. There is no justification whatsoever for this outrageous and brutal act of aggression.

A puppet regime imposed from the outside is unacceptable. The acquisition of territory by force is unacceptable. No one, friend or foe, should doubt our desire for peace, and no one should underestimate our determination to confront aggression.

Four simple principles guide our policy. First, we seek the immediate, unconditional and complete withdrawal of all Iraqi forces from

---

* Source: Executive Office of the President, Office of Administration, Washington D.C.

Kuwait. Second, Kuwait's legitimate government must be restored to replace the puppet regime. And third, my administration, as has been the case with every President from President Roosevelt to President Reagan, is committed to the security and stability of the Persian Gulf. And fourth, I am determined to protect the lives of American citizens abroad.

Immediately after the Iraqi invasion, I ordered an embargo of all trade with Iraq and, together with many other nations, announced sanctions that both froze all Iraqi assets in this country and protected Kuwait's assets. The stakes are high. Iraq is already a rich and powerful country that possesses the world's second largest reserves of oil and over a million men under arms. It's the fourth largest military in the world.

Our country now imports nearly half the oil it consumes and could face a major threat to its economic independence. Much of the world is even more dependent upon imported oil and is even more vulnerable to Iraqi threats.

We succeeded in the struggle for freedom in Europe because we and our allies remain stalwart. Keeping the peace in the Middle East will require no less. We're beginning a new era. This new era can be full of promise. An age of freedom. A time of peace for all peoples. But if history teaches us anything, it is that we must resist aggression or it will destroy our freedoms. Appeasement does not work. As was the case in the 1930s, we see in Saddam Hussein an aggressive dictator threatening his neighbors. Only 14 days ago Saddam Hussein promised his friends he would not invade Kuwait. And four days ago he promised the world he would withdraw. And twice we have seen what his promises mean. His promises mean nothing.

In the last few days I've spoken with political leaders from the Middle East, Europe, Asia and the Americas, and I've met with Prime Minister Thatcher, Prime Minister Mulroney, and NATO Secretary General Woerner. And all agree that Iraq cannot be allowed to benefit from its invasion of Kuwait.

We agree that this is not an American problem or a European problem or a Middle East problem. It is the world's problem. And that's why, soon after the Iraqi invasion, the United Nations Security Council, without dissent, condemned Iraq, calling for the immediate and unconditional withdrawal of its troops from Kuwait. The Arab world, through both the Arab League and the Gulf Cooperation Council, courageously announced its opposition to Iraqi aggression. Japan, the United Kingdom, and France, and other governments around the world have imposed severe sanctions. The Soviet Union and China ended all arms sales to Iraq.

And this past Monday, the United Nations Security Council approved for the first time in 23 years mandatory sanctions under Chapter VII of the United Nations Charter. These sanctions, now enshrined in international law, have the potential to deny Iraq the fruits of aggression, while sharply limiting its ability to either import or export anything of value - especially oil.

I pledge here today that the United States will do its part to see that these sanctions are effective and to induce Iraq to withdraw without delay from Kuwait.

But we must recognize that Iraq may not stop using force to advance its ambitions. Iraq has massed an enormous war machine on the Saudi border, capable of initiating hostilities with little or no additional preparation. Given the Iraqi government's history of aggression against its own citizens as well as its neighbors, to assume Iraq will not attack again would be unwise and unrealistic.

And therefore, after consulting with King Fahd, I sent Secretary of Defense Dick Cheney to discuss cooperative measures we could take. Following those meetings, the Saudi government requested our help. And I responded to that request by ordering U.S. air and ground forces to deploy to the Kingdom of Saudi Arabia.

Let me be clear. The sovereign independence of Saudi Arabia is of vital interest to the United States. This decision, which I shared with the congressional leadership, grows out of the longstanding friendship and security relationship between the United States and Saudi Arabia. U.S. forces will work together with those of Saudi Arabia and other nations to preserve the integrity of Saudi Arabia and to deter further Iraqi aggression.

Through their presence, as well as through training and exercises, these multinational forces will enhance the overall capability of Saudi armed forces to defend the Kingdom.

I want to be clear about what we are doing and why. America does not seek conflict, nor do we seek to chart the destiny of other nations. But America will stand by her friends. The mission of our troops is wholly defensive. Hopefully, they will not be needed long. They will not initiate hostilities, but they will defend themselves, the Kingdom of Saudi Arabia, and other friends in the Persian Gulf.

We are working around the clock to deter Iraqi aggression and to enforce U.N. sanctions. I'm continuing my conversations with world leaders. Secretary of Defense Cheney has just returned from valuable consultations with President Moubarak of Egypt and King Hassan of Morocco. Secretary of State Baker has consulted with his counterparts in many nations, including the Soviet Union. And today he heads for Europe to consult with President Ozal of Turkey, a staunch friend of the United States. And he'll then consult with the NATO Foreign Ministers.

I will ask oil-producing nations to do what they can to increase production in order to minimize any impact that oil flow reductions will have on the world economy. And I will explore whether we and our allies should draw down our strategic petroleum reserves. Conservation measures can also help. Americans everywhere must do their part. And one more thing. I'm asking the oil companies to do their fair share. They should show restraint and not abuse today's uncertainties to raise prices.

Standing up for our principles will not come easy. It may take time and possibly cost a great deal. But we are asking no more of anyone than of the brave young men and women of our Armed Forces and their families. And I ask that in the churches around the country prayers be said for those who are committed to protect and defend America's interests.

Standing up for our principle is an American tradition. As it has so many times before, it may take time and tremendous effort. But most of all, it will take unity of purpose.

As I've witnessed throughout my life in both war and peace, America has never wavered when her purpose is driven by principle. And on this August day, at home and abroad, I know she will do no less . . ."

Saddam Hussein was listening to all these developments around the globe and feeling the intense pressure build up against his regime and the occupation of Kuwait. His initial euphoria had sunk in and developed into an obstinate trait. Thinking that he could stand against the entire world and the tide of sanctions which would hurt his coffers very deeply, he snapped back and annexed Kuwait, bluntly stating that Kuwait is now Province number 19 of Iraq. His blustering and annexation did not stop the flood of U.S. and British forces from pouring into the Kingdom of Saudi Arabia, along with the imminent dispatching of many more from friendly Arab countries and other nations around the world. In his desperation, Saddam Hussein was brewing another confrontation and wicked design. With many foreigners working in Iraq and Kuwait, several thousands were now being held against their will. The Iraqi regime was calling them "guests". They were to soon become hostages and to be used as an important bargaining chip for Saddam Hussein and his Revolutionary Command Council.

No sooner than he declared the annexation of Kuwait then the U.N. Security Council voted unanimously in favor of *Resolution 662*, on Thursday, August 9. The resolution declared that the annexation of the State of Kuwait was null and void.

King Fahd Makes A Historic Move

With the historic decision taken by King Fahd of Saudi Arabia after extensive consultation with President Bush and world leaders, and after several appeals to Saddam Hussein to withdrew from Kuwait, King Fahd rose to the occasion and challenge! He exhibited tremendous valor and bravery in standing up to defend the security of the Kingdom of Saudi Arabia and to guard his people against the imminent danger poised on the borders of the Kingdom. . . all along being the dynamo in devising meticulous plans for exploring all possible peace avenues, but in the meantime amassing an enormous force backed by the entire world community to bring about the liberation of the State of Kuwait. King Fahd and the generous and courageous Saudi people were all one voice in their stand against tyranny and occupation, against the devastation and destruction of a brotherly nation. They opened their homes and hearts for the multitude of thousands and thousands of brotherly Kuwaitis who were turned into refugees overnight by the brutality of an attack perpetrated by Saddam Hussein. The official silence of Saudi Arabia which was in itself a wise move, did lull the aggressive aims of Saddam Hussein so that he would not be excited in any way nor antagonized into placing his operation into the next mode for executing his plan to occupy the Eastern region of Saudi Arabia along with his allies from the south, from the north and from the west to bring about the dismantling of the Kingdom. Now the time had come, after the long days and nights that King Fahd spent consulting with world leaders to secure all the possible support needed, and much of it was urgently needed, to confront this overwhelming force amassed against the borders of his beloved Kingdom. The silence had evaporated! The King had spoken and took a courageous stand. The world would see and realize anew that the Kingdom throughout its history stood on the side of right not might, for justice against tyranny and oppression. The world was very quick to rise solidly in support of the Kingdom, because of its policy of moderation and justice. The Kingdom never wished or bore any ill against any nation or any people on earth! While its wealth brought great progress to all Saudis across the entire spectrum, such bounty was also spread around the world to needy nations and to people of all origins, religions, colors and creeds. Its goodness and goodwill emanate and propagate across the four corners of the globe. Its wealth is spread not only on the Saudis and other needy around the world, but through a process of transfers in technology, labor, needs and basic necessities. You see in the Kingdom, as well as in Kuwait, millions of people that come from all over the world and are welcomed in the land to work, make a decent living and send their earnings to support their families at home, extending from the Philippines, the West Bank and Pakistan to Canada and the United States of America, or from France to Brazil and every Arab country in the whole Arab world.

The moderation, justice, wisdom, good hands and good deeds of the Kingdom rallied the whole world to come vigorously to its defense against an imminent attack by a man whose idols were Hitler and Stalin, a man who cursed the hand that fed him! King Fahd's deep love and devotion for his countrymen led him in the difficult times, while making his historic decision. He reaffirmed the Kingdom's demand to restore the situation in the brotherly state of Kuwait to its prior status, and called for the return of the ruling family of Kuwait. As for the Coalition Forces from friendly countries, he stated that they were of a temporary nature. They would leave Saudi territory immediately upon request by the Kingdom of Saudi Arabia.

The following are excerpts from his *speech*,* addressing the nation on August 9, 1990:

". . . You realize, no doubt, by following the course of regrettable events in the Arabian Gulf region during the last few days, the gravity of the situation faced by the Arab Nation in present circumstances. You undoubtedly know that the government of the Kingdom of Saudi Arabia has exerted all possible efforts with the governments of the Iraqi Republic and the State of Kuwait to contain the dispute between them.

In this context, I made numerous telephone calls and held fraternal talks with the brothers. As a result, a bilateral meeting was held between the Iraqi and Kuwaiti delegations in Saudi Arabia with the aim of bridging the gap and narrowing differences to avert any further escalation.

A number of brotherly leaders, thankfully, contributed to these efforts based on their belief in the unity of the Arab Nation and the cohesion of its solidarity and cooperation to achieve success in serving its fateful mission.

However, regrettably enough, the course of events took a turn for the worse, contrary to our endeavors and aspirations of the Islamic and Arab people, as well as all peace-loving nations of the world.

Nevertheless, these painful and regrettable events started in the pre-dawn hours of Thursday, August 2, 1990 (Muharram 11, 1411 A.H.). The whole world was taken by surprise when the Iraqi forces stormed the brotherly state of Kuwait, in the most sinister aggression witnessed

---

* Source: Royal Embassy of Saudi Arabia in Washington, D.C. and *Saudi Arabia*, Vol. 7, No. 3, Fall 1990, also Saudi and Arabic Newspapers.

by the Arab Nation in its modern history. Such an invasion inflicted painful suffering on the Kuwaitis and rendered them homeless.

While expressing its deep displeasure at this aggression on the brotherly neighboring state of Kuwait, the Kingdom of Saudi Arabia declares its categorical rejection of all ensuing measures and declarations which followed this aggression. These were rejected through the statements issued by Arab leaderships, the Arab League, the Islamic Conference Organizations, the Gulf Cooperation Council, as well as all Arab and international bodies and organizations.

The Kingdom of Saudi Arabia reaffirms its demand to restore the situation in the brotherly state of Kuwait to its status prior to the Iraqi occupation, as well as the return of the ruling family headed by his Highness Sheikh Jabir Al-Ahmad Al-Sabbah, the Emir of Kuwait and his government.

We hope that the Emergency Arab Summit, called for by President Mohammed Hosni Moubarak of the sisterly state of Egypt, will give results which will fulfill the aspirations of the Arab Nation and bolster its march towards solidarity and unity of opinion.

In the aftermath of this regrettable event, Iraq massed large forces on the borders of the Kingdom of Saudi Arabia. In view of these bitter realities and out of the eagerness of the Kingdom to safeguard its territory and protect its vital and economic interests, and its wish to bolster its defensive capabilities and to raise the level of training of its armed forces, in addition to the keenness of the government of the Kingdom to resort to peace and non-recourse to using force in solving disputes, the Kingdom of Saudi Arabia expressed its desire for the participation of fraternal Arab forces and other friendly forces.

Thus, the governments of the United States of America, Britain and other nations took the initiative, based on the friendly relations that link the Kingdom of Saudi Arabia and these countries, to dispatch air and land forces to sustain the Saudi armed forces in performing their duty to defend the homeland and the citizens against any aggression, with the full emphasis that this measure was not addressed against anybody. It was merely and purely for defensive purposes, imposed by the circumstances faced by the Kingdom of Saudi Arabia. It is worth mentioning in this context that the forces, which will participate in the joint training exercises with the Saudi armed forces, are of a temporary nature. They will leave Saudi territory immediately at the request of the Kingdom. . . ."

An Arab League Summit convened in Cairo, Egypt at the invitation of President Hosni Moubarak. The Conference was held August 9 and 10, 1990. On the 10th of August (19th Mouharram 1411 A.H.), a resolution was passed in favor of sending Arab military forces to join U.S. and Allied Forces in the Eastern Region of Saudi Arabia for the defense of the Kingdom. Of the 21 members of the League, twenty were in attendance. Twelve of them voted in favor of such a resolution. Those against the resolution were: Iraq, Libya and the Palestine Liberation Organization. Yemen and Algeria abstained. Jordan, Sudan and Mauritania expressed their reservations about such a resolution and did not participate in the voting. The vote was binding only on those who voted in favor. Although the resolution was not unanimous, it was the first time in three decades where an affirmative vote was taken by the Arab League for the distinct purpose of sending troops to repel aggression committed by a member state. The Arab League also condemned the aggression against Kuwait and called for immediate and unconditional withdrawal of Iraqi forces to their positions prior to the invasion of the State of Kuwait. It demanded the restoration of the legitimate government of Kuwait and declared that the annexation of Kuwait by Iraq to be null and void. The resolution reaffirmed the sovereignty, independence and security of Kuwait and deplored the numerous Iraqi threats lodged against the Arabian Gulf countries. It denounced the amassing of Iraqi troops along the Saudi border and supported the Kingdom and Gulf States in their determination to defend their territories according to the provisions of the Arab League Charter and the United Nations.

Saddam Hussein was very quick to reach in his bag of threatening tricks, and on the same day declared "a Jihad (Holy war) to defend Mecca and the Holy places against the infidels and the spears of the Americans and the Zionists." He urged all Arabs to sweep "Amirs of ill from their thrones in the Gulf." He urged the Arab masses to "burn the soil under the feet of the aggressors and invaders who want harm for your families in Iraq. Attack their interests wherever they may be." The world community received such declarations coming from Saddam Hussein particularly his declaration of a Jihad, with astonishment and surprise, especially since he had never been known to be such a religious man. Anyway, "you got to be holy to declare a holy war!" Some extremist fundamentalist Islamic forces, in the Arab land and beyond, although few in number, were vociferous in their vehemence in their attacks on the Coalition Forces, the Kuwaitis and other moderates in the Gulf. Saddam's agents fed their venom and recruited many of them. Although these extremists did not have much love for Saddam Hussein, their hatred and greed propelled them to side with him against the forces of justice and decency. But their support was lukewarm at best.

Some extremist voices were heard in Jordan and some from Iran. In fact the Iranian religious leader Ayatullah Khamenei (this is not Khomeini) said, "Anyone who fights America's aggression has engaged in a Holy War, in the cause of Allah, and anyone who is killed on that path is a martyr." These expressions of extremism and hate were really alien to the true spirit and teachings of Islam. Calling for a real Jihad emanates from the true spirit or a struggle against an oppressor, but their calls were motivated by sheer hatred, greed and a spirit which is far from anything called justice or a struggle to liberate Kuwait and defend the innocent population which was rendered homeless overnight, through the dictates and whims of a ruthless dictator. Their Jihad should have been against the aggressor Saddam Hussein! Many people wondered about this "instant love" and "friendly relations" voiced by the leadership of Iraq toward Iran, especially since the two countries had just concluded a vicious war of eight years, killing one million men, and injuring millions more. Their economies were left in havoc and devastation! The wounds of war were still fresh. How could Iran come to the aid of its arch enemy Iraq? That did not happen!

The forces reflecting the true spirit of Islam which stands for justice and goodness to mankind, were echoed on August 5, 1990, when the Organization of the Islamic Conference issued a statement in which it condemned the Iraqi aggression against Kuwait and demanded the immediate and unconditional withdrawal of the occupying forces of Iraq, as well as the restoration of the legitimate government to Kuwait. It also called on Iraq to abide by the Charter of the Organization of the Islamic Conference which calls for resolving any disputes through peaceful means and negotiations. This statement declared that the two states should respect each others independence, sovereignty, and territorial integrity.

On the 13th of August, 1990 (Muharram 22, 1411 A.H.), a milestone statement was issued by the Council of Senior Ulama of the Kingdom of Saudi Arabia. This Islamic body is a cornerstone in the interpretation and understanding of Islamic teachings. The statement issued by the council is as follows:

Statement Issued By The Council Of Senior Ulama Of The Kingdom Of Saudi Arabia August 13, 1990 (Muharram 22, 1411 A.H.)

"Praise be to God, Lord of all the worlds, ultimate success is for those who serve Him, and aggression is legitimate only against the aggressors.

May God's peace and blessings be on our Prophet Mohammed, his family, his companions and whoever follows his guidance and path.

The Council of Senior Ulama, like everyone else in the Kingdom of Saudi Arabia, has been aware of the fact that large numbers of Iraqi troops invaded a neighboring country, and are gathering on the borders of Saudi Arabia.

The Council has learned from the announcements of various news agencies, other mass media, as well as from those who fled Kuwait, of the atrocities, crimes, violations of moral values and violation of the sanctity of neighborhood which has taken place there. The reality is much worse than any description could convey. Happy is he who is warned by the example of others.

These facts prompted the leadership in the Kingdom of Saudi Arabia to take all necessary measures to protect their land, its inhabitants and its resources against anything similar to what happened to their neighboring Kuwait and to seek the help of Arab and non-Arab states to forestall the expected danger and to stand firm against an anticipated aggression. The events in Kuwait have proved that this is an enemy whose promise is not to be trusted and whose treachery is not to be ruled out.

Thus, it is necessary in this situation that the Ulama declare an Islamic ruling so that people in this country and elsewhere may be aware of the correct and clear position. Because of this, the Council of Senior Ulama decided to hold a special meeting to issue this statement in which to emphasize for our people the importance of defending the nation (Umma) and its resources with all possible means, and that it is the duty of those responsible for the affairs of the Umma to be swift in taking all necessary measures to shield off danger, stop the advance of evil, and safeguard the people's religion, lives, wealth, and honor; also, to see to it that the security and stability which they now enjoy is maintained.

The Council of the organization of Senior Ulama approves, therefore, the steps taken by the ruler (King Fahd), may God lead him to success, in inviting forces equipped with arms which frighten and deter anyone wishing to invade this land. This is a duty which the present circumstances impose on him and a decision which the painful reality makes necessary. The principles of Islamic Shari'a make it a duty of the Moslem ruler to seek the help of whoever has the power which enables them to perform the task. There is clear evidence in the Holy Qoran and the Sunna of the Prophet for the necessity of being prepared and of taking all precautionary measures before it is too late.

May God's peace and blessings be on our Prophet Mohammed, his family, and his companions."

(The Council of Senior Ulama)

The United Nations economic sanctions against Iraq just beginning to be felt, the Arab League with its historic decision to come to the aid of the Kingdom of Saudi Arabia and in defense of the occupied state of Kuwait, coupled with the entire world community being so united, (probably for the first time in the history of the United Nations and the world) all began to exhibit their tremendous pressure and impact on Iraq and the events shaping the Gulf region. Saddam Hussein began to feel the heat and the powerful impact of such a unified effort, led and orchestrated by the genius and courage of top leaders in the world. To get the United Nations solidly behind the massive efforts being exhibited to defend the Kingdom, and pave the way toward the liberation of Kuwait, is a stroke of a genius and a masterpiece of diplomacy which will be registered in the annals of political history for centuries to come. The coupling of these international forces, strengthened by condemnations from political organizations, as well as religious and humanitarian societies, all exposed most clearly and unequivocally the assertions, lies, threats and innuendos emanating from the propaganda machine of Baghdad and the utterings of deathly threats from Saddam Hussein. In the midst of all this pressure, the ruler of Iraq did not acquiesce and respond to the will of the world and the spirit of the New World Order, nor did he move in tune with logic or justice. Instead, he continued his threats and his acts of aggression and atrocities not only against the people of Kuwait but also against the innocent people who were working in Iraq and Kuwait, trying to make a living to support themselves and their families around the world. Saddam Hussein defiantly aggravated the situation by holding thousands and thousands of innocent foreign people as hostages. Hundreds of thousands of people were forced to stream out of Iraq and Kuwait as refugees moving to safety and fleeing under terrible conditions of deprivation, thirst, and scorching heat of the desert. The Kuwaitis continued to stream out of their land which had already become a land of hell and agony, when only yesterday it was a welfare state of goodness, peace and tranquility. The hostages, the refugees, and the Kuwaitis all suffered terribly because Saddam Hussein wanted to use them as pawns in his scheme of manipulating the world to serve his aims. But all his efforts in this regard were to be to no avail!

War is hell and destruction.

Chapter 5

Occupation of Kuwait and Atrocities of an Aggressor

The brutal occupation of the State of Kuwait brought with it devastation, agony, destruction and death to thousands of Kuwaitis and millions of people from all over the world. The direct aftermath of the blitzkrieg attack was the agonizing death of over 1,200 Kuwaiti citizens along with a number of innocent people who came from the four corners of the world to make a living in Kuwait and Iraq. Thousands of foreign workers who came from the Western world in a gigantic process of technology transfer in order to help in the building of Iraq and Kuwait, along with the millions of workers that came from throughout the Third World, all these people suffered badly from the ruthless occupation of the innocent State of Kuwait. In no time, foreign personnel, especially from the Western World as well as the Eastern World, became pawns in the hands of the leader of Iraq who mercilessly used them and abused them without regard to anything called human value or justice. Thousands of these people were held against their will, not only in Kuwait but also in Iraq as well.

These unfortunate innocent people were subjected to terrifying agonies and abuse, and in no time they became hostages. In fact they were hostages from day one of the invasion. The semantics and definitions were abundant, with Saddam's propaganda machine saying that they were in their homes for their own safety, then they became "guests" and gradually they became "human-shields" where they were dastardly and most inhumanely used as "sacrificial lambs" at various strategic locations, including facilities for chemical weapons, biological weapons and nuclear sites. Saddam built these facilities throughout Iraq in order to support his elaborate designs against his innocent neighbors. He showed total disregard for humanity and the will of the entire world. This was done in total disregard to international law and the very basics of civil behavior among nations of the world. This was a flagrant violation smack against any humanitarian feelings toward mankind. It was accompanied by much more vicious behavior inside the State of Kuwait, against the Kuwaitis where many of them were killed, injured, subjugated and terribly abused. All this became very clear through extensive intelligence and through documented work of world organizations, leading among them Amnesty International. It will all be described in more detail toward the latter part of the chapter. Again, parallel to these terrible events, millions of refugees leaving the theater of war from Iraq and Kuwait were flooding the borders of Saudi Arabia and Jordan, also Iran and Turkey to a lesser extent. This flood of unfortunate refugees especially from the Third World suffered miserably in the searing heat of the desert. Many died in agony from thirst and hunger after being stranded for many days and weeks with their families, youngsters, old men and women alike. That shall be described in this chapter as well. However, let us begin with the plight of the hostages and describe the way this scenario moved on with its international implications.

The Agony of the Hostages

When the occupation began, westerners in Kuwait and Iraq were held against their will. In any language, it was simple and clear that they were being held as hostages. America suffered enough during the hostage crisis with Khomeini of Iran, where 52 Americans were held 444 days against their will. This touched a very sensitive nerve and America was determined never to allow this to happen again, no matter what the cost may be. There were many, many thousands of "Western detainees" in the realm of Kuwait and Iraq, reaching nearly 20,000 people. Among them, about 2,500 Americans in Kuwait, in addition to 4,000 British, 300 Japanese, nearly 1,000 Soviets, 300 from West Germany, 300 French, 150 Italians and about 70 from Australia. While the number of hostages held in Iraq was about 600 Americans, 600 British, 230 Japanese, 8,000 Soviets, 600 from West Germany, over 200 from France, about 350 from Italy and 60 from Australia. Saddam Hussein's venomous tirades and his propaganda machine of disinformation and terror were aimed mainly at the United States of America, but to an equal degree, especially, against Saudi Arabia and the Gulf countries. Included in his scheme of hostage manipulations were people that came from England, France, the Netherlands, Brazil and all other western countries. Also thousands from the former Soviet Union were in Iraq assisting in many technical services which also included military help. The Soviets were not allowed to move freely and depart from Iraq, despite the initial denials of the Iraqi government. In fact, they became hostages just like the rest of the western hostages. Iraq and Kuwait, under the grip of Saddam Hussein became a huge prison for these thousands of people who agonized with their loved ones about their future and fate. Playing with the destiny of these people, manipulating the emotions and psychology of their loved ones caused untold agony, worry and apprehension among thousands of innocent people around the globe. These anxious, terrible feelings were compounded several times over, when many of these hostages were used as a human-shield in various strategic sites in Iraq, for the purpose of deterring any possible attack on the supposedly vital establishments which would make optimum military targets for the Coalition Forces now arrayed against the brutal dictatorship of Saddam Hussein.

Demagoguery and stalling for time became a cornerstone for his propaganda machine and sinister policy. The news media of the world was used and at times abused by the propaganda organs of Saddam. His intentions were clearly to influence America's public opinion and especially the Congress of the United States of America, along with other parliaments and leaders around the world. He did not succeed in fooling the people who read through him and understood his ill intentions and designs. He tried to manipulate the hostage dilemma to an optimum! At one time he would release women and children and thus hope that the world will reward him for this "humanitarian act!" In fact, many former leaders and distinguished men around the world began to give an attentive ear to the pronouncements of Saddam Hussein. They responded to his promise that whoever comes to Baghdad will not go back empty handed. A shameful and criminal theatrical show was not only in the making but it was being played on the world stage. A stream of dignitaries was rushing to Baghdad, appealing to him to free some of their countrymen who were held hostage in Iraq. He was at center stage, basking in the fame and glory of having world leaders at his door step appealing for the release of a trickle of hostages. All along he thought he could hold the entire world, and especially America, as a hostage as well. This was never to materialize! Although there was deep concern for the safety and security of the hostages, the United States policy and the policy of other friendly and allied nations around the world was not going to be affected, substantially, by the hostages. In fact, Saddam was made to understand that if any harm befell the hostages, he and his clique would be held responsible. Nevertheless, the hostage bargaining chip was used to an optimum. In the media campaign which was instantaneously carried on a world-wide scale, Saddam and his government made an optimum use of the situation. In fact he proved to be a master at demagoguery and use of the news media on a global scale. Every move, every pronouncement, every action by Saddam Hussein was instantaneously broadcast across the waves to the entire world community.

Threats and blackmail were uttered by the puppet government which was proclaimed in Kuwait. The Foreign Minister of the short-lived government declared on August 5, 1990, "Countries that resort to punitive measures against the provisional free Kuwait government and the fraternal state of Iraq should remember they have interests and nationals in Kuwait." Diplomats and loved ones alike were frantically working to establish contact with the thousands of hostages held in Kuwait and Iraq. Broadcasts carried by the Voice of America and the British Broadcasting Corporation (BBC) were aired to the Western people in Kuwait, advising them to stay indoors and avoid confrontation on the streets. In other words stay low and avoid being captured by the Iraqi invaders. Immediately after the occupation, an American official in Washington said, "We do not have, as far as I know, any indication of mistreatment of Americans, but there are reports of pretty brutal treatment of Kuwaitis in Kuwait." The first sign of hostages was indicated by the 38 Americans who were held in the Al-Rashid Hotel. However, the Foreign Minister Tariq Aziz said, "Hostages do not stay at hotels, drink beer and enjoy their lives."

The borders of Iraq and Kuwait were sealed and opened at the whims of Saddam Hussein. With every move, the hopes and aspirations of millions were dashed into despair and dust. The dictator thought he had a wild card with the hostages and he played it to the hilt. The speaker of his rubber-stamp parliament declared, "The people of Iraq have decided to become hosts to the citizens of these aggressive nations, as long as Iraq remains threatened with an aggressive war." He also stated that they would be housed in areas which most likely would be targets in case of war. The world was outraged at such behavior and the Foreign Secretary of Great Britain, Douglas Hurd, reflected the thought and feeling of many around the world when he said about Iraqis holding of hostages, "Disgraceful, inhumane and contrary to civilized behavior."

Scenarios of rescue missions were drawn and the possibility of overtaking Kuwait City was considered as a way for possibly rescuing the hostages in Kuwait and eventually freeing all of Kuwait. Several other options were considered, but the hope was pinned down on the chance that Saddam might release the hostages, so patience and perseverance were the good virtue.

President George Bush declared that Saddam Hussein himself would be held accountable for his behavior concerning the hostages. He stated also that, "the human-shield" strategy will not work and will not influence the allies policy in the Gulf crisis.

Other world leaders reflected this view and determination by carrying a policy which is not influenced by the manipulations of Saddam Hussein. Early in the hostage crisis, the Prime Minister of Great Britain, known as the "iron lady," Margaret Thatcher accused him of hiding behind the skirts of women and children, she said, "Saddam Hussein is now trying in his tactics to hide behind women and children and use them as human-shields and use them as part of his negotiations. We do not enter into such negotiations. These people are entitled to certain fundamental human rights, which are being totally flaunted to the repugnance of the whole civilized world." The new Prime Minister of England, John Major, continued a policy of decisiveness and determination in facing the actions of Saddam Hussein declaring that the policy of using hostages as a human shield is, "inhumane and illegal." He also stated that Saddam and others responsible with him would be held accountable and may be tried for war crimes when the war is over.

The hostage agony, suffering and fear prompted some of them to risk their lives and run for the security and safety of some neighboring countries, always fearing that knock on the door from the gestapo of Saddam Hussein. Prior to taking off into the desert in hope of seeking safety, some were warned that many have met their fate attempting such an escape. In fact, a British subject who tried to escape was killed with Iraqi bullets as he was trying to flee toward the Saudi border. Daring escapes were discouraged by western officials in Kuwait and Iraq. Some Britishers crossed the border to Syria preferring the risk of a hail of bullets to hell in Iraq and Kuwait. Such dangerous trips will never be forgotten in the lifetime of those who took them, suffering in the desert heat and fine sand along with the problems one would encounter with such car travel and being stuck in the sand, always worrying about Iraqi soldiers and the Iraqi bullets. Some of them were lucky and made it, because they bribed Iraqi soldiers either with money, food or produce. Most were able to make it to safety, but after having horrifying experiences that will linger with them and scar their life forever.

A trickle of hostages were released at a time, and at other times a number were taken away to be used as a human-shield. Out of 213 Japanese in Baghdad hotels, 20 were taken around the 27th of August to be used as human-shields, while two Japanese engineers were permitted to leave for Jordan in order to receive medical treatment. At the same time, 52 relatives of the American Diplomatic Corps crossed to Iraq and then to Turkey at a late hour on Monday, August 27. The journey from Kuwait to Iraq to Turkey is a long arduous one in the devastating heat of August where many in the best of health would suffer from such a trying journey. Once reaching the Iraqi border, another agony of bureaucracy and harassment begins. It takes several hours and some are not permitted to go through. In fact, three young men were held by the Iraqi authorities on the border. This scenario is repeated time and again, almost daily. Saddam Hussein was using his "cynical manipulation" of the hostages to the hilt. He was rewarding personalities and countries that he was hoping would not send forces to the Gulf. He was also punishing countries helping in the Gulf crisis and those who were contemplating aid of any sort to the Allied Forces. All his manipulations, maneuvers and exploitations of the world media, for the specific purpose of driving a wedge among the allied nations that are arrayed against him in the Gulf, led to nothing. He failed on all fronts!

Immediately after the call of Saddam Hussein for all British and Americans in Kuwait to assemble in three different hotels prior to transporting them to Baghdad, the United Nations was very swift in its reaction and world condemnation was imminent.

On August 18, 1990 the Security Council passed **Resolution 664,** with a unanimous vote: The United Nations Security Council, acting under Chapter VII of the United Nations Charter,

1. Demands that Iraq permit and facilitate the immediate departure from Kuwait and Iraq of the nationals of their countries and grant immediate and continuing access of counselor officials to such nationals;

2. Further demands that Iraq take no action to jeopardize the safety, security or health of such nationals;

3. Reaffirms its decision in Resolution 662 (1990) that annexation of Kuwait by Iraq is null and void, and therefore demands that the government of Iraq rescind its orders for the closure of diplomatic and consular missions in Kuwait and the withdrawal of the immunity of their personnel and refrain from any such actions in the future;

4. Requests the Secretary-General to report to the Council on compliance of this Resolution at the earliest possible time.

Instead of compliance, Saddam Hussein and his governmental organs in the Revolutionary Command Council were beaming to the world arrogance and defiance. Saddam wanted to keep the hostages and optimize their use. He decreed that, "Every citizen, regardless of nationality, harboring foreigners–who are forbidden to leave the country–will be sentenced to death." Despite the abhorrent threats, westerners stayed hidden in various apartments and locations in Kuwait. Many Kuwaitis and Arabs of other nationalities lent a compassionate, humanitarian hand and helped them in their tragic time and dilemma. Some of the unfortunate who helped westerners in their hiding were severely punished. Some were castrated and others tortured by various other means. Thousands of foreigners were living in fear and hiding–a tormenting life, devastating to the spirit and mind. Luckily, many of them were able to tune in to the British Broadcasting Corporation (BBC) and the Voice of America (VOA).

With Saddam's annexation of Kuwait, he pulled away diplomatic immunity from the Embassies in Kuwait and demanded that all personnel of the various Embassies should join the respective Embassies in Iraq, since Kuwait is now Province 19 of Iraq. Of the 68 diplomatic missions in Kuwait, many Embassies did not fold nor succumb to his pronouncements and threats. In fact, personnel of nearly twenty diplomatic missions remained under siege inside their Embassies. Among these were: Embassies of the United States of America, Saudi Arabia, Britain, West Germany and Japan, along with a number of others. The former Soviet Union evacuated the Embassy personnel but while the Embassy was not shutdown, it was empty. Brazil, India, and the Philippines, along with an assortment of other nations, especially from the Third World, had closed or were in the process of closing their embassies. This situation of siege was disturbing and frustrating to many leaders, especially President Bush who said, "The American flag is flying over the Kuwaiti Embassy (U.S. Embassy in Kuwait) and our people inside are being starved by a brutal dictator and you think I'm concerned about it? You darn right I am. And what I'm going to do about it, just wait and see! Because I have had it with that kind of treatment of Americans." Embassies were surrounded by Iraqi troops and blockaded from receiving any supplies. This was a flagrant violation of international law and the norms of diplomatic relations among civilized nations of the world. It was in fact, a direct violation of the United Nations Vienna Convention of 1961 which guarantees the sanctity of Embassies in foreign countries and stipulates the norms of diplomatic relations. Among the major points are:

The rights of a diplomatic mission are inviolable. Agents of the host country are not permitted to enter without the specific permission of the Chief of the diplomatic mission. Any belongings of an Embassy may not be acquired by the host country. As for the diplomatic personnel, they should not be subjected to detention or arrest. In fact, in case of an armed conflict certain rights of the personnel of the diplomatic mission must be respected and protected. Such a convention was signed essentially by all nations of the world and its application began in 1964.

Saddam Hussein declared officially on the 19th of August, that he would hold thousands of hostages from the West, living in Iraq and Kuwait, in flagrant disregard for the Security Council Resolution of August 18. He threatened to apprehend all British citizens in Kuwait who refused to gather at the designated three hotels. Such moves did not deter nor paralyze the world community in its determination to amass forces for confronting Saddam Hussein and eventually evicting him from Kuwait. On the contrary it strengthened its resolve.

The stream of foreign dignitaries coming to Baghdad pleading for their nationals was at full swing during the hostage crisis. The first to head the list of arrivals was the President of Austria and former Secretary General of the United Nations, Kurt Waldheim. He was the only head of state to come pleading with Saddam Hussein. The list included personalities such as: Jesse Jackson of the U.S., former Governor and former Secretary of the Treasury, John Connally, Mohammed Ali, the veteran boxer, former Chancellor Willy Brandt of West Germany, former Prime Minister of Japan, Naksone Yasuhiro, British Labor member of Parliament, Tony Benn, former British Prime Minister, Edward Heath, along with a number of other personalities from throughout the world. Saddam rewarded each one of his visitors with a handful of hostages that were freed. When President François Mitterrand of France gave his United Nations speech, Saddam was quick to release the sick and elderly among the hostages of French origin. He also apologized for the entry of Iraqi troops into the residence of the French Ambassador in Kuwait. His manipulation took him a step further, when he asked his National Assembly in late November for approving the freedom of all 327 French hostages. All these moves aimed at driving a wedge between the solid alliance did not succeed. Saddam Hussein failed!

By November 18, and again trying to manipulate deliberations taking place at the United Nations, Saddam suggested that all hostages would be released at stages during the next three months, starting with Christmas time, December 25, 1990, unless events developed in such a manner to "mar the atmosphere of peace." The offer was dismissed by U.S. officials and the world, as a propaganda ploy. However, Saddam had other intentions for his new hostage plan. Not only did he desperately want to drive a wedge among the solid alliance poised against him, he also wanted to stretch the hostage crisis as far as he could to block windows of opportunity for possible military action against him. On November 19, 1990 Secretary of State James Baker commented on Saddam's offer, he said, "He never should have taken them in the first place, and I think this is just further cynical manipulation of innocent lives." Margaret Thatcher, Prime Minister of Britain despised Saddam's tactics. On November 20, 1990 she said, "They are brutal and most people understand that evil has to be stopped. Either he withdraws, or the military option has to be used." The pressure continued to mount on him through the sanctions and other means that were brewing and about to materialize. Finally, on December 6,

1990, he used his wild card and announced the release of all foreign hostages. His ploy failed! He intended to influence world opinion and especially the debate that was gaining momentum in the United States of America, hoping that Congress would be pacified to a good degree and that military action would not be taken against him.

The hostage tragedy was reaching a conclusion and thousands of foreigners rushed to get away from the life of hell and torment they were living as hostages in constant fear and danger in Iraq and Kuwait. All along, during this Gulf Crisis and from the very beginning, another group of unfortunate people became a human tragedy in the making— a continuing saga which moved and tormented the minds and spirits of men of goodwill everywhere! This was the plight of refugees from Third World countries that were forced to flee for their safety, away from the theater of war and the grip of Saddam Hussein in Kuwait and Iraq.

The Agony of the Refugees

The human suffering of hundreds of thousands of refugees was a sad melodrama played on worldwide news media for many weeks. The world conscience was touched and moved!

The occupation of Kuwait brought along a tidal wave of refugees mainly from the Third World who streamed into the safety of neighboring countries. The scorching heat of the desert took its toll in human life and suffering! In a matter of a few days, hundreds of thousands of people were fleeing the theater of conflict in Iraq and Kuwait. Thousands upon thousands would have to take the dangerous and arduous journey through the desert, going from Kuwait to Iraq and suffering through the never ending bureaucracy and agony of waiting for exit visas; when they reach the borders between Iraq and Jordan, the long agonizing waiting period began . . . They would have to wait for a week or more, before their papers were processed for transit entry into Jordan to be stationed at one of the camps in Rouweished. More human suffering, agony and disease was to be the fate of these unfortunate people, who but a few days earlier were minding their own business, and taking pride in their work so they would earn their salary which they sent to their loved ones, to over seventy countries around the globe. Now, they were forced to leave their jobs behind. They lost their savings and left most if not all their belongings as well. They were essentially, penniless, leaving behind everything they worked hard for, giving their blood and sweat to earn an honorable living! Saddam and his troops looted not only what these unfortunate people left behind, but they plundered and looted the state of Kuwait and the innocent Kuwaiti people. A human tragedy on a global scale was in the making indeed! The world humanitarian organizations, the United Nations, the Red Crescent and the International Red Cross were all being energized to rise to the occasion and come to the aid of hundreds of thousands of refugees stranded in the desert, under terrible conditions where food, water and medical attention, along with all the minimum basic necessities for living, are either rare or non-existent.

The horror stories were coming out from those who were lucky enough to escape. Thousands of Egyptians were streaming toward Jordan; some came through the Kingdom of Saudi Arabia, where they were welcomed as Arab brothers with traditional Saudi hospitality. They were well fed, well treated, supplied with basic needs and given some money for their immediate needs, since they had fled without any money and with minimum belongings if any. Hundreds of people perished in the desert. Many of them young and some elderly. The Iraqi forces stripped them of all their belongings and any electrical equipment they could find. Many of the Egyptians who left Kuwait complained about being attacked by the aggressors and their agents. This was very disheartening and a great disappointment to those fleeing Kuwait. Many of them stated that the aggressors and their agents attacked them in their homes and helped the Iraqis in locating them as well. The fleeing Egyptians, along with thousands of other refugees, were exposed to all kinds of torment in the desert, lacking water, food and rest.

By the 20th of August, over 65,000 refugees from 70 different nationalities entered Jordan, fleeing Iraq and Kuwait since the occupation of Kuwait. Those able to leave Jordan were only 17,000, others were still being processed or waiting for help to come either from their nations or from the world humanitarian organizations. Over 17,000 were reaching the border everyday. Some Thailand nationals also came through the Saudi border and were well received by Saudi authorities; their stories supported the numerous other stories told by fleeing refugees over and over again.

What added more to this human tragedy were the ever changing policies and moods of Saddam Hussein. The borders with Jordan, Saudi Arabia, Turkey or Iran would be open one day and another they would be closed. With these fluctuations, the suffering of the people, their apprehension and worries would mount exponentially. As the borders close, the numbers of refugees pile on enormously and the suffering takes its toll in human life and misery.

The outpouring of these refugees, since early August, went on for several months. When the air war and then the ground war broke out, many more refugees joined the ranks of others who had already fled. In August, the searing heat of the desert could reach 130 degrees Fahrenheit in the shade. Water was very scarce! So was food. All this added to the agony and troubles of the refugees. Many of those who became ill were doomed for lack of basic medical needs. People from countries across the Third World: Sri Lanka, Bangladesh, Pakistan, India, the Philippines, Thailand, several other Arab countries, among them Egyptians, Lebanese, Sudanese, Yemenis and Moroccans along with several other nationalities across the world spectrum, all had a common fate of suffering in the desert, while waiting for aid to come so they could go home. Iraq had about one million Egyptian workers while Kuwait had 150,000. For a few months, an average of fifty Egyptians per month were sent in body bags from Iraq. So among all other nationalities, the Egyptians were especially, alarmed and those fleeing had chilling stories to tell. (Almost a quarter of a million Egyptian refugees were repatriated through Jordan. Many of them by plane, others shipped from the Gulf of Aqaba.)

The refugees languished in three huge tent cities named: Sha'alan 1, 2, and 3. Every now and then, the desert wind would whip the sand and spread the filth in these cities of misery and human tragedy. Animals, insects, snakes and scorpions took their toll on the populations of these camps. The President of the French relief organization, Doctors Without Borders, said, "These people are hostages of the desert." When water arrived at the border camps the refugees struggled for a drink. At times, it became the law of the jungle, everyone searching for a precious few droplets to quench their thirst. In fact, dehydration became one of the most serious problems encountered by many refugees. People waited in line, some waited for nine hours so they could have a drink of water. Not long ago many of these were professionals doing good jobs for their host country, Kuwait and Iraq. Many of them spent over two weeks at these camps and some did not have a drink for over a day or a meal for over two days. Life at the camps was not much better than the life of abuse and terror left behind in Kuwait.

Witnessing the misery of this enormous flood of refugees in a bleak, and dusty border crossing brings to question the self-styled Arab Robin Hood in the person of Saddam Hussein, supposedly robbing the rich to give the poor. At the Rouweishid and at other crossings, another story was being witnessed, all created by the ruler of Baghdad.

It is a terrible and ugly site to see people fighting over a crumb of bread or a few cups of water. But that is what actually took place at the camps. A Philippino described his horrifying experience when he spent seven days at a desert camp saying, "I still could not forget the sight of men who became like wild beasts fighting to stay alive."

While the hostages and refugees streaming into Jordan and other neighboring countries suffered a terrible fate, in the meantime another human tragedy of untold magnitude was unfolding inside Kuwait and along the treacherous desert escapes of the Kuwaitis along the Kuwaiti-Saudi border.

Atrocities Committed in Kuwait and Suffering of the Kuwaiti Refugees

This sad human tragedy was the direct outcome of the ruthless occupation of Kuwait by Saddam Hussein supposedly an Arab brother to the Kuwaitis. The occupation was swift and ruthless! Many Kuwaitis died! Thousands more were injured and many more thousands were abused and tormented. Fearing death and destruction, nearly a third of the population of Kuwait, about 300,000 were rendered homeless, destitute refugees rushing toward the border with Saudi Arabia for safety and security. But traveling in the desert, during the terribly hot month of August is a trying experience for anyone, let alone women, children and the elderly. The Kuwaitis packed their children, families and what few belongings were left and headed for the desert, sometimes in small numbers, at other times in convoys. All struggling to avoid an encounter with the invading ruthless army. Vehicles got stuck in the sand, even at times, the four-wheel drive type did not fair any better than regular transportation vehicles. A few hours in the scorching sun and dehydration would set in. Unfortunate Kuwaitis would fall ill, some died from thirst and hunger, others perished at the hands of the invading forces and still others would perish from the deadly mines strewn everywhere by the forces of the aggressor. Many went through the traumatic experience of facing their enemy and wondering what their fate would be! Their cars would be searched, looted, the occupants robbed and abused. At other times they were let go, once they paid the soldiers whatever meager sums of money they were able to bring with them, or by giving them some of the food and water they brought for their own survival. A journey of a short distance seemed like eternity! It was most frightening and tormenting when a family would be forced to give up their loved ones, because the dictates of the Iraqi army stipulated that men between the age of 17 and 40 would not be permitted to leave Kuwait. In fact, many youngsters were rounded up and taken to Iraq for indoctrination, brain washing and sometimes torture. (The Iraqi authorities would let the women go through, while holding the husbands and when some women wanted to go back to be with their husbands, they were prevented from doing so.)

Saudi Hospitality

The Kuwaitis were stripped of their passports and all their identification papers, in a campaign to confuse the host country and strip Kuwait of its legitimate population. Saudi authorities were waiting to receive their Kuwaiti brothers and sisters mainly at the border town of Khafji. Saudi hospitality, compassion and graciousness, to their fellow Kuwaiti Arabs, was exemplary.

Sites for processing human waves of Kuwaiti refugees were established. Food, water, lodging and medical supplies were made available overnight! The fear was genuine that Saddam Hussein, by stripping these refugees from their proper documents, would infiltrate the Kingdom with a number of his terrorist groups. So, the job was not an easy one for the Saudis to screen the flood of refugees in order to separate the undesirable implants of terrorism sent by Saddam and his occupying force in Kuwait. However, efficiently and meticulously, without ever losing sight of the ordeal that the unfortunate refugees had been exposed to, Saudi authorities, on direct orders from King Fahd of Saudi Arabia and the Saudi government, moved with speed and professionalism in processing the multitude of refugees to alleviate their fear and ease their pain. In a short time, thousands and thousands of Kuwaiti refugees were on their way to the four corners of the Kingdom, from the Eastern Region in Dammam and Dhahran to the Western Hijaz in Mecca, Madina and Taif, and from the north in Toubouk to Asir in the south and especially to the heart of Najd, Riyadh, to every corner of the Kingdom, the homes and hearts of the Saudis were open to receive their destitute brothers and sisters coming from Kuwait. Some Kuwaiti refugees went on to Bahrain where they were welcomed; some were offered free housing, others stayed at hotels paid for by the Kuwaiti Embassy. Other Gulf countries also helped some of the Kuwaiti refugees.

About 100 years ago, the founder of the Kingdom of Saudi Arabia, Abdulaziz was ten years old when his father Abdul Rahman was sent as a refugee from Riyadh, the heart of Najd to the hospitality of Kuwait, where he stayed for ten years and then as a young man went back to liberate the land of his forefathers in 1902. What a twist of history! Now, one hundred years later, the Kuwaitis with their ruling family who are descendants of Moubarak, the old ruler of Kuwait, came outpouring across the border to their brothers and sisters in Saudi Arabia, seeking their compassion, care, and a helping hand.

Back in the boom days of the late 70's and early 80's, the Kingdom embarked on a development program which built a great infrastructure, from super-highways to massive airports; from huge air bases, top schools, universities and hospitals, to a surplus of hundreds of multi-story apartment buildings, in the four corners of the Kingdom. With the flood of Kuwaiti refugees, hotels, private homes, and these large buildings built during the boom, for Saudi families with limited income, were filled overnight. The great infrastructure and the thousands of residential dwellings that were built by the Saudi government became very valuable indeed during the occupation and the liberation of the state of Kuwait. The generosity of the top leadership and the Saudi populace brought compassion and care to all the Kuwaitis, who felt in Saudi Arabia as if they were in their own homes, in Kuwait. They were indeed most welcome and best cared for! All their needs for food, lodging, medical services and other necessities of life were made available to them by the Saudis, free of charge and with a great spirit of care and love. Saudi authorities paid cash allowances per month as income for every family.

The Kuwaiti government in exile was operating from the summer resort town of Taif in Saudi Arabia. The Amir of Kuwait and his Crown Prince and Ministers were conducting Kuwaiti governmental affairs and making urgent contacts with world leaders seeking desperate help for the salvation and liberation of their lost land. Their government was treated with the utmost of dignity and respect. Whatever their needs may have been they were fulfilled by the Saudi host. Many of their business transactions and governmental functions were again oper-ational from Saudi Arabia and with the help and full cooperation of the Saudi government and people. With the help of Saudi newspapers and their presses, a number of Kuwaiti newspapers and magazines began their publications again from Saudi Arabia. Kuwaiti children joined their Saudi brothers and sisters in the schools and universities of Saudi Arabia, at no cost to them. This parade of goodness and care goes on and on and on, to touch every walk of life and every need the Kuwaitis may have had. Loyalty and gratitude at their best! That is what the Saudis have propagated and exhibited everywhere. They were true friends of their Arab Kuwaiti brothers. They were a true friend in need!!!

Human Suffering in Kuwait

With the brutal occupation of Kuwait came the looting and plunder-ing of the whole state. The atrocities against the Kuwaitis became well documented with time and touched the heart of every decent man and woman around the world. Eyewitness accounts multiplied in num-ber, and in a short time became well documented for the world to see! The occupiers went on a rampage of "pillage and rape." Everything was looted! The Central Bank was looted. The gold reserves were stolen and shipped to Iraq. The gold market was looted. Everything of value was being ripped, stripped and taken away by the Iraqi invaders. Hospitals were stripped of advanced medical equipment and shipped to Iraq. Medical supplies, even incubators, were taken. If infants happened to be in some of these incubators, they were put aside. A car with a woman on her way to delivery was shot at. The woman was killed and the unborn baby was also killed. All blood banks were stolen. A woman was in need of a blood transfusion. It was difficult to find relatives to help, because people were afraid; they would leave their homes and change from one place to another because they feared the grip of Saddam's Moukhabarat. When relatives were found they were not allowed to donate blood for her. The mother died leaving behind two youngsters and her newborn, who was two days old. A youngster was found writing on a wall, "We die and Kuwait will live and no to the tyrant of Baghdad." They took the youngster, tortured him for two weeks, then they brought him to his home and killed him in front of his mother while she had to watch. A medical doctor was taken from Moubarak hospital. They killed him in front of his family.

The nation was stripped bare! One car dealer lost his entire stock of tires and 4,000 cars in one day alone. The first wave of thieves was organized by the invading forces. Soon after, a great influx of marauding waves of civilians poured from Iraq into the streets and homes of Kuwait. To the soldiers and new waves of Iraqi civilians, nothing was sacrosanct! They robbed everything they could lay their hands on. None was safe from their uncivilized and amoral behavior, which is totally contrary to the spirit of Islam and Arab traditions. Soon afterward, Iraqi shops in Baghdad were full of merchandise looted from the grocery stores, supermarkets, gold markets, jewelry stores, electronics, spare parts, book stores, department stores, children's toys, cosmetics, pharmacies, hardware stores, shoes, furniture, electrical supplies, street lights, traffic lights, and an endless list of other facilities in Kuwait. All of a sudden an abundance of luxury items, refrigerators, televisions, video cassette recorders and cars were flooding the markets and streets of Baghdad. Later on, many of these items especially cars were refurbished and conveniently retitled for export and sale abroad, through the safe passage of an accommodating neighboring country. In fact, many of these cars found their way to outlet sales facilities in Amman, Jordan and other places.

At all odd hours of the night or day comes the much feared and dreaded knock on the door from the Iraqi occupiers. A knock that brought chills to the spines of thousands of families who locked their doors in total fear and despair. They were petrified from the torture and atrocities committed against them. The Iraqi soldiers came in search

of Kuwaitis who may be suspect of belonging to the resistance movement. Much of the time they were looking for foreigners who were
hiding in various locations throughout Kuwait. They were hidden and
protected by their Kuwaiti friends. As we mentioned earlier, there
was a decree by Saddam Hussein that anyone hiding or protecting a
foreigner would be condemned to death. This was not an idle threat.
It evoked fear and terror among the Kuwaiti populace. Terrified parents
had to give up their loved ones who were taken by Iraqi soldiers for
interrogation. Thousands of young men were taken from their families
to these interrogation centers, which were established in the schools
and at the university. These centers of learning were transformed overnight by Saddam Hussein into centers of terror and torture. Saddam's
much feared infamous intelligence services, called the Moukhabarat,
flooded Kuwait, and were the masterminds of his terror campaign.
The mere mention of their name evoked trembling and fear. Many
times, after interrogations, the Moukhabarat would bring a young man
back to his home; knock on the door, the parents would answer–the
intruders asked, "Is this your son?" The terrified parents would say,
"Oh, yes, this is our son!" Then, follows the brutal tragedy, where
soldiers would take their gun, shoot the young man, leave him by
the door and go back to hunt for more innocent people, where many
of them would receive a similar bleak fate. What a disgrace to the
human race? Others would be tormented and mutilated. The reports
that emanated from inside Kuwait and the eyewitness account of the
thousands that were able to flee Kuwait, and many thousands had to
go by the side desert paths in order to avoid the onslaught of Iraqi
soldiers, all carried with them horror stories of destruction and despair!!!

At one time, there were some exchange programs underlining the
friendship between Kuwait and Iraq, where some Iraqi scientists and
professionals would come and work in Kuwait for a certain duration.
For example, some doctors worked at certain hospitals, getting acquainted with the system and the latest medical equipment and technology used at these hospitals, others came and did work at the Kuwait
Institute for Scientific Research and the University of Kuwait with its
varied departments and divisions. So, when the time came for brutal
occupation of Kuwait, these people knew exactly where valuable equipment was and how to dismantle some of the sensitive equipment and
ship it to Iraq. In fact, these people were supervising the dismantling
of some of the most modern equipment in computer technology. Others
assisted and directed the dismantling and gathering of the latest medical
equipment that was all shipped to Baghdad. However, there were many
instances, where the marauding hordes of people that came from south-

ern Iraq and other parts of the country were ripping everything they could lay their hands on and in the process abusing, misusing and destroying many sensitive pieces of equipment, which they knew nothing about.

The *Kuwaiti Resistance* was formed in a short time after occupation and the people of Kuwait were all united in their disdain and hate for the invaders. They supported the Resistance by every means at their disposal. Women demonstrated in the streets, they carried messages, food and weapons for the Resistance forces. They were proud Kuwaitis as much as the men who were willing to sacrifice their lives for the Kuwait they love. The Iraqi occupation forces were very brutal in stopping demonstrations. In their fight against Kuwaiti Resistance they stepped up arrests, especially against young men who were more likely to be active in the Resistance.

One exhausted and destitute refugee said to a reporter after a grueling ordeal and hardship drive: "Please don't write that Moslems are doing this to Moslems; if the Israelis invaded, they would treat us better than this."

The courageous Kuwaiti people refused to cooperate with the occupying force. As mentioned previously, Saddam Hussein was not able to find a single Kuwaiti who would accept being a part of his "provisional government." Passive resistance continued throughout the duration of the occupation. The Kuwaitis refused to go to their jobs, or to render any services that would in any way be supportive or helpful to the occupiers. The soldiers did not stop at robbing and stealing the establishments and homes that were left behind by the refugees who fled to neighboring countries, they also robbed the poor and destitute among the Third world countries and especially their Arab brothers the Egyptians, who were struggling to make a living in the Gulf so they could support their families back home. One such unfortunate man said, "They robbed us of everything we had: our money, television set, radio, even our vacuum cleaner."

The resistance was very helpful to those foreigners who were struggling to get away from the hell created by Saddam Hussein in Kuwait. When a caravan of thirteen cars carrying over sixty British people, headed for Saudi Arabia, the Iraqi forces prevented them from continuing their trip, so they returned and were helped by the Kuwaiti Resistance in finding and selecting another route through the barren desert, where they continued their journey and arrived to the safety of Saudi Arabia. Upon completing his task, the hero who led them through the ordeal returned to Kuwait to continue the Resistance struggle against the occupiers. The determined Kuwaiti Resistance contributed extensively to the decline in the Iraqi soldiers' morale. About thirty Iraqi soldiers were being treated daily for wounds caused by the actions of the Kuwaiti Resistance. During August and September, the Resistance continued its extensive activities and impact, but with time its efforts dwindled to some degree because of the increase in the ruthlessness of the occupiers.

Later on, on Friday, March 5, 1991, U.S. Secretary of Defense, Dick Cheney said concerning the Kuwaiti Resistance: "We received extensive reports from the Kuwaiti Resistance throughout the Iraqi occupation of Kuwait. We received information on targets. We received information on activities by Iraqi forces, the status of Iraqi forces. We couldn't always tell how valid the information was, because we didn't have ways to verify, but it turned out that they did provide useful information to us. They obviously, provided a lot of assistance to our forces as soon as they arrived on the scene, and I think a number of them were probably the victims of Iraqi brutality."

On another occasion he also said regarding the Kuwaiti Resistance, "They provided a lot of help in the sense that they sheltered a number of Americans, for example, who were there in the early months of the occupation; they provided assistance in terms of intelligence on Iraqi forces–where they were located, what the morale of their troops were. So we did get useful information from the Kuwaiti Resistance inside. We did indeed get some targeting information."

The Kuwaiti government in exile was lending all the support possible to the Kuwaiti Resistance. The basic necessities of food, medication and money were distributed to the people in need through various means. Many of the workers from Third World countries were used in the distribution process, because they were not suspected by the occupiers, but all the Kuwaitis were under suspicion.

With the Iraqi Moukhabarat roaming the streets of Kuwait, with his mighty force of hundreds of thousands of troops, and around 3,500 tanks, all commanded by the notorious Ali Hassan Al-Majid, who is a cousin to Saddam Hussein, the ruthlessness in dealing with the Kuwaiti Resistance increased many fold in a matter of a few weeks, until it became very difficult and extremely dangerous for the Resistance to operate efficiently against the oppressors. License plates were changed to Iraqi plates. Names of streets and various establishments were changed. Identity cards of Kuwaitis were changed to be Iraqi identities, since Saddam Hussein declared that Kuwait is the 19th Province of Iraq. He went on a campaign of deleting altogether the identity of Kuwait and wiping the state from the face of the earth. People caught with a picture of the ruler of Kuwait were condemned to death. In fact, the head of an organization was given a picture of Saddam Hussein, and the next day when the troops checked to see if it was displayed and it was not, the man was shot and killed. Anyone suspected of cooperating with the Kuwaiti Resistance was tortured and killed. Homes of families suspected of working with the Resistance, were blown up. They exacted revenge against members of a family if they could not get hold of the one whom they sought in the Kuwaiti Resistance. Even the time zone in Iraq was to be also adopted in Kuwait. They forced the Kuwaitis to shave their beards, because the beard to the Iraqis indicated some extremism in religion.

The invaders attacked Kuwaiti homes searching for food even at the check points, they would ask for cheese and bread, like beggars. Food in storage was distributed to the people, to prevent Iraqis from expropriating it and stealing it, prior to reaching the populace. Each member of a Kuwaiti family would take turns in guarding the home, especially at night so that they would try to repel theft by Iraqi troops. But with time, the morale of the Iraqi soldiers dwindled extensively. Soldiers were saying, "We don't know why Saddam would do these things. The mistake is not ours, but we are helpless and cannot do anything."

Another Kuwaiti, witnessing the destruction of his belongings and his home, said about the Iraqi soldiers, "They destroyed everything my wife owned. Everything on the walls. They did not leave anything except the ceramic floor." Pamphlets were printed by the Resistance and distributed urging the populace not to believe the lies and propaganda of the Iraqis. Whenever they found homes with a picture of the Ruler of Kuwait, they burned the home. This same thing was done if they found any arms in the house. When the Kuwaitis demonstrated from the rooftops, saying, "Allahou Akbar–God is Great," a hail of bullets poured on them. Loud speakers in mosques were destroyed, so that the word of God would not be propagated with ease to the masses. It is ironic and hypocritical, that Saddam, after declaring a "Jihad," added the expression: "Allahou Akbar–God is Great" to the Iraqi flag!

The activities of the Kuwaiti Resistance increased with the fall of night, because Iraqi troops tried to avoid confrontation at night. The Resistance booby-trapped many of the apartment doors and Kuwaiti villas, so that the Iraqis coming to probe and steal, would be faced with an explosion, injury or death.

Saddam Hussein's big statues and huge pictures filled many strategic corners in Kuwait. They had slogans on them such as: "Saddam Hussein the Liberator;" "If Saddam wished something and said: be, it shall be." A flood of Iraqis came to settle in Kuwait tipping the demographic balance, in a dynamic process for eliminating the former existence of the State of Kuwait. A kid would be allowed to come across the border but his young father would not be allowed. The child would cry in despair for his father and his mother would do the same. But all in vain! A new bride would be allowed to go through the border but her groom would be turned back. When she tried to go back with him, she was forbidden to do so. How many families were psychologically tortured in this manner, divided and separated?

In one day in Khalidya, seven young men were killed because they were accused of belonging to the Kuwaiti Resistance.

The increase in the ferocity of the occupation force and the mushrooming of its torture methods, coupled with the flood of Iraqis into Kuwait and the ever increasing oppression by the Iraqi Moukhabarat, all were making life terribly difficult and unbearable under Iraqi occupation. It seemed to be an orchestrated campaign to force the Kuwaitis into fleeing their homeland. It is very unfortunate that some Palestinians, who were guests of the Kuwaiti people, working in Kuwait and making a living, supporting their families back in the West Bank and elsewhere in the Arab world, welcomed the Iraqi occupiers and helped them in identifying many of the Kuwaitis that were either in the military, the police or possibly in the Kuwaiti Resistance. This disloyalty and ingratitude earned the Kuwaitis contempt and hatred for those who followed such a path. This became a serious problem that led to more division, mistreatment, and abuse.

The grim scenario of atrocities committed in Kuwait became more clear to the world as the number of people fleeing increased. The Kuwaitis carried the stories of horror with them; the flood of refugees from Third World countries recited many tormenting stories which they either experienced or witnessed. Western workers who were able to flee also corroborated all these horror stories. Soon enough, the world was well aware of the atrocities committed in Kuwait and of the tragedy which befell the Kuwaiti people and millions of guest workers.

All these inhumane practices strengthened the resolve of the World community and especially the United Nations.

The United Kingdom's Ambassador to the U.N., Sir David Hannay said that, "Iraq was engaged in a determined campaign to expunge the very identity of the State of Kuwait. The Iraqis had made life so unbearable that half the indigenous population had left, public and private property had been looted and the Iraqis had even tried to destroy Kuwait's public records. All over Kuwait, Kuwaitis were being replaced with Iraqis. Iraqi soldiers had reportedly stripped Kuwaitis of all documentary evidence of their nationality, including birth certificates, marriage certificates and passports. That amounted to an attempt by Iraq to change the demographic structure of the country it occupied, in violation of the Fourth Geneva convention." Such a Convention was designed to protect people in a humane manner and this contrasted with the report which was well documented by Amnesty International. It has also been documented by the thousands of refugees who poured out of Kuwait.

The theft and willful damage to public and private property in Kuwait was evidenced by a systematic campaign to eradicate the previously booming business, social and cultural life of the State of Kuwait. Ambassador Hannay continued to say, "We have received numerous reports of private cars being seized at road blocks and buses taken. There is clear evidence that school furniture, museum exhibits, traffic signals, street lights, and electricity substation transformers are being stolen by the Iraqi forces and sent back to Iraq. When Kuwaitis are pressed into leaving, they are forced to sign documents ceding all their property to the Iraqi government."

The French Ambassador to the United Nations, Pierre Louis Blanc said, "The shocking testimony heard yesterday had confirmed the reality and the magnitude of the human rights violations committed by the Iraqi occupation force in Kuwait. Those actions were particularly revolting because many of their victims belong to vulnerable groups of the population. Kuwait was today an occupied country and the Fourth Geneva Convention was by law fully applicable. France demanded that Iraq conform scrupulously to its obligations under that Convention." The Ambassador of the United Arab Emirates to the United Nations, Mohammad Hussein Al-Sha'ali, said, "Arabs could only feel shame at the conduct of the Iraqi regime, which has betrayed the heritage and principles of Islam. Iraq's barbaric practices were driving the Kuwaiti people from their country and displacing foreign workers. Those who fled to third countries lost their livelihood and left all their possessions behind, imposing a burden on the asylum countries. The persons responsible for the atrocities must be held accountable. Iraqi civilian and military authorities must take responsibility. The international community must take action to avert a state of absolute chaos."

The Ambassador of the United States to the United Nations and at the time President of the Security Council, Mr. Thomas Pickering, submitted to the Council a document containing grave breaches of the Geneva Convention. He cited the numerous breaches committed by the Iraqi authorities including: "mass extrajudicial executions; torture, including rape, electric shock treatment, beatings, breaking of limbs and mock executions; expulsion of patients from hospitals and other public care institutions; confiscation of crucial equipment; evicting Kuwaitis from their homes and replacing them with Iraqis; unlawful deportation, unlawful confinement and taking of hostages." He went on to say, "The plunder of Kuwait is now far beyond our worst fears . . . Hospitals, mosques, schools, factories, port facilities, industrial complexes, stores, private residences and even amusement parks were looted. Anything that could be moved had been stolen. Much of what had been left behind had been destroyed." He then questioned, "What kind of policy does Iraq have to destroy so much and leave in its place only evil and misery? Certainly, none of the hospitals, schools or other public facilities in Kuwait had represented any threat to Iraq. Like the violations of human beings perpetrated by Iraqi forces, their destruction had but one sinister purpose: the destruction of Kuwaiti people, Kuwaiti society and the State of Kuwait."

The spokesman for Rumania said at the Council, "Attempts to change the demographic composition of Kuwait were aimed at erasing the country's national identity."

In this regard the Kuwaiti Ambassador to the United Nations, Mohammad Ali Abulhasan, held in his hand computer discs on which his country's population data were recorded. Such data would be invaluable, once Kuwait was liberated. The United Nations was entrusted to safeguard these data against any sinister Iraqi plans and designs.

The torture and gruesome atrocities committed in the occupied state of Kuwait were well documented in a report released on December 19, 1990 by Amnesty International. The report was entitled: "Iraq/Occupied Kuwait–Human Rights Violations Since August 2." Testimony after testimony by eye-witness people was described in this report. It is hard to believe that such atrocities would be committed by men, especially Arab men against their Arab brothers. Leaders around the world were appalled upon reading this report. President Bush was moved and his wife Barbara was unable to finish reading it because of all the gruesome, torture and inhumane treatment of the Kuwaiti people.

President Bush said that, "Iraqis have ransacked and pillaged a once peaceful and secure country." In fact such systematic "destruction" of Kuwait added to the urgency for action to liberate Kuwait from the grip of Saddam Hussein.

Amnesty International* listed 38 methods of torture and ill treatment of Kuwaitis on the hands of the occupiers. Some of the torture methods included: beatings and kickings using metal rods and rifle butts; the falaga which is the practice of beating the bottom of the feet of detainees and then forcing them to run after a terrible painful

---

* Source: Amnesty International, "Iraq/Occupied Kuwait–Human Rights Violations Since 2 August," December 19, 1990, London.

experience; detainees were suspended by their feet from a ceiling while they were beaten, others were suspended from a rotating fan; breaking of legs, ribs, arms, dislocating elbows and shoulder joints; picking up the victims and then dropping them from a certain height, where they fell on the floor and fractured their bones; pressurizing the fingers in a clamping manner; cutting arms, legs, ears, and face with knives; pulling away fingers and toenails; drilling a hole in the leg or other parts of the body; chopping a tongue or an ear; gouging the eyes of a victim; castration; hammering nails into hands; piercing the skin with pins or staplers; shooting the detainees in the legs or arms and then depriving them from any medical treatment; rape of women and young men alike, while inserting bottles and other objects into their privates; tying a string around the privates of a man and then pulling it tight; pumping air into the rectum of men; using electrical shock to the sensitive parts of the body, including tongue and genitals; using electric appliances to burn the genitals and other parts of the body; taking burning cigarettes and extinguishing them on the bodies of victims and on their eyeballs, genitals, nipples, chest or hands; using hot and cold water to shock the detainees; placing a detainee in a cold room for many hours and then immediately taking him to a hot steamy room; pouring sodium hydroxide on the eyes, causing blindness, pulling hair from the face and especially the bearded men, with pliers and pincers; using heavy weights on the body and spitting into the mouth of the detainees; exposing victims to the searing heat of the sun for several hours without water; mock executions were used as a psychological terror method, which included holding the head below the water until a point close to suffocation. The motions of mock execution take place by a firing squad, while holding a gun at the head or mouth and pulling the trigger in a Russian roulette manner; the detainees are forced to watch others that are being tortured or they are exposed to hearing their screams and appeals for mercy; torture and beatings of a relative are done so that a detainee will witness this and is threatened that his fate will be the same; a detainee will be threatened with the electric chair or with death by immersing his body in acid; when a detainee is in desperate need for medical treatment, he is deprived of receiving it, so that his torment will go on; basic necessities of life—water, food, fresh air and sleep along with sanitary facilities are made unavailable to the detainee who is deprived of his needed sleep; stripping the victim of his dignity and degrading him through the use of obscene language, abnormal sexual practices and other forms of abuse.

It is an endless list indeed! It is as if Saddam Hussein borrowed many pages from the horror chambers and practices of Hitler, Stalin and Ceausescu. While all these practices were meant to terrify, intimidate and break the will of the Kuwaiti people, along with breaking the will and unanimity of the world in its determination to eject Saddam Hussein and his barbaric practices out of Kuwait, on the contrary, all these evil acts did not deter the Kuwaitis, nor did they shake the powerful forces of the world which were energized to a mighty strata, gathering a formidable storm, which in due time will sweep away Saddam Hussein and his barbaric forces. Kuwait shall be free again!!!

Kuwait is fleeing the brutal occupation to the safety of Saudi Arabia.

The agony of the refugees!

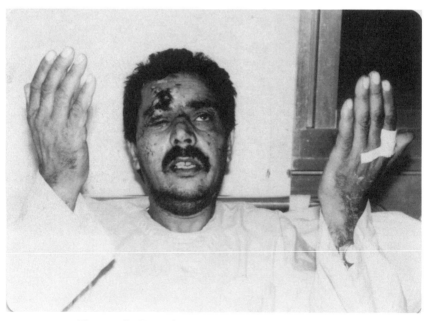

Torture in Kuwait–Humanity wept and agonized!

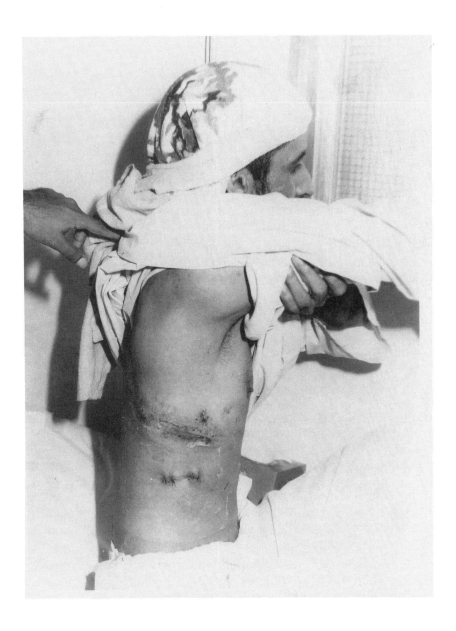

Chapter 6

Countdown to War in the Gulf

The dilemma of the hostages, their use and abuse along with the horrifying stories coming out of Kuwait regarding the atrocities committed by the occupying force, coupled with the bluster and increasing pitch of Saddam Hussein's threats, all added to the resolve of the world community to do whatever necessary to force him and his troops out of Kuwait and bring justice to all the aggrieved.

The Embargo

By now, economic sanctions were beginning to take hold, despite the fact that some nations were not honoring the United Nations Resolution. Although Jordan voted in favor of the sanctions against Iraq, nevertheless, King Hussein followed a scheme of stalling and seeking further "clarifications" and "explanations," all in line with a policy of hedging, postponing and avoiding any strict adherence to the stipulations of the U.N. Resolution. The borders between Jordan and Iraq became a sieve, where trade continued to take place, but this was not going to last for long. Soon enough, the United Nations passed another resolution allowing the Coalition members to use the force necessary for searching ships carrying goods to and from Baghdad.

Some supplies of food and materials arriving at the Gulf of Aqaba were finding their way by land to the border with Iraq and from there on transported overland to Baghdad. Breaches of sanctions were similar to breaches taking place on the border with Iran, but were not very significant.

As described earlier, Saddam used the hostages as a wild card in his international game of manipulating the world media, and for bringing pressure to bear on the respective countries with hostages held in Iraq and Kuwait. He intended to hold the world as a hostage through this policy, but he failed! The United States had already been deeply disturbed and very sensitive about hostage-taking, especially after the bitter experience of the 52 American hostages held in Iran against their will for 444 days and because of other American hostages held in Lebanon for over five years. President Bush, America, and the World were determined not to allow the hostage crisis to paralyze their policies, nor let Saddam Hussein benefit from using them as human shields or bargaining chips in his campaign for securing his hold on Kuwait.

World pressure was enormous and mounting! The United Nations has never been so unified in its history. The storm was gathering momentum and Saddam Hussein's days in Kuwait were numbered!

After the United Nations imposed economic sanctions against Iraq, the sale of Iraqi or Kuwaiti oil was not allowed on world markets. Saddam's oil outlet through Turkey was shutdown. His oil outlet through Syria was shutdown for several years and his oil outlet through a pipeline crossing Saudi Arabia from the East to Yanbu on the Red Sea was also not available for exporting his oil. The remaining possible outlet through the Arabian Gulf was easy to monitor and Iraqi ships were not allowed to carry oil for sale abroad. This brought a halt to the inflow of hard currency so desperately needed by Iraq. His economy was brought to a standstill; needed supplies were scarce. Shortages began to appear everywhere!

The United Nations Security Council, in its *Resolution 665* which was adopted on August 25, 1990, called upon member states cooperating with the government of Kuwait and deploying maritime forces in the area, to use measures commensurate to the specific circumstances as may be necessary under the authority of the Security Council to halt all inward and outward maritime shipping, in order to inspect and verify their cargos and destinations and to insure strict implementation of the provisions related to such shipping laid down in Resolution 661. It also urged all states to provide necessary assistance, cooperation and coordination of their actions in pursuit of this Resolution by using appropriate mechanisms of the Military Staff Committee. This was a unique move in the history of the Security Council. Authorizing military action to halt shipping to and from Iraq is the first move taken by this body in its 45 year history.

With a new clearance from the United Nations Security Council, U.S. warships in cooperation with other Coalition Forces, such as Britain, the Netherlands and Australia were intercepting ships and asking for identifications relating to their content and destination. Coalition personnel would decide whether to let the ships continue on their way, or most of the time they would decide to come on board to identify and search their load. No ships were immune from submitting to the will of the United Nations as enforced by the United States and the Allies. The blockade was maintained by firing shots across the bow of the ships which did not obey orders to halt and submit to search. Thus, the embargo began to have solid teeth at the entry of the Arabian Gulf, at the Gulf of Aqaba and around the Shatt Al-Arab waterway. The Gulf of Aqaba ceased to be a problem in circumventing the sanctions and economic blockade against Iraq. However, the embargo continued to be violated on a minor scale via the land route between Amman, Jordan and Baghdad. As for other borders, especially between Iran and Iraq, Iran did not rush to the aid of its arch-enemy, Iraq. Despite their declared position on these sanctions, the Iranian border also witnessed some violations; policing trade across the border with Iraq would not be an easy task. But any traffic of goods on this front was minimal and did not have much significance. On the northern front, there was Turkey, a strong ally of America, a good friend of Saudi Arabia and a member of the North Atlantic Treaty Organization (NATO). Turkey had been very supportive of U.N. Resolutions and staunchly espoused the leading role of the Kingdom of Saudi Arabia and the United States of America. Turkey was also very efficient in blocking the transport of any oil through a pipeline which normally carried Iraqi oil to the terminal in Yumurtalik. This was done at a substantial economic loss. But the Coalition Forces were quick to promise Turkey some compensation for this economic harm.

The Allied Forces were also on alert watching carefully the movement through the Suez Canal, so that Saddam would not succeed in the possibility of giving an order to sink one of his ships in this vital waterway, and thus block the canal to warships coming to the region.

The AWACS radar surveillance planes played a vital role in policing the embargo imposed by the United Nations. Spy satellites with high accuracy were able to monitor compliance with the embargo. One such plane in the Gulf region was in the air all the time, tracking all airplane traffic around the air space of Iraq. The data gathered was relayed to a ground station in Saudi Arabia, which in turn transferred the vital data to Bolling Air Force Base in Washington, D.C. Data from intelligence satellites were also beamed to the United States and then relayed to American ships and aircraft in the Gulf. The analyzed data relayed to the Commanders was of great value in their operations and for the security of their personnel.

The border with Turkey was well sealed. Any smuggling infractions were either minimal or non-existent.

Another resolution of the United Nations Security Council, namely *Resolution 666*, was adopted at a later date. It gave provisions for allowing shipments of food and medicine to Iraq but only under strict conditions supervised by the United Nations and for the purpose of humanitarian help. Thus, the noose was being effectively tightened around the Iraqi economy and around the neck of Saddam Hussein.

Still other leaks developed and the sanctions had to be tightened further. So the United Nations passed *Resolution 670* on September 25, 1990. Among the provisions of the resolution is the condemnation of Iraq's continued occupation of Kuwait, its failure to rescind its actions and reverse its purported annexation and also its holding of third state nationals against their will, in flagrant violation of previous resolutions. The U.N. further condemned the treatment of Kuwaiti nationals by Iraqi forces, including measures to force them to leave their own country and mistreatment of persons and property in Kuwait in violation of International Law. This resolution decided further that all States shall deny permission to any *aircraft* destined to land in Iraq or Kuwait, whatever its State of registration, to overfly its territory unless:

a. The aircraft lands at an air field designated by that State outside Iraq or Kuwait, in order to permit its inspection to ensure that there is no cargo on board in violation of the economic sanctions Resolution 661 or the present resolution. For this purpose the aircraft might be detained for as long as is necessary.

b. The particular flight has been approved by the Committee established by Resolution 661 on Economic Sanctions.

c. The flight is certified by the United Nations.

This Resolution also called upon all States to detain any ships of Iraqi registry which entered their ports and which are or have been used in violation of the original sanctions Resolution 661, or to deny such ships entrance to their ports, except in circumstances recognized under international law, as necessary to safeguard human life. In the event of evasion of the provisions of Resolution 661 or of the present Resolution 670 by a State or its nationals or through its territory, measures directed at the State in question will be taken to prevent such evasion. With this air-tight resolution, sanctions began to take a stronger bite. The world was hoping that these sanctions and whatever inconvenience and shortages coming with them to Saddam Hussein and his people, might do what was necessary to bring him to his senses and force him out of Kuwait. The world was anxiously waiting for a peaceful resolution to this conflict, but the economic blockade was not to be the only means used to bring Saddam to face reality.

The Coalition Forces

Military buildup was accelerating by the day. Since the occupation of Kuwait, forces from many friendly countries were pouring into Saudi Arabia, especially after the historic decision taken by King Fahd and President Bush to build up such forces for defending Saudi Arabia against any possible attack from Saddam Hussein. In due time, if mounting pressures failed to do the job, then military force would be the only avenue and the last resort for liberating Kuwait.

One of the gravest risks for the Kingdom of Saudi Arabia was the possibility of an Iraqi attack being triggered by an excited Saddam Hussein and especially if a word leaked out about the U.S. deployment plan. Once U.S. soldiers were in place, the possibility of an attack would substantially diminish, but nevertheless the region would continue to be a potentially dangerous flash point.

Aircraft carriers, and other navy ships were making their presence felt in the Arabian Gulf, with thousands of troops on board. The British Navy in the region was also strengthened. Other friendly nations sent some ships into the area. Troops from the United States, Britain, France, the Netherlands, Australia, Canada, Pakistan, Egypt, Syria, Morocco, Bangladesh, and a number of other friendly nations, all were heading east toward the front in Saudi Arabia. It was a long journey for most of them. Large numbers of men and supplies were being shipped in a massive worldwide campaign using ships, airplanes, and other modes of transportation. The civilian fleet was called upon to help in this great task of massive movement of men and supplies. The Kingdom of Saudi Arabia activated its military and supply machine to the optimum. The great *infrastructure*, which was built in the Kingdom during the boom years, became extremely useful in this emergency. The huge airfields and seaports, military and civilian alike, were able to receive the large influx of airplanes and ships pouring into the Kingdom. These huge, first rate airports were a great asset in the buildup of forces and defenses of the Kingdom of Saudi Arabia. Giant modern seaports were receiving an array of ships coming from America and other ports around the world, loaded with men and heavy equipment covering the whole spectrum of war machines from tanks to cannons, from the Patriot missiles to Cruise missiles and a vast assortment of high tech military hardware. The Kingdom warmly welcomed these troops and appreciated very deeply the mission for which they came. Saudi Arabia rolled the red carpet for them and made available everything humanely possible, so that their mission of friendship and defense would be a successful one. The Kingdom made available a whole assortment of needed supplies. Just to list a few, all the jet fuel necessary for airplanes, gasoline and other fuels needed for transport vehicles and war machines were supplied in abundance by the Saudis. The scorching heat of the desert, especially in August, made life indeed unbearable without an abundant supply of water. So the Saudis made available the fresh drinking water needed by the multitude of Coalition Forces, running into the equivalent of nearly seven liters a day per individual. Also made available were: food needed to supplement other food supplies, hospitals, living quarters, medical assistance, other facili-

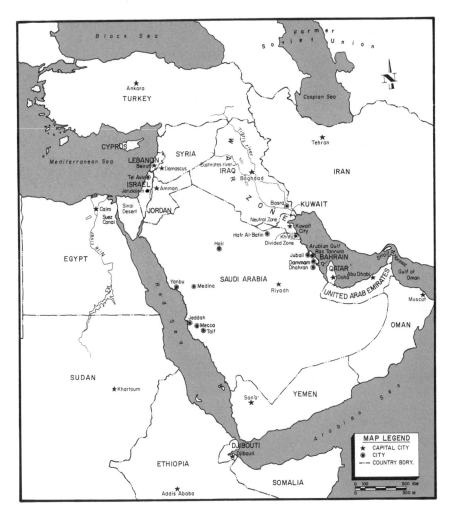

**WAR ZONE AND
SURROUNDING AREA**

ties, including at times swimming pools and a whole list of other services.

While a frenzy of diplomatic activities was gaining momentum, military buildup of *Desert Storm* was going in full swing. By the 20th of August, the United Arab Emirates agreed to the dispatch of some U.S. Forces on its territory. By this time, about 20,000 U.S. soldiers had reached Eastern Saudi Arabia. Fifty-nine U.S. ships were in the Arabian Gulf with 35,000 soldiers aboard. The military buildup was moving at full speed. So, by the end of August the military picture was as follows:

Syria made a wise decision and moved a large number of military personnel to its border with Iraq. Syrian troops began to move into the front in order to boost Saudi defenses. President Hafez Assad, carefully, observed the changing geopolitical winds and made his decisive moves to be on the side of forces fighting evil and injustice.

Former Secretary of State Henry Kissinger called the President of Syria, Hafez Assad, in 1970 "a leader of courage and relative moderation." Later on, when he was ignored by former Secretary of State George Shultz, who was trying to forge a peace treaty between Israel and Lebanon in the aftermath of the Israeli occupation of Lebanon, the pact fell through because President Assad was not included in that process.

In the third week of September 1990 and during a visit to Damascus, Syria, U.S. Secretary of State James Baker declared in a statement concerning the U.S. and Syria, "We share a common purpose with respect to problems in the Gulf." Relations improved and led to possible resolution of the conflict in Lebanon.

On the East, Saddam Hussein made peace overtures with Iran. In fact, he wrote a letter to the President of Iran, Hashemi Rafsanjani, on August 15, 1990, proposing a settlement to outstanding differences in all areas of conflict resulting from the Iran-Iraq war. In his proposal, the Iraqi ruler gave up all his claim to whatever territory had been conquered toward the end of the war. He went even further and accepted all terms of the Algiers Agreement of 1975. In other words, all that he had fought for, for eight years, losing over a quarter of a million men and destroying both Iran's and Iraq's economies, he gave back at the stroke of a pen. His act of desperation was aimed at neutralizing the eastern front of Iraq. Despite Saddam's desperate moves for striking a deal with Iran, observers around the world did not think that Iran would come to the defense of Iraq, especially on the heels of a futile war of eight years, where Iranians lost nearly one million men, and millions of Iraqi and Iranian men, women and children were maimed and injured for life.

More military enforcements were supplied. More aircraft, missiles and other weapons were added as well. They were coming from America, other U.S. bases in Germany and elsewhere in Europe. Toward the latter part of August, U.S. plans called for a quarter of a million American men and women in the Arabian Gulf and the Eastern Region of Saudi Arabia. However, such numbers were modified depending on the need and situation. On the southern front of Iraq, Saudi forces numbered about 66,000 men with 550 tanks and over 180 combat aircraft, on top of 450 artillery rocket launchers, about 20 armed helicopters, and 9CSS-2 missiles with a range of 1550 miles (2500 Kilometers). As far as Kuwaiti forces are concerned, whatever was left of them, they had 275 tanks, 90 artillery and rocket launchers and 36 combat aircraft, with 18 armed helicopters. The U.A.E. had 130 battle tanks and 155 artillery rocket launchers along with 60 combat aircraft and about 20 armed helicopters.

Thousands of American troops were pouring into Eastern Saudi Arabia. The 2,300 men of the "Ready Brigade" in the 82nd Airborne Division supported by Saudi forces were given the duty of guarding the *Dhahran Air Base* in Eastern Saudi Arabia. This major air base constituted the backbone of air operations when the war broke out. This strategic air base is 200 miles south of Kuwait, where the major defense for the oil fields would be mounted. Also, strong defenses would come from King Khaled Military City at Hafr Al-Batin. A good assortment of F-15s came from Langley Air Force Base in the U.S. to the Dhahran Air Base in Saudi Arabia. This Air base was also equipped with Tornado and AWACS aircraft. The U.S. 82nd and 101st airborne troops were there. They received powerful air support. King Faisal Air Force Academy had U.S. AWACS planes, used for aerial surveillance. These were supported by aerial tankers for refueling, and mainly operated from Riyadh.

Off the Arabian Gulf waters, U.S. battleships were in force, including the Wisconsin whose long range Tomahawk cruise missiles proved to be a decisive weapon during the war. These have a range of 1,550 miles (2500 Kilometers). The La Salle Command Ship was leading an eight-ship task force in the Gulf waters. The John F. Kennedy Aircraft Carrier was on its way to joining other flotilla in the Arabian Gulf. France had one aircraft carrier and a number of other warships. Other maritime nations also had a presence in the Gulf. A force of 45,000 Marines with their killer M-60 A1 tanks and A-6E bombers was pouring into the Kingdom. They were equipped with Harrier jets and Hornet attack aircraft. Several ships, with provisions and ammunition for supplying the mighty forces gathering in the Gulf, were en route from Guam and Diego Garcia. Some of these ships were loaded with M60 tanks and other heavy military equipment.

In the Gulf of Oman, there was the USS Independence battleship group. It included 85 combat aircraft with six fighting ships and one nuclear submarine. It also included two frigates and a destroyer. While on the west, in the Red Sea, the USS Eisenhower Carrier battle group received special permission from President Hosni Moubarak of Egypt so that it could sail through the Suez Canal into the Red Sea, on the western borders of Saudi Arabia. It had six fighting ships, 85 combat aircraft, one guided missile cruiser, one destroyer and a nuclear submarine. In the Mediterranean Sea, there was the USS Saratoga carrier group with the USS Wisconsin. Tanks and other heavy equipment shipped by sea would take a journey of nearly one month of sailing from America to the Gulf waters. The mighty U.S. Air Force was moving toward the Gulf zone with great zest. In the early days of the buildup, over 210 U.S. aircraft were in Saudi Arabia at major air fields, especially the air bases in Dhahran and Hafr Al-Batin. These included one squadron of F-15E fighters; three squadrons of A-10 antitank planes; some interceptors and F-16 bombers. The AWACS radar planes were very vital in this deployment operation, to warn against any possible attack by Iraqi aircraft.

This air power was also supported by a large number of U.S. F-111 Precision fighter bombers in Turkey and B-52 bombers stationed at the Island of Diego Garcia in the Indian Ocean. These powerful B-52 bombers are famous for their carpet-bombing. They are well known for bringing devastation to the enemy. They fly long distances and could attack major strategic targets into the very depth of Iraq itself.

In the north, at the Incirlik base in Turkey there were U.S. F-111 bombers which came from Lakenheath, England. There were also a good number of F-117A Stealth Fighters which had been redeployed to this base.

The Mediterranean Sea had ships for blockading the outlet of any Iraqi oil through the pipeline in Turkey. There were submarines of the SSN-Class attack type. There was also the USS Saratoga carrier battle group.

Other Coalition forces reaching the Gulf were British forces with two warships, a destroyer, along with three minesweepers and two air squadrons; the French had two frigates, one destroyer and an aircraft carrier with more troops from the Foreign Legion heading for the Gulf; Canada had already two destroyers and one supply ship; Australia two frigates and one supply ship; Belgium two mine sweepers, the Netherlands two frigates and West Germany five mine sweepers, the former Soviet Union was sending a guided-missile destroyer, along with two supply ships.

The Arab League voting in favor of sending troops to defend the Kingdom of Saudi Arabia gave the green light to Egypt, Syria, Morocco and others to send troops for the defense of the Kingdom. Already thousands of troops from Egypt were coming to Saudi Arabia along with a symbolic contingent of 1,300 troops from Morocco. Syria was gearing up to send several thousands for the defense of the Kingdom. Other friendly Islamic nations such as Pakistan and Bangladesh sent a few thousand soldiers. The numbers would increase . . .

Iraqi Forces

As mentioned previously, the Iraqi forces numbered one million troops with 5500 tanks and 513 combat aircraft. By August 20, 1990 they had around 200,000 troops in Kuwait and large forces amassed on the border, where the Republican Guard was stationed within close proximity.

Iraq also had large stockpiles of the much feared chemical and biological weapons. As for *chemical weapons*, the Iraqi army had abundant stocks of mustard gas and nerve gas. These were made at three different plants in the northern part of Iraq. Weather conditions, especially the seering heat of the desert, speedily dissipates nerve gas and this would lessen its impact and threat. However, the fear from it remained very real, since it is a deadly agonizing weapon. This fear could be very demoralizing for the troops and could be a terrible military threat to confront and combat in the seering heat of the desert. However, gas masks and uniforms for combating possible use of chemical weapons had been issued to the troops in the theater area. Saddam Hussein had threatened several times to use all the weapons at his disposal including chemical weapons. He had made his threats before, and he did use chemical weapons against Iran and his own people, the Kurds. In any event, the Allied Forces were prepared for such an eventuality. They practiced extensive exercises to guard against this possible nightmare!

Nevertheless, fear from the use of chemical weapons was very genuine since it is a severe burden to combat against it. But chemical weapons are a double-edged sword, because their use could also be detrimental to those unleashing them, depending on the directions of wind and other weather conditions. Thus, using them is not an easy task. Another deterrent was the strong possibility of an overwhelming reprisal which would not only include chemical weapons, but might also include small tactical nuclear weapons. The latter was especially deterring against the possible use of these vicious instruments of war.

Anyway, troops of the Coalition Forces had drilled extensively and were well prepared. In case of such an emergency, they would have to don a helmet cover and a gas mask to breathe through. Gas suits are designed to have detector strips which would show red dots when exposed to invisible poison gases. Rubber gloves would prevent any contact with them. The uniform, or gas suit, had an outer shell repellent to fluids. It covers a charcoal impregnated inner portion of the suit. This charcoal is an activated carbon with strong capacity for absorbing chemicals. The boots used also have a cover which is a rubber outer shoe. This prevents the transfer of chemical gases into the feet. The gas suit had two canteens for water. An antidote kit was also enclosed. In case of chemical attack, the Allied Forces were directed to immediately inject themselves with two drugs: one of them to counter the poisonous gas and its deadly action, the other to revive body functions. The needle in such a unit is large enough to go through all the layers of the gas suit and reach the human body in order to deliver the life-saving drugs.

Saddam's *biological weapons* were also very worrisome. In germ warfare, a quantity less than one gram (0.035 ounce) of bacterium called Tularemia can make thousands of deadly germs. Of course, the gas masks and the suits prevent the effect of germs on the soldiers. The problem is, not knowing when you may be hit. One could be caught by surprise and then it can be deadly, if the gas masks and suits are not donned in time. However, soldiers of the enemy themselves may be infected and this double-edged sword would make an enemy reluctant to use germ warfare. The major impact of germ and gas warfare is mainly psychological because it evokes terrible feelings of fear and anxiety. One possible germ that could be used by Iraq is Anthrax which causes fever and serious respiratory distress along with shock. If it is untreated, it could cause death among 80–95% of those stricken. Another agent that can be used is Botulism which causes paralysis, respiratory failure and dizziness. The Plague causes acute respiratory problems and fever. Tularemia causes acute respiratory distress, fever and chills. This can cause death up to 60% of those stricken if not treated, while for the other two, Botulism and Plague, the estimated death rate, if untreated, is 60–70%.

As for other weapons in the Iraqi arsenal, their 5500 tanks were larger in number than the total number of tanks for Britain and France combined. However, they were mostly old Soviet tanks from the sixties, T-54 and T-55. It was estimated that about 1500 Iraqi tanks were of the modern type. Aside from the fearsome chemical and biological weapons Iraq also possessed many rockets and 3700 artillery rocket launchers. They were mostly defensive but some had been modified for offensive purposes. The Soviet Scud missiles had been modified for extended range.

According to military analysts, Iraq had ballistic missiles, 25–30 Soviet Frog-7 missile launchers and 24 Scud-B missile launchers, a surface-to-surface missile launcher Al-Hussein with a range of 350 miles (550 kilometers). They also had Al-Abbas, a Scud missile launcher which had been modified to have a longer range of 550 miles (900 kilometers).

The oil fields of Saudi Arabia, as well as Dhahran and the capital city, Riyadh, could be reached with these Scud missiles from bases close to the Saudi border. Also, Iraqi bases in the western region, closer to the border with Amman, Jordan could become a launching ground for offensive action, reaching targets as far as the eastern Mediterranean. These Scud missiles can be terrifying, especially if they carried chemical warheads.

The Iraqis also had short range weapons such as the Babyl. It is a surface-to-surface launcher, but its range is not more than 60 miles (100 kilometers). This weapon could be devastating against ground troops. It can deliver cluster bombs, covering in just one salvo a larger area than a battery of Howitzers.

Iraqis also had the Exocet missiles, anti-ship weapons built by the French. They could be launched either by Mirage jet fighters or by attack helicopters. Their range does not exceed 450 miles (725 Kilometers). These had proved their accuracy and their destructive record had been noted during the Falkland war between Britain and Argentina.

The 513 combat aircraft of the Iraqi Air Force were a potent force, but they could be easily outflown, outnumbered and outmanned by the latest high tech combat aircraft in the Allied arsenal. Only a few of their fighters were top of the line. Seventy of them were modern Soviet MIG23s and 64 were French Mirage F-1 fighters. These airplanes were placed in the southern region. Iraq also had 160 armed helicopters.

The air defenses of over 4,000 anti-aircraft guns, along with 270 surface-to-surface launchers, could be a very dangerous combination that could exact a heavy toll on the Allied Forces. Nevertheless, the advanced weaponry on the Allied side was to prevail.

However, Iraq's strongest assets were its possession of 5,500 tanks and 3,000 pieces of artillery–a large and strong tank force. It could inflict heavy damage and casualties on any fighting force on the ground. But when the Gulf War broke out, this mighty tank force was pulverized by incessant air bombardment, and thus the road was paved for the next phase of the war on the ground.

Other forces in the region which must be mentioned here include the armed forces of Israel. These constitute a well trained army of 140,000 troops and many reservists, with nearly 3800 tanks, 574 combat aircraft, 1400 artillery rocket launchers, and 77 armed helicopters. It is widely believed that Israel possesses nuclear weapons and a vast array of high tech military hardware. The reservists in Israel number over half a million, while the reservists in Iraq number over 800,000, aside from the one million man army under arms. While Iraq had 66 surface to surface missiles with intermediate range, Israel had a few dozen. Many feared that if Israel was drawn into the war the whole equation and scenario would be jolted to the core. If Israel were to be attacked by chemical or biological weapons, because of sensitivities from World War II, many believed that Israel would retaliate with nuclear weapons. Then, devastation and massive destruction would surely befall the region. All out efforts were made to keep Israel out of the conflict.

Egypt, with a large army, had about 2500 tanks, 1,600 artillery rocket launchers and a combat aircraft fleet of 520, with 90 armed helicopters; Jordan had, 1130 tanks, 250 artillery rocket launchers, 110 combat aircraft and 24 armed helicopters; Syria had a strong army with a large number of tanks exceeding 4000, 2500 artillery rocket launchers and 510 combat aircraft with 130 armed helicopters.

As for Iran, it had 500 tanks, 900 artillery rocket launchers, 190 combat aircraft and 110 armed helicopters.

Possible Scenario

At this juncture, in case the war was to expand and spill over the borders of Saudi Arabia, most likely Iraqi troops would move on toward the industrial city of Jubail, the refining and oil loading town of Ras Tanura and then further down on a journey of 200 more miles south to Dhahran, the heart of oil operations in the Kingdom. Such a move by the Iraqi army would require a minimum of four armored divisions, needing infantry and air cover. In the initial stages of deploying the Allied Forces, the possibility of an Iraqi attack remained very strong. Such an attack could be preluded by the use of chemical weapons. In any event, if this scenario took place, strategic targets in Iraq would immediately have been attacked by an overwhelming air superiority. B-52 bombers would pour in from Diego Garcia with their large loads of bombs to obliterate targets deep into Iraq and paralyze Iraqi actions in the south. From the airfields of Saudi Arabia, be it in Dhahran, King Faisal Air Force Academy or the Hafr Al-Batin Air Base, latest fighting aircraft would have poured into Iraq seeking to destroy major strategic targets. Massive bombardment and the use of Cruise missiles would have come from the amphibious force that had been gathering in the Gulf; coming from the northern border in Turkey, F-111 bombers and Stealth fighters F-117A would have rained death and destruction on chemical and biological facilities, possibly refineries, nuclear facilities, military bases, missile facilities, command and control centers and other military targets. The force already in the Gulf was a great deterrent for any expansionist policies or sinister designs of Saddam Hussein. Nevertheless, the possibility still remained that out of desperation, he might strike the suicidal note and attack Saudi Arabia in order to control the oil fields and thus, if his sinister designs succeeded, become the master for over 45% of all the proven oil reserves in the world. His strike at this stage would definitely have caused havoc, heavy casualties and proved to be a difficult one. But with time, he would be soundly defeated.

The major objective would be to establish air superiority in the first few hours, if such a battle took place. The ground based A-10's and F-16's would come from the Air Base in Dhahran and attack the tanks. The F-15's would help in establishing air superiority. Many of them would be functioning from King Khaled Military City. Cruise missiles would rain destruction on the forces and strategic areas in Iraq and occupied Kuwait. Top on the target list would be radar and communication centers in order to paralyze the command structure of Saddam's army. Heavy bombardment would be applied especially by the B-52 bombers, in order to destroy, demoralize and isolate the Republican Guard in southern Iraq, and thus sever supply lines to the half million man army dug in around southern Iraq and Kuwait proper. Power and communications in Baghdad would be heavily attacked, so that the city would be thrown into darkness and confusion.

In fact, at this stage of the crisis, there was an alternative plan for taking over Kuwait City. In the event that the hostage crisis went from bad to worse, it was possible that paratroopers would have been dropped on the city after some advanced special forces had cleared the way for such an assault, supported by an amphibious landing from the Gulf. Special forces would have neutralized Iraqi command centers, and thus thrown their "military brain" into paralysis and confusion.

On the electronic side of the war, the Allies had a decisive edge. Jamming the radar of Iraqi forces would be of prime importance. Thus, the enemy would lose the edge and the skies would be controlled by the Allied Forces.

When the Iraqis invaded the Embassies of France, Canada, Belgium and the Netherlands where they briefly held five Western Consuls, one of them was an American. They also took three French citizens to an unknown spot. When President Bush heard of the incident, he called it an "outrageous break-in." When reporters pressed in to get more declarations from the President, he said, "You are trying to get me to sound like I am rattling sabers, when I rattle a saber, the man (Saddam Hussein) will know!"

Cost of Desert Shield

According to the U.S. Department of Defense, the cost for Desert Shield, from its inception in August, 1990 until the end of September, 1991, is as follows: 5.3 billion dollars for deployment of forces which includes airlift, sealift, and other deployment such as support ships and storage; fuel costs around 2 billion dollars; call up of reserves which include active duty pay, transport and support amounting to over 3 billion dollars; operating expenses for logistics support and spare parts, over 3 billion dollars; support for theater operations such as water, sanitation and housing amount to over 2 billion dollars; cost of construction, where facilities were designed for two-years use, will be about 2 billion dollars; other expenses including family separation, medical and miscellaneous, are a fraction of a billion. The total amounts to 165 million dollars. However, these costs were defrayed, because of the large sums of money donated by many Coalition partners. This amount initially totaled about 17.5 billion dollars. The countries pledging substantial sums of money for Desert Shield included: The Kingdom of Saudi Arabia, Kuwait and the United Arab Emirates (UAE), who pledged the combined total sum of 12 billion dollars which was paid by the end of the year 1990. The lion's share of this aid, equivalent to 7 billion dollars, came from Saudi Arabia and about 3 billion from Kuwait. Six billion dollars of this money went to U.S. operations and six billion went to the Middle Eastern countries who were suffering in the Gulf Crisis.

Japan pledged 4 billion dollars. Two billion went to the U.S. operations; two billion to needy Middle Eastern countries. The European community pledged 2 billion dollars. This sum went to aiding needy nations in the Middle East arena. Also West Germany pledged over 2 billion dollars.

The Gulf Crisis affected the economies of many nations around the world, especially Middle Eastern nations. Among them: Jordan claimed a loss of 2 billion dollars, because it was receiving 80% of its oil supplies from Iraq; Egypt claimed a loss of 2 billion dollars because of the loss of salaries of Egyptians working in Iraq and Kuwait; there were about one million workers in Iraq and many thousands in Kuwait. Turkey stated a loss of 3 billion dollars, due to U.N. sanctions, especially since transport of Iraqi oil through its pipeline had been halted. Yemen claimed a loss of 2.5 billion dollars, because of the economic blockade against Iraq. Yemen had strong trade relations with Iraq, but they have been scaled down because of the sanctions. Nevertheless, the blockade was violated by Yemen on a number of occasions. The Eastern European countries, the new budding democracies in Europe, claimed a loss of 4 billion dollars due to loss of debt and trade. India claimed a loss of 2.5 billion dollars because thousands of their workers fled for their safety away from Iraq and Kuwait. Also, India was forced to pay more for oil because of the increase in its cost, due to war fever. Several countries claimed money losses and hoped to receive some compensation.

More Troops

By the end of September the deployment of forces in the Gulf was as follows: Iraq had nearly 400,000 troops in Kuwait with 2,800 tanks and a large contingent of the Republican Guard on the borders between Iraq and Kuwait. The Coalition forces in the Arabian Gulf stood at 150,000 troops from the United States, along with 52 ships and 700 aircraft. The United Kingdom had over 5,000 troops, ten ships and five air squadrons. France had 5,000 troops and 9 ships. The Gulf forces were about 12,000 troops and Saudi Arabian forces were about 65,000. Egypt had dispatched 5,000 troops and Syria 4,000; Pakistan sent 2,000, Bangladesh 2,500 and Morocco around 1,300 troops. Other Allied nations: Canada, Italy, Netherlands, Greece, Spain, and Belgium supplied a total of 10 ships. By November, U.S. forces reached 210,000 and other Allies who came to the aid of Saudi Arabia and Kuwait totaled 87,000 soldiers.

Approaching January 15, 1991

With the approach of mid-January, 1991, the Iraqis had boosted their forces in the Kuwait theater until they reached half a million men. Again, they were heavily supported by the Republican Guard stationed south of Basra. By this time, the Allied Forces had been mobilized with the blessing of the United Nations, and the start of the war for liberating Kuwait was imminent. Total American forces in the Gulf theater of operations reached approximately half a million men, supported by state-of-the-art combat aircraft, approaching 1,800 in number and over 100 warships. The total number of tanks for the Allied forces was approaching 4,000. The Arabian Gulf waters had the following battle ships: the aircraft carrier Midway, Ranger, the battleship Wisconsin and the battleship Missouri. While in the Red Sea, the aircraft carriers, Saratoga, Kennedy, Theodore Roosevelt, and America were well in position and capable of unleashing Tomahawk cruise missiles into Iraqi Command Centers and other strategic targets. The Coalition Forces were as follows, Britain, 25,000 men, 60 aircraft, 15 ships and 170 tanks; France, 380 aircraft, 14 ships, 10,000 men and 40 tanks; Italy, 10 ships and 8 aircraft; Canada 18 aircraft, 3 ships; Belgium, 6 ships; Germany, 5 mine sweepers; Spain, 4 ships; former USSR, 4 ships; Australia, 2 ships; Turkey, 2 ships; Denmark, 1 ship; Greece 1 ship; Norway 1 ship; Portugal 1 ship.

Arab Allied forces included 35,000 troops and 480 tanks from Egypt along with 20,000 troops and 270 tanks from Syria. Kuwaiti forces were about 12,000 troops and the Saudi troops about 65,000 with a

strong air force of 500 airplanes. Other nations made modest contributions as follows: Bangladesh, 6,000 troops; Pakistan, 5,000; Canada,
1,700; Morocco 1,500; Nigeria 500; Senegal, 500; Czechoslovakia, 200;
Honduras, 150; the Gulf Cooperation Council had a force of 10,000
in the area. Overseeing the whole region and especially the theater of
operations were five U.S. AWACS and five Saudi AWACS.

This great armada of Allied Forces was amassed along the borders
with Kuwait and Iraq. It was ready for action on a moment's notice
to begin the operation for liberating Kuwait. The historic and great
buildup of Desert Shield was soon to give way to Desert Storm.

Frenzy of Diplomatic Activity and Worldwide Condemnation of Iraqi Aggression

From the very beginning of the tragic occupation of the State of
Kuwait on August 2, 1990, the entire world was up in arms against
such a brutal occupation of an innocent, peaceful state. The United
Nations moved with great vigor. World leaders were strongly supportive
of the U.N. moves and leading among them were the great efforts exhibited by King Fahd of Saudi Arabia, President Hosni Moubarak of Egypt
and President George Bush of the United States of America. Many
resolutions were passed in a rapid fire manner by the United Nations,
appealing to Saddam Hussein to withdraw his troops from Kuwait
and to stop his atrocities against the Kuwaitis and foreigners both in
Kuwait and Iraq.

The Foreign Minister of the former Soviet Union, at the time, Edward Sheverdnadze said, "The U.N. has the power to suppress acts
of aggression. There is ample evidence that this right can be exercised.
It will be, if the illegal occupation of Kuwait continues."

On August 4, 1990, the Foreign Minister of Italy, Gianni De Michelis,
announced the imposition of an embargo on oil imports from Iraq
and Kuwait along with a ban on arms sales to Iraq by the twelve-
member states of the European Economic Community (EEC). He declared that EEC favored applying "the strongest pressure to obtain an
immediate and unconditional withdrawal by Iraq." He also stressed
that the European Economic Community condemned "without reserva-
tion the brutal Iraqi invasion of Kuwait."

The Federal Council of Switzerland, a neutral nation, declared:
"Iraq, by invading Kuwait . . . has violated the fundamental principle
of international law. Switzerland has therefore decided unanimously
to follow the Security Council's recommendations to the non-U.N. members and take economic and financial measures against Iraq."

President George Bush of the United States and President Mikhail Gorbachev of the former Soviet Union, issued the following *joint statement* on September 9, 1990, at the conclusion of their Summit Conference held in *Helsinki*, Finland relating to the Iraqi aggression against Kuwait. Here is what they said:

- We are united in the belief that Iraq's aggression must not be tolerated. No peaceful international order is possible if larger states can devour their smaller neighbors.

- We reaffirm the joint statement of our Foreign Ministers of August 3, 1990 and our support for United Nations Security Council Resolutions 660, 661, 662, 664 and 665. Today, we once again call upon the Government of Iraq to withdraw unconditionally from Kuwait, to allow the restoration of Kuwait's legitimate government, and to free all hostages now held in Iraq and Kuwait.

- Nothing short of the complete implementation of the United Nations Security Council Resolutions is acceptable.

- Nothing short of the return to the pre-August 2 status of Kuwait can end Iraq's isolation.

- We call upon the entire world community to adhere to the sanctions mandated by the United Nations, and we pledge to work, individually and in concert, to ensure full compliance with the sanctions. At the same time, the United States and the Soviet Union recognize that U.N. Security Council Resolution 661 permits, in humanitarian circumstances, the importation of food into Iraq and Kuwait. The Sanctions committee will make recommendations to the Security Council on what would constitute humanitarian circumstances. The United States and the Soviet Union further agree that any such imports must be strictly monitored by the appropriate international agencies to ensure that food reaches only those for whom it is intended, with special priority being given to meeting the needs of children.

- Our preference is to resolve the crisis peacefully, and we will be united against Iraq's aggression as long as the crisis exists. However, we are determined to see this aggression end, and if the current steps fail to end it, we are prepared to consider additional ones consistent with the U.N. Charter. We must demonstrate beyond any doubt that aggression cannot and will not pay.

- As soon as the objectives mandated by the United Nations Security Council resolutions mentioned above have been achieved, and we have demonstrated that aggression does not pay, the

Presidents direct their Foreign Ministers to work with countries in the region and outside of it to develop regional security structures and measures to promote peace and stability. It is essential to work actively to resolve all remaining conflicts in the Middle East and Persian Gulf. Both sides will continue to consult each other and initiate measures to pursue these broader objectives at the proper time.

These appeals were repeated again and again but they fell on deaf ears in Iraq. Saddam continued his obstinate attitude ignoring the United Nations appeals, ignoring the voice of wisdom and the voices for conscience and decency around the world. He stuck to his guns declaring that Kuwait is an integral part of Iraq and he would never get out of it. In November, 1990, he said, "If an embargo would force the American people to withdraw from Hawaii, then he would consider withdrawal from Kuwait." The economic blockade, initiated and instituted by the United Nations with the support of a vast majority in the Security Council and with the approval of all permanent members, was having some serious effect and a good bite on Iraq's economy. The tougher the Resolutions were, the more the sanctions tightened the noose around the neck of Saddam Hussein, the more he resorted to stalling, lies, deceit, manipulations of the hostages and other ways and means to stall for time. He used this manipulative approach for delay and deception to an optimum. In fact he proved to be a master of manipulation and deceit, also a master of use and abuse of the news media, not only of Iraq but of the world.

On September 11, 1990, President George Bush delivered a *moving speech** to a joint session of Congress. This dynamic speech laid the foundations of U.S. policy in the Gulf crisis. Here are several excerpts from this historical landmark:

"We gather tonight, witness to events in the Persian Gulf as significant as they are tragic. In the early morning hours of August 2nd, following negotiations and promises by Iraq's dictator Saddam Hussein not to use force, a powerful Iraqi army invaded its trusting and much weaker neighbor, Kuwait. Within three days, 120,000 Iraqi troops with 850 tanks had poured into Kuwait and moved south to threaten Saudi Arabia. It was then that I decided to check that aggression.

Our objectives in the Persian Gulf are clear, our goals defined and familiar: Iraq must withdraw from Kuwait completely, immediately, and without condition. Kuwait's legitimate government must be restored. The security and stability of the Persian Gulf must be assured. And American citizens abroad must be protected.

---

* Source: The White House, Washington, D.C.

These goals are not ours alone. They've been endorsed by the United Nations Security Council five times in as many weeks. Most countries share our concern for principle. And many have a stake in the stability of the Persian Gulf. This is not, as Saddam Hussein would have it, the United States against Iraq. It is Iraq against the world.

As you know, I've just returned from a very productive meeting with Soviet President Gorbachev. And I am pleased that we are working together to build a new relationship. In Helsinki, our joint statement affirmed to the world our shared resolve to counter Iraq's threat to peace. Let me quote: "We are united in the belief that Iraq's aggression must not be tolerated. No peaceful international order is possible if larger states can devour their smaller neighbors."

Clearly, no longer can a dictator count on East-West confrontation to stymie concerted United Nations action against aggression. A new partnership of nations has begun.

We stand today at a unique and extraordinary moment. The crisis in the Persian Gulf, as grave as it is, also offers a rare opportunity to move toward an historic period of cooperation. Out of these troubled times, our fifth objective—*a new world order*—can emerge: a new era—freer from the threat of terror, stronger in the pursuit of justice, and more secure in the quest for peace. An era in which the nations of the world, East and West, North and South, can prosper and live in harmony.

A hundred generations have searched for this elusive path to peace, while a thousand wars raged across the span of human endeavor. Today that new world is struggling to be born. A world quite different from the one we've known. A world where the rule of law supplants the rule of the jungle. A world in which nations recognize the shared responsibility for freedom and justice. A world where the strong respect the rights of the weak.

This is the vision that I shared with President Gorbachev in Helsinki. He and other leaders from Europe, the Gulf and around the world, understand that how we manage this crisis today could shape the future for generations to come.

The test we face is great—and so are the stakes. This is the first assault on the new world that we seek, the first test of our mettle. Had we not responded to this first provocation with clarity of purpose, if we do not continue to demonstrate our determination, it would be a signal to actual and potential despots around the world.

America and the world must defend common vital interests. And we will. America and the world must support the rule of law. And we will. America and the world must stand up to aggression. And we will. And one thing more—in the pursuit of these goals America will not be intimidated.

Vital issues of principle are at stake. Saddam Hussein is literally trying to wipe a country off the face of the Earth. We do not exaggerate. Nor do we exaggerate when we say Saddam Hussein will fail.

Vital economic interests are at risk as well. Iraq itself controls some 10 percent of the world's proven oil reserves. Iraq plus Kuwait controls twice that. An Iraq permitted to swallow Kuwait would have the economic and military power, as well as the arrogance, to intimidate and coerce its neighbors–neighbors who control the lion's share of the world's remaining oil reserves. We cannot permit a resource so vital to be dominated by one so ruthless. And we won't.

Recent events have surely proven that there is no substitute for American leadership. In the face of tyranny, let no one doubt American credibility and reliability. Let no one doubt our staying power. *We will stand by our friends.* One way or another, the leader of Iraq must learn this fundamental truth.

From the outset, acting hand in hand with others, we've sought to fashion the broadest possible international response to Iraq's aggression. The level of world cooperation and condemnation of Iraq is unprecedented. Armed forces from countries spanning four continents are there at the request of King Fahd of Saudi Arabia to deter and, if need be, to defend against attack. Muslims and non-Muslims, Arabs and non-Arabs, soldiers from many nations stand shoulder to shoulder, resolute against Saddam Hussein's ambitions.

We can now point to five United Nations Security Council resolutions that condemn Iraq's aggression. They call for Iraq's immediate and unconditional withdrawal, the restoration of Kuwait's legitimate government, and categorically reject Iraq's cynical and self-serving attempt to annex Kuwait.

Finally, the United Nations has demanded the release of all foreign nationals held hostage against their will and in contravention of international law. It is a mockery of human decency to call these people "guests." They are hostages, and the whole world knows it.

Prime Minister Margaret Thatcher, a dependable ally, said it all: "We do not bargain over hostages. We will not stoop to the level of using human beings as bargaining chips ever." Of course, our hearts go out to the hostages and to their families. But our policy cannot change. And it will not change. America and the world will not be blackmailed by this ruthless policy.

We're now in sight of a United Nations that performs as envisioned by its founders. We owe much to the outstanding leadership of Secretary General Javier Perez de Cuellar. The United Nations is backing up its words with action. The Security Council has imposed mandatory economic sanctions on Iraq, designed to force Iraq to relinquish the spoils of its illegal conquest. The Security Council has also taken the decisive step of authorizing the use of all means necessary to ensure compliance with these sanctions.

Together with our friends and allies, ships of the United States Navy are today patrolling Mideast waters. They've already intercepted more than 700 ships to enforce the sanctions. Three regional leaders I spoke with just yesterday told me that these sanctions are working. Iraq is feeling the heat.

The response of most of our friends and allies has been good. To help defray costs, the leaders of Saudi Arabia, Kuwait and the UAE (United Arab Emirates) have pledged to provide our deployed troops with all the food and fuel they need. Generous assistance will also be provided to stalwart front-line nations, such as Turkey and Egypt.

I cannot predict just how long it will take to convince Iraq to withdraw from Kuwait. Sanctions will take time to have their full intended effect. We will continue to review all options with our allies, but let it be clear: *we will not let this aggression stand.*

Our interest, our involvement in the Gulf is not transitory. It pre-dated Saddam Hussein's aggression and will survive it. Long after all our troops come home—and we all hope it's soon, very soon—there will be a lasting role for the United States in assisting the nations of the Persian Gulf. Our role then—to deter future aggression. Our role is to help our friends in their own self-defense. And something else—to curb the proliferation of chemical, biological, ballistic missile and, above all, nuclear technologies.

Let me also make clear that the United States has no quarrel with the Iraqi people. Our quarrel is with Iraq's dictator and with his aggres-sion. *Iraq will not be permitted to annex Kuwait. That's not a threat, that's not a boast, that's just the way it's going to be* . . .

In the final analysis, our ability to meet our responsibilities abroad depends upon political will and consensus at home. This is never easy in democracies—for we govern only with the consent of the gov-erned. And although free people in a free society are bound to have their differences, Americans traditionally come together in times of adversity and challenge.

Once again, Americans have stepped forward to share a tearful good-bye with their families before leaving for a strange and distant shore. At this very moment, they serve together with Arabs, Europeans, Asians and Africans in defense of principle and the dream of a new world order. That's why they sweat and toil in the sand and the heat and the sun.

If they can come together under such adversity; if old adversaries like the Soviet Union and the United States can work in common cause; then surely we who are so fortunate to be in this great chamber–Democrats, Republicans, liberals, conservatives–can come together to fulfill our responsibilities here.

Thank you. Good night. And God bless the United States of America."

The United Nations Secretary General Javier Perez de Cuellar did his utmost, trying to find a peaceful resolution to the crisis. In fact, when he was visiting Iraq, Saddam Hussein made him wait until the next day before granting him an audience. The Secretary General, patiently used every possible means trying to convince Saddam Hussein to get his troops out of Kuwait and abide by the U.N. resolutions. Despite all his genuine and honorable efforts, the Secretary General did not succeed in making any headway with him. He continued to stall for time and tried to do his very best to drive a wedge between the world Alliance poised against him. But the Coalition Forces were gathering a storm that was eventually to sweep him out of Kuwait altogether!

Saddam tried to manipulate the French public opinion, the American public opinion and other democracies' public opinions. For example, he released a few hostages from one country or the other, trying to gain some favors from the respective nations of the world. He tried to make some rapprochement with the French, hoping for some division to materialize between the Alliance and the French. Of course, on all these fronts, where he tried to drive a wedge, he failed!

The President of the French Republic, François Mitterrand, said, "Not one jesture, not one word from the President of Iraq has given us a glimpse, a hope of reconciliation." On September 15, 1990, he said that Iraq is a, "bellicose state, that poorly estimates the risks of its actions." At a later date he said, "Iraq should know that she definitely can not count on the breaking up of the coalition which had taken on the responsibility of implementing United Nations Resolutions."

A rapid succession of condemnations reverberated across the four corners of the globe. Some of these powerful statements follow:

President Hosni Moubarak of Egypt said on October 31, 1990 that the Gulf Crisis became so dangerous "it could explode at anytime . . . With the greatest concentration of military force I have ever seen in this area, I hope our brothers in Iraq will understand well that the situation is very dangerous . . . If war comes, Iraq will be ruined."

The President of Yugoslavia, Borisav Jovic, said on September 28,

1991: "Yugoslavia individually and as chairman of the Non-Aligned Movement, resolutely condemns the annexation of Kuwait, supports the legitimate Kuwaiti government and demands an unconditional withdrawal of Iraq from this country . . . it is in the interest of the entire international community . . . that the situation which preceded the invasion be restored."

Margaret Thatcher, then Prime Minister of Britain, said on November 7, 1990: "Time is running out for Saddam Hussein . . . either he gets out of Kuwait soon or we and our allies will remove him by force and he will go down to defeat and all its consequences. He has been warned! This man is a despot and a tyrant and must be stopped."

German Chancellor, Helmut Kohl, said on November 9, 1990: "We noted with great concern that the Iraqi government still refuses to comply with the demand of the international community to release all hostages of all nationalities and withdraw completely from Kuwait."

Mikhail Gorbachev, President of the former Soviet Union said on November 9, 1990: Iraq's actions in the state of Kuwait are "against the norms of ethics. If Iraq really wants to avoid the worst, it must openly declare and show in actions that it is leaving Kuwait . . . this is not Vietnam; this is not Afghanistan. This is extremely dangerous. All of us, the world community of nations . . . must act firmly and resolutely in the spirit of the decisions of the United Nations and its Security Council. Let no one hope to undermine this unity to drive a wedge . . . if we should prove to be unable to work together in the solution of problems . . . this would have adverse consequences . . . we must remain united."

Qian Qichen, Foreign Minister of China, said on November 9, 1990 that his government, "opposes the invasion of Kuwait and calls on Iraq to withdraw its troops from Kuwait unconditionally."

Stalling for Time

The Iraqi leader wanted to optimize the use and abuse of innocent hostages held in the big prison of Iraq. He was to cause untold agony and fear among these innocent people and their loved ones. He declared that all women and children were free to go. With the pressure of world opinion mounting against his acts, which were alien to international law and contrary to any decent diplomatic behavior among nations, he then declared that the hostages could leave at stages beginning in December and stretching on through March. He was trying very hard to make use of them, so that any possible military action against him would be postponed until sometime beyond March. Thus, he was aiming not only at driving a wedge against the Alliance, but very desperately trying to block any windows of opportunity for the possible military action, which would have to be taken to liberate Kuwait, if he did not get out peacefully. And indeed, time was of the essence! Saddam Hussein thought the longer he could prevail and postpone action against him, the better his chances would be for his survival and for the permanent occupation of Kuwait, thus becoming not only the master of the Gulf but the hero of the Arab masses.

Weather conditions of the Gulf region make a unique desert climate. It is very hot in the summer and temperatures could be upward of 130 degrees Fahrenheit, although most of the time they range between 110 to 120 degrees F. Hot and humid conditions around the Gulf, especially in the months of August, September and portions of October, make it very uncomfortable. The weather improves tremendously around November, December and January. At this time of year, during the day and at night, the weather is very pleasant in the region.

By the time one approaches February and March, the weather takes a change for the worse and desert storms start whipping fine sand and dust creating clouds of particulate matter which are very bad for man and machine alike. The Shamal wind (coming from the north) is the culprit for creating these sandstorms. In some regions, the highways and streets will have masses and piles of sand, very fine sand, reminiscent of the snow storms up in the north. This fine sand will complicate the situation! While it would be bad for flying missions, it has also serious negative effects on military equipment from cannons, to rifles, to helicopters and airplanes. So, it was understandable why Saddam Hussein was so desperately trying to stretch and postpone military action against him until this period of time, when weather conditions will significantly interfere with military operations.

Also, by the time March approaches, Ramadan begins. It is the Holy month for all Moslems; there are one billion of them around the world who face Mecca in their prayers five times a day. Mecca and Madina are the Holy sites for Islam and Saudi Arabia is the focal point for all Moslems around the globe. While wars have been fought during Ramadan, it did not seem logical nor proper to start a war of eviction during this month against Saddam Hussein, especially since most of the Allied Forces are non-Moslem and despite the fact that these forces arrayed against the borders in Kuwait and Iraq were over 700 miles (1134 Km.) away from the holy sites of Islam.

The International Islamic Conference of September 10–12, 1990, condemned Saddam Hussein and his religious exploitations. The statements of resolutions and recommendations are included here.

Resolutions & Recommendations
Of The International Islamic Conference
On The Situation In The Gulf
Held in Mecca, Saudi Arabia, September 10–12, 1990 (Safar 21–23, 1411 A.H.)

Praise be unto God, Lord of the worlds. Peace and blessings be upon our Prophet Mohammed, his family and all his companions.

In view of the perilous events that have taken place in the Gulf region as a result of Iraq's occupation of Kuwait, the direct threat to the Kingdom of Saudi Arabia and the other Arabian Gulf countries and the subsequent Arab, Islamic and foreign military build-up to defend the Arabian Gulf states, the Moslem World League held an international conference of Moslem scholars and thinkers on September 10–12, 1990 (Safar 21–23, 1411 A.H.).

Mindful of their religious duty and humanitarian as well as historic responsibilities, the participants have carefully examined the various dimensions of these serious events.

Realizing the significance of observing and enhancing the bonds of brotherhood and neighborliness . . . Gravely concerned at the menace and challenges that threaten the very existence of the Nation (Umma) . . . After three days of objective and frank deliberations in an atmosphere of Islamic brotherhood, the Conference adopted the following resolutions and recommendations:

1. Since the text of the Holy Qoran and Sunna ordain that the life, property and honor of a Moslem are a sacred trust unto his fellow Moslem, the Conference strongly condemns the Iraqi invasion of Kuwait and the subsequent looting of properties, demolition of public and private institutions and other inhuman practices of the Iraqi invading forces. The Conference also denounces the amassing of the Iraqi forces on the borders of Saudi Arabia–an act which threatens the territorial integrity and security of the Gulf states.

2. The Conference calls upon the Iraqi regime to immediately and unconditionally withdraw its troops from Kuwait, pull back to Iraq its forces stationed on the borders with Saudi Arabia and end all consequences of occupation, with a pledge to pay compensation for the pillage and destruction it has caused.

3. The Conference demands the restoration of Kuwait's legitimate government to power.

4. In view of Shari'a's binding rules which stipulate the respect of covenants, treaties with Moslems and non-Moslems alike, protection of life and properties of emissaries, diplomats, residents in Moslem countries and in accordance with international conventions and diplomatic norms, the Conference calls upon the Iraqi regime to respect and abide by these covenants and treaties.

5. With respect to the military assistance of foreign troops, the Conference, having examined the scholarly papers presented by the Ulama (Moslem scholars), resolves that out of necessity, the Kingdom of Saudi Arabia acted in self-defense as permitted by Islamic Shari'a. Whenever the cause for their presence has been totally removed, through the Iraqi withdrawal from Kuwait and cessation of threats to the Kingdom and the Gulf countries, these foreign forces must leave the region.

   The Conference appeals to the Islamic states to create a permanent Islamic military force under the direction of the Organization of Islamic Conference (OIC), which would be deployed in the event of similar conflicts between two member states.

6. The Conference envisages that all Moslems should renew their repentance, return to God's commandments and correct their path in all life's affairs, according to the Holy Qoran and Sunna. They should also infuse the Moslem youths with faith fully and militarily in order to prepare them for defending the Umma of Islam against any possible threat.

   The Conference also resolves that it has become an obligatory duty on Moslems to equip themselves with whatever strength they can afford, in order to safeguard their own security and to defend themselves against any potential danger.

7. The Conference appeals to Islamic states and organizations to exert their effort to prevent war and restore security and peace to the region.

8. The Conference appeals to Islamic states, organizations and Moslem peoples at large to strive for a meaningful Islamic unity by creating an Islamic economic community and concluding a joint defense treaty.

9. The Conference appeals to Islamic states to enforce Shari'a in every walk of life, be it legal, political, economic or social, and to establish the principle of consultation (Shoura) in government and purge their societies of such evils as usury and their mass media of all that is at variance with Islam.

10. The Conference shall continue in session and shall have a

follow-up committee to pursue the situation, coordinate with the Islamic organizations, send goodwill delegations to explain the serious impact of the present crisis on the future of Islam and affirm the necessity of solving the problem before it gets worse.

The Conference also requests the participants to contribute toward solving the problem as they deem appropriate and within the framework of their individual or organizational specialties.

11.   The Conference calls upon the Islamic bodies to organize similar conferences and symposia to enlighten the Moslem public on various topics covered by the conference and enable them to benefit from the scholarly papers presented.

12.   The Conference reaffirms the necessity of participation of the Islamic relief agencies, especially the International Islamic Relief Organization and the International Red Crescent Association, in aiding all those affected by the calamity in the Gulf, wherever they may be.

13.   The Conference insists that this tragedy should not divert the attention of Moslems from their major and basic problems i.e. the Al-Aqsa Mosque in Al-Qods (Jerusalem), Palestine, Afghanistan, Kashmir and the oppressed Moslem minorities in the world.

14.   With the conclusion of its work, the Conference extends its gratitude to those Moslem governments, institutions and peoples who have expressed solidarity with the people of Kuwait in their time of distress and who have condemned the barbaric Iraqi invasion and supported the measures adopted by the Kingdom of Saudi Arabia. A special reference of thanks is due the Custodian of the Two Holy Mosques (King Fahd), the people of Saudi Arabia and other Moslems for the support and loving care they have shown to the brotherly people of Kuwait.

The Conference also thanks the Secretariat General of the Moslem World League for organizing the conference and for the excellent arrangements which enabled the conference to conclude its deliberations, successfully, within the allotted time.

Finally, peace and blessings be upon our Master and Prophet Mohammed, his family and all his companions.

You recall that Saddam Hussein tried to use religion to his advantage, although he had never been a religious man. He declared that the infidels were defiling the Holy places of Islam, when in reality they were far away from them. So, for a number of reasons, it would not have been advisable to initiate war around this Holy month of Ramadan.

Saddam was thinking, again, down the road, by the time he reaches March and no military action had taken place against him, then soon after there will be the Hajj. This is the pilgrimage season, where two million Moslems come for pilgrimage to Mecca and Madina. This is a duty upon every Moslem, who is capable of doing it; to exercise such a duty once in his or her lifetime. This period is very spiritual and holy to all Moslems, especially the pilgrims. Thousands and thousands of them come from the four corners of the earth and pour toward the Holy Moslem sites in Mecca and Madina. It did not seem either logical nor politically feasible to start a war during the pilgrimage. That would be a very counter-productive folly since the whole Moslem world would be focusing on this Holy event.

Extremist Moslem Fundamentalists

Of course, all these maneuvers used by Saddam Hussein were not lost on the leaders and commanders of the Allied Forces. By a stroke of luck, he was hoping that he could postpone military action against him, so he would take advantage either of the hostages, the Shamal wind, Ramadan or the Pilgrimage. If he succeeded in this endeavor and out of global circumstances, frustration, or absolute necessity, the Allies were forced to attack him during this Holy season, he would have appealed with great manipulation and zeal to the extremist Moslem Fundamentalist forces which were brewing in the Moslem land. These forces, while small in number in the Arab world, were vociferous and strong on zeal, but lacking in principle and compassion to fellow men, be it in the Moslem religion, or men of other religions of the world. These extremists were numerous in Iran. After the Khomeini Revolution came to power in 1979, the world was witness to their fanaticism and their message of hate for their fellow men. In fact these extremist forces were the backbone of the Khomeini Revolution in Iran. While they terrorized thousands and murdered thousands of their own population, they also spread hate and terrorized many people around the globe: businessmen flying from one continent to the other, innocent people traveling in a train, a man with his family in a cafe somewhere in Europe, Paris or London and many, many more across the globe, all suffered from the terrorist activities of these extremist groups. They were the spear and backbone of Khomeini's terrorism which he spread around the world. These same forces that hated Saddam because of his war with Iran for eight years, turned against America simply because they hated America more.

Such forces were gaining momentum in some parts of the Arab land. For example, in Algeria, on the Western flank of the Arab world in Africa, these forces were increasing in number and the moderate leadership of the former President of Algeria, Chadli Benjadid, was paying close attention to these developments. The buildup of these forces and their increasing influence on the masses were worrisome. They were sympathetic to Saddam Hussein, certainly far more than their extremist brothers in Iran; but they were blind and insensitive to the fact that Kuwait was ripped and raped by a ruthless dictator. Their double standards were an injustice to the good spirit of Islam.

They turned a deaf ear and closed their eyes to the atrocities committed against the innocent people of Kuwait. They forgot about the mothers that were raped and lost their children, the fathers who have been abused and tortured and the children that have been brain-washed then tortured and killed. All these are human beings! They are fellow Moslems. The Moslem religion preaches goodness, decency, justice and tolerance! Any such abuse, torture, and ruthless aggression are all condemned by the religion of Islam and the Ulama of Islam.

Despite their influence, for example, in Algeria, the Algerian leadership tried to steer a moderate course. In fact, former President Chadli Benjadid made several appeals to Saddam Hussein in hopes that he would listen to reason and get out of Kuwait before it was too late. Benjadid visited Iraq and used all possible means for convincing Saddam Hussein, but all to no avail! Algeria tried to follow a moderate course, but in some instances, there was a tilt toward the Iraqi position. Nevertheless, the tilt was very minor. This is usually the policy of Algeria. In fact, during the Iran-Iraq war, Algeria kept the lines open with Khomeini and was very helpful during the American hostage crisis. Algeria was able to mediate and help in securing the release of the 52 American hostages which were held in Iran against their will for 444 days. So, despite the number of extremist fundamentalists that have developed in the latter decade in Algeria, they were held in check and were not able to go much beyond the noisy demonstration in favor of Saddam Hussein's ruthlessness and occupation of Kuwait. However, Benjadid has since resigned and genuine fears remain about a possible civil war ignited by extremist fundamentalists.

In neighboring Morocco, King Hassan II has always been a man of moderation and wisdom. He supported the Coalition Forces. He is a good friend of Saudi Arabia and voted in favor of sending Arab troops and Allied Forces to the defense of the Kingdom. In the first few days of the occupation, he sent a symbolic force to support Saudi

Arabia and the Kuwaitis. On the diplomatic side, he used his good offices, trying to bring about a peaceful solution to the conflict. Despite the fact that his country had extremist fundamentalists, their numbers were small. However, with the world media focusing its total attention on the Arabian Gulf region, any symbolism, demonstration, or actions relating to the war, although at times orchestrated and paid for by agents of Saddam Hussein, were propagated across the waves instantaneously, for the whole world to see! So when a demonstration of a hundred thousand or three hundred thousand took place for example in Morocco, the news medias of the world were quick to instantly pick up such an event and start their rumor mill and analysis machine. With people focusing their attention on such events, some of the Allied nations around the world began to worry. Sometimes the media gave such demonstrations much more weight than they actually deserve. What is one hundred or three hundred thousand out of a population of 27 million?

Reporting from Amman, Jordan

If we cross the Arab land from the west or the Maghreb and move on east until we reach Jordan, here you will find a very interesting story that influenced world opinion to some degree. It certainly is worthy of some description and analysis. Jordan is a small Arab country with a population of nearly three and a half million, 60% of which are Palestinian. The Monarchy has been in power for several decades. King Hussein has been a statesman for over thirty years and earned such a reputation because of his diplomacy and moderation in the Arab land. While the Monarchy has a good grip over the population, a certain degree of democracy and freedom has been in existence for several years. Not long ago, when an election took place for a parliament, about 40% of the seats gained were occupied by extremist Islamic Fundamentalists. Thus, they became a power to be reckoned with.

Since one of Saddam Hussein's maneuvers and ploys was to link the Palestinian question with the possibility of his evacuation from Kuwait, the Palestinian masses, out of desperation, along with their leadership in the person of Yasser Arafat, put their solid support behind Saddam Hussein. In the process, they forgot the abundant aid and great sacrifices made by the Kuwaitis, the Saudis, and other nations in the Arabian Gulf. Hundreds of millions of dollars went to the coffers of the Palestine Liberation Organization (PLO) to help the Palestinians for their livelihood and for securing a permanent home. Also, Kuwait had about 300,000 Palestinians working there and sending much of their money to support their families in the West Bank and elsewhere in the Arab land. The same situation was in Saudi Arabia and other Gulf countries, where large numbers of Palestinians were working and sending their remittances to their families elsewhere.

Despite all this, Yasser Arafat was very enthused and exuberant about the occupation of Kuwait by Saddam Hussein's forces. Every time he journeyed to Iraq during the crisis, he was very excited about meeting Saddam! He greeted him in the warmest possible ways, for all people around the world to see! He tried his utmost to delay any possible political or military moves against Saddam Hussein. His diplomatic maneuvers in the Arab League, especially prior to the tenth of August Resolution, are well known and documented. In fact, he voted against this resolution. He was definitely against condemning Iraq for its occupation of Kuwait and against sending any troops to the defense of Saudi Arabia. The whole world was astonished by the position taken by someone like Yasser Arafat, who represented the Palestinian cause, where the Palestinians lost their home and have been struggling for decades to gain a homeland. The world watched in amazement that this man would be on the side of a ruthless occupation of a small innocent state such as Kuwait. On top of this, those who knew Arafat knew that he had lived in Kuwait for many years.

Another astonishment for moderate leaders around the world was the fact that King Hussein of Jordan, the moderate man, the one who had been looked upon as a statesman for so many decades, threw his lot with Saddam Hussein. He did his best to present himself as a man of peace. He visited a number of Arab countries and visited Saddam several times, trying to forge some peace plan which he then carried around. He also visited President George Bush in the United States for the same purpose. He was beating the drums for an Arab solution to the conflict, when it became obvious that an Arab solution was not possible nor feasible. Arab solution or not, Saddam Hussein must get out of Kuwait immediately and unconditionally! Simply and clearly, he was too powerful for any Arab force or a combination of Arab forces to stop him from the possible attack and occupation of the oil fields in the Eastern Region of Saudi Arabia, let alone drive him out of his complete stranglehold on Kuwait and the Kuwaiti population.

King Hussein mystified many people around the world for the position he had taken, since he had been receiving enormous aid from Saudi Arabia, Kuwait and the other Arabian Gulf countries. Keeping in mind that, lately, he developed a very cozy relationship with Saddam Hussein, especially where 80% of his trade was with Iraq. It was certainly difficult for the world to understand that such a man, who has been known for his moderation and political acumen, would stand on the side of a tyrant, against an innocent state that had been raped and pillaged. What happened to decency, integrity and justice? His peaceful moves and busy trips around the world seeking a possible peaceful solution to the crisis, in fact, had the potential of leading to sinister and counterproductive results. By his so called peace maneuvers he was trying to postpone and delay any possible action against Saddam Hussein. Delaying this inevitable possibility would fall into the direct line of Saddam's policy of stalling, demagoguery, and manipulation. . . . always hoping for the Arab masses to rise and support him, always waiting for a window of opportunity to come his way! Any actions helping him in this endeavor, while bolstering his ploys for postponement and delays, were all contrary to the spirit of United Nations Resolutions. Such maneuvers stood against the resolve and determination of the world, which was united in a very unique way, never witnessed before in the history of the U.N.. Saddam Hussein had to come to his senses and get out of Kuwait or be faced with a mighty force that would throw him out and destroy his aggressive forces.

Demonstrations were filling the streets in Amman, Jordan. Reporters from all around the world were represented there, where they had relative freedom of expression and action. The streets were flooded with demonstrators. Palestinians, who have been very frustrated with American policy in the Middle East vis-a-vis the Arab-Israeli conflict, were having a field day with the world news media paying special attention to their demonstrations, their grievance, and their great zeal for Saddam Hussein. Expressions of adulation for him and hate for the West and especially America, were instantaneously picked up and transmitted across the world to millions of homes in America and elsewhere. The extremist Islamic Fundamentalists in Jordan threw their lot entirely with Saddam Hussein. King Hussein of Jordan was watching all these events and waiting to see which direction the wind would blow while he kept preaching his so called peaceful moves, many times waiting for explanations of certain sections of U.N. Resolutions relating to the sanctions or other matters. Special unique methods were used for playing with words, killing time, and trying to avoid facing an issue or essentially confusing the issue. Wild demonstrations took place and threats were expressed against the Western forces and the Allied Arab forces as well. Praises of Saddam Hussein were filling the waves; but in reality all the noise was nothing but a *vociferous lip service show*. It has been analyzed by thoughtful commentators that when the chips are down such lip service will not be good on delivery. Threats and promises were made that floods of the demonstrators, Palestinians and Jordanians, would come to the aid of Saddam Hussein in his hour of need, when in reality none of this materialized.

In fact, when the war broke out, Amman's streets were very silent and somber. The waves of extremist fundamentalists did not rush to volunteer for the defense of Saddam Hussein!!!

The King of Jordan welcomed forces from the PLO, including various rival factions to come and hold a two-day Conference in his capital.

Many reports were coming from the theater in the Arabian Gulf, but a great abundance of them were emanating from Amman, Jordan. These were way out of proportion! They were beamed across the world, especially the Arab world. Because of such heavy bombardment of reports from Amman, some people were misled as to the actual weight that Jordan carried as far as the political and military situation in the region. The might of the Arab land is not in the Jordanian realm by any stretch of the imagination. The economic might of the Arab land is in Saudi Arabia and the Arabian Gulf countries, where most of the proven oil reserves exist. The demographic might of the Arab world is centered in Egypt with a population of 55 million out of 150 million Arab population. The spiritual might of the Arab land emanates from Mecca and Madina in Saudi Arabia, not in Jordan. The reports that were spread across the world originating from Amman, Jordan gave the impression that all the Arab masses were solidly behind Saddam Hussein and would be volunteering in the hundreds of thousands to defend and rescue him from imminent disaster. This image was very erroneous and misleading to many! When in reality, the majority of the Arab masses were with the Coalition Forces. On the scale of economic might of the Arab world, Jordan's economy is miniscule. On the scale of the Arab world, the population in Jordan is a small fraction of the total population of the Arabs. However, King Hussein and the majority of the population in Jordan were solidly on the side of Saddam Hussein.

On several occasions, King Hussein of Jordan, who was supposedly a good friend of America for many decades and not only a friend but a brother to the Saudis and Kuwaitis for many, many years, made pronouncements that were distinctly in the camp of Saddam Hussein. Early in the Gulf Crisis, he declared that the Allied Forces were there to be used against the Arabs and Islam. He was reflecting accusations that came from the camp of Saddam Hussein, the aggressor. In reality, his peace overtures were nothing but policies that were totally subservient to the aims and goals of Saddam Hussein. The possibilities, which he was exploring, tended to reward Saddam for his atrocities and for his aggression against the State of Kuwait. To let Saddam procrastinate and stall for time until his occupation became a fait accompli and to possibly reward him by giving him territory, money and oil, would be a flagrant case of appeasement. This approach would have led to the subjugation of the Kuwaiti people to the whims of the dictator in Baghdad. In no time, if Saddam Hussein was to strengthen his position and make his occupation permanent, he would have moved into the second stage of preparing and maneuvering until he found the ripe atmosphere to strike again and occupy the Eastern Region of Saudi Arabia and the entire Arabian Gulf. Then his dream would come true, where he would become a master of a precious source of energy, and thus hold a stranglehold over the lifeline to America and the lifeline of the Western world and Japan. With such a stranglehold, he could become the master of the Arab World, dictating his terms not only to the Arabs, but to the world community as well. But why the world community? Because with the great oil resources of the region comes great wealth which would strengthen his war machine enormously and propel him into the nuclear club, where he could threaten whoever did not fall in line and follow the fold!

Oil Power and Moderation

The Arabian Gulf region floats on a sea of oil. Saudi Arabia alone has proven oil reserves in excess of 255 billion barrels. This constitutes over 25% of all the proven oil reserves of the entire world. Kuwait, a small nation, essentially floats on a lake of oil with proven oil reserves in excess of 94 billion barrels and Iraq itself has about 100 billion barrels. Now, with his solid grip on Kuwait, Saddam Hussein controlled 20% of the oil reserves of the world. The region as a whole has 65% of all the proven oil reserves of the world. Thus, the strategic importance of this area is of paramount importance to the interests of the United States of America and its allies. The United States has only 27 billion barrels, other allies have small amounts and yet many more have none; the numbers speak for themselves! As far as the dependence on energy needs, the United States has been importing over 45% of its energy needs from around the world. Nowadays, out of 16 million barrels per day of oil needed, the U.S. imports half of that amount, about 8 million barrels per day. While the Arabian Gulf countries did not supply the largest portion of this oil needed, that was expected to increase with the years. Prior to the Gulf Crisis, the U.S. was importing less than 20% of its oil needs from the region. This number had increased upward to 30% and before the year 2,000 it will move toward 50% or more. Oil production in the U.S. has been on the decrease for a number of years because oil reserves are limited, while imports are on the increase.

On the other hand, an important economic power like Japan, imports nearly 90% of its energy needs from the Gulf countries. Such a mighty economic power has great dependence on the stability of these oil resources. Any disruption or wide fluctuation in the prices of oil would affect its economy and thus indirectly or directly affect the economies of countries all around the world. Nations like France and India depend greatly on their imports of oil from the region. For example, the French import about 60% of their energy needs from the oil region of the Middle East, while the balance of their energy needs are filled with their advancements in nuclear technology and nuclear powered generation. India imports most of its oil energy needs from the Gulf countries. This constitutes a vast drain on their hard currency and in the best of circumstances, it is a strong influential factor on the state of their economy and the standard of living for the vast masses of India. Thus any fluctuation in oil prices leaves a strong negative effect on the Indian continent and other Third World countries around the globe. Leading among these: Pakistan, Bangladesh, the Philippines, Lebanon, Jordan, Thailand, and many more . . .

As you recall, the Gulf Crisis was fabricated in a way relating to the price of oil. Saddam Hussein stated that Kuwait and the United Arab Emirates were producing far more oil than allotted under the agreement stipulated by the Organization of Petroleum Exporting Countries (OPEC). This organization, normally, studies world markets and allots the rate of production for its thirteen members. Allotting the rate of production will control to some degree the price of oil. OPEC had great sway over oil markets and prices for several years, however, since the mid 80s their sway and control of world oil prices had diminished substantially for several reasons, leading among these is the rivalry that exists between member states of OPEC. Some of them produced more than their allotted share and others were inclined to do so because of internal economic needs. Thus, in a way, some members added to the overproduction of oil, where there had already been an oil glut for some time. The over-supply of oil led to some decrease in its price which, essentially, broke down in 1986, until it reached 10 dollars per barrel. Of course, the price of oil had gained with time and currently oil is selling around twenty dollars a barrel. Among other factors influencing the price of oil one must also list production from North Sea Oil facilities and other oil producing nations who are not members of OPEC. New discoveries added a few million barrels per day to the world oil supply. These certainly contributed, to some degree, toward stabilization of oil prices around the world.

Severe fluctuations in the price of oil lead to serious disruptions and dislocations in world economies, everywhere in the world. Thus, stabilization of oil markets are a healthy policy to follow. Such a policy is good for the consumers and the producers alike. The leading nation preaching such a policy and practicing it through the decades is an oil giant named the Kingdom of Saudi Arabia. In fact, immediately after the occupation of the State of Kuwait and the increase in the possibility of war in the Middle East, the price of oil on world markets was propped up instantly. In a very short time, oil was selling for twenty five dollars a barrel and by October, it reached a maximum of nearly forty dollars a barrel. At such a price, the world economy would receive terrible jolts that would cause serious setbacks to the nations dependent on oil, and would lead to breakdown of the economies of many Third World countries. It would also lead to a good degree of paralysis for the economies of the industrialized nations of the world. Thus, when such prices were reached, counter forces came into play. Many nations practiced policies of conservation and began to experience some stagnation; that leads to less use of oil. Oil producing countries would like for other nations to use more oil, not less, in order to have more hard currency for their development. Thus, excessively high prices of oil are essentially counterproductive to the interests of the oil producing nations themselves, and it is certainly clear that this is contrary to the interests of the oil consuming nations as well.

A happy medium and an optimum solution should be reached for the benefit of all. Pioneering and moving along this line of moderation and optimum pricing for oil is the wise and moderate policy of the oil rich Kingdom of Saudi Arabia. In fact, to counter these pressure forces due to war psychology which propelled the price of oil, the Kingdom of Saudi Arabia came to the forefront and increased its oil production in order to fill the shortfall which resulted from the decrease in oil supply, since the entire oil productions of Iraq and Kuwait were brought to a halt. This was done because of the occupation of Kuwait. The world community acted by shutting down the Iraqi oil pipeline in Turkey with its outlet to the Mediterranean Sea and the other pipeline transporting oil through Saudi Arabia to the Red Sea at Yanbu. Thus, the economic sanctions against Iraq took their immediate bite against the Iraqi economy, although, indirectly, it caused negative impact on other economies of the world. However, the world was willing to pay the price and be subjected to substantial economic loss, because the world stood on the side of justice and decency in its defense of Kuwait and strong condemnation of the brutal aggression committed by Iraq. Nearly four and a half million barrels of oil per day were removed from the world market due to the Gulf Crisis. Saudi Arabia energized its oil machine and started pumping more oil. Facilities that had been mothballed for some time because of the oil glut that had existed and because of restrictions from OPEC on the individual production of various members. These facilities were dusted off and put back into action in order to alleviate the shortage and ease the pain of the world and its thirst for oil. The Kingdom of Saudi Arabia started producing more oil in order to help the economies of the industrialized nations and third world countries around the globe. Within a short period of time, Saudi production jumped from about four and a half million barrels a day to about six and half and then increasing until it reached nearly 8 million barrels per day. Other countries came to the aid of world markets. For example, Venezuela started producing more oil on a relatively smaller scale. North Sea facilities pumped more oil. But the oil giant of the world which really made a very serious and significant impact on world markets and prices was the Kingdom of Saudi Arabia. It practiced a policy of moderation since the discovery of oil way back in 1938. The oil policy takes into top priority and serious consideration the interests of the parties involved: namely, the oil producing and oil consuming nations of the world.

This policy is in tune with the international approach which is taken and practiced by the moderate and wise leadership of the Kingdom of Saudi Arabia. Since the Kingdom has very strong relations around the world, it has a mission of peace, friendship and goodness to all members of the world community and since it has special relations with a number of western countries, Arab brotherly nations and Moslem nations, the Kingdom feels that these countries' welfare is very important. If their economies are well served and are prospering, so in turn the Kingdom and its people will also be thriving and prospering. The Kingdom has special and intertwined diplomatic relations with several nations around the world. Anything that affects these nations will most directly and immediately affect the welfare of the Kingdom of Saudi Arabia. This intertwining of interests creates an atmosphere of responsibilities and interdependence in the world community. In fact, such policies that take into account the welfare of other people around the globe, along with the policy of wisdom, moderation, and compassion for mankind, and the intertwining of interests of Saudi Arabia with the interests of other nations around the world, were dynamic factors in energizing the conscience and spirit of the world to rise and come to the aid of the Kingdom of Saudi Arabia, and to stand against the aggression and oppression committed in Kuwait.

The price of oil declined until it stabilized around 25 dollars a barrel, where it would not drastically or substantially affect world economies in a negative way. In fact, such a price is essentially fair to all concerned, producers and consumers alike. Immediately after the hostilities broke out in the Gulf, the price per gallon of gasoline jumped very steeply. Within a week or two, a gallon of gasoline jumped something like 45 cents in the United States and even more in other countries around the world. The price per gallon of gasoline is still much cheaper in the United States than it is elsewhere in the world, especially the European countries and Japan. A round figure like a dollar per gallon in America, is many times this in other countries. It can be as high as three or four dollars a gallon in a number of countries. In any event, such a jump in gasoline prices affects the pocketbook of every single individual around the globe. Not only in America, but more so in the Third World nations who need the hard cash and a good shot in their economy, more than the advanced industrialized nations. Thus, a crisis of this nature brings more disaster and agony to the populations of the Third World than it would to the other well-to-do industrialized nations and their people.

It is very evident that Saddam Hussein would have loved to control the lifeline for the world. Imagine a madman who earned his reputation in blackmail, threats, murder, torture and deceit! Imagine him holding the lifeline to the world in one hand and weapons of mass destruction, be it biological, chemical or nuclear, in the other hand! Such a man would not look after the interests of the common man, nor the interests of the people around the world. He would have been more of a tyrant that would have extensively followed the path of past brutal dictators.

Appeasement Would Not Work

In any event, appeasement did not pay with former dictators in the world, especially Hitler, nor would it pay in the case of Saddam Hussein. To grant him the islands of Boubayan, Warba and other bonuses for his aggression, including the Roumeila oil field, would be nothing but appeasement that would not quench his thirst for acquiring more territory, for threatening and blackmailing his neighbors, and for annexing neighboring areas progressively, just as Hitler did in the late 1930s and early 1940s. Appeasement with Hitler did not work! The more he was given and the more concessions were made by the West, especially the French and the British, the more he wanted. As it is recalled in history, after Hitler absorbed Sudetenland then Czechoslovakia and more, Neville Chamberlain, then the Prime Minister of England, came back from signing concessions with Hitler. He came back to London declaring that peace was at hand, "peace for our time." Hitler promised that his ambitions were satisfied and that he would not encroach on his neighbors anymore! While these events were unfolding a statesman of vast experience and courage was observing and analyzing. With the mistaken belief that peace was at hand, Winston Churchill declared to the world that the Munich agreement was "a total and unmitigated defeat." Because of it, peace was not at hand, but war instead, a disastrous war was awaiting the world as a result of appeasing Hitler. Winston Churchill was absolutely right! He rose to the challenge! Then, the British appealed to him to become their leader and the Prime Minister of Great Britain in its hour of destiny. With great courage, brain power, vast stature and determination, he, America and the Allies fought the overwhelming hoardes of Hitler. The Allies were the victors after a long arduous and vicious war that swept Hitler out of power into the dustbin of history. But what a price? Economies of nations in shambles, progress and infrastructures destroyed and millions of people killed. Appeasement did not pay with Hitler. Appeasement would not pay with Saddam Hussein!!!

Decisive Action by the U.N.

Several experts thought that Article 51 of the United Nations Charter approves the use of force in self-defense, only in the absence of action by the U.N. Security Council; but others say it recognizes the right of self-defense against armed attack on a victimized nation, and also for others who come to its aid. Thus, Washington and the Allies could have used this as justification for initiating the war against Saddam Hussein, if they so desired.

With the mounting buildup of mighty forces gathering from around the world and pouring into the Gulf area, with the barrage of threats, counter threats, stalling and manipulations coming from Saddam Hussein and his obstinate refusal to abide by the U.N. Resolutions, the world community was now geared to bring a stop to all these exercises in futility. The United Nations, on November 29, 1990, voted a milestone resolution of far reaching consequences. The U.N. Security Council, in no uncertain terms, called on the Iraqi dictator to get out of Kuwait within a period not later than *January 15, 1991*, or else! If not, members of the United Nations desiring to use whatever means necessary to evict him out of Kuwait would be at liberty to do so. This was a very strong warning to Saddam Hussein! The international community meant business! He was either to get out of Kuwait or else he would be routed out. Military action would be spearheaded by the might of the United States of America, the dominant superpower in the world, which had been well armed with the legalities and approval of the world community. In fact, the energizing of the United Nations was a masterly achievement that had been led by President George Bush, King Fahd and other friendly nations. These two leaders, along with the support of other friendly leaders in the world, made contacts and mounted diplomatic campaigns of the largest magnitude, bringing about a unity which had never been witnessed in the history of the U.N.

Coordination of great effort was established not only among the 34 Coalition nations but also for serious diplomatic contacts with other major powers of the world, leading among them members of the Security Council and nations of the Eastern Block. The former Soviet Union and China who were at the time the mighty powers of the communist forces in the world, both were supportive of the U.N. initiative. In fact, the East and West were one in this mission for stopping the designs of a dictator and for gearing world forces toward ejecting him from Kuwait.

U.N. Resolution 678, November 29, 1990

The Security Council,

Recalling and reaffirming its resolutions 660 (1990) of August 2, 1990, 661 (1990) of August 6, 1990, 662 (1990) of August 9, 1990, 664 (1990) of August 18, 1990, 665 (1990) of August 25, 1990, 666 (1990) of September 13, 1990, 667 (1990) of September 16, 1990, 669 (1990) of September 24, 1990, 670 (1990) of September 25, 1990, 674 (1990) of October 29, 1990 and 677 (1990) of November 28, 1990,

Noting that, despite all efforts by the United Nations, Iraq refuses to comply with its obligation to implement resolution 660 (1990) and the above-mentioned subsequent relevant resolutions, in flagrant contempt of the Security Council,

Mindful of its duties and responsibilities under the Charter of the United Nations for the maintenance and preservation of international peace and security,

Determined to secure full compliance with its decisions,

Acting under Chapter VII of the Charter,

1. Demands that Iraq comply fully with resolution 660 (1990) and all subsequent relevant resolutions, and decides, while maintaining all its decisions, to allow Iraq one final opportunity, as a pause of goodwill, to do so;

2. *Authorizes* Member States co-operating with the Government of Kuwait, *unless Iraq on or before January 15, 1991 fully implements, as set forth in paragraph 1 above, the foregoing resolutions, to use all necessary means to uphold and implement resolution 660 (1990) and all subsequent relevant resolutions* and to restore international peace and security in the area;

3. *Requests* all States to provide appropriate support for the actions undertaken in pursuance of paragraph 2 of the present resolution;

4. *Requests* the States concerned to keep the Security Council

regularly informed on the progress of actions undertaken pursuant to paragraphs 2 and 3 of the present resolution;

5. *Decides* to remain seized of the matter.

Despite the urgency of the situation and the very clear warnings to Saddam Hussein, he continued on the same path of stalling and trying to manipulate world opinion through his sinister acts and the use of the world media. When he declared that he was going to let all hostages free, this did not help him in the U.N., nor did it help him with the American public, although he thought that his decision would have some positive impact by attempting to change American thinking about the Gulf Crisis. He thought he could undermine President Bush and thus undermine the whole Coalition by stopping the tide that had been moving very rapidly against him. In a last ditch effort, the Soviets tried again to come up with a peaceful resolution to the crisis. In a flurry of activities geared toward this end, Saddam Hussein was not phased. He did not make any concessions, always declaring that Kuwait was an integral part of Iraq. There had been hints of giving him some control over the two islands and the Roumeila oil field, and that he would progressively move out of Kuwait on a condition that the United Nations and the world community would solve the Palestinian problem. He tied this issue, completely, to the possibility of his withdrawal from Kuwait. The two had no connection whatsoever! If he wanted to liberate some portions of Palestine, he did not need to occupy Kuwait or any other Arab country. Where is the connection? If he was serious about such a liberation why did he not liberate one square mile of Israeli territory or Israeli occupied territory. The logic does not stand!

The killing of several Palestinians around mid October at Jerusalem's Temple Mount and wounding of 140 gave new ammunition to Saddam Hussein for linking the Palestinian problem to the occupation of Kuwait. It also increased the dangers of the Gulf Crisis and some feared possible strains on the Alliance poising against Iraq. But the U.N. soothed the atmosphere, somewhat, by condemning Israel for this act.

However, the shortsightedness of some leaders in the Palestinian movement led to a blind attitude which welcomed pronouncements of the Iraqi leader and treated him as the hero of the Arab land, the potential liberator of Palestine. He was clearly a desperate man trying to cling to anything that would bring the deluge of appeal to the Arab masses. So he exploited the Palestinian cause. Of course, in their desperation, the Palestinians rallied behind him and behind their leader, Yasser Arafat who was very much in support of Saddam Hussein.

Their emotions carried them a bit too far into his camp and their interests were badly served by taking such a position. Many people were terribly disappointed because of this sway toward the brutal occupier of Kuwait. This tilt brought many doubts and disappointments to the hearts of millions who consecrated their lives for the defense of the Palestinian cause!

Right after U.N. Resolution 678, President Bush, after consulting with King Fahd and leaders of the Coalition around the world, in a gesture of peace and as a last ditch effort to avoid direct military confrontation which was about to become a reality, proposed that Secretary of the United States, James Baker would go to Baghdad and meet with Saddam Hussein. Also, the Foreign Minister of Iraq, Tariq Aziz would come to Washington to meet with President Bush. Several dates were proposed for this meeting, but after three days of silence, came the word from Baghdad that Secretary Baker could come on January 12. Tariq Aziz was welcome to come to Washington on a number of other dates. Negotiations back and forth went on, but all were only an exercise in futility. Saddam stuck to his guns and in his well known style of playing for time, he decided that January 12 was the only date when Baker could come to Baghdad. The purpose for this last minute arrangement was again to stall for time and to force the world community to go beyond the deadline that had been set by the U.N. for Saddam to get out of Kuwait. He thought that if the meeting was to take place on January 12, then he would probably throw an olive branch or two saying that he may withdraw, with many ifs and buts and then stall until the situation went beyond the U.N. deadline. But this was not going to happen! In fact, the exchange of visits did not take place. Finally, a date was set for a meeting to be held in *Geneva on January 9, 1991*, between Secretary of State James Baker and the Foreign Minister of Iraq, Tariq Aziz. This meeting took several hours and the whole World community was focusing on the Intercontinental Hotel in Geneva. A letter was delivered by Secretary Baker from President Bush to President Saddam Hussein. The letter was laid on the table, but the Iraqi delegation refused it. Here are some excerpts from it: "There can be no reward for aggression. Nor will there be any negotiation. Principle cannot be compromised. However, by its full compliance, Iraq will gain the opportunity to rejoin the international community . . . More immediately, Iraq and the Iraqi military establishment will escape destruction. But unless you withdraw from Kuwait completely and without condition, you will lose more than Kuwait. You may be tempted to find solace in the diversity of opinion that is American democracy. You should resist any such temptation. Diversity ought not to be confused with division. Nor should you underestimate, as others have before you, America's will."

The positions of the United States and the United Nations were reiterated to Tariq Aziz and the spirit of the President's letter reflected this also. James Baker warned the aggressors saying, "Don't miscalculate the resolve of the American people." However, the Iraqi delegation and its spokesman, Tariq Aziz, refused to budge one inch. They went into lengthy tirades and speeches denouncing the Allied Forces and thus standing against the will and conscience of the entire world. Tariq Aziz went into a lengthy speech in front of the world press, where the previous positions of Iraq were restated. His various demands were contrary to the spirit of the United Nations Resolutions. This policy of demagoguery and playing for time did not work, and the Geneva Conference between the two Foreign Ministers failed miserably. The world community was dismayed, disheartened, and disappointed because the glooms of devastation and destruction were imminent. In a matter of days, the war in the Gulf would break out. Saddam's forces would be routed! Kuwait would be liberated!

On January 12, 1991, King Fahd made a speech to the Executive Council of the Islamic Popular Conference. He said, "The real cause for the invasion is only an Iraqi ambition in Kuwait, no more no less, and ambitious expansionist Iraqi designs extending to the Gulf countries, beginning with Kuwait and the Kingdom of Saudi Arabia, Bahrain, Qatar, The United Arab Emirates and possibly Oman. There are proofs for this; when Iraqi forces attacked Kuwait they attacked in great numbers . . . It has been proven to the Kingdom of Saudi Arabia, that the *second round, after a few days, was the occupation of a portion of the Kingdom* and after that, if Iraq is capable, then it would continue the journey . . . The independent State of Kuwait was never linked to Iraq. It is just greed and the coveting of Kuwait, an independent and peaceful state which the Almighty God had endowed with petroleum. But Iraq also has tremendous wealth and natural resources, including the two rivers: the Tigris and the Euphrates. Also Iraq has the best fertile cultivated soils of the Arab world. It also has the people who are able to develop the lands and natural resources. What is the crime of Kuwait and the Kingdom of Saudi Arabia? The two countries did their best in supporting Iraq without any conditions . . . After all this, brothers, someone could demand that all forces deployed in the Kingdom of Saudi Arabia should return to their countries! I'm sorry to say that this is a shameful demand.

Why does he (Saddam Hussein) say this and neglect the main cause which compelled these forces to respond to the wishes of the

Kingdom of Saudi Arabia and the Gulf countries? They did not come by force, but in response to our wishes and desires, when we officially declared, after the invasion of Kuwait by a day or two, that we desire first of all for the Arab countries to send their forces to the Kingdom of Saudi Arabia to defend the Kingdom from an Iraqi invasion, because Iraq has a massive army. We did not impose our will on these Arab, Islamic and friendly countries!

Since all these nations responded to the requests of the Kingdom of Saudi Arabia and the Gulf countries, I believe that this is the will of God! I don't believe that anyone has the right to say to the Kingdom of Saudi Arabia: why are you seeking support from forces of the Arab, or Islamic, or friendly nations? (We are right), based on Shari'a which is the base and foundation, and based on other legal matters. We all know that the Prophet Mohammed also requested help from non-Moslems for the benefit of Islam and Moslems . . ."

Over a decade ago, when King Fahd was visiting Baghdad and Saddam Hussein was complaining about the Iranians stating that they had mistreated Iraq and that they were causing some skirmishes along the Iraqi border and placing explosives in Baghdad, he asked for advice from his visitor! King Fahd said, "Would you like to hear my advice?"

Saddam said, "Yes." Then King Fahd said, "Do not antagonize Iran . . . I tell you that it is not in the interest of Iraq that you interfere in the affairs of Iran."

Saddam then said, "Iran is now in turmoil." King Fahd replied, "Does this mean if turmoil takes place in any country, logic and wisdom give you the right to interfere when the country is minding its own affairs? But what actually happened, he interfered! And what was the benefit after eight years of war? Cities and villages were destroyed in Iran and Iraq; millions were killed and the lives of millions of people were disrupted along with billions of dollars squandered; then he returned to the 1975 agreement which he tore up and canceled completely (previously) . . . Matters between Iran and Iraq have been settled by the United States. Each party accepted Security Council Resolutions of the United Nations and they were about to sign an agreement without a need for Iraq to make any concessions. In a matter of a few minutes, the Iraqi President took unilateral decisions to reinstate the 1975 (Algiers Agreement) and conceded all territories which Iran wanted to remain in or control, even if it was under the control of the Iraqi army. I don't object to the Iraqi President, nor would I say why he returned to the 1975 agreement and conceded these territories, because this is his business and I have no right to interfere or say anything.

However, is withdrawal of his troops from Kuwait more difficult than the reinstatement of the 1975 agreement? And more so from territories claimed by Iraq and gained by the Iraqi army, then returned to Iraq? . . .

And now, what prevents him from applying the same logic and returning to his senses to announce his withdrawal from Kuwait, without any conditions? Then, the problem will terminate and the fighting will end with it."

The Monarch also stated, "They said (Saddam and his propagandists) the two Holy Mosques were in the hands of foreign troops and even their administration and the religious functions, including the visit to the Prophet's Mosque in Madina and Mecca–these are being organized by Western girls who prepare all arrangements . . . to whom do you say this? Do you direct the lies toward Mecca and Madina? The Holy Mosque in Mecca and the Prophet's Mosque in Madina are 1,500 kilometers away (926 miles)–a flight of nearly two and a half hours."

Debate in America and the World

The vast impact of the Gulf Crisis on economies of the world and world opinion was very much felt in America. The United States and its people were directly affected by the Gulf Crisis. American public opinion and the American conscience were both very sensitive to the unfolding of events in the region and more so to the use and abuse of hostages by Saddam Hussein. The agony of refugees fleeing areas of conflict and the atrocities committed against the people of Kuwait all touched the hearts not only of people around the world, but especially people in America.

On another scale, the occupation of Kuwait brought instant rise to the price of oil everywhere. In a matter of days, the price of gasoline jumped nearly 50% and this touched the pocketbook of every single American. Thus, America had very genuine interests in the region: first of all, a small peaceful Kuwait was occupied by an aggressor who amassed a vast army along the borders with the Kingdom of Saudi Arabia, secondly, his deployment of forces as seen by spy satellites were in a position to strike a blitzkrieg attack against the Eastern Region of Saudi Arabia with its great oil resources. Saudi Arabia had been good friends of America for several decades, going back to the era of King Abdulaziz, known in the West as Ibn Saud.

On November 30, 1990, President Bush gave the following statement concerning the Gulf Crisis:

"We are dealing with a dictator all too willing to use force, who has weapons of mass destruction and is seeking new ones . . . the developing countries are being victimized by this dictator's rape of his neighbor, Kuwait. Those who feel that there is no down side to waiting months and months must consider the devastating damage being done everyday to the fragile economies of those countries that can afford it least . . . The increase in oil prices resulting directly from Saddam's invasion is hurting our country too . . . no nation should rape, pillage and brutalize its neighbor. No nation should be able to wipe a member state of the United Nations and the Arab League off the face of the earth."

He also said, "This aggression will not and must not stand . . . Hitler revisited . . . Should military action be required, this will not be another Vietnam."

On a visit to the Kingdom of Saudi Arabia, the Vice President of the United States, Dan Quayle while addressing American troops on December 30, 1990, sent a simple message to Saddam Hussein. "Either get out of Kuwait peacefully or leave by force." He made it clear that although the United States and other members of the Coalition Forces would very much like a peaceful resolution to the crisis created by Iraqi aggression, "If force is necessary, it will be quick, massive, and decisive . . . this will not be another Vietnam . . . the whole world will be grateful when the allies have achieved their objectives of getting Saddam out of Kuwait . . . Unless (he) is stopped today, a nuclear-armed Iraq will control the world's energy supply tomorrow, thereby threatening the security and welfare of all nations."

When Prime Minister of Britain, John Major, visited Riyadh, Saudi Arabia on January 7, 1991, he addressed the British troops in Dhahran and strongly condemned the brutal aggression committed by Iraqi forces against the peaceful nation of Kuwait. He emphatically stated that, "We do not thirst for anything other than a peaceful settlement." However, if solving the crisis becomes impossible, the Coalition Forces would use all other available options which include a massive force to guarantee that, "Iraq is ejected by force from Kuwait." He went on to say that Kuwait has become "a massive prison camp . . . there are still appalling atrocities being perpetrated in Kuwait. Murders, attacks on wholly innocent women, brutality of one form or another . . . ."

After meeting the Amir of Kuwait Sheikh Jabir Al-Ahmad Al-Sabbah in Taif, Saudi Arabia, Prime Minister Major stated that the United Kingdom and the Allies remain committed to the implementation of all U.N. Security Council Resolutions relating to the Iraqi-Kuwaiti problem. He then declared, "Saddam Hussein must leave Kuwait either voluntarily or be expelled forcibly . . . any partial withdrawal will not be accepted in the case of Kuwait . . . there will be no negotiations. The Iraqi regime must pull out from all the Kuwaiti lands."

The world media was up in arms against the brutal invasion of

Kuwait. Newspaper, radio and television commentaries around the world were almost unanimous in their condemnation of Saddam Hussein's behavior and ruthless policies. In Great Britain the Times of London said, "The world's disgust should be expressed in the strongest terms, but with no illusion that words will be treated with other than contempt by a man in command of one of the world's most ruthless tyrannies . . . Iraq should be treated as pariah, deprived of all diplomatic and economic contact and assistance . . . in a worldwide expression of anger at a small nation's sovereignty rudely shattered by brute force."

As for the news media in the Arab world, some of it reflected the opinion of the extremist Fundamentalists and others who betrayed the trust and were ungrateful for the help they received. Nevertheless, they were in the minority. Their noisy protests amounted to nothing but lip service. Coming from the demographic and political might of the Arab world in Egypt, the leading newspaper Al-Ahram said concerning this brutal occupation: "President Saddam Hussein is mistaken in his reading of the succession of events in the Gulf Crisis and the great dangers they hold in store for him. He is isolated internationally, in the Arab world, and even in his own country. Saddam, mistakenly, believes that he has mastered the region and the world." ". . . Megalomania and self-deception led Saddam to commit small but murderous mistakes. But he will not pay for his errors alone, rather his people and the Arab peoples will pay the price."

Also, another influential Egyptian newspaper, Al-Akhbar said: ". . . Nobody trusts Saddam Hussein anymore, and nobody will ever believe him again . . . The days of Hitler will not return . . . It shows that Saddam Hussein reads only the first few pages of his history books and is unaware of the fate in store for tyrants who violate the independence of nations."

Even the Eastern Block joined the chorus of condemnation. In this regard the leading newspaper in the former USSR, Izvestia, condemned the annexation of Kuwait and said ". . . The U.S.S.R. and the U.S. have come out against the Iraqi annexation of Kuwait, increasing the chances that Saddam Hussein's regime, following an instinct for self-preservation, will submit to the will of the world community. One of the principal levers that can lift us out of the crisis is now seen in new relations of cooperation and coordination with the United States in particular. Political and practical benefits from this direction will more than compensate for the loss of (Soviet) friendship with Saddam."

The Secretary General of the United Nations Javier Perez De Cuellar made certain remarks at a luncheon on September 18, 1990, held at the Dag Hammarskjold Memorial Scholarship Fund. He spoke of, "The pervasive effects of this crisis on the world economy, on the citizens of many nations, and not least in its devastating effects on many developing countries of the world." He went on to say, "For the United Nations, this is the first full scale test of its capacity to deal with an act of invasion and annexation through collective action." Although Chapter VII of the U.N. Charter was originally considered to be its greatest innovation–the "teeth" of the Charter have "never before been applied so comprehensively or with such full backing from member states." He also stated that tragic humanitarian emergencies and massive economic stresses have resulted from the crisis. However, the cold war brought an end to the paralysis of the Security Council due to the rivalry between the major world powers, which went on for forty years.

The Secretary General had a meeting with the Foreign Minister of Iraq on the 31st of August and the first of September in Amman, Jordan. He said, "On my own initiative, I had invited him to meet with me personally and urgently in the hope that his government could be persuaded to comply with the resolutions adopted by the Security Council and thereby to defuse the tension in that region which, throughout the month of August, had heightened to an alarming degree. I told him that, in my view, the best way of promoting a peaceful resolution of the conflict would be for Iraq to declare its commitment to withdraw immediately from Kuwait and to begin the process without delay, in accordance with the position taken by the Security Council. Regrettably, my talks with Mr. Tariq Aziz did not lead to this outcome."

Then the Secretary General made an appeal for justice and dialogue saying, "I have witnessed war, global war. And that is the tremendous threat that we are facing now, because injustice was done against a small country which was one of the most faithful and loyal countries of our organization. But please do not give the floor to arms; give the floor to dialogue." It is indeed a sad commentary on international diplomacy. A dialogue with Saddam Hussein was a dialogue with the deaf!

The Secretary General continued his contacts with Baghdad and other leaders, seeking a possible peaceful solution to the conflict. He even went to Baghdad January 12, 1991, on the eve of the war and he again met the Foreign Minister, Tariq Aziz and the Iraqi President on January 13, 1991. He stated to the President that, "Our efforts to avert the unfolding tragedy will fail unless Iraq could signify its readiness to comply with the relevant resolutions of the Security Council, beginning with Resolution 660 (1990)."

Saddam Hussein was lending a very attentive ear to the mounting debate taking place, not only in the United States of America but throughout the World. He intended to optimize and make use of the great freedoms and democracies in America, France and Britain. He made every possible effort to exploit these freedoms of expression. The war of words was not only heating up, but reaching new heights, because of all the modern achievements in communication. News items and the creation of news, sometimes for information but at other times for disinformation, were propagated around the globe in a matter of seconds. America became a focal point during the Gulf Crisis, since President Bush was spearheading the campaign through the United Nations and throughout the world community, for ejecting Saddam Hussein from Kuwait.

President George Bush is a Republican, but the U.S. Congress, both in the House of Representatives and the Senate, had a majority of Democrats; so special attention was paid to matters that might influence and sway the opinion in Congress. Through a presidential order, American troops were dispatched to the Gulf region almost immediately after the invasion. Simultaneously, voices across America were raised against the possibility of war which might result from the pouring of American troops and other Allied forces into the Gulf theater of operations. What added more heat to the debate in America and the war of information and words around the world, was the fact that by November 6, 1990, there was a mid-term election for all the members of the House of Representatives and a third of the Senate. These elections could change the make-up and the balance of power in the Congress. Initially, the democrats lobbed several accusations against the President. Some of them accused him of raising the rhetoric concerning the Gulf Crisis for possible gains during the election; others were against sending any large numbers of American troops to the Arabian Gulf. Voices of doubt and doom were reverberating across the freedom waves of America. They were instantly transmitted throughout the world into the listening and attentive ears of Saddam Hussein. Senator Patrick Moynihan of New York said, "We will lose, one way or the other," Senator Sam Nunn of Georgia invoked the gruesome images of G.I.s coming back from the Arabian Gulf "in body bags." Senator Bob Kerrey of Nebraska said, "Bush has not thought this through."

The major outcry was related to some interpretation of the Constitution that the President of the United States could not by himself declare war or commit troops into an area of potential explosion without the expressed and written consent of Congress. However, the President of the United States is allowed under the law to send troops anywhere to respond to an emergency as long as this emergency may not exceed 60 days.

The War Powers Resolution

This is sometimes referred to as the War Powers Act. It is a controversial piece of legislation, passed by Congress in 1973 during the last days of the Vietnam War. It was, essentially enacted as a reaction to that war. It murkied the picture on committing American troops abroad. Congress wanted to exercise more authority in this regard at the expense of the expressed authority invested in the President who is the Commander in Chief of the Armed Forces. So, anytime there is a crisis abroad, the same ritual and debate over who has authority on committing American troops becomes almost an exercise in futility. The President has vast powers. In fact, during the past two centuries, American presidents committed troops several times and continue to do so. However, Section 2(c) of the War Powers Resolution attempts at limiting presidential authority in committing U.S. troops "only pursuant to: 1. a declaration of war, 2. specific statutory authorization, or 3. a national emergency created by attack upon the United States, its territories or possessions, or its Armed Forces." President Bush explained that the Armed Forces were not in a situation of "imminent" hostility. In fact, their presence deterred against the spread of hostilities, and thus at this stage, he did not need approval from Congress.

Although Congress was not in session when U.S. troops were dispatched to the Gulf, the President consulted with congressional leadership and briefings were given to nearly 150 legislators. On the second of August, 1990, the Senate adopted a resolution, with a vote of 97 in favor and zero against, supporting the President's actions and recommending that he "acts immediately, using unilateral and multilateral means to seek the full and unconditional withdrawal of all Iraqi forces from Kuwaiti territory." As mentioned in a previous chapter, the House of Representatives passed a similar resolution condemning the invasion of Kuwait and demanded an embargo against the state of Iraq.

Despite all this initial support, the debate went on, and many still questioned the authority of the President, vis-a-vis the War Powers Resolution. This Act stipulates that the President must withdraw within 60 days American forces subjected to a situation of actual or imminent hostilities. This duration could be extended to 90 days. After that, Congress must specifically authorize continued deployment of American troops. The whole scenario led to lively debate, but the President prevailed!

Strong objections and doubts were expressed by powerful senators such as Ted Kennedy of Massachusetts and Sam Nunn of Georgia, who headed the powerful Armed Services Committee. He went on to hold public hearings concerning the Gulf Crisis. These public hearings, while legal and legitimate under the law, along with the freedom of expression which prevails in America, tended to give the wrong message to Saddam Hussein and his supporters. He miscalculated again and misjudged the spirit of debate and freedom of the word! He had mistaken this for weakness and he had wrongly taken it to indicate deep division in America. He energized his propaganda machine and his varied acts of threats and manipulations in order to feed into any possible flames of division and dissension. By manipulating the hostages the way he did–allowing a few of them to depart Iraq at different intervals–he thought that Congress would mellow in its opposition to his occupation, and with enough propaganda and disinformation, a majority in Congress would block the moves and policies of President Bush, and thus force him into halting the flow of troops and armament into the region. This scenario would bring about a total collapse of his policy in the Gulf region.

As election day, on November 6, approached, the debate got more heated by the day and the hour. However, President Bush, armed with vast support from the world community and with strong United Nations Resolutions, was not going to budge one inch. He met head on with any dissension and gave the debate an extra notch or two.

On the 5th of November, 1990, President Bush went to Houston, Texas, since this is his home base, in order to cast his vote the next day in the election. On that drizzling day, the towering figure of President George Bush was at a tennis court hitting the ball hard and giving his opponent a swift defeat. These authors happened to be walking around the exercise track of the Houstonian Club and the President attracted their immediate attention. One of the co-authors stepped by the green hedge and greeted the President, then said, "Mr. President! We are very proud of your policy in the Gulf and we think you are absolutely on target." The President replied, "Thank you, thank you very much." Then, when the drizzle turned into more steady rain the President stopped his match and said concerning the policy in the Gulf, *"We've got to stay the course!"* Watching his features and the manner in which this expression was uttered, one could not help but have full faith that the President meant every word he said. He certainly stayed the course!

That same evening, there was a rally for the Republican Party and for the Republican candidates in the State of Texas. Clayton Williams was running for governor of the state, and a number of other Republicans were seeking positions at various levels of government. President George Bush was the main speaker at the rally. Again, one of the co-authors happened to be at that gathering. The President's speech was very well received by the audience and transmitted by the news media not only across the state of Texas or America, but to many parts of the world. He stated in very clear unequivocal terms the policy of the United States of America in the Gulf Crisis. His statements were reinforcements for the speeches and other statements of policy which had been enunciated on a number of occasions be it in Washington, D.C. or other parts of America and Europe. The audience was electrified with the seriousness, sincerity and determination of the message delivered by the President. But again, in the spirit of debate which was going on across America, about three people in the audience lifted some placards and started chanting: "No blood for oil! No blood for oil!" Secret Service was everywhere and immediately wanted to apprehend those causing the fracas. However, the President intervened saying, "No, no, no, please let them talk. Let me explain why we are in the Gulf." And then he went on, not only to address them but to address the nation as well, saying that we were in the Gulf to help a friend in need and stop the aggression and torture being practiced by a ruthless dictator named Saddam Hussein. The Saudis and Kuwaitis have been friends with America for many, many decades and we were there to defend innocent people against the aggressive designs and the atrocities committed by the Iraqi dictator and his forces. He stated that our primary objectives were to uphold justice while defending our friends and interests in the Gulf. It happened that America's dependence on oil and its economic interests dictate that American policy should not be held hostage either by Saddam Hussein or anyone else, and certainly should not allow someone like him to have control over our lifeline and the vital interests of our allies around the world. The President promised to continue his utmost toward the possible peaceful resolution of the conflict and certainly did not want to lose one single precious American life or the life of any soldiers from the Allied Forces. Thus, he promised to work ceaselessly toward peace!

Voices were expressed during the heat of the debate in America, stating that President Bush and his Administration did not yet rise to the occasion and explain clearly and eloquently the wisdom of his policy in the Arabian Gulf. Knowing very well the power of the media, the President went on the offensive. Not long ago, when he was running for election for the Presidency of the United States of America in 1988, a strong and vicious campaign was waged against him. Innuendos, accusations, dirty tricks and much more were beamed across the waves to discredit him. This was a campaign carried by a minority and also by a number of Democrats who are on the other side of the aisle in American democratic elections. In fact, a negative message was propagated and stuck in the ears, minds and hearts of many people, it was: "George Bush is a wimp!" Listening to this man as we both specifically have on a number of occasions, and meeting this man in person, presenting his views on world order and other sensitive issues of the time, you cannot help but be charmed by his delivery, his decisiveness and conviction. He is anything but a vacillating or indecisive man! In fact, once you meet him and you listen to him in person, you cannot help but admire the courage and great sense of leadership that this man commands, both based on his personal character, personal belief, and the decades of experience he earned through the years. Despite all this, the power of the word–the power of the media was certainly enormous, so the negative slogan stuck into the minds of many across the land. Thus, it was his job and his job alone to dismiss such accusations. No matter how much support he got from his capable advisors, he was the only one that could dismiss such serious accusations against his personality. George Bush rose to the occasion and challenged his critics with enthusiasm and dedication. He crisscrossed the country; he delivered speeches in the far corners of America, until he was able to reach every home and every hamlet. Soon enough, he reached every heart in the land, and when election time came, he won the Presidency by a landslide.

In the debate of the Gulf policy, he gave it all his energies and dedication as well; and in the final analysis, as events will prove, he won the race and the affection and admiration of leaders around the world. He gave speeches, interviews, press releases, and certainly worked the phones, in a mission for bringing the public to his side and to rally the Coalition leaders to a solidly unified front with America.

The results of the elections were not entirely favorable to the Republican candidates. Immediately, Saddam Hussein and his Revolutionary Command Councils seized on the occasion, thinking that a rift had developed in America, and thus Congress would tie the hands of President Bush. So Saddam increased his normal activities of manipulations and stalling. Again, he miscalculated the resolve of the American public which was solidly behind the President (nearly 75% of them approving his Gulf Policy), and he misinterpreted the atmosphere of freedom and democracy in the nation. While many voters did not agree with a number of candidates, nevertheless, it was clear to analysts and world leaders alike that the American public was with the President–Congress would have to reflect the will of the people.

One issue of major and lasting disturbance to the American psyche and public opinion was the Vietnam War. It left permanent scars in America and there was a wave of genuine fear that the situation in the Gulf might evolve into another Vietnam. Many people worried about such a possibility, and again Saddam Hussein and his propaganda organs paid special attention to nurturing such a fear. His bombastic expressions and threats about "pools of blood" and "body bags" became household words in America. The gruesome threats egged on the worry of the Vietnam era.

There was a heavy and far reaching participation in this debate. Men of justice, conviction and good conscience propagated the good word across America, be it in interviews with television, radio stations, or newspapers that spread the message and beamed it to millions of Americans across the land or through a series of lectures and speeches. All this left its impact and helped in easing the mind of Americans.

The Gulf region, if it was to explode into war, would never be another Vietnam. The reasons were many! In the Vietnam era, the cold war was at its peak. The North Vietnamese were having ample supply lines from the Communist Bloc, especially the mighty power of the former Soviet Union. The Chinese and a number of other Eastern European nations who were then under the grip of Communism, came to the aid of North Vietnam. With these vast supply lines and the dedication of communist cadres in Vietnam, the battle there was not an easy one to wage, unless there was a solid determination and a unified front at home. Public opinion in America was then very divided. Americans were coming back in "body bags" by the thousands. The dedication of the enemy and his good supply lines took their toll on American lives and the American psyche as well. The determination to fight in Vietnam was at best lukewarm. There was never a final decision to get into the war and give it what it would take to win. In fact, the policy was vacillating and indecisive, moving forward one step and going backward two! This led to nothing but more confusion and more debacle on the battlefield. Very importantly, the North Vietnamese communists were infiltrating every corner and every hamlet in South Vietnam. It became very difficult at times to distinguish friends from foe. The casualties mounted in the jungles of Vietnam and gradually a defeat was imminent. It was not a defeat of the great mighty American machine and ingenuity, it was a defeat of willpower. As President Bush declared on a number of occasions, the Gulf Crisis "will not be another Vietnam!" Vietnam was never to be again! It was explained to the millions of Americans that the current world situation was a very different one indeed.

The dawn of the *New World Order* had come! The vicious rivalry that existed during Vietnam, between the two superpowers, namely the United States and the former Soviet Union was no longer there. A new era had come, where close cooperation and understanding existed between the two superpowers. The communist regimes in Eastern Europe and the former Soviet Union have vanished. Glasnost and Perestroika were moving with vigor. The possibility of working one against the other and thriving on the rivalry between the superpowers was no longer there. In this atmosphere of close cooperation and understanding, Saddam Hussein was standing against the world. In case of war, he certainly had no supply lines from the Eastern Block, nor any nation in the world. With no supply lines, coupled with a strong economic embargo against Iraq, where would he get his supplies and support? In the case of Hitler, Germany was a mighty technological power during World War II. The great industries of Germany had mass production for his war machines from airplanes to tanks, artillery pieces and other military equipment. Where were all these manufacturing facilities in Iraq? They were essentially non-existent. Iraq depended on the world for its supplies. While it produced and exported oil, Iraq had to import at least 90% of everything the Iraqis need! In case the Gulf was to explode into war, because of the obstinacy of Saddam Hussein, the Iraqi army would receive a heavy blow from the Allied Forces, it would lose its communications centers, tanks, trucks, airplanes and the rest . . . How many pieces of equipment could the Iraqis replace? They could not replace any through imports, because of the grip of the embargo, nor could they produce any of these heavy war machines.

Again, another point of importance that was conveyed to the American mind, was the fact that America was in the Gulf with the total support of the world community, through ironclad resolutions enacted by the United Nations Security Council, in a unanimous way, never witnessed in the history of the United Nations. American and Allied Forces were in the Gulf at the invitation of the Kingdom of Saudi Arabia and they were warmly received and appreciated for the mission of defense and liberation they carried with them. They were supported in every sense of the word. They were supplied with everything they needed: water, fuel, transportation and much more. They were in the open desert of Saudi Arabia, not in the jungles of Vietnam. The vast open spaces of the desert certainly would not lend themselves to anything like the guerrilla warfare that took place in the jungles, nor were there any Vietcong-like people in Saudi Arabia. With all these convincing explanations conveyed to the American public, it became clear that whatever fear may have existed about getting the nation embroiled in the quagmire of another Vietnam, such a fear had vanished! The public began to understand that another Vietnam, would never be!

Opposition to the war was never strong, because President Bush had behind him the solid American support in excess of 70% of the population, giving him a green light to carry his policy for defending Saudi Arabia and liberating Kuwait. Nevertheless, this vocal opposition continued to drum support around the United States and other parts of the world. Some demonstrations took place in the U.S., France,

England, Germany and other nations. The critics of the President's policy resorted to computer predictions, trying to spread again fear among the populace and stating that thousands of Americans would come back in "body bags." Some computer predictions were saying probably 60,000 Americans would be killed if the war broke out. Others were predicting that a war breaking out against the fortified positions of the Iraqis would result in a U.S. toll of five thousand dead and probably fifteen thousand wounded in a matter of ten days only. On November 2nd, the Iraqi leader declared that if Iraq was attacked, "its foes will curse their destiny." America cannot afford to lose such numbers! Losing anything in the thousands would be disastrous to American policy and the American Administration. Serious analysts and observers of the events and facts that existed about Iraq, its capabilities and the mighty powerful Armada that had been amassed to confront Saddam Hussein, would know that the possibility of losing several thousands of the Allied Forces was very remote indeed, nearly impossible! Then a strong and compelling message went out to the American public, stating that the war, should it break out, would be a short one. It would deal a decisive blow to Saddam's forces in Kuwait . . . In fact, as it will be seen in later chapters, war losses to the Coalition Forces were minimal. The outcome was miraculous, despite the mighty war machine of Saddam Hussein and the millions of land mines which covered the desert and the beaches of the Gulf.

The battle for influencing the minds and emotions of senators and congressmen raged on. Accusations by some politicians in the opposition went on unabated. Some accused President Bush of running away from difficult problems at home to more appealing matters abroad. Even conservatives were expressing some doubts. For example, columnist Patrick J. Buchanan said, "Before we send thousands of American soldiers to their death, let us make damn sure America's vital interests are threatened." He also said, "There are lots of things worth fighting for, but an extra ten cents for a gallon of gas is not one of them." These dissenting voices did not help in presenting a solid front, since Americans normally rally around the flag and support the President in cases of a national emergency. Many Conservatives warned against America's involvement in the Arabian Gulf. Former U.S. Attorney General Ramsey Clark visited Baghdad for nearly a week at the invitation of an Iraqi Friendship, Peace and Solidarity Organization. He arrived there on Sunday, November 11, 1990. He was very adamant in his opposition to any possible military action against Iraq. His views were beamed on a number of news networks, but their impact was counterproductive. After week-long discussions by Secretary of State James Baker with America's major partners in the Coalition, he gave a press conference in Paris around November 10, 1990, and said after a meeting with the President of the French Republic François Mitterrand: "As we wrap up this trip, I feel that we have very strong consensus on our collective aims and on the need, particularly, to resist partial solutions." Commenting on the possibility of a military option, he said, "There are some different views with respect to some of those issues, but generally speaking, there is an extraordinary unanimity and cohesiveness. There are differing opinions with respect to how long it would take sanctions to work. Indeed, there are some different opinions on whether sanctions are already having some bite."

Propagators of doom and negativism declared that if war would flare up in such a volatile region of the world, it would disrupt oil supplies and would poison Western interests for decades. A Palestinian intellectual warned in Baghdad, "If there is war, your men (American) won't be able to walk the streets of the Arab world safely for two hundred years."

Soviet Moves

The Soviet envoy Yevgeni Primakov, who is an advisor to former President Gorbachev and who visited Saddam Hussein in Baghdad around the first week of October 1990, came and exchanged views with President Bush in the latter part of October. He stated that the Iraqi leader would not withdraw from Kuwait, prior to negotiations. The President's reply was simple and clear, "Tell him I am not flexible either."

Yevgeni Primakov, Soviet envoy to the Middle East is well acquainted with the region. He was the personal envoy of former President Gorbachev who was seeking a peaceful resolution to Saddam Hussein's invasion of Kuwait. Beginning on February 27, 1991, Primakov wrote a series of articles in Pravda, a widely circulated Soviet newspaper. His articles were entitled, "The War Which Did Not Need to Happen."

When he first met the Iraqi leader and his Foreign Minister in 1969, he noticed the abundance of guns hanging on the walls. He also noticed Saddam's toughness which was transferred into brutality and his decisiveness which became obstinacy. He was the type of man who had the aptitude of reaching what he wanted no matter what the cost might be. All this was compounded with another danger: that is, no one knew what next step Saddam might take at any moment.

On his first trip during the Gulf Crisis, Primakov's first goal was to find an agreement by which Soviet advisers could leave Iraq. The second part of his mission was to assure Saddam Hussein that there were no ways by which he could escape from submitting to the U.N.

Security Council Resolutions, and no way to refuse them! Also, the Soviets wanted to explore possibilities for the Iraqi forces to withdraw from Kuwait through diplomatic means.

The Soviet's plane first landed in Amman, Jordan in order to exchange ideas with King Hussein and the Jordanian leaders, along with the leader of the PLO, Yasser Arafat, who was heading the Palestinian delegation. Yevgeni Primakov said, "King Hussein and especially the Palestinians supported Saddam Hussein's position and counted themselves as his allies."

On the 4th of October, 1990, Primakov arrived in Baghdad, where he was received by the Iraqi Foreign Minister. The Soviet envoy stated, "Tariq Aziz concentrated on proving that Kuwait belonged historically, politically and economically to Iraq. A month earlier, he also explained this to us in Moscow and stated situations, dates, numbers and events relating to this way of thinking. He also gave a historical briefing to justify the legality of invading Kuwait by using Iraqi forces. I sensed in his discussion a vibrance of not being comfortable and not accepting the Soviet position. He said that the (former) Soviet Union should have followed a different path and should have taken into consideration the treaty which was signed between Iraq and the Soviet Union. But Tariq Aziz avoided answering the question which we addressed to him: "Why did Iraq not inform Moscow about its intention of occupying Kuwait?"

Prior to their arrival to Baghdad, many attempts were made to obtain the release of Soviet citizens. But all attempts failed! While Iraq did not outright refuse, their answer was never clear and in reality they never took any practical step to release Soviet citizens. At that time, thousands of hostages from other countries: Americans, Europeans, Japanese and others were held in Iraq against their will. Primakov and his party met Saddam Hussein on October 5, 1990. He repeated everything that was presented before by Tariq Aziz. The Soviets strongly demanded clarification concerning the situation of Soviet specialists in Iraq. Saddam answered by saying, "Whoever wants to leave Iraq is able to leave; but in the coming two months, Iraq will permit only one thousand specialists to travel, so that work on projects will not be interrupted." Saddam reiterated to the Soviets that there was a conspiracy against Iraq and that the Kingdom of Saudi Arabia and the Gulf Emirates were parties to it. According to him, this conspiracy also used economic weapons. He said Kuwait and Saudi Arabia did not abide by oil production quotas. Prior to this, he had already stated that Kuwait was historically part of Iraq . . .

Primakov made it a point to bring to Saddam Hussein's attention the severe consequences which would result from his refusal to remove his forces from Kuwait. He was concerned about the fact that Saddam's advisors were only giving him the rosy side and neglecting the ominous side of his occupation. Saddam was informed that if he did not get out of Kuwait, he was going to be exposed to attack; but Primakov told him that the purpose of his visit was not to threaten him. However, he stated that, most likely, there was no other exit for Saddam except withdrawal. Saddam replied, saying that he would use all means at his disposal if the war broke out and he would expand the fires of war to neighboring countries, especially Israel. On the other hand, the Iraqi leader said, "I am a practical man and I believe that it is possible to withdraw, but I can not do this if withdrawal is not accompanied with a solution to all matters in the region." At another discussion, Saddam said "You know that on the 15th of August, I relinquished all that I have gained during the war with Iran, which went on for eight years. Now, the people of Iraq will not forgive my withdrawal from Kuwait without any conditions. And they will ask me: what are we to do concerning an outlet for us to the sea?" Primakov said, "If the Iraqi people accepted what you have relinquished from the outcome of the war with Iran, without a doubt, they will agree on a withdrawal decision from Kuwait."

On October 19, 1990, Primakov met with President George Bush in Washington to brief him on his discussions with Saddam Hussein. He also met with Prince Bandar Bin Sultan, Ambassador of the Kingdom of Saudi Arabia in Washington, D.C. Primakov then said, "This meeting was very interesting. It was very much like seeing matters from within, from one of the important sources of information to the White House, concerning developments of the Gulf Crisis. Prince Bandar refused categorically to accept the idea that a military solution would lead to very tragic results." He said, "You exaggerate very much! I am a military pilot, and I can assure you through experience and knowledge that in case a strike takes place–if Iraq refuses to withdraw its forces–everything will end in a matter of hours. Don't exaggerate the number of possible casualties! The attack will be accomplished with modern electronic means and it will be more like a surgical strike." According to Primakov, Prince Bandar did not refuse a political solution. In fact, he said that the former Soviet Union was the only one capable and qualified to influence the Iraqi position in a positive manner.

When the Soviet envoy met the "Iron Lady," former Prime Minister of England, Margaret Thatcher, he noted her solid convictions. She said, "We should not be satisfied with the Iraqi forces withdrawing from Kuwait, a decisive strike against Iraq must take place in order "to break the back" of Saddam Hussein and to destroy all his military capabilities and even possibly his industrial capabilities as well." According to Primakov, "with difficulty" he was able to ask her this question, "Then you do not see any alternative to the military option?" Thatcher answered, "Yes, there is no other alternative!" Then he said, when will military operations begin? She answered, "I can not tell you this, because this should be a surprise to Iraq."

On another trip, in the latter part of October, Primakov met with the President of Syria. According to him, Hafez Assad has a special ability for listening to his visitors. He asked about the possibility of convening an Arab Summit Conference with an invitation for Saddam Hussein, and asking him to withdraw his forces from Kuwait for the good of Arab interest; with an indication in the invitation saying that the Iraqi withdrawal could open the road toward a solution of the Palestinian question, which is desired by all Arabs. When the Soviet envoy met President Hosni Moubarak in Cairo, Egypt, he was assured by the Egyptian President that there was no one who wished war! He concurred with the thought that if Saddam Hussein agreed to withdrawal he could be given assurances of securing proper circumstances for future discussions with Kuwait. When he was asked another question regarding the Kingdom of Saudi Arabia, President Moubarak said, "I can tell you with certainty that the Kingdom of Saudi Arabia will be on the side of such assurances."

After this, Primakov went to Baghdad and met with Saddam Hussein on the 28th of October, 1991. Saddam said, "I invited my colleagues, especially, so they can listen to our conversation, and among them there are the 'hawks' and the 'doves.' " According to Primakov, "This type of conversation was intentional so that Saddam Hussein could show that not only one person decides everything. The only appearance of freedom of thought was that some of those present were shaking their heads as a sign of agreement for whatever Saddam Hussein was saying, some others were shaking their heads also, but with less enthusiasm . . ." In comparing our conversation at this time with a conversation held previously with Saddam, we found out that Saddam, on the 5th of October, concentrated on the conviction that Kuwait was historically part of Iraq, "but during this meeting of the 28th of October, he did not resort to discussing the subject at all." Saddam said, "Would I be able to withdraw my forces from Kuwait without knowing about the mechanism of withdrawal of American forces from the Kingdom of Saudi Arabia? And would the penalties of the Security Council continue after withdrawal or not? And how would I guarantee the interest of my nation for finding an exit to the sea? And is there a suggested mechanism for connecting my withdrawal from Kuwait with the Palestinian question?" During these conversations, Saddam Hussein said, "The Kingdom of Saudi Arabia is the major Arab party, if not the only one, and that I was willing to send a personal emissary to meet with the Saudi leaders any place at any time." But Saddam Hussein did not positively give an answer relating to the major question about occupation and withdrawal. "For this reason, I told him in a private meeting: You have known me for a long time, and you are aware that I speak to you truthfully and because of this, I say to you, if you do not declare your withdrawal from Kuwait and you do not withdraw, the aerial strike (against you) will be a certainty and it will be severe." Answering this, Saddam said he would not be able to do anything and for him withdrawal would be suicidal, especially if he did not receive an answer relating to the questions put forth concerning guarantees and other matters.

After this, *Primakov visited the Kingdom of Saudi Arabia*, for the first time. His meeting took place at a round table in the presence of King Fahd and other leaders of the Royal Family. Present at the meeting were: Crown Prince Abdullah, Prince Sultan, the Minister of Defense, and the Foreign Minister Prince Saud Al-Faisal. Primakov said in the meeting, "The (former) Soviet Union takes the position that Iraqi forces must withdraw and return matters to what they were prior to August 2nd, 1990. We will not retreat from this position one single inch. In the meantime, we seek help to achieve this goal through political means." When King Fahd heard this, he applauded this position. Primakov said, the Saudis, in general, are distinguished in the fact that they do not like anything fake. Also, good intentions, decency and smoothness are overwhelming in their humane character.

According to Primakov, King Fahd and others welcomed the suggested ideas relating to conversations with Saddam Hussein. The King stated his main concern and questioned if Saddam Hussein understood these suggestions and wondered if he would use them for stalling until he strengthened his position in Kuwait. Primakov stated, "Most of the Saudi leaders indicated their concern about Saddam Hussein's maneuvers for changing the demographic situation in Kuwait and for bringing Iraqis to replace the original inhabitants of Kuwait. Naturally, some members of the Royal Family were leaning toward an immediate military solution, based on the premise that time was on his side; but I believe that King Fahd was taking a balanced position. In fact, I can certify that King Fahd was hoping very sincerely for the possibility of getting Iraq out of Kuwait without resorting to military force." Saudi leaders expressed their disappointment because Iraq did not appreciate the help received from Saudi Arabia, Kuwait and the United Arab Emirates, during the Iran-Iraq war. King Fahd suggested certain ideas concerning the possibility of establishing some security arrangements, which would prevent Iraq from threatening its neighbors anew, after the present crisis was solved. King Fahd said, "If such a security system does not get established, the Gulf countries will be forced to arm themselves, buy more arms, and spend more money on armament." Then he added, "We do not wish this at all, and I don't think that an arms race is either in the interest of Saudi Arabia nor the (former) Soviet Union." Primakov said, he was in full agreement with King Fahd . . .

Efforts continued, unabated, but Saddam Hussein remained adamant and obstinate to the end!!!

By the 29th of October, the House and Senate adopted a resolution which endorsed the policies of President Bush in the Gulf, but made it very clear that it did not confer an advanced approval for the President to carry on an actual fight. The chairman of the Senate Armed Services Committee, Senator Sam Nunn of Georgia indicated that the real power of the Congress at this juncture was its ability to shut off funds for a war. Attacks were repeated again by Congressman Richard Gephardt on December 29, 1990. The War Powers Act has an inherent weakness, where it fails to specify who should be consulted or exactly when. Congressmen were worried that the fighting might start in mid-November when Congress was in adjournment.

If a terrorist act were to take place similar to the tragedy of Pan Am flight 103 over Scotland in December, 1988, it would lead to action against Iraq, if such a terrorist act could be traced exactly to Iraqi designs and instigations. By mid-October, Rifa'at Al-Mahgoub, who was speaker of Egypt's parliament and the second ranking official in the country, was shot and killed in Cairo. The Iraqi leader was accused of engineering the assassination.

During the debate, Bush worried about the possibility that support for this Arabian Gulf policy was ebbing due to the possible failure of explaining his goals in very clear, convincing terms.

President Bush was praised for welding the great international alliance, but he was accused of stumbling when he was called upon to explain the strategy and the reasons for being in the Gulf. President Bush explained that if the U.S. was to get engaged in war in the Gulf, it would go in with an overwhelming superior force, instead of the gradual escalation of the forces in conflict as was done in Vietnam. A blitzkrieg attack and a quick knockout would pull the rug from under the critics. A swift victory would not allow much credible opposition. The U.S. learned an expensive lesson–to make sure that when going to war, it must have the overwhelming support of the public and the Congress as well.

Secretary of State James Baker gave a pragmatic explanation for the operations in the Gulf, he said, "If you want to sum it up in one word, it is jobs!" Meaning that the control of oil operations in the region and the increase in oil prices would mean loss of jobs to millions of Americans.

The antiwar movement that was energized, orchestrated and at times inspired from the propaganda machine of Saddam Hussein, was never like anything which had taken place during the Vietnam war. At that time, protests were massive and contagious. With the roll of years, they brought about the debacle and failure of U.S. policy in Vietnam.

On the eve of the air war, the United States had four hundred and thirty thousand soldiers in the Arabian Gulf region. The Arab and Moslem Coalition Forces exceeded a total of two hundred thousand. This great armada was opposing the forces of Saddam Hussein and were ready to take a blitzkrieg action, unless he withdrew by midnight January 15, according to United Nation's Resolution 678.

When the newly elected 102nd Congress met in Washington on the 3rd of January, few lawmakers thought that a majority could be gathered in either house of Congress that would favor resorting to the use of force in the Gulf. The Democratic leadership and Democratic forces in the House and Senate were fighting to give sanctions more time. House majority leader Richard Gephardt and Georgia Senator Sam Nunn both energized matters to attract more wavering Democrats and Republicans.

After the failure of the Geneva talks, Congress took up the question of war and peace in the Gulf. Prior to the critical vote and during the worldwide debate, the President's Gulf policy was staunchly supported by many distinguished senators. Among them, the forthright and courageous articulations of Senator John Warner of Virginia, Senators: Bob Dole of Kansas, Strom Thurmond of South Carolina, Jack Danforth and Kit Bond of Missouri, Jesse Helms of North Carolina, Richard Lugar of Indiana, Phil Gramm of Texas, Don Nickles of Oklahoma and a few more. In the House of Representatives, the Gulf policy was strongly supported and defended by key members such as Congressmen: Newt Gingrich, Minority Whip from Georgia, Bob Michel, Minority leader from Illinois and Mel Hancock from Missouri.

During the Senatorial debate, Bob Dole, the Republican leader in the Senate spoke against Senator Sam Nunn's Resolution and reflected the views of the vast majority of the American public and the Administration. The following are excerpts from his remarks on January 11, 1991.

". . . But I do believe, with all my heart, that a vote for the Nunn Resolution will turn out to be a vote for a greater chance of war, greater carnage if a war does happen, and the possibility that we will not achieve all of the important goals we have laid out.

Passing the Nunn Resolution does not avoid a war. In fact, I am convinced it makes war–Which, tragically, is likely in any case–it makes that war nearly inevitable.

And I believe with the very same conviction that a vote for the Resolution that *Senators Warner and Lieberman* have offered, on behalf of many of us from both sides of the aisle, is a vote to maximize the chance of peace; to minimize the risk that any lives must be lost, and minimize the numbers of those who do lose their lives in the event that we end up in war.

It is a vote to achieve America's goals, at the least risk to America . . .

On January 12, 1991, he said:

It is ironic that, when the Senate votes in a few moments, it will be just after eleven o'clock. Because truly, we are also at the eleventh hour in the Persian Gulf.

Time is running out–time is running out for Saddam Hussein; and time is running out for peace in the Persian Gulf.

No one wants war. Certainly those of us who have personally experienced the horror of war–myself, many of us here, President Bush, and the countless others around this nation–We do not want war.

We want peace.

But we also want Saddam Hussein out of Kuwait.

And that, Mr. President, is what is wrong with the Nunn Resolution . . .

Under the Guise of *"Giving sanctions time to work,"* it actually gives Saddam Hussein a holiday from the threat that we might use force.

The *Nunn Resolution* wipes out that credible threat, and tells Saddam Hussein: We will not use force for many months.

He will use the Nunn Resolution holiday to dig in ever more deeply inside Kuwait . . .

In the next few days, Saddam Hussein–not George Bush, but Saddam Hussein–will make the decision as to whether we have war, or whether we have peace.

Let us make sure, as he makes that decision, that he understands exactly where America stands, and exactly what America is prepared to do.

Let us make sure that he understands that America stands united, and determined to do whatever we must, to achieve our vital national goals.

I urge all Senators to vote against the Nunn Resolution . . ."

After heated debate, Congress passed a resolution giving President George Bush the authority to conduct his policy in the Gulf and use force if necessary to evict Saddam Hussein from Kuwait. On January 12, 1991, by a vote of 250 to 183, the House of Representatives approved the resolution and the Senate also approved it by a lower margin of 52 to 47 votes. Thus, the President was authorized to use military force after January 15, 1991. The resolutions supported by Congress were tantamount to a declaration of war. Both houses of Congress defeated a resolution which was sponsored by the Democratic leadership, and which called for a delay in military action until sanctions had been given more time to be more effective. The alternative resolution lost in the Senate by a margin of 53 to 46. At a press conference held by President George Bush after this vote he stated that the outcome was "a clear signal that Iraq cannot scorn the January 15 deadline." It was reported that this outcome was a clear victory for President Bush, and a stunning turn around for congressional sentiment.

The Senate opened the debate where majority leader George Mitchell led the antiwar camp. He warned that "The grave decision for war is being made prematurely." Congressman Richard Gephardt stated in the House, "The only debate here in the Congress is over whether we slowly strangle Saddam with sanctions or immediately pursue a military solution. The choice is really over tactics." The minority leader in the House for the G.O.P., Robert Michel, countered that those Congressmen seeking to rein the President's war power were creating indecision, doubt and confusion.

It was a heated battle for votes indeed and the White House did not leave a stone unturned in its campaign to gain the necessary votes so that President Bush would have a clear hand in handling the Gulf Crisis. However, the close vote in the Senate gave a confusing signal to Saddam Hussein who thought that if he stalled a bit longer, he might be able to sway the vote of a few senators and thus bring about another vote if needed to tie the hands of the President of the United States and change the course of history. Again, his assessment and miscalculation prevailed! He continued to think along the same line of his earlier assessment when he met with Ambassador April Glaspie. He did not think that the U.S. has the resolve and stomach for war. He miscalculated again!!!

All the appeals to Saddam Hussein to use reason and get out of Kuwait went unheeded. All world leaders appealed to him, leading among them, right on the eve of the war was King Fahd of Saudi Arabia, who sent the following open letter to the Iraqi leader refuting his charges and appealing to him to get out of Kuwait and make a bold decision for peace. Here is this important document:

King Fahd Answers An Open Letter From Saddam Hussein

The Custodian of the Two Holy Mosques, King Fahd Bin Abdulaziz, issued on January 15, 1991, a response to an open letter by Iraqi President Saddam Hussein carried on Baghdad radio. Here is the King's message:

"In the name of God, the Compassionate, the Merciful. According to the Holy Qoran, "There is a type of man whose sayings about this world's life may dazzle thee and he calls God to witness about what is in his heart, yet he is the most contentious of enemies. When he turns his back, his aim everywhere is to spread mischief through the earth and destroy crops and cattle. But God loveth no mischief."

President Saddam Hussein, despite the disparaging style in your message to me, it is not our custom or tradition to address anyone except through the good manners and demeanors we learned from our Islamic teachings, for, according to the Holy Qoran, "When the ignorants address them, they say 'peace.' "

Based on that noble Islamic teaching, and on a keenness to clarify the facts to those who were exposed to the contents of your message, we hereby respond to some of the fallacies and slanders contained in it.

First—*Why do you ignore the direct cause* of what happened and is currently happening in the Arab region in terms of divisions, disturbances and tragedies, which inflicted the Arab nation as a result of your treacherous aggression on an Arab Moslem neighbor at peace with itself, and which sustained you during your times of trouble by extending its support to you with all possible means?

Why did you betray your pledge, when you assured me personally and my brother President Hosni Moubarak (of Egypt) that you would not attack or inflict any harm on Kuwait? Only a few days after your pledge, *you committed the most abhorrent crime in history*, when your forces attacked Kuwait under the shadow of darkness, shedding innocent blood, violating all that is sacred and forcing an entire population to flee for the wilderness of the desert.

Why did you deploy your armies and weaponry towards the Saudi borders, when Saudi Arabia was the nation that stood strongly with you during your eight-year war (with Iran), the fruits of which you squandered in eight minutes? You squandered, as well, the blood of one million people in Iraq and Iran. After all this, you question the presence of brotherly and friendly forces on Saudi soil, while ignoring all the crimes and evil you have inflicted.

Second–I tried through our past mutual friendship and affinity to use my good offices to mediate matters wisely and diligently. I tried hard to accommodate your concerns during the dispute that erupted between you, Kuwait and the United Arab Emirates on oil production and prices. I made the necessary contacts with our brothers in Kuwait and the United Arab Emirates and we were able to accommodate your wishes then. Later, with the cooperation of President Moubarak, I was able to contain the renewed dispute regarding your borders with Kuwait. I arranged for the *meeting in Jeddah* between your delegate (Vice President) Izzat Ibrahim and the Kuwaiti delegate His Highness Sheikh Sa'ad Al-Abdullah (Al-Sabbah), the Crown Prince of Kuwait, to discuss your differences and achieve a solution satisfactory to both parties. The meeting took place, and the two delegations discussed their differences without any intervention on our part. The two delegations left the Kingdom in the hope of convening another session of talks in Baghdad.

Yet a few hours later we were surprised by the grave incidents which took place at one o'clock in the morning of Thursday, August 2, 1990, when you invaded Kuwait for the whole world to see and hear. It was this action which triggered all these tragedies and agonies. I called you immediately, trying to contain the situation, but you sent me Izzat Ibrahim, who came to say that Kuwait is part of Iraq and has been restored to it.

Third–President Moubarak took the initiative and called for an emergency *Arab League Summit in Cairo,* to provide you with a chance to change your mind through the most dignified Arab venue and the largest Arab gathering. Together with other leaders of the Arab nation, we exerted all possible efforts to solve the problem, lift the oppression and restore normalcy. We were driven by a keen desire to preserve the march of Arab solidarity and unity, so as to avail the time for the leadership to serve the important causes of the Arab nation, of which the Palestinian cause is paramount.

Apparently you had already had your implicit intentions. We were then shocked by the dangerous division in the ranks of the Arab League, when some members went astray to support oppression, sustain aggression and stand for wrong against right. This painful incidence had the worst impact on the faithful leaders and peoples of the Arab Nation. This deep wound which you inflicted upon the Arab Nation shall last for years to come.

Fourth—Through Arab, Islamic and international resolutions, *the world at large agreed* to the necessity of your immediate and unconditional withdrawal from Kuwait, and the restoration of its legitimacy, as well as the withdrawal of your forces deployed on the border of the Kingdom of Saudi Arabia. Mediators from many parts of the world exerted continued and concentrated efforts to convince you to lift the oppression befalling Kuwait, and the restoration of the status quo which prevailed prior to August 2, 1990. The initiatives and appeals of leaders seeking to achieve the withdrawal of your forces from Kuwaiti territory continued.

Nonetheless, you insisted on continuing your determination to carry on the aggression, and repeating the gross slander that Kuwait is part of Iraq. Almighty God and history are witness that Kuwait was never under the rule of Iraq and that the Al-Sabbah family has been and still is ruling Kuwait for more than 250 years. Therefore, by what right do you make those claims and absurdly try to convince people of them.

Fifth–You question in your message, in a style we find disdainful, our authority to summon to the Kingdom the Arab, Islamic and friendly forces. You may, or may not discern that our authority stemmed from our duty to *defend our soil*, our means of life and that which is sacred to us. It is our people who bestowed upon us the trust to defend their life, honor, security and possessions. God Almighty inspired us to make the right decision at the right time. As a result, *we were able to undermine your predetermined, treacherous, vicious and deceitful intentions.*

In turn, we ask you the same question. Who authorized you to involve the Iraqi army and people in a bloody and losing war with Iran? Who authorized you to end the lives of one million citizens of Iraq and Iran? Who authorized you to destroy all the gains you fought for in the blink of an eye? Finally, the most important question: who authorized you to occupy Kuwait, kill its citizens, rape its women, transgress its honor, pillage its fortunes and destroy its civilization?

Undoubtedly you have been inspired by the whims of desire, evil and greed, as well as your hegemonic designs to dominate your neighbors in the Gulf. It is those neighbors who were proud of the Iraqi army, and who pinned their hopes on it–after God–for the defense of the region against any aggression.

Sixth–According to the Holy Qoran, "Those who invent a lie against God will never prosper."

You mentioned in your message that we granted you nothing but the equivalent of 11.53 million Iraqi dinars (37.1 million dollars) as a contribution to the reconstruction of Basra and that we offered only certain aid not exceeding one million dinars (3.2 million dollars) for the reconstruction of Fao. Startled by what you said, we believe that it is high time to expose the facts and figures. Saudi Arabia has provided you–ruler of Iraq–with a total amount of 25,734,469,885.80 U.S. dollars in aid as follows:

Item	Amount in U.S. Dollars
Non-remitted assistance	5,843,287,671.23
Soft cash loans	9,246,575,342.46
Development loans	95,890,410.95
Transport & Military Supplies	3,739,184,077.66
Oil assistance	6,751,159,583.00
Industrial products for reconstruction of Basra	16,772,800.00
Amounts due Saudi Arabian Basic Industries Corp. (Sabic)	20,266,667.00
270 trucks, tractors, trailers and other vehicles	21,333,333.50
Total	25,734,469,885.80

Seventh–You claimed that there are numerous conventions and agreements signed by both of us that fall within the framework of non-aggression nor the use of force, or the interference in the internal affairs of each other. Have you complied with these conventions when you deployed your forces in an offensive posture against Saudi Arabia?

How could we trust a man who breached his promise, betrayed his pledge and occupied a peaceful country? A man who used senseless arguments and relied on marginal differences to justify his actions at a time when efforts were well underway to secure proper solutions. Where are the conventions and trust when your intentions have been unveiled and your lack of credibility has been unmasked?

Eighth–Finally, you said in your message that you are willing to consider the past a nightmare, which does not preclude the restoration of relations between our two countries in their proper frame, where there is no aggression, no hostility and no foreigners, judged by the Holy Qoran and the national brotherly and spiritual linkage between our people, based on the values of virtue, affinity and compassion. "Nothing strains the bilateral relationship but the presence of foreigners," you argue.

Our reply to you is easy and simple, represented in a verse from the Holy Qoran: "Produce your proof if ye are truthful."

The proof that we seek and the whole world demands and requires is that you *declare your immediate withdrawal* from Kuwait in word and deed, so it is restored to its normal situation under the leadership of Sheikh Jabir Al-Ahmad Al-Sabbah, the Amir of Kuwait and his government, as well as the withdrawal of all your forces, deployed against the borders of the Kingdom of Saudi Arabia. Only then, all misunderstandings between us due to your occupation of Kuwait will disappear.

In conclusion, I renew and confirm our just demand that you take the bold decision and prove to the whole world that you are up to the level of responsibility you shoulder in governing Iraq. By doing so, you will have made an eternal stand which history will record for you as you will spare bloodshed, preserve innocent lives, conserve the fortunes of the Arab and Islamic nations and fulfill all their hopes.

Finally, I invoke God's saying in the Holy Qoran: "Never will God change the condition of a people until they do it themselves." God the great–God the truth."

The Secretary General of the United Nations Javier Perez de Cuellar, on January 15, 1991, gave the following statement to the press. The next day it was also addressed to the President of the Security Council.*

Statement by the Secretary-General to the Press on 15 January 1991

"As January 15 advances, and the world stands poised between peace and war, I most sincerely appeal to President Saddam Hussein to turn the course of events away from catastrophe and towards a new era of justice and harmony based on the principles of the Charter of the United Nations.

All our efforts in this direction will fail unless Iraq can signify its readiness to comply with the relevant resolutions of the Security Council, beginning with Resolution 660 (1990).

If this commitment is made, and clear and substantial steps taken to implement these resolutions, a just peace, with all its benefits, will follow. I therefore urge President Saddam Hussein to commence, without delay, the total withdrawal of Iraqi forces from Kuwait.

Once this process is well under way, I wish to assure him, on the basis of understandings that I have received from Governments at the highest level, that neither Iraq nor its forces will be attacked by those arrayed in the international coalition against his country.

Further, with the commencement of withdrawal, as Secretary General of the United Nations, I would, with the consent of the parties concerned, and the agreement of the Security Council, be prepared immediately to deploy United Nations observers and, if necessary, United Nations forces to certify the withdrawal and to ensure that hostilities do not erupt on the ground.

---

* Source: The United Nations, New York, U.S.A.

In addition, with compliance of the resolutions, I would urge the Security Council to review its decisions imposing sanctions against Iraq. I would also encourage a process whereby foreign forces deployed in the area would be phased out.

Peace in the region requires that all its problems be resolved justly and equitably, in accordance with the principles of the Charter of the United Nations.

I have every assurance, once again from the highest levels of government, that with the resolution of the present crisis, every effort will be made to address, in a comprehensive manner, the Arab-Israeli conflict, including the *Palestinian* question. I pledge my every effort to this end.

As I stated to the Council last night, all of us are aware of the extreme gravity of the decisions to be made in the period ahead. No one and no nation can—except with a heavy heart—resort to the other "necessary means" implied by Resolution 678 (1990), knowing in advance that tragic and unpredictable consequences can follow.

I trust, in the circumstances, that wisdom and statesmanship will prevail in all quarters in order to move decisively away from conflict. In appealing to President Saddam Hussein today, I wish him to know that I will readily devote my every capacity to working with him, and with all others concerned, to this end.

In the tenth and final year of my tenure as Secretary General of the United Nations, no cause would give me greater satisfaction than to set the Middle East as a whole on the road to just and lasting peace. And no disappointment would be greater and more tragic than to find the nations of the world engaging in a conflict that none of their peoples want."

Saddam Hussein remained true to his name: stubborn and short-sighted to the end. Now, the mighty force of Allied Coalition was ready to move and pulverize his communications, command posts, major airports, and many more targets inside Iraq.

If Saddam Hussein, during all these appeals which stretched from the 2nd of August 1990, until January 15, 1991, would have responded to the voices of moderation and peace, and had withdrawn from Kuwait, he would have saved tens of thousands of Iraqi lives. He would also have saved his military might, which would have been intact but would have continued to be a threat to his neighbors and to world peace. In a number of interviews, concerned statesmen said on many occasions that if the Iraqi leader decided to turn tail and get out of Kuwait, he would get out as a victor! Because, most likely, in a very short time

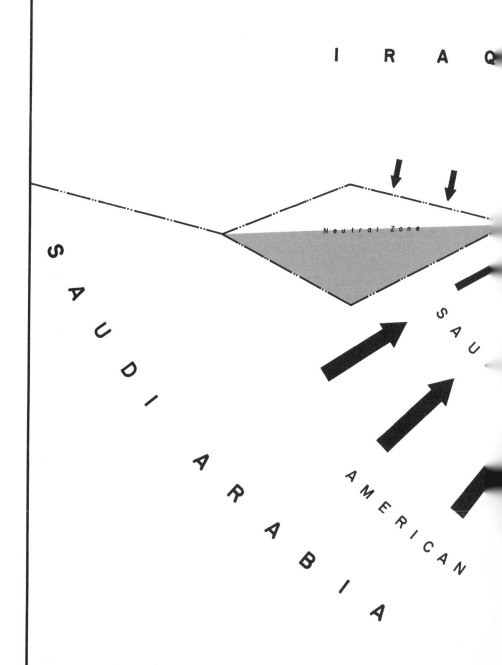

DEPLOYMENT OF COALITION FORCES
BETWEEN AUGUST 7, 1990 AND JANUARY 17, 1991

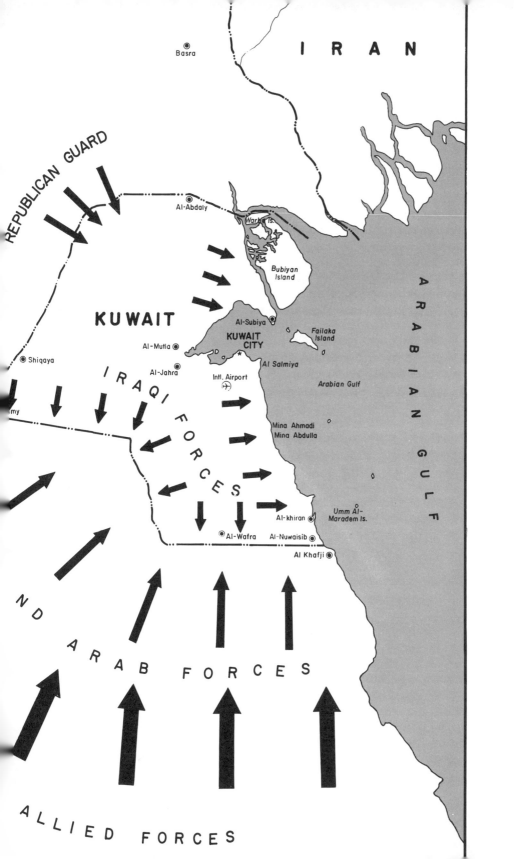

he would have used his threatening tactics again to extract many concessions from Kuwait and neighboring countries in the Gulf. Furthermore, he would have waited for the opportune time when the world was busy with another crisis or when America was involved in a heated election campaign, then he would have moved in a blitzkrieg fashion, not only against Kuwait but against the Eastern Region of Saudi Arabia and most of the Arabian Gulf as well. In a way, people of vision and decision were not very excited about the idea that Saddam Hussein might come to his senses and get out of Kuwait without a fight. His military machine was a serious threat to world peace and must be clearly pulverized. So, by not budging one inch, he did not prove to be the intelligent man that Senator Howard Metzenbaum of Ohio declared him to be on April 12, 1990. In fact, he proved to be just himself, the tyrant, the ruthless dictator who had no regard for human life—a man who isolated himself from the real world. Now, he had to face not only the might of America, but the might of the powerful nations in the Western world, the Arab world and the curse of the Moslem world and people of conscience, decency and justice everywhere!

The hour of reckoning is near! Aggression will not be rewarded!

Chapter 7

The Air War Begins

"The liberation of Kuwait had begun" on January 16, 1991, around 6:40 P.M. U.S. Eastern Standard Time (EST). This corresponded to January 17, 1991, around 2:40 A.M. local Iraqi time. The U.N. Security Council deadline had already passed at midnight of January 15. After exhausting all efforts to avoid war, President George Bush of the United States of America did not pull the trigger until he received the approval of King Fahd of Saudi Arabia, especially since the Kingdom was the host country for nearly half a million American soldiers and about a quarter of a million men from other Coalition Forces. Armed with a strong support from Riyadh and other Allies, the United States of America, with a clear mandate from the United Nations, began massive air strikes against Iraqi targets. In this endeavor it was supported by the Royal Saudi Air Force, the British Air Force and others, who joined shortly after the initial blitz.

Initial Air Attacks

From the Arabian Gulf, Tomahawk Cruise Missiles led the attack on major Iraqi targets, especially, in Baghdad and vicinity. They brought instant devastation to key targets with pinpoint accuracy. Showering Baghdad with these deadly weapons triggered the vast arsenal of defenses which dotted the city of four million inhabitants. Iraqi antiaircraft batteries and Sam Missiles were unleashed with a vengeance. The Tomahawk Cruise Missiles were fired for a dual purpose: first to cause massive destruction with pinpoint accuracy and equally important to trigger the Iraqi radar so that it would light up and reveal its location, thus enabling the Allies to identify and destroy it before it could cause massive damage to Allied Forces. Destroying the radar system was a top priority. The Cruise Missiles did their job of revealing and destroying the radar sites. Stealth bombers came into play to finish the job of destroying much of the Iraqi radar system. A vast armada of sophisticated aircraft were preceded by Cruise Missiles and about two dozen Stealth fighters, which pounded the communication centers in Iraq with great effectiveness because of their invisibility to enemy radar. Iraqi antiaircraft guns proved to be totally ineffective against the *Stealth bomber.* Other jets were loaded with radio equipment for the sole purpose of misleading and neutralizing the radar of the enemy. As an example, a formation of twelve F-16s striking enemy targets would be guarded by nearly eight electronic counter-measure aircraft and about four escort jet fighters. High powered transmitters were used for jamming. Airplanes of the type EF-11 carried ten such pieces of sophisticated equipment. These could jam radar installations as far away as a hundred miles from their targets. Unleashing Desert Storm brought with it over one hundred such planes to do the superb job of silencing Iraqi radar and air defenses.

The wave of attacking planes over Baghdad was witnessed throughout the world on prime time T.V. Foreign reporters were at the Al-Rashid Hotel on the West bank of the Tigris River in Baghdad when the first wave of attacking planes came and antiaircraft guns lit up the sky. Reporters who were broadcasting to their television networks around the world were instantaneously reporting the attack minute by minute. Vivid flashes in the sky were beamed to the world audience. After nearly ten minutes of attack, a lull and deathly quiet prevailed, but not for long. Shortly thereafter, lights in the city were off, since power plants were hit, along with a number of sensitive targets including command and communication centers. Another wave of attacking planes came in the darkness of a clear and moonless night. These planes were at very high altitudes. They hit their targets from heights in excess of 20,000 feet (6,100 meters).

By now the Stealth F-117 bombers had done their job on the radar system, and thus paralyzed the Iraqi air defenses. Bombs were unleashed from the sky, away from the reach of Iraqi artillery and safe from other sophisticated missile systems. Because of the paralysis of their radar guidance, Smart bombs were able to hit their targets with deadly accuracy. The attack on Baghdad and other key targets throughout Iraq and Kuwait was a great success. It was miraculous that no losses were suffered by the Allied Forces, especially around Baghdad. In fact, the success of this massive air bombardment against Iraqi targets is unparalleled in the annals of air warfare. Top priority targets were command and control centers, radar systems, presidential headquarters, Ministry of Defense, headquarters of the Ba'ath Party, airfields throughout the country, chemical, biological and nuclear facilities, Scud missiles–stationary and mobile sites, power plants, reinforced airplane bunkers and some oil facilities (in order to deprive the Iraqi ruler and his army from having the necessary fuel to energize his war machine). The Allies knocked out Baghdad's electrical grid plunging the city into darkness.

All the bluster and threats of Saddam Hussein vanished and proved to be hollow in very short moments indeed! The relentless air bombardment continued unabated. The Tomahawk Cruise Missiles proved their worth with tremendous accuracy. They were to continue pouring on key targets in Baghdad and elsewhere in Iraq. The Arabian Gulf was saturated with great American ships of war, supported by the Coalition Forces and the Navies of Britain and France especially, who continued their punch and devastating attacks on Iraqi targets.

Since Dhahran was within range of Iraqi Scud missiles, air warning sirens were whaling there and later on in Riyadh. People were advised to put their gas masks on, out of fear that Saddam Hussein might shower the two cities with his poison gas. His Scud missile, the SS-1 Scud, has a 186 mile-range and a 5 Mach speed, meaning five times the speed of sound. Since he had a very modern Soviet bomber known as the SU-24, he had the capability of delivering chemical weapons with this plane, if he was to succeed in evading Allied defenses.

In this air attack, U.S. forces were supported by the Saudi Royal Air Force, the Kuwaiti Air Force, as well as the British and French Air Forces.

The famous Tomahawk Cruise Missiles were launched from warships in the Arabian Gulf and also from the Red Sea, traveling several hundred miles, hitting their targets with pinpoint accuracy and destroying command centers and Scud missile launchers.

Waves of attacking bombers took off from the Arabian Gulf, the Red Sea, the Dhahran Air Base, the Riyadh Air Base, and the Hafr Al-Batin Military City. The Allied Central Command sent into the air the five U.S. AWACS and the five Saudi AWACS which monitored the air activity in the theater of war. This aerial blitz was superbly coordinated. Despite the massive number of airplanes in combat and the extensive number of sorties, *the first day went without a hitch and without losses to Allied Aircraft.*

F-14 fighters escorted Intruders F-6E and F/A-18s which went on bombing missions deep into Iraq. While F-4G Wild Weasels destroyed the radar system for SAM missiles, and the EF-111 airplanes jammed radar, the F-111 bombers went into action. K-10 tankers and KC-135s stood ready for mid-air refueling. The F-4G Escort planes accompanied the Tornado GR-1s which were actively attacking air fields and destroying their radar systems. The Apache helicopters and the A-10 tank busters carried their mission into Kuwaiti targets. All these massive activities were well coordinated, with great precision and great success.

As a precautionary measure and prior to the execution of the air attack, civilians were evacuated from the front line Saudi city of Khafji on the Kuwait border. These people were transferred to other locations outside the artillery range of the Iraqi forces who retaliated and bombed the Khafji area with heavy artillery. Some fires erupted, but were quickly extinguished. The artilleries which attacked the town were promptly silenced.

After a brief announcement at 7:00 P.M., by the Press Secretary of the White House which declared "the Liberation of Kuwait has begun", the President of the United States, George Bush issued a statement from the Oval office of the White House at 9:00 P.M. EST, on January 16, 1991. The following is the Presidential statement:

"Just two hours ago, Allied Air Forces began an attack on military targets in Iraq and Kuwait. These attacks continue as I speak. Ground forces are not engaged.

This conflict started August 2nd when the dictator of Iraq invaded a small and helpless neighbor. Kuwait—a member of the Arab League and a member of the United Nations—was crushed; its people brutalized. Five months ago, Saddam Hussein started this cruel war against Kuwait. Tonight, the battle has been joined.

This military action, taken in accord with United Nations resolutions—and with the consent of the United States Congress—follows months of constant and virtually endless diplomatic activity on the part of the United Nations, the United States and many, many other countries. Arab leaders sought what became known as an Arab solution—only to conclude that Saddam Hussein was unwilling to leave Kuwait. Others traveled to Baghdad in a variety of efforts to restore peace and justice. Our Secretary of State, James Baker, held an historic meeting in Geneva—only to be totally rebuffed. This past weekend, in a last ditch effort, the Secretary General of the United Nations went to the Middle East, with peace in his heart—his second such mission. And he came back from Baghdad with no progress at all in getting Saddam Hussein to withdraw from Kuwait.

Now the 28 countries with forces in the Gulf area, have exhausted all reasonable efforts to reach a peaceful resolution, have no choice but to drive Saddam from Kuwait by force. We will not fail.

As I report to you, air attacks are underway against military targets in Iraq. We are determined to knock out Saddam Hussein's nuclear bomb potential. We will also destroy his chemical weapons facilities. Much of Saddam's artillery and tanks will be destroyed. Our operations are designed to best protect the lives of all the coalition forces by targeting Saddam's vast military arsenal. Initial reports from General Schwarzkopf are that our operations are proceeding according to plan.

Our objectives are clear. Saddam Hussein's forces will leave Kuwait. The legitimate government of Kuwait will be restored to its rightful place and Kuwait will once again be free. Iraq will eventually comply with all relevant United Nations resolutions. And then, when peace is restored, it is our hope that Iraq will live as a peaceful and cooperative member of the family of nations, thus, enhancing the security and stability of the Gulf.

Some may ask, why act now? Why not wait? The answer is clear: The world could wait no longer. Sanctions, though having some effect, showed no signs of accomplishing their objective. Sanctions were tried for well over five months, and we and our allies concluded that sanctions alone would not force Saddam from Kuwait.

While the world waited, Saddam Hussein systematically raped, pillaged and plundered a tiny nation, no threat to his own. He subjected the people of Kuwait to unspeakable atrocities–and among those maimed and murdered innocent children.

While the world waited, Saddam sought to add to the chemical weapons arsenal. He now possesses an infinitely more dangerous weapon of mass destruction–a nuclear weapon.

And while the world waited, while the world talked peace and withdrawal, Saddam Hussein dug in and moved massive forces into Kuwait.

While the world waited, while Saddam stalled, more damage was being done to the fragile economies of the Third World, the emerging democracies of Eastern Europe, to the entire world including our own economy.

The United States, together with the United Nations, exhausted every means at our disposal to bring this crisis to a peaceful end. However, Saddam clearly felt that by stalling and threatening and defying the United Nations he could weaken the forces arrayed against him.

While the world waited, Saddam Hussein met every overture of peace with open contempt. While the world prayed for peace, Saddam prepared for war.

I had hoped that when the United States Congress, in historic debate, took its resolute action, Saddam would realize he could not prevail and would move out of Kuwait in accord with the United Nation Resolutions. He did not do that. Instead, he remained intransigent, certain that time was on his side.

Saddam was warned over and over again to comply with the will of the United Nations. Leave Kuwait or be driven out. Saddam has arrogantly rejected all warnings. Instead he tried to make this a dispute between Iraq and the United States of America.

Well, he failed. Tonight, 28 nations–countries from five continents: Europe and Asia, Africa and the Arab League–have forces in the Gulf area standing shoulder to shoulder against Saddam Hussein. These countries had hoped the use of force could be avoided. Regrettably, we now believe that only force will make him leave.

Prior to ordering our forces into battle, I instructed our military commanders to take every necessary step to prevail as quickly as possible and with the greatest degree of protection possible for American and Allied servicemen and women. I've told the American people before, that this will not be another Vietnam. And I repeat this here tonight. Our troops will have the best possible support in the entire world, and they will not be asked to fight with one hand tied behind their back.

I'm hopeful that this fighting will not go on for long, and that casualties will be held to an absolute minimum.

This is an historic moment. We have, in this past year made great progress in ending the long era of conflict and Cold War. We have before us the opportunity to forge, for ourselves and for future generations, a new world order—a world where the rule of law, not the law of the jungle, governs the conduct of nations.

When we are successful, and we will be, we have a real chance at this *new world order*—an order in which a credible United Nations can use its peacekeeping role to fulfill the promise and vision of the U.N.'s founders.

We have no argument with the people of Iraq—indeed, for the innocents caught in this conflict, I pray for their safety.

Our goal is not the conquest of Iraq—it is the liberation of Kuwait. It is my hope that somehow the Iraqi people can, even now, convince their dictator that he must lay down his arms, leave Kuwait, and let Iraq itself rejoin the family of peace-loving nations.

Thomas Paine wrote many years ago: "These are the times that try men's souls." Those well-known words are so very true today. But even as planes of the multinational forces attack Iraq, I prefer to think of peace, not war. I am convinced not only that we will prevail, but that out of the horror of combat will come the recognition that no nation can stand against a world united. No nation will be permitted to brutally assault its neighbor.

No president can easily commit our sons and daughters to war. They are the nation's finest. Ours is an all volunteer force—magnificently trained, highly motivated. The troops know why they're there. And listen to what they say, for they've said it better than any president or prime minister ever could.

Listen to "Hollywood" Huddleston, Marine Lance Corporal. He says, "Let's free these people so we can go home and be free again." He's right. The terrible crimes and tortures committed by Saddam's henchmen against the innocent people of Kuwait are an affront to mankind and a challenge to the freedom of all.

Listen to one of our great officers out there, Marine Lieutenant General Walter Boomer. He said, "There are things worth fighting for. A world in which brutality and lawlessness are allowed to go unchecked isn't the kind of world we're going to want to live in."

Listen to Master Sergeant J. P. Kendall of the 82nd Airborne: "We're here for more than just the price of a gallon of gas. What we're doing is going to chart the future of the world for the next hundred years. It's better to deal with this guy now than five years from now."

And finally, we should all sit up and listen to Jackie Jones, an Army Lieutenant, when she says, "If we let him get away with this, who knows what's going to be next?"

I have called upon "Hollywood" and Walter and J. P. and Jackie and all their courageous comrades in arms to do what must be done. Tonight, America and the world are deeply grateful to them and to their families. And let me say to everyone listening or watching tonight: when the troops we've sent in finish their work, I am determined to bring them home as soon as possible.

Tonight, as our forces fight, they and their families are in our prayers. May God bless each and every one of them, and the Coalition Forces at our side in the Gulf–and may He continue to bless our nation, the United States of America."

Shortly after the presidential statement, a news conference was held by U.S. Secretary of Defense Dick Cheney and General Colin Powell, Chairman of the Joint Chiefs of Staff. The Secretary of Defense stated that he signed the execute order on the afternoon of January 15, 1991 for undertaking such an operation. However such signature was subject to certain conditions, leading among them was meeting the terms of the resolution passed last Saturday by the Congress of the United States of America. Equally important, the military operation according to Cheney, "Was not to take place if there had been any last minute diplomatic breakthroughs. . . The operation underway, taking place in the pre-dawn darkness of the Persian Gulf, involves Allied Air Forces of four nations: the United States, the United Kingdom, Saudi Arabia and Kuwait.

As they undertake their missions, they do so after months of careful planning. At the direction of the President, great care has been taken to focus on military targets, to minimize U.S. casualties and to do everything possible to avoid injury to civilians in Iraq and Kuwait.

The targets being struck tonight are located throughout Iraq and Kuwait. Our focus is on the destruction of Saddam Hussein's offensive military capabilities—the very capabilities that he used to seize control of Kuwait and that make him a continuing threat to the nations of the Middle East. . . Our goal, the same one we have maintained throughout Operation Desert Shield, is to liberate Kuwait and to enforce the Resolutions of the U.N. Security Council. . .

I believe I can speak for all of us at the Pentagon tonight when I say that we had hoped to settle this matter peacefully. This has clearly been an agonizing decision for the President and the Congress of the United States, and we've reached the point of committing our forces to battle very reluctantly, only after the most careful consideration. But no one should doubt our ability and our resolve to carry out our mission and to achieve our objectives.

I have great confidence in the professionalism, the dedication and the determination of the men and women of our Armed Forces. They are, without question, the finest young sailors, soldiers, airmen, and marines this nation has ever sent in harm's way."

In the same press conference, General Colin Powell stated, "The air part of the campaign will continue until the whole campaign is completed. It does not end." This strong statement put an end to any speculation that the air campaign was to send a signal to Saddam Hussein about the enormity and seriousness of the attack, so he would have second thoughts and time to decide to pull out of Kuwait. The attacks were to continue until the backbone of his army was broken and his means of producing weapons of mass destruction were destroyed. General Powell further stated that hundreds of U.S. and Coalition strikes were directed against missiles and antiaircraft targets in Iraq and Kuwait with a distinct purpose to "destroy Saddam Hussein's offensive military capabilities." According to the Secretary of Defense, reports from the front indicated that, "initial attacks appear to have gone very, very well."

Les Aspin, Chairman of the House Armed Services Committee, said, "I think the plan is going pretty much the way it was laid out in our hearings. The object is to take Kuwait. It is being done with phases, beginning with the air war, particularly the air war against the strategic targets and ultimately if necessary we go in with the ground forces. I think it sounds pretty much the way we expected it."

Operation Desert Storm was initiated with a clear mandate from the United Nations Security Council, which issued twelve resolutions supporting the Coalition Forces. It was also supported by Resolutions from both houses of the United States Congress. The clear go-ahead signal came from the Kingdom of Saudi Arabia which was very pivotal in this air war of Desert Storm. Other major Coalition Forces were all in accord and fully behind such an operation.

With the unleashing of the air war, King Fahd of Saudi Arabia described the massive military operations against the aggressors as, *"the sword and voice of truth."* During an emergency meeting of the Council of Ministers held in Riyadh, Saudi Arabia on January 17, 1991, King Fahd extended his warm greetings to all the Coalition Forces and bid them good wishes for a decisive victory. He then stated, "the need has arisen for putting matters in their right course and for the implementation of the United Nations Security Council Resolutions concerning the liberation of Kuwait. We pray to Almighty God to grant victory to our soldiers. . . I repeatedly appealed to President Saddam Hussein to return to a righteous path in order to save the blood and souls of innocents, but he displayed arrogance. . . He turned a deaf ear to all calls of peace and justice."

Commanders of the Coalition Forces, be it from the U.S., Saudi Arabia, France, England and Egypt along with others all were very capable men and got along admirably well. The course of the war moved on with precision, wholehearted support and a unified approach. This happened in unison and with full cooperation of the various generals. In fact, this was one of the unique secrets of success of the war against the aggressor.

In regard to the cooperation between General Schwarzkopf and the Commander of the Saudi forces, Lt. General Khaled Bin Sultan said, "We meet all the time. Many people had doubts before, and that was in the first few months, but I think what happened until now proved that we are not only working together, but we are working and making decisions as one person." This reflected the great degree of cooperation and understanding among the commanders of the forces.

High tech played a very important and major role in the initial air attacks, especially due to the superb ability for jamming the electronics on the Iraqi side. The United States and the major Coalition Forces developed already advanced electronic jamming equipment which was aimed against the former Soviet Union and had been researched and developed for many years. This came into good use against Iraqi electronic systems which are no match or nowhere as sophisticated as those of the former USSR. Thus, the U.S. ability in jamming Iraqi communications was very impressive, indeed. Due to this and other effective results from the Cruise Missiles, one concludes that the Iraqi response was minimal to non-existent. Although some analysts indicated that the air attack came as a surprise to the Iraqis, it is very hard to believe that such is the case. This is the first time in the history of warfare where the lines have been distinctly drawn and the dates were almost specific as to the initiation of war activities. In fact, the Iraqis were anticipating this and they had massive air defenses which were absolutely no match for the high tech performance of the Allies' military equipment. High technology was a key player in Desert Storm.

High Tech in Desert Storm

Sophisticated technology played an important role in the liberation of Kuwait. The air war made extensive use of high technology equipment and other great advances in military research and development. The list is endless, but some highlights of high tech practices and achievements will be briefly described here.

Intelligence

United States satellites played a key role in the miraculous success of Operation Desert Storm from its very beginning to the very end. According to General D. J. Kutyna, United States Air Force (USAF), Commander in Chief of U.S. Space Command, in an article he wrote in Defense magazine, issue of July/August, 1991, he said, "While we did not war in space, Desert Storm was the first campaign-level combat operation in which space was solidly integrated into combat operations and was vital to the degree of success achieved in the conflict. Communications, navigation, environmental monitoring and space-base surveillance systems were on scene and available to our theater forces from the moment the crisis began, until the last shot was fired." American satellites gave pinpoint accuracy for every Iraqi troop movement and were able to pick up electronic signals from enemy units across the theater of war operations. These satellites proved their worth during Desert Storm and were very instrumental in giving the Allies a decisive edge. With Iraqi command and control centers in total ruin and being deprived of satellite intelligence, the aggressors were essentially moving in the dark. For this reason among others, their air space was under the dominance and total control of the Coalition Air Forces, who were able to move freely and at will.

Military satellite communication systems proved to be very effective for the command and control of Coalition Forces. Without them, it would have been impossible to achieve the great coordination and organization that were inherent in the Allied Forces operations. Satellites, way up in space, provided photographic details of key enemy maneuvers and targets. About six keyhole U.S. satellites with latest photo technology were providing these pictures from a distance, varying between 350 to 600 miles in space. Other critical functions, provided by these valuable state-of-the-art satellites, include military navigation. Nearly a dozen such U.S. satellites were orbiting above the earth. They are Navstar satellites which broadcast navigational data to soldiers in combat and others who make optimum use of such information. They orbit above the earth's atmosphere about 12,000 miles high in space. The U.S. military and Allied Forces were provided with a variety of critically important command and control data along with communications, navigation, environmental and other scientific information. As an example, a person with a portable receiver can make excellent use of the *Global Positioning System* (GPS). He can instantly determine his location, wherever he may be on the globe. He could calculate his longitude and latitude within 35 feet. Such information in a desert environment becomes very critical, since a flat and barren desert does not lend itself to landmarks which could help in defining a position. Thus, the Global Positioning System was a great innovation that was well used in Operation Desert Storm. Since the Iraqis did not have such capabilities and satellite systems which could guide their Scud ballistic missiles, they were essentially operating in the dark, and their Scud missiles were terror weapons with no strategic value. They were highly inaccurate, incapable of causing the military damage desired by Saddam Hussein. If he had that navigational capability, his Scud missiles would have caused extensive damage in the Eastern Region of Saudi Arabia, Riyadh, Tel Aviv, Haifa and other cities of his choice. Other satellites in space provided communication and vital weather information.

According to a U.S. General, "Effective command and control of U.S. and Coalition Forces simply would have been impossible without military satellite communication systems. Over 90% of the communications to and from the area of operations were carried over satellite systems, and thousands of satellite communications receivers were used in the theater, down to unit level."

The featureless desert environment made the Global Position System (GPS) a very popular one among the troops of Desert Storm and Desert Shield as well. It became "the most popular new piece of equipment in the desert." Iraq did not have the military hardware equipped with smart weapons which make use of the GPS in their guidance systems. So, these were doubly efficient in helping to destroy enemy targets.

The LAND SAT imaging satellites were used to gather mapping information and related data for use in Desert Shield and Desert Storm operations. The Commerce Department loaned these satellites for use by the Department of Defense during the Gulf Crisis. High quality maps were prepared from LAND SAT. These maps were made available to the troops as soon as they were deployed to Saudi Arabia. During Desert Shield the Coalition Forces received thousands of high quality maps and charts which were based on imagery from LAND SAT. Although this was sponsored by the Department of Commerce, its military usefulness proved itself very clearly during the Gulf Crisis and Gulf War. The lack of air surveillance capability of the Iraqis dealt a mortal blow to their Republican Guard and their forces in the Kuwait Theater of Operations, when the ground war began.

A radar reconnaissance satellite known as Lacross operated above the earth at a distance of 460 miles and had a great capacity for seeing enemy installations even at night and during bad cloudy weather as well. It could see up to a range of 1,200 miles distance.

Eavesdropping on enemy communications was essential. A number of satellites with sophisticated electronic equipment operated from 22,300 miles above the Equator. These included the giant magnum and sent intelligence signals from a geosynchronous orbit.

This satellite far up in space scanned the entire Arabian Gulf area, twenty-four hours a day from its stationary position. This gave credible and critical warnings about missile firings, anywhere in the region. It has a telescope of the infared type which detects heat from the exhaust of any missiles fired in the region. Such detection is accomplished within seconds of any such firings, anywhere in the theater of operations.

The Patriot Missile

It performed admirably during the Gulf War. This had been a great success story and saved thousands of lives, especially of innocent citizens. It was originally an antiaircraft weapon, but it was modified and became a ballistic missile interceptor, after some computer softwares were modified to improve and expand its capabilities. The Patriot Missile is about seventeen feet long; it is very effective against missiles or any threatening aircraft. When launched from the ground, the Patriot could reach a speed of approximately three times the speed of sound. Its efficiency is superb and its performance during the Gulf War was a great one, indeed! A radar station searches the space above for possible targets and when a Scud missile is launched it is quickly detected. Once a Scud attack is detected, either an operator in the Control Station or a computer launches the Patriot Missile against the incoming Scud. Once the Patriot is launched, it has a radar receiver in the nose cone, which in coordination with information received from the ground-based radar, will guide the Control Station to the path of the Patriot Missile. Once the Patriot reaches the Scud missile, and it explodes either on the target or in proximity, the Scud falls harmlessly to the ground. A radar beam illuminates the oncoming Scud or other targets. The antenna of the Patriot Missile picks up the beam reflections and data is relayed to the ground where the information is transmitted to the guidance system of the Patriot. A Patriot battery has eight launchers; each one has four missiles. The total cost of the system is 123 million dollars.

The Tomahawk Cruise Missile

These missiles are long range and can be launched from warships and submarines. They have a 1,500 mile range and can fly under radar. Their cost is about one million dollars apiece. They carry a one thousand pound warhead and hit their targets with great accuracy, within a few feet. The Tomahawk is a 20 feet long, air-to-ground cruise missile. Its path is planned way in advance prior to its use. Satellites give detailed maps and photographs of selected areas along its path. The Tomahawk computers are preprogrammed with a definite flight plan. The radar system compares landmarks with the prerecorded maps in order to guide the missiles to their targets. The missile adjusts its path as it flies over territory and compares the ground with the computerized information already stored in its computers. Based on the comparison of what it sees and what is stored, the Tomahawk Cruise Missile adjusts its path and homes in on its target. The route followed by the Tomahawk Cruise Missiles is not a direct path between two points, but rather a tortuous path at times, in order to avoid enemy radar. Its success during the Gulf War was fabulous. It destroyed the intended targets with very impressive accuracy. It can be programmed to fly at very low altitudes, as low as 100 feet above ground. Of the first 52 Tomahawk Cruise Missiles fired in the initial hours of the air war, fully 51 of them were absolutely on target.

The Stealth Fighter Bomber

The F-117A Stealth Fighter is a radar evading tactical fighter which slips behind enemy lines and reaches its targets unseen. The outside surface of this plane is coated with radar-absorbent material. The engines of this fighter bomber are positioned in such a way as to minimize their infrared image on any detectors. It has great maneuverability and it is very highly accurate when delivering its payload on enemy targets. This is the first airplane in the world which is invisible to enemy radar. It is bat-like in shape, entirely constructed of flat surfaces. It is a very valuable aircraft, especially in night time operations. The Stealth does not have electronic countermeasures on board and this is purposely done to insure that it would be invisible to radar. In any event, it looks like a bird or a baseball on a radar screen. This state-of-the-art fighter plane was the first to follow the Tomahawk Cruise Missiles and unleash its deadly accurate bombs on Iraqi targets during the beginning of the air war. This Lockheed fighter bomber has composite skin panels on its wings which reflect the oncoming radar signals in multiple directions. The signals which are not reflected are then absorbed by the special coating on the surface of this plane. This characteristic makes the Stealth F-117A nearly invisible to "enemy radar." The plane delivers mainly laser guided smart bombs and is capable of causing severe damage to enemy ground targets. This twin engine, single-seat plane was, along with the Tomahawk Missiles the most effective in hitting Iraqi targets. In fact, in the first hours of the battle, 27 of these planes rained destruction on the Command and Control Centers in Iraq. They destroyed several fixed Scud missile sites.

The cost of each Stealth bomber is over 100 million dollars.

Jammers in Electronic Warfare

The most advanced Electronic Counter Measure (ECMs) systems are used on several of the U.S. planes.

While electronic jamming is not new, since it has been widely used by the British and American forces in World War II in blanketing German radar screens, however the new versions are very advanced and sophisticated. Top secret electronic equipment was effectively used against the Iraqi defenses causing paralysis, confusion and deception.

The radars, being the heart of modern weapons, are the main target of jamming. In order to counter enemy radar, a jet fighter would eject a cloud of shaff (small strips of aluminum). To enemy radar, these would look like another aircraft. If the cloud of shaff is a large one, it will act as an electronic curtain which protects the Allied Forces aircraft from enemy attack. The jet fighter may eject a flare or a decoy missile to confuse the enemy radar and give them the false impression of having another target or two in the air, rather than the original target. Also in a game of radar deception, the jammers will record radar pulses coming from the enemy, then will transmit back after a fraction of a second delay, thus creating the impression that another target which is more distant is in the air.

The jammers also play a very important role in deflecting incoming radar-guided missiles. As the enemy missile homes in, the radar continuously scans back and forth, always zeroing in on the target. When an echo comes back from one side, the guidance system of the missile will send instruction so its steering fins will turn to the right if the signal is coming from the right. In order to prevent a missile from being confused by echos from very distant objects, the radar includes "a range gate" which is a circuit which dismisses echos that come after the main one emanating from the target. This circuitry can be fooled by sending a strong false echo a very short time, just a fraction of a second before the real echo makes its journey back to the radar. This fools the radar system into thinking that the target is moving closer. The latest sophisticated radars have counter-measures which will show the distinction between false and real echos. However, the confusion caused from jamming or from aluminum shaff will throw the missiles coming from the enemy off course.

Radio gear, employed for jamming, is used extensively to delete enemy ground to ground communications as well as ground to air communications. This kind of jamming will sever communications between the commanders in the field and their troops, and thus cause apprehension and a state of confusion among enemy forces. Jamming communication signals between ground stations and the enemy air force, essentially paralyzes their missions and causes confusion and disarray among their air forces as well.

Electronic wizardry was extensively used during Operation Desert Storm. Allied Aircraft containing such electronic devices were among the very first to fly over Iraq and Kuwait in order to paralyze their air defenses and jam their radars, thus crippling the enemy's ability to perform in the air battle, and rapidly curtailing its capacity for detecting the enormous number of attacking planes. Among the ECM aircraft operating in the air were the Navy's EA-6B Prowler (a 32 million dollar plane), the Air Force's F-4G Wild Weasel and several others.

Smart Bombs

High precision bombing was achieved by these Smart Bombs which were carried on most Allied fighter bombers, including the B-52s. These high tech bombs allowed attacking aircraft to stay at very high safe altitudes, away from the range of enemy antiaircraft weapons and SAM Missiles. These Smart bombs are guided by laser beams or television cameras, or infrared rays. Images relayed from the unleashed bomb will allow the pilot to keep it on course by a simple steering mechanism. These bombs hit their targets with pinpoint accuracy, moving toward the hair cross and hitting their target's bullseye.

Night Vision Capabilities

These devices amplify light many times over. For example, they can amplify starlight as much as 25,000 times more than actually received by the naked eye. The goggles used for night vision allow soldiers to see when it is pitch dark. Pilots of jet fighters, among them the F-15-E Eagle which was used in the initial strikes against targets in Iraq and Kuwait, used these night vision goggles extensively. On very dark nights, the pilots were able to see objects as far as seven miles away. A night vision capability outfitted on a jet fighter bomber cost in the neighborhood of two hundred thousand dollars. The night vision goggles cost between four to five thousand dollars. Desert Shield training exercises were done mostly at night. Soldiers were able to shoot by looking through infrared goggles, which were far superior to anything used anywhere else. Combat planes were outfitted with night vision devices, such as the Forward-Looking Infrared (FLIR) equipment.

This night vision capability helped enormously in carrying the lightning air attack on Iraq and Kuwait during the first hours of the air battle, and certainly helped extensively throughout the entire Gulf War. Many of the critical battles, be it during the air war or the ground war, were carried on at night. Iraqi capabilities for fighting at night were abysmal. Any reinforcement or resupply of Iraqi forces at night, where they thought they were undetected and unseen by the Coalition Forces, were not to succeed simply because night vision and other high tech equipment helped in detecting them and thus rendering them ineffective or obliterating them altogether.

Fuel-Air Explosives

Fuel is sprayed in a very fine mist, either from a Tomahawk Cruise Missile or a bomb, creating a blanket which covers several square feet of area and when detonated, creates a massive explosion destroying everything in the area it has covered. Fuel-air explosions (FAE) have been generated in such enormity as to correspond to a small nuclear weapon's explosion. Huge blasts of FAE could devastate an enemy target and create valuable electromagnetic pulses and thus paralyze all electronic devices within its reach. When fuel air explosions take place close to troops, the enormity of the explosion consumes all the oxygen in the atmosphere and even the oxygen breathed by soldiers inside their bunkers or tanks, leading to their annihilation.

Tactical Nuclear Weapons

Although these weapons have been ruled out by the leadership in the United States of America, the possibility for using them remained. They were a deterrent! In fact, if a tragic scenario developed, where Saddam Hussein was to use his chemical and biological weapons on a massive scale and cause death and destruction to thousands and thousands of the Allied Forces, then chances were that he would be subjecting his troops and his nation to a nuclear holocaust. In fact, it is believed that Saddam Hussein was warned in no uncertain terms that if he was to use poison gas he would be paying a very heavy price. Most likely, if such a terroristic weapon was to be used by the tyrant of Baghdad, tactical nuclear strikes or other weapons of mass destruction would have been used directly against him and his head-quarters wherever they might be. Without any doubt this must have played a role in shaping the thinking of Saddam Hussein. Although everyone worried that he might use poison gas, he must have been swayed by the gravity of the situation and the seriousness of the threat against him personally. Since he has been known to be a survivor, and one who prized his survival above and ahead of the interest of anything and everything, with the threat of destruction to his own being and his presidency, he must have heeded the warning and was restrained from using weapons of mass destruction. While President George Bush ruled out the use of nuclear weapons, nevertheless some thought was given to the use of small tactical nuclear weapons, way above the atmosphere of Iraq. This was an attractive proposition, since it would paralyze all the electronic devices operating in the Iraqi realm. In any event, the U.S. armada had no less than one hundred nuclear armed Cruise Missiles on board in the Arabian Gulf, just in case!

Initial Reactions

The success of the operation fundamentally depended on the strong and unequivocal support from Arab forces. That is why the Secretary of Defense, Dick Cheney solicited and strongly received the support of Saudi Arabia and Kuwait Air Forces. They were important forces in this air battle, both from a military point of view as well as tactical and symbolic for the Arab support which was very critical in this war. In fact, reports indicated that the Royal Saudi Air Force performed admirably and at least 150 Saudi fighters participated in the initial phase of the air war. This number increased and Saudi sorties proved to be potent and very effective. It was very important and very critical that America should not be perceived as conducting this war alone against Iraq and against the atrocities of its ruler. The participation of the Allies, and especially Arab Allies, was very important indeed. This was also the view of key military and political leaders of the Coalition Forces.

While there was much sympathy for Saddam Hussein in Jordan, after the breakout of the air war there were no demonstrations in the streets of Amman. Many people were surprised and shocked, but statesmen who knew better had already stated that their support was nothing more than *lip service*, although some of it emanated from hate and frustration which led to siding with injustice against right. In fact, no one is jubilant or chanting in Amman today! However, people in the street continued to express their hate for the Allies and support for Saddam in a quiet verbal way.

Saddam Hussein was defiant until the end. Upon the unleashing of Desert Storm, he stated, "War started today and we will teach America a lesson." A lesson was not going to be taught to America, but to this man who never learns. In fact, Pentagon officials indicated that cluster bombs and Cruise Missiles had paralyzed nearly 80% of Iraq's combat aircraft. Many of these planes were destroyed and their runways dotted with craters. Command and Control Centers were heavily damaged and thus communication from senior commanders and troops in the field became very difficult, thus adding to the paralysis of the Iraqi forces wherever they were. Chemical, biological and nuclear facilities suffered extensive damage as well.

The Secretary of Defense Dick Cheney said, "We have now flown over 1,000 air sorties in the first thirteen hours of the operation and over 100 Tomahawk Cruise Missiles have been launched as well." In fact the U.S. Administration said there will be no let up, no pause in the air operation. If Saddam Hussein wants to stop the fighting, the White House said, "he must surrender."

The initial attack was extremely successful, because strategists spent several months preparing a coordinated plan and training the Coalition Forces for over five months. The air war moved according to a definite plan, designed much earlier, but updated as the time drew closer to executing air action against Iraq. The all-out heavy bombing continued relentlessly. In a briefing, Lt. General Charles Horner said, "Every morning there is a 600 page detailed plan which outlines the assignment of every single plane that is involved and its mission . . . That plan comes out of the computer like a sheet of music everyday, they simply played it." In fact, the U.S. high tech aircraft were successful in jamming Iraq's early detection systems, while the Tomahawk Cruise Missiles knocked out many radar and several air defense establishments. The Stealth bombers succeeded in evading Iraqi radar and destroyed their intended targets. The massive B-52 bombers, A-10 attack planes and Apache helicopters attacked Iraqi troops and tanks in southern Iraq where the Republican Guard was dug in. They also attacked several key targets in Kuwait. This was intended to throw the Iraqi forces off balance and prevent them from counterattacking on the ground, thus forcing the Allies to engage in a ground war contrary to their designs and plans. The choice for the time and place of the ground war was to be decided by the Coalition Forces not Hussein.

While the Iraqi defenses were very spectacular due to their number and intensity, their effect was nil. All the boasting about their air defenses did not bring any positive results to the Iraqis. By daybreak the mayhem was silenced for a brief period and the whizzing of Cruise Missiles stopped for awhile. It was an eerie calm! The lull before the storm!

When Saddam Hussein said his forces have met the best of the

Allied Coalition had to offer during the initial stages of the air war, General Schwarzkopf said, "The best is yet to come."

Baghdad was shocked and stunned by the enormity of the attack and the speed with which it had been executed. The thoroughfares were empty. While it was difficult to determine how much fight was left in the Iraqi war machine, one could guess that more pounding would be necessary. But it was feared that Saddam, in his desperation, might decide to enlarge the war zone by attacking Israel and the major oil centers in Saudi Arabia.

In order to prevent the repairs of runways demolished and destroyed by the air attacks, some bombs with delaying explosive effect were dropped; they became booby traps for those who came to repair the runways. This way, repairs could not take place as fast as the enemy desired. In the attempt to avoid civilian casualties and when the weather particularly interfered with identifying targets, Allied planes returned with their loads intact.

Oil Markets Response

When the United States declared on the 4th of January, 1991, that the January 15 deadline would not be extended, the price of oil jumped from about 25 dollars a barrel to 28 dollars a barrel. This is the price of West Texas intermediate crude oil. When the deadline of January 15, 1991 passed without a peaceful solution in sight, again the price of oil jumped from 30 dollars to 32 dollars a barrel.

While the immediate reaction upon the initiation of the air war was just an increase in the price of oil for a few hours, nevertheless the overall reaction for oil prices was to move downward. In fact, the price per barrel lost about 33% of its value and the stock markets of the world moved upward.

When Coalition Forces succeeded in their air attack on enemy targets on January 16 (U.S. time), the price of oil plummeted from 32 dollars a barrel until it reached on January 18, a price of 19 dollars per barrel. The financial and oil markets reflected a special confidence about the outcome of the war. The predictions essentially were that the Iraqi ruler would fail miserably and the Allied Forces would succeed beyond belief; in reality Saddam's bluster and threats would not succeed in destroying oil wells in Saudi Arabia. On the contrary, major supply lines continued, and the oil market had an abundance of oil supplies. This economic news created a positive reaction to Operation Desert Storm. The fear of attack from Iraq against Saudi oil facilities still existed. However, it is generally believed that they were well defended. Any possible attack on these oil facilities would fail. The world economies breathed a sigh of relief! That is why stock market reaction and oil prices were in the positive as far as consumer's interests were concerned.

After a day and a half of war, President Bush declared, "We are now some 37 hours into Desert Storm and the liberation of Kuwait— so far so good!"

Two days after the war began, a poll was taken in the United States of America. It indicated that 83% of all Americans supported the President in his Gulf War policy. Only 14% disapproved. 65% of those polled believed that the final objective should be forcing Saddam Hussein out of power altogether. However, this objective was not included in the U.N. Resolutions.

Terrorist Option

Saddam Hussein threatened to spread terrorism throughout the world against America's and Allied interests, mainly in Europe. He even threatened to bring terrorism to the heart of America and thus jeopardize the interests of Arab Americans. The Federal Bureau of Investigation (FBI), interested in identifying any who might commit such a dastardly act, interrogated a number of Arab Americans and became more active in tracing three thousand Iraqis whose visas had expired in the United States. The U.S. Government obtained some evidence verifying that terrorists, supported and inspired by Iraq, were planning to mount serious attacks against America's interests throughout the world. For this reason, security had been tightened in many parts of the United States, especially at various airports throughout the country and elsewhere in the world such as France and England. Large cities joined Federal authorities in setting up Command Centers in order to gather and analyze intelligence. President George Bush warned very explicitly: "We will hold Saddam Hussein directly responsible for any terrorist actions." Since Iraq was no match for American and Coalitions military might, Saddam's only wild card seemed to be his terror tactics which he might try to use to break America's resolve in the Gulf.

Airline business had fallen dramatically, because people were fearing to travel. In fact, TWA cut overseas service by half and laid off nearly 5,000 employees.

Security measures were extensive, especially in Europe. British troops and tanks were out in force at Heathrow Airport and other major sensitive facilities. Intelligence reports indicated that terrorist groups had deployed a number of their agents in various European countries. It was feared that terrorists would take action against a major target, which would attract worldwide attention.

Leaders of the Coalition Forces and political analysts did not forget Saddam's veiled threats during his meeting with April Glaspie in Iraq on the 25th of July, 1990, saying, "If a war broke out, we cannot reach America militarily, but there are other ways to reach America." Although it would be very difficult for him or other terrorists to reach America, he was alluding to the use of some Arab Americans to carry his ill deeds. In that he also failed miserably!

Many terrorist threats were made against the Coalition partners. Saddam Hussein trained and sent his terrorist emissaries across the world to strike at key targets which were symbols of the American government. They would also seek to attack airports or mass transit facilities in order to create more havoc and bigger headlines. People throughout the Western World were concerned about such threats and many of them were worried and apprehensive. Many people were buying gas masks just as an extra precaution. In just a couple of days, a New York City store sold over 500 gas masks. Many people became safety and security conscious. Wireless video systems became popular. These gadgets allowed people to see inside their offices or homes prior to entering, in order to be sure there were no terrorists waiting inside. Several other items were sought, such as metal detectors and resistant vests. It was just a wave of psychological warfare, where terrorism was at center stage. However, leaders and experts were reassuring people that the chances of being struck by a terrorist were far less than any risk one would take from just driving a car.

Saddam Hussein's terrorist hordes were dispatched to the major capitals of the Western world such as London, Paris and other European cities, reaching far beyond the seas into the United States of America, and certainly covering a number of Arab countries, leading among them, Egypt and its capital, Cairo. These terrorist cells were dispatched shortly after his occupation of Kuwait. They were told to lay low for use immediately upon notification. Each of these terrorist groups had a special assignment to execute upon receiving the secret Code word which would be broadcast from Iraq and carried by the news organs of the international community. The Iraqi dictator even proclaimed a presidential ruling which stated that whoever might be killed in action against the interests of the Coalition Forces would be declared as a martyr, no matter where his terrorist action had taken place around the globe. Saddam also cooperated with other terrorist organizations specializing in terrorism for several years.

Terrorists working for the Iraqi dictator were arrested in Egypt. The information gathered from those arrested revealed that he was planning to use some of the Egyptians working in Iraq who were indoctrinated by the Ba'ath party to do his dastardly deed and execute his terrorist missions in Egypt. Some of these reaching Egypt gave themselves up to the authorities because they did not want to carry on his wicked designs and create terror and havoc in their own country. At a press conference held in Riyadh, Saudi Arabia on January 30, 1990, President Hosni Moubarak of Egypt answered rumors about the possibility of an attack on the Aswan High Dam in Egypt saying, "The strike on the High Dam is a formidable task. There are rumors suggesting that (Saddam Hussein) deployed missiles in Sudan and that he will launch an attack from there, where he also had deployed military aircraft.

An attack on the High Dam is not that easy. He or others would never succeed! Threats will not save him! We are able to trace whoever tries to attack the High Dam. We will never let him get away with it. We will compel him to pay a high price, whatever the sacrifices we may have to pay!"

Several acts of terrorism took place in Turkey against America's interests and the interests of other Coalition Forces. At least eight such terrorist acts took place in the span of a week, among these, bombs were exploded in the airline bureaus of France and Japan. Terrorist activity even reached the Philippines where some bombs exploded causing minor damage. Military leave for American forces and their families in the Philippines was suspended for 40,000 soldiers in the bases there, out of the fear that radical groups might carry terrorist activities against them. This threat became more prevalent, especially after a bomb attack took place against the American Library in the financial district of the capital city, Manila. French and British interests received some threats and bomb damage from Saddam's terrorist agents operating in Lebanon.

Special measures were taken to guard against terrorism and terrorist attacks. In fact, the White House was using several helicopters when the President was moving from one spot to another, so that the helicopter carrying the President would not be easily detected. Strong precautionary measures for guarding against terrorist acts were practiced whenever the President was moving from one place to another, and then wherever activities took him outside the White House. Instead of having one official car with the American flag, other similar cars were used with the American flag in order to confuse any would-be attackers.

Huge reinforced concrete blocks were put in place in front of major governmental buildings, especially the White House, in order to guard against any possible truck bombing by a lunatic supporting Saddam Hussein. Even in Japan, French companies were advised to take precautionary measures and to watch their cars and not leave them unattended. They were also advised to change the course of their daily routine to avoid being an easy target for a possible terrorist attack. The French school in Japan took security measures to make sure that all the attendees were indeed students and that the school was not being infiltrated by anyone else. Other nations of the Coalition took similar precautionary measures. The government of South Korea beefed up airport security after receiving intelligence information about a possible terrorist attack. Threats of terrorism reached several countries of the world, including Italy, Australia, and the entire European theater. An explosion took place in Italy where one woman was killed, another explosion took place in front of the French newspaper, "Parisien," which injured three guards. This newspaper supported the French President and the Coalition Forces for their actions in the Gulf. In Lima, Peru a car bomb exploded, killing one person, injuring several and destroying some property. An attack on the U.S. Embassy took place from a passing car without causing any severe damage. Also, in response to Saddam Hussein's call for a Jihad, some terrorist activities took place in Australia.

Because of the great concern about terrorism, a major U.S. carrier refused to transport Iraqis, even if they were permanent residents of the United States. This policy was practiced for some time, until it was later reversed. Some extremist groups responded to Saddam's calls and cooperated with him in spreading terrorism, as desired and dictated by his regime. However, all the terrorist activities he generated did not help him in modifying the decisive Coalition policy against his aims and sinister designs. On the contrary, this scenario strengthened the resolve of the Allied Forces and accelerated their action toward the obliteration of his occupying forces in Kuwait and the disintegration of his defenses inside Iraq.

Military Balance and the First Week of War

The U.S. troop strength* on the eve of the war, January 16, 1991 was 425,000 in the Gulf area. Among them were 60,000 in the Navy, 75,000 Marines and 45,000 in the Air Force. The Iraqi forces had more than 545,000 troops in the Kuwaiti Theater of Operations (KTO). The Iraqis had about 4,200 tanks. Their armored personnel carriers and infantry fighting vehicles were estimated at 2,800, while their artillery pieces were estimated at 3,100. "Again, in Kuwait, a westward expansion of Iraqi defense lines had taken place. However, their fundamental posture remained of a defensive nature, which could become offensive

---

* Source: U.S. Department of Defense, All Hands, Desert Storm special issue, the Navy–Marine Corps Team, April 11, 1991.

on a very short notice. At this time, there was no evidence of them pulling out of Kuwait. Quite the contrary from our last briefing, the number of forces, tanks, artillery pieces, and so forth have gone up, which is certainly not consistent with withdrawal."

U.S. Navy ship strength in the Gulf was 108 in total: 37 in the Arabian Gulf, 35 in the North Arabian Sea and the Gulf of Oman, 26 in the Red Sea and 13 in the Eastern Mediterranean. Ships in the Arabian Gulf consisted of the air carriers Midway and Ranger, also the battleships Wisconsin and Missouri, then two command ships, the Blue Ridge and the La Salle, five cruisers, five destroyers, three frigates, four mine warfare ships, seven amphibious ships and seven auxiliary ships. These do not include the non-combatant hospital ships, Comfort and Mercy. Midway was the latest carrier to enter the Arabian Gulf.

In the Red Sea there were 26 ships, which included four U.S. aircraft carriers: the America, the Theodore Roosevelt, the Saratoga and the John F. Kennedy. In addition there were eight cruisers, four destroyers, two frigates, and eight auxiliary ships. The Theodore Roosevelt battle group entered the Red Sea the weekend of January 11, 1991, and the America battle group came through the Suez Canal one week later.

The blockade against Iraq, which had been in effect for five months continued. So far, there were 6,913 intercepts; 823 boardings and 36 ships diverted since the beginning of the embargo. The United States conducted 485 of these boardings, while the Allies boarded 315 ships. There were 23 combined U.S. and Allied boardings.

Seventeen mines were found in the Gulf, since December 21, 1990. Sixteen of them were confirmed to be planted by Iraqi forces. One old mine may have been placed prior to August 2, 1990.

Nineteen countries among the Coalition Forces deployed ground forces and fourteen of them participated in Naval operations, in cooperation with the United States of America.

As mentioned earlier, the initial air bombardment was accomplished by the U.S. Air Force, the Royal Saudi Air Force and the Kuwaiti Air Force, along with the Air Forces of Britain and France. On the second wave of attacks, the massive air bombardments were carried by the United States of America, the Kingdom of Saudi Arabia, Kuwait, Britain, France, Italy and Canada.

On Friday, January 18, 1991 the Iraqis were firing antiaircraft artillery and shoulder-fired SAM Missiles from eleven Kuwaiti oil platforms in the Northern Arabian Gulf. U.S. forces, supported by a Kuwaiti patrol boat, neutralized the Iraqi forces. Five Iraqis were killed, three were wounded and twenty-three were taken as Enemy Prisoners Of

War (EPWs). Wave after wave of planes were wreaking havoc on Iraqi forces, especially in Baghdad and at other major targets throughout Iraq and Kuwait. There was *no bombing pause* for Saddam Hussein to take a message and make up his mind on withdrawal from Kuwait. The relentless bombardment, nonstop around the clock, was extremely successful. The success was truly unparalleled in the history of warfare.

The Iraqi Ambassador in Paris branded the air operation as "high altitude cowardly bombing." This was in reference to the attacking airplanes maintaining a high altitude while using their smart bombs to zero in on targets with pinpoint accuracy, without risking the heavy barrage of fire coming from the ground. It was truly miraculous that the *Allied Forces did not lose a single man or a single airplane in the first night of massive bombardment*, especially over the capital city, Baghdad.

It was not until the second night of the air war that the Iraqis scored any hits. Much of the time, it was due to the huge number of antiaircraft guns shooting aimlessly in the air and at times hitting some targets by sheer luck and accident. By the second night of the bombing, on January 18, 1991, local time, the losses were one U.S. plane, one British plane, one Kuwaiti plane, and four French planes were damaged. This happened after more than 1,000 sorties had taken place. The whole world was amazed at the low number of hits by the Iraqis, especially, after the tremendous blusters and threats emanating from Baghdad and since Iraq had thousands and thousands of antiaircraft weapons and SAM Missiles. However, good planning, high technology, and determination of the Coalition Forces brought a devastating blow to Iraqi defenses and paved the way to speedy paralysis of their air force.

Iraqi citizens reacted swiftly. They were fleeing Baghdad by the thousands, and cars were jamming the streets all in search of an outlet for the neighboring towns and countryside. Refugees began to pour out of Baghdad and Iraq toward Jordan. Radio Baghdad became alive again in the predawn hours of January 17, and nearly two hours after the air war began, defiantly proclaimed to the Iraqis that *"the mother of all battles"* had just begun, predicting victory for Iraq and defeat for the Allied Forces. The same day, Saddam Hussein staged a street demonstration while he was greeting the "adoring" Iraqi public as their "sole leader." Bodyguards were surrounding him and practically outnumbered the demonstrators. The "spontaneous" demonstration of affection and devotion was beamed across the airwaves of the world through the television media, which was grabbing on more than ever before to anything uttered or shown by Saddam Hussein and his Revolutionary Command Council. He was defiant and in no time, his Information Minister declared victory saying, "the battle was settled in our favor." Reports of great Iraqi successes were beamed through the airwaves of Iraq from Radio Baghdad and their television station, but all in a campaign of deceit to mislead the public. Much rhetoric along religious lines was propagated as well, for the sinister and distinct purpose of branding the conflict as being between Islam and the "infidels." The Iraqi ruler was borrowing a few pages from the recent history of other brutal dictators and was banking on what he learned from the eight year war with Iran. However, this devious scheme did not fool anyone, and the pious Moslems of the world did not buy his accusations nor his exploitations in his desperate hours. Vehement and vicious attacks were launched against King Fahd of Saudi Arabia and especially President George Bush of the United States of America. Declarations were made that, "Najd and Hijaz will be liberated, the invaders will be defeated; Palestine will be liberated from the filth of the zionists; Israel will disappear forever." He warned of inflicting high casualties among the Western powers and their Allies, declaring, "not a few drops of blood, but rivers of blood would be shed. Then, Bush would have been deceiving America, the American public opinion, the American people, and the American constitutional institutions."

Will Israel Enter the War?

In his desperation, Saddam Hussein used his wild card on the second day of the air war. On Friday, the 18th of January, 1991, at 3:30 in the morning local time, Saddam Hussein lobbed five Soviet made Scud missiles on Israel. Three of the ballistic missiles fell on Tel Aviv and the other two hit the northern part of Haifa. The Israeli defense systems were not equipped nor capable of intercepting these missiles, and thus they hit residential areas and caused some minimal damage. A number of people were injured and some living quarters were destroyed. There was a great eerie feeling of worry and concern that these missiles may carry with them poison gas. This sent shock waves through Israel, the Middle East and the rest of the World for that matter. There was great concern that Israel might retaliate for the actions of Saddam Hussein and this would bring a dynamic change in the equation and scenario of the air war which had so far been carried with great precision and great success. From the start, Saddam's major goal was to bring Israel into the melee so that he would inflame the Arab masses to side with him and rise against regimes friendly to the West. If Israel had responded to these attacks, it would have fallen into the trap established by him; it would be essentially responding to his wishes and serving his aims. Nevertheless, the temptation was very strong! Long ago Israel had established a policy of swift retaliation, sometimes provoked, at other times with the very minimum of provocation. This policy added to the escalation of the Arab-Israeli conflict, and helped in fueling four wars between the Arabs and the Israelis, since the establishment of Israel in May of 1948.

Saddam's designs were to embarrass the Arab Coalition Forces, especially, Saudi Arabia, Egypt and Syria. President George Bush was extremely concerned about the new developments. He worked the telephones and exercised statesmanship and tremendous pressure in order to stop Israel from exacting revenge on Saddam Hussein and thus threatening the Alliance that had been engineered and properly organized to face the atrocities of Saddam Hussein. This impressive Coalition was gathered after expanding tremendous efforts—It was a stroke of political genius. The Coalition leaders were very concerned that a derailing of such a Coalition because of Israeli action would be extremely counter-productive and would certainly help the Iraqi leader in his vicious designs. The pressures exercised by President Bush on Israel prevailed, at least for the time being and after several promises were exacted by the Israeli government, leading among these was the promise of prompt delivery of Patriot Missiles manned by U.S. forces to defend against any possible Scud missile attack in the future. Also a promise was made that a special effort and heavy air power concentration would be delegated to destroy the mobile Scud launchers which were active in the Western part of Iraq, not far from the Jordanian border. Being in this region placed the Scuds at a strategic position close to their targets. Once they were fired from western Iraq over Jordan, it would be a short distance to reach the populated Israeli cities.

It had been reported that nearly 15% of the air strikes against targets in Iraq and Kuwait were aimed at destroying these Scud missiles. The mobile launchers proved to be elusive and many times more difficult to track. They hid by day and became active by night. Sophisticated high technology was used to trigger the radars and attack them, although at times some decoy mobile launchers were in the field in order to confuse the mission of planes searching for them. These Scud missiles were very inaccurate. Their value from a military point of view was essentially negligible, but they were powerful as a terror and psychological weapon. The Israelis were terrified from the thought that these Scud missiles may have warheads with chemical weapons. In fact, prior to these attacks, the Israelis practiced the use of gas masks. So, as soon as Scud missiles were launched and detected, air raid sirens warned the Israeli population to don their gas masks and head for the highest floor in a building, not to the bomb shelters in basements and underground. This is due to the fact that poison gas, being heavier than air, would settle toward the ground and lower residential areas. This sent waves of terror through the populations; reporters stationed in Israel were filing their reports while having their gas masks on. These images were distributed instantously throughout the world, and brought vivid reminiscence of the poison gas used by Saddam Hussein against the Iranians and also against his own people at Halabja; it also brought vivid memories of the poison gas used during World War I and the gas chambers of Hitler in World War II. People were warned to go to a sealed room so that in the event the warhead carried poison gas, the deadly substance would not seep into this air tight room. In fact, every time there was an air raid siren, families huddled in such sealed rooms hoping to avoid the agonizing death from poison gas.

Initially, with the first Scud missile attack, false rumors spread and it was reported that a chemical weapon was used, but that turned out to be not true.

The Israeli Minister of Defense, Moshe Arens, said, "We have said publicly and to the Americans, that if we were attacked, we would react; we were attacked, certainly. We have to defend ourselves." However, in this case, restraint had overtaken the policy decision of Israel, which reserved the right to retaliate at the right time, at the right place.

Serious analysts and statesmen in America realized that, despite the complexity of the situation and even if Israel was to enter into the war, the Coalition Forces would prevail and the Arab Coalition would remain solidly behind the goals set by the United Nations Resolutions. It would be very unfortunate, irritating and disturbing to the Arab Coalition Forces, but certainly they were not going to fall for the wicked designs of Saddam Hussein and the Coalition was to endure and prevail. Although, without a shred of a doubt, it was preferred by all members of the Coalition and especially the Arab Coalition Forces, that Israel should not initiate any reprisals because of the enormity of the situation and the potential of complicating matters further and expanding the realm of the war. In this strategic goal, Saddam Hussein failed! The Syrians were not moved by his actions, nor were they willing to be drawn into a conflict not of their choosing, which would be of benefit to him. Moustafa Tlass, the Syrian Minister of Defense said addressing Saddam, "You are free to fight the whole world alone. But you are not free to claim wisdom and reason. You are especially not free to call on other people to join you in this folly." In fact, the Foreign Minister of Syria, Farouk Al-Shara'a assured Ambassadors of the Coalition Forces that Syria would not be tricked into war with Israel so that Saddam would achieve his goals. Even if Israel was to retaliate against Iraq, Syria would not be dragged into a war against Israel for the sake of its arch enemy, Saddam Hussein.

Scud Missile Attacks on the Kingdom

In Saudi Arabia, the pitch of worry and fear that the Iraqi ruler might send his Scud missiles their way, was getting very high indeed! There was lots of fear and concern that such an attack was imminent. Cities like Dhahran, Dammam, Ras Tannura, Jubail, Riyadh and along the military cities and air bases, military and civilian personnel were all alerted for the possibility of such an attack. Gas masks were used off and on with every air raid siren. The whole exercise was nerve-racking and essentially devastating to the psychology of people, especially the civilians.

True to his name and character, Saddam Hussein launched his Scud missile attack on the Abdulaziz Air Base in Dhahran, Saudi Arabia. People rushed for their gas masks. It was fired in the pre-dawn hours of January 18, 1991, on the Holy Moslem day, Friday. The Soviet made Scud missile was detected by the AWACS covering the entire war theater, immediately on its take off. People had enough time to put on their gas masks and hurry to their airtight sealed rooms for safety. It was a devastating eerie feeling of fear and despair, an agonizing worrisome feeling about the terrible and tragic effects of poison gas and what it had done to other people who were unfortunate enough to receive the deadly poison gas weapons of Saddam Hussein. Again, high technology prevailed! The Patriot Missiles had been ready and operational in Saudi Arabia at the base in Dhahran, Riyadh and other strategic air bases in the Kingdom, also at other nerve oil centers in the Eastern Region of Saudi Arabia. They were ready to prove their high accuracy! Just as soon as the Scud approached its target, the Patriot homed in on the oncoming Scud and up in the air disintegrated it into pieces that fell harmlessly on to the ground. No injuries or damage were reported. Everyone breathed a sigh of relief! Knowing that the Scud missile is far from being accurate, Saddam Hussein intended to cause harm to wherever the Scud missile would fall, be it on the Air Base or on civilians. It could have killed or maimed men, women and children, but the conscience of this man was not in the least worried about this. He had apparently forgotten the great support and aid received from the Kingdom of Saudi Arabia during his eight year war with Iran.

During another meeting of the Council of Ministers held on January 19, 1991 in Riyadh, King Fahd clearly stated, "We have made every possible effort at all levels to avoid the critical circumstances which the Arab Nation is passing through at the present. We have *knocked on every door for peace!* We followed every path for fraternal dialogue and understanding. (But Iraq repeatedly) refused to listen to the voice of reason." This forced the entire world to set a deadline and implement the Arab, Islamic, and international U.N. Resolutions for the withdrawal of the aggressor's forces from the State of Kuwait. He then concluded that Saddam Hussein must "face the responsibility of his stand alone in front of the Iraqi people and army."

On the third day of operations, air to air engagements took place with eight Iraqi MiG-29s and Mirage F-1s. All the Iraqi planes were destroyed. In fact, every Iraqi airplane that dared to challenge the Allied Forces was shot down and the Allies lost none in air to air combat with any Iraqi planes. Around 8:00 P.M. of the third day of action, the Iraqi forces launched a number of ground to ground tactical Soviet Frog missiles against the Eastern Region of the Kingdom, but they fell in the desert and caused no harm. Allied air power silenced the sources that launched these Frog missiles. On this day a Saudi plane developed mechanical trouble over Saudi territory after completing its mission. The two pilots ejected safely from their plane. A Marine OV-10 reconnaissance plane was downed by Iraqi SAM missiles. The two crewmen were missing. Up to this date and since the beginning of the air war, ten Iraqi aircraft were destroyed, six of them were MiG-29s, three were Mirage F-1s and one MiG-23; these were due to air engagement with the Coalition Forces. The United States lost six aircraft and seven personnel were listed as missing in combat. During the three days of air operation against Iraqi forces, the Coalition conducted 5,000 sorties against strategic targets in Iraq and Kuwait. Losses were miraculously minimal with 11 planes lost during these operations.

On the fourth day of air operations, heavy bombardment continued on strategic targets and other targets of significance. The Iraqi military was thrown in confusion and the Iraqi air force was obliterated. The skies of the war theater were dominated by the Coalition Air Forces. Air supremacy prevailed and the Allied airplanes were attacking at will. The submarine-launched Tomahawk Cruise Missile was fired for the first time in combat history, while submerged in the Red Sea. The launch took place from the USS Louisville (SSN724). Much effort was made to locate and destroy the mobile Scud missiles which brought terror to Tel Aviv, Dhahran and Riyadh. The Iraqi military was receiving more heavy air bombardment.

The Royal Saudi Air Force performed admirably and carried 510 sorties against strategic targets in Iraq and Kuwait out of a total of 8,323 sorties carried by the Coalition Forces. Three more Scud missiles were launched by Saddam Hussein against the Eastern Region of Saudi

Arabia, but they were all intercepted and destroyed by the Patriot Missile in mid-air. They never reached their destined targets. At the beginning of Monday, January 21, 1991, at 12:40 A.M., the tyrant of Baghdad launched four more ground to ground Scud missiles toward Riyadh, the capital city of Saudi Arabia. However, the great high tech star of the war, the Patriot Missile, intercepted the Scud missiles of terror and psychological warfare and destroyed them before they were able to cause any damage to the innocent population. One of the Scud missiles dug a deep, wide hole in a certain area of Riyadh, without causing any serious damage. The population was terrified by these random acts of terror against men, women and children of a brotherly Arab Nation.

In contrast, the Allied Forces went the extra mile to be extremely careful about their targets. They did everything humanely possible to avoid injury to civilians; with high tech equipment at their disposal, they were very successful in destroying their specific targets with great accuracy. Another three Scud missiles were launched against the Eastern Province in Saudi Arabia. Two of them were intercepted by the Patriot Missile and destroyed. The third one fell in the Arabian Gulf. As expected the population was extremely apprehensive and very worried about the possibility of these Scud missiles carrying nerve gas and other chemical warfare substances. This was nerve-racking! Every time the air raid sirens came on to warn of an attack, Saudis and workers in their country were deeply disturbed and rushed for their gas masks and their sealed rooms. The population never imagined that such terrible fate would befall them from an Arab brother in Iraq. Saddam Hussein intended to cause harm to the population and the Arab masses in Saudi Arabia out of vengeance and terrible greed. But on all fronts he failed!

Scud missile activity remained at a high pitch. In fact, at 11:00 P.M. in the evening of January 21, a Scud missile was launched toward the Eastern Province. It was detected and then traced until it was destroyed on impact in the Arabian Gulf waters. These missiles carried conventional warheads, and their military impact was insignificant. However, they continued to constitute a psychological and terrorist threat.

Up to this day, the Royal Saudi Air Force carried 608 air sorties against the enemy, out of a total of 10,000 sorties by the Allied Forces. The Air Force of Qatar, for the first time, participated in the air attacks against the enemy and in support of the Allies. The Saudi Air Force did not lose any airplanes in the last 24 hours. Saudi pilots effectively participated in successful raids destroying command and control centers, military bases, air strips, missile launching facilities, ammunition dumps and other strategic targets in both Iraq and Kuwait. With great worry about Scud missile attacks, the Allied Forces focused a good bit of their air operations on neutralizing both fixed and especially mobile Scud launch sites. Iraqi troop concentrations also received heavy bombardment.

As of January 21, 1991, Coalition aircraft losses totaled eight. This included two non-combatant related losses. Thirteen U.S. personnel were listed as missing. The Coalition Maritime Forces destroyed three mines in the Arabian Gulf waters.

At 3:45 in the morning of January 22, 1991, two more Scud missiles were launched by the aggressive forces of Iraq. One of them was destroyed by a Patriot Missile. Debris from the other fell in a residential area. It was examined to determine whether or not it was destroyed by a Patriot Missile or from its impact on the ground. In any case, damage from these Scuds was extremely minor in nature. In the early morning hours of the same day, three more Scud missiles were launched against the Eastern Region of Saudi Arabia. One of them was destroyed by Patriot Missiles, while the other two were traced until they were destroyed on impact in a remote area.

Since the regime in Baghdad began parading war prisoners on television, and threatened mistreatment, contrary to the Geneva Convention, the United States warned Saddam Hussein that he would be held personally accountable for any mistreatment of U.S. and Allied prisoners of war (POWs). This warning came immediately after the Iraqi government announced that the captured Americans and other Allied prisoners of war would be placed at various strategic target sites and would be used as "human shields."

On January 22, 1991, the Iraqi forces in Kuwait set on fire some oil storage tanks in Wafra, Al-Shuaiba and Mina Abdullah. Four Navy A-6s attacked and disabled an Iraqi T-43-class ship which was capable of laying 20 mines in the northern Arabian Gulf. The U.S. ships also attacked three Iraqi patrol boats, disabling one and chasing off the other two. Three additional mines were found and destroyed. On that date, the United States troop strength was set at 474,000. The Iraqis had 545,000 in the Kuwait Theater of Operations (KTO).

By Wednesday, January 23, 1991, the Bahraini Air Force joined the Coalition Forces in their massive air operations. By this time these operations had reached 14,000 sorties and the Royal Saudi Air Force had conducted very successfully 1,007 of them.

Thus, the first week of massive air bombardment against enemy targets in Iraq and Kuwait was a gigantic success, unparalleled in the history of warfare. The Coalition Forces achieved much beyond their goals. They essentially achieved air superiority throughout the theater of war operations both in Iraq and Kuwait. High Tech weapons tipped the balance very decisively in favor of right, which in this case also meant might against tyranny and occupying forces. However, Iraqi Scud missiles remained elusive. Fixed launchers were destroyed, but mobile Scud launchers were sought very energetically and anytime they were detected they were destroyed. Despite all the extensive effort to silence them, they continued to be a source of irritation and psychological warfare throughout the duration of the Gulf War. As mentioned previously, these Scud missiles are highly inaccurate and from a military point of view, they did not tip the balance in favor of Iraq one bit. In any event, Saddam Hussein continued to have the earnest desire to fulfill his basic goal of engaging Israel in the war and thus, expanding Desert Storm to engulf other countries in the region. His dreams were not to come true! Showering Israel and Saudi Arabia with Scud missiles did not trigger the desired vengeful response from Israel. He was hoping that an attack by Israel would inflame Arab masses because of the old enmities and problems of the Arab-Israeli conflict. Failing here and elsewhere, he then reached into his magic bag on instruments of terror, and found what proved to be a shock for the world and a disaster for the environment. He committed an unforgivable act of environmental terrorism, where he dumped millions of barrels of oil in the waters of the Arabian Gulf. This proved to be only the beginning! The worst environmental disaster is yet to come . . . Now, the second week of the war begins!

Double Kill in the Sky

On January 24, 1991, an impressive dog fight developed in the skies over the Gulf. This air to air engagement attracted international attention, especially in military circles around the world. Captain Ayedh Al-Shamrani scored a first hit for the Allied Forces. He shot down two Iraqi war-planes flying southward to unload their bombs on Allied Forces. The attentive and alert Saudi ace pilot zeroed in to a distance of 3,000 feet from a formation of the three Iraqi Mirage F-1 jet fighter bombers which were heading toward the ships of the Allies in the Gulf.

Within seconds the two enemy jets were destroyed, one after the other. The third turned tail and ran away after ditching its Exocet missile which caused no harm. This was the first and only double kill in the air war against Iraq. It was a great display of courage and skill by the Saudi pilot. This was the result of high training, superior military expertise and high tech equipment. It was a credit to the Royal Saudi Air Force, a testimonial to their level of performance, courage and professionalism. The pilot was proud of his U.S. made F-15 Eagle jet and its superior performance. He was equally proud of the warning which came in the nick of time from the AWACS reconnaissance planes, flying the skies over the theater of war operations. The proud Saudi pilot stated, "We got one, we got both destroyed . . . it was very easy mission for me; you know the F-15 nobody can beat it! I just rolled behind him; I saw Iraqis and shot them."

This remarkable feat reflected the true state of preparedness of the Royal Saudi Air Force. Saudi pilots performed admirably since the outbreak of the war against the enemy. Saudi pilots and Saudi forces are well disciplined, motivated and very dedicated to the defense of their homeland. Moreover, they exhibit a great spirit of comradery, cooperation and appreciation toward the Allied Forces who came to help the Saudis and the Kuwaitis in their hour of need. This great performance of a double kill was not only of paramount military importance but it had political and other implications, as well as lifting the morale of other pilots and forces in the Arabian Gulf. On the ominous side, if low flying Iraqi jets succeeded in unloading their Exocet French-made missiles on some of the Allied warships in the Gulf it could have led to a major disaster and probably killed hundreds, if not thousands, of the Allied Forces. The alertness and speed of action of the Saudi pilot prevented a possible tragedy from happening. For that the entire forces of the Coalition were grateful. His performance certainly brought credit not only to the Saudi forces, but to the Allies as well.

Television and news media around the world picked up this fascinating story and dispersed it for the whole world to see.

A Saudi military source stated, "The two Iraqi planes penetrated Saudi air space where the battle took place." He also said, "The Iraqi planes were carrying anti-ship Exocet missiles. Neither of the Iraqi pilots were seen parachuting, because of the high speed and short duration of the dog fight, which took just a few seconds."

The *Royal Saudi Air Force* (RSAF) was established in 1950 by order of the founder of the Kingdom, the late King Abdulaziz, known in the West as Ibn Saud. Prior to that period, air operations were under the realm of the army. Initially, the British helped in providing aircraft and training. As British influence declined in the region and U.S. interests increased, American aircraft and training personnel were used by the Royal Saudi Air Force (RSAF). Several state-of-the-art huge air bases dot the Kingdom and contribute extensively to its defense and the defense of the Arabian Gulf. These air bases proved to be of paramount importance to the Multinational Coalition Forces and to the miraculous success of the air war against the oppressor.

Squadrons of American F-15 planes and British Tornados along with F-5s carried an impressive combat punch. The AWACS gave early warning and provided a reliable umbrella of safety and protection. Jet intercepters, air defense radar, SAM missiles from the British and the Americans, along with Maverick air to ground missiles helped in making the Royal Saudi Air Force a deterrent to be reckoned with in the Middle East, and a very valuable force in performing miracles and exhibiting great courage during the air war of Desert Storm.

Captain Shamrani's performance is a vivid testimonial to the level of professionalism, dedication and courage of the Saudi forces.

Continuing Second Week of the War

By January 24, 1991, 15,000 sorties were carried against enemy targets. 8,000 of these were combat and 7,000 support missions. Over 220 Tomahawk Cruise Missiles had been launched at several targets. These massive air strikes continued to be aimed at Scud missile launchers, communication and transportation facilities, control centers and various air fields. Three Soviet-built TU-16 Badger heavy bombers were caught on the grounds of the Ai-Kuara West Air Field. They were ready to take off but were instantly attacked and rendered useless. Around 6:00 in the evening, Navy A-6s attacked and destroyed an Iraqi mine layer. A second one was sunk; it was a Zhuk patrol boat. While another Iraqi mine sweeper was evading the attack, it hit a mine laid by the perpetrators themselves. Eleven Iraqi marines were picked from the waters around each of the two boats. A total of 22 survivors were taken by a Helo from USS Curts, near the island of Qourah. The Helo of the rescue operation came under attack. Fire was returned and three were killed. Twenty-nine more Iraqi prisoners of war surrendered. A total of 51 enemy prisoners of war (EPWs) were taken into custody by the Helo crew from USS Leftwich. The island of Qourah was reclaimed and became the first liberated soil of Kuwait. In the same day A-6s and F/A-18s attacked the Omm Qasr Naval Base. Four Iraqi ships were damaged. Multiple operations were carried out by U.S. Navy ships. These included locating and destroying twenty-five mines laid up to this date by the Iraqis in the northern Arabian Gulf.

On January 24, more Scud missiles fell on Israel. It was reported that seven of them were launched from Iraq against the Jewish State. Patriot Missiles were fired against them but some damage nevertheless had occurred. The damage could have been from the falling debris or from the Scuds themselves upon disintegration. Several houses in a residential area in Tel Aviv were destroyed. Apartment blocks were smashed and some cars were burning. Several people were injured and some of them were killed. The same concern remained! Do these Scuds carry chemical warheads or will the future ones have poison gas? The question remained, when will the patience of the Israelis give to retaliation and revenge? When will the pressures from George Bush and the Alliance fail to prevail on the Israelis?

By the 25th of January, a record 2,700 sorties were flown, which brought the total number of sorties to 17,500. The number of Tomahawk Cruise Missiles unleashed against enemy targets amounted to 236. The Royal Saudi Air Force had flown 1,138 sorties out of this total. The Iraqis had lost 43 aircraft since the beginning of the air war; nineteen of them were lost in air to air engagements, while 24 were destroyed on the ground. The United States had lost ten aircraft to ground fire, while Coalition Forces lost seven. A total of 17 aircraft losses represented only two tenths of one percent of all the combat missions flown to this date.

An Iraqi vessel caught laying mines near the Sea Island terminal was attacked by U.S. Navy warships; part of the terminal was set on fire. By this date, U.S. troop strength in the Gulf stood at 482,000.

Around January 25, 1991, the organized resistance by the Kuwaitis had been severely hampered for all practical purposes, because of the brutal responses of the Iraqi occupying force. For every ten Iraqis killed, scores of Kuwaitis were executed. While all smuggling trips from Saudi Arabia to Kuwait had been stopped, the propaganda activities were in full gear. The U.S. Psychological Operations Team from Fort Bragg, North Carolina went to Riyadh, Saudi Arabia, for the sole purpose of conducting a special information campaign. A very critical goal had been to devise ways and means that would effectively contribute to breaking the spirit and the morale of the Iraqi soldier. Over fifteen million leaflets were distributed in the Theater of Operations. These urged the Iraqis to give up or risk death. They gave them clear instructions to follow when surrendering. However, the problem of surrendering is not an easy one, especially since Saddam Hussein had sent to the Kuwaiti Theater of Operations death squads who were given orders to shoot anyone attempting to defect. Faced with these threats some of the Iraqi soldiers were shot on the spot and others hunkered deeper in their bunkers waiting for a terrible fate if they resisted but hoping for an opportune time to come out and flee for their lives.

The fourth Scud missile attack on the Saudi capital city of Riyadh took place on Friday, January 26, 1991. Air raid sirens were wailing at 10:30 P.M. Moments later Patriot Missile batteries fired their salvo at the oncoming Scud missile. By an act of God, the damage was minimal. Friday was the holiday in Riyadh and few people were in the streets where the Iraqi Scud missile hit causing some damage. While the Patriot Missile's effectiveness has been lavishly praised by Saudi officials and the Coalition, however this night, the Patriot seemed to have missed the target and this made it a bit less invincible.

Reporting on January 27, 1991, Military Communique #10 states: "so far there have been 22,528 aerial sorties since the beginning of Desert Storm." The Royal Saudi Air Force had conducted 1,431 of these missions. The Bahraini Air Force 20 missions, the Kuwaiti Air Force 131 missions and now the Qatari Air Force 8 missions.

Environmental Terrorism

By the 25th of January, a huge oil slick was forming next to the Al-Ahmadi port in Kuwait. Iraqi authorities had committed a despicable act against the environment by dumping millions of barrels of oil into the Gulf waters from the Sea Island crude oil loading terminal, which is located off the coast of the State of Kuwait. Five Iraqi tankers were purposely placed in the port of Mina Al-Ahmadi, and their oil was dumped into the Gulf, creating a grave environmental situation. But this was not the first time Saddam Hussein committed his act of terrorism against the environment. Back in 1983 his planes attacked and destroyed the offshore Norruz oil field, spilling large quantities of oil into the Gulf. In their desperation, the Iraqi forces resorted to this new brand of terrorism. Crude oil from the pumping stations at Mina Al-Ahmadi was purposely dumped into the Gulf waters. Huge amounts of oil, exceeding two million barrels per day, were released as an act of war, severely polluting the ecosystem of the Gulf. This war strategy proved to be of no practical value from a military point of view, while ecologically it caused terrible damage to the environment as a whole and was especially destructive to marine life.

On January 26, 1991, it was estimated that 120 million gallons of oil had been deliberately spilled into the Arabian Gulf from the Sea Island terminal. This oil slick was partly ablaze from a January 25 engagement between the Allied ships and an Iraqi patrol boat. The oil slick grew to 31 miles long and 8 miles wide. The United States sent a team of oil pollution experts to assist the Saudi Arabian effort in combating this major oil spill. The organizations included in this were the Environmental Protection Agency, the Coast Guard and the National Oceanographic and Atmospheric Administration. On January 27, 1991, Air Force F-111s attacked the pipelines feeding the Sea Island terminal. The Air Force used GBU-15 Laser-guided bombs in order to interrupt the flow of oil into the Gulf. The attack also was meant to ignite some of the oil. This system of pipes was specifically targeted because it regulated the oil flow from storage tanks to the terminal known as the manifolds. The operation was successful and the oil flow was essentially stopped.

As a result of this futile act against mankind and environment, nearly, eleven million barrels of oil were deliberately released. This is equivalent to 462 million gallons, about 1.7 million tons of spilled oil, compared to only 11 million gallons of crude oil spilled during the 1989 Exxon Valdez Oil Spill.* This makes it the largest oil spill in history! Some of it was burned, but the oil slick thinned out rapidly, moving southward with prevailing winds and Gulf currents at a speed of nearly 12 miles per day. Within four days the slick was 50 miles long, 12 miles wide and three millimeters thick (about ¹⁄₁₀th of an inch).

Kuwaiti oil is rich with light components which rapidly evaporated to the atmosphere, leaving heavier components which after several days became "Chocolate Mousse". Picking up particles from the air caused some of this "mousse" to settle to the bottom of the Gulf and some ended up reaching the shores.

The main concern was pollution of the intake (10 to 16 feet below the water surface) for the water desalination plants dotting the Arabian Gulf. These must be well protected along with the water cooling supplies to the electric generation plants. The Saudis and other affected Arabian Gulf nations had gained some experience in this regard during the eight-year Iran-Iraq war of 1980–1988, where a number of oil spills occurred during the crippling of several oil tankers and oil terminals.

Booms, extending three feet below the surface, were used to contain the slick and to protect important sites and sensitive facilities. Intake waters were carefully observed and controlled around the clock. Some ships were used to pick up the oil held by the booms. Efforts were made to save some wildlife and keep the beaches clean. The world community rendered a helping hand in minimizing the damage despite the raging war.

Compared to the Exxon Valdez Oil Spill, where the water of Prince William Sound rejuvenates itself nearly every month, the isolated waters of the Gulf, with one narrow outlet of 34 miles (55 kilometers) across the Strait of Hormuz, cleanses itself, on the average, once every four years. Moreover, the average water depth in the Sound is 330 feet, while in the Gulf, the average depth is around 110 feet. Thus, after ravaging the Gulf during the Iran-Iraq war, another environmental

---

* By early March, 1991, this spill was estimated to be around five million barrels of oil.

tragedy struck.* Its reverberating impact will linger on for many years. Hopefully, the Arabian Gulf will not become a dead sea!

The oil slick threatened to cause extensive environmental damage to Gulf waters for many years to come. It was feared that this deliberate pumping of oil into the Gulf waters could cause serious problems to the intakes of desalination plants in the region, and especially in Saudi Arabia.

First sightings of an oil slick were reported to Saudi Aramco around two o'clock in the morning, on Friday, the 25th of January, 1991. This spill was increasing by the moment and someone dubbed it "the mother of all oil spills." Saudi Arabia was facing the *worst ecological disaster in environmental history.*

Saudi Arabia was very keen on developing good safeguards against environmental pollution. Back in the 1980s it had established the National Commission for Wildlife Conservation and Development. It also established the Meteorological and Environmental Protection Administration (MEPA). This latter organization was established along similar lines of the United States Environmental Protection Agency (EPA), with specific missions for safeguarding the environment and combating pollution on all fronts. The functions of these organizations are complimentary to one another, and they all cooperated with other companies and governmental agencies for the sake of a cleaner environment. Thus, in this environmental catastrophe, coordination and cooperation prevailed throughout.

The eleven-member Oil Spill Committee of Saudi Aramco held an emergency session at its headquarters in Dhahran, Saudi Arabia, on the 26th of January in order to discuss this tragic situation. The chairman of the committee declared, "We knew the Iraqi government had been threatening to turn the Gulf into flames. They planned to release oil and ignite it in an attempt to stop any amphibious landings. We had met about that threat and were getting prepared for such an event." But no one imagined an oil spill of such magnitude! Initial reports indicated that the oil spill could be as large as ten million barrels. However, this was estimated downward to nearly 5 million barrels. It certainly was far larger than the oil spill which occurred off the Gulf of Mexico in 1979, where over four million barrels of oil spilled in the span of 40 days, due to a well blowout. . . The Global Oil Spill Coordinator for Saudi Aramco, Abdullah Zaindin remarked,

---

* Between February 23–27, 1991, another unique act of environmental terrorism was committed against the State of Kuwait by burning over 700 of its oil wells. These well fires were burning about six million barrels of oil per day. It took eight months to put them under control.

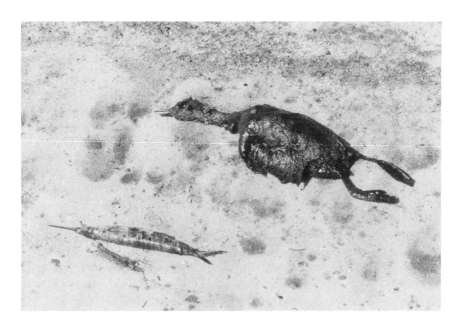

Environmental terrorism led to the worst environmental disaster in history.

"I was prepared in my mind for something large, but not for an oil spill of anything like that size." Saudi Aramco went into action and began the massive job of dispatching booms and acquiring the necessary equipment and material for combating this gigantic oil spill.

In the meantime, a task force was established and directed by Dr. A. Al-Gain, President of MEPA, and NCWCO Secretary-General Dr. A. Zinada. At King Fahd University of Petroleum and Minerals, computer models were established to predict the movement and behavior of the oil slick. This was to help the Saudi and International team in devising the plans necessary to succeed in combating such a gigantic oil spill. Top oil spill experts from throughout the world rendered their assistance. Experts and critically needed equipment came from the United States of America, Britain, France, Germany, Canada, New Zealand, the Netherlands, Norway, Japan and the former Soviet Union.

The U.S. Coast Guard had representatives in the Arabian Gulf region who assessed response techniques and provided the necessary technical aid to the responsible Saudi authorities. The Coast Guard Aireye carried daily flights and made good use of its special electronic sensors, which gave periodic updates relating to this massive oil slick. These data helped Saudi authorities in devising proper strategies for combating the spill. Booms were set to protect sensitive areas, and especially water desalination plants. Initially, about 100 pilings were set in the sea floor, in order to secure these booms from adverse weather and wave action. The oil finally reached Saffaniya in the first week of February. The dispersant chemicals which had been sprayed on the oil spill in its initial stages had not done the job, simply because the light components of the oil slick had evaporated quickly and the thicker remaining oil proved to be hard to penetrate by dispersants. Booms, absorbent booms and skimmers were the most valuable line of defense. Saudi Aramco activated its offices throughout the world especially, in Dhahran, Houston, New York, and Leiden to search for and acquire the necessary oil spill equipment.

Special urgent arrangements had to be made to transport the needed equipment, especially, since commercial flights to Riyadh and Dhahran had been canceled because of the war. By the afternoon of the fourth of February, some thick brown oil, similar to chocolate mousse, was reported outside the diversion booms in Saffaniya. When the weather turned for the worst and waves were up to six feet high, a frenzy of activities dominated the atmosphere in a race to prevent oil from seeping into the intakes of desalination plants. All this was being done under unusual and dangerous circumstances, since the area was right in the midst of the war zone.

Transporting the massive equipment needed, and in a hurry, was a giant job indeed, requiring a massive transport system which needed none other than the giant Antonov-124. This Soviet plane is the world's largest transport aircraft. It landed in early February in Houston, Texas where the acquisition and transport operation was directed by the Houston based Aramco Services Company (ASC), whose president, Hamad Juraifani, personally directed the massive and impressive transport operations. The AN-124, with its four engines, had a payload of 330,700 pounds (150 metric tons) of massive booms and needed equipment for combating a massive oil spill on board, along with two large skimmer boats. One of these came from Seattle, Washington and the other from Long Beach, California; their size is a hefty 40 by 14 feet (12 by 4 meters).

The gigantic efforts spearheaded and coordinated by Saudi Aramco in cooperation with other environmental agencies, energized an impressive force of nearly 450 men at its peak, supported by 49 vacuum tank trucks, 35 skimmer boats, 20 vessels and 40 pieces of an assortment of construction equipment. Work continued until late February, where berm constructions were accelerated and boom replacement and repairs continued to be done. By this time, the oil spill had been practically stopped. Only a small amount escaped, on the order of 2,500 barrels of oil per day, which were coming from various damaged oil tankers in the Kuwait area. As the oil spill moved South, a good bit of it gathered at Manifa Bay. Another shallow bay known as Dawhat Al-Dafi on the southern fringe of Tanajib caught much of this oil and its southerly movement. Although these were unspoiled bays, now they caught over half a million barrels of oil. They became the sacrificial lamb in this massive oil spill, and they saved the rest of Saudi Arabia's East coast from further environmental damage. Efficient recovery teams activated their operations around these bays and much of the oil was skimmed. Skimming operations also took place in the open waters of the Arabian Gulf.

The volunteer effort of many concerned citizens and organizations helped very much in the cleanup operation and in rescuing many birds and animals of the Gulf.

In all, about twenty miles of offshore booms and an equal length of oil absorbent booms along with sixteen skimmers were used. It took 24 chartered planes to transport the urgently needed cargo to Dhahran, Saudi Arabia, and from there further north to the scene of the tragic oil disaster. The oil recovered from these massive operations amounted to nearly one million barrels. The complete stop to any oil spill was finally achieved in the first week of May, 1991.

Saddam Hussein's terrorism, be it against men or his environment, did not shake the solid front against him, nor did it reshape his image . . .

Presidential Address

At a press conference held on January 25, 1991, when answering a question as to why the Coalition did not directly target the Iraqi ruler, President George Bush said, "because we are not in the business of targeting Saddam Hussein . . . no one will weep when he is gone . . . we have no argument with the people of Iraq. We don't want to see a destabilized Iraq when this is all over, but we also don't want to see a continuation of this aggression. We will not tolerate a continuation of this brutality and so we have a mix of problems, but the problems are not with the Iraqi people in the streets of Baghdad."

In the U.S., time was getting near for the presentation of the yearly State of the Union message. At the same time the worry about terrorism was reaching new heights. During the above mentioned press conference a reporter asked, "Why not give the State of the Union message quietly from the White House?" By doing so, the reporter meant that the President would avoid being exposed to danger from any possible terrorist act which could be executed through the orders of Saddam Hussein. President George Bush answered: "Well, many presidents have given a State of the Union message by post messenger; sent it up there, and I don't know that any of them have been done from the White House; but when I go to the capitol, let me put it that way, I will have total confidence in the security apparatus in this country. It doesn't bother me one single bit, and I know that this man (Saddam Hussein) has sponsored terrorism and we continue to be safeguarding in every way we can against it. But the capitol of the United States will be secure and the people that are there will be safe and so it doesn't worry me . . . Yes, every once in a while you find some outbreak (of terrorist violence), none quite like that though, that was probably the most, but it does not concern me. I will be standing up there giving that speech with total confidence in the men and women of our security system, they are the best. I haven't considered changing. I am not going to be held a captive in the White House by Saddam Hussein of Iraq and you can make a note of that one. We are going about our business and the world goes on. Somebody asked me a while back about the Super Bowl! Do you think we ought to cancel the Super Bowl because of this situation: one, the war is serious business and the nation is focused on it and two, life goes on, and parading of

American prisoners, and boy that one has hit me right square in the heart. I tell you!"

President George Bush of the United States of America delivered on January 29, 1991 at 9:09 P.M. EST a speech on the State of the Union, delivered to a joint session of Congress. Here are some excerpts:

"Mr. President, and Mr. Speaker, and members of the United States Congress. I come to this House of the people to speak to you and all Americans, certain that we stand at a defining hour. Halfway around the world, we are engaged in a great struggle in the skies and on the seas and sands. We know why we're there. We are Americans–part of something larger than ourselves. For two centuries, we've done the hard work of freedom. And tonight, we lead the world in facing down a threat to decency and humanity.

What is at stake is more than one small country; it is a big idea: *a new world order*, where diverse nations are drawn together in common cause to achieve the universal aspirations of mankind–peace and security, freedom, and the rule of law. Such is a world worthy of our struggle and worthy of our children's future.

The community of nations has resolutely gathered to condemn and repel lawless aggression. Saddam Hussein's unprovoked invasion–his ruthless, systematic rape of a peaceful neighbor–violated everything the community of nations holds dear. The world has said this aggression would not stand–and it will not stand.

Together, we have resisted the trap of appeasement, cynicism, and isolation that gives temptation to tyrants. The world has answered Saddam's invasion with 12 United Nations Resolutions, starting with a demand for Iraq's immediate and unconditional withdrawal and backed up by forces from 28 countries of six continents. With few exceptions, the world now stands as one . . .

The triumph of democratic ideas in Eastern Europe and Latin America, and the continuing struggle for freedom elsewhere all around the world all confirm the wisdom of our nation's founders.

Tonight, we work to achieve another victory–a victory over tyranny and savage aggression.

We in this Union enter the last decade of the 20th century thankful for our blessings, steadfast in our purpose, aware of our difficulties, and responsive to our duties at home and around the world.

The conviction and courage we see in the Persian Gulf today is simply the American character in action. The indomitable spirit that is contributing to this victory for world peace and justice is the same spirit that gives us the power and the potential to meet our toughest challenges at home.

We are resolute and resourceful. If we can selflessly confront evil for the sake of good in a land so far away, then surely we can make this land all that it should be. If anyone tells you that America's best days are behind her, they're looking the wrong way. . .

This nation was founded by leaders who understood that power belongs in the hands of people. And they planned for the future. And so must we–here and all around the world.

As Americans, we know that there are times when we must step forward and accept our responsibility to lead the world away from the dark chaos of dictators, toward the brighter promise of a better day.

Almost 50 years ago we began a long struggle against aggressive totalitarianism. Now we face another defining hour for America and the world.

There is no one more devoted, more committed to the hard work of freedom, than every soldier and sailor, every Marine, airman, and Coastguardsman–every man and woman now serving in the Persian Gulf. Oh, how they deserve–and what a fitting tribute to them.

You see–what a wonderful, fitting tribute to them. Each of them has volunteered–volunteered to provide for this nation's defense–and now they bravely struggle, to earn for America, for the world, and for future generations, a just and lasting peace.

Our commitment to them must be equal to their commitment to their country. They are truly America's finest.

The war in the Gulf is not a war we wanted. We worked hard to avoid war. For more than five months we, along with the Arab League, the European Community, the United Nations, tried every diplomatic avenue. U.N. Secretary General Perez de Cuellar; Presidents Gorbachev, Mitterrand, Ozal, Moubarak, and Bendjadid; Kings Fahd and Hassan; Prime Ministers Major and Andreotti–just to name a few–all worked for a solution. But time and again, Saddam Hussein flatly rejected the path of diplomacy and peace.

The world well knows how this conflict began and when: It began on August 2nd, when Saddam invaded and sacked a small, defenseless neighbor. And I am certain of how it will end. So that peace can prevail, we will prevail.

Tonight, I am pleased to report that we are on course. Iraq's capacity to sustain war is being destroyed. Our investment, our training, our planning–all are paying off. Time will not be Saddam's salvation.

Our purpose in the Persian Gulf remains constant: to drive Iraq out of Kuwait, to restore Kuwait's legitimate government, and to ensure the stability and security of this critical region.

Let me make clear what I mean by the region's stability and security.

We do not seek the destruction of Iraq, its culture, or its people. Rather, we seek an Iraq that uses its great resources, not to destroy, not to serve the ambitions of a tyrant, but to build a better life for itself and its neighbors. We seek a Persian Gulf where conflict is no longer the rule, where the strong are neither tempted nor able to intimidate the weak.

Most Americans know instinctively why we are in the Gulf. They know we had to stop Saddam now, not later. They know that this brutal dictator will do anything; will use any weapon; will commit any outrage, no matter how many innocents suffer.

They know we must make sure that control of the world's oil resources does not fall into his hands, only to finance further aggression. They know that we need to build a new, enduring peace–based not on arms races and confrontation, but on shared principles and the rule of law.

And we all realize that our responsibility to be the catalyst for peace in the region does not end with the successful conclusion of this war.

Democracy brings the undeniable value of thoughtful dissent–and we've heard some dissenting voices here at home–some, a handful, reckless–most responsible. But the fact that all voices have the right to speak out is one of the reasons we've been united in purpose and principle for 200 years.

Our progress in this great struggle is the result of years of vigilance and a steadfast commitment to a strong defense. Now, with remarkable technological advances like the Patriot Missile, we can defend against ballistic missile attacks aimed at innocent civilians.

Looking forward, I have directed that the SDI program be refocused on providing protection from limited ballistic missile strikes–whatever their source. Let us pursue an SDI program that can deal with any future threat to the United States, to our forces overseas, and to our friends and allies. . .

The courage and success of the RAF pilots, of the Kuwaiti, Saudi, French, the Canadians, the Italians, the pilots of Qatar and Bahrain–all are proof that for the first time since World War II, the international community is united. The leadership of the United Nations, once only a hoped-for ideal, is now confirming its founders' vision.

I am heartened that we are not being asked to bear alone the financial burdens of this struggle. Last year, our friends and allies provided the bulk of the economic costs of Desert Shield. And now, having received commitments of over $40 billion for the first three months of 1991, I am confident they will do no less as we move through Desert Storm.

But the world has to wonder what the dictator of Iraq is thinking. If he thinks that by targeting innocent civilians in Israel and Saudi Arabia, that he will gain advantage, he is dead wrong. If he thinks that he will advance his cause through tragic and despicable environmental terrorism, he is dead wrong. And if he thinks that by abusing the coalition prisoners of war he will benefit, he is dead wrong.

We will succeed in the Gulf. And when we do, the world community will have sent an enduring warning to any dictator or despot, present or future, who contemplates outlaw aggression.

The world can, therefore, seize this opportunity to fulfill the long-held promise of a *new world order,* where brutality will go unrewarded and aggression will meet collective resistance.

Yes, the United States bears a major share of leadership in this effort. Among the nations of the world, only the United States of America has both the moral standing and the means to back it up. We're the only nation on this Earth that could assemble the forces of peace. This is the burden of leadership and the strength that has made America the beacon of freedom in a searching world.

This nation has never found glory in war. Our people have never wanted to abandon the blessings of home and work, for distant lands and deadly conflict. If we fight in anger, it is only because we have to fight at all. And all of us yearn for a world where we will never have to fight again.

Each of us will measure within ourselves the value of this great struggle. Any cost in lives—any cost—is beyond our power to measure. But the cost of closing our eyes to aggression is beyond mankind's power to imagine.

This we do know: Our cause is just. Our cause is moral. Our cause is right.

Let future generations understand the burden and the blessings of freedom. Let them say we stood where duty required us to stand.

Let them know that, together, we affirmed America and the world as a community of conscience.

The winds of change are with us now. The forces of freedom are together, united. We move toward the next century more confident than ever that we have the will at home and abroad to do what must be done, the hard work of freedom.

May God bless the United States of America. Thank you very, very much."

At a press conference held in Riyadh on January 30, 1991, King Fahd said,

"On this occasion, I would like to express my sincere thanks to our friends who did not hesitate in responding to the Kingdom of Saudi Arabia's call for help from the Arab countries, the Islamic countries, and friendly nations. I, hereby, repeat what I had said before that the Arab States and the Islamic countries and our friends in the United States, Britain, and France have offered the largest striking force which could be offered at this time, be it ground, air or marine forces. A number of countries from Europe and other parts of the world have also offered what they could offer including the fleets which we witnessed today, whether in the Arabian Gulf waters, the Mediterranean Sea, or the Indian Ocean." He continued to say that the occupation of Kuwait by Iraqi forces was, "a prelude to the occupation of Saudi Arabia and possibly other countries."

Also at the same occasion, King Fahd said, "I wish to make this clarification. Our aim in the Kingdom, or Kuwait, in assisting Iraq was not to invade Iran, but it was supporting Iraq so that it would not be invaded by Iran. . . Iran is an Islamic country and it will be in the interest of Iran and the Gulf countries to forget the past and live together in a friendly atmosphere."

At the same press conference, President Moubarak of Egypt said, "We have tried in vain to avoid the war and fighting. I had sent him (Saddam Hussein) about twenty-seven appeals to withdraw to enable us to seek a cease-fire. I am still saying this. I hope he would order his forces to withdraw and begin withdrawing from Kuwait, so that we all, would be able to seek a cease-fire as soon as possible to prevent the shedding of more bloodshed.

Today, we are very much concerned about the Iraqi people in the same way we are concerned about the Egyptian and Saudi people and mankind at large. We never like to fight with each other. Whenever I sent an appeal to Saddam Hussein, in return I received many insults."

The Battle of Khafji

On the 29th of January, 1991, the Coalition Forces reached a strength in excess of 700,000. Over 110 ships were engaged in the theater of operations and U.S. troops reached a staggering number of 490,000.

Iraqi forces mounted a four-pronged raid from Kuwait. A mechanized Iraqi battalion was engaged near the Kuwaiti town of Al-Wafra. U.S. and Allied Forces used Cobra gunships and other fighting aircraft to repulse the attack and decimate enemy forces; in that engagement, several tanks were destroyed. This was a diversionary move by the Iraqi forces, because their aim was not the incursion in that area of the Kuwait-Saudi border, but they were shooting for a bigger prize in the deserted coastal Saudi city of Khafji (also known as Al-Khafji or

Ra's Al-Khafji). This Saudi town on the Arabian Gulf is to the southeast of Wafra just across the border from Kuwait. An Iraqi battalion crossed the border to Khafji, their tanks moving with turned turrents which is a known gesture for surrender. Suddenly, they aimed their guns at anything they could hit in the city of Khafji, located only six miles inside the Saudi border. The attacking force comprised over 80 tanks. They hit Saudi positions; marines in the neighboring area took cover. A ferocious and bloody battle was in the making. Fortunately the city of Khafji had been evacuated several days prior to the Iraqi invasion. Forces from the Saudi National Guard, the Royal Saudi Marines and Qatari forces poured into the city in order to engage enemy forces and destroy them. A column of United States marines moved closer to the battle area. Already a few marines were inside the city for lookout. Light armored vehicles and anti-tank TOE Missiles were sent in with the marines. While the battle raged on between the Saudi Forces and the Iraqis, army Cobra helicopters joined the melee and helped in destroying enemy tanks; in the heat of the battle the Army Blackhawks and AC-130s were pounding the enemy. From a northern air field in Saudi Arabia came the A-10 tank killers. The protective shield from the artillery of the Coalition Forces coupled with the impeccable air strikes by Saudi and U.S. forces, combined to throw the enemy into total confusion and disarray.

One soldier stated, "I think it is more of a harassing move; they know that we don't have a whole lot of forces up in Khafji." At the Central Command Headquarters in Riyadh, Saudi Arabia, General Norman Schwarzkopf, Commander of the U.S. and Allied Forces in Saudi Arabia was asked if he was surprised about the cross-border attack, he said, "I would tell you, I don't think that battle is over by a long shot. I expect a lot more fighting will occur tonight. I would tell you that, obviously we have been talking and we are ready for whatever comes in there. I don't think we were surprised." He also said, downplaying the significance of the initial Iraqi performance, as being "about as significant as a mosquito on an elephant."

The battle to retake the city was fought viciously. Saudi and Qatari forces fought with great zeal and valor. While the area was generally controlled by Arab Coalition Forces, a few marine units were also posted nearby.

The battle was so ferocious, it was fought "house to house and tank to tank." Saddam Hussein desperately wanted to have a foothold on Saudi territory, so he could use it extensively for his propaganda machine to state to the world that despite the massive air bombardment of the great armada of Allied Forces, and despite the might of the Saudi Air Force and armed forces, he was able to occupy Saudi territory!

On this score, again, he failed miserably! "At one point the Iraqi fire power was so intense, the Saudi and Qatari forces had to temporarily retreat." But it was not for long. They regrouped and hit the Iraqi attacking force with vengeance. The Iraqi forces were firing rockets, which hit dangerously close to positions of the marines on the southern fringes of Khafji. The U.S. Marines fired back with gusto using heavy machine guns. However, they were ordered to stop the firing when the U.S. reconnaissance team was being hit from friendly fire in the heat of the battle. Two of the teams were moved out from the city proper. One of the team said, "When we got to the gates of the city, it was like all hell broke loose and there were tracers flying everywhere, and we abandoned our vehicle and got into a garage."

On Thursday morning, January 31, 1991, around 2:30 A.M., the Saudi and Allied Forces started their counterattack against the Iraqi occupiers. Enemy forces were besieged. They were estimated to be a brigade. The strategy was to cut off the enemy from the north and to launch a counterattack from the south.

The tide of the battle began to turn when tanks of the Saudi and Qatari forces attacked a water tower which was occupied by Iraqi artillery spotters. The Saudis then requested help from U.S. helicopter gunships to destroy the enemy on the tower. Finally, after a vicious battle that raged on for a couple of days, the enemy forces were defeated and retreated in a hurry, leaving behind tanks and armored personnel carriers—mostly destroyed and some intact. Many of their dead remained behind and several others were taken as prisoners of war. Thus, within 48 hours, the Saudi town of Khafji was liberated from the Iraqi occupiers. Mop-up operations were accomplished by 3:00 P.M. on Thursday afternoon, January 31, 1991. An eyewitness report said, "There is no doubt that the Saudis are in control of Khafji tonight. At least, they were when I was there a few hours ago and there is absolutely no doubt that there was a big battle there."

Prince Khaled Bin Sultan Bin Abdulaziz, Commander of the Multinational Arab Forces in Saudi Arabia answered a question relating to the infiltration of Iraqi troops into Khafji on February 9, 1991, he said, "We were expecting such infiltration and accordingly we evacuated civilians from the city." He then said, "When the aggressor tried to infiltrate into Khafji, we set up a National Guard battalion along with a Qatari battalion and successfully cut the aggressors supply lines. Since last Wednesday (January 30) afternoon, Khafji has been liberated and the aggressors' soldiers have become prisoners of war." He also stated that any delay in the liberation of Khafji was due to the fact that the joint forces were very keen on minimizing their casualties and inflicting the aggressor with heavy losses.

The rumble of air strikes and flashes of artillery continued in the distance. The road to Khafji was now lined with heavy armored vehicles mostly Saudi and some of it from the Allied Forces. "The battle-scarred town was filled with the stench of war and littered with the debris of war." The Iraqi armored personnel carriers and their tanks were still smoldering, many ripped apart by the defending forces and by the support they received from the U.S. marines.

Lt. General Khaled Bin Sultan Bin Abdulaziz, said regarding the battle of Khafji, "The Iraqis were easy prey. I think they were pushed for this. It is like a suicide mission. Most of them surrendered without a fight after we surrounded them."

While some sporadic small elements remained, they were swiftly neutralized and some small mopping operations continued. The Iraqi forces were continually being pounded from the air.

The town of Khafji was a deserted town and Saddam Hussein's forces did not have any air coverage whatsoever; they were essentially easy prey, not only for the Saudi armor but also to the American and Allied Forces. Despite all this, Saddam Hussein in his desperation and utter disregard for the safety of his men, ordered the attack on Khafji in order to grab the headlines. He wanted this to be a psychological boost, and he always wanted to speed up the time table for the ground war so that he could cause severe casualties among the Allies; hoping that heavy casualties would cause an uproar among the populations of the Allied nations and thus would exert their pressure on their governments to ease out and stop the war of liberation. But on this and all other fronts, Saddam Hussein failed!

While the Iraqis occupied Khafji for nearly two days, the significance of such an occupation was downplayed by General Norman Schwarzkopf who said, "I have already heard that is being counted as a major military victory on the battlefield. You know, moving into an unoccupied village, six miles inside the friendly lines, when there is nobody there, I don't consider that a major military victory. However, if they want to consider it one, that's fine. However, that's just one battle, that's not the war."

An Iraqi armored column attempting to reinforce Iraqi elements north of Khafji was attacked by the Saudi Royal Air Force flying F-5s and Tornados. Iraqi forces had to retreat.

Saudi forces took 420 Iraqi prisoners of war from the battle of Khafji. They destroyed nearly 100 armored vehicles and Iraqi tanks. About 93 armored vehicles and transports were captured along with enough equipment to meet the needs of an entire armored battalion. An Allied soldier who captured some Iraqis said, "I don't think the reservist (Iraqi) individuals want to fight. I don't think they know how

The Battle of Al-Khafji.

to fight! They were just thankful, quite frankly they were very happy that I was saving them from this situation." Iraqi prisoners of war were receiving only one meal a day in the Kuwaiti Theater of Operations. The Iraqis also lost 40 soldiers killed in battle and 33 were injured. The Saudis and other Allied Forces lost 18 soldiers killed, 29 wounded and 4 missing. Eleven U.S. marines were killed, eight of them were from friendly fire. These were the first casualties of a ground battle.

For those who doubted the Saudi determination to defend their homeland, the world was saying, "Come to Khafji!" Prior to this battle some biased reporting alluded that the Americans and British had been hired by the Saudis to do their battle. This was far from the truth, as expressed by U.S. Colonel John Noble who was well acquainted with the Khafji battle. He said, "It wasn't that way at all, just the opposite. They wanted this. This is Saudi Arabia." He then continued to say to an American reporter, "We had been working with them and you never know until you are in the battle. I mean I was in Vietnam and even the Americans you think you know, soldiers, but until you have actually fought with them, you don't know them. And when they attacked, it surprised me! Honestly! Because they did it with such force. We thought about closing with the enemy and the soldiers went straight at the enemy, past the enemy, even under fire. I could not have asked for any American to do any better!"

Shortly after the decisive Saudi victory in the battle of Khafji, General Norman Schwarzkopf stated, "I played down Khafji as militarily insignificant (for Iraq) and I still say that but subsequently, results have shown that politically it was very significant. Everybody said the Arabs wouldn't fight. The Arabs fought and they fought very well. They acquitted themselves magnificently well and it turned out, I think, Saddam tried to start out for a great propaganda victory and in fact took a bad, bad licking. So that may have backfired on him."

Colonel Jack Petri, of the U.S. Central Command said regarding this decisive battle, "They (the Saudis) acquitted themselves terribly well."

The aggressors described their attack on Khafji as, "A lightening strike into the Kingdom of Evil." They indicated that President Saddam Hussein visited his troops in the southern portion of Iraq in Basra just a few days prior to the battle of Khafji. Saddam, along with the Revolutionary Command Council issued the orders for their military to attack the coastal city.

"Radio Baghdad declared that the first signs of dawn on January 30, began to illuminate the battlefield on the ground, giving hope to all Arabs, honest men in the world and believers." According to the same reference, on January 31, Iraqi mechanized divisions, with some

250 tanks and nearly 60,000 soldiers, were gathering in the southwestern Kuwaiti border in Al-Wafra. Also, a ten mile long Iraqi column was making its way through Kuwait. Both of these units were subjected to furious assaults from the Allied Air Force. They exacted heavy casualties from the aggressor's forces and aborted any possible attack by them.

Saudi Forces performed exceptionally well in the Battle of Khafji. Here is a brief background on the National Guard and other Saudi Forces participating in this battle:

National Guard

The National Guard of Saudi Arabia and Crown Prince Abdullah Bin Abdulaziz have been truly intertwined for decades. The Crown Prince has taken special interest in various internal affairs. He has been head of the National Guard from 1963 until the present day. His keen interest in developing and making it a potent force, truly essential to the security of the Kingdom, was achieved through his deep and total dedication to the Guard. Considerable precious time was spent with the traditional groups of the Saudi society, especially tribal leaders who helped in providing the capable troops for the National Guard, which became highly trained and modernized. This made it a strong force in internal security matters and a power to be reckoned with in case of serious emergency. This is not a reserve force like its American counterpart. Most of the National Guard personnel are on active duty. It is a parallel and separate force from the regular armed forces. It remains the most powerful internal security force. Due to extensive training and modernization, it has become very valuable for reinforcing the regular armed forces in case of a major emergency or an invasion. Such an emergency presented itself when the aggressors came to occupy the Saudi town of Khafji upon the direct orders of Saddam Hussein and his Revolutionary Command Council. The National Guard's performance under the unified command of Lt. General Khaled Bin Sultan was very admirable indeed. The Cavalry of the National Guard is a crack regiment that carries with it an emotional and historical appeal. Being the descendents of those men who swept out of the desert of Arabia in support of King Abdulaziz, their presence always brings cherished memories of the long struggle for unifying the Kingdom. Aside from the Cavalry, the motorized battalions are equipped with modern tanks, half-tracks, and mobile artillery designed for desert conditions.

The great expanse of Saudi Arabia, a country as large as the United States of America east of the Mississippi River, requires a strong deterrent to any potential aggressors. The Ministry of Defense commanding under its realm the Army, Navy and Air Force (described previously), and in cooperation with other security forces, sees to it that any potential aggressor is doomed to defeat.

His Royal Highness Prince Sultan Bin Abdulaziz, second Deputy Prime Minister, Minister of Defense and Aviation and Inspector General has contributed extensively in the modernization of these forces. Military training is modern and sophisticated. It has made strong headway in improving Saudi military capabilities and thus boosting self-confidence. The primary mission of the Ministry of Defense is to defend the nation through the use of military forces.

Army

The army has become a strong force in size and deterrence. It includes mechanized armored infantry and airborne brigades. A number of artillery battalions and anti-aircraft artillery batteries, along with surface-to-air missile batteries, also are a major part of the army. The Royal Guard Regiment is part of the Saudi combat units.

About forty kilometers from Riyadh, King Abdulaziz Military Academy is the major source for second lieutenants for the Army. It replaced the Royal Military College. This facility was designed for accommodating 1,500 cadets. It is a self-sufficient small city, having family housing for staff and faculty. Military and academic subjects are taught. The duration of study is three years. Graduates earn a Bachelor of Military Science upon completion of the program. The newly commissioned Second Lieutenant officers attend advanced school for further specialization in armor, artillery, infantry, airborne, air defense, engineering communications, maintenance or military administration. Competition is keen for students to attend the Command and Staff College in Riyadh. It offers a Master's Degree program in military science. It is patterned after its counterpart in the U.S.A. Officers are chosen to be sent for higher military education in the United States, France, Britain, West Germany and other friendly countries.

Royal Saudi Navy

The Royal Saudi Navy was very effective and cooperative with the U.S. and Allied Navies in the Arabian Gulf, especially in combating the spread of mines by enemy forces. Thousands of Saudi personnel had received training abroad, mainly in the United States, Britain and France. Naval equipment was built and supplied from various sources. Some of these came from America at the yard of the Tacoma Boat Building Company of Washington, and the Peterson Builder of Wisconsin. Certain Torpedo boats were built in West Germany along with other patrol craft. Some coastal patrol craft was built by Cnim of Cherbourg, France. Other craft was built by Halter Marine of New Orleans, USA.

Saudi Naval expansion programs provided for the establishment of a deep water port in Jeddah on the Red Sea and Jubail on the Arabian Gulf, along with the construction of various major bases at both Jeddah and Jubail. The United States Army Corps of Engineers was assigned to oversee this construction in its capacity as the provider of engineering and construction management services to the government. Smaller naval bases also exist at Ras Tannura, Ras Al-Mishab, Yanbu and Dammam.

The War Continues

On the 29th of January, U.S. marines captured the island of Omm Al-Maradim, which is twelve miles off the Kuwaiti coast. The Kuwaiti flag was hoisted and antiaircraft weapons destroyed. This reclaimed Kuwaiti territory is the second island liberated so far. Navy Helos, while investigating reports about some Iraqis willing to surrender, were fired upon by approximately 20 Iraqi small craft, using automatic weapons and rocket propelled grenades. Four of the boats were sunk and twelve were damaged.

Again two weeks after the beginning of the air war, on January 30, over 32,000 sorties had taken place and on this day itself 2,600 were carried out. Air to air losses so far had been zero as far as U.S. aircraft are concerned. The Coalition Forces now totaled 705,000 and U.S. troops were now over half a million.

Despite the great success of the air war and heavy losses on the Iraqi side, all appeals to Saddam Hussein to withdraw from Kuwait went unheeded. On January 30, 1991, the Secretary General of the United Nations, Javier Perez de Cuellar, wrote a letter to the Foreign Minister of Iraq in which he said,

"I have read your letter of 24 January, 1991, (S/22154) with regret and cannot but reject its connotations.

When we met at Amman on 31 August, 1990 and at Baghdad on 12 January, 1991, and again when I met President Saddam Hussein on 13 January, 1991, I stated that our efforts to avert the unfolding tragedy would fail unless Iraq could signify its readiness to comply with the relevant resolutions of the Security Council, beginning with resolution 660 (1990). On each occasion, after returning to New York, I reported the views of your Government to the Security Council.

As you know, on 15 January, 1991 (see S/22091), I appealed again to President Saddam Hussein to indicate his readiness to proceed in the manner I had suggested to him, so that the course of events could be turned away from catastrophe and towards a new era of justice and harmony, based on the principles of the Charter of the United Nations. I pledged, in such circumstances, to work with him, and with all others concerned, to bring just and lasting peace to the Middle East as a whole.

Today, I reiterate my 15 January appeal, as I did on 22 January, 1991, when I also expressed my profound grief and anxiety at the increasing severity of the war, the widening of the area of hostilities and my fear that the toll in death and destruction would escalate unless my appeal received a positive response. I continue to believe that such a response is needed in order to find a peaceful solution to this grave and tragic conflict and to save human lives. In the mean time, in order to alleviate the present suffering which is causing me deep anguish, I have already asked the main humanitarian agencies of the United Nations system to co-ordinate their efforts with a view to ensuring that help is provided to those afflicted by the conflict as soon as circumstances permit.

You will recall, Mr. Minister, that when speaking in the formal meeting of the Security Council after the adoption of resolution 678 (1990), I stressed that, in requiring compliance with the resolutions of the Council, the United Nations sought not surrender but the most honorable way of resolving a crisis in a manner that respected all legitimate interests and was conducive to the wider peace and the rule of law. I also underlined that the actions of the United Nations in the present crisis must be perceived as part of the larger endeavor of the Organization to establish *peace through justice*, whenever the one was imperiled and the other denied.

That remains my view today and I would therefore urge your Government to make a serious effort to put this tragic situation on the road to a peaceful solution."

Of course, the Secretary General's appeal did not trigger any positive response. On the contrary, on the 31st of January, 1991, Saddam Hussein, in an interview, was just himself, arrogant, stubborn and evasive. Asked if he had any doubts about the outcome of the war, he was quick to respond by saying, "not one in a million, whoever attacks the men in Kuwait will be beaten." He was fully convinced that the "mother of all battles" would prevail on his side—he and his troops would be the victors! His world was so far removed from reality, one cannot but wonder about the state of mind which governs such tyrants who commit their people to national suicide! Anything can be sacrificed, be it the people, the army, the nation, as long as Saddam Hussein prevailed! What a tragedy!

By the second of February, 35 Iraqi naval ships were mostly destroyed and some severely damaged. On the third of February, 1991 an Iraqi Scud missile was launched toward Riyadh at 12:50 A.M. Part of the missile was intercepted by a Patriot Missile and destroyed while the second part fell in a residential area. Some damage occurred: two homes were destroyed and 29 people were slightly injured. Fourteen of these were Saudis, six Jordanians, four Syrian, three from Yemen, one from Kuwait and one from Pakistan. This included women and small children.

On this day the battleship Missouri fired its huge guns against prefabricated concrete command and control bunkers which were being moved by Iraq into the Kuwaiti theater. The sixteen-inch guns of this famous ship fired eight 2,000-pound shells against these targets and destroyed them. This battleship was active during the Korean War and this is the first time its huge guns pounded targets since that time. The barrage of these high explosives continued to cause devastation and annihilation of enemy targets in the Gulf War. Also for the first time, a Remotely Piloted Vehicle (RPV) was used for gunfire spotting when the environment was too hostile for other means to be effective.

In the Aftermath of Khafji

Shortly after the decisive defeat of the aggressor's forces in Khafji, President George Bush stated,

"Coalition Forces continued to perform their assigned missions with great professionalism and thankfully with only modest casualties on our side. We are going to extraordinary, and should I say, extra lengths to avoid damage to civilians and Holy Places. We do not seek Iraq's destruction, nor do we seek to punish the Iraqi people for the decisions and policies of their leaders. In addition, we are doing everything possible and with great success to minimize collateral damage, despite the fact that Saddam is now relocating some military functions such as Command and Control Headquarters in civilian areas such as schools. I would also emphasize that our goals have not changed. We continue to seek Iraq's full compliance with the 12 relevant U.N. Security Resolutions. . .

There is strong support in many Arab countries. And I am staying in very close touch with our Coalition partners. I am also encouraged when I talk to them about the support in their countries and in other parts of the Arab world for what we are doing. . . Yes, I have seen the demonstrations in Amman (Jordan). I have seen some of the demonstrations in the Maghrib (Morocco). . . They will not influence my decision-making on the timing involved, say for the use of ground forces. Saddam Hussein will not set the timing for what comes next.

We will do that and I will have to make that decision if we go to ground forces and I will do it upon serious consideration and recommendations of our military, including our Secretary of Defense and Chairman, of course, but also of our Commanders in the field. I see those demonstrations and I understand that some look at this, some of the more fundamentalists, particularly differently. But I am also gratified with the support in the Arab world and I think it is strong. I think a lot of them want to see this man (Saddam Hussein) comply with these resolutions fully and not see this aggression rewarded, no matter what is happening in the streets."

On the second of February, the Iraqi military newspaper Al-Qadisiya declared, "We will use whatever power and whatever weapons that are at our disposal from kitchen knives to weapons of mass destruction."

King Hussein of Jordan, delivered a bitter speech in which he attacked the Coalition Forces, especially the United States of America. He declared that the U.S. sought regional dominance, "It is waging war against all Arabs and all Moslems, not just against Iraq alone." It was an angry and shaking speech, indeed, from someone who had received substantial aid from both countries, the U.S. and the Kingdom, for several decades!

Secretary of State, James Baker, declared upon hearing of the speech, "We find it very sad that the King omitted in this rather long speech any reference whatsoever, not one single reference to Iraq's invasion of Kuwait!"

On February 3, 1991, in an interview with David Brinkley, King Hussein was totally evasive in his responses. Nevertheless, the truth existed that he threw his lot entirely behind Saddam Hussein and the extremist fundamentalist and Palestinian forces in his country. When President Bush heard of the King's speech, he openly expressed his disappointment and said, "We have always had a historically good relationship with Jordan. This complicates things."

Senator Richard Lugar, of Indiana, former chairman of the powerful Senate Foreign Relations Committee stated in this regard, "We should not give any unauthorized aid to Jordan while we are at war; and Jordan has amply discussed the situation and decided that they are against us. I appreciate Hussein (King) but I appreciate likewise constance of friendship."

King Hussein not only supported Saddam Hussein but blamed the Allies for, "committing war crimes under the disguise of U.N. Resolutions."

By February 4, 1991, over 44,000 sorties had been flown by the Coalition Forces. This was nearly one bombing sortie for every minute of Desert Storm operations. These included 250 sorties and six B-52 strikes on the Republican Guard stationed in southern Iraq on the fringes of the Kuwaiti border. These attacks caused softening and weakening of this elite group of the Iraqi forces. More Scud missiles were destroyed. Three of them were hit on this day; some tanks and truck convoys were hit and damaged.

So far on the 4th of February, 1991, the total Iraqi prisoners stood at 742 in the Kingdom of Saudi Arabia. These prisoners of war included 43 officers.

The Saudi Air Force had been effectively targeting armored aircraft shelters, hangers, air bases, the Republican Guard in the Kuwaiti Theater of Operations and the aggressor's forces in Kuwait, along with the air defenses and military installations in Kuwait proper.

By the fifth of February, Marine Harriers bombed and strafed a 25-truck convoy which caused several secondary explosions. Resupply convoys, which were trying to cross the bombed out bridges connecting Baghdad to Basra, were hit by repeated air strikes.

At 2:40 P.M. on February 4, Saudi time, Saudi Naval forces spotted two enemy sea targets near Omm Al-Maradim Island, then directed Royal Saudi Naval airplanes to identify them. When they were identified, two of the four boats were bombed and destroyed, while a repair and a support ship was set on fire.

Also, on this day, the Saudi Minister of the Interior, Prince Naif Bin Abdulaziz, announced the arrest of those responsible for shooting at a bus carrying military men in Jeddah. The attackers were non-Saudis working in the Kingdom.

On February 5, 1991, at 9:30 P.M., the enemy attempted to sneak into Khafji again. This time coming from the Arabian Gulf waters. An exchange of fire with the Saudi Navy marines sent the enemy running for cover. Two Iraqi boats escaped, while another one was hit and sunk. The battleship Missouri continued to fire its powerful sixteen-inch guns with their high explosive bombs. It fired 112 of the 2,000-pound shells and twelve 5-inch rounds in a 48 hour period. After the devastating attack by the Missouri, came the battleship Wisconsin to pound enemy targets, coming into action for the first time since its participation in the Korean War. Its sixteen-inch guns dealt enemy forces in Kuwait a heavy destructive blow and threw them into despair and confusion. The USS Wisconsin fired a salvo of eleven rounds at an Iraqi artillery battery in southern Kuwait destroying it completely.

The U.S. casualties so far totaled 35. Twelve killed in action, twenty-three non-combatant deaths; eleven were wounded in action, while twenty-four were missing in action and eight were prisoners of war.

On February 6, 1991, seven Iraqi MiG-21 planes were detected flying to neighboring Iran. The Coalition Forces shot four of them while the other three escaped and reached Iran.

Thirty-two nations now had forces in place supporting Desert Storm operations. Some of these nations having sizable forces, others symbolic. They are: Argentina, Australia, Bahrain, Bangladesh, Belgium, Canada, China, Czechoslovakia, Denmark, Egypt, France, Germany, Greece, Hungary, Italy, Kuwait, Morocco, the Netherlands, New Zealand, Niger, Norway, Oman, Pakistan, Poland, Qatar, Saudi Arabia, Senegal, Spain, Syria, United Arab Emirates, United Kingdom and the United States of America.

On February 7, 1991, A-6 planes of the U.S. Navy pounded two Iraqi patrol boats which were spreading mines near Al-Fao Peninsula in the northern Arabian Gulf waters. At 1:48 A.M. February 8, 1991, local time, Iraqi forces launched another Scud missile on Riyadh which was intercepted and destroyed by the Patriot Missile.

By February 11, 1991, the number of Iraqi prisoners of war reached over one thousand. And on this day a three hundred-member contingent of the Afghan Moujahidine fighters became the (33rd) Coalition partner in support of Desert Storm.

By February 9, 1991, Operation Desert Storm had carried more than 57,000 air sorties against enemy targets in both Iraq and Kuwait. These sorties included over 3,700 successfully executed by the Royal Saudi Air Force, 330 by the Kuwaiti Air Force, 21 by Qatar and 126 by the small state of Bahrain. Also, on this day, 6 aircraft of the U.S. forces bombed a Silkworm rocket site at Mina Abdullah in Kuwait. Three launchers and a control vehicle were destroyed in the attack. More sea mines were detected and destroyed.

On February 11, 1991, at 10:22 P.M., Iraqi forces launched a Scud missile on the capital city of Riyadh. Again it was intercepted and destroyed in mid-air. Some of its debris fell on residential areas. Two residents were slightly injured.

The Baghdad Bunker and More U.N. Discussions

On February 13, 1991, two laser-guided bombs were fired on a target in Baghdad. This was "identified as a camouflaged Command and Control bunker. It was located in the residential area of the Al-Ameriah district of Baghdad, Iraq. This attack caused hundreds of casualties. The Iraqi leadership claimed that this was a bomb shelter inhabited by civilians. The number of those killed approached 300. Immediately, Saddam Hussein's propaganda machine went into high gear broadcasting to the world the results of this attack and the gruesome display of several bodies killed in this bunker. It was, indeed, a crucial propaganda coup scored by the Iraqi regime. This was a golden opportunity to portray to the world that the Multi-national Forces were aiming at destroying Iraq. When in reality, these forces did everything humanely possible to avoid the unnecessary loss of civilian life in Iraq. In this endeavor they made excellent use of high tech equipment to achieve pinpoint accuracy and minimize unnecessary losses.

According to U.S. military sources, this bunker was a military one. It was a command and control facility. U.S. and Allied Forces had been systematically attacking such bunkers since the beginning of Desert Storm. According to these authorities, "The U.S. had evidence from satellite photos and electronic intercepts to prove that the facility was military. The roof had been reinforced and camouflaged. The building was also surrounded by fencing and military guards . . . we are not going after civilian targets. It was an active Command and Control structure . . . from a military point of view, nothing went wrong. The target was struck as designated. From a personal point of view, I am outraged that civilians might have been placed in harm's way."

U.S. Secretary of Defense, Dick Cheney, said, "I think you all know that we sincerely regret any damage or any death caused to civilian population. We have done everything we can to avoid that. Our forces, I think, have done an excellent job of targeting military targets and avoiding collateral damage to non-military targets." In fact, the Secretary of Defense went further, suggesting that Saddam Hussein may have consciously and deliberately mingled civilians with military targets. It has been pointed out that messages from the bunker went out on cables which connected with antennas somewhere down a distance from the bunker. The U.S. Secretary of Defense went on to say, "We went after those facilities because they are military targets, because they plugged into the communications network, because we have seen them used to support the military effort."

Thus, according to defense officials, the bunker was attacked because it was sending a barrage of electronic messages. While satellite photos and electronic devices picked up the exchange of these messages, tragically they did not identify the scores of civilians that were placed in harm's way.

General Thomas Kelly, Director of Operations for the Joint Chiefs of Staff, stated that the bunker episode must be "a cold blooded decision on the part of Saddam Hussein to put civilians without our knowledge into a facility and have them bombed. He had to know we knew this was a military facility."

The Foreign Secretary of Great Britain, Douglas Hurd, said in this regard, "There is no doubt that war has its tragedies and sometimes these can be great, even with the greatest possible care and precision."

The Iraqi leader and his Revolutionary Command Council saw this as a boon not a boondoggle. He energized his propaganda machine and was pleased to hear suggestions that the ground war may be on the way sooner than the Allies desired. In the meantime, a flurry of diplomatic activities revived. Some were emanating from Moscow and others from the United Nations. On the afternoon of February 13, 1991, the Security Council of the United Nations convened regarding the Iraqi-Kuwait situation. After some procedural discussion, the Council voted 9 in favor and 2 against with 4 abstentions, relating to discussing the matter in a formal private meeting which was scheduled for 11:00 A.M. on February 14. The two voting against were Cuba and Yemen. The four abstentions were: China, Ecuador, India and Zimbabwe. The members voting in favor of holding the debate behind closed doors were: Austria, Belgium, Côte d'Ivoire, France, Rumania, the former Soviet Union, United Kingdom, United States, and Zaire. The meeting was convened in response to requests made a month earlier by representatives of Cuba, Yemen and the Arab Maghreb Union which is made of Algeria, Libya, Mauritania, Morocco and Tunisia. These nations were asking that the Council hold a public meeting regarding the situation in the Arabian Gulf. The United Kingdom's representative said, "Such a format would allow a careful consideration of all developments away from the glare of publicity. The Council should do nothing to detract from its unity of purpose or to blur the signal being sent to the outside world."

The Yemeni delegate to the United Nations stated, "All small countries supported the right of Kuwait to territorial integrity and sovereignty, but it was legitimate to question the objectives of the military operations now under way. When the Council had authorized the use of all means to implement its resolutions, had it intended to exclude peaceful means? Military operations were taking place in northern Iraq and targeting civilians. Did delegations not have the right to question the purpose of such actions?" He then said, "There had been a failure of diplomatic efforts, but with the visit of Mr. Primaqov to Baghdad yesterday (February 12, 1991), there was a new opportunity for diplomatic initiatives." Of course, Yemen was vigorously trying to hold a public meeting of the United Nations Security Council. However, the majority voted against such a public meeting because it might send the wrong signals to Saddam Hussein and add to his intransigence.

On February 14, 1991, Ambassador Samir S. Shihabi, permanent representative of the Kingdom of Saudi Arabia to the United Nations who became President of the U.N. General Assembly in September, 1991, said, "As for the justifiers, the apologists and the pretenders who said that duty dictates that more chance should have been given to him (Saddam Hussein); we say to them that no usurper in all history was given the chance and time which was given to the Iraqi regime to desist from its adventures and to evacuate Kuwait. How many emissaries marched to him advising and guiding, enlightening and promising, warning and threatening? How many emissaries marched to Baghdad for five and a half months, until the middle of January, explaining the consequences of insisting on oppression and continuing the invasion of Kuwait?

Have you forgotten the game of the guest hostages when each leader or mediator who arrived in Baghdad was given a number of persons to take back to his country, satisfying his visit? To those who call today for excuses and apologies for Iraqi aggression while they know that in this manner *they are sacrificing Kuwait* as a State and a people, and who threaten the whole region, we ask them: what would be your attitude today if your people and country were in the position of Kuwait and its people, invaded by one who does not fear the creator and does not value a human being? He ransacks, destroys, kills its sons, and violates its women, yesterday, today, and tomorrow. Or is the Kuwaiti blood for you permissible for the greedy! Generosity with and sacrifice of the countries of other peoples, is a losing exercise which backfires on its perpetrators. . .

The Iraqi regime bares all responsibility, with all its dimensions for this war. . . Those who support the Iraqi invasion will share in bearing this historic responsibility. . .

I do not object to raising any subject in the U.N. but I ask you, what do you want today by raising this subject here? Do you want the whole region to submit to oppression on someone else's account? This is the reality of the demand of whoever seeks to dilute the United Nations stand for the implementation of Security Council Resolutions at this stage. We know and you know, that the Coalition Forces are proceeding on their way to liberate Kuwait and restore legitimacy to it and to deter oppression from the region. If the justifiers and apologists have a case for the subject of the continuation of war or peace, words here instead of Baghdad are a hypocrisy which we refuse, and a deception whose dimensions we know. The question, Mr. President, should be addressed to Baghdad, will the Iraqi regime withdraw from Kuwait, every inch of Kuwait, and carry out all Security Council Resolutions? Or are the dreams and hopes of expansion and aggression still their objective."

Thomas R. Pickering, Ambassador of the United States to the United Nations, also expressed the hope that a meeting of the Security Council should offer the opportunity for serious and constructive discussion in private. This way it would be free from the glare of instantaneous publicity and possible misinterpretations. He said, "The Security Council had been compelled to authorize the use of force to confront unprovoked aggression and to achieve a return to international legality. A few nations still found it all too easy to turn to violence and aggression to achieve their ends, counting on the acquiescence of others. Unfortunately Iraq had given the world no reason to believe that it ever intended to comply with the Council's Resolutions and the will of the international community.

No one liked the fact that the international community had been compelled by Saddam Hussein to respond to force with force. There were no greater advocates of peace than those who were called upon to pay the price for defending the principles of international law and conduct as contained in the Charter. The United States again called upon Iraq to withdraw immediately from Kuwait, and to comply with the twelve relevant Security Council Resolutions. By doing so and only by doing so–Iraq could end the bloodshed right now, today." He also stated that efforts were made by all Coalition members to avoid any civilian casualties. This was a policy in stark contrast to Iraq's own policy of deliberately targeting civilians in terrorist attacks. Also Saddam Hussein had increased the danger to his own population by moving military equipment and placing it in populated areas. He was essentially, now using his own population as human shields. He also declared that thousands of people throughout the world, in dozens of ministries and institutions, had exerted every effort to avoid the conflict. "All wanted it ended as soon as possible. However, Iraq's refusal to leave Kuwait, and its many deeds and contravention of international law, made it an "outlaw" state. In fact, as early as February 10, 1991, Radio Baghdad "had declared that Iraq rejected the idea of a cease-fire, and still insisted that Kuwait was an integral part of Iraq."

With Iraqi's continued intransigence, "the Council must not do anything which would prolong the conflict, particularly sending signals to Iraq that the Council was not firm in its decisions and was not intent on seeing them implemented. The Council refused to tolerate the unprovoked seizure and attempted obliteration of a member State and would not tolerate the outrageous behavior of occupying forces in Kuwait. The Council would not tolerate indiscriminate terror attacks against civilians in Saudi Arabia and Israel, flagrant violation of the Geneva Conventions on the treatment of prisoners of war, or mindless attacks on the environment."

Baghdad didn't waste any time in launching two more Scud missiles toward the Kingdom of Saudi Arabia at 11:45 in the morning of February 14, 1991. The two missiles exploded in the air, when hit by Patriot Missiles. Some debris fell on Hafr-Al-Batin, four people were slightly injured. Some cars were burned. A house and a workshop were destroyed. Despite the flurry of diplomatic action more than 70,000 sorties were flown by the Allied forces and the Royal Saudi Air Force implemented more than 4,600 of the sorties. The Saudis have flown more missions than any other country in the Coalition except the U.S.

More Political Maneuvering

Saddam Hussein with his mastery of manipulation and deceit decided that the time was opportune for moving in to either provoke the ground war which he wanted to begin sooner than later, or better yet, exploit the situation to come up with a proper diplomatic initiative, where he could secure a cease-fire by optimizing activities at the U.N. Security Council. So he and his Revolutionary Command Council decided to strike while the iron was hot. On the 15th of February, 1991, the decision of the Iraqi leadership was made stating, "Iraq is ready to deal with Security Council Resolution 660 of 1990, with the aim of reaching an honorable and acceptable solution including withdrawal." This announcement sent shock waves through the world which was eagerly waiting for some outlet from the escalation of war in the Gulf. Some political leaders were initially hopeful, because this was the first time since the 5th of August, 1990, that Saddam Hussein was signaling the possibility of withdrawing from Kuwait. However, the initial euphoric reaction of the Iraqi people and a number of politicians around the world hoping that finally a possible solution to the war in the Gulf might be in the offing had hopes dashed away, because the Iraqi proposal had many conditions contrary to the spirit and letter of the twelve resolutions of the United Nations regarding Iraqi aggression in Kuwait. *On the 15th of February, 1991* (29 Rajab A.H. 1411) a lengthy Iraqi announcement made several attacks against the Coalition Forces and their supporters and finally, made the following declaration, sounding as if the Iraqis were the victors:

"The *Revolutionary Command Council** has decided to announce the following:

". . . On the basis of this strongly entrenched feeling and of this assessment of the character of the conflict, in order to deprive the vicious United States, Zionist and NATO alliance of the opportunity to achieve its planned destructive goals, in appreciation of the initiative of the Soviet Union conveyed by the envoy of the Soviet leadership, and in keeping with the principles set forth in the initiative of President

---

* Source: United Nations, New York.

Saddam Hussein, announced on 12 August 1990, the Revolution Command Council has decided to announce the following:

I. Iraq's readiness to deal on the basis of Security Council resolution 660 (1990) with a view to reaching an honourable and acceptable political solution, including withdrawal. The first step that must be taken, as a commitment on Iraq's part with regard to the matter of withdrawal, is linked with the following:

(a) A complete and comprehensive cease-fire on land, at sea and in the air;

(b) That the Security Council should decide to annul, with full retroactive effect, its Resolutions 661, 662, 664, 665, 666, 667, 669, 670, 674, 677 and 678 and all the consequences to which they have given rise. Similarly, the annulment of all decisions and measures of boycott and embargo and the other detrimental decisions and measures adopted by certain States against Iraq, jointly and severally, prior to 2 August 1990, and which were the true cause of the Gulf Crisis, so that the situation may be restored to normal, as if nothing had happened, and without any detrimental consequences for Iraq for any reason whatever;

(c) The United States, the other States participating in the aggression and all States that have dispatched forces to the region shall withdraw from the Middle East region and the Arabian Gulf region all the forces, armaments and matériel that they introduced before and after 2 August 1990, whether they are on land, at sea, in the oceans or in the gulfs, including the weapons and matériel provided by certain States to Israel on the pretext of the crisis in the Gulf, it being understood that the withdrawal of such forces, armaments and matériel shall take place within a period not to exceed one month from the date of the cease-fire;

(d) That Israel should withdraw from Palestine and from the Arab territories it is occupying in the Golan and in Lebanon, in implementation of the resolutions of the Security Council and the General Assembly of the United Nations. In the event that it should refuse to do so, the Security Council shall apply against Israel the same resolutions that it adopted against Iraq;

(e) The guarantee of Iraq's full and undiminished historical territorial and maritime rights in any political solution;

(f) The political arrangement to be agreed upon shall be based on the will of the people in accordance with genuine democratic practice and not on the acquired privileges of the House of Al Sabah. On this basis, national and Islamic forces must participate in a fundamental manner in the political arrangement to be agreed upon.

II. Those States that have participated in the aggression and in financing it shall undertake to rebuild that which the aggression has destroyed in Iraq, in accordance with the highest specifications for each of the activities, projects and installations targeted by the aggression, at their own expense and without Iraq's incurring any financial outlays.

III. Cancellation of all the debts incurred by Iraq, as well as by the States of the region damaged by the aggression which have not participated in it either directly or indirectly, to the Gulf States and those foreign States which participated in the aggression; the establishment of relations between the poor and wealthy States of the region and of the world based on justice and fairness so as to confront the wealthy countries with unequivocal obligations for the achievement of development in the poor countries and for the elimination of their economic sufferings, on the basis of the principle that the poor have a right to share in the resources of the wealthy; and a halt to the use of double standards in dealing with issues affecting peoples and nations, whether on the part of the Security Council or on the part of one State or another.

IV. The States of the Gulf, including Iran, shall be left free to undertake the task of devising security arrangements in the region and to regulate relations among themselves without any external interference.

V. The declaration of the Arabian Gulf region as a zone free of foreign military bases and of any form of foreign military presence; and commitment by all to that effect.

This is our clear and evident case, which we have brought against the perfidious traitors and their imperialist masters and which we have stated to the whole world. Our fundamental assurance, having placed our trust in the One and Only God, is in our mighty Iraqi people, in its combatant and valiant armed forces, and in those who believe in the road that we are taking in resisting oppression and the oppressors. In the coming days, victory over the oppressors shall be assured, just as it was assured in former days. God is most great. May the infamous be driven out."

Revolution Command Council

29 Rajab A.H. 1411
15 February 1991

The Iraqi decision was transmitted to the President of the Security Council to be distributed as a document from the Revolutionary Command Council of the Republic of Iraq.

Saddam Hussein and his RCC were making extensive demands and a string of conditions linking the Palestinian issue to the occupation of Kuwait and covering a wide range of questions. These demands are self-explanatory as stipulated in the previous few paragraphs. The initial euphoria of the world for possible peace dissipated and disappeared rather quickly. President George Bush of the United States said, "Regrettably, the Iraqi statement now appears to be a *cruel hoax*." The Iraqi representative to the United Nations, was quick to declare, "We would have no choice but to resort to weapons of mass destruction." The situation was accelerating toward the initiation of a ground war and President Bush promised the Kuwaitis that their nightmare will be coming to an end "very, very soon."

The Iraqi Ambassador to France said, "We are saying that we will defend Iraq, we will keep defending it, and we will never surrender unconditionally."

President Gorbachev of the former Soviet Union had been in constant touch with President Bush. Telephone conversations at times dragged on for over an hour. At one time, the former Soviet President talked to President Bush by phone for nearly an hour and a half, regarding a possible solution to the Gulf War prior to a major ground explosion.

Brandt Scowcroft, National Security Advisor to President Bush said, "We have a certain tempo in the military operation now and that tempo is important to maintain to save Allied lives."

The air campaign in Kuwait and Iraq continued without any interruptions despite the fact that about fifty oil field fires were raging, creating heavy smoke clouds which at times complicated the air missions, mainly in Al-Wafra region of Kuwait. The Iraqi aim was to complicate the situation further, but the high tech equipment of the Allies prevailed. Also, Iraqis intended to cloud the theater of war and hide their troop movements, but to no avail! Sporadic border fires and clashes continued and were on the increase. All signs were pointing to the imminent ground war which would bring with it the final stage of liberation for the State of Kuwait.

By the 13th of February, the United States had lost 28 aircraft. Eighteen of these were fixed-wing and lost in combat, three fixed-wing were non-combat mishaps and seven helicopters were lost to non-combat as well. The other Coalition Forces lost 10 aircraft. Forty Iraqi aircraft and four Helos had been shot down in air to air engagements. The U.S. did not lose a single airplane in air to air combat. By this time 136 Iraqi aircraft had escaped to safety in Iran. Also about 1,300 Iraqi tanks, 1,100 artillery pieces, and 800 armored vehicles of the enemy forces were confirmed destroyed as verified by bomb damage assessments. The Department of Defense declared on February 14, 1991, that "Iraq's military situation is precarious."

More millions of leaflets were distributed over enemy territory and Iraqi soldiers were urged to defect. Loud speakers and radio broadcasts told the Iraqi soldiers, "You have suffered enough under Saddam Hussein's oppression." Their soldiers were urged to grab a white piece of cloth and give themselves up to Coalition Forces. However, for the Iraqis to defect was not an easy task. It had many obstacles, leading among them, the mine fields and the execution squads sent by Saddam Hussein to the Kuwaiti Theater of Operations and also the swift retaliations against the families of would-be defectors.

On February 16, 1991, at 2:00 A.M., a Scud missile was launched by Iraq against the Kingdom of Saudi Arabia. It fell into the waters of the Arabian Gulf, just off the coast of the Industrial city of Jubail, in the Eastern Region of Saudi Arabia. By this date a total of 33 Scud missiles had been launched on Saudi Arabia.

By February 18, 1991, the United Arab Emirates joined, for the first time, the Coalition Forces in carrying some air missions against enemy targets using their Mirage planes. Also, on this date, the USS Tripoli and the USS Princeton both *struck mines* within three hours of each other, while engaged in operations in the northern region of the Arabian Gulf. Very extensive minesweeping operations were being conducted. The Tripoli sustained a sixteen by twenty foot hole in the forward starboard side below the water line. Minor flooding took place. Only four crew members were injured. Military authorities declared that the amphibious assault ship remained fully capable of carrying out other missions. The USS Princeton was also damaged and developed a crack in the super structure. Three crewmen of the ship were injured.

The next day, on February 19, 1991, the USS Beaufort and minesweeper escort USS Adroit maneuvered through an uncharted minefield to reach the Princeton and proceeded to tow the cruiser to nearby Bahrain for further repairs.

Again, on February 19, the two Saudi minesweepers, the Safwi and the Wadifah, joined U.S. minesweepers in operations in the northern region of the Arabian Gulf. The U.S. minesweepers were also accompanied by the Saudi ships: Khadim Al-Haramein, Abdulaziz and Tabuk. They discovered twenty-two sea-mines. This raised the total to 153.

During the Jihad Convention, King Fahd stated in Riyadh on February 19, 1991,

"Certain Arab and Islamic States hastened to provide support. We do thank them for this brotherly gesture. So did some friendly states, after we were sure that the next phase (of Saddam's invasion) will take place within days, which will lead to the occupation of a part of the Kingdom of Saudi Arabia, namely the Eastern Region.

Information available to us made us quite sure that the targets of Saddam Hussein may continue until the Strait of Hormuz–this will involve Kuwait, Saudi Arabia, Bahrain, Qatar, the United Arab Emirates and Oman. . . We thank all countries that sided with the Kingdom of Saudi Arabia and Kuwait. . .''

King Fahd went on to say, "Nowadays, we are hearing about a settlement! What kind of settlement? There will be no settlement without Iraq's total and unconditional withdrawal from Kuwaiti territory and bearing in mind all the consequences of its invasion of Kuwait including losses, damages, destruction, looting, destruction of the oil wells, also insulting the Kingdom and the debts incurred by Iraq because of this invasion. We will charge Saddam Hussein for all this . . . if Saddam is crying over this pounding (air attacks), what is his justification for launching 34 destructive missiles against the Eastern Region, Riyadh, Hafr Al-Batin and other regions? Are human beings here different from human beings in Iraq? And (is our) region a battlefield not inhabited by human beings? Saddam killed women, children and men; he destroyed homes.

If it wasn't for the intercepting anti-missiles (Patriots), his missiles would have inflicted greater casualties and damage!''

The King concluded his address by saying, "I hope that our next meeting will be in Kuwait City; I have the feeling this will happen soon, God willing."

The tempo of the possible and imminent ground war had picked up momentum and artillery units from the Arab Coalition of Saudi Arabia, Egypt, Syria and Kuwait, along with support from the Air Force of the Coalition partners, heavily bombarded enemy targets and destroyed several of their military equipment and facilities. This had been one of the most productive artillery and air bombardments of the recent days. By now the Theater of Operations in Kuwait and especially, the Republican Guard, were receiving concentrated bombing for the purpose of destroying enemy targets and throwing Iraqi forces in disarray and total confusion.

So far, U.S. fatalities were 55; 17 killed in action, 38 non-combatant fatalities, 25 wounded in action, 27 missing in action, and 9 prisoners of war. The U.S. troop strength reached 527,000. U.S. aircraft losses in the war were 36. The Coalition had lost 11 aircraft. The Iraqis had lost 42 aircraft and 6 Helos had been shot down in air to air engagements with *no U.S. air to air losses during the entire air war.*

At 2:30 in the morning on February 22, 1991, one Scud missile was fired from Iraq in the direction of Dhahran and Bahrain. A Patriot Missile intercepted and destroyed this Scud. The debris from the Scud fell in the Arabian Gulf.

Another Scud was launched at 5:00 in the morning of February 23, 1991. It was launched in the direction of the Eastern Region. It fell harmlessly in the desert of the Kingdom.

Ultimatum Is Imminent

The Foreign Minister of Iraq visited the former Soviet Union and accepted a Soviet brokered 8-point peace plan. Such a proposal fell very short of fulfilling U.N. Resolutions. It continued to have a number of conditions which were unacceptable and contrary to the spirit of these Resolutions. The United States had very serious reservations about such a peace proposal. In fact, the jittery waves of worry propagated throughout the world. Many people wondered if Saddam Hussein was pulling another trick and whether he would order a partial withdrawal and get by without the full destruction of his military machine. . . Border engagements continued to increase.

President George Bush consulted extensively with the Coalition partners and then rejected the Iraqi peace plan, declaring that he would not tolerate any more delaying tactics. President Bush then declared on the 22nd of February,

"We will give Saddam Hussein until noon Saturday, February 23, 1991 EST (8:00 in the evening, Iraqi time) to do what he must do, begin his immediate and unconditional withdrawal from Kuwait. We must hear publicly and authoritatively his acceptance of these terms."
The terms stipulated by the President were:

- Large-scale, immediate withdrawal; complete within one week.
- Within 48 hours, leave Kuwait City and allow prompt return of the legitimate government of Kuwait.
- Withdraw from all prepared defenses along the Saudi-Kuwait and Saudi-Iraq borders.
- Return troops to Iraqi position of August 1, 1990.
- Cooperate with the International Red Cross and release all POWs and remains of servicemen within 48 hours.
- Remove all explosives or booby traps and provide data on location and nature of any land or sea mines.
- Cease all combat airfire, aircraft flights over Iraq and Kuwait except for transport aircraft carrying troops out of Kuwait.
- Cease all destructive action against Kuwaiti citizens and property, and release all Kuwaiti detainees.

U.S. and Coalition Forces agree not to attack retreating Iraqi forces and will exercise restraint as long as withdrawal proceeds within the guidelines. Any breach of the terms will bring an instant and sharp response from the Coalition in accordance with U.N. Security Council Resolution 678.

Saddam Hussein's answer to the Coalition demands was swift and decisive. He launched more Scud missiles and moved on at an accelerated pace with a *scorched earth policy* in Kuwait. The Iraqi forces of

Saddam Hussein while setting fires to hundreds of oil fields in Kuwait, went on an orgy of executions of innocent Kuwaiti citizens. U.S. intelligence satellite photos indicated that at least 25% of the Kuwaiti oil wells were set aflame within a 24 hour period.

President Bush announced on February 22, that Iraq had "launched a scorched–earth policy destroying the entire oil production system of Kuwait."

On February 23, 1991, the White House office of the Press Secretary, Marlin Fitzwater, issued a statement. Here are some excerpts from it:

"CENTCOM (Central Command) reports that they have detected no military activity which would indicate any withdrawal of Saddam Hussein from Kuwait. Similarly, there has been no communication between Iraq and the United Nations that would suggest a willingness to withdraw under the conditions of the Coalition plan. Iraq continues its scorched earth policy in Kuwait, setting fire to oil facilities. It's a continuing outrage that Saddam Hussein is still intent upon destroying Kuwait and its people, still intent upon destroying the environment of the Gulf, and still intent upon inflicting the most brutal kind of rule on his own population; yet appears to have no intention of complying with the U.N. Resolutions. Indeed, his only response at noon was to launch another Scud missile attack on Israel.

The Coalition Forces have no alternative but to continue to prosecute the war.

As we indicated last night, the withdrawal proposal the Soviets discussed with Tariq Aziz in Moscow was unacceptable because it did not constitute an unequivocal commitment to an immediate and unconditional withdrawal. Thus, the Iraqi approval of the Soviet proposal is without effect."

Conclusion

Saddam Hussein remained true to his name and character! Manipulation and deceit were finally catching up with him, but despite all the appeals, he was always ready to sacrifice his entire nation and thousands upon thousands of lives so that he could remain in power. For some time now, he had been pushing for the ground war to begin, so he would deal a deadly blow to the Coalition Forces and declare his victory in the "mother of all battles." How blind can someone be? How remote could one become from the world of reality? How could his inner circle and Revolutionary Command Council all be a chorus reverberating the echo of Saddam Hussein and follow him in a dark blind alley that would bring more tragedy and disaster to their own people, the Iraqis? Only if there was a shade of democracy and

Briefings by Lieutenant General Khaled Bin Sultan and Commander Norman Schwarzkopf.

freedom in their land, tyrants and their clique of demagogue yes-men could not even dream of being at the helm of their tortured land!

Again, Saddam Hussein will fail in his obstinacy and wicked designs. The hour of decision is ticking! The moment of truth had come! The final blow to his occupation of Kuwait was nearing by the second. Desert Storm would yield to Desert Sabre, and coordination of air and land power was to rain disaster and decimation to Saddam's forces in Kuwait and Southern Iraq.

Chapter 8

The One Hundred-Hour Ground War

Rejecting President Bush's ultimatum and the will of the United Nations and Coalition Forces, Saddam Hussein sealed his fate in Kuwait! His abhorrent atrocities in this small country picked up vicious momentum, coupled with a spree of raging oil well fires and destruction. The world could not wait any longer to put an end to this tragedy! President George Bush of the United States of America, with a strong United Nations mandate, supported by strong Coalition Forces of the world community, and the overwhelming majority of the world public opinion, coupled with an avalanche of popular support from the American people—nearly 82% on the eve of the Ground War were supporting his Gulf policies—with all this and a strong understanding with King Fahd of Saudi Arabia, President Bush followed his ultimatum by unleashing the might of a massive armada poised to strike from the air, from the sea, and from the ground, for a final push to drive the forces of a tyrant out of Kuwait in one of history's speediest and most decisive miraculous victories against a huge army, well entrenched in the desert!

Ejection Order and War Scenarios

The deadline for Saddam Hussein to get out of Kuwait was noon, Saturday, February 23, 1991 (EST). At 8:00 o'clock in the evening Washington time, corresponding to 4:00 o'clock in the morning of February 24, local Iraqi time, President George Bush ordered the Commander of U.S. and Allied Forces in the Gulf to use all force necessary to eject the Iraqi occupiers from the State of Kuwait. Here is his brief, but historic statement:

"Good evening. Yesterday, after conferring with my senior national security advisors, and following extensive consultations with our coalition partners, Saddam Hussein was given one last chance, set forth in very explicit terms, to do what he should have done more than six months ago—withdraw from Kuwait without condition or further delay and comply fully with the resolutions passed by the United Nations Security Council.

Regrettably, the noon deadline passed without the agreement of the government of Iraq to meet demands of United Nations Security Council Resolution 660, as set forth in the specific terms spelled out by the coalition to withdraw unconditionally from Kuwait. To the contrary, what we have seen is a redoubling of Saddam Hussein's efforts to destroy completely Kuwait and its people.

I have, therefore, directed General Norman Schwarzkopf, in conjunction with Coalition Forces, to use all forces available, including ground forces, to eject the Iraqi army from Kuwait. Once again, this was a decision made only after extensive consultations within our coalition partnership.

The liberation of Kuwait has now entered a final phase. I have complete confidence in the ability of the Coalition Forces swiftly and decisively to accomplish their mission.

Tonight, as this coalition of countries seeks to do that which is right and just, I ask only that all of you stop what you are doing and say a prayer for all the Coalition Forces, and especially for our men and women in uniform who this very moment are risking their lives for their country and for all of us.

May God bless and protect each and every one of them. And may God bless the United States of America. Thank you very much."

British Prime Minister John Major said upon the initiation of the ground war, "It will not, I believe, be a long conflict. But it may be a furious one. There is no doubt in my mind that it is an absolutely justifiable conflict and that we will win it."

With a final thrust into the liberation of Kuwait at full swing, the Kuwaiti Ambassador to the United States Sheikh Saud Al-Sabbah said, "We should give credit where credit is due, and that is that man in the White House, President George Bush, and to his administration and to the people of this great nation and to King Fahd of Saudi Arabia and all our Allies in France that have rallied behind us in the cause. We are deeply grateful to all those who are in Desert Storm, and we pray and we hope that we can see the conclusion of this operation with the minimum loss of life."

The final push for liberating Kuwait from Saddam Hussein had already begun!

Subjected to five weeks of intensive air bombardment and optimum use of high technology, the forces of Saddam Hussein were in a state of shock. Their morale was at a low ebb! Their communications, Command and Control Centers, their military equipment, their supplies of food, water, you name it, were all in a state of disarray. The heavy and concentrated bombing in the South, specifically the frontal line with Saudi Arabia, knocked out many of the enemy guns. There was a genuine concern that Iraqi artillery might fire poison gas shells on the attacking Coalition Forces. Thus, orders were to decimate these front artillery guns and they were! In fact, by February 19, 1991, General Schwarzkopf had already stated, "Iraq's military is hurting and hurting very badly. Our assessment is that they are on the verge of collapse." A long time before the Ground War began, the Iraqi leader lost his air force. Much of it was destroyed. About 147 fighter planes fled to safety in Iran, where they were grounded and removed from the theater of war. The Coalition Forces had air superiority just a few days after the Air War began. On top of this, they had access to the most advanced technology in warfare. Their reconnaissance airplanes, the AWACS, the spy satellites, along with a long string of other advanced military technology, all gave the Allies the edge of total superiority and a clear view of everything going on, be it in the Iraqi realm or in the Kuwaiti Theater of Operations. Saddam Hussein and his commanders were quickly deprived of any reconnaissance. Thus, enemy forces were operating mostly in the dark, being at a total loss as to what the Coalition Forces were planning to do next. In fact, they misjudged the intentions and designs of the mighty force that was unleashed against them. The Iraqi commanders were not able to detect the massive movements of Allied Forces nor were they able to exercise any mobility, since they were hunkered in their bunkers along the entire war operations theater. Their tank forces were obliterated, especially in the last days of the heated air campaign. The Republican Guard suffered severe losses prior to the ground blitzkrieg attack.

So, while Saddam was acting literally in the blind where he could not see what was happening on the other side of the border, massive numbers of the Coalition Forces moved far west along the border and then swept way north into Iraqi territory. All along, Saddam Hussein was expecting a frontal attack across the border from Saudi Arabia. He was certain that an amphibious landing would come from the Arabian Gulf waters. All along, the commanders of the Coalition Forces meant for him to make this assessment. That was one reason for the number of practiced landings and the very heavy bombardment from the battleships, especially, the Wisconsin and the Missouri. Certainly, the eastern shores of Kuwait, sown with mines and boobytraps, were heavily defended. The Allies planned this scenario so that thousands of his troops would be busy trying to defend the eastern shores of Kuwait, when in the final analysis an amphibious landing was being ruled out. The Iraqi ruler miscalculated about the amphibious landing and the frontal attack. He was totally blind to the massive armada moving west along the borders of Saudi Arabia for a distance of nearly

300 miles and then swiftly moving north way into Iraqi territory, then east, establishing bases of operation and severing any possible routes of supply for the enemy or any possible avenue of escape.

The intensity of the air campaign was very formidable, indeed, especially, in the two days prior to the ground operation. The number of sorties approached nearly 3,000 a day just prior to the Ground War. Heavy concentration of air power, at least 1,000 sorties over the Kuwait Theater of Operations, was intended to isolate KTO. This goal was achieved by knocking out bridges and damaging other lines of transport, so that supply lines would be severed for good and Saddam would not be able to support his troops. His front lines became much weaker and the Allied Forces continued the amphibious rehearsals; all part of a scheme to confuse the enemy and strengthen his belief that an amphibious landing was imminent and thus occupy substantial numbers of these forces along the eastern shores of Kuwait. Operation Imminent Thunder relating to amphibious operations was not entirely a deceptive move. It was going to be used if it became very necessary. And the rehearsals were very real rather than imaginary.

As mentioned previously, prior to the massive movement of troops way out to the western region of the front line, Saddam's air force was decimated. General Norman Schwarzkopf said in a Central Command *news briefing* in Saudi Arabia on Wednesday, *February 27, 1991,* "Very early on we took the Iraqi Air Force. We knew that he (Saddam Hussein) had very limited reconnaissance means. Therefore, when we took out his air force, for all intents and purposes, we took out his ability to see what we were doing down here in Saudi Arabia. . . When we knew that he couldn't see us anymore, we made a massive movement of troops all the way out to the West, to the extreme West . . . because at that time we knew that he was still fixed in this area (the southern border of Kuwait) with the vast majority of his forces, and once the air campaign started, he would be incapable of moving out to counter this move, even if he knew we made it. So on the eve of the ground war, the front lines extended from the Gulf westward, a distance reaching 300 miles." Moving over 200,000 U.S., British and French troops, secretly and swiftly far to the West, was not an easy task. However, good planning and excellent cooperation and determination made it all possible. The logistics were enormous. Not only thousands of troops had to be moved for such a long distance, but enormous quantities of fuel, spare parts, munitions, food and water supplies had to be moved along, to support these massive numbers of troops. General Schwarzkopf opted to have enough supplies to last for two months, just to be on the safe side, in case the battle got very heated and unforeseen conditions prevailed, where fighting took longer than expected.

In such a case, anything the troops needed would be there at the newly established bases. Regarding this gigantic logistics accomplishment, the General said, "I can't give credit enough to the logisticians and the transporters who were able to pull this off, for the superb support we had from the Saudi government, the literally thousands and thousands of drivers of every national origin who helped us in this move out here. Credit goes to the commanders of the units who were also able to maneuver their forces out here and put them in this position."

Schwarzkopf was a master at the history of military art which he studied very well at West Point. He recalled the battle of El-Alamein where in 1942, during World War II, the British Field Marshal Bernard Montgomery effectively used decoy operations, so that the Germans would be misled about the intention and main attack plans of the British. Thus, the plan worked and Montgomery was the victor in the famous battle of El-Alamein in the deserts of North Africa. General Schwarzkopf, followed more or less a similar tactic in capitalizing on the obsession of Saddam Hussein that an amphibious Marine landing was imminent. The General stated, "I was worried about the barrier they (Iraqi forces on the shores of Kuwait) were building and the troops that were digging in behind them. The worst case would be for our troops to go in there and get hung up on the wire and have chemicals dumped on them. As long as they weren't moving troops out to the West, as long as they weren't sending that barrier out to the West, we were in great shape. I knew we had the ability to defeat them by this turning movement."

Ingenuity at the Front

Crossing the heavily defended front lines between Kuwait and Saudi Arabia was not an easy task by any means. Mine-fields were everywhere. Ditches were filled with oil. Saddam Hussein intended to set these oil filled trenches ablaze, so he would confuse the attacking forces and destroy or slow down the tanks. However, this system was attacked and knocked out three days prior to the ground operation. Much of the oil in the ditches was burned with napalm.

On top of this and starting on Thursday, February 21, Iraqi forces had already put the torch to the oil fields in Kuwait and unleashed a campaign of destruction; the oil fields became an inferno. Within a day it was estimated that 25% of the over 1,000 oil wells of Kuwait were ablaze. Also refineries, storage tanks and pipelines were being systematically destroyed. Wellheads were loaded with explosives in order to destroy their controls and valves. When oil gushed out it was set afire. Flames shot way up into the air and clouds of smoke

Nearly 700 Kuwaiti oil wells were torched by the fleeing forces of Saddam Hussein–another tragic act.

covered the Kuwaiti Theater of Operation turning days into nights. Despite all his evil deeds, Saddam's humiliating defeat was imminent.

The Coalition Forces also had to contend with high walls of sand berms and trenches which were specifically designed to attract the Coalition Forces into certain channels that would lead them to "killing fields." This tactic was very successfully used with the Iranians but the commander of the Coalition Forces was not about to make a kind of "Cannon Fodder" of his troops, nor fall for the designs of Saddam Hussein.

The probing attacks increased in the few days prior to G-Day (ground day). About 3,000 Marines had crossed the border and moved about ten miles inside Kuwait in order to prepare for the onslaught of the ground war. B-52s and helicopter gunships pounded enemy lines, especially in the front positions. These night operations contributed to destroying, not only the artillery at the front, but also the morale of the troops which was already at a low ebb. Bombardment from the air included multiple-launch rocket systems, unleashing thousands of shrapnel-like bomblets which rained over the trenches of enemy forces.

Drone planes which do not have pilots on board, and remotely piloted vehicles (RPV) were used to guide the Allied soldiers into areas which were lightly defended by the enemy.

At the peak of air and ground bombardment, just before the start of the Ground War, Allied engineers, under cover of rocket and artillery fire, reached into their large bag of technical tricks in order to devise practical means for destroying the highly lethal mines abundantly spread in Kuwait and especially the front lines. They used fuel air explosives, where parachute bombs ignited a spray of fuel above the ground level. The enormity of the blast exerts a downward pressure and causes the mines to explode whether they are on the surface or under it. Engineers also fired small rockets flying at a distance of about 360 feet while trailing a line full of explosives. Then the charges were detonated. The explosions cleared large areas about 325 feet wide. Specially designed tanks moved on to push away any remnants in the field.

Allied engineers used armored bulldozers to punch needed openings in the sand berms which stood as high as ten feet in a front line described by Saddam Hussein as impenetrable. Not an easy task by any means, especially since the remnants of the Iraqi artillery were frantically pounding the forces trying to open the way for the deluge of ground forces that were soon to liberate Kuwait.

Some refitted tanks were equipped with chain-wrapped rollers which detonated the mines as the tanks moved on. Then bulldozers moved afterward to smooth the road and make it passable for the oncoming troops. There was also serious concern about the possibility that some of the mines were laden with chemical agents. So vehicles used in these operations were equipped with chemical gas detectors to give the troops the necessary warning to use their protection gear against chemical weapons.

Navy Seals (NS) began moving into Kuwait as soon as the Iraqis occupied it. They slipped into Kuwait City, where the U.S. Embassy was surrounded by Iraqi troops. They were observing and gathering information for a possible rescue of American hostages. Navy Seals provided vital information about the hostages and enemy actions inside Kuwait. They were conducting very valuable information as "forward spotters" for U.S. air pilots. They used hand held laser beams to pinpoint certain key Iraqi targets. Missiles fired by the Allied Forces then followed the laser beam path and destroyed these targets.

Seal Commandos were the ones who liberated the tiny small island off the shores of Kuwait where they killed three Iraqis and took 29 prisoners of war.

General Norman Schwarzkopf was prompted later on to say: "I shouldn't forget these fellows. That S.F. stands for special forces. We put special forces deep into enemy territory. They went out on strategic reconnaissance for us, and they let us know what was going on out there. They were the eyes that were out there and it is very important not to forget those folks."

The General also said, "Any student of military strategy will tell you that in order to attack a position, you should have a ratio of approximately 3 to 1 in favor of the attacker. In order to attack a position that is heavily dug in and barricaded such as the one we had here, you should have a ratio of 5 to 1 in the way of troops in favor of the attacker. . . We had to come up with some way to make up the difference."

Unleashing the Ground War

The final putsch for liberating the state of Kuwait from the grip of Saddam Hussein and his occupying forces was unleashed at 4:00 in the morning, on Sunday, February 24, 1991, Iraqi time. The massive armada was anxiously waiting for the go signal and moved with tremendous zeal and force across the entire front line extending from the eastern shores of Kuwait, way west three hundred miles along the entire border of Saudi Arabia with Kuwait and Iraq. After nearly six and a half months of extensive training and preparation, and over five weeks of intensive air bombardment, Coalition Forces were in top condition for the fight, while enemy forces were at their lowest ebb; clearly demoralized and thousands of them were waiting for the opportune time, not to fall as martyrs in defense of the tyrant of Baghdad, but waiting to seize the moment and dash across the front lines to become prisoners of war, in the thousands–a fate they preferred over remaining in their bunkers of hell or under the thumb of execution squads sent by Saddam Hussein to spread terror and fear among them. How on earth could an army like this put up a fight for such a dastardly cause?

At the same moment, massive energetic forces swept across the defensive lines declared by Saddam as being impenetrable whatever the attacking force may be! Leading in this fight along the eastern shores of Kuwait were two Saudi task forces, comprised of the elite of Saudi defenses and including Kuwaiti forces that had been eagerly waiting for a long time to exact revenge from the occupiers that brought disaster and destruction to their homeland. The Saudis were also supported by forces from the Gulf Cooperation Council. They moved against strong defenses and barriers that were breached by their sheer courage and determination to contribute their fair share for the defense and liberation of their brotherly state of Kuwait.

The United States First Marine Division was on the left of the Saudi Forces, along with the U.S. Second Marine Division and the U.S. Tiger Brigade of the Second Armored Division. They moved with massive force through the barrier system. Their penetration of the barrier was swift and decisive. Marines had been impatiently and anxiously waiting for the assault. Regiments of the First Marine Division–First Battalion, Fifth and Seventh Marines, supported by third Tank Battalion, and Second Marine Division, Sixth Marines and Armor moved with vigor and easily breached the enemy's defensive assortment of mine fields, barbed wire, berms and bunkers. Some units were outfitted with chemical protective gear, since the commanders of the Allied Forces were genuinely concerned about the threats that Saddam Hussein would use poison gas against the liberating forces. While this was cumbersome, it was nevertheless a must, especially in the first hours of battle.

Another powerful Saudi Task Force was launched slightly west of the U.S. Marines. They pushed forward breaching barriers and achieving their goals with great rapidity. Right next to them, the Commander of the Coalition Forces unleashed an Arab Force which was mainly composed of Egyptian and Syrian troops. This force moved impressively against the barriers established by the Iraqi forces. All this was in accordance with the main aim to convince the Iraqi leader that the Coalition Forces were moving in a frontal attack against his force on

THE GROUND WAR
FEBRUARY 24-28, 1991

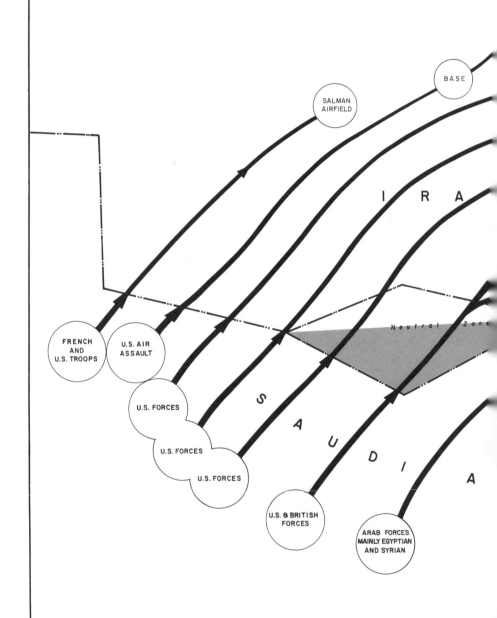

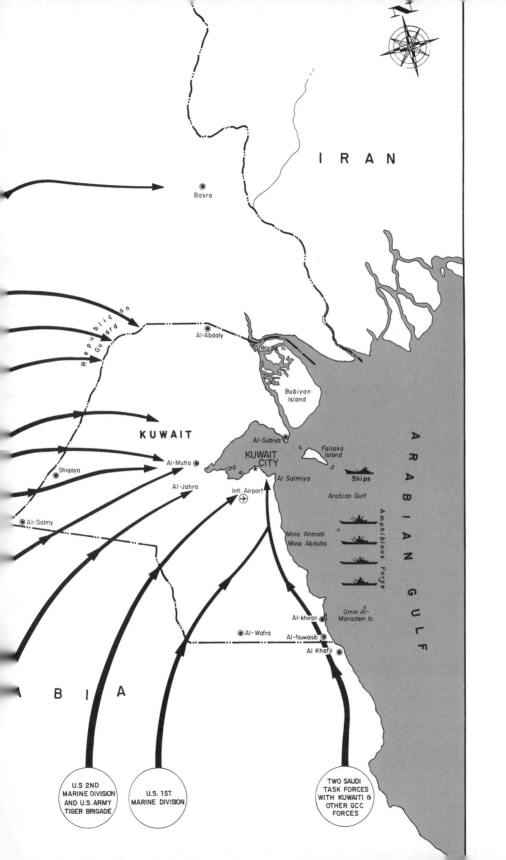

IRAN

Basra

Republican Guard

Al-Abdaly

Warba Is.

Bubiyan Island

KUWAIT

Al-Subiya

Failaka Island

KUWAIT CITY

Al Salmiya

Ships

Shiqaya

Al-Mutla

Al-Jahra

Intl. Airport

Arabian Gulf

A R A B I A N

Al-Salmy

Mina Ahmadi
Mina Abdulla

Amphibious Force

G U L F

Umm Al-Maradem Is.

Al-khiran

Al-Wafra

Al-Nuwaisib

A B I A

Al Khafji

U.S 2ND MARINE DIVISION AND U.S. ARMY TIGER BRIGADE

U.S. 1ST MARINE DIVISION

TWO SAUDI TASK FORCES WITH KUWAITI & OTHER GCC FORCES

the Kuwaiti–Saudi border, just as he thought it would be. In the meantime, to convince him further of the deceiving plan, the battleships in the Arabian Gulf were pouring a hail of bombardment, bringing destruction and havoc to his fortified forces on the eastern shores of Kuwait. The Marines in the Gulf were pounding him with vengeance and this added to his conviction that an amphibious landing was imminent. The plan worked perfectly!

The wide reporting of opinions expressed by retired military men and other military analysts and experts was broadcast across the waves of the world for Saddam Hussein to observe and digest. Many of these views indicated that his army would be isolated in Kuwait and obliterated, thus, calling for an outflanking move to surround his Republican Guard and other forces in the southern realm of the war theater. Despite all this, the flanking move by Commander Schwarzkopf, and the massive movement of nearly a quarter million men with a two months supply, was essentially a surprise to Saddam Hussein and his field commanders!!!

The Saudi and Arab forces encountered a very, very tough barrier system. ". . . a very, very tough mission indeed." But they overcame all difficulties and performed admirably.

Again at 4:00 in the morning of February 24, far into the west and according to the deception plan using the flanking maneuver, the Sixth French Armored Division and a brigade of the U.S. 82nd Airborne launched an attack across Iraqi territory and in no time reached the Al-Salman airfield. The three brigades of the 82nd Airborne took positions to defend supply bases for the Coalition Forces, while the French further west formed a defensive line protecting against any possible attack from the enemy which could come from the west, although this area was very lightly defended by the Iraqis.

The weather changed for the worse. There was heavy rain, which interfered to some degree with air assault in this area. However, by 8:00 in the morning the 101st Airborne launched a very concentrated air attack on enemy territory in the far west region which is deep into southern Iraq and established a base near Al-Salman airfield located about 150 miles southwest of Baghdad and 70 miles within Iraqi territory. This was an important base for supplies such as fuel, ammunition, spare parts, water and all necessary materials for the support of the troops in this region of southern Iraq. At this stage, the 101st Airborne, after establishing their forwarding base, launched their attacks into the valleys of the Euphrates and the Tigris rivers, knocking out bridges and roads, making it impossible for the enemy to resupply his troops in the war theater of operations. Still the intention was not to capture Iraq. In this regard, Commander Schwarzkopf declared emphatically,

"There are a lot of people still saying that the object of the United States of America was to capture Iraq and cause the downfall of the entire country of Iraq. Ladies and gentlemen, when we were here (where the base was established deep into Iraq), we were 150 miles away from Baghdad, and there was nobody between us and Baghdad. If it had been our intention to take Iraq, if it had been our intention to overrun the country, we could have done it unopposed, for all intents and purposes, from this position at that time. That was not our intention, we have never said it was our intention. Our intention was purely to eject the Iraqis out of Kuwait and destroy the military power that had come in here."

As later on narrated by Commander Schwarzkopf, "An attack was then launched on the part of the entire 7th Corps where the First Infantry Division went through, breached an obstacle and minefield barrier here, established quite a large breach where we passed the First British Armored Division. (This was right to the left of the Arab force operating at the corner where the Kuwaiti, Saudi and Iraqi borders meet). At the same time, we launched the First Armored Division, the Second Armored Cavalry Division and the Third Armored Division and because of our deception plan and the way it worked, we didn't even have to worry about a barrier. We just went right around the enemy and were behind him in no time at all. The 24th Mech. Division was also launched out here in the far west (so was the Third Armored Cavalry Regiment)." This was the situation by the afternoon of February 24, 1991. All Coalition Forces had made unbelievable progress across all front lines.

The performance of the Coalition Forces was best described by the Commander, General Schwarzkopf. Concerning the Saudi Task Forces, he said, "First of all, the Saudis over here on the east coast did a terrific job. They went up against the very, very tough barrier system; they breached the barrier very, very effectively; they moved out aggressively; and continued their attacks up the coast."

On the performance of the British forces and their commander, General Norman Schwarzkopf stated, "The British, I've got to tell you, have been absolutely superb members of the Coalition from the outset. I have a great deal of admiration and respect for all the British that are out there and particularly General Sir Peter De la Billière, who is not only a great General, but he has also become a very close personal friend of mine. They played a very, very key role in the movement of the main attack."

As for the performance of the French forces, he said, "I would also like to say that the French did an absolutely superb job of moving out rapidly to take their objective out here (in the far west), and they were very successful, as was the 101st." He then elaborated further and said, "So the French mission was to go out and not only seize Al-Salman, but to set up a screen across our left flank which was absolutely vital to insure that we weren't surprised. So they definitely did not stop fighting. They continued to perform their mission, and they performed it extraordinarily well." The Commander was certainly very pleased with the performance of all the Allied Forces. When he spoke of the performance of the Marines operating between the Saudi Task Forces, he was very effusive in his praise. He said, "I can't say enough about the two marine divisions. If I used words like brilliant, it would really be an under-description of the absolutely superb job that they did in breaching the so-called impenetrable barrier. It was a classic, absolutely classic, military breaching of a very, very tough minefield, barbed wire, fire trenches type barrier. They went through the first barrier like it was water. They went across into the second barrier line, even though they were under artillery fire at the time– they continued to open up that breach. Then they brought divisions streaming through that breach. Absolutely superb operation, a textbook, and I think it will be studied for many, many years to come as the way to do it."

Performance of the 101st Airborne, in establishing the base and moving deeper inside Iraq reaching the Euphrates river, was compared by some to the performance of the 101st during the Normandy invasion in June, 1944, during World War II. According to Major Robert Sellers, "The only difference is, there is no water below and we are moving in helicopters not gliders."

After the massive breaching of obstacles and destruction of the initial defense lines, the Iraqi troops began to surrender in the thousands. Many of these troops were waiting for the opportunity to leave their bunkers and flee to the possible safety on the other side, away from the tyranny of Saddam Hussein and his death squads. Many of these unfortunate soldiers were brought to the Kuwaiti Theater not knowing that they were pawns for Saddam's wicked designs for occupying Kuwait and terrorizing Arab brothers and sisters. The Iraqi soldiers were haggard and beat, hungry and demoralized. Many of them were ever grateful to be in the hands of their supposed enemy. Barely fed one meal a day, many streamed out of their bunkers, barefoot, and in a state of shock. One Iraqi soldier spoke for all his fellow Iraqi prisoners of war, saying to his captor, "May God save you, you saved us from the grip of Saddam Hussein!"

The British forces, being an important member of the flanking maneuver, had the First Armored Division anxiously moving to meet head on with the Republican Guard of Saddam Hussein. This division comprised the 7th Armored Brigade, descendents of the famous World War II Desert Rats. These performed admirably at the battle of Al-Alamein and were the courageous forces that drove the Germans out of the realm of North Africa.

The surrendering Iraqis, essentially, treated the Coalition Forces as liberators not enemies or occupiers. This was indeed strange in the history of warfare!

After twelve hours of the ground offensive, over 6,000 prisoners were captured. Many more were in the process of surrendering. This became also a logistical problem to transport all these thousands of prisoners away from the front into safe camps. Buses and trucks began streaming in and loading, then moving them to camps and interrogation centers, where they were well fed, clothed and treated according to the Geneva Convention rules regarding prisoners of war.

According to Commander Norman Schwarzkopf, the casualties were extremely light, "As a matter of fact remarkably light. So far, the offensive is progressing with dramatic success. The troops are doing a great job, but I would not be honest with you if I did not remind you that this is the very early stages, we are a little more than 12 hours into the offensive and the war is not over yet."

One reporter said, "There was no flaming oil threatened by Saddam Hussein, no Iraqi resistance, hundreds of Saudi tanks and armored personnel carriers poured nose to tail through breaches in the barrier and fanned out across the desert." An Arab soldier said, "We drive to liberate Kuwait from Saddam Hussein and we will try to follow him until we kill him!"

A reporter with the British troops said, "The tanks and the APCs rolled across without any resistance. That was the remarkable thing."

The frightened and exhausted Iraqi prisoners of war asked to surrender to anything in sight, including helicopters flying above them or journalists in rented vehicles. One unique instance was the sight of some Iraqi troops trying to surrender to a drone reconnaissance plane, which was operating under remote control. Doubtless, this is probably the first and only recorded time in the history of warfare when troops attempted to surrender to a pilotless machine.

On the 25th of February, 1991, Lt. General Prince Khaled Bin Sultan Bin Abdulaziz stated that orders were not given for the forces to attack the occupiers until after all possible means were explored, hoping to bring the tyrant back to his senses. "He caused enough destruction and looting, then obliged us to wage a war of liberation in order to recover the right and impose justice whatever the price or the sacrifices may be. We have no enmity or evil designs against the people of Iraq, but we were forced to fight and let the liberation of Kuwait be a means for the liberation of Iraq's army and people from a tyrant. I know that some soldiers among the Iraqis were misled and their minds were filled with lies by the tyrant and they committed crimes and disgraced honors. To those, I send a warning that anyone who commits any sabotage, killing, or an act of aggression will be tried as a war criminal and will come under the international laws and norms and we shall not let him escape the punishment." He then went on to say, "Before I end my speech, I would like to express my thanks and gratitude to the 33 sisterly and friendly nations who joined us in the fight, and for their support to our forces and our cause. I wish to greet every mother whose son is standing in the ditch of right, every wife whose husband is fighting for peace, and every child whose father is supporting the oppressed."

By Monday, the 25th of February, 1991, the number of Iraqis surrendering reached 18,000. Coalition Forces continued to make great progress and were extremely successful along all fronts. They had, by now, destroyed over 270 Iraqi tanks. The Saudi task forces and the marines continued their thrust forward toward Kuwait City, with tremendous success. U.S. ground casualties were miraculously low, only 4 killed in action and 21 wounded. Only four U.S. aircraft were lost so far during this ground offensive.

The Allied Naval forces continued their heavy bombardment of the eastern shores of Kuwait, leading among them were the battleships, Wisconsin and Missouri. The battleship Missouri alone fired 533 rounds, equivalent to 125 tons of ordinance, on enemy targets. The Coalition mine sweepers, especially from the U.S., Britain, Saudi Arabia and Kuwait, were busy clearing more areas in the Gulf, so the battleships could carry their support mission closer to the shores. More Scud missiles were launched against Israel beginning at 1:30 in the morning, local time of February 25, then later on, at 3:30 in the morning, which made it the 39th Scud missile attack to date against Israel.

On this day (Monday, February 25) and around 9:30 A.M., a Silkworm missile was targeting the battleship Missouri. The HMS Glouscester which was escorting this battleship in the Arabian Gulf waters destroyed the incoming Iraqi missile, using two C-Dart missiles. Another Silkworm missile was fired by the Iraqis, but it missed its target and fell into the waters of the Arabian Gulf.

On the same day and around 8:40 P.M., local time, a Scud missile was launched by Iraq from a position way behind the front lines, nearly two hundred miles inside Iraq. Its destination was the Eastern Region of Saudi Arabia and specifically the Dhahran Air Base. These Scud missiles had been very erratic in the past and every time were dealt a heavy blow by the great performance of the Patriot Missile. However, at this very moment when the defeat of the aggressor was only hours away, this Scud missile broke up in flight and scattered debris over a U.S. housing compound in suburban Al-Khobar, near Dhahran. This was a warehouse which was turned into a U.S. military barracks. Maybe because of the disintegration of the Scud missile, the Patriot Missile was not fired. In any event, a tragedy occurred. Twenty-eight U.S. Army Reserve personnel involved in the logistics and support missions were killed, and over 100 others were wounded.

Saddam Begins His Retreat

Radio Baghdad was quick to blare that his attack was aimed directly against "coward traitors who mortgage the sacred places of the nation and turn Arab youths into shields of flesh." How ironic?

Saddam Hussein felt the inferno and realized that a military catastrophe was befalling him and his wicked designs. He finally felt that he should move and move fast before the onslaught of the Coalition Forces not only sealed his humiliating defeat and forced him out of Kuwait, but also dealt him a heavy blow that would sweep him out of power, or existence altogether. Sweep him out of power? This is the forbidden threshold that Saddam would do anything and everything to avoid! When it came to his survival at the helm, Saddam Hussein would do anything and everything–bar none–to save his tyrannical rule!

Thus, on Monday, February 25, 1991 around 5:35 P.M. (EST) in Washington corresponding to 11:35 P.M. Iraqi time, Radio Baghdad announced that the Iraqi "Foreign Minister informed the Soviet Ambassador (of the Iraqi Plan) which constitutes a practical compliance with U.N. Security Council Resolution 660, that President Saddam Hussein has ordered his troops to make a fighting withdrawal from Kuwait and return to the position they occupied before August 2, 1990."

The radio announcement also stated, "our armed forces which have proven their ability to fight and stand fast, will confront any attempt to harm them while carrying out their order."

Saddam's salvaging attempt was quickly rebuffed. Despite Soviet interests in bringing about a cease-fire, which for all practical purposes would have robbed the Coalition Forces from imminent victory, despite the appeals of Mikhail Gorbachev of the former Soviet Union and the maneuvers of Saddam Hussein, the Coalition Forces were not buying his stance. White House spokesman, Marlin Fitzwater, stated, "We do not consider there is anything to respond to, the war goes on! Also, the announcement was made by Radio Baghdad not by Saddam Hussein. The United States of America and the Coalition Forces are not in the mood to negotiate with a radio announcer. President George Bush demanded that Saddam Hussein must "personally and publicly" agree to all the terms of the ultimatum which was previously given, and he must accept and fully comply with all the twelve U.N. Security Council Resolutions." That would have been too much loss of face for Saddam Hussein, who preferred to sacrifice his troops in the face of certain defeat.

On the 26th of February, 1991, Lt. General Khaled Bin Sultan stated, "The Coalition casualties after two days (of ground war), remain remarkably light. Joint forces have 5 killed and 20 wounded in action. Many Iraqi soldiers have surrendered to us. We will treat them in accordance with our high Islamic and Arabic standards and the Geneva Convention. We have now about 20,000 Iraqi prisoners of war in our care or en route. Many Iraqi units we faced until now, will not be fighting another day. They are casualties or prisoners of war. For the benefit of innocent civilians, the Coalition has deliberately tied its own hands, with what I call the Golden Rule of Desert Storm. The Golden Rule is to avoid if we possibly can, any harm to Iraq's innocent people. This is in clear contrast to Saddam's killing of innocent civilians, including thousands of Kuwaitis who have been tortured and murdered. This war need never have occurred! King Fahd, President Bush, President Moubarak, President Assad and nearly all other world leaders appealed to Saddam repeatedly to abide by the United Nations Resolutions; instead he began to systematically destroy Kuwait and murdered its people. From here, I would like to say, we warn all who have taken part in the many crimes against the innocent civilians in Kuwait, whether by rape, murder or torture, that they will be held responsible before an international court of justice and will be treated as criminals of war.

Before I take any questions, I would like to end my remarks by thanking all the 33 countries who are participating in this historic Coalition. I also thank the brave fighting soldiers who are here and their parents, spouses, and families, for joining our Coalition effort to liberate Kuwait."

On February 26, Saddam Hussein announced on Radio Baghdad that his troops had begun withdrawing from Kuwait and that their withdrawal would be complete in one day. In his speech, he maintained that, "Kuwait was a part of Iraq which was separated from it in the past, and current circumstances are such that armed forces are forced to withdraw."

Never admitting defeat, he declared that the Iraqi withdrawal was a victory. He went on to say, "Applaud your victories, my fellow countrymen. You have faced thirty countries and the evil they have brought here. You have faced the whole world, oh great Iraqis! You have won! You are victorious! How sweet victory is?" He then asserted that, "the gates of Constantinople were not open before the Moslems in their first struggling attempt. . . The Iraqis will remember and will not forget that on August 8, 1990, Kuwait became part of Iraq legally, constitutionally, and actually. They remember and will not forget that it continued in this state for a period of time between August 8, 1990 and until last night, when withdrawal began." Trying to snatch hollow victory from the jaws of defeat! How can anyone around the globe buy these defeatist pronouncements? After all the bluster of war and threatening his attackers to "swim in their own blood"–after impatiently waiting for the "mother of all battles," Saddam Hussein was now being handed a decisive and swift defeat, that would be the mother of all defeats indeed!

The world community was shocked with his speech, especially, when he was harnessing disaster to his forces and more agony to his country. People around the world were appalled. President George Bush was especially incensed. He considered Saddam Hussein's speech as an outrage and promised to continue to prosecute the war with undiminished intensity. From the Rose Garden at the White House, the Presidential statement was televised to the nation and the world. Here is what President Bush said on Tuesday evening, February 26, 1991:

"I have a brief statement to make today. Saddam's most recent speech is an outrage. He is not withdrawing. His defeated forces are retreating. He is trying to claim victory in the midst of a rout, and he is not voluntarily giving up Kuwait. He is trying to save the remnants of power and control in the Middle East by every means possible. And here too Saddam Hussein will fail.

Saddam is not interested in peace, but only to regroup and fight another day, and he does not renounce Iraq's claim to Kuwait. To the contrary, he makes clear that Iraq continues to claim Kuwait. Nor is there any evidence of remorse for Iraq's aggression or any indication that Saddam is prepared to accept the responsibility for the awful consequences of that aggression.

He still does not accept U.N. Security Council Resolutions or the coalition terms of February 22, including the release of our POWs–all POWs–third-country detainees, and an end to the pathological destruction of Kuwait. The coalition will therefore continue to prosecute the war with undiminished intensity.

As we announced last night, we will not attack unarmed soldiers in retreat. We have no choice but to consider retreating combat units as a threat and respond accordingly. Anything else would risk additional United States and coalition casualties.

The best way to avoid further casualties on both sides is for the Iraqi soldiers to lay down their arms as nearly 30,000 Iraqis already have. It is time for all Iraqi forces in the theater of operation, those occupying Kuwait, those supporting the occupation of Kuwait, to lay down their arms. And that will stop the bloodshed.

From the beginning of the air operation nearly six weeks ago, I have said that our efforts are on course and on schedule. This morning I am very pleased to say that coalition efforts are ahead of schedule. The liberation of Kuwait is close at hand.

And let me just add that I share the pride of all of the American people in the magnificent heroic performance of our armed forces. May God bless them and keep them."

In the meantime, according to General Schwarzkopf, "The 24th Infantry Division made an unbelievable move all the way across into the Tigris and Euphrates valley, and proceeded in blocking this avenue of egress out, which was the only avenue of egress left, because we continued in this area, and the 101st continued to operate in here (to the left and above the 24th Mechanized Infantry)."

The Special Forces operated small boats in the Arabian Gulf waters off the shores of Kuwait and supported the Navy and Coalition Forces in clearing the abundance of mines in the area. They did their duty in convincing the Iraqis that Coalition Forces were indeed threatening to carry out their amphibious operations.

Tremendous progress had been made. Forces moving from the south and from the eastern shores of the Arabian Gulf were within a short distance of their final destination–Kuwait City. Again on the performance of the Saudi and Arab forces General Norman Schwarzkopf said, "It is a tough mission because these people were being required to fight the kind of fight that the Iraqis wanted them to fight. It is a very, very tough mission. I would point out, it wasn't only the Saudis, it was the Saudis, the Kuwaitis, the Egyptians, the Syrians, the Emiris from United Arab Emirates, the Bahrainis, the Qataris and the Omanis, and I apologize if I ever left anybody out, but it was a great Coalition of people, all of whom did a fine job." Forces that were outflanking the Iraqis in a special maneuver and deceptive plan were now pouring into the east, after destroying bridges and any possible exit roads for the Iraqi military. These forces were now zeroing in on the Republican Guard. On the 26th of February, they were essentially, engaging, out-flanking and outmaneuvering the armed and retreating Iraqi troops.

Fully twenty-one Iraqi divisions had been so far destroyed or rendered ineffective.

In fact, General Schwarzkopf accelerated the ground war by 24 hours, especially, after enormous numbers of Iraqi forces surrendered and after hearing about terrible atrocities being committed in Kuwait City.

Kuwait Is Liberated

Now, the Kuwait Theater of Operations (KTO) was totally isolated from any possible reinforcement, and the Iraqi army was cut off. His escape route, the one he used to invade Kuwait, was now entirely cut off. There was nowhere to go but surrender!

A large tank battle of the war erupted when U.S. Marines faced the Iraqi 3rd Armored Division at the Kuwait International Airport. The sky above was pitch black from the clouds of smoke generated from the burning of Kuwaiti oil wells. At the height of day, soldiers needed a flashlight to read their maps. Before the day was over, all Iraqi tanks, numbering over a hundred, were systematically destroyed by the onslaught of the Marines.

Around 10:20 in the morning of February 26, 1991, the Coalition Forces began entering the outskirts of Kuwait City. Prior to that, the Iraqi forces were fleeing the city en mass. Around 11:50 in the morning, the vast majority of the occupying force had grabbed trucks, other vehicles, loot, some military equipment and had fled on the highway north toward Basra. Saudi and Arab forces were the first to enter Kuwait City.

A Marine reconnaissance unit also entered Kuwait City and took control of the U.S. Embassy. The capital city of Kuwait was spared further horrors and destruction since Iraqi troops were rapidly fleeing the city. The Kuwaitis and the Coalition Forces were saved from vicious house to house fighting, which would have resulted in a heavy toll for all sides.

With the certain defeat that had befallen the Iraqi forces, Saddam Hussein continued his obstinacy. He did not order them to surrender, but rather to withdraw. Thus, for all practical purposes the war was continuing. The flood of Iraqi troops with their trucks, buses, other vehicles, and some military equipment and huge amount of loot, ranging from vacuum cleaners to television sets, video cassette recorders, along with a number of tanks, jeeps, armored vehicles, cars, and tractor-trailers–all this loot-gathered by the fleeing soldiers who stole anything they could carry from the homes and streets of Kuwait, did not go too far. The powerful armor of the Coalition Forces and Navy A-6E of Ranger's Attack Squadron 155 and marine aircraft bombed the fleeing, but trapped Iraqi forces. They were systematically destroyed . . . The super highway which was supposed to reflect the friendship between Iraq and Kuwait became a highway of death for the invaders. The heavy bombing and destruction of bridges and roads by the Allied Forces led to the mammoth traffic jam which trapped, not only the soldiers, but their tanks, APCs (Armored Personnel Carriers) and their loot. They all became a very attractive target for the Allies. Mile after mile of burned and destroyed equipment littered the multi-lane highway.

It was indeed a graveyard for man and machine—it was a grotesque sight—a testimony to the old saying, "war is hell." The ferocity of the attack raised some eyebrows! But nevertheless, the Iraqi dictator refused to accept in very clear terms the conditions for a cease-fire as stipulated by the United Nations Security Council Resolutions. Also, as mentioned previously, he did not order his fleeing troops to surrender. If this was done, the terms of the Geneva Convention relating to prisoners of war would have been applied and the fleeing troops would have been saved from the death grip of the Coalition Forces led by the United States of America. Fleeing from the battlefield is not the equivalent of surrender!!!

Finally, on the evening of February 26, 1991, corresponding to the 30th anniversary of the State of Kuwait, and after an occupation by a ruthless dictator which lasted for nearly seven months, the flag of liberated Kuwait was proudly flying again, over Kuwait City. By 1:30 A.M. on February 27, 1991, Kuwait City was fully under control by Saudi and Arab Forces along with U.S. and Coalition Forces. The liberating Arab and Allied Forces were elated, so were, indeed, the Kuwaitis who had suffered untold misery and atrocities under the occupation.

By now, over 30,000 prisoners of war have been taken and handed to Saudi authorities. U.S. ground casualties were 45 killed in action, 21 wounded and 2 were missing. The overall total since the beginning of Desert Storm was 55 killed in action, while 155 were wounded, 30 were missing and 9 were prisoners of war. The U.S. Department of Defense reported that over 100,000 sorties had been flown by Coalition Forces in the war theater.

The Missouri and Wisconsin fired more than 1,000 rounds from their sixteen inch guns, in support of ground operations. The two battleships used RPVs and Marine Spotters ashore in order to guide them for homing on their targets which included mortar and missile positions, ammunition dumps, artillery, and a Silkworm missile site. The battleship Missouri alone fired over one million pounds of ordinance.

At the height of the Iraqi rout, oddly enough, a classical tank battle was in the making between the Coalition Forces and the Republican Guard.

On February 26, 1991, nine British were killed from friendly fire, specifically, two U.S. A-10 aircraft came and attacked by mistake two Scout British armored cars. Death from friendly fire was a terrible tragic mistake, but with the multitude of maneuvers, several different forces, extreme conditions of weather, many different languages and sometimes bad judgement, all of these contributed to causing a few tragic accidents. Of course, extraordinary measures were taken to avoid such terrible tragedies.

While bombing of northern Iraq continued, the night of February 26, 1991, Coalition pilots had a very successful afternoon and night when they attacked mobile erector launchers for Scud missiles which were located in western Iraq. However, by this date, Iraq had launched a total of 41 Scud missiles against Saudi Arabia, one against Bahrain, one against Qatar, and 38 against Israel.

Battling the Republican Guard

Powerful Coalition Forces, operating from inside Iraqi territory, had formed a solid wall attacking the Republican Guard straight in the easterly direction.

According to Schwarzkopf, the Arab Forces coming from the east and the west had moved into Kuwait City and were now completely securing the capital, conducting whatever mop-up operations were needed to make sure that the control of the city was absolute. The First Marine Division continued its hold on the Kuwait International Airport. Any egress or escape from Kuwait City was now blocked by the Second Marine Division, so no one could escape. Essentially, the whole city was now under the total control of the Allied Forces. No one could enter or leave without their permission. By this date, the Coalition Forces had rendered totally ineffective more than 29 Iraqi Divisions out of 42, in the Theater of Operations.

The final decisive battle with the elite Republican Guard was now shaping up. This was the climax of the Gulf War! The Allies were ready and extremely eager for this fateful moment. They wanted to meet head on with the best Saddam Hussein had to offer. The battle with the Republican Guard, or more precisely the remnants of it, raged on. On February 27, 1991, the elite Republican Guard had no place to go. It had been under siege surrounded from every side. East, west, north and south, there was nowhere to go but fight! Three Divisions fought, and fought very hard, but they were no match for the overwhelming might of the attacking forces. It was a classical tank battle.

The Republican Guard had no air cover; Iraqi troops had no air cover either. Eight hundred U.S. tanks of the 101st Airborne, 24 Mechanized Infantry and 3rd Armored Division attacked about 300 tanks of the Guards including the Medina & Hammurabi Armored Divisions. As for numbers, this tank battle was the world's largest tank battle since the Soviet-German combat at Kursk, fought during World War II in 1943. Also the Soviet built T-72 tanks of the Iraqi army were no match for the U.S. M-1 A-1 tanks.

Saddam Hussein stationed his elite Republican Guard on the northern fringes of Kuwait, inside Iraqi territory, thinking they would be out of harm's way when the frontal attack came from the Saudi border across Kuwait sweeping with speed, courage and valor toward the liberation of Kuwait City and the entire state of Kuwait. However, the Coalition Forces and their brilliant commanders beat him to the punch and used the outflanking maneuvers to trap his elite troops and decimated them in the climactic "classic tank battle" of the Gulf War. The trapped forces were boxed in by a wall of Coalition Forces from every direction. The outcome of the battle was sealed. The elite forces of Saddam Hussein were defeated, losing over 200 tanks, 50 armored vehicles and 20 artillery pieces.

U.S. casualty count prior to the last battle with the Republican Guard was as follows:

Between January 17 and February 23, 1991, those killed in action were 23; wounded 34 and missing in action 39. Casualties from the Scud attack were 28 dead and 100 injured. As far as the ground war was concerned, the casualties between February 24 and February 27, 1991 were respectively 28 killed, 89 injured, and 5 missing in action. The total casualties of the war since the beginning were respectively: 79, 213, and 44 missing in action. As for the Iraqi prisoners of war between January 17 and February 23, there were 2,720 and between February 24 to February 27, 1991, there were around 48,000 and the total by February 27, was over 51,000. As for the Kuwaiti Theater of Operations, the ground war destroyed nearly 3,700 tanks of the original Iraqi tanks operating in the area which amounted to 4,230, according to General Schwarzkopf. About 1,856 armored vehicles were destroyed out of a total of 2,870. Also, 2,140 artillery pieces were destroyed or captured out of a total of 3,110.

The Republican Guard, or remnants of it, did not really have much of a chance! Especially since the strategic targeting of the air attacks conducted by the Allies shifted to the Republican Guard in the few days prior to the ground war. The Republican Guard was a mechanized armor force which was, according to Schwarzkopf, "very, very well dug in, and very, very well spread out. So in the initial stages of the game, we were hitting the Republican Guard heavily, but we were hitting them with strategic type bombers, rather than pinpoint precision bombers." When the air campaign shifted from the strategic phase into the Kuwait Theater of Operation, the Coalition Forces wanted to avoid at all costs a nightmare scenario, where the Allied Forces would be pinned down by enemy artillery, which could rain chemical weapons on them. So, heavy concentration on attacking the enemy troops in the Kuwait theater and destroying their artillery was an absolute necessity. The area of the Republican Guard was punished very severely and attrited heavily prior to the ground war. By doing this, the Coalition Forces then reached a state where they would be fighting their own kind of war, not the war of dug-in trenches of Saddam Hussein.

The remnants of the Iraqi forces did not constitute any offensive regional threat any longer, especially, after the defeat that was dealt the Republican Guard. The Iraqi army, north of the Tigris and Euphrates valley, up from Basra, was an infantry. It was not an armored one. In military language this meant it was not an army which could carry on an effective offense. So, for all practical purposes, the offensive capabilities of Saddam Hussein were now finished. His wings had been clipped, and if anything, his lingering on to power was only by a thread. His position was very precarious!

Relating to the attacks on the retreating Iraqi forces, some people wondered why this should continue? General Norman Schwarzkopf responded to this in his famous February 27 news briefing by saying, "In the business of the military, of a military commander, my job is not to get ahead and at some point say that's great, they've just now pulled out of Kuwait–even though they are still shooting at us, they are moving backward and therefore, I have accomplished my mission! That's not the way you fight it. And that's not the way I would ever fight it."

In the ferocious tank battle with the Republican Guard, attack helicopters and bomber aircraft supported the Coalition Forces and targeted the enemy with devastating blows and accuracy. Again, high technology played a role. Despite the fact that weather conditions were anything but ideal. During the last three days of the ground war, there was heavy rain, dust, smoke and a haze in the atmosphere surrounding the Theater of Operations. However, infantrymen operate best under conditions of this nature and they usually perform very well. Also, high tech night vision worked admirably under these severe conditions of haze, dust and smoke. Enemy targets were sighted efficiently, while enemy forces did not have much luck with their vision equipment. They were surprised to see their tanks explode once they were sighted by Coalition Forces.

As for the military capabilities of the commander in chief of enemy forces, General Norman Schwarzkopf said, "As far as Saddam Hussein being a great military strategist, he is neither a strategist, nor is he schooled in the operational arts, nor is he a tactician, nor is he a general, nor is he a soldier. Other than that, he's a great military man. I want you to know that!" On rating Saddam's army, the General said, "Rating an army is a tough thing to do. A great deal of the capability of an army is its dedication to its cause and its will to fight. You can have the best equipment in the world, you can have the largest numbers in the world, but if you're not dedicated to your cause, if you don't have the will to fight, then you're not going to have a very good army."

As for the performance of the Iraqis on the front lines, Lt. General Walter Boomer said, "I expected them to fight harder than they did . . . My view is that their heart wasn't in it."

The *Special Forces* were very vital to the Coalition, not only because of the important reconnaissance missions they carried out, but equally important, some of them were with every Arab force combating to liberate Kuwait during the ground war. They served as communicators between the Arab forces and the English speaking Coalition Forces. Communication was extremely important because of the diversity of languages in the theater of war. They also, called in for air strikes when these were needed. Essentially, they helped in coordinating air strikes and helicopter attacks. They also were in charge of the combat search and rescue. These are tough dangerous missions which exposed them to extreme danger, mainly in enemy territory, while they were seeking to rescue pilots of the Coalition Forces who were shot down, or other soldiers who had been trapped in dangerous situations. Many times, operating behind enemy lines, they conducted direct action operations against enemy targets in strategic locations.

When all gates were shut on the enemy forces, innocent civilians were allowed to go through these gates and also the unarmed Iraqis were allowed to move on. However, the gates were completely shut for war machines and those manning them.

The 100 Hour War Stops! Saddam Is Defeated

Concerning President George Bush who is the Commander in Chief of the United States Forces, General Norman Schwarzkopf said, "I am very thankful for the fact that the President of the United States has allowed the United States military and the Coalition military to fight this war exactly as it should have been fought, and the President in every case has taken our guidance and our recommendations to heart, and has acted superbly as the Commander in Chief of the United States."

After consulting with the Allies, the generals in the field and assessing the war situation, and the total capitulation of Saddam's forces, on February 27, 1991, President George Bush addressed the nation. Here is his speech:

"Kuwait is liberated. Iraq's army is defeated. Our military objectives are met. Kuwait is once more in the hands of Kuwaitis, in control of their own destiny. We share in their joy—a joy tempered only by our compassion for their ordeal.

Tonight the Kuwaiti flag once again flies above the capital of a free and sovereign nation. And the American flag flies above our Embassy.

Seven months ago, America and the world drew a line in the sand. We declared that the aggression against Kuwait would not stand. And tonight, America and the world have kept their word.

This is not a time of euphoria; certainly not a time to gloat. But it is a time of pride—pride in our troops; pride in the friends who stood with us in the crisis; pride in our nation and the people whose strength and resolve made victory quick, decisive and just. And soon we will open wide our arms to welcome back home to America our magnificent fighting forces.

No one country can claim this victory as its own. It was not only a victory for Kuwait, but a victory for all the coalition partners. This is a victory for the United Nations, for all mankind, for the rule of law, and for what is right.

After consulting with Secretary of Defense Cheney, the Chairman of the Joint Chiefs of Staff General Powell, and our coalition partners, I am pleased to announce that at midnight tonight Eastern Standard Time, exactly 100 hours since ground operations commenced and six weeks since the start of Desert Storm, all United States and Coalition Forces will suspend offensive combat operations.

It is up to Iraq whether this suspension on the part of the coalition becomes a permanent cease-fire. Coalition political and military terms for a formal cease-fire include the following requirements:

Iraq must release immediately all coalition prisoners of war, third country nationals and the remains of all who have fallen. Iraq must release all Kuwaiti detainees. Iraq also must inform Kuwaiti authorities of the location and nature of all land and sea mines. Iraq must comply fully with all relevant United Nations Security Council Resolutions. This includes a rescinding of Iraq's August decision to annex Kuwait, and acceptance in principle of Iraq's responsibility to pay compensation for the loss, damage and injury its aggression has caused.

The coalition calls upon the Iraqi government to designate military commanders to meet within 48 hours with their coalition counterparts at a place in the theater of operations to be specified, to arrange for military aspects of the cease-fire. Further, I have asked Secretary of

State Baker to request that the United Nations Security Council meet to formulate the necessary arrangements for this war to be ended.

This suspension of offensive combat operations is contingent upon Iraq's not firing upon any Coalition Forces and not launching Scud missiles against any other country. If Iraq violates these terms, Coalition Forces will be free to resume military operations.

At every opportunity, I have said to the people of Iraq that our quarrel was not with them, but instead with their leadership—and above all, with Saddam Hussein. This remains the case. You, the people of Iraq, are not our enemy. We do not seek your destruction. We have treated your POWs with kindness. Coalition Forces fought this war only as a last resort, and look forward to the day when Iraq is led by people prepared to live in peace with their neighbors.

We must now begin to look beyond victory and war. We must meet the challenge of securing the peace. In the future, as before, we will consult with our coalition partners. We've already done a good deal of thinking and planning for the postwar period, and Secretary Baker has already begun to consult with our coalition partners on the region's challenges. There can be, and will be, no solely American answer to all these challenges. But we can assist and support the countries of the region and be a catalyst for peace. In this spirit, Secretary Baker will go to the region next week to begin a new round of consultations.

This war is now behind us. Ahead of us is the difficult task of securing a potentially historic peace. Tonight, though, let us be proud of what we have accomplished. Let us give thanks to those who risked their lives. Let us never forget those who gave their lives. May God bless our valiant military forces and their families. And let us all remember them in our prayers.

Good night. And may God bless the United States of America."

On February 27, 1991 U.S. time (February 28, 1991 Baghdad time), Tariq Aziz, Foreign Minister of Iraq addressed the following letter (S22276) to the President of the Security Council:

I have the honor to inform you officially that the Government of Iraqi agrees to comply fully with Security Council Resolution 660 (1990) and all the other Security Council Resolutions.

You are kindly requested to transmit this letter to the members of the Security Council and to have it circulated as an official document of the Security Council.

(Signed) Tariq AZIZ
Deputy Prime Minister
Minister for Foreign Affairs
of the Republic of Iraq

The Commander of the British forces, General Sir Peter De la Billi-ère, attributed the swift defeat of the Iraqis to "A meticulously planned campaign, designed to soften up the battlefield before committing ground troops, by using tremendously superior air power."

Exactly 100 hours from the time the Ground War began and six weeks since the start of Operation Desert Storm, U.S. and Coalition Forces suspended offensive military operations. A *statesman* predicted as far back as day one of Iraqi occupation of Kuwait, that "the mother of all battles" will reveal the truth about Saddam Hussein. Simply said, he was just like a balloon, from the first hit he'll bust. And bust he did! His "mother of all battles" became a mother of all defeats.

The United Nations formally requested compliance by the Iraqi government with the cease-fire terms. Shortly thereafter, Iraq delivered a letter to that effect. However, the cease-fire was not final at this stage. Air bombardments and sporadic ground attacks continued until the last hour of the deadline, which was 12:00 midnight February 27, 1991, Washington time, corresponding to 8:00 o'clock in the morning, February 28, Iraqi time. Over 103,000 sorties had been flown so far. Over 6,500 of these were conducted by the Saudi Royal Air Force, 738 by Kuwait, 266 by Bahrain, 55 by Qatar, and 68 by UAE. A staggering number of 3,000 sorties had been flown on this very day alone (February 27). Many of them, "focusing on battlefield air interdiction and close–air support. Navy and Marine pilots have flown more than 26,000 combat sorties to date."

George Bush held a news conference, the day after he declared the cease-fire. He said to a reporter who was wondering why the President didn't look very jovial and exuberant about the occasion: "Well, to be honest with you, I haven't yet felt this wonderful euphoric feeling that many of the American people feel. I think it is that I want to see an end. Now, we have Saddam Hussein still there, the man who wreaked this havoc upon his neighbors. I just need a little more time to sort out in my mind how I can say to the American people, it is over, finally. Last t is crossed, last i is dotted."

On February 28, 1991, reconnaissance flights continued. While the Coalition Forces were in defensive positions, several incidents with Iraqi troops took place, where Iraqi forces, remote from the main actions and cut off from communications, were not aware that a cease-fire had taken effect. When they fired on Coalition troops, they were silenced or captured. The temporary cease-fire continued to hold despite these minor infractions. On the 1st of March, 1991, after a bombardment of a trench line on Faylaka Island off the shores of Kuwait, hundreds of Iraqi soldiers waving white flags surrendered to an RPV (Remotely Piloted Vehicle) flying overhead on a mission from the battleship Missouri. Again, on this very day, the United States Embassy opened in Kuwait City, after it had been thoroughly searched and carefully examined for possible mines and booby traps. Also, Western Embassies of the British, French, Canadian and a few others opened on this same day. The Kuwait International Airport started its operations again, after it had been sealed by the occupiers for nearly seven months.

As soon as victory was decisively achieved against Saddam Hussein, Jordan's King Hussein, who supported him, was quick to reach out to the United States of America and Arab nations as well, seeking to make peace. He gave a speech to his subjects saying, "Jordan extends its arms wide open to all those who wish to establish friendly relations, based on mutual respect and cooperation." However, Arab nations, who were fighting for the liberation of Kuwait, as well as their safety and security, were not very impressed with the change of color and policy of King Hussein once his ally was defeated in battle. In fact, Kuwait, which was viciously destroyed by Saddam's forces and his supporters, was in no mood for reconciliation with King Hussein. The newly liberated nation rising from the ashes of a ruthless occupation responded with a scathing attack on King Hussein of Jordan and his betraying policies. Kuwait stated that the man could not be trusted and he was accused of supporting Saddam Hussein in capturing the State of Kuwait. Later on, in July, 1991, King Hussein was asked if he had any regrets about refusing to join the Coalition Forces. His answer was quick, "None whatsoever."

In order to consolidate the temporary and possibly fragile cease-fire, the United Nations Security Council moved with determination to consolidate the peace. On the 2nd of March, 1991, and by a vote of 11 to 1 with three abstentions, it passed Resolution 686, which specified the conditions that Iraq must meet before, a final and formal cease-fire was established. Iraq's response to this Resolution and some others was documented as follows:

Letter dated 3 March 1991 from the Deputy Prime Minister and Minister for Foreign Affairs of Iraq addressed to the President of the Security Council (S/22320)

I have the honour to inform you that the Iraqi Government has taken note of the text of Security Council resolution 686 (1991) and that it has agreed to fulfill its obligations under the said resolution. We hope that the Council, in its turn, will interact in an objective and honourable manner, pursuant to the provisions of international law and the principles of equity and justice, with our faithful and to the extent that we are able–speedy fulfillment of those obligations.

You and the members of the Security Council are well aware of the manner in which the American forces and their partners in the military operations against Iraq have implemented Security Council Resolution 678 (1990), and of the major losses which Iraq has suffered to its infrastructure, economic, civilian, cultural and religious property, basic public services such as electricity, water, telephones, transport, fuel and other essential requirements of everyday life.

Despite these facts, Resolution 686 (1991) has ignored the Iraqi people's suffering and the imposition on Iraq alone of a long series of obligations. A number of members of the Security Council referred to this fact, leading one of them (Cuba) to vote against the Resolution, while three States—India, Yemen and China, the latter being a permanent member of the Council—abstained.

We record these facts for history and for the attention of those members of the Security Council and the international Organization—and those elements of international public opinion—who have a conscience. Our agreement to fulfill our obligations under this Resolution stems from our determination to refute the pretexts which some may employ in order to persist in their aggression against Iraq and to inflict further harm on its people.

Iraq hopes that the Security Council will ensure the adoption of a resolution proclaiming an official cease-fire and the cessation of all military operations on land, at sea and in the air, as well as the immediate withdrawal of the foreign military forces stationed without any justification in various regions of Iraq. Iraq also hopes that the Security Council will proceed to declare, with all possible speed, the bases for its adoption of Security Council Resolutions 661 (1990), 665 (1990) and 670 (1990) as having lapsed, with the result that the Resolutions become null and void.

Accept, Sir, the assurances of my highest consideration.

(Signed) Tariq AZIZ
Deputy Prime Minister
Minister for Foreign Affairs

Baghdad, 3 March 1991

On his way to meeting with the Iraqi Generals to formalize the temporary cease-fire and surrender of the Iraqi forces, General Norman Schwarzkopf flew over Kuwait. Here he described to Barbara Walters of ABC television what he saw and how he felt: "We flew into Kuwait to land and because you fly obviously into the wind, all the black smoke was blowing directly at the airplane and we descended into this black smoke where you couldn't see anything, and then suddenly I was looking out the window and you could just make the ground out and there were the huge balls of fire. I was totally unprepared for this scene. The first thing to pass through my mind was, if I ever visualized what hell would look like, this is it. The oil fields burning south of Kuwait City! It was so senseless! Absolutely was senseless destruction! By every definition, it would accomplish nothing; and so by the time I landed at Safwan, I was angry. Why would anyone do something like this?"

The place chosen for the meeting was Safwan in Iraq; it is less than five miles northwest of the Kuwaiti border. The Iraqis would have preferred the meeting to be in Kuwait, not on Iraqi occupied territory. The symbolic choice of this site was purposely made so the Iraqi leadership would clearly understand who won the war!

Finally, on the 3rd of March, 1991, General Norman Schwarzkopf and Joint Forces Commander, Lt. General Prince Khaled Bin Sultan Bin Abdulaziz met military Commanders of the defeated Iraqi forces at a captured air strip in the southeastern region of Iraq, Safwan Air Field in the occupied portion of southern Iraq. A tent was erected for this special occasion with no frills of any kind. Upon arrival, General Schwarzkopf said, "Now, I don't want to embarrass them (Iraqi military representatives) in any way, alright! And I don't want them humiliated. I am not here to give them anything. I am here to tell them exactly what we expect them to do."

The Iraqi military representatives arrived under very heavy guard from the army's first division. Their weapons were left behind. There were eight in total, six of them without identifications. Their leader was Deputy Chief of Staff Lt. General Sultan Hashem Ahmad. The meeting lasted for two hours, during which the Iraqi military formally accepted all the Coalition demands for a permanent cease-fire, including the speedy release of Allied prisoners of war. When General Norman Schwarzkopf emerged from the meeting, he stated, "I am very happy to tell you that we agreed on all matters. Some of the subjects that were discussed were control measures to ensure that armed units of the Coalition would not come in contact with armored units of the Iraqi military so that there would be no deaths. The most important point that we discussed was the immediate release of all prisoners of war. We have all agreed that this release should be immediate." The terms of surrender were dictated at this meeting. Saddam Hussein can call it whatever he wants, but it sure was a far cry from the victory he dreamed of achieving in "the mother of all battles!"

When the Iraqi U.N. Ambassador was using double talk concerning the "logistical problems" in dealing with the number of Allied prisoners of war, the U.S. Secretary of Defense, Dick Cheney said, "I think we have reached the point where the Iraqis would do very well to listen very carefully to what we say, and then do it. We have destroyed their army, we have destroyed much of their infrastructure, we have turned the lights out in Baghdad, we have shutdown their petroleum system, we have shutdown their transportation system. Unless and until they comply explicitly with U.N. Security Council Resolutions, return our prisoners immediately, they are going to have more grief. The effort of the Iraqi Ambassador to the U.N. or anybody else to fuzz it up, simply is intolerable, will not be accepted. The President has made it clear, there will not be a permanent cease-fire until they have satisfied our conditions."

Saddam would go on to tell his people, "You have won, Iraqis. Iraq is the one that is victorious, Iraq has succeeded in demolishing the aura of the United States, the empire of evil, terror and aggression. Iraq has punched a hole in the myth of American superiority and rubbed America's nose in the dust. . . We are confident that President Bush would have never accepted a cease-fire, had he not been informed by his military leaders of the need to preserve the forces fleeing the fist of the heroic men of the Republican Guard."

His army and especially his elite Republican Guard had been decimated. His war machine pulverized! His country in ruin and disarray, and yet the man was claiming victory in the mist of a rout and utter defeat!

After the surrender agreement at the historic site in occupied Iraq, Baghdad Radio went on the blare, "Iraq has been victorious because it stood for right against evil and because Iraqis did not bow to the political demands of the West." However, those who suffered in this war and saw hell, hunger and defeat were returning in the thousands back to their hamlets and towns. They carried with them a sad saga of defeat and humiliation. Soon enough many will rise against the tyrant of Baghdad!

At the conclusion of the war, here are some statistics from Lt. General Thomas Kelly, U.S.A., Monday, March 4, 1991, 3:00 P.M. EST. "Presently, U.S. forces are 540,000 troops in the theater, 98 killed, 308 wounded, 35 MIAs. 63,000 EPWs in Saudi Arabia, 3,000 in Turkey, 800 Iraqi EPWs are in U.S. medical facilities—80% of them were wounded in action; two died of malnutrition or dehydration. Tanks destroyed, 3,300 is what we are sure of, 3,300+; 2,100 armored vehicles, 2,200+ artillery pieces, 1,400 EPWs taken from naval operations around Faylaka Island without Iraqi resistance. With regard to Boubiyan and Warbah Islands, we have not taken them, but reconnaissance has been conducted over them and no Iraqis were noted, so that ought to be a fairly simple thing to do." The Iraqis released 10 POWs on March 4, 1991. On the 5th of March, 1991, the Iraqis released 35 prisoners of war, 15 of them were Americans and the revised U.S. casualty list included 115 killed in action, 65 non-combat fatalities, 330 wounded in action, 37 missing in action and 6 POWs.

By March 6, 1991, 116,000 sorties had been flown over Iraq and Kuwait. The United States of America lost 57 aircraft, 35 of these were fixed wing. Of these 27 were lost in combat and 8 in non-combat, while 22 Helos were lost, 5 in combat, 17 in non-combat.

On the 6th of March, 1991, President George Bush of the United States of America *addressed a joint session of Congress*, in which he reported to the nation and the world that aggression had been defeated. The war was over. Here are excerpts from his historic speech:

". . . Members of Congress. Five short weeks ago, I came to this House to speak to you about the State of the Union. We met then in time of war. Tonight, we meet in a world blessed by the promise of peace.

From the moment Operation Desert Storm commenced on January 16th until the time the guns fell silent at midnight one week ago, this nation has watched its sons and daughters with pride–watched over them with prayer. As Commander-in-Chief, I can report to you our Armed Forces fought with honor and valor. And as President, I can report to the nation aggression is defeated. The war is over.

This is a victory for every country in the Coalition–for the United Nations. A victory for unprecedented international cooperation and diplomacy–so well led by our Secretary of State James Baker. It is a victory for the rule of law–and for what is right.

Desert Storm's success belongs to the team that so ably leads our Armed Forces: our Secretary of Defense and our Chairman of the Joint Chiefs, Dick Cheney and Colin Powell.

And while you're standing–this military victory also belongs to the one the British call the "Man of the Match"–the tower of calm at the eye of Desert Storm–General Norman Schwarzkopf.

And let us–recognizing this was a coalition effort, let us not forget Saudi General Khaled, Britain's General de la Billière, or General Roque-joffre of France–and all the others whose leadership played such a vital role. And most importantly, most importantly of all, all those who served in the field. . .

The recent challenge could not have been clearer. Saddam Hussein was the villain–Kuwait the victim. To the aid of this small country came nations from North America and Europe, from Asia and South America, from Africa and the Arab world–all united against aggression.

Our uncommon coalition must now work in common purpose–to forge a future that should never again be held hostage to the darker side of human nature.

Tonight in Iraq, Saddam walks amidst ruin. His war machine is crushed. His ability to threaten mass destruction is itself destroyed. His people have been lied to–denied the truth. And when his defeated legions come home, all Iraqis will see and feel the havoc he has wrought.

And this I promise you: For all that Saddam has done to his own people, to the Kuwaitis, and to the entire world, Saddam and those around him are accountable.

All of us grieve for the victims of war, for the people of Kuwait– and the suffering that scars the soul of that proud nation. We grieve for all our fallen soldiers and their families–for all the innocents caught up in this conflict. And, yes, we grieve for the people of Iraq–a people who have never been our enemy. My hope is that one day we will once again welcome them as friends into the community of nations. . .

Now, we can see a new world coming into view. A world in which there is the very real prospect of a new world order. In the words of Winston Churchill, a world order in which "the principles of justice and fair play protect the weak against the strong. . ." A world where the United Nations–freed from Cold War stalemate–is poised to fulfill the historic vision of its founders. A world in which freedom and respect for human rights find a home among all nations. . .

We went halfway around the world to do what is moral and just and right. We fought hard and, with others, we won the war. We lifted the yoke of aggression and tyranny from a small country that many Americans had never even heard of–and we shall ask nothing in return.

We're coming home now–proud; confident–heads high. There is much that we must do, at home and abroad. And we will do it. We are Americans. . ."

In a message to his forces, General Schwarzkopf addressed all Desert Storm forces on March 6, 1991, saying, "I asked you to be the thunder and lightening of Desert Storm. You were all of that and more. Through your courageous acts, your dedicated service, your determination, and your love of country, you have written history in the desert sands that can never be blown away by the winds of time."

The Allies insisted on more concrete responses from Iraq. Saddam Hussein himself and through his Revolutionary Command Council (RCC) had to respond on the 5th of March. His response was conveyed to the U.N. Security Council on March 8, 1991. The following is the official document:

S/22342

Identical Letters Dated 8 March 1991 from the Permanent Representative of Iraq to the United Nations Addressed Respectively to the Secretary-General and the President of the Security Council
On instructions from my Government, and further to its acceptance of Security Council Resolution 686 (1991), as indicated in the letter

addressed to you by the Minister for Foreign Affairs of my Government, dated 3 March 1991, I have the honour to transmit to you a copy of Revolution Command Council decision No. 55 of 5 March 1991 concerning the application of paragraph 2 (a) of Resolution 686 (1991).

I should be grateful if you would have this letter and its annex circulated as a document of the Security Council.

(Signed) Abdul Amir A. AL-Anbari
Ambassador
Permanent Representative

Annex

Revolution Command Council decision No. 55 dated 17 Sha'ban A.H. 1411 (5 March A.D. 1991)

In accordance with the acceptance by the Iraqi Government of Security Council Resolution 686 (1991) and with its previous declarations regarding acceptance of the other Security Council resolutions, and pursuant to the provisions of article 42, paragraph (a) of the Constitution,

The Revolution Command Council has decided as follows:

1. All Revolution Command Council decisions subsequent to 2 August 1990 regarding Kuwait are null and void.
2. All laws, decisions, regulations, instructions, directives and measures issued by virtue of the decisions of the Council referred to in paragraph 1 above are abrogated and all the effects arising therefrom are nullified.
3. No text which is contradictory to the provisions of this decision shall have any effect.
4. This decision shall be published in the Official Gazette and shall take effect from 3 March 1991.
5. The competent ministries and authorities shall undertake the implementation of this decision.

(Signed) Saddam HUSSEIN
Chairman of the Revolution
Command Council

Since the defeat of the Iraqi army and the liberation of Kuwait, a vast number of soldiers and volunteers were trying desperately to make Kuwait City a safe place again. They were dismantling booby traps and mines by the thousands. Minesweeping operations were carried with diligence and absolute care. Finally, by March 8, 1991, the port of Kuwait City was safe enough, and was reopened for the first time since the occupation of Kuwait. Another major Kuwaiti port, Ash-Shuai-

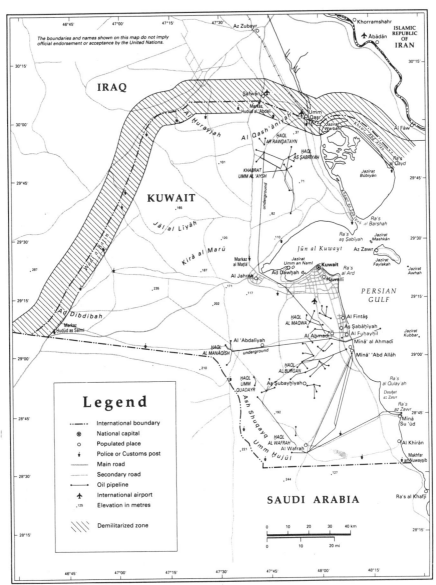

U.N. OBSERVER UNIT AND
DEMILITARIZED ZONE

bah was reopened. Over one hundred Coalition divers cleared a path of the deadly mines and thus created a safe channel for two tankers steaming through to bring badly needed supplies of drinking water and food to the Kuwaiti populace. On March 14, 1991, the Amir of Kuwait Sheikh Jabir Al-Ahmad Al-Sabbah returned from his exile in Saudi Arabia.

On March 20, 1991, one Iraqi SU-22 Fighter jet was shot down near Tikrit, hometown of the Iraqi dictator; another plane landed on its own after an engagement with the Coalition Forces. An announcement by the U.S. Department of Defense stated that these two aircraft were flying in violation of the terms agreed upon by the Iraqi military officials. Specifically, no fixed wing aircraft was allowed to fly by the Iraqis in the skies of Iraq or elsewhere for that matter. Again on March 22, 1991, an Iraqi SU-22 Fighter was shot down near Kirkuk, Iraq. Another aircraft crashed after its pilot ejected. This was again in violation of the cease-fire terms. By March 26, 1991, the number of naval maritime interceptions was 8,379 challenges, 1,055 boardings and 53 diversions.

While the blockade continued, on April 2, the update for Maritime interceptions was as follows: 8,598 challenges, 1,110 boardings and 58 diversions.

On the 3rd of April, 1991, the U.N. Security Council passed the *landmark Resolution 687* (See Appendices) by a vote of twelve in favor, one against from Cuba and two abstentions from Ecuador and Yemen. Resolution 687 stresses the "restoration to Kuwait of its sovereignty, independence, and territorial integrity and the return of its legitimate government." It also relates to the status of sanctions and it sets specific conditions for a formal cease-fire. It was sponsored by: Belgium, France, Romania, United Kingdom, United States and Zaire.

The temporary cease-fire was initially observed, but it took Iraq until April 6, to accept United Nations terms for a permanent and formal cease-fire. On the 9th of April, 1991, the United Nations Security Council approved Resolution 689 whereby it established a United Nations' Iraq–Kuwait Observer Mission in order to monitor the permanent cease-fire between Iraq and the Coalition Forces. On April 11, 1991, the United Nations Security Council announced that a formal cease-fire had been established and declared an end to the Gulf War.

More on Atrocities in Kuwait

When Kuwait was liberated, Kuwaitis received with jubilation, great joy and open arms the liberators from the Arab Forces and Coalition Forces–gallant warriors who fought with exemplary courage and valor to free them from the grip of the tyrant of Baghdad. All the stories told by those who escaped torture and destruction in Kuwait were certainly true. Kuwait City was systematically plundered and looted by the occupiers. Luxury hotels and modern government buildings were looted and destroyed. When the Iraqi troops were leaving the city in a hurry, they looted what they could find and set torch to anything they desired. They abducted thousands of young Kuwaiti men and took them to Basra and Baghdad. This massive operation of abduction began even a week before Kuwait was liberated.

In his historic briefing from Riyadh on February 27, 1991, General Schwarzkopf spoke about these *atrocities*. He said, "There was a very, very large number of young Kuwaiti males taken out of that City (Kuwait City) within the last week or two. But that pales to insignificance compared to the absolutely unspeakable atrocities that occurred in Kuwait in the last week. They are not a part of the same human race, the people that did that, that the rest of us are. I've got to pray that that's the case."

Reporters and eyewitnesses driving around the city also witnessed the remnants of war; Iraqi tanks destroyed, military vehicles burning, the stench of death in the gloomy air. The skies were pitch black from more than 700 burning oil wells. They were torched by Saddam Hussein, turning the height of day into pitch black of night. When a Kuwaiti was asked about confirming any abductions, he went on to say that on Friday, right after prayer, his neighbor was taken away. Then he went on to describe the ugly scene with tears streaming down his face and said, "They stopped people with their families, I swear to God, with their families, wives and children; took husbands, young men . . . my neighbor is gone with them. We don't know where he is now! Last night, it was like hell for the Iraqi forces! There is no way they can be Arabs! They are not Moslems at all. They destroyed the people!"

On Thursday, February 21, and only just a couple of days before the ground war was unleashed, Iraqi soldiers roamed the streets, picking up men from their homes and their cars, taking them as hostages.

When the Iraqi soldiers came knocking on the door, an uncle hid some youngsters in the water tank above the bathroom, since it was empty. Five young men were hidden there to avoid the onslaught and terror of the Iraqi soldiers. What a terrifying moment? What an atrocity of man against his fellow man? During these last few days, mosques were an attractive target for the Iraqi forces. They surrounded the mosques and then picked up the men they wanted and took them away. Stories of rape and all forms of torture abound! Six women were found with their breasts cut off! People across all walks of life were missing.

Their loved ones in agony and despair, not knowing what happened to them! A mother was crying over the disappearance of her son, who was taken away as soon as the ground war began. She said, "Collaborators with the Iraqis stopped my son's car, then turned him over to Iraqi soldiers. I jumped onto the car, I kissed him (the soldier in charge) begging him to let my son go. He pushed me away. I don't know where my son is now!"

On the outskirts of Kuwait City mounds of dirt were discovered. They constituted a gruesome sight, a cemetery for many of the people tortured and killed by the occupying forces of Saddam Hussein. It has been reported that in August and September of 1990, tortured bodies were arriving there at a rate of 40 per day. Digging went on leading to more gruesome sights and more tortured bodies. Cemetery records showed 2,797 Kuwaitis had been buried here since the occupation of Kuwait by the Iraqi aggressors. Many tortured victims could not be recognized. Some cemetery staff members took secret photos of the victims. These were smuggled out of the country to provide substantiated proof concerning the terrible atrocities committed by the occupiers. Another large graveyard contained 56 bodies from those babies killed in hospitals when the Iraqis "tore the respirators from their incubators." Over 5,000 Kuwaiti men were taken away by the fleeing Iraqi soldiers. They wanted to use these unfortunate people as hostages and for bargaining chips. Schools and sport complexes became notorious torture centers. Evidence of electric wires in torture chambers used by the Iraqis to torment their victims, gave an eerie feeling and a chill to the bone! Neighbors living near these torture sites, could hear the agony and screams of these unfortunate Kuwaiti victims.

Conclusion

With a temporary cease-fire declared, a wave of fleeing Iraqi soldiers flooded the southern Iraqi city of Basra and spread further upward reaching Iraqi cities and hamlets. The wave of haggard soldiers, devastated refugees, dead and wounded in a useless futile war, initiated and executed by Saddam Hussein, were all testimony to the obstinacy and ill designs of a tyrant—their ruler, Saddam Hussein! In a matter of hours, after the temporary cease-fire, a state of chaos and confusion prevailed in the southern city of Basra. The Shi'ite rebellion against the rule of Saddam Hussein had begun with gusto! Soon after, it spread further north, until it reached Baghdad and way into the northern reaches of Iraq, where the Kurdish rebellion began, again. Another chapter in the atrocities of Saddam Hussein had already begun, almost before another tragic chapter had begun to fold!!!

Kuwait is liberated!

Saddam Hussein and his forces are routed and defeated.

Unclassified

Multinational Personnel Strengths

**These figures are peak personnel strengths
of the countries listed and included air,
ground and naval forces.**

1.	Afghanistan	300	22.	Norway	50
2.	Argentina	300	23.	Oman	6,300
3.	Australia	700	24.	Pakistan	4,900
4.	Bahrain	400	25.	Philippines	UNK
5.	Bangladesh	2,200	26.	Poland	200
6.	Belgium	400	27.	Qatar	2,600
7.	Canada	2,000	28.	Romania	UNK
8.	Czechoslovakia	200	29.	Saudi Arabia	100,000
9.	Denmark	100	30.	Senegal	500
10.	Egypt	36,000	31.	Sierra Leone	200
11.	France	14,600	32.	Singapore	UNK
12.	Germany	UNK	33.	South Korea	200
13.	Greece	200	34.	Spain	500
14.	Hungary	50	35.	Sweden	UNK
15.	Italy	1,200	36.	Syria	19,000
16.	Japan	UNK	37.	Thailand	UNK
17.	Kuwait	9,900	38.	Turkey	UNK
18.	Morocco	1,300	39.	UAE	4,300
19.	Netherlands	600	40.	UK	45,400
20.	New Zealand	UNK	41.	Zaire	UNK
21.	Niger	480			

U.S. Forces   541,400

Coalition Forces   255,080
_____
796,480

(35,146 of that number were
women, cincbrif, CPV,
Unclassified, J1-10 Jun 91)

*Source: U.S. Department of Defense, United States Central Command, Macdill Air
Force Base, Florida, USA, and other sources.

Cost of the Gulf War

	Amount in Billions of Dollars for the year	
	1990	**1991**
Direct War Costs to the U.S.	11.100	36.400
Revised Additional cost to the U.S.		13.500
Pledges by the Allies		
Saudi Arabia	3.339	13.500
Kuwait	2.506	13.500
Japan	1.740	9.000
Germany	1.072	5.500
United Arab Emirates	1.000	2.000
Korea	0.080	0.305
	9.737	43.805
Revised Miscellaneous Additional Pledges		

Total U.S. Cost   =   61 billion dollars   (According to ABC TV, as of November 8, 1991)

"   Allied Pledges   =   58   "   "

Actual U.S. War Cost   =   3   "   "

War damage to Kuwait including destruction to oil wells is estimated to be over   100 billion dollars

War damage to Iraq, due to Saddam Hussein's occupation of Kuwait, is estimated to be around   100 billion dollars

Source: Various Journals, Defense Budget Project, ABC TV.

KILLED IN ACTION

UNITED STATES	148
SAUDI ARABIA	47
UNITED KINGDOM	25
EGYPT	12
UAE	10
SYRIA	2
FRANCE	2
TOTAL	246

KUWAITIS KILLED BY IRAQI FORCES AND DURING THE
WAR OF LIBERATION ARE ESTIMATED TO BE ABOUT 3,000

IRAQIS KILLED IN THE GULF WAR ARE ESTIMATED TO
BE IN EXCESS OF 100,000

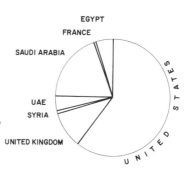

SOURCE : (Except for Kuwait and Iraq) U.S.
DEPARTMENT OF DEFENSE, UNITED
STATES CENTRAL COMMAND, MAC-
DILL AIR FORCE BASE, FLORIDA,
U.S.A. AND OTHER SOURCES.

WOUNDED IN ACTION

UNITED STATES	467
SAUDI ARABIA	220
EGYPT	95
UNITED KINGDOM	45
FRANCE	38
UAE	17
SENEGAL	8
BAHRAIN	2
SYRIA	1
OMAN	1
TOTAL	894

KUWAITIS INJURED AND TORTURED ARE ESTIMATED
TO BE ABOUT   5,000
(Many are still missing)

IRAQIS INJURED ARE ABOUT   250,000

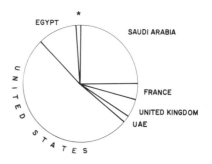

* —OMAN, BAHRAIN, SYRIA, SENEGAL

SOURCE : (Except for Kuwait and Iraq) U.S.
DEPARTMENT OF DEFENSE, UNITED
STATES CENTRAL COMMAND, MAC-
DILL AIR FORCE BASE, FLORIDA,
U.S.A. AND OTHER SOURCES.

Chapter 9

The Never Ending Atrocities of a Tyrant

While the propaganda machine of Saddam Hussein was busy declaring victory to the Iraqi people, thousands upon thousands of defeated soldiers, demoralized, hungry, and wounded, were streaming into the southern cities of Iraq and then way beyond to reach the four corners of the Iraqi nation. They brought with them stories of a horrifying defeat and abandonment by their leadership which invited their slaughter and agonizing defeat because of its arrogance and obstinacy. Such leadership refused surrender in the face of overwhelming odds, then decided at the last moment to withdraw, although it had seven months of appeals from all leaders of the world to get out of Kuwait! All the appeals fell on deaf ears. When the soldiers retreated with their trucks, loot, and war machines, they were pulverized. And they have only Saddam Hussein to blame! The stories of betrayal and defeat spread across the land like a wildfire. No sooner had the Shi'ite masses met with the defeated soldiers, than a bloody uprising developed in Basra, the Iraqi southern town with a large population of Shi'ite Moslems.

The Shi'ite Rebellion

Relations were never warm between Saddam Hussein and the religious leadership of the Shi'ites in Iraq. In fact, as you recall, Ayatollah Khomeini, tried to excite the Shi'ite Fundamentalists' zeal in Iraq, by appealing to his fellow religionists to rise and topple the rule of the Ba'ath Party in Iraq. The core of the rebellion centered around the extremist Islamic Fundamentalists who were always at odds with Saddam Hussein. Several others in the population joined in the rebellion because of their hatred to the Iraqi regime and in no time, the masses of Basra were desperately trying to fulfill a dream of toppling the tyrant of Baghdad.

The religious overtones were strong and ominous, especially since the Mullahs of Iran were again supporting their brotherly Shi'ites who constitute about 55% of the Iraqi population . . . Their (over a decade) dream of toppling Saddam Hussein and his Sunni government from power was now being revived and the hopes were very high indeed!

This background religious information is essential here to shed some light on the underlying currents and causes contributing to this uprising.

After the rise and great conquests of Islam, rivalries later developed and resulted in dividing the Moslem religion into Sunni and Shi'a (Shi'ite) sects. After the murder of the third Caliph, Outhman, his cousin, Ali, who was a son-in-law to the Prophet, became the fourth Caliph but Mouaweeia, the governor of Syria, accused Ali of complicity in the murder of Outhman, and finally, gained the Caliphate after Ali was assassinated.

With this came the major division in the Moslem faith: the *Sunni*, who believed that the Caliphate was an elective office, and the *Shi'a*, who believed that the heirs of Prophet Mohammed, namely his daughter, Fatima, and her husband, Ali were entitled to the Caliphate.

One more attempt was made to wrest the Caliphate for Ali's son, Hussein. But he and his followers were murdered at Karbala, Iraq, in October, 680 A.D. The most important Shi'a shrines are at Karbala and Al-Najaf in southern Iraq.

This division and schism were buried for centuries. In fact, a few years ago, people from across the Arab land, be it in the Arab world or those studying abroad at American Universities, European Universities, or the former Soviet Union, all did not think of someone being either a Sunni Moslem or a Shi'a Moslem. Then, came the Iranian Revolution which was engineered and led by Ayatollah Khomeini and his brand of *extremist Islamic Fundamentalism*. This led to the polarization and resurfacing of old divisions which trace their history back hundreds of years. This was also at the core of the rebellion in southern Iraq.

The Iraqi leader gave bonuses and pay raises to his military, especially the remnants of his Republican Guard. He also fired the Interior Minister and replaced him with a relative, his cousin Ali Hassan Majid, who was the notorious governor of occupied Kuwait and also the one who supervised the use of poison gas against the rebellious Kurds in Halabja in 1988.

Saddam Hussein was very quick to order the expulsion of international journalists, so they would not be eyewitnesses to the oncoming blood bath. Many Iraqis saw this as an ominous sign of things to come!

The spiritual leader of the Shi'ite Rebellion was the religious Iraqi cleric Ayatollah Mohammed Bakr Al-Hakim, who was living in exile in neighboring Iran. He immediately predicted that the Iraqi dictator was facing "a dark and bitter end." Thus, the Shi'ite upheaval was aiming at creating an Islamic Republic in Iraq, along the lines of the Islamic Republic created by Ayatollah Khomeini in Iran.

As for the position of the United States of America, as well as the Coalition countries, the choice between Saddam Hussein or an extremist Fundamentalist Republic in Iraq was not a choice at all! No moderate country in the world aspired to see the extremist revolution of Iran exported to other borders. So, taking sides in this rebellion was not in the cards. The United States and the Coalition Forces did not want to get involved in a exploding civil war in Iraq. Besides, not long ago, the extremist Fundamentalists in Iran held 52 Americans as hostages for 444 days. They were also accused of orchestrating through their proxies in Lebanon, the brutal kidnapping and inhumane holding of innocent American and European hostages for several years– all contrary to the spirit of Islam. There was no way that the American administration or the American public opinion would be excited or in favor of a Shi'ite extremist rebellion to be supported by America's might, so that the road would be paved for an Islamic Republic in Iraq, along the lines of the Iranian revolution. After all, the vacillating American leadership of the late 70s contributed to paving the way for Ayatollah Khomeini to come to power and the price for such vacillation was exorbitantly high, indeed! That policy and behavior shall never be repeated again and won't.

The Shi'ites continued their uprising with vengeance. They were joined by a few thousand disgruntled and disheartened soldiers fleeing from the humiliation and disaster that befell them in Kuwait and southern Iraq. The combination of the rebelling civilian population and army deserters attacked government buildings, headquarters of the hated Ba'ath Party, military establishments and threw wide open the gates to prison cells and torture chambers. In the first few days of March, the uprising was gaining tremendous momentum and spreading fast to other southern cities of Iraq. This eruption began on the 2nd of March, 1991 and with it began a flood of refugees heading to Safwan which was under the control of the American and Allied Forces.

The rebels wearing distinct green headbands, carried with them pictures of the deceased Ayatollah Khomeini and also pictures of Al-Hakim, who is head of the Supreme Council of the Islamic Revolution, based in exile, in the Iranian capital, Tehran. Weapons captured from Iraqi soldiers and others smuggled from Iran were used to carry the fight. Many people were killed and whole families were murdered. The ruthless crackdown was on the way but before Saddam's forces would succeed in crushing the rebellion, the fires of the revolt spread wildly in the Shi'ite cities of southern Iraq covering the ancient valley of the Tigris and Euphrates rivers. Hostilities, strife and fires moved from Basra to Nasra and Siriya, Amarah, Samawah, Kumayt, Diwaniya, Al-Kut and the Holy Shi'ite cities of Najaf and Karbala. The revolt even reached certain Shi'ite quarters in the capital city, Baghdad.

In a few critical days, Saddam Hussein and the Revolutionary Command Council rallied the forces supporting them, especially the remnants of the Republican Guard, and fought back to stop the wave of revolt. Some army units with their T-55 tanks who sided with the rebels, fought brief battles. However, the few army soldiers did not prevail and soon enough the Republican Guard, supported by remaining army units, moved ferociously against the revolt. They used tanks, artillery and deadly helicopter gunships. These were very devastating to the civilian uprising against the Iraqi ruler.

It was feared that Saddam Hussein in his desperate hours might resort to the use of chemical weapons which he had done before, on a number of occasions, against both the Iranians and the Iraqi Kurds. For this reason, the United States and some Coalition partners warned him that he must desist from using chemical weapons against his population or else air attacks would be resumed against his forces and other Iraqi targets. The warning was explicit and it gave the desired effect. He did not dare to use his chemical weapons again. Nevertheless, he used Phosphorus bombs and still had enough military power and military equipment to cause devastation to his enemies in Iraq.

While his wings were severely clipped and his potential for aggression against his neighbors was not only diminished but eliminated, he still had the might of a strong internal security and police force whereby he began to prevail against the rebelling forces in several cities. Saddam Hussein intended to crush his opponents mercilessly, so his forces rained their rockets and instruments of death on the revolting population, killing indiscriminately thousands and thousands of those rebelling against his tyrannical regime. Much devastation and destruction was caused especially by the French–built helicopters which poured their rockets, incendiary bombs, and napalm on the Shi'ites.

While Saddam and his forces were desperately trying to control the situation in the southern cities and towns of Iraq, another rebellion was gaining momentum. This time, the Kurds in northern Iraq were trying their luck again, against the regime of Saddam Hussein–their arch enemy from way back when he fought them in the early 70s and then again used poison gas against them in Halabja in 1988. This part of the brief civil war will be discussed in more detail as we move on in this chapter.

Destruction, havoc and fires from Saddam Hussein raged on the civilian populations of the Iraqi cities in the South. The disorganized revolt did not have a chance against the avalanche and onslaught from Saddam's remaining forces. Thousands of artillery rounds and short-range Frog-7 missiles charged with white phosphorus were used to add to the casualties and destruction. Despite the fact that Saddam's forces were stretched to the limit, his commanders were able to leap-frog the remnants of their forces moving them from one heated battle to another. The situation was touch and go! But the seesaw battles began to tip in his favor. Although winged Iraqi aircraft was not allowed to fly, according to the temporary cease-fire agreement, nevertheless, Saddam made optimum use of *helicopters* which rained devastation on his opposing forces.

While the Allies did their utmost to avoid any accidental attack on the Holy cities of Karbala and Al-Najaf, Saddam and his troops did not hesitate to rain havoc and destruction on the two Holy Shi'ite cities. Refugees were streaming from the southern region of Iraq to neighboring Kuwait and Iran. At the border town of Safwan close to the Kuwaiti border, Iraqi children, fleeing the hell and destruction in the south, lined the roads begging for food and water. This area which was occupied by the American and Allied Forces received a constant stream of refugees running for the safety of this zone. Many Iraqi soldiers fled south hoping that they could be taken as prisoners of war, but many were turned back north. Southern cities were covered with the stench of death. People were desperately looking for food and medicine. Many of the destitute refugees had been injured. Some small children were injured in the fighting and others from stumbling on mines or small bombs that exploded in their hands. Hundreds of thousands of people were suffering terribly from the attacks of Saddam Hussein who crushed their revolt in the southern cities.

Many of the refugees in the camps of southern Iraq were moved to the Saudi camp in Rafha in the northwest region of Saudi Arabia. This camp included over 22,000 people. Many of them were destitute Iraqis, but some were from other nationalities who were working in Iraq. The Kingdom did everything possible for their safety and welfare.

The rebellion was spontaneous and disorganized. In fact, the various factions fighting against his regime met in Beirut around mid-March in order to forge out some common grounds in facing their enemy. Too many deep animosities prevailed. Various groups were represented, including various factions of the Shi'ites, the Kurds, the Communists, the Sunni Nationalists, and members of the Ba'ath Party who are loyal to the Syrian wing of the party. Much strife and discord existed between these groups. So instead of coming up with a unified position for the world to see, they did not portray this image. They certainly failed in either forming a government in exile or establishing a decisive leadership organization in opposing Saddam Hussein and in seeking the sorely needed support from the world community.

The Bush Administration and the Allies were dead set against the dismemberment of Iraq. It was genuinely feared that Iraq would be "Lebanonized," whereby the Shi'ites in the South would set their brand of Islamic Fundamentalist regime, while the Kurds in the North would establish their basic seed for their dream of Kurdistan, and the remainder of Iraq might be absorbed by the neighboring countries. For this reason, Iran was specifically warned not to interfere in the raging civil war in Iraq. In fact, President Bush warned that any invasion of Iraq by Iran would be "the worst thing it could do."

The U.S. and Coalition Forces were especially alarmed about the possible and imminent disintegration of Iraq and what this would entail as far as instability in the region, especially, since the Kurds simultaneously rose up in arms and were making progress in their revolt against their arch enemy, Saddam Hussein.

Brief History of the Kurds

It is essential to give a brief historical background about the Kurds, prior to dwelling into their recent uprising against the regime in Baghdad. Way back in history, the Kurds were mountain people who were converted to Islam in the dawn of the seventh century. The main Kurdish populations in the world reside in the northern area of Iraq, the western side of Iran, northeastern Syria, the southern side of eastern Turkey and a small portion of the southern fringes of the former Soviet Union. The whole region is mainly mountainous. While it had been called *Kurdistan* for several centuries, this region has never been independent. Kurdistan means the land of the Kurds. While this sect of people live there, they have never had the separate entity and defined boundaries of the modern, independent states in the new world or the old world for that matter. However, the Kurds kept their separate identity in these respective countries. Their aspiration is for autonomy and down deep they very much desire to have an independent state called Kurdistan, which would be treated like any other member state of the United Nations. This remains to be a long shot and a dream. Its realization remains very remote, indeed, if at all possible.

The Kurdish people speak the Kurdish language which is related to the Hindu-European family of languages. It has two main dialects. The language does not have special letters. In Iraq, the Kurds use Arabic letters for their languages as well as in Iran and Syria. While in Turkey, they use Roman letters and in the former Soviet Union the Russian alphabet is used. The vast majority of the Kurds are Moslem Sunni.

There was never a census to determine the actual number of Kurds in the world. However, estimates vary between 15 and 28 million. The latest estimates are as follows. Iraq had a Kurdish population close to 4 million, mostly in the northern part of Iraq. Iran had over 6½ million, while Syria had around 1½ million, Turkey about 8½ million and the former Soviet Union about ½ million. This gives a total Kurdish population of nearly 21 million.

The word Kurdistan was first used by the Saljuc Sultan in the twelfth century. Kurdistan is mainly mountainous with heights extending from 6,000 feet in Turkey to 14,000 feet in Iran. The Zagrous mountains in Iran reach a height of 10,000 feet and mountains around the borders with Iraq reach over 12,000 feet.

The wars that erupted in the sixteenth century between the Ottoman Empire and the Safawid in Iran brought division and war to the Kurds caught in between. The Kurds were used by the two warring powers and allegiance swayed between the two major powers. From time to time, some Kurdish municipalities were established, but lost their presence depending upon who gained the upper hand among the major warring factions.

The Kurds are known through history for their toughness and sometimes brutality. They have been warriors, farmers and very much lacking in education. In fact, illiteracy was predominant among them for many decades. The most famous Kurd was a great warrior and a hero to the Arabs named Salah Al-Din Al-Ayyubi known to the west as *Saladin*. This great military leader was able to capture Jerusalem and a vast portion of Palestine from the invading Crusaders between the years 1187 and 1192. Although he was a Kurd, he gained his fame defending the Arab land. Saladin was famous for his bravery and magnanimity. This is synonymous with chivalry known in Arabic as Mourouwwah. When the Fatimid Caliph died in the year 1171, Saladin proclaimed himself the Sultan of Egypt. Saladin was successful in uniting Egypt and Syria under the rule of his family known as the *Ayyubid dynasty*.

The Kurds remained conservative, religious and loyal to their traditional leadership. When World War I erupted, they were urged by their tribal leadership to respond vigorously to Turkey's call for a Jihad. Initially, they responded favorably, but as soon as it became clear that Turkey was destined to be defeated at the conclusion of the war, their enthusiasm dampened. They were very much encouraged by the declarations of *President Woodrow Wilson* of the United States of America. Among the principles he enunciated in his 14-Point Plan was *self-determination* for people around the world, among them the Kurds and the Arabs. The best opportunity for establishing a nation for the

Kurds came at the conclusion of World War I, after 1918. The Treaty of Sèvre in 1920 supported an autonomy for the Kurds which could have led to possible independence. However, this treaty was never ratified and the hopes for an independent or autonomous Kurdistan evaporated. Although Great Britain installed initially, some acceptable local Kurdish leaders to manage the affairs of the Mosul Wilayat (district), however, Britain was not very serious about an autonomous region for the Kurds, which might lead to independence. Their basic interests were in establishing an independent Arab state in Iraq which included the oil rich region in Kirkuk and Mosul.

Finally, the state of Iraq was founded and it included Basra and Baghdad. It was placed under a British mandate as designed and approved by the League of Nations. This was according to the San Remo Agreement of April, 1920. When the British needed a treaty with Iraq which would safeguard their interests, the Iraqis and their parliament were reluctant. So the British revived the hopes of the Kurds again with promises of autonomy. Based on these encouragements and some promises, a Kurd named Sheikh Mahmoud returned from exile and was used to combat Turkish influence and desire for absorbing Mosul. But he was too quick to take advantage of this unique opportunity. He gathered his well armed men on the 18th of October, 1922 and declared the establishment of a Kurdish Independent Kingdom in Souleimaniya which was to be governed by him. This again, presented an opportunity for Britain to support Iraq in this new challenge and thus earned some points in its favor. In February, 1923, British forces took action to put an end to the Kingdom of Sheikh Mahmoud. Tribal division among the Kurds contributed to his downfall, and the British occupied the Souleimaniya region in May, 1923.

Most of the Mosul Wilaya was given to Iraq and Turkey was granted some monetary compensation. This decision of the League of Nations, reached in December, 1925, also had some guarantees for the Kurds. A new treaty between Britain and Iraq was enacted, which also stated that the mandate of Britain would go on for 25 years, unless Iraq was accepted as a member of the League of Nations prior to the expiration of that period. The government of Iraq was required to respect and guarantee the rights of the Kurds living in the Wilaya. When Iraq applied to become a member of the League of Nations in 1930, Britain supported Iraq in this regard and in return this facilitated the passage of a new treaty between Iraq and Britain by the Iraqi Parliament. In this new spirit, Britain did not insist on any special treatment for the Kurds, for fear that such an insistence would lessen chances of the treaty passage in the Iraqi Parliament.

Immediately after this, the Kurds demonstrated and rebelled against the *Iraqi-British treaty*. However, the uprising was lacking in organiza-tion and leadership. From there on, the history of the Kurds in northern Iraq was a *history of uprising and rebellion* and much of the time discourse with the central Iraqi government. Of course, Turkey with its large Kurdish population was not immune from Turkish rebellions. The Kurdish rebellions through the years have been crushed whether in Iraq or other realms of Kurdistan. Division among the Kurds always played a role which was inherent to the defeat of their revolts and dissipation of their dreams. Turkey definitely did not favor any separat-ist movement among the Kurds and considered those living in Turkey as Turkish citizens, certainly not entitled to a national entity. The same reasoning was adopted in Iran and other countries with a strong Kurdish population.

Among the noted leaders of the Kurds in Iraq was the late Mullah Moustapha Barazani. During World War II, the former Soviet Union conquered the northern part of Iran, while Britain conquered the rest. Russia encouraged the formation of a party which included the various national and leftist currents; it was called the *Democratic Kurdish Party*. Its main center of activity was in Mahbad, Iran. The leader of the party declared on December, 1945, the establishment of the Mahbad Kurdish Republic. This was joined by Mullah Moustapha Barazani, the Barazan tribes and others who were Kurdish Iraqi refugees in Iran. Barazani was one of its four generals and the tribe of Barazan was considered the army of the new Republic. However, the former Soviet Union withdrew from Iran after World War II and the Central Govern-ment in Tehran attacked the Kurdish Republic in Mahabad which crum-bled very quickly. There was then cooperation between Iran and Iraq to suppress the Kurdish national movement and to oppose its activities both in Iraq and Iran.

After the Monarchy was toppled in Iraq, on July 14, 1958, most of the Kurds who were in exile in Iran returned and were allowed to practice their political activities under the Democratic Kurdish Party. The Kurdish population was initially given some relative freedom, during the rule of the Revolution that toppled the Monarchy. In fact, the Kurdish leader, *Mullah Moustapha Barazani*, his family and other followers returned on the 5th of October, 1958 from the former Soviet Union, where they were in exile. By the 16th of April, 1959, hundreds of Kurds from the Barazan tribe returned to Iraq. However, the honey-moon did not last for long. Barazani traveled back to the former Soviet Union on the 5th of October, 1960 to participate in the socialist festivi-ties. He remained there until nearly mid-January, 1961. Shortly after his return, strife and attacks began between the competing tribes of the Iraqi Kurds. He accused the government police of supporting the

Zibaryyin who are competitors and enemies of the Barazan tribe. They were both Kurds, but they were competing for leadership of the Kurdish population. It was stated that enemies of the Barazan tribe attacked, with Iraqi police in Mosul, about fifteen villages belonging to the Barazan Clan. These villages were devastated.

The Mullah Moustapha Barazani had his special *connections with the former Soviet Union and leftist forces* where he received financial and military support. Within a brief period, the conservative Sheikhs and feudal leaders of the Kurds also combined forces with the leftists against the Iraqi government. Several clashes occurred between the Kurds and the Iraqi army and many atrocities were committed. Soon after September 23, 1961, more clashes took place and the Kurds started receiving support, military and otherwise from the government of the Shah of Iran. At times, Iraqi forces attacked nearby Iranian villages where the Kurds sought refuge. Abdul Karim Qassem accused the United States and Britain of fomenting the Kurdish rebellion. By March 11, 1970, a special manifesto was declared relating to Kurdish autonomy. Supposedly, the Kurds were granted rights they had struggled for, for decades. Because of this arrangement with the central government, the fighting ceased, but the Ba'athist regime in Iraq used this time to consolidate its forces and plans for the Kurds. By 1974, the Kurdish autonomy agreed upon in 1970 collapsed. War exploded again! This time the Kurdish revolt, while widespread, was met head on with tough vicious forces, with much devastation to the towns of Zakho and Qala'at Diza. Due to the ferocity of the attack, hundreds of thousands of the Kurdish population in these cities fled the scene of brutality and death. At this stage, the Iranian government under the Shah was supporting the rebellion of the Kurds. Their attacks continued, but the treaty of Algiers concluded in 1975 reflected a deal between the Shah and Saddam Hussein of Iraq. It gave Iran much of what it had requested, especially regarding sovereignty over the Shatt Al-Arab Waterway. In return, the Shah stopped his support for the Kurds and their rebellion crumbled immediately thereafter. The Kurdish leader Mullah Moustaph Barazani died in exile in 1979.

In March, 1988, Saddam Hussein exacted revenge from the Kurds for their leaning toward Iran during the Iran-Iraq war. He viciously and ruthlessly attacked Kurdish towns and villages. The most infamous attack was on Halabja, where he devastated the Kurdish population by using poison gas. He killed over 5,000 people. The Kurds were also uprooted and moved elsewhere in the country.

This brief review of Kurdish history and their affinity for a homeland of their own played a key role in seizing a new golden opportunity to rise against their arch enemy Saddam Hussein.

The Kurdish Revolt

When the Shi'ite uprising in the south became very threatening to the Ba'athist regime in Iraq, Saddam Hussein moved with venomous determination to crush this new challenge to his authority, especially, after he felt that he survived the onslaught of the Allies. He transferred some of his troops from the northern Kurdish regions of Iraq so that his troops embattling the Shi'ites would have the upper hand and certainly, in a short time, they did. No sooner had he realized this goal, than the Kurdish Iraqis in the north rose up in arms and moved with tremendous dedication and determination against the local forces of Saddam Hussein. In this endeavor they were strengthened by the many deserters from Saddam's army who came streaming into their hamlets in northern Iraq, bringing with them the horror stories which were the creation of Saddam Hussein and his obstinacy. Also, many Kurds that were moved from their villages some time ago in a campaign to dilute their identity, found their way back to their old villages and towns. With the Shi'ite rebellion in full swing in the south and with the great initial thrust made by the Islamic Fundamentalists in the first week of March, the Kurds found the time to be very opportune indeed, to attack the forces of their arch enemy, who had brutalized them and used poison gas against them. With his forces spread thin and juggled in between northern Iraq and southern Iraq, initially, the Kurdish fighters made substantial progress in a very short time. This rebellion started only a week after the Shi'ite rebellion began in the south.

Mas'oud Barazani, son of Moustapha Barazani was leading the revolt. He had been amazed as to the speed with which the Kurdish population made tremendous progress in their new insurgence. The uprising started around March 4, 1991 in the town of Rania and from there on it spread like wildfire across the Kurdish hamlets and towns of northern Iraq. The fighting forces of the Kurdish population are called the Peshmerga, meaning the self-sacrificing ones or those who face death; one of their trademarks was sporting the AK-47 rifle and their unique khaki baggy trousers. They are tough fighters and well seasoned in uprisings against the central authority in Iraq. They attacked military headquarters in the region and had overtaken military depots. This way they were able to claim a good bit of military equipment from the Iraqi forces. They threw doors to jails wide open and thus, their ranks swelled with more support from the liberated prisoners and the defecting soldiers. While Saddam Hussein was still struggling for his very existence in suppressing the Shi'ites in the south and bombarding the Shi'ite cities, including the Holy sites in Karbala and Najaf, he began to have the upper hand in the south. Thousands and thousands of Shi'ite refugees flooded the southern borders with Kuwait and Iran. They were prevented from entering Kuwait but the American and Allied Forces in the southern region of Iraq fed them and gave them water and shelter until moved to camps in Saudi Arabia where they were well cared for.

The initial stages of the Kurdish rebellion were very successful. Whatever Iraqi forces were in the northern region had to flee for their lives, although many of them did not make it to safety. The Kurdish leader Mas'oud Barazani was granting interviews held in none other than the luxurious villa of Saddam Hussein in the town of Saladin. He stated, "We realized that an independent Kurdistan is out of the question . . . All we want is the right to till our land in peace, the right to local government, the right to speak our language and have it taught in our schools.: He then went on to say, "We were all taken by surprise at the swiftness of our victory."

The Kurds were vastly predominant in the northern Iraqi towns of Irbil, Mosul, Dahuk, Kirkuk, Souleimaniya, Zakhu, and others.

By the 20th of March, 1991, the Kurdish leaders were asserting that nearly all Iraqi Kurdistan was now free from the grip of Saddam Hussein. The Kurds were very jubilant for having liberated their territory. Although they claimed their desire was for autonomy within Iraq, but given the chance, they definitely and very determinedly would like to have the seed for their nationhood of Kurdistan and thus would desire an independent realm in northern Iraq. Such a dream will cause immediate worry and threats to neighboring countries with sizable Kurdish populations. All these countries, including the major powers, do not desire to support the creation of a new state of Kurdistan. The geopolitical atmosphere was not conducive to this undertaking, nor would it contribute to the stability of the area.

By March 26, 1991, Jalal Talabani, the Damascus-based Kurdish leader of the *Patriotic Union of Kurdistan*, returned from a three year exile to the liberated Kurdish territory in northern Iraq, in order to share in the struggle and the joy of the liberation achieved by the Kurdish rebelling forces. The U.S. State Department confirmed that the Kurdish rebels controlled a large segment of the northern region of Iraq and Secretary of State, James Baker, stated that he did not wish to see Iraq dismembered. "We do not desire to see a Lebanonization of the country. We do not want to see a power vacuum there." In fact, the unleashing of these forces in the north and south were a double-edged sword that had to be watched very carefully. The situation became very precarious by opening a Pandora's box, with ethnic, religious and linguistic deep divisions. If this broke up into many segments, chaos would prevail and destabilization would result in the Arabian

Gulf. All this would be contrary to the goals and designs of the new world order.

Kurdish jubilation at their newly won freedom did not last for long. After crushing the rebellion in the south, the Iraqi leader juggled his troops and moved them swiftly to the north. He attacked the Kurdish rebels with vengeance. He still had a substantial force which was to be reckoned with, especially, in any internal uprising. Despite the devastating defeat that befell his army, both in Iraq and Kuwait, he was able to gather nearly a quarter of a million men, ready to fight with whatever military equipment they had, including nearly 2,000 tanks. This was far more than what was needed to crush the rebellion and that is precisely what he did. He used his tanks, artillery, missiles, napalm, phosphorus and the most devastating and feared *helicopter gunships*, against the Kurdish forces. The deeply wounded and humiliated Saddam Hussein attacked his people viciously. Both armed rebels and civilians were equally slaughtered by his superior war machine. Kurdish forces were vastly outnumbered and out-gunned. His hatred for them was deep and went back over two decades.

As the month of March neared its end, the forces of Saddam Hussein had the upper hand over the rebellious Kurds. In fact, by March 31, 1991, his forces were decisively crushing the Kurdish rebellion. The Peshmerga and their Guerrilla supporters staged a strategic retreat. The Commander in Chief, Barazani, who just a few days before was gloating victory, now realized that he could not hold on to the cities which were liberated by his forces. He realized that his supporters could not stand up to the onslaught of Saddam's forces. The remnants of the Republican Guard were still a potent force that remained loyal to Saddam Hussein in dishing out death blows to his rebelling citizens. Barazani advised his forces and people to leave as quickly as possible. He said, "The battle for the plains is over. Now we must continue the battle in the mountains." The memories of atrocities committed by the Iraqi ruler against the Kurds were very fresh, indeed!

Kurdish Plight and International Aid

Once they sensed that their insurgency was falling apart, the Kurds were not going to depend on the "magnanimity" of Saddam and his forces. They recalled vividly the poison gas attacks, the killing and slaughter they received at the hands of Saddam and his forces for the last two decades or more. The Kurds en mass moved from their northern villages and towns northward to the mountains bordering Iraq and Turkey, and some went eastward toward Iran. Men, women and children; sick, healthy and elderly all fled the region, fearing the onslaught and death from Saddam Hussein and his forces. This mass migration was enormous indeed, the likes of which are very few in the history of mankind! This *forced mass migration was a human catastrophe* in the making! Hundreds of thousands of unfortunate Kurds fled their homes and earthly belongings, carrying with them their little children, blankets, little food, and ran for the safety of the mountains on the borders with Turkey and Iran. Columns of fleeing Kurds with trucks, cars, tractors, animals (sheep and goats), frontend loaders, you name it–all loaded with their families and whatever meager belongings they could carry. These stretched for several miles at times. Sixty mile jams developed in attempts to reach the safety in the mountains in Turkey, away from the venomous reach of Saddam Hussein who was ferociously unleashing death and destruction against his citizens; not for the first time, but after practicing such death scenarios in real life many times over, and not long ago. In about one day, thirty thousand Kurds were crossing the border with Turkey, clinging on to the safety of the Turkish border. Turkey, of course, was alarmed at this massive exodus. In a matter of two more days, two hundred thousand Kurds were amassed by the borders and many more hundreds of thousands followed them. Turkey was not essentially very sympathetic to the autonomy dreams of the Kurds, especially since they themselves have a Kurdish population in excess of 8 million people (some estimates put this number at 14 million). Also, Turkey had been fighting Kurdish aspirations for autonomy, or independence of Kurdistan, for over eight years. Thus, Turkey had reason to be alarmed at the avalanche of humans, destitute and desperate, pouring toward its borders. It appealed for international help and especially to President Bush of the United States of America.

The plight of the Kurds was a tragedy of the human race, on a massive proportion. This exodus, being in March, a cold time of the year in the mountains, led to many tragic consequences. First of all, the fleeing Kurds were attacked by the much hated helicopter gunships which remained operational. Some of the warplanes, at the initial stage of the uprising, were used but the Allied Forces quickly downed one plane then another and gave the message to Saddam Hussein that he could not use fixed wing aircraft in his fight with the Kurds. The use of helicopter gunships was contrary to the spirit of the temporary cease-fire agreement. But nevertheless, the Allied Forces did not see fit to get involved in a quagmire of a civil war in Iraq, and they did not stop him from using his gunships. Some military authorities indicated that stopping him from using his helicopters would not have made much difference as far as the outcome of the battle with the Kurds. But nevertheless, if he was prevented from using them, many innocent lives would have been saved.

Fleeing the plains of the north, the Kurds reached the mountainous region, and those who were unfortunate did not make it through the long journey. Many died on the way, especially the young children and the elderly. When they reached the mountains, another tragedy was taking place already. Many of these unfortunate destitute people, especially the weak, the young and the elderly perished. These mountains are *hostile, cold and rugged*. While the streams were a welcome sign of life, snow was another story that brought with it shivering cold. Many of the babies and elderly could not take the severity of the cold and the frostbites. They died in agony!

With a flood of nearly one million men, women and children clinging on to the heights and mountains on the border with Turkey, sanitary conditions were anything but ideal. Human waste polluted the waters and some of the scarce food supplies. Diarrhea was a serious cause of death, again especially for the young and elderly. Nearly one thousand people were killed every day, most of them in that category. Loved ones were buried in shallow graves, dug in the rugged terrain. The heartache and agony of the people was devastating and indescribable. Saddam Hussein intended to drive the Kurds away from their homeland, so in turn they would become a problem for his neighboring countries and not to the Iraqi regime anymore. While he succeeded in causing untold agony and tragedy to the Kurds, he did not succeed in keeping them from their homeland. Again, he failed!

The world was witnessing this tragedy played again and again on television screens and across their air waves. The conscience of the world was stirred to action. With nearly 30,000 refugees in the camps of the Allied Forces in the south and hundreds of thousands crossing into Iran, and now in the north, nearly one million Kurds fleeing to the harsh mountains and another million fleeing across to Iran with large numbers going to Syria and Turkey, the time for massive aid to save these unfortunate people was now overdue.

Crossing into Syria was a treacherous mission. The banks of the Tigris river were mined. In fact, thousands of mines were placed along the Iraqi side of the river. Iraqi shells were falling regularly, in order to prevent any supplies which may come from the Syrian side by crossing the waters of the river. So the refugees, trying to flee Iraq, boarded some small boats to cross the river, holding their lives in their hand and trying to overcome the possible devastation from the mines in the waters, or the destruction from the Iraqi shells falling at random on the river. Such an escape path was extremely dangerous. The Iraqis succeeded in closing it most of the time.

The tragedy mounted by the hour and by the day! The "iron lady," Margaret Thatcher, declared on April 3, 1991, "The Kurds don't need talk, they need practical action. It should not be beyond the wit of man to get planes there, with tents, food and warm blankets. It is not a question of standing on legal niceties. We should go now." The French President, François Mitterrand sent his Secretary of State for humanitarian action to the northern region of Iraq. With him, he brought two planeloads of aid to the destitute Kurdish refugees. The niceties of sovereignty of nations was slightly put aside in the case of Iraq, because of the gravity of the situation and the butcher approach that Saddam Hussein had been practicing. After the appeal of the former Prime Minister, Margaret Thatcher, the British pledged forty million dollars for a first installment to help the Kurdish refugees. Right after her appeal, the British sent three planeloads of blankets and tents for the Kurdish refugees along the Turkish border. The Germans and other nations followed suit. By Friday, April 5, 1991 the White House ordered American authorities to dispatch planeloads of food, clothing and blankets to be air-dropped to the refugees. Another ten million dollars was promised as emergency aid and more to come.

Finally, massive aid was organized. Many countries contributed to this aid effort. Leading among them Britain, France, the United States of America, and a number of other countries around the world. Supplies were air-lifted from bases in Saudi Arabia to the Kurdish refugee camps along the Turkish border. Once the decision was made, the emergency relief effort of the United States was described as, "The largest U.S. relief effort in modern military history." Because of the huge number of destitute refugees, this gigantic effort still was not enough. The desperately needed supplies were air-lifted in a hit–or–miss operation, where crates of these supplies were dropped from the air, falling everywhere along the rugged terrain. Some of it was damaged, and others yet caused damage to the refugees who rushed with desperation to grab whatever food they could find. There was a lot of suffering and agony for all these refugees and their families. Tempers flared and fights developed among destitute people over water, clothing, medicine and food.

The rugged mountains were so dangerous for the helicopters to land, that is why food, clothing, tents, blankets and medicine were dropped from the air and some of it disintegrated. In other areas which are relatively flat, and where helicopters landed, the refugees nearby mobbed the helicopters and that created a dangerous scene for the Kurds and the personnel in the helicopters.

Reaching the refugees who made it to the peaks was not an easy task. Some trucks with food and medical supplies snaked through the muddy roads bringing a shred of life and hope to the terrified, ragged, cold and starved refugees.

Some deals were being worked out with Saddam Hussein but no

one believed or trusted him among the Kurdish community. The autonomy talks led to some understanding but they had been broken in the past and these promises again were not being taken seriously.

Any delay in President Bush's response was because he did not want to go beyond the U.N. Mandate, nor did he want to get American and Allied Forces involved in an Iraqi civil war. President George Bush stated, "I made very, very clear from day one, that it was not the objective of the Coalition to get Saddam Hussein out of there by force. And I don't think there is a single parent of a single man or woman that has fought in Desert Storm that wants to see United States forces pushed into the situation, brutal, tough, deplorable as it is."

Thus, he was extremely cautious in this regard. But when the refugee situation became very grave and appeals from certain allies and friends were made for America to come with its might and aid the Kurds in their plight, the President moved efficiently and compassionately with massive aid. This became the worst refugee crisis in the modern history of man and especially, since World War II.

Secretary of State, James Baker, who made a brief visit to the border between Iraq and Turkey said concerning the Kurdish refugees, "You look at this and you can't help but think it is nothing less than a *crime against humanity.*"

However, despite the massive help from major allies and international relief organizations, the situation was so grave, it called for other measures and means of aid and distribution. The Prime Minister of Britain, John Major, proposed a plan which was first urged by the Turkish President, Turgut Ozal, as a possible solution to the gigantic refugee problem on the borders with Turkey. The Turkish President, a staunch friend and ally of the West became alarmed at the possibility of unrest and destabilization on the Turkish-Iraqi border. The plan called for United Nations-sanctioned *"safe havens,"* which would be created inside Iraq. These "havens" would be protected from any encroachment or attacks from Saddam Hussein's soldiers. However, this approach was not an easy one to be accepted by some permanent members of the Security Council such as, China, the former Soviet Union and India. To set a precedent of this nature would cause concern for these nations with large numbers of ethnic groups. Creation of these safe spots were not called safe enclaves in order not to give the impression that these will be the seeding for a Kurdish State, which was definitely opposed by the neighboring countries having substantial Kurdish populations, as well as major powers of the world which would see it as a destabilizing force in the region. Insisting on any formal establishment of enclaves, sponsored by the United Nations, could be construed as a prelude to forming a small Kurdish State within

Iraq and thus would lead to the disintegration of the Iraqi Republic. This was avoided and semantics played a role in the choices of "safe havens."

However, the presence of the International Relief Agencies and their workers should, along with the presence of Allies, be deterrent enough for Saddam not to interfere with the relief work nor should he dare to mess again with the Allied Forces, since the lessons were very fresh in his mind and since his miscalculations brought him and his people humiliation and disaster.

With the unified plan supported by the United States, Britain and France, the Iraqi ruler was clearly warned not to use any fixed-wing aircraft or helicopters north of the 36 parallel. Any use of forces or violation of this warning or any interference with relief operations would lead to immediate and swift action by the Allies against his forces and aircraft. The area north of this line constitutes almost ten percent of Iraqi territory. This region of northern Iraq, which is the traditional home of the Iraqi Kurds became a "safe haven," where U.N. relief organizations and other international relief groups, along with the U.S., British, French and other governments could operate freely, safely and without fearing the onslaught of Saddam Hussein. It was a risky proposition to some degree, but the Tyrant of Baghdad had his wings already severely clipped and it was believed that he would not dare to commit any suicidal acts by interfering with relief operations.

The stage was set for massive organized aid, supported by sheer force to guarantee the safety of personnel and success of the distribution system so the agony of the Kurds could be eased. By the end of April, a large force was dispatched to guarantee the safety of the refugee camps, which would be erected in various areas, north of the 36th parallel. The United States sent a force in excess of 10,000 soldiers, the British sent a force of over 5,000 and the French over 1,300. Also, Italy and the Netherlands sent 1,000 soldiers each, for the same purpose. This approach essentially treats the Kurdish problem as a humanitarian one. The political situation of the Kurds would have to be addressed later between the Iraqis and the Kurdish leadership. The 36th parallel did not include Kirkuk, Souleimaniya or Halabja. Kirkuk is an important oil center; much of Iraqi oil production comes from that region. North of the 36th parallel are the cities of Irbil, Mosul, Dohuk, Zakhu and others.

The campsites were to be built to house the Kurdish refugees and attract them to come back to the safety of the zone, north of the 36th parallel. President George Bush said, "All along, I have said that the

United States is not going to intervene militarily in Iraq's internal affairs and be drawn into a *Vietnam-style quagmire*. This remains the case. Nor will we become an occupying power, with U.S. troops patrolling the streets of Baghdad. . . We intend to turn over the administration and the security of these sites as soon as possible to the United Nations, just as we are fulfilling our commitment to withdraw our troops and hand over responsibility to U.N. forces along Iraq's southern border–the border with Kuwait. But we must do everything in our power to save innocent lives and this is the American tradition and we will continue to live up to that tradition.''

The United States military and its Allies began establishing encampments north of the 36th parallel. These campsites were built in flat areas, where aid could be administered with organization and much less difficulty than previously. Although there are about 3,000 Iraqi troops on the fringes of the area, the Allied Forces were far superior and they did guarantee the safety of the camps and security of the supply lines from any possible attack. Also, nearby in Turkey there could be a quick deployment force of Marines and Air Cavalry troops which could act very swiftly against any encroachment or breach in the security by any Iraqi forces. The Kurds would not be permitted to use these camps as bases for any guerrilla activity. Any Kurds returning to the camps would not be allowed to bring arms with them. Security inside the camps would be carried out by U.S. and Allied Military Police. Seven campsites in the Zakhu area and vicinity were erected. Each one capable of accommodating 100,000 refugees. These were built on flat terrain, about twelve miles inside northwestern Iraq.

As soon as the campsites were finished, the U.S. and its Allies accelerated their campaign to convince the Kurdish refugees that these camps were safe and secure. Their safety and security were guaranteed by the might of the U.S. forces, supported by the British, the French and others. It was not an easy task to convince the terrified Kurdish refugees. But the Allied campaign prevailed, since they brought down a number of Kurdish leaders to show them the camps and to prove that they were secure. Kurdish leaders went back and convinced their fellow Kurds to move to these campsites. Kurds in the mountain region began streaming to the safety of these camps. The tent city was declared safe and sound! The weakest were flown down, the youngest, ill and elderly were helped in their return, while others made it back on their own. While the Iraqi army was forced to leave the mountain-top positions they had in northern Iraq, not far from the campsites a few hundred Iraqi soldiers were stationed. These evoked fear and terror in the hearts of the Kurdish refugees, who remained skeptical to some degree about the safety and security of their loved ones, especially, after the American and Allied Forces were to leave. They certainly and earnestly hoped that these forces would remain.

A great network of *supply and distribution lines* was established, stretching all the way from the Mediterranean to Turkey, and then to the needy refugees in Iraq. Some of the relief came by air. Not long ago, about a thousand unfortunate refugees were dying every day from hunger, diarrhea and exposure to the elements. Now, it is estimated that about 500 are still dying every day. This was taking place at the biggest camp near the Turkish city of Cukurca. People were dying from stomach problems and respiratory ailments.

Although the Iraqi government sent a letter to the United Nations Security Council where it stated that the refugee camps built by the U.S. and its Allies, "are a flagrant violation of Iraq's sovereignty," the campsites were built and they are being used by the refugees. U.S. authorities and their allies wanted the United Nations to take over. The U.N. was initially reluctant. Iraq then demanded that the United Nations take these campsites over. So, as soon as the mechanism was worked out and order established, safety and security guaranteed for the camps and their occupants, with the proper supply lines for food, medicine, clothing and other necessities of life, the U.S. and their Allies were ready to turn the campsites over to the U.N. In fact, they were delighted to do so, since none of them wanted to get involved in a long term arrangement, which could have undesirable consequences or might drag them into an internal problem from which they could not extract themselves easily. There was always the worry of getting involved in a quagmire of a civil war, or a Vietnam syndrome situation.

At the same time, talks between Saddam Hussein and the Kurdish leaders, namely, Barazani and Talabani were going on trying to arrange some understanding and some partial solution to the dilemma and tragedy of the Kurds. The Iraqi government, finally, promised amnesty to those involved in the revolt. Excepted from this amnesty were those who committed murder, robbery, or rape.

Badly needed supplies came by sea to the Turkish port of Iskandaroun on the Mediterranean Sea. Other supplies came by air to the Incirlik Air Base and also to Diyar Bakir Air Base in Turkey. A 24-hour a day truck convoy was moving the supplies from the Mediterranean ports across Turkey closer to the refugee areas, for immediate distribution. This land transport was around 800 miles. The Military kept this commitment for some time, until the situation came under control. Lives were saved and the Kurds were in the safety of the campsites.

Kurdish leaders stated that an agreement in principle was achieved and further negotiations would pave the way for autonomy for the Kurds. These talks between Saddam Hussein and the Kurdish leaders apparently led to possible free elections, a national assembly and freedom of the press for the Kurds in the future. As soon as an elusive peace accord was signed, then U.S. troops were to leave Iraq. Many Kurds were elated at the news, but many more were skeptical, because Saddam Hussein had broken many promises in the past and would not hesitate to break them again and he did!

The people who lived in the camps were either too afraid to go back to their own homes since these were under the control of the Iraqi army or there were no homes left to go back to. Thousands of homes were destroyed by the Iraqi forces when they attacked the Kurds. The United Nations assumed humanitarian responsibilities for the "safe havens" in the early part of June. Many of the refugees who fled to Iran had returned, but still hundreds of thousands remained. A mountain strip which is about 30 miles (48 kilometers) inside Iraq was under the control of the Kurdish Peshmerga guerrillas. Several thousands of refugees were camping in the rubble of their homes. Previously, over 4,000 Kurdish villages were destroyed and the Kurds were spread elsewhere so that these borders with Iran would be more secure and the Kurdish problem would be diminished. Doctors Without Borders, which is a French charitable group, did their good share in giving medical services and aid, especially to many of the victims that acquired their injuries from exploding land mines.

After reaching proper arrangements and understanding with the U.N. *team* and after establishing safety guarantees, the Allied troops began withdrawing from the northern Iraq region. Thousands of Kurds demonstrated against their withdrawal. They wanted the Allied Forces to remain. Although many Kurds tried to block the withdrawing forces, however, the pullout continued.

The Allied leaders who helped in the mercy mission and aid to the Kurdish refugees announced that all the troops would be out of Iraq by Monday, July 15, 1991.

Jay Garner, Commander of the Allied Forces and a U.S. Army Lt. General in the Security Zone, stated that the Iraqi military forces would not be allowed to enter the *3,600 square mile* zone. He stated, "We have told (Saddam Hussein) not to come back in here. And he won't come back here. If he comes, he knows that we will come back." The Kurds were grateful for the great help they received and they carried Garner on their shoulders prior to their dispersal.

The Commander of the forces in the zone, Garner and a number of other Allied Forces were to be on hand in the Turkish border town of Silopi. A good force was stationed there just in case it was needed. A force of nearly 3,000 troops were to be stationed in Turkey for rapid deployment, if needed to prevent any violence by Saddam Hussein against the Kurdish refugees. Talks between Kurdish leaders and the Iraqi regime continued on the possible autonomy for the Iraqi Kurds. Again on Saturday, July 13, 1991, Saddam Hussein met with the Kurdish leader, Mas'oud Barazani, who is the leader of the Democratic Party of Kurdistan. Jalal Talabani, head of the rival Patriotic Union of Kurdistan met with him on Thursday, July 11, 1991. They were all optimistic for a tentative solution to the Kurdish problem.

After the departure of the Allies from the campsites some incidents occurred where a clash took place between some Iraqi forces and Kurdish guerrillas. Several people were killed or injured. The Kurdish rebel leader, Barazani who was in Baghdad for the autonomy talks, stated that the fighting took place because of some misunderstanding. He further said that the Kurds who opposed his negotiations took advantage of the matter and aggravated the situation. He said, "there was a misunderstanding between the Peshmergas (Kurdish guerrillas) and some soldiers in one of the checkpoints near Souleimaniya. It was not a problem between the Kurdish front and the government; it was a misunderstanding first, but after that, some people tried to use it against us, to use it against the agreement, to use it against the negotiations." There were about 73 U.N. guards in Souleimaniya and 54 in the town of Erbil, according to the agreement signed in April for the protection of Kurdish minority. . . A temporary solution for the Kurdish tragedy had been achieved, but the nightmare and agony of the Iraqi people continue unabated! Saddam and the Kurds remain at odds. He had been blockading their region and cutting their food supplies whenever he could.

The Rope Is Getting Shorter

With the refugee situation in northern and southern Iraq temporarily stabilized, Saddam Hussein and his regime were now carrying a game of hide and seek, "cheat and retreat" with the United Nations team charged with supervising the destruction of Iraq's nuclear, chemical and biological weapons. Despite the explicit requirement by the U.N. Resolution 687, which authorizes U.N. Inspectors to find and destroy all Iraqi weapons of mass destruction, the Iraqi ruler continued to obstruct their mission. With the wealth of satellite intelligence which gave much information about Iraqi nuclear facilities and other weapons of mass destruction, came an unsolicited source of great wealth of information. This came from an Iraqi defector who showed up at the

American lines in the northern part of Iraq. This good source gave very valuable information about the nuclear facilities and capabilities of Iraq. The Iraqi regime was threatened time and again to give full cooperation with the U.N. team or else face air attacks by the Allies against Iraqi targets. Despite these threats, Saddam continued to obstruct the U.N. mission and he essentially ordered his men to shuttle equipment, facilities and files away from the U.N. searching team. Finally, United States officials said that Iraq could face military strikes if it failed to disclose the full extent of their nuclear potential. That was what the cease-fire accords stipulated. These must be respected and honored. The nuclear game of hide and seek had to stop and finally, President George Bush warned Saddam Hussein to allow the complete inspection of his nuclear facilities within ten days from July 14, 1991 or else face resumption of air raids against Iraqi targets. With these serious threats, he was forced to produce the necessary evidence which showed that Iraq was indeed trying to join the nuclear club. This response averted another crisis, which would have spelled the end of Saddam Hussein altogether.

By mid July, Iraq submitted a 29 page report to the United Nations and the International Atomic Energy Agency, revealing that it possessed more than four and a half pounds (2 kilograms) of enriched uranium. These were developed in a clandestine nuclear facility. All along, Iraq had denied any interest in developing a nuclear bomb, but finally, they were forced to admit it. Their admission was certainly contrary to all their declarations in this regard and counter to their signature on the Non Proliferation Treaty.

On July 17, 1991, Saddam and his regime celebrated the 23rd anniversary of the 1968 revolution which brought the Ba'ath Party back to power in Iraq. He stated, "that the United Nations sanctions are a plot to destroy the nation." He urged his people to "unite to rebuild the nation. Stating also, "We are soon going to enter the phase of experiencing a multi-party system with its open door policy. Let us all work together to rebuild a great and prosperous Iraq." He continued to portray the Gulf Crisis as a battle "of good against evil." However, his normal threats did not materialize this time, nor his rhetoric about the infamous "mother of all battles," which turned out to be a mother of all surrenders and defeats.

The game of "cheat and retreat" continued. Finally, on March 21, 1992, after the U.N. warned Saddam Hussein, and after the entry of the U.S. warship America into the Gulf, the head of the U.N. Special Commission Rolph Ekeus announced the Iraqi ruler's compliance with U.N. Resolution 687 for eliminating his weapons of mass destruction. The game of deception will go on! But the end is near!

Concluding Episode

The list of atrocities committed by Saddam Hussein is endless. The people that have been touched by his ruthlessness are in the millions. The agony of refugees streaming from Kuwait and Iraq and then other refugees driven from their homes in southern Iraq and northern Iraq run into the millions. His blood thirsty ways were strengthened by the *vengeance of a wounded tyrant*. The torture chambers discovered in Kuwait, in the south of Iraq and in the north of Iraq, all speak to the evil embodied in this man. His atrocities did not stop only against women, children, old men and innocent refugees from all walks of life and all nations of the world, but they extended against nature in a most dastardly gruesome way. The millions of barrels of oil he purposely pumped into the Arabian Gulf waters, and later the torching of over seven-hundred oil wells which burned about six million barrels of oil per day to the tune of burning nearly 120 million dollars per day, all were a waste! This was *environmental terrorism* on a massive scale. The pall of smoke hanging over Kuwait turned day into night and will cause much damage to the health of men and women, especially, the young and elderly for many years to come.

When his power grew aggressively and abnormally to unacceptable levels, where he was on the verge of becoming a nuclear power, he ventured his aggression on Kuwait and humanity was not able to tolerate his tyranny and aggression. His power was broken, but he remained in power and the Iraqis failed in their attempts to delete his tyranny. One wonders why?

First of all, the U.N. Mandate did not call for the removal of Saddam Hussein and the Gulf War ended a few days early–"*a job well done but incomplete*"–so it was left for the Iraqis to remove him from power– not an easy task by any stretch of the imagination! Why? The security precautions taken by this ruthless man are enormous. Even his ministers are thoroughly searched and decontaminated before meeting with him.

He is surrounded by circles of security men–almost an army in itself–who are well fed and who receive special privileges. These men are his *partners in crime;* his fate becomes their fate! Special streets and special roads are designated for his personal use. When he moves he uses a caravan of 40 vehicles to camouflage his personal, heavily armored and exactly identical car. His living quarters are an intricate maze of several palaces connected with a maze of access roads surrounded by high walls and secret underground access tunnels. Each of these palaces is ready to receive him anytime–complete with everything he needs. When a foreign dignitary brings a message, his security staff makes a copy and hands it to him. Journalists interviewing him are thoroughly searched and stripped except of their clothing. Their hands are also decontaminated.

All these extraordinary precautions and more have given Saddam Hussein some additional survival time. His atrocities will catch up with him and his luck shall run out!

The United Nations continued to play a key role by passing more resolutions regarding Iraq and its responsibilities. One resolution allowed Iraq to sell some oil for an equivalent sum of about 1.6 billion dollars so that this money would pay claimants and the U.N. team supervising the demolition of Iraqi weapons of mass destruction and, also buy some badly needed food and medicine to be closely supervised and distributed to the Iraqi population. However, despite their dire need, the regime of Saddam Hussein was still hedging, delaying, circumventing and refusing to comply. But they will have no choice but respect, observe and apply all U.N. Resolutions in the vivid spirit of the new world order. Saddam will not succeed in dodging his responsibilities. He will be forced to pay for all the destruction and evil he caused.

Since the 20th of May, several U.N. Security Council Resolutions have been passed. Here is a brief summary of them:

Resolution 692–20 May, 1991

Relating to the funds to be paid by Iraq for damages to natural resources, environments, injury to foreign governments, nationals and corporations as a result of its unlawful invasion and occupation of Kuwait.

Resolution 699–17 June, 1991

Relating to the destruction of Iraq's biological and nuclear weapons and specifies that the government of Iraq shall be liable for full costs involved.

Resolution 700–17 June, 1991

Relating to the establishment of a Committee for monitoring the prohibitions against the sale or supply of arms to Iraq and related sanctions.

Resolution 705–15 August, 1991

Relating to and stating that compensation paid by Iraq (from section E of Resolution 687) shall not exceed 30 percent of the annual value of the exports of petroleum and petroleum products from Iraq.

Resolution 706–15 August, 1991

Relating to the decision to allow importing of petroleum and petroleum products originating in Iraq, sufficient to produce the sum required to pay some reparations, but not to exceed 1.6 billion U.S. dollars;

the requirement for the International Committee of the Red Cross to report on activities undertaken in connection with facilitating repatriation or return of all Kuwaiti and 3rd country nationals or their remains present in Iraq on or after 2 August, 1990; and requiring Iraq to supply monthly to the Secretary General a statement of the gold and foreign currency reserves held in Iraq and elsewhere.

Resolution 707–15 August, 1991
Relating to condemnation of Iraq's violation of U.N. Resolutions and non-compliance with its obligations under the safeguards agreement with the International Atomic Energy Agency and demands full, final, and complete disclosure regarding weapons of mass destruction and missiles with a range of over 150 km and all holdings of such weapons. It further demands unrestricted access to inspection teams, immediate cessation of attempts at concealment, making available to inspecting teams any items previously denied access, allowing flights throughout Iraq for inspection and surveillance purposes, halting all nuclear activities, safety for inspection teams, facilitation of transportation, medical, or logistical support for teams, and full response to any questions.

Resolution 712–19 September, 1991
Relating to authorization for the Security Council Committee to release funds to finance the purchase of foodstuffs, medicines, materials and supplies for essential civilian needs; calling for Iraq to allow full freedom of movement and all necessary facilities to United Nations representatives.

Resolution 715–11 October, 1991
Relating to the plan of the Director General of the International Atomic Energy Agency (IAEA) to continue designation of locations for inspections and overflights, and demands that Iraq unconditionally meet all its obligations under the plans approved by the present resolution and cooperate fully with the Special Commission and the Director General of the (IAEA).

The raging fire of the oil wells and the spewing of millions of gallons of oil from the high pressured ones took a gigantic international effort to put them under control. Ten thousand firefighters from thirty-four nations around the world participated in this gigantic effort. With determination, ingenuity and perseverance, the great international cooperation in fighting these fires of environmental terrorism finally, on November 8, 1991, succeeded in capping them all and placing them under control within eight months. It was previously estimated that it would take at least a year or more. The job remains to get these wells functional after they have been capped. Kuwait has been producing about one fifth of its oil production capabilities prior to the war. Its current production is nearing one million barrels per day. This will progressively move toward 2 million barrels per day, but it will take some time.

All the men of decency and justice around the world hoped that Saddam Hussein would be deleted from power. In fact, the Allies were hoping that the Iraqis would rise up and topple him and his regime. But when the Shi'ites and Kurds revolted, there was fear of Iraqi dismemberment and the hope was that someone in the military from Saddam's inner circle would muster enough courage to end his dictatorial rule, so that it could be replaced by someone who would have compassion and care in his heart for his people, and who could be civil enough to join the family of nations and remove Iraq from being the pariah of a nation that it had become. Several times, his headquarters have been bombed, whether he was targeted or not, the spots where he could have been were centers of communication command and control, but nevertheless, he survived the numerous and repeated attacks.

In the aftermath of the Gulf War, the former Prime Minister of Britain was awarded, in March 1991, the Medal of Freedom. This is the highest award given by President George Bush to a civilian. The President recalled her words and advice to him, while meeting together in the summer of 1990, at the time Saddam Hussein invaded and occupied Kuwait. He said, "These words of caution, words that guided me through the Gulf Crisis, words that I will never forget as long as I am alive. "Remember George!" She said, "this is no time to go wobbly!"

In fact, President Bush and the "Iron Lady" had identical opinions concerning the Gulf Crisis. Concerning George Bush, Thatcher said, "He was staunch and he has never faltered from the first moment; that's a true test of leadership. It was a clear case of aggression. It was a clear case of a bully saying you are small, you must do as I want, if I wish to take you, then you must just endure it. Once we allowed him to get away with that, he wouldn't have stopped there. It was one of the most clear cut decisions, I think, that one has ever been faced with."

Acknowledging her honorable stand and unwavering support, King Fahd of Saudi Arabia awarded the "Iron Lady" on September 17, 1991, the Abdulaziz Order of Merit, which is the highest award in the Kingdom.

Reminiscent of Winston Churchill's farsightedness, Margaret

Thatcher said on an interview with Kuwaiti television on August 2, 1991: "It has been my hope and expectation that the question and position of Saddam Hussein would have been dealt with in the cease-fire agreement. We should not have had a cease-fire agreement unless as a condition on it, Saddam had been handed over by the Iraqi people for international trial."

Legal authorities around the world agree with her. A prominent Saudi legal scholar published a series of articles relating to the conditions for trying war criminals. Saddam Hussein, his accomplices and inner circle meet all the conditions and requirements of international law and Islamic law, Shari'a *for trial as war criminals!*

In his speech to a joint session of Congress on March 6, 1991, President Bush said, ". . . And this I promise you: For all that Saddam has done to his own people, to the Kuwaitis, and to the entire world, Saddam and those around him are accountable."

A ruthless tyrant like Saddam Hussein could never be trusted whether by his people or the world community. The United Nations has ironclad resolutions and especially Resolution 678. He must abide by it or else! The sanctions are ironclad and they remain in effect and shall remain as long as Saddam Hussein is in power. His days are numbered; if anything, the numbering has been going on for too long! It is indeed a puzzle to see someone like him at the helm after the mountain of atrocities he committed against mankind in general, and the Kuwaiti and Iraqi people in particular. All men who preach terror and hate will eventually meet their fate, so will Saddam Hussein!

Appendices

Appendix A

Chronology

Date	Event
B.C.	
7000	Early civilizations flourished between the regions extending from Egypt to Mesopotamia. Arabia, the beating heart of this region was called "The Cradle of Civilization." The Southern portion of Arabia was known to the Romans as "Arabia Felix," which means "Happy Arabia."
5000–2000	Sumerian culture flourishing in Mesopotamia
A.D.	
570	The Prophet Mohammed was born in Mecca, present day Saudi Arabia. By July 16, 622 A.D., the Prophet migrated to Medina; this is the beginning of the Hijra year. Thus, it is A.H. 1. The Prophet died in 632 A.D.
610–632	The Holy Qoran was revealed to Prophet Mohammed in Mecca. The birth of Islam made the Arabian Peninsula the focal point for the Arab World as well as all Moslems around the globe.
660–750	The Oumayyad family of the Qoureish tribe had the Caliphate. Their rule originated from Damascus, present day Syria.
750–1258	The Abbasids took the Caliphate and established their rule in Baghdad. They are the descendents of Abbas, an uncle to the Prophet. Prosperity reached its greatest peak during the reign of the Caliph Horoun Al-Rashid (786–809 A.D.). The Abbasid dynasty continued to rule from Baghdad until its shattering by the Mongols in the year 1258 A.D.
969	Fatimids conquer Egypt and establish their rule in Cairo.
970	The Seljuk Turks occupy Persia.
1055	The Seljuks take over Baghdad.
1079	The Crusaders from Europe began their invasion of Syria.

Date	Event
1099	The Crusaders held Jerusalem until its capture by Salah Eddine Al Ayyoubi (Saladin) in the year 1187 A.D.
1258	Mongols ransacked Baghdad and toppled the Abbasid Caliphate.
1453	Ottomans captured Constantinople.
1517	Ottomans conquer Syria and Egypt. Their rule throughout the Middle East is strengthened.
1534	The Ottoman Turks conquer Baghdad.
1720	Saudi ancestors came from the Qatif region in the east and settled in the historical community of Diriya. Saud Ibn Mohammed Ibn Moqrin became the ruler of Diriya from 1720 until his death in 1725.
1798	Napoleon Bonaparte invades Egypt. He was expelled in 1801.
1869	Opening of the Suez Canal in Egypt.
1880	Abdulaziz Ibn Saud was born on December 2, at the Amir's Palace in Riyadh.
1882	A popular uprising in Egypt was followed by the British invading and occupying Egypt.
1890	Ibn Rashid conquered the city of Riyadh. Abdul Rahman Al-Saud and his family were forced into exile. The men wondered in the Empty Quarter while his wife and some servants went to Bahrain. Finally, permission came for the Al-Saud family to have refuge in Kuwait, where they would be in the hospitality of Al-Sabbah family for nearly ten years. Among these refugees was a young man barely ten years of age, named Abdulaziz Ibn Saud.
1899	An agreement has been reached between Britain and the Sheikh of Kuwait. This placed the Sheikdom under British protection.
1902	January 15, Abdulaziz Ibn Saud conquers Riyadh and begins his long arduous struggle for unifying the land.
1916	Sykes-Pickot Agreement reached between France and Britain for dividing the Middle East region into spheres of influence, once Turkey is defeated in World War I.
1917	Britain, through the Balfour Declaration, supports

Date	Event
	the establishment of a home for the Jews in Palestine.
1918	Defeat of the Axis; Germany and Turkey surrender—end of World War I. The Ottoman Empire is dismantled.
1920	The British mandate over Palestine is established.
1920	July 24, French forces occupy Damascus; the French mandate over Syria begins.
1921	Faisal, son of Sherif Hussein of Mecca, is enthroned as King of Iraq on August 27. He was installed by the British who gained a mandate over Iraq from the League of Nations.
1923	Another son of Sherif Hussein is declared by the British as King of the newly created Trans-Jordan.
1932	September 23, Abdulaziz Ibn Saud proclaimed King of the Kingdom of Saudi Arabia. This became the national day for the Kingdom.
1932	October 3, Iraq declared its independence and is formally admitted to the League of Nations.
1936–38	The Arabs revolt against British occupation in Palestine.
1937	April 28, Saddam Hussein is born in a desert town named Tikrit.
1938	Oil discovered in the Eastern region of Saudi Arabia; the Arabian American Oil Company (Aramco) was formed. It is now called Saudi Aramco. Oil was also discovered in Kuwiat.
1941	France declared Lebanon a sovereign state.
1943	Independence is declared in Syria; it was completed in 1946.
1945	February 10, President Roosevelt meets in the Suez Canal, with Ibn Saud, founder of the Kingdom of Saudi Arabia. Saudi-American friendship is cemented. Also in February, Ibn Saud met with Prime Minister Churchill of Great Britain. Saudi-British relations remain on track.
1947	The British mandate over Palestine ends, the United Nations votes for partitioning the country between the Arabs and the Jews. The Arabs refuse partition.
1947	April, the first congress of the Ba'ath party is held in Damascus, Syria. The ideas of the party began

Date	Event
	to transmit to Iraq and organized campaigns of the party began in early 1951.
1948	The first Arab-Israeli war begins. The State of Israel is established after winning a short war.
1952	King Farouk of Egypt was overthrown.
1956	Gamal Adul Nasser nationalizes the Suez Canal. Egypt is invaded by Britain, France and Israel.
1957	Saddam Hussein joins the Iraqi branch of the Ba'ath party.
1958	July 4, about two hundred free officers overthrow the Monarchy in Iraq. General Abdul Karim Qassem emerges as the new ruler.
1959	October 7, a hit team of the Ba'ath party failed in its attempt to assassinate General Qassem. Saddam Hussein, then twenty-two years of age, was a part of the assassination squad; he escapes to Syria and then moves on to Cairo, Egypt. Over 62 belonging to the party and implicated in the assassination plot are brought to trial before the People's court of Mahdawi.
1960	Organization of Petroleum Exporting Countries (OPEC) is founded.
1961	On June 19, Britain and Kuwait, by mutual agreement, terminated their treaty and Kuwait declared its sovereignty and independence. A few days later, on June 25, General Qassem, ruler of Iraq declared his intention to annex Kuwait. Britain and Saudi Arabia came to the aid of the newly independent nation and deterred an imminent attack from Iraq. In August, British troops were replaced by forces from some Arab countries as sponsored by the Arab League.
1961	September 8, first major attack by the Iraqi army against the Kurdish population of Iraq.
1962	In July, the Kurdish guerilla war gains momentum.
1963	February 8, a coup by the Ba'ath party overthrows the Qassem regime after several days of vicious street fighting. This new regime lasted barely nine months. On November 18, 1963, Abdul Salam Aref became President of Iraq and Ahmad Hasan Al-Bakr Vice President.

Date	Event
1963	October 4, international boundary and the allocation of islands were set out in the "Agreed Minutes between the State of Kuwait and the Republic of Iraq regarding the restoration of friendly relations, recognition and related matters," signed in Baghdad by both parties in the exercise of their sovereignty. The agreement was registered with the United Nations and was published by it in Document 7063–United Nations Treaty Series, 1964.
1964	February, Michel Aflaq, founder of the Ba'ath party and head of its Iraqi wing, recommended the elevation of Saddam Hussein to the regional command of the party in Iraq.
1967	In June, the six day Arab-Israeli war brings a catastrophic military defeat to the Arab world.
1968	On July 30, a carefully planned coup brings the Ba'ath party (ABSP)–meaning the Arab Ba'ath Socialist Party–to power. The supreme authority is vested in the Revolutionary Command Council (RCC) which was chaired by Ahmad Hasan Al-Bakr who was the Secretary General of the party and became President of Iraq and Commander of the Army. The Assistant Secretary General of the Party, Saddam Hussein, became Deputy Chairman of the Revolutionary Command Council and was placed in charge of internal security.
1969	January 5, A public trial of a number of "spies" was held; seventeen of them were sent to the gallows.
1969	August 8, A Kurdish village called Dakan and the city of Mosul are places where a major army atrocity was committed. The war against the Kurds was intensified.
1970	January 21, An alleged conspiracy against the regime is thwarted. Within a week forty-four people met the firing squad.
1970	March 11, the Ba'ath regime reaches an agreement on Kurdish autonomy. Fighting stops and the Ba'athist government consolidates its grip on power.
1972	April, Iraqi-Soviet Friendship Treaty is declared

Date	Event
	and the communists enter the government for the first time in May, 1972. Also, in June, 1972, the Iraqi Petroleum Company was nationalized.
1973	Chief of Iraqi Internal Security is executed along with more than thirty-five others, in the aftermath of an attempted Coup d' Etat; the October War, also called Ramadan, Yom Kippur War, between Israel and the Arabs began. An oil embargo takes place.
1974	March, the Kurdish autonomy accords of 1970 collapse, an all-out-war begins. Zakho and Qala'at Oiza, two Kurdish towns are destroyed. Hundreds of thousands of Kurds run for their lives; many atrocities are committed.
1974	December, five Ulama of the Shi'a sect are killed.
1975	March 6, Algeria mediates an agreement between Iraq and the Shah of Iran. Iraq concedes to Iranian territorial demands along Shatt Al-Arab and the Shah agrees to stop his support for the Kurds. Kurdish resistance collapses. The Iraqi Ba'athist regime carries a policy of mass deportation and resettlement of the Kurdish population.
1975	April 13, the Lebanese civil war begins, lasting nearly sixteen years.
1977	February, religious men of the Shi'a sect carry on a demonstration in the city of Karbala. The government responds repressively, eight more Ulama were executed. Mass deportations from Iraq to Iran of the Shi'a; about 200,000 were deported to Iran.
1977	President Anwar Sadat of Egypt visits Israel seeking peace.
1978	October, Ayatollah Khomeini is expelled from Iraq after being there in exile for over thirteen years.
1979	Egypt and Israel sign a peace treaty at Camp David, in the U.S.A.
1979	February, the Islamic revolution in Iran takes hold. The Shah is sent into exile; an Islamic Republic is formed and led by Ayatollah Khomeini.
1979	June, Saddam Hussein becomes President of Iraq replacing Ahmad Hasan Al-Bakr who was stripped of any authority and then placed under house arrest.
1979	July, massive purges of the Ba'athist party

Date	Event
	leadership took place; by August 1, 1979 about five hundred top brass of the Ba'ath party have been murdered.
1979–81	On Sunday, November 4, 1979, Iranian "students" supported by the Khomeini regime took over the American Embassy in Tehran and held 66 Americans as hostages. Fourteen women and blacks were released later; but 52 Americans were held hostage for 444 days, until the beginning of the Reagan Presidency.
1980	September 22, Saddam Hussein invaded Iran in a full scale war–a very destructive war lasting eight years.
1981	June 7, Israel destroys the French built nuclear reactor Osirak (named after Osirisa the Egyptian god of the dead) by executing a daring and lightning air attack. Eight Israeli F-16 jet fighters and six F-15 fighter interceptors were used.
1982	Israel invades Lebanon in hopes of driving the Palestinian Guerillas out and establishing friendly relations.
1983	October 23, in a suicide attack, a truck laden with explosives destroys a building in Beirut where American Marines were sleeping. They were part of a peacekeeping force. 241 U.S. servicemen were killed instantly. Islamic extremist fundamentalists claimed responsibility.
1988	March, the Iraqi army, under orders from Saddam Hussein, uses poison gas against his countrymen: the Kurds in the northern part of Iraq. Thousands of people are killed and maimed. This constituted the first time ever chemical weapons were used by a State against its own citizens.
1988	August 8, the Iran-Iraq war ended.

EVENTS IN THE YEAR 1990

Date	Event
February 12,	John Kelly of the U.S. State Department meets Saddam Hussein, President of Iraq, expressing U.S. desire for developing good relations with Iraq.
February 21,	U.S. State Department published a report on human rights violations around the world. Twelve pages dealt with Iraq. Authorities in Iraq were described as the "worst violators of human rights."
February 23,	Arab Cooperation Council (ACC) met in Amman, Jordan. Saddam Hussein's message to the gathering was broadcast on Jordanian television. The main diatribe was aimed against America. He stressed to his audience that the U.S. is beatable.
April 2,	An announcement by Saddam Hussein states that Iraqi scientists have developed an advanced arsenal of chemical weapons, adding, "we will make the fire eat up half of Israel, if it tries to do anything against Iraq."
May 28,	Arab Summit Conference held in Baghdad, Iraq. In a closed session, the Iraqi ruler denounced his fellow Arabs, stating that the Gulf States were keeping the price of oil too low; in his opinion, this was an economic war against Iraq.
July 15,	Iraqi Foreign Minister Tariq Aziz wrote a public memorandum which was delivered to the Arab League on July 16. He vehemently accused Kuwait of violations for its oil production quotas and for "stealing" Iraqi oil from the Roumeila field. He warned of terrible consequences which might take place.
July 17,	The ruler of Iraq delivers a fierce attack on Kuwait on this Revolution Day, the 22nd anniversary of the Ba'ath takeover in Iraq. He also attacks other Arabian Gulf countries for exceeding their oil production quotas, asserting that they are "stabbing Iraq in the back."
July 18,	The Iraqi Foreign Minister informs the Arab League that Kuwait has "stolen" 2.4 billion dollars worth of oil from the Roumeila field and it has also built some military posts on Iraqi soil. The United Arab Emirates promised to cut its oil production and

Date	Event
	the Kuwaitis denounced Iraq's vicious attack against Kuwait.
July 24,	The U.S. State Department sent a confidential cable advising a number of American Ambassadors to inform their host governments that the United States was worried about the threats enunciated by the Iraqi President Saddam Hussein, and that he may use military force.
July 25	The Iraqi army moves south toward Kuwait. Over 30,000 Iraqi troops are deployed on the border with Kuwait and in close vicinity of Saudi Arabia. American warships in the Gulf were put on a state of alert. Egyptian President Hosni Moubarak visited Iraq, Kuwait and Saudi Arabia. Iraq demands that oil prices rise to $25 per barrel; the Iraqi government demands 2.5 billion dollars in compensation from Kuwait and President Hosni Moubarak of Egypt announced that Iraq would meet in Jeddah with Kuwait. Iraq has given Egypt assurances that it will not attack Kuwait; the meeting of U.S. Ambassador Ms. April Glaspie with Saddam Hussein took place. He warned that America should not oppose his aims in the Middle East. According to the Iraqis, her response was to reassure the Iraqi leader that the United States had no official position on Iraq's border dispute with Kuwait. "We have no opinion on the Arab-Arab Conflicts, like your border dispute with Kuwait . . ."
July 26,	OPEC Ministers meeting in Geneva agreed to limit the over-production of oil and thus decided to give a push to oil prices. Kuwait pledged to abide by this agreement.
July 28,	Satellite photos taken by the U.S. detect Iraqi preparations for an offensive. The Pentagon and the Central Intelligence Agency of the United States both estimated that an attack was highly likely. However, many diplomats throughout the world believed that Saddam Hussein was only trying to frighten Kuwait into territorial concessions without resorting to an outright invasion . . . President Bush sent a message to the Iraqi President stating that

Date	Event
	the United States wanted better relations with Iraq, but was deeply concerned about Saddam's threats to use force against neighboring countries.
July 31,	U.S. Assistant Secretary of State for Near-Eastern and South Asian Affairs, John Kelly, gave a testimony before Congress essentially stating that the United States does not have a defense treaty or arrangement with Kuwait. Representative Lee Hamilton responded, "he left the impression that it was the policy of the United States not to come to the defense of Kuwait." On this date, the Kuwaiti Crown Prince and his delegation met with the Iraqi Vice President Izzat Ibrahim and his delegation in Jeddah, Saudi Arabia in order to discuss their differences. The Kuwaiti army of 20,000 troops is faced with a threat of 100,000 Iraqi troops amassed on the border with Kuwait.
August 1,	The talks in Jeddah between Iraq and Kuwait did not succeed but a further meeting planned for Saturday was to take place in Baghdad, Iraq.
August 2, (Thursday)	Iraqi troops and tanks cross the border with Kuwait and a blitzkrieg attack on Kuwait begins about two o'clock in the morning local time. Kuwait is occupied within five hours. The Kuwaiti ruler Sheikh Jabir Al-Ahmad Al-Sabbah, along with his government, flee for their safety to the Kingdom of Saudi Arabia. King Fahd called Saddam Hussein and urged his withdrawal from Kuwait. Saddam Hussein sent a delegation to explain the situation. When they arrived to meet with the King, they said, "the matter is over! Kuwait is now part of Iraq." The United Nations Security Council condemned Iraq's occupation of Kuwait and demanded its unconditional and immediate withdrawal. The vote regarding Resolution 660 was fourteen in favor and zero against, one member, Yemen did not participate in the vote. Shortly afterward, President Bush spoke to King Fahd of Saudi Arabia by telephone; about thirty B-52 bombers were ordered to the Indian Ocean Island of Diego Garcia. President Bush and Prime Minister of Britain,

Date	Event
	Margaret Thatcher met in Aspen, Colorado and pressed for collective efforts by members of the United Nations.
August 3, (Friday)	Prince Bandar Bin Sultan, Saudi Ambassador to the United States, arrived Friday for a 7A.M. breakfast discussion with President George Bush, topic: the Gulf Crisis. President Bush ordered the Defense Department and the CIA to give Prince Bandar a detailed briefing, including satellite pictures of Iraqi military moves in Kuwait and toward the border of the Kingdom of Saudi Arabia. President Bush reiterated his pledge to help the Kingdom of Saudi Arabia when he talked again to King Fahd. President Bush and King Fahd agreed that Secretary of Defense, Dick Cheney, should leave for the Kingdom. 120 Iraqi military officers were executed by Saddam Hussein for refusing to participate in the invasion of Kuwait. All Kuwaiti and Iraqi assets are frozen in the United States. The former Soviet Union condemns the invasion and suspends arms shipments to Iraq. Meeting in Cairo for the second straight day, the Arab League condemned the Iraqi invasion. Fourteen countries voted for the resolution; Jordan, Sudan, Mauritania, Yemen and the PLO abstained. Libya and Tunisia did not participate in the voting.
August 4, (Saturday)	After two days of detailed intelligence meetings, Prince Bandar Bin Sultan flew to Saudi Arabia, so that he could provide the Saudi leaders with necessary briefings prior to Cheney's arrival. The Secretary of State for the United States, James Baker and the Soviet Foreign Minister, Sheverdnadze, issued a joint statement condemning the Iraqi invasion of Kuwait and urging the world to halt all arms shipments destined for Iraq.
August 5, (Sunday)	President Bush of the United States dispatches Secretary of Defense Dick Cheney to Saudi Arabia to discuss the possible responses necessitated by the Gulf Crisis: "While Bush dispatched Cheney and top aids to Saudi Arabia Sunday, it was widely reported that their mission was to gain Saudi Arabia's concurrence for U.S. military forces to

Date	Event
	enter the country. But, said a senior official, the deal was essentially done in Bush's conversations with the King." Secretary of Defense, Cheney returned to the U.S. carrying with him King Fahd's approval for dispatch of U.S. forces to Saudi Arabia. Saddam Hussein met with a U.S. Embassy official and told him, "the invasion was a done deal–Kuwait now belongs to Iraq."
August 6, (Monday)	The United Nations Security Council voted Resolution 661 approving a worldwide embargo on Iraq. Thirteen members of the Council approved the embargo. Only Yemen and Cuba abstained. On his way to the U.S., Cheney meets in Egypt and Morocco with the respective leaders in an attempt to add Arab forces to the defense of Saudi Arabia.
August 7, (Tuesday)	The Saudi government invites U.S. troops to the Kingdom of Saudi Arabia.
August 8,	President George Bush addresses the nation declaring the dispatching of American troops to Saudi Arabia as a wholly defensive mission. "A line has been drawn in the sand . . . the mission of our troops is wholly defensive. They will not initiate hostilities but they will defend themselves and the Kingdom of Saudi Arabia and other friends in the Persian Gulf." Saddam Hussein annexes Kuwait as U.S. forces poured into the Kingdom of Saudi Arabia. The agony of hostages has already begun. The Iraqi regime calls them "guests". They are in the thousands.
August 9, (Thursday)	The United Nations Security Council votes unanimously in favor of Resolution 662 declaring the annexation of Kuwait by Iraq as null and void.
August 9, 10,	Arab League Summit convened in Cario, Egypt at the invitation of President Hosni Moubarak. The Conferees voted in favor of sending Arab military forces to join U.S. forces in the Eastern Region of Saudi Arabia to defend the Kingdom. Twelve of the twenty members voted in favor of the Resolution. A first contingent of Egyptian forces arrives in the Kingdom. Saddam Hussein calls for a Jihad (A Holy War) to defend Mecca against the

Date	Event
	infidels and the "spears of the Americans and the Zionists." He urged all Arabs to sweep "Amirs of ill from their thrones in the Gulf." The friendly Coalition Forces are over 1,500 kilometers (793 miles) away, East of the Holy places.
August 14, (Tuesday)	Troops from Syria join other Arab forces in Saudi Arabia.
August 15, (Wednesday)	President Hashemi Rafsanjani of Iran receives a letter from Saddam Hussein of Iraq, offering to meet all Iranian conditions for a final settlement of the Iran-Iraq war. This entails withdrawal from Iranian territory and the release of prisoners of war.
August 18, (Saturday)	The U.N. Security Council unanimously passes Resolution 664 condemning Iraq for holding foreign nationals as hostages and demands the immediate release of everyone.
August 20, (Monday)	United Arab Emirates agreed to the dispatch of some U.S. forces on its territory. By now, about 20,000 U.S. soldiers have reached Saudi Arabia with 59 U.S. ships in the Arabian Gulf area, having on board 35,000 soldiers and more on the way from the U.S.; the Iraqi regime announces a plan for placing Western hostages in vital military installations to be used as human shields against possible attack.
August 22, (Wednesday)	A flood of refugees swells the desert border with Jordan. Overwhelmed by these large numbers, Jordan chooses to close the border. The agony and tragedy of hungry and thirsty people by the thousands goes on for a number of weeks. The border opens again on August 24. People–many women, children and elderly have died. These refugees are workers of many nationalities from third world countries who were making a living in Kuwait and Iraq, and had to flee for their lives. Many of them came from the Philippines, Pakistan, Bangladesh, India, Sri Lanka, Lebanon, Egypt and a number of other countries. They earned their living from the Gulf states and sent money to their families back home to support their livelihood.
August 25, (Saturday)	The U.N. Security Council passed Resolution 665 allowing navies of the world to use force in order

Date	Event
	to enforce trade sanctions against Iraq. This is the first time in the United Nations' 45 year history that the Security Council permitted the use of these forces without being under the U.N. flag. Sanctions begin to take their bite, and the noose is tightened around the neck of the aggressor. Yemen and Cuba abstained while thirteen other nations voted in favor.
August 26, (Sunday)	Kurt Waldheim, President of Austria, arrived to Iraq and rescued 96 Austrian hostages. 52 Americans, wives and children of diplomats from the U.S. Embassy in Kuwait, arrived to Turkey. The hostages' agony will go on for a few months. A number of dignitaries stream into Baghdad pleading for their nationals; Iraqi leader basks in the fame emanating from these pleas of world leaders. Everytime, the reward was to free a trickle of hostages.
August 28, (Tuesday)	Saddam Hussein, declares Kuwait the 19th province of Iraq; he orders release of all women and children held hostage in Iraq and Kuwait.
September 9 (Sunday)	A Summit Conference was held in Helsinki, Finland, between President George Bush of the U.S. and former President Mikhail Gorbachev of the former Soviet Union; Iraqi Foreign Minister visits Tehran.
September 11, (Tuesday)	President Bush addresses a joint session of Congress. In his speech he states commitment to annull annexation of Kuwait by Iraq.
September 13, (Thursday)	The Moslem League approves Saudi Arabia's decision to call on U.S. troops for helping in the defense of Saudi Arabia. "A Mecca Declaration" states that Iraqi President Saddam Hussein violated Tenets of the Faith of Islam in his invasion of the State of Kuwait. U.N. Resolution 666 is passed with 13 votes in favor and two against–Yemen and Cuba. This Resolution sets the type of limits on humanitarian food supplies sent to Iraq and occupied Kuwait and gives the Security Council power to determine whether such shipments are justified.

Date	Event
September 16, (Sunday)	Foreign Minister of Saudi Arabia, Prince Saud Al-Faisal visits Moscow. The U.N. Security Council adopts Resolution 667, in which Iraq's violation of diplomatic premises in Kuwait are condemned in a unanimous vote of 15 to 0; the Foreign Minister of Iran visits Iraq. A meeting of King Hussein of Jordan with leftist Palestinian leaders, George Habash and Naif Hawatma, takes place in Amman, Jordan. They attended the Conference of Popular Arab Movements held September 15–17; all foreign Ambassadors in Kuwait are told by the Iraqi Embassy to get out of Kuwait or face harsh measures.
September 17, (Monday)	After 52 years, Saudi Arabia and the former Soviet Union establish diplomatic relations and agree to work together to help assure that Iraq would get out of Kuwait; the pro-Iraqi Conference held in Jordan decides to "strike against American interests everywhere, if the United States was to attack Iraq and its forces in Kuwait." The U.S. Air Force Chief of Staff, General Michael J. Dugan, is fired by the Secretary of Defense, Dick Cheney, because of his public pronouncements detailing U.S. plans in case of war with Iraq.
September 19, (Wednesday)	The U.N. Security Council agrees to extend the embargo against Iraq to cover the air corridors leading to Iraq.
September 20, (Thursday)	The Sudanese News Agency states that Sudan joins Iraq in calling for Jihad against the non-Islamic western forces. All oil deliveries to Jordan coming from Saudi Arabia are stopped by midnight Thursday, because Jordan has been following a policy favoring Iraq in its occupation of Kuwait.
September 22, (Saturday)	King Hussein of Jordan calls for the withdrawal of U.S.–led Coalition forces from the Kingdom of Saudi Arabia. This was done in a televised message to the American people.
September 25, (Tuesday)	President Hafez Assad of Syria told reporters upon ending his visit to Tehran: "We are in full agreement that aggression must be eliminated and foreign presence must be terminated." The price of oil reaches nearly $40.00 per barrel. The U.N. Security

Date	Event
October 1,	Council passes Resolution 670 tightening the economic embargo against Iraq and cutting off air traffic to and from Iraq and also Iraqi-occupied Kuwait. The vote was 14 to 1, with Cuba opposing. The U.S. House of Representatives voted 380 in favor to 29 against, to support the moves of President Bush in the Gulf Crisis. However, the House emphasized that diplomacy must be used to resolve the standoff resulting from Iraq's invasion of Kuwait.
October 2,	The Senate, by a vote of 96 to 3, endorsed President Bush's efforts to "deter Iraqi aggression." Some members were concerned that such a move could be interpreted as giving President Bush broad authority to wage war; King Hussein of Jordan said that Iraq would not leave Kuwait as long as thousands of U.S. and other foreign forces were in the Arabian Peninsula. "Iraq is willing and ready to discuss the problem and all other Arab problems . . . but Iraq is clearly unwilling to do so facing a military threat to itself and its future." The French peace initiative, linking the Palestinian problem with the occupation of Kuwait, was dismissed by the Saudi Foreign Minister Saud Al-Faisal who said: "There is no place for alternative proposals."
October 7, (Sunday)	A PLO commander predicted that Arab troops in the multi-national force would switch sides if U.S. forces attacked Iraq. Diplomats from twelve EC (European Community) nations declared that the pressure must be kept on Iraq, so that President Saddam Hussein would be forced to withdraw his forces from Kuwait. They agreed that there could be no compromise with Iraq over U.N. Resolutions concerning the occupation.
October 8, (Monday)	A bloody clash on Temple Mount, Jerusalem, between Israeli soldiers and Palestinian demonstrators led to the death of 19 Arabs.
October 13, (Saturday)	Lebanese forces loyal to the government supported by Syrian forces, attacked the stronghold at Ba'abda, Lebanon. The rebel General took refuge in the French Embassy and told his troops to surrender;

Date	Event
	President Bush is determined not to allow a linkage between the Gulf Crisis and the Arab-Israeli dispute. Such a linkage could allow Saddam Hussein to remain in Kuwait until the Palestinain-Israeli problem is solved.
October 15, (Monday)	The Kuwaitis, exiled from their homeland and now in Saudi Arabia, met in Jeddah for three days and strongly denounced the PLO (Palesine Liberation Organization) for its support of Iraq and its occupation of Kuwait. They called upon the U.N. Security Council to use all available means to free their nation. The 1962 Kuwaiti Constitution will be honored, guaranteeing parliamentary elections.
October 22, (Monday)	Former British Prime Minister Edward Heath returns from Baghdad with 33 British hostages. The British debate consequences of such a move.
October 29,	The U.N. Security Council passes Resolution 674, holding Iraq legally responsible for financial damages and any human rights violations caused during its invasion of Kuwait. The vote was thirteen to zero. The two abstentions were Yemen and Cuba. During a visit to France, Soviet President Mikhail Gorbachev said: "I think it is unacceptable to have a military solution to this problem." He was addressing the possibility of military attack to eject Iraq from Kuwait. Peace moves carried by the Soviet envoy Primakov were downplayed by many officials.
October 31,	When asked about the treatment of U.S. Embassy personnel in Kuwait, President Bush said, "I have had it. Do you think I am concerned about it? You're darn right I am. And what am I going to do about it? Let us just wait and see." President Hosni Moubarak of Egypt said, the situation "could explode at any time."
November 5, (Monday)	According to an ABC poll, most Americans believed that the U.S. should attack Iraq if any of the hostages are mistreated; they also favor military action against Iraq if the sanctions do not bring about the liberation of Kuwait.

Date	Event
November 18, (Friday)	U.S. Secretary of State, James Baker said that another reason for the United States involvement is that the Administration will thwart Iraq's future ability to intimidate neighboring countries with chemical, biological and conventional forces. Saddam Hussein made an offer for freeing hostages over a period of three months beginning December 25, 1990, unless events develop in such a manner to "mar the atmosphere of peace." The offer was dismissed by U.S. officials as a propaganda ploy.
November 21, (Wednesday)	President Bush met with King Fahd of Saudi Arabia and other Saudi and Kuwaiti officials. Secretary of State James Baker said upon emerging from the session with King Fahd that "Saudis were in total accord in opposing 'the siren song of partial solution.'" In a statement read by his spokesman, King Fahd said that "he and Bush both agree that aggression must not be rewarded. Thus, the only way to solve this crisis peacefully–an objective we both support, is unconditional Iraqi withdrawal." King Fahd also said that he and President Bush agreed that the U.S. Forces would leave Saudi Arabia immediately when the crisis was resolved or at the request of the government of Saudi Arabia.
November 22, (Thursday)	President George Bush and leaders of the Senate and House visit U.S. troops in the Eastern Region of Saudi Arabia for the occasion of Thanksgiving. Margaret Thatcher, Prime Minister of Britain resigns.
November 26, (Monday)	King Fahd declares to the Saudi editors that Iraq must withdraw from Kuwait. "No other solution will be accepted." The King warns that failing to do so would be "a tragedy for Iraq."
November 28, (Wednesday)	The U.N. Security Council introduces Resolution 677 which condemns the Iraqi attempts to change the demography of Kuwait and for the destruction of Kuwait's civil records.
November 29, (Thursday)	U.N. Security Council passes yet another landmark Resolution, 678, demanding that Iraq comply with all previous resolutions regarding the invasion of

Date	Event
	Kuwait and most importantly it authorizes member states to use all necessary means to secure the compliance of Iraq in case Iraq fails to do so by a *deadline of January 15, 1991.*
November 30, (Friday)	In a last ditch effort for peace, President Bush invites Iraqi Foreign Minister Tariq Aziz to visit Washington and suggests that Secretary of State James Baker will be sent to visit Baghdad to secure Iraq's compliance with the U.N. Security Council Resolutions.
December 3,	The United Nations General Assembly Committee votes 131 in favor to one against, condemning Iraq for human rights violations in Kuwait. Iraq was the only dissenting vote.

EVENTS IN THE YEAR 1991

1991

January 9,	U.S. Secretary of State James Baker met in Geneva, Switzerland, with Tariq Aziz, Foreign Minister of Iraq. The meeting failed; the Gulf War was imminent.
January 12	After a heated debate, the congress of the United States gave President Bush a de facto declaration of war, setting January 15 as the deadline for Saddam's withdrawal from Kuwait. The Senate voted 52–47 in favor and the House of Representatives vote was 250–183 in favor. Most of the Democrats were in opposition.
January 16, (6:30 P.M. EST)	Desert Shield turned into Desert Storm. The *Air War* against Saddam Hussein began. The Iraqi Air Force is devastated and air supremacy of the coalition forces is imminent. Air strikes with pinpoint accuracy continue for several days.
February 15,	The Soviets, through their emissary Primakov, are maneuvering for compromise and peace in the Gulf. Saddam Hussein still continues to stall for time and sets several unacceptable conditions. His peace offers prove to be "a cruel hoax." The Allied forces are demanding total unconditional withdrawal of

Date	Event
	Iraq and acceptance of all U.N. Resolutions without any exception.
February 23, (Saturday) 8:00 P.M. (EST)	The *Ground War* against Iraq began after obliteration of the Iraqi air force along with the destruction of their communications and control centers. The Republican Guard is dealt a heavy blow. The air war goes on for 100 hours. Saddam's army is defeated and thrown out of Kuwait. Prior to their rout, environmental terrorism was committed by Hussein's forces spilling over 5 million barrels of oil in the Gulf and leaving over 700 oil wells burning.
February 27,	President George Bush declares "Kuwait is liberated; Iraq's army is defeated." He declared a temporary cease-fire at 12:00 midnight EST (8:00 o'clock in the morning of February 28, Iraqi time). He said, "Exactly 100 hours since ground operations commenced and six weeks since the start of Operation Desert Storm, all U.S. and Coalition Forces will suspend further offensive combat operations." U.N. requests Iraqi compliance; Iraq delivers a letter indicating its intention to comply with cease-fire conditions.
March 2,	The U.N. Security Council passes Resolution 686 relating to the suspension of offensive combat operations and to the importance of Iraq taking the necessary measures which would permit a definitive end to the hostilities.
March 9,	The Shi'ites in the south of Iraq and, a week later, the Kurds in the north, revolt against Saddam Hussein. Both make initial gains in their uprising, but their defeat and tragedy followed soon after.
April 3,	U.N. Security Council Resolution 687 is passed, relating to the restoration to Kuwait its sovereignty, independence and territorial integrity and the return of its legitimate government; the sanctions remain and specific conditions for a formal cease-fire are set.
April 6,	Iraq accepts U.N. terms for the formal cease-fire as stipulated in Security Council Resolution 687.
April, 1991	Defeat of the Kurds and the Shi'ites is final.

Date	Event
	Hundreds of thousands of Shi'ites flee for their safety in Iran and millions of Kurds flee to the barren mountains in northern Iraq and some of them to Turkey and Iran. It is a human tragedy! Thousands of people were killed, especially the young and elderly. The United States, France and Britain moved to establish safe havens for the Kurds in the north and to prevent Saddam Hussein from using his army and aircraft against his own people. After their tragic plight in the mountains and once assured of safety, the Kurds gained some confidence from the Allied Forces and began to stream down to the plains. The United Nations takes action to cooperate and help ease this tragedy.
May–July	Safe havens secured; the Kurds are back in their region. Autonomy talks between the Iraqi Government and the Kurds falter. Allied forces leave northern Iraq July 13, 1991. No Iraqi flights or forces beyond the 36 parallel. A quick strike force is stationed nearby in Turkey to keep an eye against any violations; the sanctions against Iraq are continuing; its nuclear capability is being checked by a U.N. team. Its weapons of mass destruction are being destroyed; Saddam Hussein is still in power. Trials for war crimes not initiated yet.
April 9–Oct. 11 1991	The U.N. Security Council passes nine more Resolutions relating to Iraq and the aftermath of the Gulf War.
November 8, 1991	Oil well fires in Kuwait are under control.
Dec. 25, 1991	Dismantling of the former Soviet Union.
March–April 1992	Kuwait is being rebuilt, necessary services are re-established; Saddam Hussein is still in power. Many wonder if the war was stopped sooner than it should have been. The game of "cheat and retreat" continued. Finally, on March 21, 1992, after the U.N. warned Saddam Hussein, and after the entry of the U.S. warship America into the Gulf, the head of the U.N. Special Commission Rolph Ekeus announced the Iraqi ruler's compliance with U.N. Resolution 687 for eliminating his weapons of mass destruction. The game of deception will go on! But the end is near!

Appendix B

United Nations Security Council Resolutions* Relating to the Situation Between Iraq and Kuwait

The Resolutions

Between 2 August 1990, the date of the invasion of Kuwait by Iraq, and 9 April 1991, the Security Council adopted 15 resolutions relating to the situation between Iraq and Kuwait, beginning with resolution 660. The full text of these 15 resolutions is reproduced on the following pages.

The Council

The United Nations Security Council is composed of 15 members. Five are permanent: China, France, Soviet Union,** United Kingdom, United States. The ten non-permanent members are elected by the General Assembly to serve two-year terms. At the time the first 12 resolutions were adopted, the non-permanent members of the Security Council were: Canada, Colombia, Côte d'Ivoire, Cuba, Ethiopia, Finland, Malaysia, Romania, Yemen and Zaire. On 1 January 1991, Austria, Belgium, Ecuador, India and Zimbabwe replaced Canada, Colombia, Ethiopia, Finland and Malaysia for two-year terms.

Summary

Resolution 660   2 August 1990
Relating, inter alia, to the Council's condemnation of the Iraqi invasion of Kuwait.
Adopted by a vote of 14 in favour and 0 against. One member, Yemen, did not participate in the vote.
Sponsors: Canada, Colombia, Côte d'Ivoire, Ethiopia, Finland, France, Malaysia, United Kingdom, United States.

Resolution 661   6 August 1990
Relating, inter alia, to the imposition of mandatory sanctions and to the establishment of a Committee to undertake certain tasks regarding the implementation of the resolution.

* Source: United Nations Department of Public Information, New York, U.S.A.
** Former Soviet Union; Russia occupied this seat in early 1992.

Adopted by a vote of 13 in favour, 0 against and 2 abstentions (Cuba and Yemen).
Sponsors: Canada, Colombia, Côte d'Ivoire, Ethiopia, Finland, France, Malaysia, United Kingdom, United States, Zaire.

Resolution 662   9 August 1990
Relating, inter alia, to the non-validity of the Iraqi annexation of Kuwait.
Adopted by unanimous vote.
Prepared in the course of the Council's consultations.

Resolution 664   18 August 1990
Relating, inter alia, to the nationals of third countries in Iraq and Kuwait and to diplomatic and consular missions in Kuwait.
Adopted by unanimous vote.
Prepared in the course of the Council's consultations.

Resolution 665   25 August 1990
Relating, inter alia, to measures to ensure implementation of resolution 661.
Adopted by a vote of 13 in favour, 0 against and 2 abstentions (Cuba and Yemen).
Sponsors: Canada, Côte d'Ivoire, Finland, France, United Kingdom, United States, Zaire.

Resolution 666   13 September 1990
Relating, inter alia, to the determination of humanitarian circumstances.
Adopted by a vote of 13 in favour and 2 against (Cuba and Yemen).
Sponsors: Canada, Finland, France, Soviet Union, United Kingdom, United States.

Resolution 667   16 September 1990
Relating, inter alia, to diplomatic and consular personnel and premises.
Adopted by unanimous vote.
Sponsors: Canada, Côte d'Ivoire, Finland, France, United Kingdom, Zaire.

Resolution 669   24 September 1990
Relating, inter alia, to requests for assistance under the provisions of Article 50 of the Charter.
Adopted by unanimous vote.
Prepared in the course of the Council's consultations.

Resolution 670   25 September 1990
Relating, inter alia, to the applicability of sanctions to all means of transport, including aircraft. Thirteen of the 15 members of the Council were represented by their Foreign Ministers at the meeting during which this resolution was adopted.
Adopted by a vote of 14 in favour and 1 against (Cuba).
Sponsors: Canada, Côte d'Ivoire, Finland, France, Romania, Soviet Union, United Kingdom, United States, Zaire.

Resolution 674   29 October 1990
Relating, inter alia, to the situation of Kuwaiti and third-State nationals in Kuwait and Iraq, to further measures in the event of non-compliance by Iraq with Security Council resolutions and to the good offices of the Secretary-General.
Adopted by a vote of 13 in favour, 0 against and 2 abstentions (Cuba and Yemen).
Sponsors: Canada, Finland, France, Romania, Soviet Union, United Kingdom, United States, Zaire.

Resolution 677   28 November 1990
Relating, inter alia, to attempts by Iraq to alter the demographic composition of the population of Kuwait.
Adopted by unanimous vote.
Sponsors: Canada, Côte d'Ivoire, Ethiopia, Finland, Kuwait, Romania, United Kingdom, Zaire.

Resolution 678   29 November 1990
Relating, inter alia, to the use by Member States of "all necessary means to uphold and implement [Security Council] resolution 660 (1990) and all subsequent relevant resolutions and to restore international peace and security in the area." This resolution *sets January 15, 1991 as the deadline for Iraq to comply with all U.N. resolutions.* Thirteen of the 15 members of the Council were represented by their Foreign Ministers at the meeting during which this resolution was adopted.
Adopted by a vote of 12 in favour, 2 against (Cuba and Yemen) and 1 abstention (China).
Sponsors: Canada, France, Romania, Soviet Union, United Kingdom, United States.

Resolution 686   2 March 1991
Relating, inter alia, to the suspension of offensive combat operations and to the importance of Iraq taking the necessary measures which would permit a definitive end to the hostilities.

Adopted by a vote of 11 in favour, 1 against (Cuba) and 3 abstentions (China, India, Yemen).
Sponsors: Belgium, France, Romania, Soviet Union, United Kingdom, United States, Zaire.

Resolution 687   3 April 1991

Relating, inter alia, to the restoration to Kuwait of its sovereignty, independence, and territorial integrity and the return of its legitimate government, to the status of sanctions and to the setting of specific conditions for a formal cease-fire.
Adopted by a vote of 12 in favour, 1 against (Cuba) and 2 abstentions (Ecuador, Yemen).
Sponsors: Belgium, France, Romania, United Kingdom, United States, Zaire.

Resolution 689   9 April 1991

Relating to the establishment of the United Nations Iraq-Kuwait Observation Mission (UNIKOM).
Adopted by unanimous vote.
Prepared in the course of the Council's consultations

Resolution 692   20 May 1991

Relating to the funds to be paid by Iraq for damages to natural resources, environments, injury to foreign governments, nationals and corporations as a result of its unlawful invasion and occupation of Kuwait.

Resolution 699   17 June 1991

Relating to the destruction of Iraq's biological and nuclear weapons and specifies that the government of Iraq shall be liable for full costs involved.

Resolution 700   17 June 1991

Relating to the establishment of a Committee for monitoring the prohibitions against the sale or supply of arms to Iraq and related sanctions.

Resolution 705   15 August 1991

Relating to and stating that compensation paid by Iraq (from section E of resolution 687) shall not exceed 30 percent of the annual value of the exports of petroleum and petroleum products from Iraq.

Resolution 706   15 August 1991

Relating to decision to allow importing of petroleum and petroleum products originating in Iraq sufficient to produce the sum required to pay some reparations, but not to exceed 1.6 billion U.S. dollars; the requirement for the International Committee of the Red Cross to report on activities undertaken in connection with facilitating repatriation or return of all Kuwaiti and 3rd country nationals or their remains present in Iraq on or after 2 August 1990; and requiring Iraq to supply monthly to the Secretary-General a statement of the gold and foreign currency reserves held in Iraq and elsewhere.

Resolution 707   15 August 1991

Relating to condemnation of Iraq's violation of U.N. resolutions and non-compliance with its obligations under the safeguards agreement with the International Atomic Energy Agency and demands full, final, and complete disclosure regarding weapons of mass destruction and missiles with a range of over 150 km and all holdings of such weapons. It further demands unrestricted access to inspection teams, immediate cessation of attempts at concealment, making available to inspecting teams any items previously denied access, allowing flights throughout Iraq for inspection and surveillance purposes, halting all nuclear activities, safety for inspection teams, facilitation of transportation, medical, or logistical support for teams, and full response to any questions.

Resolution 712   19 September 1991

Relating to authorization for the Security Council Committee to release funds to finance the purchase of foodstuffs, medicines, materials and supplies for essential civilian needs; calling for Iraq to allow full freedom of movement and all necessary facilities to United Nations representatives.

Resolution 715   11 October 1991

Relating to the plan of the Director General of the International Atomic Energy Agency (IAEA) to continue designation of locations for inspections and overflights, and demands that Iraq unconditionally meet all its obligations under the plans approved by the present resolution and cooperate fully with the Special Commission and the Director General of the (IAEA).

Complete Resolutions

Resolution 660   2 August 1990

The Security Council,

Alarmed by the invasion of Kuwait on 2 August 1990 by the military forces of Iraq,

Determining that there exists a breach of international peace and security as regards the Iraqi invasion of Kuwait,

Acting under Articles 39 and 40 of the Charter of the United Nations,

1. Condemns the Iraqi invasion of Kuwait;

2. Demands that Iraq withdraw immediately and unconditionally all its forces to the positions in which they were located on 1 August 1990;

3. Calls upon Iraq and Kuwait to begin immediately intensive negotiations for the resolution of their differences and supports all efforts in this regard, and especially those of the League of Arab States;

4. Decides to meet again as necessary to consider further steps to ensure compliance with the present resolution.

Resolution 661   6 August 1990

The Security Council,

Reaffirming its resolution 660 (1990) of 2 August 1990,

Deeply concerned that that resolution has not been implemented and that the invasion by Iraq of Kuwait continues with further loss of human life and material destruction,

Determined to bring the invasion and occupation of Kuwait by Iraq to an end and to restore the sovereignty, independence and territorial integrity of Kuwait,

Noting that the legitimate Government of Kuwait has expressed its readiness to comply with resolution 660 (1990),

Mindful of its responsibilities under the Charter of the United Nations for the maintenance of international peace and security,

Affirming the inherent right of individual or collective self-defence, in response to the armed attack by Iraq against Kuwait, in accordance with Article 51 of the Charter,

Acting under Chapter VII of the Charter of the United Nations,

1. Determines that Iraq so far has failed to comply with paragraph 2 of resolution 660 (1990) and has usurped the authority of the legitimate Government of Kuwait;

2. Decides, as a consequence, to take the following measures to secure compliance of Iraq with paragraph 2 of resolution 660 (1990) and to restore the authority of the legitimate Government of Kuwait;

3. Decides that all States shall prevent:

a) The import into their territories of all commodities and products originating in Iraq or Kuwait exported therefrom after the date of the present resolution;

b) Any activities by their nationals or in their territories which would promote or are calculated to promote the export or transshipment of any commodities or products from Iraq or Kuwait; and any dealings by their nationals or their flag vessels or in their territories in any commodities or products originating in Iraq or Kuwait and exported therefrom after the date of the present resolution, including in particular any transfer of funds to Iraq or Kuwait for the purposes of such activities or dealings;

c) The sale or supply by their nationals or from their territories or using their flag vessels of any commodities or products, including weapons or any other military equipment, whether or not originating in their territories but not including supplies intended strictly for medical purposes, and, in humanitarian circumstances, foodstuffs, to any person or body in Iraq or Kuwait or to any person or body for the purposes of any business carried on in or operated from Iraq or Kuwait, and any activities by their nationals or in their territories which promote or are calculated to promote such sale or supply of such commodities or products;

4. Decides that all States shall not make available to the Government of Iraq or to any commercial, industrial or public utility undertaking in Iraq or Kuwait, any funds or any other financial or economic resources and shall prevent their nationals and any persons within their territories from removing from their territories or otherwise making available to that Government or to any such undertaking any such funds or resources and from remitting any other funds to persons or bodies within Iraq or Kuwait, except payments exclusively for strictly medical or humanitarian purposes and, in humanitarian circumstances, foodstuffs;

5. Calls upon all States, including States nonmembers of the United Nations, to act strictly in accordance with the provisions of the present resolution notwithstanding any contract entered into or licence granted before the date of the present resolution;

6. Decides to establish, in accordance with rule 28 of the provisional rules of procedure of the Security Council, a Committee of the Security Council consisting of all the members of the Council, to undertake the following tasks and to report on its work to the Council with its observations and recommendations:

a) To examine the reports on the progress of the implementation of the present resolution which will be submitted by the Secretary-General;
b) To seek from all States further information regarding the action taken by them concerning the effective implementation of the provisions laid down in the present resolution;

7. Calls upon all States to co-operate fully with the Committee in the fulfilment of its task, including supplying such information as may be sought by the Committee in pursuance of the present resolution;

8. Requests the Secretary-General to provide all necessary assistance to the Committee and to make the necessary arrangements in the Secretariat for the purpose;

9. Decides that, notwithstanding paragraphs 4 through 8 above, nothing in the present resolution shall prohibit assistance to the legitimate Government of Kuwait, and calls upon all States:
a) To take appropriate measures to protect assets of the legitimate Government of Kuwait and its agencies;
b) Not to recognize any regime set up by the occupying Power;

10. Requests the Secretary-General to report to the Council on the progress of the implementation of the present resolution, the first report to be submitted within thirty days;

11. Decides to keep this item on its agenda and to continue its efforts to put an early end to the invasion by Iraq.

Resolution 662   9 August 1990

The Security Council,

Recalling its resolutions 660 (1990) and 661 (1990),

Gravely alarmed by the declaration by Iraq of a "comprehensive and eternal merger" with Kuwait,

Demanding, once again, that Iraq withdraw immediately and unconditionally all its forces to the positions in which they were located on 1 August 1990,

Determined to bring the occupation of Kuwait by Iraq to an end and to restore the sovereignty, independence and territorial integrity of Kuwait,

Determined also to restore the authority of the legitimate Government of Kuwait,

1. Decides that annexation of Kuwait by Iraq under any form and whatever pretext has no legal validity, and is considered null and void;

2. Calls upon all States, international organizations and specialized agencies not to recognize that annexation, and to refrain from any action or dealing that might be interpreted as an indirect recognition of the annexation;

3. Further demands that Iraq rescind its actions purporting to annex Kuwait;

4. Decides to keep this item on its agenda and to continue its efforts to put an early end to the occupation.

Resolution 664   18 August 1990

The Security Council,

Recalling the Iraqi invasion and purported annexation of Kuwait and resolutions 660, 661 and 662,

Deeply concerned for the safety and well being of third State nationals in Iraq and Kuwait,

Recalling the obligations of Iraq in this regard under international law,

Welcoming the efforts of the Secretary-General to pursue urgent consultations with the Government of Iraq following the concern and anxiety expressed by the members of the Council on 17 August 1990,

Acting under Chapter VII of the United Nations Charter,

1. Demands that Iraq permit and facilitate the immediate departure from Kuwait and Iraq of the nationals of third countries and grant immediate and continuing access of consular officials to such nationals;

2. Further demands that Iraq take no action to jeopardize the safety, security or health of such nationals;

3. Reaffirms its decision in resolution 662 (1990) that annexation of Kuwait by Iraq is null and void, and therefore demands that the government of Iraq rescind its orders for the closure of diplomatic and consular missions in Kuwait and the withdrawal of the immunity of their personnel, and refrain from any such actions in the future;

4. Requests the Secretary-General to report to the Council on compliance with this resolution at the earliest possible time.

Resolution 665   25 August 1990

The Security Council,

Recalling its resolutions 660 (1990), 661 (1990), 662 (1990) and 664 (1990) and demanding their full and immediate implementation,

Having decided in resolution 661 (1990) to impose economic sanctions under Chapter VII of the Charter of the United Nations,

Determined to bring an end to the occupation of Kuwait by Iraq which imperils the existence of a Member State and to restore the legitimate authority, and the sovereignty, independence and territorial integrity of Kuwait which requires the speedy implementation of the above resolutions,

Deploring the loss of innocent life stemming from the Iraqi invasion of Kuwait and determined to prevent further such losses,

Gravely alarmed that Iraq continues to refuse to comply with resolutions 660 (1990), 661 (1990), 662 (1990) and 664 (1990) and in particular at the conduct of the Government of Iraq in using Iraqi flag vessels to export oil,

1. *Calls upon* those Member States cooperating with the Government of Kuwait which are deploying maritime forces to the area to use such measures commensurate to the specific circumstances as may be necessary under the authority of the Security Council to halt all inward and outward maritime shipping in order to inspect and verify their cargoes and destinations and to ensure strict implementation of the provisions related to such shipping laid down in resolution 661 (1990);

2. *Invites* Member States accordingly to cooperate as may be necessary to ensure compliance with the provisions of resolution 661 (1990) with maximum use of political and diplomatic measures, in accordance with paragraph 1 above;

3. *Requests* all States to provide in accordance with the Charter such assistance as may be required by the States referred to in paragraph 1 of this resolution;

4. *Further requests* the States concerned to coordinate their actions in pursuit of the above paragraphs of this resolution using as appropriate mechanisms of the Military Staff Committee and after consultation with the Secretary-General to submit reports to the Security Council and its Committee established under resolution 661 (1990) to facilitate the monitoring of the implementation of this resolution;

5. *Decides* to remain actively seized of the matter.

Resolution 666   13 September 1990

The Security Council,

Recalling its resolution 661 (1990), paragraphs 3 (c) and 4 of which apply, except in humanitarian circumstances, to foodstuffs,

Recognizing that circumstances may arise in which it will be necessary for foodstuffs to be supplied to the civilian population in Iraq or Kuwait in order to relieve human suffering,

Noting that in this respect the Committee established under paragraph 6 of that resolution has received communications from several Member States,

Emphasizing that it is for the Security Council, alone or acting through the Committee, to determine whether humanitarian circumstances have arisen,

Deeply concerned that Iraq has failed to comply with its obligations under Security Council resolution 664 (1990) in respect of the safety and well-being of third State nationals, and reaffirming that Iraq retains full responsibility in this regard under international humanitarian law including, where applicable, the Fourth Geneva Convention,

Acting under Chapter VII of the Charter of the United Nations,

1. Decides that in order to make the necessary determination whether or not for the purposes of paragraph 3 (c) and paragraph 4 of resolution 661 (1990) humanitarian circumstances have arisen, the Committee shall keep the situation regarding foodstuffs in Iraq and Kuwait under constant review;

2. Expects Iraq to comply with its obligations under Security Council resolution 664 (1990) in respect of third State nationals and reaffirms that Iraq remains fully responsible for their safety and well-being in accordance with international humanitarian law including, where applicable, the Fourth Geneva Convention;

3. Requests, for the purposes of paragraphs 1 and 2 of this resolution, that the Secretary-General seek urgently, and on a continuing basis, information from relevant United Nations and other appropriate humanitarian agencies and all other sources on the availability of food in Iraq and Kuwait, such information to be communicated by the Secretary-General to the Committee regularly;

4. Requests further that in seeking and supplying such information particular attention will be paid to such categories of persons who might suffer specially, such as children under 15 years of age, expectant mothers, maternity cases, the sick and the elderly;

5. Decides that if the Committee, after receiving the reports from the Secretary-General, determines that circumstances have arisen in which there is an urgent humanitarian need to supply foodstuffs to Iraq or Kuwait in order to relieve human suffering, it will report promptly to the Council its decision as to how such need should be met;

6. Directs the Committee that in formulating its decisions it should bear in mind that foodstuffs should be provided through the United Nations in co-operation with the International Committee of the Red Cross or other appropriate humanitarian agencies and distributed by them or under their supervision in order to ensure that they reach the intended beneficiaries;

7. Requests the Secretary-General to use his good offices to facilitate the delivery and distribution of foodstuffs to Kuwait and Iraq in accordance with the provisions of this and other relevant resolutions;

8. Recalls that resolution 661 (1990) does not apply to supplies intended strictly for medical purposes, but in this connection recommends that medical supplies should be exported under the strict supervision of the Government of the exporting State or by appropriate humanitarian agencies.

Resolution 667   16 September 1990

The Security Council,

Reaffirming its resolutions 660 (1990), 661 (1990), 662 (1990), 664 (1990), 665 (1990) and 666 (1990),

Recalling the Vienna Conventions of 18 April 1961 on diplomatic relations and of 24 April 1963 on consular relations, to both of which Iraq is a party,

Considering that the decision of Iraq to order the closure of diplomatic and consular missions in Kuwait and to withdraw the immunity and privileges of these missions and their personnel is contrary to the decisions of the Security Council, the international Conventions mentioned above and international law,

Deeply concerned that Iraq, notwithstanding the decisions of the Security Council and the provisions of the Conventions mentioned above, has committed acts of violence against diplomatic missions and their personnel in Kuwait,

Outraged at recent violations by Iraq of diplomatic premises in Kuwait and at the abduction of personnel enjoying diplomatic immunity and foreign nationals who were present in these premises,

Considering that the above actions by Iraq constitute aggressive acts and a flagrant violation of its international obligations which strike at the root of the conduct of international relations in accordance with the Charter of the United Nations,

Recalling that Iraq is fully responsible for any use of violence against foreign nationals or against any diplomatic or consular mission in Kuwait or its personnel,

Determined to ensure respect for its decisions and for Article 25 of the Charter of the United Nations,

Further considering that the grave nature of Iraq's actions, which constitute a new escalation of its violations of international law, obliges the Council not only to express its immediate reaction but also to consult urgently to take further concrete measures to ensure Iraq's compliance with the Council's resolutions,

Acting under Chapter VII of the Charter of the United Nations,

1. *Strongly condemns* aggressive acts perpetrated by Iraq against diplomatic premises and personnel in Kuwait, including the abduction of foreign nationals who were present in those premises;

2. *Demands* the immediate release of those foreign nationals as well as all nationals mentioned in resolution 664 (1990);

3. *Further demands* that Iraq immediately and fully comply with its international obligations under resolutions 660 (1990), 662 (1990) and 664 (1990) of the Security Council, the Vienna Conventions on diplomatic and consular relations and international law;

4. *Further demands* that Iraq immediately protect the safety and well-being of diplomatic and consular personnel and premises in Kuwait and in Iraq and take no action to hinder the diplomatic and consular missions in the performance of their functions, including access to their nationals and the protection of their person and interests;

5. *Reminds* all States that they are obliged to observe strictly resolutions 661 (1990), 662 (1990), 664 (1990), 665 (1990) and 666 (1990);

6. *Decides* to consult urgently to take further concrete measures as soon as possible, under Chapter VII of the Charter, in response to Iraq's continued violation of the Charter, of resolutions of the Council and of international law.

Resolution 669   24 September 1990

The Security Council,

Recalling its resolution 661 (1990) of 6 August 1990,

Recalling also Article 50 of the Charter of the United Nations,

Conscious of the fact that an increasing number of requests for assistance have been received under the provisions of Article 50 of the Charter of the United Nations,

Entrusts the Committee established under resolution 661 (1990) concerning the situation between Iraq and Kuwait with the task of examining requests for assistance under the provisions of Article 50 of the Charter of the United Nations and making recommendations to the President of the Security Council for appropriate action.

Resolution 670   25 September 1990

The Security Council,

Reaffirming its resolutions 660 (1990), 661 (1990), 662 (1990), 664 (1990), 665 (1990), 666 (1990), and 667 (1990),

Condemning Iraq's continued occupation of Kuwait, its failure to rescind its actions and end its purported annexation and its holding of third State nationals against their will, in flagrant violation of resolutions 660 (1990), 662 (1990), 664 (1990) and 667 (1990) and of international humanitarian law,

Condemning further the treatment by Iraqi forces of Kuwaiti nationals, including measures to force them to leave their own country and mistreatment of persons and property in Kuwait in violation of international law,

Noting with grave concern the persistent attempts to evade the measures laid down in resolution 661 (1990),

Further noting that a number of States have limited the number of Iraqi diplomatic and consular officials in their countries and that others are planning to do so,

Determined to ensure by all necessary means the strict and complete application of the measures laid down in resolution 661 (1990),

Determined to ensure respect for its decisions and the provisions of Articles 25 and 48 of the Charter of the United Nations,

Affirming that any acts of the Government of Iraq which are contrary to the above-mentioned resolutions or to Articles 25 or 48 of the Charter of the United Nations, such as Decree No. 377 of the Revolution Command Council of Iraq of 16 September 1990, are null and void,

Reaffirming its determination to ensure compliance with Security Council resolutions by maximum use of political and diplomatic means,

Welcoming the Secretary-General's use of his good offices to advance a peaceful solution based on the relevant Security Council resolutions and noting with appreciation his continuing efforts to this end,

Underlining to the Government of Iraq that its continued failure to comply with the terms of resolutions 660 (1990), 661 (1990), 662 (1990), 664 (1990), 666 (1990) and 667 (1990) could lead to further serious action by the Council under the Charter of the United Nations, including under Chapter VII,

Recalling the provisions of Article 103 of the Charter of the United Nations,

Acting under Chapter VII of the Charter of the United Nations,

1. Calls upon all States to carry out their obligations to ensure strict and complete compliance with resolution 661 (1990) and in particular paragraphs 3, 4 and 5 thereof;

2. Confirms that resolution 661 (1990) applies to all means of transport, including aircraft;

3. Decides that all States, notwithstanding the existence of any rights or obligations conferred or imposed by any international agreement or any contract entered into or any licence or permit granted before the date of the present resolution, shall deny permission to any aircraft to take off from their territory if the aircraft would carry any cargo to or from Iraq or Kuwait other than food in humanitarian circumstances, subject to authorization by the Council or the Committee established by resolution 661 (1990) and in accordance with resolution 666 (1990), or supplies intended strictly for medical purposes or solely for UNIIMOG;

4. Decides further that all States shall deny permission to any aircraft destined to land in Iraq or Kuwait, whatever its State of registration, to overfly its territory unless:
a) The aircraft lands at an airfield designated by that State outside Iraq or Kuwait in order to permit its inspection to ensure that there

is no cargo on board in violation of resolution 661 (1990) or the present resolution, and for this purpose the aircraft may be detained for as long as necessary; or

b) the particular flight has been approved by the Committee established by resolution 661 (1990); or

c) The flight is certified by the United Nations as solely for the purposes of UNIIMOG;

5. *Decides* that each State shall take all necessary measures to ensure that any aircraft registered in its territory or operated by an operator who has his principal place of business or permanent residence in its territory complies with the provisions of resolution 661 (1990) and the present resolution;

6. *Decides further* that all States shall notify in a timely fashion the Committee established by resolution 661 (1990) of any flight between its territory and Iraq or Kuwait to which the requirement to land in paragraph 4 above does not apply, and the purpose for such a flight;

7. *Calls upon* all States to co-operate in taking such measures as may be necessary, consistent with international law, including the Chicago Convention, to ensure the effective implementation of the provisions of resolution 661 (1990) or the present resolution;

8. *Calls upon* all States to detain any ships of Iraqi registry which enter their ports and which are being or have been used in violation of resolution 661 (1990), or to deny such ships entrance to their ports except in circumstances recognized under international law as neces-sary to safeguard human life;

9. *Reminds* all States of their obligations under resolution 661 (1990) with regard to the freezing of Iraqi assets, and the protection of the assets of the legitimate Government of Kuwait and its agencies, located within their territory and to report to the Committee established under resolution 661 (1990) regarding those assets;

10. *Calls upon* all States to provide to the Committee established by resolution 661 (1990) information regarding the action taken by them to implement the provisions laid down in the present resolution;

11. *Affirms* that the United Nations Organization, the specialized agen-cies and other international organizations in the United Nations system are required to take such measures as may be necessary to give effect to the terms of resolution 661 (1990) and this resolution;

12. *Decides* to consider, in the event of evasion of the provisions of resolution 661 (1990) or of the present resolution by a State or its

nationals or through its territory, measures directed at the State in question to prevent such evasion;

13. Reaffirms that the Fourth Geneva Convention applies to Kuwait and that as a High Contracting Party to the Convention Iraq is bound to comply fully with all its terms and in particular is liable under the Convention in respect of the grave breaches committed by it, as are individuals who commit or order the commission of grave breaches.

Resolution 674   29 October 1990

The Security Council,

Recalling its resolutions 660 (1990), 661 (1990), 662 (1990), 664 (1990), 665 (1990), 666 (1990), 667 (1990) and 670 (1990),

Stressing the urgent need for the immediate and unconditional withdrawal of all Iraqi forces from Kuwait, for the restoration of Kuwait's sovereignty, independence and territorial integrity and of the authority of its legitimate government,

Condemning the actions by the Iraqi authorities and occupying forces to take third-State nationals hostage and to mistreat and oppress Kuwaiti and third-State nationals, and the other actions reported to the Security Council, such as the destruction of Kuwaiti demographic records, the forced departure of Kuwaitis, the relocation of population in Kuwait and the unlawful destruction and seizure of public and private property in Kuwait, including hospital supplies and equipment, in violation of the decisions of the Council, the Charter of the United Nations, the Fourth Geneva Convention, the Vienna Conventions on Diplomatic and Consular Relations and international law,

Expressing grave alarm over the situation of nationals of third States in Kuwait and Iraq, including the personnel of the diplomatic and consular missions of such States,

Reaffirming that the Fourth Geneva Convention applies to Kuwait and that as a High Contracting Party to the Convention Iraq is bound to comply fully with all its terms and in particular is liable under the Convention in respect of the grave breaches committed by it, as are individuals who commit or order the commission of grave breaches,

Recalling the efforts of the Secretary-General concerning the safety and well-being of third-State nationals in Iraq and Kuwait,

Deeply concerned at the economic cost and at the loss and suffering caused to individuals in Kuwait and Iraq as a result of the invasion and occupation of Kuwait by Iraq,

Acting under Chapter VII of the Charter of the United Nations,

Reaffirming the goal of the international community of maintaining international peace and security by seeking to resolve international disputes and conflicts through peaceful means,

Recalling the important role that the United Nations and its Secretary-General have played in the peaceful solution of disputes and conflicts in conformity with the provisions of the Charter,

Alarmed by the dangers of the present crisis caused by the Iraqi invasion and occupation of Kuwait, which directly threaten international peace and security, and seeking to avoid any further worsening of the situation,

Calling upon Iraq to comply with the relevant resolutions of the Security Council, in particular its resolutions 660 (1990), 662 (1990) and 664 (1990),

Reaffirming its determination to ensure compliance by Iraq with the Security Council resolutions by maximum use of political and diplomatic means,

A

1. Demands that the Iraqi authorities and occupying forces immediately cease and desist from taking third-State nationals hostage, mistreating and oppressing Kuwaiti and third-State nationals and any other actions, such as those reported to the Security Council and described above, that violate the decisions of this Council, the Charter of the United Nations, the Fourth Geneva Convention, the Vienna Conventions on Diplomatic and Consular Relations and international law;

2. Invites States to collate substantiated information in their possession or submitted to them on the grave breaches by Iraq as per paragraph 1 above and to make this information available to the Security Council;

3. Reaffirms its demand that Iraq immediately fulfil its obligations to the third-state nationals in Kuwait and Iraq, including the personnel of diplomatic and consular missions, under the Charter, the Fourth Geneva Convention, the Vienna Conventions on Diplomatic and Consular Relations, general principles of international law and the relevant resolutions of the Council;

4. Also reaffirms its demand that Iraq permit and facilitate the immediate depature from Kuwait and Iraq of those third-State nationals, including diplomatic and consular personnel, who wish to leave;

5. Demands that Iraq ensure the immediate access to food, water and basic services necessary to the protection and well-being of Kuwaiti nationals and of nationals of third States in Kuwait and Iraq, including the personnel of diplomatic and consular missions in Kuwait;

6. Reaffirms its demand that Iraq immediately protect the safety and well-being of diplomatic and consular personnel and premises in Kuwait and in Iraq, take no action to hinder these diplomatic and consular missions in the performance of their functions, including access to their nationals and the protection of their person and interests and rescind its orders for the closure of diplomatic and consular missions in Kuwait and the withdrawal of the immunity of their personnel;

7. Requests the Secretary-General, in the context of the continued exercise of his good offices concerning the safety and well-being of third-State nationals in Iraq and Kuwait, to seek to achieve the objectives of paragraphs 4, 5 and 6 above and in particular the provision of food, water and basic services to Kuwaiti nationals and to the diplomatic and consular missions in Kuwait and the evacuation of third-State nationals;

8. Reminds Iraq that under international law it is liable for any loss, damage or injury arising in regard to Kuwait and third States, and their nationals and corporations, as a result of the invasion and illegal occupation of Kuwait by Iraq;

9. Invites States to collect relevant information regarding their claims, and those of their nationals and corporations, for restitution or financial compensation by Iraq with a view to such arrangements as may be established in accordance with international law;

10. Requires that Iraq comply with the provisions of the present resolution and its previous resolutions, failing which the Security Council will need to take further measures under the Charter;

11. Decides to remain actively and permanently seized of the matter until Kuwait has regained its independence and peace has been restored in conformity with the relevant resolutions of the Security Council;

B

12. Reposes its trust in the Secretary-General to make available his good offices and, as he considers appropriate, to pursue them and to undertake diplomatic efforts in order to reach a peaceful solution to the crisis caused by the Iraqi invasion and occupation of Kuwait on the basis of Security Council resolutions 660 (1990), 662 (1990) and 664 (1990), and calls upon all States, both those in the region and others, to pursue on this basis their efforts to this end, in conformity with the Charter, in order to improve the situation and restore peace, security and stability;

13. Requests the Secretary-General to report to the Security Council on the results of his good offices and diplomatic efforts.

Resolution 677   28 November 1990

The Security Council,

Recalling its resolutions 660 (1990) of 2 August 1990, 662 (1990) of 9 August 1990 and 674 (1990) of 29 October 1990,

Reiterating its concern for the suffering caused to individuals in Kuwait as a result of the invasion and occupation of Kuwait by Iraq,

Gravely concerned at the ongoing attempt by Iraq to alter the demographic composition of the population of Kuwait and to destroy the civil records maintained by the legitimate Government of Kuwait,

Acting under Chapter VII of the Charter of the United Nations,

1. Condemns the attempts by Iraq to alter the demographic composition of the population of Kuwait and to destroy the civil records maintained by the legitimate Government of Kuwait;

2. Mandates the Secretary-General to take custody of a copy of the population register of Kuwait, the authenticity of which has been certified by the legitimate Government of Kuwait and which covers the registration of the population up to 1 August 1990;

3. Requests the Secretary-General to establish, in co-operation with the legitimate Government of Kuwait, an Order of Rules and Regulations governing access to and use of the said copy of the population register.

Resolution 678   29 November 1990

The Security Council,

Recalling and reaffirming its resolutions 660 (1990) of 2 August 1990, 661 (1990) of 6 August 1990, 662 (1990) of 9 August 1990, 664 (1990) of 18 August 1990, 665 (1990) of 25 August 1990, 666 (1990) of 13 September 1990, 667 (1990) of 16 September 1990, 669 (1990) of 24 September 1990, 670 (1990) of 25 September 1990, 674 (1990) of 29 October 1990 and 677 (1990) of 28 November 1990,

Noting that, despite all efforts by the United Nations, Iraq refuses to comply with its obligation to implement resolution 660 (1990) and the above-mentioned subsequent relevant resolutions, in flagrant contempt of the Security Council,

Mindful of its duties and responsibilities under the Charter of the United Nations for the maintenance and preservation of international peace and security,

Determined to secure full compliance with its decisions,

Acting under Chapter VII of the Charter,

1. Demands that Iraq comply fully with resolution 660 (1990) and all subsequent relevant resolutions, and decides, while maintaining all its decisions, to allow Iraq one final opportunity, as a pause of goodwill, to do so;

2. Authorizes Member States co-operating with the Government of Kuwait, unless Iraq on or before 15 January 1991 fully implements, as set forth in paragraph 1 above, the foregoing resolutions, to use all necessary means to uphold and implement resolution 660 (1990) and all subsequent relevant resolutions and to restore international peace and security in the area;

3. Requests all States to provide appropriate support for the actions undertaken in pursuance of paragraph 2 of the present resolution;

4. Requests the States concerned to keep the Security Council regularly informed on the progress of actions undertaken pursuant to paragraphs 2 and 3 of the present resolution;

5. Decides to remain seized of the matter.

Resolution 686   2 March 1991

The Security Council,

Recalling and *reaffirming* its resolutions 660 (1990), 661 (1990), 662 (1990), 664 (1990), 665 (1990), 666 (1990), 667 (1990), 669 (1990), 670 (1990), 674 (1990), 677 (1990), and 678 (1990),

Recalling the obligations of Member States under Article 25 of the Charter,

Recalling paragraph 9 of resolution 661 (1990) regarding assistance to the Government of Kuwait and paragraph 3 (c) of that resolution regarding supplies strictly for medical purposes and, in humanitarian circumstances, foodstuffs,

Taking note of the letters of the Foreign Minister of Iraq confirming Iraq's agreement to comply fully with all of the resolutions noted above (S/22275), and stating its intention to release prisoners of war immediately (S/22273),

Taking note of the suspension of offensive combat operations by the forces of Kuwait and the Member States cooperating with Kuwait pursuant to resolution 678 (1990),

Bearing in mind the need to be assured of Iraq's peaceful intentions, and the objective in resolution 678 (1990) of restoring international peace and security in the region,

Underlining the importance of Iraq taking the necessary measures which would permit a definitive end to the hostilities,

Affirming the commitment of all Member States to the independence, sovereignty and territorial integrity of Iraq and Kuwait, and *noting* the intention expressed by the Member States cooperating under paragraph 2 of Security Council resolution 678 (1990) to bring their military presence in Iraq to an end as soon as possible consistent with achieving the objectives of the resolution,

Acting under Chapter VII of the Charter,

1. Affirms that all twelve resolutions noted above continue to have full force and effect;

2. Demands that Iraq implement its acceptance of all twelve resolutions noted above and in particular that Iraq:
a) Rescind immediately its actions purporting to annex Kuwait;
b) Accept in principle its liability under international law for any loss, damage or injury arising in regard to Kuwait and third States, and their nationals and corporations, as a result of the invasion and illegal occupation of Kuwait by Iraq;
c) Immediately release under the auspices of the International Committee of the Red Cross, Red Cross Societies, or Red Crescent Societies, all Kuwaiti and third country nationals detained by Iraq and return the remains of any deceased Kuwaiti and third country nationals so detained; and
d) Immediately begin to return all Kuwaiti property seized by Iraq, to be completed in the shortest possible period;

3. Further demands that Iraq:
a) Cease hostile or provocative actions by its forces against all Member States, including missile attacks and flights of combat aircraft;
b) Designate military commanders to meet with counterparts from the

forces of Kuwait and the Member States cooperating with Kuwait pursuant to resolution 678 (1990) to arrange for the military aspects of a cessation of hostilities at the earliest possible time;

c) Arrange for immediate access to and release of all prisoners of war under the auspices of the International Committee of the Red Cross and return the remains of any deceased personnel of the forces of Kuwait and the Member States cooperating with Kuwait pursuant to resolution 678 (1990); and

d) Provide all information and assistance in identifying Iraqi mines, booby traps and other explosives as well as any chemical and biological weapons and material in Kuwait, in areas of Iraq where forces of Member States cooperating with Kuwait pursuant to resolution 678 (1990) are present temporarily, and in the adjacent waters;

4. *Recognizes* that during the period required for Iraq to comply with paragraphs 2 and 3 above, the provisions of paragraph 2 of resolution 678 (1990) remain valid;

5. *Welcomes* the decision of Kuwait and the Member States cooperating with Kuwait pursuant to resolution 678 (1990) to provide access and to commence immediately the release of Iraqi prisoners of war as required by the terms of the Third Geneva Convention of 1949, under the auspices of the International Committee of the Red Cross;

6. *Requests* all Member States, as well as the United Nations, the specialized agencies and other international organizations in the United Nations system, to take all appropriate action to cooperate with the Government and people of Kuwait in the reconstruction of their country;

7. *Decides* that Iraq shall notify the Secretary-General and the Security Council when it has taken the actions set out above;

8. *Decides* that in order to secure the rapid establishment of a definitive end to the hostilities, the Security Council remains actively seized of the matter.

Resolution 687   3 April 1991

The Security Council,

Recalling its resolutions 660 (1990), 661 (1990), 662 (1990), 664 (1990), 665 (1990), 666 (1990), 667 (1990), 669 (1990), 670 (1990), 674 (1990), 677 (1990), 678 (1990) and 686 (1991),

Welcoming the restoration to Kuwait of its sovereignty, independence, and territorial integrity and the return of its legitimate government,

Affirming the commitment of all Member States to the sovereignty, territorial integrity and political independence of Kuwait and Iraq, and noting the intention expressed by the Member States cooperating with Kuwait under paragraph 2 of resolution 678 (1990) to bring their military presence in Iraq to an end as soon as possible consistent with paragraph 8 of resolution 686 (1991),

Reaffirming the need to be assured of Iraq's peaceful intentions in light of its unlawful invasion and occupation of Kuwait,

Taking note of the letter sent by the Foreign Minister of Iraq on 27 February 1991 (S/22275) and those sent pursuant to resolution 686 (1991) (S/22273, S/22276, S/22320, S/22321 and S/22330),

Noting that Iraq and Kuwait, as independent sovereign States, signed at Baghdad on 4 October 1963 "Agreed Minutes Regarding the Restoration of Friendly Relations, Recognition and Related Matters," thereby recognizing formally the boundary between Iraq and Kuwait and the allocation of islands, which were registered with the United Nations in accordance with Article 102 of the Charter and in which Iraq recognized the independence and complete sovereignty of the State of Kuwait within its borders as specified and accepted in the letter of the Prime Minister of Iraq dated 21 July 1932, and as accepted by the Ruler of Kuwait in his letter dated 10 August 1932,

Conscious of the need for demarcation of the said boundary,

Conscious also of the statements by Iraq threatening to use weapons in violation of its obligations under the Geneva Protocol for the Prohibition of the Use in War of Asphyxiating, Poisonous or Other Gases, and of Bacteriological Methods of Warfare, signed at Geneva on 17 June 1925, and of its prior use of chemical weapons and affirming that grave consequences would follow any further use by Iraq of such weapons,

Recalling that Iraq has subscribed to the Declaration adopted by all States participating in the Conference of States Parties to the 1925 Geneva Protocol and Other Interested States, held at Paris from 7 to 11 January 1989, establishing the objective of universal elimination of chemical and biological weapons,

Recalling further that Iraq has signed the Convention on the Prohibition of the Development, Production and Stockpiling of Bacteriological (Biological) and Toxin Weapons and on Their Destruction, of 10 April 1972,

Noting the importance of Iraq ratifying this Convention,

Noting moreover the importance of all States adhering to this Convention and encouraging its forthcoming Review Conference to reinforce the authority, efficiency and universal scope of the Convention,

Stressing the importance of an early conclusion by the Conference on Disarmament of its work on a Convention on the Universal Prohibition of Chemical Weapons and of universal adherence thereto,

Aware of the use by Iraq of ballistic missiles in unprovoked attacks and therefore of the need to take specific measures in regard to such missiles located in Iraq,

Concerned by the reports in the hands of Member States that Iraq has attempted to acquire materials for a nuclear-weapons programme contrary to its obligations under the Treaty on the Non-Proliferation of Nuclear Weapons of 1 July 1968,

Recalling the objective of the establishment of a nuclear-weapon-free zone in the region of the Middle East,

Conscious of the threat which all weapons of mass destruction pose to peace and security in the area and of the need to work towards the establishment in the Middle East of a zone free of such weapons,

Conscious also of the objective of achieving balanced and comprehensive control of armaments in the region,

Conscious further of the importance of achieving the objectives noted above using all available means, including a dialogue among the States of the region,

Noting that resolution 686 (1991) marked the lifting of the measures imposed by resolution 661 (1990) in so far as they applied to Kuwait,

Noting that despite the progress being made in fulfilling the obligations of resolution 686 (1991), many Kuwaiti and third country nationals are still not accounted for and property remains unreturned,

Recalling the International Convention against the Taking of Hostages, opened for signature at New York on 18 December 1979, which categorizes all acts of taking hostages as manifestations of international terrorism,

Deploring threats made by Iraq during the recent conflict to make use of terrorism against targets outside Iraq and the taking of hostages by Iraq,

Taking note with grave concern of the reports of the Secretary-General of 20 March 1991 (S/22366) and 28 March 1991 (S/22409), and conscious of the necessity to meet urgently the humanitarian needs in Kuwait and Iraq,

Bearing in mind its objective of restoring international peace and security in the area as set out in recent Council resolutions,

Conscious of the need to take the following measures acting under Chapter VII of the Charter,

1. *Affirms* all thirteen resolutions noted above, except as expressly changed below to achieve the goals of this resolution, including a formal cease-fire;

A

2. *Demands* that Iraq and Kuwait respect the inviolability of the international boundary and the allocation of islands set out in the "Agreed Minutes Between the State of Kuwait and the Republic of Iraq Regarding the Restoration of Friendly Relations, Recognition and Related Matters," signed by them in the exercise of their sovereignty at Baghdad on 4 October 1963 and registered with the United Nations and published by the United Nations in document 7063, United Nations Treaty Series, 1964;

3. *Calls on* the Secretary-General to lend his assistance to make arrangements with Iraq and Kuwait to demarcate the boundary between Iraq and Kuwait, drawing on appropriate material including the map transmitted by Security Council document S/22412 and to report back to the Security Council within one month;

4. *Decides* to guarantee the inviolability of the above-mentioned international boundary and to take as appropriate all necessary measures to that end in accordance with the Charter;

B

5. *Requests* the Secretary-General, after consulting with Iraq and Kuwait, to submit within three days to the Security Council for its approval a plan for the immediate deployment of a United Nations observer unit to monitor the Khor Abdullah and a demilitarized zone, which is hereby established, extending 10 kilometres into Iraq and 5 kilometres into Kuwait from the boundary referred to in the "Agreed Minutes Between the State of Kuwait and the Republic of Iraq Regarding the Restoration of Friendly Relations, Recognition and Related Matters" of 4 October 1963; to deter violations of the boundary through its presence in and surveillance of the demilitarized zone; to observe any

hostile or potentially hostile action mounted from the territory of one State to the other; and for the Secretary-General to report regularly to the Council on the operations of the unit, and immediately if there are serious violations of the zone or potential threats to peace;

6. Notes that as soon as the Secretary-General notifies the Council of the completion of the deployment of the United Nations observer unit, the conditions will be established for the Member States cooperating with Kuwait in accordance with resolution 678 (1990) to bring their military presence in Iraq to an end consistent with resolution 686 (1991);

C

7. Invites Iraq to reaffirm unconditionally its obligations under the Geneva Protocol for the Prohibition of the Use in War of Asphyxiating, Poisonous or Other Gases, and of Bacteriological Methods of Warfare, signed at Geneva on 17 June 1925, and to ratify the Convention on the Prohibition of the Development, Production and Stockpiling of Bacteriological (Biological) and Toxin Weapons and on Their Destruction, of 10 April 1972;

8. Decides that Iraq shall unconditionally accept the destruction, removal, or rendering harmless, under international supervision, of:

a) all chemical and biological weapons and all stocks of agents and all related subsystems and components and all research, development, support and manufacturing facilities;

b) all ballistic missiles with a range greater than 150 kilometres and related major parts, and repair and production facilities;

9. Decides, for the implementation of paragraph 8 above, the following:

a) Iraq shall submit to the Secretary-General, within fifteen days of the adoption of this resolution, a declaration of the locations, amounts and types of all items specified in paragraph 8 and agree to urgent, on-site inspection as specified below;

b) the Secretary-General, in consultation with the appropriate Governments and, where appropriate, with the Director-General of the World Health Organization (WHO), within 45 days of the passage of this resolution, shall develop, and submit to the Council for approval, a plan calling for the completion of the following acts within 45 days of such approval:

i) the forming of a Special Commission, which shall carry out immediate on-site inspection of Iraq's biological, chemical and missile capabilities, based on Iraq's declarations and the designation of any additional locations by the Special Commission itself;

ii) the yielding by Iraq of possession to the Special Commission for destruction, removal or rendering harmless, taking into account the requirements of public safety, of all items specified under paragraph 8 (a) above including items at the additional locations designated by the Special Commission under paragraph 9 (b) (i) above and the destruction by Iraq, under supervision of the Special Commission, of all its missile capabilities including launchers as specified under paragraph 8 (b) above;

iii) the provision by the Special Commission of the assistance and cooperation to the Director-General of the International Atomic Energy Agency (IAEA) required in paragraphs 12 and 13 below;

10. *Decides* that Iraq shall unconditionally undertake not to use, develop, construct or acquire any of the items specified in paragraphs 8 and 9 above and requests the Secretary-General, in consultation with the Special Commission, to develop a plan for the future ongoing monitoring and verification of Iraq's compliance with this paragraph, to be submitted to the Council for approval within 120 days of the passage of this resolution;

11. *Invites* Iraq to reaffirm unconditionally its obligations under the Treaty on the Non-Proliferation of Nuclear Weapons, of 1 July 1968;

12. *Decides* that Iraq shall unconditionally agree not to acquire or develop nuclear weapons or nuclear-weapons-usable material or any subsystems or components or any research, development, support or manufacturing facilities related to the above; to submit to the Secretary-General and the Director-General of the International Atomic Energy Agency (IAEA) within 15 days of the adoption of this resolution a declaration of the locations, amounts, and types of all items specified above; to place all of its nuclear-weapons-usable materials under the exclusive control, for custody and removal, of the IAEA, with the assistance and cooperation of the Special Commission as provided for in the plan of the Secretary-General discussed in paragraph 9 (b) above; to accept, in accordance with the arrangements provided for in paragraph 13 below, urgent on-site inspection and the destruction, removal, or rendering harmless as appropriate of all items specified above; and to accept the plan discussed in paragraph 13 below for the future ongoing monitoring and verification of its compliance with these undertakings;

13. *Requests* the Director-General of the International Atomic Energy Agency (IAEA) through the Secretary-General, with the assistance and cooperation of the Special Commission as provided for in the plan of the Secretary-General in paragraph 9 (b) above, to carry out immediate on-site inspection of Iraq's nuclear capabilities based on Iraq's declarations and the designation of any additional locations by the Special Commission; to develop a plan for submission to the Security Council within 45 days calling for the destruction, removal, or rendering harmless as appropriate of all items listed in paragraph 12 above; to carry out the plan within 45 days following approval by the Security Council; and to develop a plan, taking into account the rights and obligations of Iraq under the Treaty on the Non-Proliferation of Nuclear Weapons, of 1 July 1968, for the future ongoing monitoring and verification of Iraq's compliance with paragraph 12 above, including an inventory of all nuclear material in Iraq subject to the Agency's verification and inspections to confirm that IAEA safeguards cover all relevant nuclear activities in Iraq, to be submitted to the Council for approval within 120 days of the passage of this resolution;

14. Takes note that the actions to be taken by Iraq in paragraphs 8, 9, 10, 11, 12 and 13 of this resolution represent steps towards the goal of establishing in the Middle East a zone free from weapons of mass destruction and all missiles for their delivery and the objective of a global ban on chemical weapons;

D

15. Requests the Secretary-General to report to the Security Council on the steps taken to facilitate the return of all Kuwaiti property seized by Iraq, including a list of any property which Kuwait claims has not been returned or which has not been returned intact;

E

16. Reaffirms that Iraq, without prejudice to the debts and obligations of Iraq arising prior to 2 August 1990, which will be addressed through the normal mechanisms, is liable under international law for any direct loss, damage, including environmental damage and the depletion of natural resources, or injury to foreign Governments, nationals and corporations, as a result of Iraq's unlawful invasion and occupation of Kuwait;

17. Decides that all Iraqi statements made since 2 August 1990, repudiating its foreign debt, are null and void, and demands that Iraq scrupulously adhere to all of its obigations concerning servicing and repayment of its foreign debt;

18. Decides to create a Fund to pay compensation for claims that fall within paragraph 16 above and to establish a Commission that will administer the Fund;

19. Directs the Secretary-General to develop and present to the Council for decision, no later than 30 days following the adoption of this resolution, recommendations for the Fund to meet the requirement for the payment of claims established in accordance with paragraph 18 above and for a programme to implement the decisions in paragraphs 16, 17, and 18 above, including: administration of the Fund; mechanisms for determining the appropriate level of Iraq's contribution to the Fund based on a percentage of the value of the exports of petroleum and petroleum products from Iraq not to exceed a figure to be suggested to the Council by the Secretary-General, taking into account the requirements of the people of Iraq, Iraq's payment capacity as assessed in conjunction with the international financial institutions taking into consideration external debt service, and the needs of the Iraqi economy; arrangements for ensuring that payments are made to the Fund; the process by which funds will be allocated and claims paid; appropriate procedures for evaluating losses, listing claims and verifying their validity and resolving disputed claims in respect of Iraq's liability as specified in paragraph 16 above, and the composition of the Commission designated above;

F

20. Decides, effective immediately, that the prohibitions against the sale or supply to Iraq of commodities or products other than medicine and health supplies, and prohibitions against financial transactions related thereto, contained in resolution 661 (1990) shall not apply to foodstuffs notified to the Committee established by resolution 661 (1990) or, with the approval of that Committee, under the simplified and accelerated "no-objection" procedure, to materials and supplies for essential civilian needs as identified in the report of the Secretary-General dated 20 March 1991 (S/22366), and in any furhter findings of humanitarian need by the Committee;

21. Decides that the Council shall review the provisions of paragraph 20 above every sixty days in light of the policies and practices of the Government of Iraq, including the implementation of all relevant resolutions of the Security Council, for the purpose of determining whether to reduce or lift the prohibitions referred to therein;

22. Decides that upon the approval by the Council of the programme called for in paragraph 19 above and upon Council agreement that Iraq has completed all actions contemplated in paragraphs 8, 9, 10, 11, 12, and 13 above, the prohibitions against the import of commodities and products originating in Iraq and the prohibitions against financial transactions related thereto contained in resolution 661 (1990) shall have no further force or effect;

23. *Decides* that, pending action by the Council under paragraph 22 above, the Committee established under resolution 661 (1990) shall be empowered to approve, when required to assure adequate financial resources on the part of Iraq to carry out the activities under paragraph 20 above, exceptions to the prohibition against the import of commodities and products originating in Iraq;

24. *Decides* that, in accordance with resolution 661 (1990) and subsequent related resolutions and until a further decision is taken by the Council, all States shall continue to prevent the sale or supply, or promotion or facilitation of such sale or supply, to Iraq by their nationals, or from their territories or using their flag vessels or aircraft, of:
a) arms and related matériel of all types, specifically including the sale or transfer through other means of all forms of conventional military equipment, including for paramilitary forces, and spare parts and components and their means of production, for such equipment;
b) items specified and defined in paragraph 8 and paragraph 12 above not otherwise covered above;
c) technology under licensing or other transfer arrangements used in the production, utilization or stockpiling of items specified in subparagraphs (a) and (b) above;
d) personnel or materials for training or technical support services relating to the design, development, manufacture, use, maintenance or support of items specified in subparagraphs (a) and (b) above;

25. *Calls upon* all States and international organizations to act strictly in accordance with paragraph 24 above, notwithstanding the existence of any contracts, agreements, licences, or any other arrangements;

26. *Requests* the Secretary-General, in consultation with appropriate Governments, to develop within 60 days, for approval of the Council, guidelines to facilitate full international implementation of paragraphs 24 and 25 above and paragraph 27 below, and to make them available to all States and to establish a procedure for updating these guidelines periodically;

27. *Calls upon* all States to maintain such national controls and procedures and to take such other actions consistent with the guidelines to be established by the Security Council under paragraph 26 above as may be necessary to ensure compliance with the terms of paragraph 24 above, and calls upon international organizations to take all appropriate steps to assist in ensuring such full compliance;

28. *Agrees* to review its decisions in paragraphs 22, 23, 24, and 25 above, except for the items specified and defined in paragraphs 8 and 12 above, on a regular basis and in any case 120 days following passage of this resolution, taking into account Iraq's compliance with this resolution and general progress towards the control of armaments in the region;

29. *Decides* that all States, including Iraq, shall take the necessary measures to ensure that no claim shall lie at the instance of the Government of Iraq, or of any person claiming through or for the benefit of any such person or body, in connection with any contract or other transaction where its performance was affected by reason of the measures taken by the Security Council in resolution 661 (1990) and related resolutions;

G

30. *Decides* that, in furtherance of its committment to facilitate the repatriation of all Kuwaiti and third country nationals, Iraq shall extend all necessary cooperation to the International Committee of the Red Cross, providing lists of such persons, facilitating the access of the International Committee of the Red Cross to all such persons wherever located or detained and facilitating the search by the International Committee of the Red Cross for those Kuwaiti and third country nationals still unaccounted for;

31. *Invites* the International Committee of the Red Cross to keep the Secretary-General apprised as appropriate of all activites undertaken in connection with facilitating the repatriation or return of all Kuwaiti and third country nationals or their remains present in Iraq on or after 2 August 1990;

H

32. *Requires* Iraq to inform the Council that it will not commit or support any act of international terrorism or allow any organization directed towards commission of such acts to operate within its territory and to condemn unequivocally and renounce all acts, methods, and practices of terrorism;

I

33. *Declares* that, upon official notification by Iraq to the Secretary-General and to the Security Council of its acceptance of the provisions above, a formal cease-fire is effective between Iraq and Kuwait and the Member States cooperating with Kuwait in accordance with resolution 678 (1990);

34. Decides to remain seized of the matter and to take such further steps as may be required for the implementation of this resolution and to secure peace and security in the area.

Resolution 689   9 April 1991

The Security Council,

Recalling its resolution 687 (1991),

Acting under Chapter VII of the Charter of the United Nations,

1. Approves the report of the Secretary-General on the implementation of paragraph 5 of Security Council resolution 687 (1991) contained in document S/22454 and Add.1-3 of 5 and 9 April 1991, respectively;

2. Notes that the decision to set up the observer unit was taken in paragraph 5 of resolution 687 (1991) and can only be terminated by a decision of the Council; the Council shall therefore review the question of termination or continuation every six months;

3. Decides that the modalities for the initial six-month period of the United Nations Iraq-Kuwait Observation Mission shall be in accordance with the above-mentioned report and shall also be reviewed every six months.

Resolution 692 (1991)
Adopted by the Security Council at its 2987th meeting, on 20 May 1991

The Security Council,

Recalling its resolutions 674 (1990) of 29 October 1990, 686 (1991) of 2 March 1991 and 687 (1991) of 3 April 1991, concerning the liability of Iraq, without prejudice to its debts and obligations arising prior to 2 August 1990, for any direct loss, damage, including environmental damage and the depletion of natural resources, or injury to foreign Governments, nationals and corporations, as a result of Iraq's unlawful invasion and occupation of Kuwait,

Taking note of the Secretary-General's report 2 May 1991 (S/22559), submitted in accordance with paragraph 19 of resolution 687 (1991),

Acting under Chapter VII of the Charter of the United Nations,
1. Expresses its appreciation to the Secretary-General for his report of 2 May 1991;[1]

---

[1] S/22559

2. *Welcomes the fact* that the Secretary-General will now undertake the appropriate consultation requested by paragraph 19 of resolution 687 (1991) so that he will be in a position to recommend to the Security Council for decision as soon as possible the figure which the level of Iraq's contribution to the Fund will not exceed;

3. *Decides* to establish the Fund and the Commission referred to in paragraph 18 of resolution 687 (1991) in accordance with section I of the Secretary-General's report, and that the Governing Council will be located at the United Nations Office at Geneva and that the Governing Council may decide whether some of the activities of the Commission should be carried out elsewhere;

4. *Requests* the Secretary-General to take actions necessary to implement paragraphs 2 and 3 above in consultation with the members of the Governing Council;

5. *Directs* the Governing Council to proceed in an expeditious manner to implement the provisions of section E of resolution 687 (1991), taking into account the recommendations in section II of the Secretary-General's report;

6. *Decides* that the requirement for Iraqi contributions will apply in the manner to be prescribed by the Governing Council with respect to all Iraqi petroleum and petroleum products exported from Iraq after 3 April 1991 as well as such petroleum and petroleum products exported earlier but not delivered or not paid for as a specific result of the prohibitions contained in Security Council resolution 661 (1990);

7. *Requests* the Governing Council to report as soon as possible on the actions it has taken with regard to the mechanisms for determining the appropriate level of Iraq's contribution to the Fund and the arrangements for ensuring that payments are made to the Fund, so that the Security Council can give its approval in accordance with paragraph 22 of resolution 687 (1991);

8. *Requests* that all States and international organizations cooperate with the decisions of the Governing Council taken pursuant to paragraph 5 of the present resolution, and also requests that the Governing Council keep the Security Council informed on this matter;

9. *Decides* that, if the Governing Council notifies the Security Council that Iraq has failed to carry out decisions of the Governing Council taken pursuant to paragraph 5 of the present resolution, the Security Council intends to retain or to take action to reimpose the prohibition against the import of petroleum and petroleum products originating in Iraq and financial transactions related thereto;

10. Decides also to remain seized of this matter and that the Governing Council will submit periodic reports to the Secretary-General and the Security Council.

Resolution 699 (1991)
Adopted by the Security Council at its 2994th meeting, on 17 June 1991

The Security Council,

Recalling its resolution 687 (1991),

Taking note of the report of the Secretary-General of 17 May 1991 (S/22614), submitted to it in pursuance of paragraph 9 (b) of resolution 687 (1991),

Also taking note of the Secretary-General's note of 17 May 1991 (S/22615), transmitting to the Council the letter addressed to him under paragraph 13 of the resolution by the Director-General of the International Atomic Energy Agency (IAEA),

Acting under Chapter VII of the Charter,

1. Approves the plan contained in the report of the Secretary-General;

2. Confirms that the Special Commission and the IAEA have the authority to conduct activities under section C of resolution 687 (1991), for the purpose of the destruction, removal or rendering harmless of the items specified in paragraphs 8 and 12 of that resolution, after the 45-day period following the approval of this plan until such activities have been completed;

3. Requests the Secretary-General to submit to the Security Council progress reports on the implementation of the plan referred to in paragraph 1 every six months after the adoption of this resolution;

4. Decides to encourage the maximum assistance, in cash and in kind, from all Member States to ensure that activities under section C of resolution 687 (1991) are undertaken effectively and expeditiously; further decides, however, that the Government of Iraq shall be liable for the full costs of carrying out the tasks authorized by section C; and requests the Secretary-General to submit to the Council within 30 days for approval recommendations as to the most effective means by which Iraq's obligations in this respect may be fulfilled.

Resolution 700 (1991)
Adopted by the Security Council at its 2994th meeting, on 17 June 1991

The Security Council,

Recalling its resolutions 661 (1990) of 6 August 1990, 665 (1990) of 25 August 1990, 670 (1990) of 25 September 1990 and 687 (1991) of 3 April 1991,

Taking note of the Secretary-General's report of 2 June 1991 (S/22660) submitted pursuant to paragraph 26 of resolution 687 (1991),

Acting under Chapter VII of the Charter of the United Nations,

1. *Expresses its appreciation* to the Secretary-General for his report of 2 June 1991 (S/22660);

2. *Approves* the Guidelines to Facilitate Full International Implementation of paragraphs 24, 25 and 27 of Security Council resolution 687 (1991), annexed to the report of the Secretary-General (S/22660);

3. *Reiterates* its call upon all States and international organizations to act in a manner consistent with the Guidelines;

4. *Requests* all States, in accordance with paragraph 8 of the Guidelines, to report to the Secretary-General within 45 days on the measures they have instituted for meeting the obligations set out in paragraph 24 of resolution 687 (1991);

5. *Entrusts* the Committee established under resolution 661 (1990) concerning the situation between Iraq and Kuwait with the responsibility, under the Guidelines, for monitoring the prohibitions against the sale or supply of arms to Iraq and related sanctions established in paragraph 24 of resolution 687 (1991);

6. *Decides* to remain seized of the matter and to review the Guidelines at the same time as it reviews paragraphs 22, 23, 24 and 25 of resolution 687 (1991) as set out in paragraph 28 thereof.

Resolution 705 (1991)
Adopted by the Security Council at its 3004th meeting, on 15 August 1991

The Security Council,

Having considered the note of 30 May 1991 of the Secretary-General pursuant to paragraph 13 of his report of 2 May 1991 (S/22559) which was annexed to the Secretary-General's letter of 30 May 1991 to the President of the Security Council (S/22661),

Acting under Chapter VII of the Charter,

1. *Expresses its appreciation* to the Secretary-General for his note of 30 May 1991 which was annexed to his letter to the President of the Security Council of the same date (S/22661);

2. *Decides* that in accordance with the suggestion made by the Secretary-General in paragraph 7 of his note of 30 May 1991, compensation to be paid by Iraq (as arising from section E of resolution 687) shall not exceed 30 per cent of the annual value of the exports of petroleum and petroleum products from Iraq;

3. *Decides further,* in accordance with paragraph 8 of the Secretary-General's note of 30 May 1991, to review the figure established in paragraph 2 above from time to time in light of data and assumptions contained in the letter of the Secretary-General (S/22661) and other relevant developments.

Resolution 706 (1991)
Adopted by the Security Council at its 3004th meeting, on 15 August 1991

The Security Council,

Recalling its previous relevant resolutions and in particular resolutions 661 (1990), 686 (1991), 687 (1991), 688 (1991), 692 (1991), 699 (1991) and 705 (1991),

Taking note of the report (S/22799) dated 15 July 1991 of the inter-agency mission headed by the executive delegate of the Secretary-General for the United Nations inter-agency humanitarian programme for Iraq, Kuwait and the Iraq/Turkey and Iraq/Iran border areas,

Concerned by the serious nutritional and health situation of the Iraqi civilian population as described in this report, and by the risk of a further deterioration of this situation,

Concerned also that the repatriation or return of all Kuwaitis and third country nationals or their remains present in Iraq on or after 2 August 1990, pursuant to paragraph 2 (c) of resolution 686 (1991), and paragraphs 30 and 31 of resolution 687 (1991) has not yet been fully carried out,

Taking note of the conclusions of the above-mentioned report, and in particular of the proposal for oil sales by Iraq to finance the purchase of foodstuffs, medicines and materials and supplies for essential civilian needs for the purpose of providing humanitarian relief,

Taking note also of the letters dated 14 April 1991, 31 May 1991, 6 June 1991, 9 July 1991 and 22 July 1991 from the Minister of Foreign

Affairs of Iraq and the Permanent Representative of Iraq to the Chairman of the Committee established by resolution 661 (1990) concerning the export from Iraq of petroleum and petroleum products,

Convinced of the need for equitable distribution of humanitarian relief to all segments of the Iraqi civilian population through effective monitoring and transparency,

Recalling and reaffirming in this regard its resolution 688 (1991) and in particular the importance which the Council attaches to Iraq allowing unhindered access by international humanitarian organizations to all those in need of assistance in all parts of Iraq and making available all necessary facilities for their operation, and in this connection stressing the important and continuing role played by the Memorandum of Understanding between the United Nations and the Government of Iraq of 18 April 1991 (S/22663),

Recalling that, pursuant to resolutions 687 (1991), 692 (1991) and 699 (1991), Iraq is required to pay the full costs of the Special Commission and the IAEA in carrying out the tasks authorized by section C of resolution 687 (1991), and that the Secretary-General in his report to the Security Council of 15 July 1991 (S/22792), submitted pursuant to paragraph 4 of resolution 699 (1991), expressed the view that the most obvious way of obtaining financial resources from Iraq to meet the costs of the Special Commission and the IAEA would be to authorize the sale of some Iraqi petroleum and petroleum products; *recalling further* that Iraq is required to pay its contributions to the Compensation Fund and half the costs of the Iraq-Kuwait Boundary Demarcation Commission, and *recalling further* that in its resolutions 686 (1991) and 687 (1991) the Security Council demanded that Iraq return in the shortest possible time all Kuwaiti property seized by it and requested the Secretary-General to take steps to facilitate this,

Acting under Chapter VII of the Charter,

1. *Authorizes* all States, subject to the decision to be taken by the Security Council pursuant to paragraph 5 below and notwithstanding the provisions of paragraphs 3 (a), 3 (b) and 4 of resolution 661 (1990), to permit the import, during a period of 6 months from the date of passage of the resolution pursuant to paragraph 5 below, of petroleum and petroleum products originating in Iraq sufficient to produce a sum to be determined by the Council following receipt of the report of the Secretary-General requested in paragraph 5 of this resolution but not to exceed 1.6 billion United States dollars for the purposes set out in this resolution and subject to the following conditions:

a) Approval of each purchase of Iraqi petroleum and petroleum products by the Security Council Committee established by resolution 661 (1990) following notification to the Committee by the State concerned;

b) Payment of the full amount of each purchase of Iraqi petroleum and petroleum products directly by the purchaser in the State concerned into an escrow account to be established by the United Nations and to be administered by the Secretary-General, exclusively to meet the purposes of this resolution;

c) Approval by the Council, following the report of the Secretary-General requested in paragraph 5 of this resolution, of a scheme for the purchase of foodstuffs, medicines and materials and supplies for essential civilian needs as referred to in paragraph 20 of resolution 687 (1991), in particular health related materials, all of which to be labelled to the extent possible as being supplied under this scheme, and for all feasible and appropriate United Nations monitoring and supervision for the purpose of assuring their equitable distribution to meet humanitarian needs in all regions of Iraq and to all categories of the Iraqi civilian population, as well as all feasible and appropriate management relevant to this purpose, such a United Nations role to be available if desired for humanitarian assistance from other sources;

d) The sum authorized in this paragraph to be released by successive decisions of the Committee established by resolution 661 (1990) in three equal portions after the Council has taken the decision provided for in paragraph 5 below on the implementation of this resolution, and notwithstanding any other provision of this paragraph, the sum to be subject to review concurrently by the Council on the basis of its ongoing assessment of the needs and requirements;

2. *Decides* that a part of the sum in the account to be established by the Secretary-General shall be made available by him to finance the purchase of foodstuffs, medicines and materials and supplies for essential civilian needs, as referred to in paragraph 20 of resolution 687, and the cost to the United Nations of its roles under this resolution and of other necessary humanitarian activities in Iraq;

3. *Decides further* that a part of the sum in the account to be established by the Secretary-General shall be used by him for appropriate payments to the United Nations Compensation Fund, the full costs of carrying out the tasks authorized by Section C of resolution 687 (1991), the full costs incurred by the United Nations in facilitating the return of all Kuwaiti property seized by Iraq, and half the costs of the Boundary Commission;

4. *Decides* that the percentage of the value of exports of petroleum and petroleum products from Iraq, authorized under this resolution to be paid to the United Nations Compensation Fund, as called for in paragraph 19 of resolution 687 (1991), and as defined in paragraph 6 of resolution 692 (1991), shall be the same as the percentage decided by the Security Council in paragraph 2 of resolution 705 (1991) for payments to the Compensation Fund, until such time as the Governing Council of the Fund decides otherwise;

5. *Requests* the Secretary-General to submit within 20 days of the date of adoption of this resolution a report to the Security Council for decision on measures to be taken in order to implement paragraphs 1 (a), (b) and (c), estimates of the humanitarian requirements of Iraq set out in paragraph 2 above and of the amount of Iraq's financial obligations set out in paragraph 3 above up to the end of the period of the authorization in paragraph 1 above, as well as the method for taking the necessary legal measures to ensure that the purposes of this resolution are carried out and the method for taking account of the costs of transportation of such Iraqi petroleum and petroleum products;

6. *Further requests* the Secretary-General in consultation with the International Committee of the Red Cross to submit within 20 days of the date of adoption of this resolution a report to the Security Council on activities undertaken in accordance with paragraph 31 of resolution 687 (1991) in connection with facilitating the repatriation or return of all Kuwaiti and third country nationals or their remains present in Iraq on or after 2 August 1990;

7. *Requires* the Government of Iraq to provide to the Secretary-General and appropriate international organizations on the first day of the month immediately following the adoption of the present resolution and on the first day of each month thereafter until further notice, a statement of the gold and foreign currency reserves it holds whether in Iraq or elsewhere;

8. *Calls upon* all States to cooperate fully in the implementation of this resolution;

9. *Decides* to remain seized of the matter.

> **Resolution 707 (1991)**
> **Adopted by the Security Council at its 3004th meeting, on 15 August 1991**

The Security Council,

Recalling its resolution 687 (1991), and its other resolutions on this matter,

Recalling the letter of 11 April 1991 from the President of the Security Council to the Permanent Representative of Iraq to the United Nations (S/22485) noting that on the basis of Iraq's written agreement (S/22456) to implement fully resolution 687 (1991) the preconditions established in paragraph 33 of that resolution for a cease-fire had been met,

Noting with grave concern the letters dated 26 June 1991 (S/22739), 28 June 1991 (S/22743) and 4 July 1991 (S/22761) from the Secretary-General, conveying information obtained from the Executive Chairman of the Special Commission and the Director-General of the IAEA which establishes Iraq's failure to comply with its obligations under resolution 687 (1991),

Recalling further the statement issued by the President of the Security Council on 28 June 1991 (S/22746) requesting that a high-level mission consisting of the Chairman of the Special Commission, the Director-General of the IAEA, and the Under-Secretary-General for Disarmament Affairs be dispatched to meet with officials at the highest levels of the Government of Iraq at the earliest opportunity to obtain written assurance that Iraq will fully and immediately cooperate in the inspection of the locations identified by the Special Commission and present for immediate inspection any of those items that may have been transported from those locations,

Dismayed by the report of the high-level mission to the Secretary-General (S/22761) on the results of its meetings with the highest levels of the Iraqi Government,

Gravely concerned by the information provided to the Council by the Special Commission and the IAEA on 15 July 1991 (S/22788) and 25 July 1991 (S/22837) regarding the actions of the Government of Iraq in flagrant violation of resolution 687 (1991),

Gravely concerned also by the evidence in the letter of 7 July 1991 from the Minister of Foreign Affairs of Iraq to the Secretary-General and in subsequent statements and findings that Iraq's notifications of 18 and 28 April were incomplete and that it had concealed activities, which both constituted material breaches of its obligations under resolution 687 (1991),

Noting also from the letters dated 26 June 1991 (S/22739), 28 June 1991 (S/22743) and 4 July 1991 (S/22761) from the Secretary-General that Iraq has not fully complied with all of its undertakings relating to the privileges, immunities and facilities to be accorded to the Special Commission and the IAEA inspection teams mandated under resolution 687 (1991),

Affirming that in order for the Special Commission to carry out its mandate under paragraph 9 (b) (i), (ii) and (iii) of resolution 687 (1991) to inspect Iraq's chemical and biological weapons and ballistic missile capabilities and to take possession of them for destruction, removal or rendering harmless, full disclosure on the part of Iraq as required in paragraph 9 (a) of resolution 687 (1991) is essential,

Affirming that in order for the IAEA, with the assistance and cooperation of the Special Commission, to determine what nuclear-weapons-usable material or any subsystems or components or any research, development, support or manufacturing facilities related to them need, in accordance with paragraph 13 of resolution 687 (1991), to be destroyed, removed or rendered harmless, Iraq is required to make a declaration of all its nuclear programmes including any which it claims are for purposes not related to nuclear-weapons-usable material,

Affirming that the aforementioned failures of Iraq to act in strict conformity with its obligations under resolution 687 (1991) constitutes a material breach of its acceptance of the relevant provisions of resolution 687 (1991) which established a cease-fire and provided the conditions essential to the restoration of peace and security in the region,

Affirming further that Iraq's failure to comply with its safeguards agreement with the International Atomic Energy Agency, concluded pursuant to the Treaty on the Non-Proliferation of Nuclear Weapons of 1 July 1968, as established by the resolution of the Board of Governors of the IAEA of 18 July 1991 (GOV/2532),[1] constitutes a breach of its international obligations,

Determined to ensure full compliance with resolution 687 (1991) and in particular its section C,

Acting under Chapter VII of the Charter,

1. *Condemns* Iraq's serious violation of a number of its obligations under section C of resolution 687 (1991) and of its undertakings to cooperate with the Special Commission and the IAEA, which constitutes a material breach of the relevant provisions of resolution 687 which established a cease-fire and provided the conditions essential to the restoration of peace and security in the region;

2. *Further condemns* non-compliance by the Government of Iraq with its obligations under its safeguards agreement with the International Atomic Energy Agency, as established by the resolution of the Board

---

[1] A/45/1037; S/22812, appendix.

of Governors of 18 July, which constitutes a violation of its commitments as a party to the Treaty on the Non-Proliferation of Nuclear Weapons of 1 July 1968;

3. **Demands** that Iraq

(i) provide full, final and complete disclosure, as required by resolution 687 (1991), of all aspects of its programmes to develop weapons of mass destruction and ballistic missiles with a range greater than 150 km, and of all holdings of such weapons, their components and production facilities and locations, as well as all other nuclear programmes, including any which it claims are for purposes not related to nuclear-weapons-usable material, without further delay;

(ii) allow the Special Commission, the IAEA and their Inspection Teams immediate, unconditional and unrestricted access to any and all areas, facilities, equipment, records and means of transportation which they wish to inspect;

(iii) cease immediately any attempt to conceal, or any movement or destruction of any material or equipment relating to its nuclear, chemical or biological weapons or ballistic missile programmes, or material or equipment relating to its other nuclear activities without notification to and prior consent of the Special Commission;

(iv) make available immediately to the Special Commission, the IAEA and their Inspection Teams any items to which they were previously denied access;

(v) allow the Special Commission, the IAEA and their Inspection Teams to conduct both fixed wing and helicopter flights throughout Iraq for all relevant purposes including inspection, surveillance, aerial surveys, transportation and logistics without interference of any kind and upon such terms and conditions as may be determined by the Special Commission, and to make full use of their own aircraft and such airfields in Iraq as they may determine are most appropriate for the work of the Commission;

(vi) halt all nuclear activities of any kind, except for use of isotopes for medical, agricultural or industrial purposes until the Security Council determines that Iraq is in full compliance with this resolution and paragraphs 12 and 13 of resolution 687 (1991), and the IAEA determines that Iraq is in full compliance with its safeguards agreement with that Agency;

(vii) ensure the complete implementation of the privileges, immunities and facilities of the representatives of the Special Commission and the IAEA in accordance with its previous undertakings and their complete safety and freedom of movement;

(viii) immediately provide or facilitate the provision of any transporta-

tion, medical or logistical support requested by the Special Commission, the IAEA and their Inspection Teams;

(ix) respond fully, completely and promptly to any questions or requests from the Special Commission, the IAEA and their Inspection Teams;

4. *Determines* that Iraq retains no ownership interest in items to be destroyed, removed or rendered harmless pursuant to paragraph 12 of resolution 687 (1991);

5. *Requires* that the Government of Iraq forthwith comply fully and without delay with all its international obligations, including those set out in the present resolution, in resolution 687 (1991), in the Treaty on the Non-Proliferation of Nuclear Weapons of 1 July 1968 and its safeguards agreement with the IAEA;

6. *Decides* to remain seized of this matter.

Resolution 712 (1991)
Adopted by the Security Council at its 3008th meeting, on 19 September 1991

The Security Council,

Recalling its previous relevant resolutions and in particular resolutions 661 (1990) of 6 August 1990, 686 (1991) of 2 March 1991, 687 (1991) of 3 April 1991, 688 (1991) of 5 April 1991, 692 (1991) of 20 May 1991, 699 (1991) of 17 June 1991, and 705 (1991) and 706 (1991) of 15 August 1991,

Expressing its appreciation for the report dated 4 September 1991 submitted by the Secretary-General pursuant to paragraph 5 of resolution 706 (1991),[1]

Reaffirming its concern about the nutritional and health situation of the Iraqi civilian population and the risk of a further deterioration of this situation, and underlining the need in this context for fully up-to-date assessments of the situation in all parts of Iraq as a basis for the equitable distribution of humanitarian relief to all segments of the Iraqi civilian population,

Recalling that the activities to be carried out by or on behalf of the Secretary-General to meet the purposes referred to in resolution 706 (1991) and the present resolution enjoy the privileges and immunities of the United Nations,

---

[1] S/23006.

Acting under Chapter VII of the Charter of the United Nations,

1. *Confirms* the figure mentioned in paragraph 1 of resolution 706 (1991) as the sum authorized for the purpose of that paragraph, and reaffirms its intention to review this sum on the basis of its ongoing assessment of the needs and requirements, in accordance with paragraph 1 (d) of resolution 706 (1991);

2. *Invites* the Security Council Committee established by resolution 661 (1990) to authorize immediately, pursuant to paragraph 1 (d) of resolution 706 (1991), the release by the Secretary-General from the escrow account of the first one-third portion of the sum referred to in paragraph 1 above, such release to take place as required subject to the availability of funds in the account and, in the case of payments, to finance the purchase of foodstuffs, medicines and materials and supplies for essential civilian needs that have been notified or approved in accordance with exiting procedures, subject to compliance with the procedures laid down in the report of the Secretary-General as approved in paragraph 3 below;

3. *Approves* the recommendations in the Secretary-General's report as contained in its paragraphs 57 (d) and 58;

4. *Encourages* the Secretary-General and the Security Council Committee established by resolution 661 (1990) to cooperate, in close consultation with the Government of Iraq, on a continuing basis to ensure the most effective implementation of the scheme approved in the present resolution;

5. *Decides* that petroleum and petroleum products subject to resolution 706 (1991) shall while under Iraqi title be immune from legal proceedings and not be subject to any form of attachment, garnishment or execution, and that all States shall take any steps that may be necessary under their respective domestic legal systems to assure this protection, and to ensure that the proceeds of sale are not diverted from the purposes laid down in resolution 706 (1991);

6. *Reaffirms* that the escrow account to be established by the United Nations and administered by the Secretary-General to meet the purposes of resolution 706 (1991) and the present resolution, like the Compensation Fund established by resolution 692 (1991), enjoys the privileges and immunities of the United Nations;

7. *Reaffirms* that the inspectors and other experts on mission for the United Nations, appointed for the purpose of the present resolution, enjoy privileges and immunities in accordance with the Convention

on the Privileges and Immunities of the United Nations, and demands that Iraq allow them full freedom of movement and all necessary facilities;

8. *Confirms* that funds contributed from other sources may if desired, in accordance with paragraph 1 (c) of resolution 706 (1991), be deposited into the escrow account as a sub-account and be immediately available to meet Iraq's humanitarian needs as referred to in paragraph 20 of resolution 687 (1991) without any of the obligatory deductions and administrative costs specified in paragraphs 2 and 3 of resolution 706 (1991);

9. *Urges* that any provision to Iraq of foodstuffs, medicines or other items of a humanitarian character, in addition to those purchased with the funds referred to in paragraph 1 of the present resolution, be undertaken through arrangements that assure their equitable distribution to meet humanitarian needs;

10. *Requests* the Secretary-General to take the actions necessary to implement the above decisions, and authorizes him to enter into any arrangements or agreements necessary to accomplish this;

11. *Calls upon* States to cooperate fully in the implementation of resolution 706 (1991) and the present resolution, in particular with respect to any measures regarding the import of petroleum and petroleum products and the export of foodstuffs, medicines and materials and supplies for essential civilian needs as referred to in paragraph 20 of resolution 687 (1991), and also with respect to the privileges and immunities of the United Nations and its personnel implementing the present resolution, and to ensure that there are no diversions from the purposes laid down in these resolutions;

12. *Decides* to remain seized of the matter.

Resolution 715 (1991)
Adopted by the Security Council at its 3012th meeting, on 11 October 1991

The Security Council,

Recalling its resolutions 687 (1991) of 3 April 1991 and 707 (1991) of 15 August 1991, and its other resolutions on this matter,

Recalling in particular that under resolution 687 (1991) the Secretary-General and the Director General of the International Atomic Energy Agency were requested to develop plans for future ongoing monitoring and verification, and to submit them to the Security Council for approval,

Taking note of the report and note of the Secretary-General,[1] transmitting the plans submitted by the Secretary-General and the Director General of the International Atomic Energy Agency,

Acting under Chapter VII of the Charter of the United Nations,

1. ***Approves,*** in accordance with the provisions of resolutions 687 (1991), 707 (1991) and the present resolution, the plans submitted by the Secretary-General and the Director General of the International Atomic Energy Agency;[1]

2. ***Decides*** that the Special Commission shall carry out the plan submitted by the Secretary-General,[2] as well as continuing to discharge its other responsibilities under resolutions 687 (1991), 699 (1991) and 707 (1991) and performing such other functions as are conferred upon it under the present resolution;

3. ***Requests*** the Director General of the International Atomic Energy Agency to carry out, with the assistance and cooperation of the Special Commission, the plan submitted by him[3] and to continue to discharge his other responsibilities under resolutions 687 (1991), 699 (1991) and 707 (1991);

4. ***Decides*** that the Special Commission, in the exercise of its responsibilities as a subsidiary organ of the Security Council, shall:

a) Continue to have the responsibility for designating additional locations for inspection and overflights;

b) Continue to render assistance and cooperation to the Director General of the International Atomic Energy Agency, by providing him by mutual agreement with the necessary special expertise and logistical, informational and other operational support for the carrying out of the plan submitted by him;

c) Perform such other functions, in cooperation in the nuclear field with the Director General of the International Atomic Energy Agency, as may be necessary to coordinate activities under the plans approved by the present resolution, including making use of commonly available services and information to the fullest extent possible, in order to achieve maximum efficiency and optimum use of resources;

---

[1] S/22871/Rev.1 and S/22872/Rev.1 and Corr.1.

[2] S/22871/Rev.1.

[3] S/22872/Rev.1 and Corr.1.

5. Demands that Iraq meet unconditionally all its obligations under the plans approved by the present resolution and cooperate fully with the Special Commission and the Director General of the International Atomic Energy Agency in carrying out the plans;

6. Decides to encourage the maximum assistance, in cash and in kind, from all Member States to support the Special Commission and the Director General of the International Atomic Energy Agency in carrying out their activities under the plans approved by the present resolution, without prejudice to Iraq's liability for the full costs of such activities;

7. Requests the Committee established under resolution 661 (1990), the Special Commission and the Director General of the International Atomic Energy Agency to develop in cooperation a mechanism for monitoring any future sales or supplies by other countries to Iraq of items relevant to the implementation of section C of resolution 687 (1991) and other relevant resolutions, including the present resolution and the plans approved hereunder;

8. Requests the Secretary-General and the Director General of the International Atomic Energy Agency to submit to the Security Council reports on the implementation of the plans approved by the present resolution, when requested by the Security Council and in any event at least every six months after the adoption of this resolution;

9. Decides to remain seized of the matter.

Annex

The Charter of the United Nations   Chapter VII
Action with Respect to Threats to the Peace, Breaches of the Peace, and Acts of Aggression

Article 39
The Security Council shall determine the existence of any threat to the peace, breach of the peace, or act of aggression and shall make recommendations, or decide what measures shall be taken in accordance with Articles 41 and 42, to maintain or restore international peace and security.

Article 40
In order to prevent an aggravation of the situation, the Security Council may, before making the recommendations or deciding upon the measures provided for in Article 39, call upon the parties concerned

to comply with such provisional measures as it deems necessary or desirable. Such provisional measures shall be without prejudice to the rights, claims, or position of the parties concerned. The Security Council shall duly take account of failure to comply with such provisional measures.

Article 41

The Security Council may decide what measures not involving the use of armed force are to be employed to give effect to its decisions, and it may call upon the Members of the United Nations to apply such measures. These may include complete or partial interruption of economic relations and of rail, sea, air, postal, telegraphic, radio, and other means of communication, and the severance of diplomatic relations.

Article 42

Should the Security Council consider that measures provided for in Article 41 would be inadequate or have proved to be inadequate, it may take such action by air, sea, or land forces as may be necessary to maintain or restore international peace and security. Such action may include demonstrations, blockade, and other operations by air, sea, or land forces of Members of the United Nations.

Article 43

1. All Members of the United Nations, in order to contribute to the maintenance of international peace and security, undertake to make available to the Security Council, on its call and in accordance with a special agreement or agreements, armed forces, assistance, and facilities, including rights of passage, necessary for the purpose of maintaining international peace and security.

2. Such agreement or agreements shall govern the numbers and types of forces, their degree of readiness and general location, and the nature of the facilities and assistance to be provided.

3. The agreement or agreements shall be negotiated as soon as possible on the initiative of the Security Council. They shall be concluded between the Security Council and Members or between the Security Council and groups of Members and shall be subject to ratification by the signatory states in accordance with their respective constitutional processes.

Article 44

When the Security Council has decided to use force it shall, before calling upon a Member not represented on it to provide armed forces in fulfilment of the obligations assumed under Article 43, invite that Member, if the Member so desires, to participate in the decisions of the Security Council concerning the employment of contingents of that Member's armed forces.

Article 45

In order to enable the United Nations to take urgent military measures, Members shall hold immediately available national air-force contingents for combined international enforcement action. The strength and degree of readiness of these contingents and plans for their combined action shall be determined, within the limits laid down in the special agreement or agreements referred to in Article 43, by the Security Council with the assistance of the Military Staff Committee.

Article 46

Plans for the application of armed force shall be made by the Security Council with the assistance of the Military Staff Committee.

Article 47

1. There shall be established a Military Staff Committee to advise and assist the Security Council on all questions relating to the Security Council's military requirements for the maintenance of international peace and security, the employment and command of forces placed at its disposal, the regulation of armaments, and possible disarmament.

2. The Military Staff Committee shall consist of the Chiefs of Staff of the permanent members of the Security Council or their representatives. Any Member of the United Nations not permanently represented on the Committee shall be invited by the Committee to be associated with it when the efficient discharge of the Committee's responsibilities requires the participation of that Member in its work.

3. The Military Staff Committee shall be responsible under the Security Council for the strategic direction of any armed forces placed at the disposal of the Security Council. Questions relating to the command of such forces shall be worked out subsequently.

4. The Military Staff Committee, with the authorization of the Security Council and after consultation with appropriate regional agencies, may establish regional sub-committees.

Article 48

1. The action required to carry out the decisions of the Security Council for the maintenance of international peace and security shall be taken by all the Members of the United Nations or by some of them, as the Security Council may determine.

2. Such decisions shall be carried out by the Members of the United Nations directly and through their action in the appropriate international agencies of which they are members.

Article 49

The Members of the United Nations shall join in affording mutual assistance in carrying out the measures decided upon by the Security Council.

Article 50

If preventive or enforcement measures against any state are taken by the Security Council, any other state, whether a Member of the United Nations or not, which finds itself confronted with special economic problems arising from the carrying out of those measures shall have the right to consult the Security Council with regard to a solution of those problems.

Article 51

Nothing in the present Charter shall impair the inherent right of individual or collective self-defence if an armed attack occurs against a Member of the United Nations, until the Security Council has taken measures necessary to maintain international peace and security. Measures taken by Members in the exercise of this right of self-defence shall be immediately reported to the Security Council and shall not in any way affect the authority and responsibility of the Security Council under the present Charter to take at any time such action as it deems necessary in order to maintain or restore international peace and security.

Appendix C
Oil and Gas Statistics

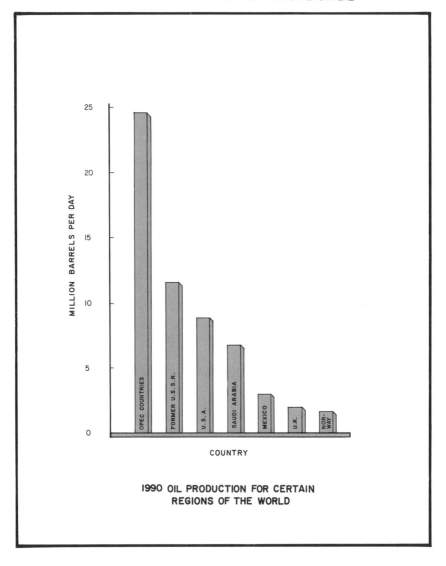

1990 OIL PRODUCTION FOR CERTAIN
REGIONS OF THE WORLD

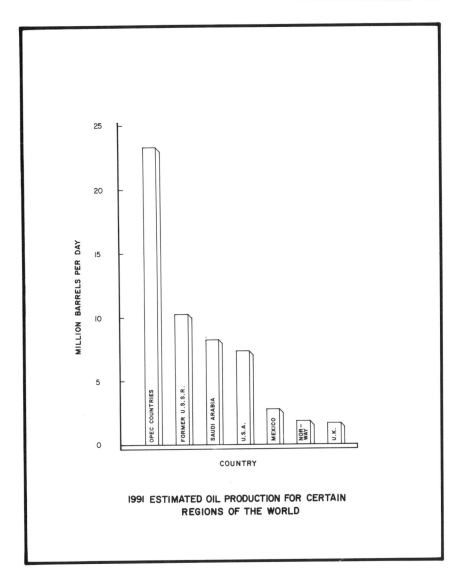

1991 ESTIMATED OIL PRODUCTION FOR CERTAIN
REGIONS OF THE WORLD

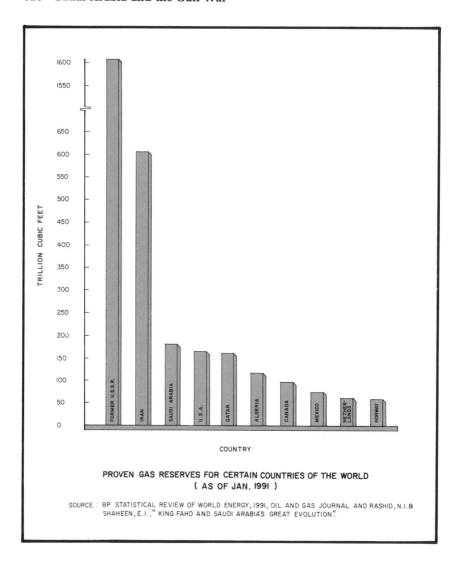

PROVEN GAS RESERVES FOR CERTAIN COUNTRIES OF THE WORLD
(AS OF JAN. 1991)

SOURCE : BP STATISTICAL REVIEW OF WORLD ENERGY, 1991, OIL AND GAS JOURNAL AND RASHID, N.I. &
SHAHEEN, E.I.," KING FAHD AND SAUDI ARABIA'S GREAT EVOLUTION".

Appendix D

Background Information On Certain Arab Countries

The Kingdom of Saudi Arabia (KSA)

Area: About 900,000 square miles (2.25 million square kilometers), approximately equal to the size of the United States of America east of the Mississippi River. Most of the land is desert. Some steep mountains are near Taif. Also, mountains are encountered in other parts of Saudi Arabia including the Asir region along the southern portion of the Red Sea.

Major Cities: Riyadh is the capital of Saudi Arabia. It has a population in excess of one and a half million. Other important cities are as follows: Jeddah, with its large seaport, Mecca and Medina, the Holy cities for Islam, Taif, the summer resort city of Saudi Arabia, Hail the bride of the North and Dammam, Khobar and Dhahran in the Eastern region of Saudi Arabia. Dammam has a large seaport on the Arabian Gulf and Dhahran has a large air base. It is also the oil capital not only for Saudi Arabia, but for the world. It is the center of oil operations in the Kingdom. It is home for KFUPM.

Government: It is a Monarchy aided by a Council of Ministers, and guided by the Holy Qoran (constitution of the land) and Shari'a. On the 29th of February 1992 (26 Sha'aban, 1412 A.H.), the Custodian of the Two Holy Mosques, King Fahd Bin Abdulaziz made a historic move by announcing new constitutional reforms. King Fahd Bin Abdulaziz ascended to the Throne on June 13, 1982. While King Abdulaziz, known in the West as Ibn Saud, was the founder of the Kingdom of Saudi Arabia, King Fahd is truly the father of modernization in the Kingdom. A famous Saudi institution is called the Majlis, where any citizen with any grievance, or suggestion or request may address the governor, the Amir or the King himself. This way, every citizen has access to the leaders of the nation.

All education and medical care are provided free of charge to the populace. It is a benevolent leadership where every citizen's rights are protected under the laws of Shari'a and the social welfare system assures a comfortable standard of living for all Saudi citizens.

Climate: The annual rainfall in the Kingdom varies between two and four inches of precipitation. The only exception to this is in the Southwest area of Asir where the rainfall may reach twelve to twenty inches per year. The climate is very humid along the shores of the Arabian Gulf in the regions of Dhahran, Dammam, Jubail and Ras Tannura as well as on the Red Sea at Jeddah and Yanbu. Summer temperatures during the day can reach 100 to 115 degrees Fahrenheit (°F.) and at night it can become chilly to cold. Winter temperatures tend to be pleasantly moderate. During the winter nights, the central and northern regions may experience some freezing temperatures. As a whole, the weather in Saudi Arabia is very pleasant from September to January. The city of Taif is the summer resort of Saudi Arabia. It has low humidity in the summer and comfortable day temperatures in the 70s.

Population: There are an estimated 12 million Saudi citizens, mostly of the Moslem Sunni faith. There are about 200,000 Shi'ites. The Saudis are a conservative society where the Holy Qoran is the constitution of the land. The Shari'a, inspired by and based on the Holy Qoran, is the law of the land.

Modern History: King Abdulaziz, known as Ibn Saud, unified Arabia from many warring factions. On September 23, 1932, which is also the National Day of the Kingdom, the unified land became known as the Kingdom of Saudi Arabia (KSA). The present Monarch of the Kingdom is King Fahd who energized the evolution of the Kingdom into the modern age. His official title is also: Custodian of the Two Holy Mosques.

Resources and Industry: Saudi Arabia is the oil giant of the world, with proven oil reserves in excess of 255 billion barrels. This constitutes over 25% of all the proven reserves of the world. Saudi Arabia has the potential of being the largest producer in the world. It is the largest exporter of oil in the world. The Kingdom is currently producing about 8.5 million barrels per day and it will be producing about 10 million barrels per day in the near future. The gas reserves in Saudi Arabia are estimated at about 180 trillion cubic feet. Other resources include: Gypsum, Copper, Manganese, Gold, Lead, Silver and Iron.

Major Crops: Dates, Wheat, Barley, Fruits and Vegetables. The desert nation of Saudi Arabia now exports wheat to a number of countries around the world.

Restrictions: Alcohol and narcotics are forbidden (prescription drugs must be verified). Not long ago, in the Kingdom of Saudi Arabia, according to Shari'a, it was decreed that the death penalty will be meted out for drug peddlers. In addition to the above, weapons, ammunition, pork or pornography are not allowed to enter the country. Only members of the Islamic faith are allowed to enter the two Holy Moslem cities: Mecca and Madina.

Special Calendar/Customs: Thursday and Friday are the weekend for Saudis. The Holy month of Ramadan is the month of fasting where every Moslem should fast from dawn till dusk. During the Hajj season, or Pilgrimage, nearly two million Moslems come to the Holy sites in Mecca and Madina. Every Moslem around the globe is supposed to make the pilgrimage once in his or her lifetime if he is capable of doing so. The Hajj is culminated with Eid Al-Adha which is a period of sacrifice. The pilgrims will sacrifice lambs and these are distributed to the needy in Saudi Arabia and the poor abroad. Government offices are closed during the official holidays of Eid Al-Fitr (breaking of the feast of Ramadan), and also Eid Al-Adha during the Hajj, or Pilgrimage. Business hours vary. Many businesses are open between 8:00 A.M. in the morning and 1:00 P.M. in the afternoon, with an intermission between one and four P.M. They reopen again between four and seven P.M. This way, the timing for the afternoon is essential to coincide with doing business with the Western World. When it is four o'clock in the afternoon in Saudi Arabia it is eight o'clock in the morning in Washington D.C. However, government offices are usually open between eight o'clock in the morning and 2:00 o'clock in the afternoon. This schedule of business changes dramatically during the Holy month of Ramadan. All shops and businesses are closed during prayer time. Christians and people of other faiths must respect these traditions and practices. Also, women of all faiths are required to dress conservatively. Saudi women particularly, dress with the black Abaya.

Kuwait

Area: 6,800 square miles, slightly smaller than the state of New Jersey in the U.S. Kuwait is located on the northeast corner of the Arabian Peninsula. It is a desert country. Iraq borders Kuwait on the North and West, while Saudi Arabia borders Kuwait on the South; on the eastern side of Kuwait, there is the Arabian Gulf. Kuwait includes the islands of Boubayan, Warba and Failaka.

Capital/Major Cities: The Capital of the State of Kuwait is Kuwait City. Other cities include: Burgan, Mina Abdullah, Mina Al-Ahmadi, Shouaiba, Jahra, Rawdatein and Al-Abdaly.

Government: The head of state is an Amir from the Sabbah family. It is a constitutional Emirate with a national assembly. The constitution was adopted shortly after independence. The Al-Sabbah family have been ruling the Emirate of Kuwait since 1756. The ruling Amir appoints a Council of Ministers and a Prime Minister who is the Crown Prince. Kuwait is a highly developed welfare state, where free medical services, free education and other social benefits are provided for the people who do not have to pay taxes and who derive the pleasures and benefits from a free economy. A modern legal code inspired from the Shari'a of Islam is enforced.

Climate: The realm of Kuwait is a desert land where summer temperatures can be as high as 130 degrees Fahrenheit in the shade. Winter temperatures are relatively mild and are around 60 degrees Fahrenheit. The Arabian Gulf waters help in tempering the climate. In the summertime, it is humid along the shores. Rainfall is scarce with an annual average around 4–5 inches.

Population: Kuwaiti citizens number less than one million. There are about two and a half million expatriates who come to Kuwait from many countries around the world in order to earn a living. Kuwait is an Islamic State where the Sunnis are a majority and the Shi'ites constitute about 30% of the population.

Modern History: Around the year 1716 A.D., several people of the Utaiba tribe migrated from the Uneiza region in Saudi Arabia to what is today known as Kuwait. These tribesmen emigrated from Najd in Central Arabia in search of water and livelihood and settled on the shores of the Arabian Gulf and present day Kuwait City; building a fort in the area and thus the name of Kuwait or little fort is mentioned. Kuwait is the diminutive for "Kut" which means "Fort." With the dawn of the year 1756 the settled tribesmen chose a leader from the Sabbah family; thus the present Sabbah ruling dynasty was founded. Although the Turks had occupied the Arab land for many years, their control over Kuwait was minimal. Prior to the time when Sheikh Moubarak Al-Sabbah ruled between 1896 and 1915, he feared that his nation might be annexed either by the Ottomans or other major powers. He was very concerned and had some rapprochement with the British. An agreement was signed in 1899 between the British and the ruler of Kuwait, where Britain would guarantee the protection and defense of the Arab Emirate. When oil exploration began in Kuwait around 1934, it brought with it special attention and increased importance to the Emirate. It also brought special worries and sinister designs on the small state, which had the potential of becoming very rich. The small, but very rich, State of Kuwait was declared independent by the British on June 19, 1961. Not more than six days later, on June 25, 1961, the Iraqi government, under the leadership of General Abdul Karim Qassem, declared Kuwait an integral part of Iraq. His designs were fouled by assistance from Great Britain and the Kingdom of Saudi Arabia. Kuwait became a member of the Arab League and a member of the United Nations. Upon the overthrow of the Qassem regime, Kuwait and Iraq reached a border agreement, on October 4, 1963. This agreement became an official document of the United Nations–Treaty

Series 1964. During the Iran-Iraq war, Kuwait sided with Iraq out of fear from the zealous Islamic Fundamentalist Revolution in Iran. Despite this aid, in the early morning hours of August 2, 1990, Saddam Hussein invaded Kuwait in a blitzkrieg and occupied the peaceful Arab neighbor for nearly six months, until it was liberated by the Allied Forces on February 27, 1991.

Resources: Oil and natural gas are the main resources of Kuwait. The Emirate has about one hundred billion barrels of proven oil reserves. This constitutes about 10% of all the proven oil reserves in the world. Also, some fishing, trading and pearling are commercial industries from ancient times. Since many decades ago, the Kuwaitis have built small sailing vessels known as dhows.

Restrictions: Importation of alcohol and narcotics is forbidden. In fact, very heavy penalities are meted out for narcotic peddlers. Prescription drugs must be verified.

Special Calendar/Customs: Islamic holidays are observed. Conservative dress is desired in public.

Iraq

Area: 168,000 square miles, slightly larger than the state of California. This is the land of ancient Mesopotamia. There are mostly plains and desert with mountains in the North. Iraq has the two famous rivers, namely, the Tigris and Euphrates flowing from the North, southward to the Arabian Gulf, meeting at Shatt Al-Arab Waterway which is mainly marsh land between Iraq and Iran.

Capital and Major Cities: Baghdad is the capital city of The Republic of Iraq. Other cities of importance are Basra in the South, the Holy Shi'ite cities of Karbala and Najaf also in Southern Iraq, Mosul in the North, Kirkuk which is an oil center in the North of Iraq and Souleimaniya which is heavily inhabited by Iraqi Kurds. Other Kurdish towns in the North include: Erbil, Oahuk and Zakhu. These are all in the Northern realm of Iraq and closer to the Turkish and Iranian border.

Government: The official name of the state is The Republic of Iraq. The President of the Republic is the highest authority in the land. He is supported by a ruling Council known as the Revolutionary Command Council (RCC). Iraq was a Monarchy up to July 14, 1958; since that time it has become a Republic. However, democracy did not flourish in Iraq and all the presidents have been military men, the product of coup d'etats—coming one on the heel of another. The Ba'ath Party has been the dominant force in Iraq since 1968.

Population: Of the 18 million Iraqi people, nearly 55% of them are Moslem Shi'ites, the Moslem Sunni Arabs are 20%, the Kurds, who are also Moslem Sunni are about 15%, and there is a small Christian minority in Iraq amounting to about 5% of the population.

Climate: Temperature in the summer could reach 120 degrees F. In January it could fall to below freezing. There is rainfall varying between four to seven inches annually and occuring between December and April.

Modern History: After World War I and the defeat of Turkey, the British had a mandate over Iraq. A King was installed as the ruler of Iraq in 1921. It was granted independence in 1932. On July 14, 1958 a revolution toppled the Monarchy and established a Republic. The Ba'ath Party has ruled Iraq with an iron fist since 1968. Saddam Hussein became president of Iraq in 1979. Since Iraqi independence, the Kurds have rebelled several times. Their revolts have been crushed. Saddam Hussein used poison gas against them in 1988. Iraq and Iran fought a war for eight years from 1980 to 1988. Although Kuwait has been a separate national entity from way back in 1756, and more recently in the early 20th century, Iraq has continued to have some claim on this land. Even during the Monarchy, there was some claims on Kuwait. After Kuwait became independent in 1962, Abdul Karim Qassem, then the President of Iraq, moved his troops toward the border and prepared to attack Kuwait. However, Britain and Saudi Arabia came to the rescue and deterred him from any attack. After he was deposed and killed in a coup d'etat, the new Iraqi government recognized the independence of the State of Kuwait in a formal document which was registered with the United Nations. Kuwait became a member of the United Nations and a member of the Arab League. Despite all the international guarantees for its independence, and despite all the aid given to Iraq during its war with Iran, Saddam Hussein attacked Kuwait on August 2, 1990, in a blitzkrieg war. He occupied the State of Kuwait until he was evicted with his occupying force on February 27, 1991. There was an air war against the occupying forces of Saddam Hussein which began on January 17, 1991 (Iraqi time), followed by a one hundred-hour land war which started on February 24, 1991 and ended with his total capitulation and humiliation. Kuwait became independent again!

Resources and Industry: Iraq is a rich country, well endowed with great water resources from the Tigris and Euphrates. It has great oil resources to the tune of over 100 billion barrels of proven reserves. This is about 10% of all the proven oil reserves of the world. It also has textiles, cement, grain, rice, dates, cotton and wool. However, in the last couple of decades, the agricultural production dwindled severely and the Republic of Iraq under the Ba'ath regime has depended mainly on oil resources and has imported nearly 90% of Iraqi needs.

Huge sums of money were spent on armament and development of weapons of mass destruction which have been thoroughly inspected and then destroyed by a United Nations team of experts according to Resolution 687 of the United Nations which concluded the Gulf war and led to a permanent cease-fire.

Egypt

Area: About 387,000 square miles. Egypt has lots of desert land, with high plains, rugged hills and some mountains on the east along the Red Sea and some along the valley of the River Nile. This river is the lifeline for Egypt stretching from the Aswan High Dam to the capital city, Cairo, a distance of about 550 miles. Southern Sinai has the highest point of 8,600 feet. The lowest point is the Qattara depression which is a basin in the western desert of Egypt, covering an area of nearly 10,000 square miles and it is about 400 feet below sea level.

Capital/Major Cities: The capital of Egypt is the historic city of Cairo with a huge population exceeding 13 million people. Other cities include Port Said, Suez, Az-Zaqaziq, Ismaila, Alexandria, Al-Arish in Northern Sinai and Sharm Ash-Sheikh in Southern Sinai, on the Red Sea.

Government: The official name is the Arab Republic of Egypt. It is headed by a President. It has a democratic form of government and a parliament. Prior to 1952, it was a Monarchy.

Climate: It has a warm, arid climate with winter temperatures in Cairo ranging between 40 to 65 degrees Fahrenheit. Summer temperatures range between 70 to 100 degrees Fahrenheit. The North coastal areas receive some rainfall, averaging about 8 inches per year. The region South of Cairo receives less than one inch of rainfall per year.

Population: Egypt is the largest Arab country. Its population is nearly 55 million. 90% of them are Sunni Moslems. There are over six million Christians belonging to the Coptic Church.

Modern History: Egypt was ruled by the Mamlukes between the year 1250–1517 when the Ottoman Turks took over and ruled the Arab land for over 400 years. Egypt became a British protectorate after World War I and the fall of the Ottoman Empire. Nationalist movements gained momentum in Egypt through the years and were searching for independence from the British. This required a long struggle which finally culminated with Egypt becoming independent. Egypt was ruled by a Monarchy which was toppled in 1952 by a coup led by free officers of the Armed Forces. General Mohammed Naguib was placed as Head of State but for a very short time. He was eased out by Colonel Gamal Abdul Nasser who became President and ruled Egypt from 1954 until his death in September 1970. His fervent nationalist appeals touched many corners of the Arab world. He nationalized the Suez Canal in 1956. This triggered an attack by France, England and Israel. However, they were all forced to withdraw after pressure from the President of the United States of America, General Dwight D. Eisenhower. Also, the former Soviets played some role in this regard. In 1967, the June 6 War broke out between the Arabs led by Egypt, and Israel. Its outcome was in Israel's favor. When President Nasser died in September, 1970 he was succeeded by President Anwar Sadat, who led Egyptian forces in crossing the Suez Canal to fight Israeli occupation of the Sinai. This took place during the Ramadan war with Israel in October, 1973. President Sadat signed the Camp David Agreement with Israel. After his assassination, Hosni Moubarak became the President of Egypt. He carries a wise, moderate policy and he strongly supported Saudi Arabia and Kuwait in their defense against the invading forces of Iraq. He played a pivotal role in tilting the balance of power in favor of the moderate Arab forces against aggression. His forces performed well in the war of liberation for the State of Kuwait and in the defense of the Kingdom of Saudi Arabia.

Resources/Industry: Egypt has modest oil reserves, some phosphates, iron ore; it has the strategic Suez Canal. It also has some agriculture: cotton, rice, onions and beans. Tourism is important for Egypt. Visitors are fascinated with its ancient history including the Pharaohs, King Tut remains and the monuments such as the Pyramids, Sphinxes and others.

Restrictions: Narcotics are forbidden and prescription drugs must have proper verification.

Special Calendar/Customs: Egypt is an Islamic country and Islamic holidays are observed. Christian holidays are celebrated by the Christian minority.

Syria

Area: 71,500 square miles. Syria is about the size of the State of North Dakota in the U.S. It is bordered by Turkey on the North, Iraq on the East, Jordan and Israel on the South and Lebanon and the Mediterranean Sea on the West. While Syria has some desert land, as well as good fertile land. The Euphrates river crosses the country from the North to the Southeast. Some plateaus and plains dot the land. The famous anti-Lebanon mountains are along the Western borders with Lebanon. The Alawite mountains also parallel the Mediterranean Sea and the Jabal Al-Druze mountain is in the South.

Capital/Major Cities: The capital of the Syrian Arab Republic is Damascus. Other cities include: Qouneitra, Tartus, Homs, Hama, Latakia, Aleppo, Dair Azzour, Al-Hasakah.

Government: Syria is a Republic with a parliament. It has a Socialist government headed by the Ba'ath Socialist Party. The President of Syria is Hafez Al-Assad. There is a Council of Ministers and a Prime Minister. The military has been in control on and off since the late 1940s.

Climate: The climate is hot during the summertime with average temperatures in the 80s and above. Winter temperatures are seldom below freezing. Annual rainfall averages 10 inches in the arid areas and about 30 inches along the Mediterranean coast. The rainy season is from September to April. It seldom if ever rains in the summertime.

Population: Over 11 million, about 70% of them are Sunni Moslems, 16% other Moslem sects and about 13% Christians. Syrians are Arabs with minorities including: Armenians, Kurds, Circesians and Turks.

Modern History: Syria was ruled by the Turks for over four centuries prior to World War I. After the collapse of the Ottoman Empire, Lebanon and Syria became a French mandate. The struggle for independence was long and at times arduous. Finally, Syria gained independence on April 17, 1946. Since the creation of the State of Israel in May, 1948, there has been a continuing conflict between the Jewish state and the Arab countries. Since that time, Syria endured a number of wars with Israel. Syria became a focal point for Arab nationalist movements and several coup d'etats took place. On February 1, 1958, Syria merged with Egypt under the United Arab Republic headed by President Gamal Abdul Nasser of Egypt. The union did not last for long and a military coup d'etat on September 28, 1961 caused Syria to secede from the United Arab Republic. It was reestablished again as the Independent Syrian Arab Republic. Syria supported Egypt during the Suez Canal War and again during the June 6 War of 1967, as well as the Ramadan War of June, 1973. Israel occupies the Golan Heights of Syria and the West Bank of Jordan. When the civil war broke out in Lebanon on April 13, 1975, Syria was very concerned about such a development on its back door. The internal Lebanese conflict invited foreign influences to feed the flames of the civil war. This caused more concern and apprehension in Syria, since Lebanon and Syria had long standing historical relations and events in Lebanon could seriously affect the security of Syria. Finally, Syria was invited to interfere in the Lebanese affair, hoping they would contribute to stopping the civil war. First, they worked under the umbrella of the Arab League, but within a short time they were the main power that remained in Lebanon trying to control the fighting. With the Palestinian stranglehold on the internal affairs of Lebanon, it became very difficult to exercise basic control over developments in the civil war. The situation deteriorated, and then Israel invaded Lebanon in 1982. Armed Palestinians of the Palestine Liberation Organization (PLO) were forced to leave the country and establish their headquarters in Tunis, Tunisia. Later on, events developed which forced Israel to withdraw from Lebanon, and Syria remained the major power broker there. Finally, after some rapprochement between the U.S. and Syria, along with the great help that came from the Arab League through the good offices of the Kingdom of Saudi Arabia, Morocco and Algeria, after sixteen years of destruction, the Lebanese civil war finally stopped, according to the terms of the Taif Agreement which was engineered and devised in the Kingdom of Saudi Arabia with enormous efforts and encouragement from King Fahd and under the auspices of the Arab League. According to these terms a special relationship was strengthened between Lebanon and Syria . . . During the Iran-Iraq War Syria tilted toward Iran. The support was symbolic but not military. During the invasion and occupation of Kuwait by the forces of Saddam Hussein, President Hafez Al-Assad of Syria played a key role in shaping the Arab forces on the side of might and justice. Syria contributed forces to the Allies in their defense of Saudi Arabia and liberation of Kuwait.

Resources/Industry: Syria has some petroleum reserves, good textile industry, cement, glassware, brassware, some iron ore and agricultural products including: tobacco, sugar, cotton, grain, olives, fruits and vegetables. A few years ago, Syria was a very productive agricultural country. However, with time the production of grain has dwindled.

Restrictions: Narcotics are forbidden. Prescription drugs must be verified.

Special Calendar/Customs: Moslem holidays are observed, in addition Christmas holidays are celebrated by a number of the population.

Morocco

Area: 172,000 square miles. It is divided basically into five regions; mountains, plains, alluvial plains, plateaus and desert. It has about 1,200 miles of coastline stretching from the Mediterranean through Gibraltar and far along the Atlantic Ocean. The High Atlas and Middle Atlas ranges rise over 13,000 feet. It is bordered on the East by Algeria, on the North by the Mediterranean Sea and on the West by the Atlantic

Ocean, while on the South by the Sahara. The Strait of Gibraltar separates Morocco from Europe. Morocco is about the combined size of the states of Oregon and Washington in the Western United States of America.

Capital/Major Cities: The capital city of Morocco is Rabat. Other cities are: Casablanca, Tangier, Fes, Meknes, Marrakech and Agadir.

Government: It is a Constitutional Monarchy headed by King Hassan II who acceded to the throne on March 3, 1961. The government is headed by a Prime Minister.

Climate: The climate is semi-tropical along the Atlantic side of the Atlas mountains. A mild sunny climate predominates the Mediterranean coast region. The dry months are April through October.

Population: About 27 million Arabs of Berber extraction. 99% Moslem Sunni, the balance are Christians and Jews. Coastal plains are densely populated and economically advanced. Most major cities are in this part of the country.

Modern History: The Spanish ruled Morocco in the 18th century. The French ruled it in the early 1900s until it became independent on March 2, 1956 after a long struggle. King Hassan II became ruler after the death of his highly respected father, King Mohammed V. The constitution of a representative government under a strong monarchy was approved by referendum on December 7, 1962 and elections were held in 1963. A new constitution was approved in July, 1970. Morocco has a multi-party system. King Hassan II of Morocco follows a policy of moderation and farsightedness. During the Gulf war, he sent a symbolic force in support of the Coalition forces for the defense of the Kingdom Saudi Arabia and the liberation of the State of Kuwait.

When Spain withdrew in February, 1976 from the Spanish Sahara located on the southern border with Morocco, King Hassan claimed 70,000 square miles of the former Spanish Sahara. This region is very rich in phosphate. The annexation took place on April 14, 1976. Two thirds of this land was claimed by Morocco, while the remainder was annexed by Mauritania. This led to a guerrilla movement led by the Polisario supported by some leftists forces and by neighboring Algeria. While Morocco controls the main urban areas, the Polisario Front moves more freely in open desert areas. Lately, some political compromise, sponsored by the United Nations, was developed along the lines of a free plebiscite.

Resources/Industry: Morocco has modest oil resources. It has also, coal, lead, antimony, cobalt, phosphates, manganese; carpets, clothing and leather goods are of attractive quality. Morocco is a tourist country and agriculturally it produces grain, fruits, dates and grapes.

Restrictions: The monetary unit of Dirham may not be imported or exported. Respect for Islamic and religious traditions must be exercised. Narcotics are forbidden and prescription drugs must be verified.

Special Calendar/Customs: Islamic holidays are observed. Some Christian communities observe Christmas holidays as well.

Bahrain

Area: 260 square miles. Bahrain is four times the size of Washington D.C. Its capital city is Manama.

Population: 503,022 (1990 estimate) Two thirds are Bahrainis, the balance are expatriates.

Geography: The State of Bahrain is an archipelago of 33 islands covering an area of 692.5 square kilometers. The largest island is also called Bahrain. It is here that the capital city, Manama and the largest residential towns, are located. The main island is linked by causeway to Muharraq, the second largest island and the home of Bahrain International Airport. Likewise some of the smaller islands are joined by roadways or are so tiny that they are inhabited by nothing more than a rich variety of migrating birds that visit during the year. These islands can be reached by boat and make superb picnic areas.

Most of Bahrain is low-lying and barren. A limestone surface covered with varying densities of saline sand supports some interesting, hardy desert vegetation. The northern section of the island is green and fertile, lush in date palms, almond, pomegranate, banana and fig trees, as well as numerous varieties of vegetables.

Bahr in Arabic means sea. "Ain" is a local slang for two when put on the end of the object and also means spring when literally translated. Hence it is said that the name Bahrain, meaning two seas, is reference to the sweet water that springs from the middle of the salty sea waters and helps produce the fertile strip of land in the north.

Brief History: Bahrain's first inhabitants lived here several centuries ago and extensive archaeological excavations have unearthed bones and relics that assist in piecing together a rich past.

Excavations have shown that the island had been occupied by a variety of tribes and nationalities over centuries past. Many scholars believe that Bahrain was once the ancient Dilmun, the land of immortality described in Sumerian, Babylonian and Assyrian inscriptions as a major port on the sea trade routes between Mesopotamia and India.

Today Bahrain is ruled by the Al Khalifa family, headed by the

Courtesy, Embassy of the State of Bahrain in Riyadh, Saudi Arabia.

current Amir, His Highness Sheikh Isa bin Salman Al-Khalifa. He succeeded his father, the late Sheikh Salman bin Hamad. (Bin means "son of" in Arabic and children automatically carry their father's name, hence making it fairly easy to match direct descendants. Bint is 'daughter of' and female children also inherit the father's name).

Language: Arabic. English is widely spoken.

Religion: Islam, Roman Catholic and protestant churches are available for worship.

Air Travel: Bahrain International Airport is handling up to 4.5 million passengers per year.

Roads: The King Fahd Causeway links Bahrain to the Arabian Peninsula at Al-Khobar in the Eastern Province of Saudi Arabia. The internal road system is modern and efficient.

Telecommunications: It is possible to direct-dial to 155 countries from Bahrain. The island has an efficient telephone system.

Passport & Visa Requirements: Visas are required by all except nationals of the GCC states and UK. Non-Bahraini visitors may apply for 72 hour or a seven day visa on arrival at the airport or at Bahrain embassies abroad. Alternatively, the hotel or local tour operator can handle visa requests on your behalf. Extensions are available from the department of immigration in Manama.

Health Regulations: Yellow fever immunization is required if traveling from an infected area. Cholera innoculation is recommended but not required.

Customs Regulations: 400 cigarettes; 50 cigars; half pound of tobacco; 2 bottles of alcoholic beverages for non-moslem passengers only; 8 oz perfume, personal and used goods together with sales samples are admitted duty free. Gifts up to the maximum 50 Bahraini Dinars.

Climate: Bahrain is hot, dry and humid in the summer and cool in the winter months. Rainfall averages 60mm a year occuring mainly from October to January. October–November and April to May are pleasant months with temperatures ranging from 14–24°C, although humidity often rises to 90 percent. The prevailing wind at this time is the 'shamal', a damp, northwesterly bringing occasional dust storms. In summer, the hot, dry 'Qaws' winds may bring sand storms from the southwest, but June is sometimes relieved by the cool, northerly 'Bara' wind. The summer months of June to September can be very hot with temperatures rising as high as 45°C, but on average remain in the 38–41°C range with humidity at 75–95 percent.

Electricity: Electric supply is 220 volts, 50 HZ AC.

Water Supply: The local tap water is clear, odorless and free from bacteriological contamination; it is hard and brackish. Some areas already have demineralized water available on tap.

Driving License Regulations: Holders of a valid license from certain countries are only required to validate their licenses at the Traffic Directorate. International driving licenses are obtainable at the Police Fort for license holders recognized by the State of Bahrain. Nationals of GCC countries may use their local license.

Resources/Industry: Oil, aluminum, fish and tourism. Bahrain's location, adjacent to one of the world's busiest shipping lanes, makes it ideal for repairing ships. This important role was played at peace times and during the Gulf War.

Bahrain's banking and financial services have grown steadily since the mid-seventies. The state became a major financial center.

Qatar

Geography: The State of Qatar is situated halfway along the western coast of the Arabian Gulf. It is a peninsula covering an area of 11,437 sq. km. jutting northwards into the sea. Its highest altitude is 40 meters above sea level.

The landscape of Qatar is generally flat and low lying except for some modest hills and higher ground to the northwest, such as Dukhan, the rocky outcrops in the north and some scattered sandstone hills in Umm Sa'id and southeast of the peninsula. Green areas have been increasing in the past few years due to agricultural activities and landscaping sponsored by the government.

Capital: Doha is the capital city; other towns: Musa'id, Al-Khor, Al-Wakra, Madinat Al-Shamal, Ruwais.

Population: Qatar being a part of the Arabian Peninsula, its people are descendents of ancient Arab origin.

The 1992 population of Qatar is about 372,000 inhabitants, the majority of whom live in the capital city of Doha. The highest population density of Doha and its suburbs stems from the fact that the city is the country's financial and commercial center. Recent national planning has encouraged more people to settle in the surrounding cities and towns.

History: Archaelogical discoveries show that Qatar was inhabited far back into the year 4000 B.C. The Obaid culture, which was established in southern Iraq and the northern Arabian Gulf, also reached Qatar.

After the fall of the Ottoman Empire, the British Government recognized Sheikh Abdullah Ibn Jasim Al-Thani as the ruler of Qatar. His family had resided here for two hundred years. Oil was discovered in 1940 at Dukhan located on the shores of western Qatar.

Courtesy, Embassy of the State of Qatar in Riyadh, Saudi Arabia

Oil exports began in 1949. The delay was due to World War II. The oil income was used to bring economic prosperity and industry.

Britain declared in 1968 and reaffirmed in March 1971 its policy to terminate its protectorate treaty relationships with Sheikhdoms of the Arabian Gulf. Qatar became independent on September 3, 1971.

The State of Qatar is a moslem Arab country and is an active member of the Gulf Cooperation Council, the Arab League and the United Nations. His Highness Sheikh Khalifa Bin Hamad Al-Thani, Amir of the State of Qatar, acceded on the 22nd of February 1972. In 1977, the Amir appointed his eldest son Sheikh Hamad Bin Khalifa Al-Thani as Heir Apparent, Minister of Defense and Commandar-in-Chief of the Armed Forces. The ruler is supported by a Council of Ministers and an Advisory Council. The Prime Minister or Head of Government is appointed by the Amir.

Language: Arabic is the official language, but English is widely spoken and understood. French and Urdu are also spoken. The ability to speak a little Arabic and know the normal greetings is highly appreciated.

Weights and Measures: The metric system is in general use in Qatar.

Electricity: Electric supply is 240/215 volts AC, 50 Hz.

Holidays: The major holidays observed in Qatar are as follows:
The Amir's Accession Day on the 22nd of February;
Eid al-Fitr, about 4 days;
Eid al-Adha, about 4 days;
Independence Day, 3rd of September;
Hijra New Year, 1st. of Muharram;

Business Hours: Government offices are open from 6 A.M. to 1 P.M. (Saturday through Thursday), commerical offices are normally open from 7:30 A.M. to 12:30 P.M. and then from 2 to 6 P.M. Banks are open from 7:30 to 11:30 A.M.

Local Time: GMT + 3 hours.

Entry Regulations: All visitors to Qatar should possess a valid passport. Visa requirements should be checked well in advance. The Qatari government allows four types of visas.

1. A 48 hour transit visa.
2. A 7 days visa granted to visitors for business purposes. For this, the visitor must have a valid passport and a return ticket. In addition, a letter signed by a registered Qatari sponsor stating that the visit is for business only, must be submitted to the immigration authorities at the airport 48 hours prior to the visitor's arrival.
3. A visitor's visa for up to 3 months obtained only upon application by a sponsor residing in Qatar.

4. A residence visa renewable from 1 to 3 years granted to persons holding employment contracts to work in Qatar.

Entry Points:
1. By land through two main border points at Abu Samra, frontier point with Saudi Arabia, and Sauda Nathil on the joint border with U.A.E.
2. By air through Doha International Airport.
3. By sea through the ports of Doha and Umm Sa'id.

Customs Regulations: Alcoholic beverages are prohibited, unless imported through a registered Qatari import license. Up to one pound of tobacco is allowed. There is no limit to the amount of currency brought into or taken out of Qatar.

Health Regulations: Vaccination and innoculation certificates against smallpox and cholera are not compulsory. A yellow fever vaccination certificate is required if a person arrives from an infected area.

Climate: Qatar has a desert climate with a long hot summer and a mild winter with little rain. Due to Qatar's land altitude, the average humidity especially in the inland is lower compared with neighboring regions in the Arabian Gulf. In April, May, October and November, the weather is generally pleasant. The hottest time of the year is between June and September.

Resources/Industry: Crude oil, refining, fishing, cement.

United Arab Emirates (UAE)

Area: The UAE which lie on the southern shores of the Arabian Gulf, with a small coastline on the Gulf of Oman, has an area of about 30,000 square miles. The Emirates range in size from Abu Dhabi, by far the largest, with an area of some 26,000 sq. miles, to Ajman, a mere 100 sq. miles. Dubai's area is 1,500 sq. miles. Sharjah's 1,000 sq. miles. And the other three, Ras Al-Khaimah, Fujairah and Umm Al-Qaiwain, are all under 1,000 sq. miles.

Population: The total population at the last national census, in 1985, was 1,622,464, of whom over 670,000 lived in the Emirate of Abu Dhabi, mainly in its two cities, Abu Dhabi, the federal capital, and the inland oasis-city of Al-Ain. Over 400,000 lived in the Emirate of Dubai, mainly in the twin towns of Dubai and Deira, the commercial centers of the UAE, with the remainder in the smaller Emirates. Estimated population for 1992 is about 1.8 million.

Courtesy, Embassy of the United Arab Emirates (UAE) in Riyadh, Saudi Arabia.

Language: The official language is Arabic, although English is widely used by expatriate communities and in commerce.

Religion: The state religion is Islam which also provides the underlying inspiration of the legal system. It first took root in the area that now comprises the UAE, during the lifetime of the Prophet Mohammed. Minority communities of expatriate Christians and members of other religious denominations are permitted to practice their religion freely and without hindrance.

Climate and Terrain: The UAE's climate is hot and humid from May to September, with temperatures reaching 45°C. It is temperate during the other months, however, with occasional rainfall, sometimes heavy, especially in the winter months.

The country is made up primarily of arid deserts and salt-flats, with a major part of its coastline on the Arabian Gulf, although there is also a short coastline on the Gulf of Oman, running from northeast to southwest. There are also several dozen offshore islands.

History: The Principal Sheikhs of the coast agreed in 1835 not to engage in hostilities at sea. They signed in 1853 a treaty with the British, under which the coastal Sheikhs agreed to a "perpetual maritime truce." Disputes were settled by the British. By 1892, the British agreed to protect the Trucial Coast from all aggression by sea and to use its good offices in case of any other threat.

The United Arab Emirates (UAE) is a federation of seven individual Emirates, formerly known as the Trucial States, which came together after British withdrawal from East of Suez in December 1971 to form the Arabian Peninsula's youngest country. UAE became fully independent on December 2, 1971. Largest and most populous is the Emirate of Abu Dhabi, which provides the federal capital, while the other members, in order of size, are: Dubai, Sharjah, Ras Al-Khaimah, Fujairah, Umm Al-Qaiwain and Ajman. For around a century and a half, from 1820, the sheikhdoms, or Emirates, had treaties with Britain, which controlled their foreign affairs and external defense, although they retained their own individual autonomy and sovereignty. Since 1971, the country has been an active member of International organizations like the United Nations and its specialized agencies, the League of Arab States, the Non-Aligned Movement and the Organization of the Islamic Conference. The Gulf Cooperation Council (GCC), whose six members are: the Emirates, Kuwait, Saudi Arabia, Bahrain, Qatar and Oman, was founded at a summit conference held in Abu Dhabi in May 1981.

The Head of State, the President, is His Highness Sheikh Zayed Bin Sultan Al-Nahyan, also ruler of Abu Dhabi, who was elected in 1971, and has been re-elected at subsequent five-year intervals by his colleagues on the seven-member Supreme Council of Rulers. The Vice President, who is also Prime Minister, is the Ruler of the second largest Emirate, Dubai, His Highness Sheikh Maktoum bin Rashid Al-Maktoum, succeeded his father Sheikh Rashid in October 1990.

The supreme Council of Rulers is the country's top policy-making body. It is made up of the UAE President and Ruler of Abu Dhabi, H.H. Sheikh Zayed Bin Sultan Al-Nahyan; Vice President and Prime Minister and Ruler of Dubai H.H. Sheikh Maktoum Bin Rashid Al-Maktoum, along with five other Supreme Council Members and Rulers from the rest of the individual Emirates. The Crown Princes in the UAE are: H.H. Sheikh Khalifa Bin Zayed Al-Nahyan, Crown Prince of Abu Dhabi and Deputy Supreme Commander of the Armed Forces; others are in the respective individual Emirates.

The day to day affairs of state are handled by the Cabinet, headed by the Prime Minister.

The Deputy Prime Minister is Sheikh Sultan Bin Zayed Al-Nahyan.

Resources/Industry: Oil, fish, pearls.

Oman

Geography: Oman is located in the extreme southeast corner of the Arabian Peninsula with a total land area of 300,000 sq.km. of mountainous terrain with wadis and green valleys where the efforts of man have both created and cultivated arable land. It has a coastline extending for 1700 Km.

A mountain range extends from Ras al Hadd in the northeast to join other ranges that extend from Ras Musandam. The height of the mountains varies from 1,000 to 3,075 meters at Jabal Al-Akhdar, the 'Green Mountain', which is covered with vegetation and where many fruit trees grow. To the east of the mountain ranges lies the fertile Batinah coastal plain which extends for 300 km between the sea and the mountains, all the way from Muscat to the boundary with the Emirates.

In land area, Oman is the second largest country in the Arabian Peninsula. It is about the size of the state of Kansas.

Population: The population estimate for 1992 is approximately two million people.

Capital/Major Cities: Muscat is the capital; other cities are: Matrah, Nizwa, Salalah.

Courtesy: Embassy of the Sultanate of Oman in Riyadh, Saudi Arabia

History: The Sultanate of Oman is one of the oldest cradles of civilization in the Arabian peninsula and its history can be traced back to almost 12,000 yrs. B.C.

Some light has been shed on the fact that the country was inhabited by the Samaritans around 4000 B.C., followed by the Phoenicians, the Assyrians, the Babylonians, the Shabeans and finally the Persians. By this time Oman had become famous for its trade of copper and frankincense throughout the Arab world.

By the year 630 A.D. Islam was established in Oman and the religion quickly spread.

The year 1741 saw Ahmed bin Sa'id founding the present Al-Sa'id dynasty, which later radiated into the titles of Imam and Sultan, divided between his two sons.

Since 1970 the Sultanate of Oman is ruled by His Majesty Sultan Qaboos Bin Sa'id.

Religion: Islam.

Language: The national language is Arabic. However, English is widely spoken and understood; some Farsi, Urdu, and Indian dialects are also used.

Culture: Like all the Arab Gulf countries, Arab Islamic culture dominates the style of life in Oman. However, other cultures of various nationalities are also widely visible.

Climate: Oman is a large country and has different weather conditions from region to region. Generally, temperatures are less tropical in the Northern areas during winter months. The country is very hot and humid during summer, especially on the coastal plains where temperatures up to 33 degrees centigrade and humidity of up to 85% are recorded. Light rain falls from June to September. November to March are pleasant months and simply the best time to visit Oman.

The Sultanate is also subject to frequent cyclones, especially in the Southern region. Salalah, lying on the edge of the monsoon belt, greatly benefits from seasonal showers. It is very green and ideal for vacations and getaways.

Resources and Industry: Fish, asbestos, marble, copper, crude oil and gas.

After many years of fruitless exploration, oil was finally discovered in commercial quantities in Oman in 1964 and went into production in 1967. In 1962, the first oil find was made at Yibal, followed by the Fahud field in 1964, which remains the largest single discovery in the country. Oman has primarily an oil-based economy and this will continue into the foreseeable future. The rapid development of the country over the last twenty two years has been made possible by the production and export of oil. However, diversification of the economy has been, for many years, the policy of the Government and remains so. The proven oil reserves of the country have risen by 1992 to 4.5 billion barrels. Because of the Gulf crisis and the cessation of oil exports from Iraq and Kuwait, Oman increased its output of oil in line with other oil producers.

An Example of Aid Granted by the Kingdom of Saudi Arabia (about 2.7 Billion US$ to Sudan)

Breakdown:

(A)	*Free Aid:*	*U.S. Dollars*	
	(1)	359,000,000	Petroleum Aid, up to 1991
	(2)	418,000,000	Military Aid
	(3)	572,000,000	Support for Sudan's Economy and other social and humanitarian endeavors
(B)	*Loans:*		
	(1)	1,049,620,000	Cash loans
(C)	*Development Loans:*		
	(1)	26,340,000	Water Project to Rahd
	(2)	25,490,000	Hyya-Kasla Road
	(3)	9,800,000	Port Sudan Airport
	(4)	4,410,000	Development of West Safana
	(5)	9,110,000	Satellite Communication
	(6)	6,340,000	Communication Network
	(7)	1,170,000	Ministry of Education
	(8)	23,180,000	Niala-Kas-Zalingi Road
	(9)	32,920,000	Sikr Canana
	(10)	4,190,000	Rahd Agricultural Road
	(11)	15,560,000	Rebuilding Al-Jazirah
	(12)	29,410,000	Building Sugar Plants
	(13)	18,900,000	Rebuilding Al-Jazirah (second loan)
	(14)	11,730,000	Supporting the Agricultural Sector
	(15)	9,600,000	Equipment for Sudan's Railway
	(16)	14,530,000	Building Sugar Plants (second loan)
	(17)	50,000,000	Covering Monetary Deficits in Development Projects
Total		About 2.7 Billion	

On top of this, humanitarian aid is substantial. As an example, in August, 1988, an aerial bridge of 121 planes and several ships carried badly needed supplies to the Sudanese people. Add to this many Islamic and humanitarian initiatives personally taken by King Fahd and the Saudi citizens in support of the Sudanese, then you will realize the magnitude of this aid offered by the Kingdom, in line with its policy of compassion and goodwill.

An Example of Aid Granted by the Kingdom of Saudi Arabia (Approximately 6.7 Billion US$ to Jordan)

Breakdown:

(A)　　*Free Aid:*　*U.S. Dollars*

	(1)	4,340,000,000	up till 1980
	(2)	509,000,000	Military Aid
	(3)	414,570,000	Budgetary Aid Covering Deficit and Oil Supply
	(4)	275,428,000	Social and Health Aid
	(5)	214,285,000	Aid for the Government of Jordan 1990
	(6)	107,143,000	Economic Aid 1990
	(7)	214,285,000	Economic Aid 1991
	(8)	160,000,000	Oil Supply (March 1984)

(B)　　*Loans:*

	(1)	100,000,000	Cash loan 1981
	(2)	50,000,000	Cash loan 1989/1990
	(3)	41,000,000	Loan for Oil Supply
	(4)	23,142,000	For Al-Aqaba Port Expansion 1977

(C)　　*Loans Provided by Saudi Development Fund:*

	(1)	48,714,000	Amman Water Supply Project
	(2)	20,034,000	Aghwar Irrigation Project
	(3)	23,965,000	For Vocational Secondary Schools
	(4)	20,000,000	To finance road Construction (Zarah-Ghor)
	(5)	28,000,000	Al-Hussein Electrical Project
	(6)	7,500,000	Al-Aqaba Electrical Project
	(7)	25,708,000	Al-Aqaba Electrical Project
	(8)	11,000,000	Al-Hasakah Railroad
	(9)	17,500,000	Al-Aqaba Industrial Port
	(10)	20,000,000	College of Medicine
	(11)	14,245,000	Al-Aqaba Water Supply
	(12)	9,428,000	Irbid Industrial City
	(13)	11,428,000	Road Construction South of Aqaba
	(14)	11,428,000	Al-Zarga River Basin Development

Total　　6,773,875,000

Appendix E

References

A'ssah, A., Miracle on the Sand, Domestic Lebanese Press, Beirut, 1965, (in Arabic).

Abdallah, M. S., The Middle East, MacDonald & Co., Ltd., London, 1985.

Abdeen, A. M., Shook, D. N., The Saudi Financial System, John Wiley & Sons, New York, 1984.

Abou-Ayyash, A., "Personal Communication," General Manager, Rashid Engineering, Riyadh, 1990–1992.

Abu Jaber, K. S., The Arab Ba'ath Socialist Party: History, Ideology and Organization, Syracuse University Press, New York, 1966.

Adler, Bill, The Generals, Avon Book, New York, 1991.

Aflaq, M., Fi Sabil al-Ba'ath, Dar al-Tali'ah, Beirut, 1959.

Ajami, F., The Arab Predicament: Arab Political Thought and Practice Since 1967, Cambridge University Press, Cambridge, 1981.

Al-Arif, I., The Secrets of The 14th of July Revolution and Establishment of The Republic in Iraq, Lana Publications, London, 1986 (in Arabic).

Al-Azami, W., The Political History of Kuwait Through British Documents, Riad El-Rayyes Books Ltd., London, 1991 (in Arabic).

Al-Baharna, H. M., The Legal Status of Iraq's Claim of Sovereignty Over Kuwait, Ministry of Information, Bahrain, 1991 (in Arabic).

Al-Dakheel, F., "Personal Communication," Formerly, Educational Mission, Royal Embassy of Saudi Arabia; presently, Communications Department, King Saud University, Riyadh, 1990–1992.

Al-Farsy, Fouad, Modernity and Tradition: The Saudi Equation, Kegan Paul International, London, 1990.

Al-Farsy, F., Saudi Arabia, A Case Study in Development, Kegan Paul International, London, 1982.

Al-Gosaibi, G., Gulf Crisis: Attempt at Understanding, Dar Al-Saqi, Beirut, London, 1991 (in Arabic).

Al-Gosaibi, G. A., Arabian Essays, KPI, London, 1982.

Al-Kabisy, M., Fahd In Pictures, Dar El-Ard, Riyadh, 1984 (in Arabic).

Al-Khalil, Samir, Republic of Fear (in English and Arabic), Pantheon Books, New York, 1989.

Al-Mana, M., Arabia Unified: A Portrait of Ibn Saud, Hutchinson Benham, London, 1980.

Al-Naqib, K. H., Society and State in the Gulf and Arabia, Center of Studies For Arab Unity, 2nd printing, Beirut, 1989 (in Arabic).

Al-Nashashibi, N., The Talk of the Great (Hadith Al-Kibar), Novograph, Madrid, 1986 (in Arabic).

Al-Rashid, N. I. and Shaheen, E. I., "Oil Spill: Impact and Abatement," presented at the American Institute of Chemical Engineer's Symposium: Oil Pollution Abatement: Onshore, Offshore, On the High Seas, paper No. 73a, Philadelphia, Pa., U.S.A., Aug. 20, 1985.

Al-Rihani, Amin, History of Najd & Annexed Territory, and the Story of Abdulaziz, fourth printing, Dar Rihani, Beirut, 1970 (in Arabic).

Al-Sha'er, A., Kingdom of Saudi Arabia, History, Civilization and Development (60 Years of Progress), Ministry of Information, Riyadh, 1991, (in Arabic).

Alani, Mustafa M., Operation Vantage: British Military Intervention in Kuwait, Laam, Ltd., Surrey, England, 1990.

Alawi, H., Iraq, State of the Secret Organization, Al-Madina Publishing, Jeddah, 1990.

Allen, Robert C., "Regional Security in the Persian Gulf," Military Review, 63, pp. 2–11, Dec. 12, 1983.

Amnesty International, "Iraq/Occupied Kuwait-Human Rights Violations Since 2 August" Amnesty International, London, December 19, 1990.

Amnesty International, "Iraq: Evidence of Torture," Amnesty International Publications, London, 1981.

Anderson, I. H., Aramco, the United States, and Saudi Arabia: A Study of the Dynamics of Foreign Oil Policy, 1933–1950, Princeton University Press, Princeton, N.J. 1981.

Anthony, J. D., Middle East; Oil Politics & Development, American Enterprises, 1975.

Antonious, G., The Arab Awakening, Gordon Press Publishing, New York, 1976.

Asad, M., The Road to Mecca, Dar Al-Andalus Ltd., Gilbraltar, 1980.

Atiyyah, G., "Iraq 1908–1921, The Emergence of a State," Laam Ltd., London; Beirut, 1988 (in English and Arabic).

Bakalla, M. H., Arabic Culture Through Its Language and Literature, Kegan Paul International, London, 1984.

Baker, R., King Hussein and the Kingdom of Hejaz, The Oleander Press, Cambridge, England, 1979.

Batatu, H., The Old Social Classes and the Revolutionary Movements of Iraq, Princeton University Press, Princeton, 1978.

Beling, W. A., editors, King Faisal and the Modernization of Saudi Arabia, Westview Press, London, 1980.

Benson, L. G., Saudi-American Relations, Dar Al-Jeel, Beirut, Sinai Publication, Cairo, 1981 (in Arabic).

Brittain, Victoria, Editor, The Gulf Between Us, Cox and Wyman, Ltd., Reading Berkshire, 1991.

Bureau of Public Affairs, U.S. Department of State, Background Notes on the Countries of the World, April, 1975.

Bustani, Emile, Doubts and Dynamite–The Middle East Today, Allen Wingate, London, 1958.

Caroe, O., Wells of Power, The Oilfields of South-Western Asia, A Regional and Global Study, Macmillan, London, 1976.

Carter, Jimmy, The Blood of Abraham, Houghton Mifflin Co., Boston, MA., 1985.

Chubin, S., Iran and its Neighbours, The Impact of the Gulf War, Centre for Security and Conflict Studies, London, 1987.

Chubin, Shahram, and Tripp, Charles, Iran and Iraq at War, I. B. Tauris and Co., Ltd., London, 1991.

Churchill, Winston, The Second World War, Abridged Edition to Mark the Fiftieth Anniversary of the Outbreak of the War, Cassell, London, 1989.

Cleron, J. P., Saudi Arabia 2000: A Strategy for Growth, St. Martin's Press, New York, 1978.

Collegiate Encyclopedia, Vol. 10, Grolier, New York, 1969.

Collier's Encyclopedia, "Saudi Arabia," pp. 450–457, 1982.

Committee Against Repression and For Democratic Rights in Iraq (Cardri), Saddam's Iraq: Revolution or Reaction, Zed Books, Ltd., London, 1990.

Cordesman, A., "Saudi Arabia AWACS, and America's Search for Strategic Stability in the Near East," International Security Studies Program Working Papers, #26A, Washington, 1981.

Cordesman, A., "Iran-Iraq War and Western Security: 1984–87," Jane's, London, 1987.

Crabb, Cecil V., Jr., American Foreign Policy in the Nuclear Age, Fourth Edition, Harper and Row, Publishers New York, 1983.

Daghistany, Mohamed F., and Saqqaf, Mohamed A., The Economist, Saudi Cario Bank, Jeddah, Saudi Arabia, issues 1991.

Darwish, Adel, and Alexander, G., Unholy Babylon, Victor Gollanoz, Ltd., London, January 9, 1991.

Devlin, J., The Ba'ath Party: A History From Its Origins to 1966, Hoover Institution Press, Stanford, 1976.

Directorate-General of Propaganda, Iraq–Today, Ministry of Interior, Baghdad, May, 1953.

Djalili, M. R., Diplomatie Islamique: Strategie Internationale du Khomeynisme, Presses Universitaires de France, Paris, 1989.

Dupuy, T. N., Johnson, C., Bongard, D. L., Dupuy, A. G., How to Defeat Saddam Hussein, Warner Books, New York, 1991.

Eckbo, P. L., The Future of World Oil, Ballinger Publishing Co., Cambridge, MA., 1976.

Eddy, William A., FDR Meets Ibn Saud, American Friends of the Middle East, Inc., New York, 1954, Translated by al-Uqba, Ahmad Hussain, under the title: Secrets of the Meeting of King Abdul Aziz and President Roosevelt (Expanded Study), King Abdulaziz University, Jeddah, 1984, (in Arabic).

El-Mallakh, R., and D., Saudi Arabia: Energy, Developmental Planning and Industrialization, Lexington Books, Lexington, MA., 1982.

Ellis, W. S., "The New Face of Baghdad," Vol. 167, #1, National Geographic, January 16, 1985.

Encyclopedia Americana, "Kuwait," pp. 561–562, Vol. 16, American Corp., 1964.

Encyclopedia Americana, "Saudi Arabia," Vol. 24, pp. 316–316b, American Corporation, U.S.A., 1965.

Encyclopedia Britanica, "Iran, Iraq, Kurds," 1985.

Encyclopedia Americana, "Ibn Saud," Vol. 14, p. 618, American Corp., New York, 1965.

Farid, Abdel M., editor, Oil and Security in the Arabian Gulf, St. Martin's Press, New York, 1981.

Fernea, R. A., and Louis, Wm. R., The Iraqi Revolution of 1958: The Old Social Classes Revisited, I. B. Taurus & Co., Ltd., London, 1991.

Findley, P., They Dare to Speak Out, Lawrence Hill & Co., Westport, Connecticut, 1985.

Fisher, E. M., Bassiouni, M. Cherif, Storm Over the Arab World: A People in Revolution, Follett Publishing Co., Chicago, 1972.

Forbes Magazine, "Saudi Arabia Yesterday and Today," reprinted from the August 7, 1989 issue.

Forbes Magazine, "Saudi Business," reprint, March, 1990.

Freedman, R. O., editor, The Middle East from the Iran-Contra Affair to the Intifada, Syracuse University Press, New York, 1991.

Frieddrich, O., Editor and Editors of Time Magazine, Desert Storm–The War in the Persian Gulf, Time Warner Publishing Co., 1991.

Friedman, T. L., From Beirut to Jerusalem, Anchor Books Doubleday, New York, August, 1990.

Ghaith, A., Editor, Saudi Economic Survey, Vol. XXV No. 1223, Jeddah, Saudi Arabia, July 10, 1991.

Glass, C., Tribes With Flags, The Atlantic Monthly Press, New York, 1990.

Glubb, J., Short History of the Arab Peoples, Stein & Day, 1970.

Goldschmidt, A., Jr., A Concise History of the Middle East, Westview Press, Boulder, Colorado, 1979.

Grayson, B. E., Saudi–American Relations, University Press of America, Washington, 1982.

Graz, Liesl, The Turbulent Gulf, I. B. Tauris & Co., Ltd., London, 1990.

Grolier Universal Encyclopedia, "Saudi Arabia," Vol. 9, Grolier Universal Encyclopedia, pp. 119–123, American Book, Stratford Press Inc., New York, 1966.

Grolier Universal Encyclopedia, "Ibn Saud," Vol. 5, Grolier Universal Encyclopedia, p. 338, American Book, Stratford Press Inc., New York, 1966.

Guernsey, I. S., A Reference History of the War, Dodd, Meed and Co., New York, 1920.

Hariri, R., Personal Communication, Chairman of the Board, Saudi Oger, Riyadh, 1990–1992.

Helms, C. M., The Cohesion of Saudi Arabia, Johns Hopkins University Press, Baltimore, MD and London, 1981.

Helms, C. M., Iraq: Eastern Flank of the Arab World, The Brookings Institute, Washington, D.C., 1984.

Hewins, R., A Golden Dream: The Miracle of Kuwait, W. H. Allen, London, 1963.

Hitti, P. K., History of The Arabs, 10th edition, St. Martin's Press, New York, 1974.

Hobday, Peter, Saudi Arabia Today, St. Martin's Press, 1978.

Hourani, A., A History of the Arab Peoples, Faber and Faber, Ltd., London, 1991.

Howarth, D. A., The Desert King: A Life of Ibn Saud, Collins, London, McGraw-Hill, New York, 1964.

Hurewitz, J. C., Middle East & North Africa In World Policies: A Documentary Record, Yale Univ. Press, 1975.

Hyma, A., Ancient History, Barnes & Noble, Inc., New York, 1962.

Ibrahim, A. G., British Peace In The Arabian Gulf 1899–1947–Documentary Study, Dar Al-Madina, Riyadh, 1402 A.H., 1981 (in Arabic).

Ibrahim, A. Al-Moneef, Transfer of Management Technology to Developing Nations: The Role of Multinational Oil Firms in Saudi Arabia, Brouchey, Stuart, editors, Ayer Co., 1980.

Information Office of the Royal Embassy of Saudi Arabia, "Saudi Arabia," Several Volumes, Washington, D.C., 1983–1991.

Jackh, E., Background of the Middle East, Cornell University Press, Ithaca, New York, 1952.

Jawad, Abdul G. M., Investment Climate and Opportunities in the GCC Region, Saudi Cairo Bank, Jeddah, Saudi Arabia, 1990.

Jawad, S. N., Iraq And The Kurdish Problem, 1958–1970, Laam Ltd., London, 1990, (in Arabic).

Johany, Ali D., Berne, Michel & Mixon, J. Wilson Jr., The Saudi Arabian Economy, Croom Helm, London, 1986.

Kabadaya, S., Desert Storm, Intl. Saudi Research and Marketing Co., London, January 17–February 28, 1991 (in Arabic).

Karsh, Efraim, and Rautisi, Inari, Saddam Hussein, A Political Biography, Brassey's (UK), 1991.

Karsh, Efriam, Editor, The Iran/Iraq War: Impact and Implications, Jaffee Center for Strategic Studies, Tel-Aviv University, 1987.

Keegan, John, The Second World War, Hutchinson, London, 1989.

Kemp, Ian, "100-Hour War to Free Kuwait," Jane's Defense Weekly, London, March 9, 1991.

Khadduri, M., The Gulf War: The Origins and Implications of the Iraq-Iran Conflict, Oxford University Press, New York, 1988.

Kienle, Eberhard, Ba'ath vs. Ba'ath: The Conflict Between Syria and Iraq 1968–1989, I.B. Taurus & Co., Ltd., London, 1990.

Koury, Enver M., Nakhleh, Emile A., & Mullen, Thomas W., editors, The Arabian Peninsula, Red Sea, & Gulf: Strategic Considerations, Institute of Middle Eastern & North African Affairs, Maryland, 1979.

Koury, Enver M., The Saudi Decision-Making Body: the House of Saud, Institute of Middle East & North Africa, 1978.

Kuwaiti Information Centre, The Crime: Iraq's Invasion of Kuwait, Cairo, April 1991 (in Arabic and English).

Lebkicher, Roy, Rentz George, Steinke Max, Aramco Handbook, Arabian American Oil Co., Netherlands, 1960.

Lee, W. F., "U.S.-Arab Economic Ties: An Interdependent Relationship," Journal of American-Arab Affairs, pp. 5–13, Winter, 1982–83.

Mansfield, P., Arab World, T. Y. Crowell, 1976.

McCaslin, J., & Farrar, G. L., et Al Staff editors, International Petroleum Encyclopedia, Petroleum Publishing Co., Tulsa, OK., 1976–1991.

McMillen, D. H., Asian Perspective on International Security, St. Martin's Press, New York, 1984.

Mechin-Benoist, Ibn Saud, Ou la Naissance d'un Royaume, Editions Albin Michel 1955, translated from the French by Laund, Ramadan, Dar Aswad for Publishing, Beirut, 1976 (in Arabic).

Miller, J., Mylroie, L., Saddam Hussein and the Crisis in the Gulf, Times Books, New York, 1990.

Ministry of Finance & National Economy, Real Estate Development Fund, Annual Report 1403/04, Obeikan Co., Riyadh, 1985.

Ministry of Higher Education, Statistical Index On Progress of Higher Education From 1969/70 to 1983/84, issue #2, Directorate General for the Development of Higher Education, King Saud University Press, 1985.

Ministry of Information, Kuwait, Facts and Figures 1988, The State of Kuwait, 1988.

Ministry of Information, Kuwait, Spotlight On Kuwait–1. Education, 2–91.

Ministry of Information, A Decade of Progress, Kingdom of Saudi Arabia, Obeikan Printing Co., 1985 (in English and Arabic).

Ministry of Information, Saudi Press Agency, The Echos of the Saudi Position During the Events of the Arab Gulf, Ministry of Information, The Kingdom of Saudi Arabia, June, 1991.

Ministry of Information, The Royal Message by the Custodian of the Two Holy Mosques King Fahd Ibn Abdulaziz Al-Saud and H.R.H. Crown Prince Abdullah Ibn Abdulaziz Al-Saud, Deputy Prime Minister and Head of the National Guard, to the Pilgrims to the Holy House of Allah in the Year 1411 A.H. (1991), Printed by Dar Al-Asfahani, Jeddah, 1991.

Ministry of Information, This Is Our Country, Dar Al Sahra for Publishing and Distribution, Riyadh, 1991, (1411 A.H.), (in Arabic).

Ministry of Information, This Is Our Country, Kingdom of Saudi Arabia, Obekan for Printing and Publishing, Riyadh, 1988.

Ministry of Information, Twenty Years of Achievements in Planned Development 1970–1989 (1390–1410 A.H.), Dar Al-Mawsou'a Al-Arabia for Publishing and Distribution, Riyadh, 1991 (1411 A.H.), (in Arabic).

Ministry of Information, Victory of Truth, Kingdom of Saudi Arabia, Nebras, 1991.

Ministry of Petroleum & Mineral Resources, Petroleum Facts In Saudi Arabia 1972–1981, Al-Mutawwa Press Co., Dammam, Saudi Arabia, 1981.

Ministry of Planning, Fifth Development Plan 1990–1995 (1410–1415 A.H.), Ministry of Planning, Riyadh, 1990.

Ministry of Planning, Achievements of the Development Plans 1390–1409 (1970–1989), Kingdom of Saudi Arabia, Ministry of Planning Press, Riyadh, 1990.

Ministry of Planning, Summary of the Fourth Development Plan, Riyadh, April, 1985.

Moslem World League, The International Islamic Conference on the Current Situation in the Gulf: Declarations, Resolutions and Recommendations, Makkah Al-Mukarramah, Sept. 10–12, 1990.

Nawwab, Ismail I., Speers, P. C., & Haye, P. F., editors, Aramco and Its World: Arabia and the Middle East, Dhahran, 1981.

Nakhleh, E. A., The United States and Saudi Arabia: A Policy Analysis, American Enterprise Institute For Public Policy Research, 1975.

Nakhleh, E. A., Arab–American Relations in the Persian Gulf, American Enterprise Institute, Washington, 1975.

Neff, W. E., Planner, M. G., World History for a Better World, The Bruce Publishing Co., Milwaukee, Wis. 1958.

Newsweek, Issues relating to the Gulf War, August 1990–August 1991.

Nyrop, R. F., editor, Saudi Arabia–A Country Study, Area Handbook Series, American University, Washington, Superintendent of Documents, U.S. Government Printing Office, Washington, 1985.

Nyrop, R., editor, Iraq: A Country Study, American University, Washington, D.C.: Foreign Area Studies, 1979.

People for a Just Peace, The Proliferation of Chemical Warfare: The Holocaust at Halabja, People for a Just Peace, Washington, D.C., 1988.

Peresh (Abbreviations), Iraq: A State By Force-The Story of Kurdish Resistance 1918–1937, Kurdologia Publications No. 2, London, 1986.

Peterson, J. E., editor, The Politics of Middle East Oil, Middle East Institute, Washington, 1983.

Philby, H., St. John B., Arabian Oil Ventures, Middle East Institute, Washington, 1964.

Philby, H., St. John B., The Heart of Arabia, Constable, London, 1922.

Philby, H., "Sa'udi Arabia," World Affairs series National & International Viewpoints, Ayers Co., 1955, (reprint 1972).

Plastic World, "Saudi Arabia May Soon Replace the U.S. and Japan as One of the Biggest Exporters of Plastics to World Markets," pp. 56–57, March, 1985.

Polk, W. R., The Arab World, Harvard University Press, Cambridge, MA., 1980.

Polk, W. R., The Elusive Peace: The Middle East in the Twentieth Century, St. Martin's Press New York, 1979.

Porter, J., Under Siege in Kuwait: A Survivor's Story, Victor Gollancz Ltd., London, 1991.

Price, D. L., Oil & Middle East Security, Sage, 1977.

Princeton University Press, The Arabs; A Short History, Princeton University Press, Princeton, New Jersey, 1949.

Quandt, W. B., Saudi Arabia In The 1980's, The Brookings Institution, Washington, 1982.

Quandt, W. B., Saudi Arabia's Oil Policy, The Brookings Institution, Washington, 1981.

Rashid Engineering, Riyadh, 1990–1992.

Rashid, N. I. and Shaheen, E. I., King Fahd and Saudi Arabia's Great Evolution, International Institute of Technology, Inc., Joplin, Missouri U.S.A., 1987 and 1991 (in English and Arabic).

Rashid, N. I. and Shaheen, E. I., "The Great Academic Evolution in the Kingdom of Saudi Arabia," presented at the Annual meeting of AIChE in New York, U.S.A., Nov. 1987.

Ridgeway, J., Editor, The March To War, Four Walls Eight Windows, New York, April, 1991.

Rihani, Ameen F., Maker of Modern Arabia, Greenwood, reprint of 1928 edition, Washington, 1983.

Roth, Stephen J., editor, The Impact of the Six-Day War, Macmillan Press, Institute of Jewish Affairs, London, 1988.

Routledge & Kegan P., Ibn Battuta Travels In Asia and Africa 1325–1354, Routledge & Kegan Paul Ltd., 1983.

Royal Embassy of Saudi Arabia, "A Guide to Doing Business in the Kingdom of Saudi Arabia, Washington, D.C., 1991.

Royal Embassy of Saudi Arabia, "Saudi Arabia," Vol. 3, #6, Several issues up to Aug., 1986 and Vol. 7, #3, Fall, 1990, Washington, D.C.

Salinger, Pierre, Secret Dossier, (English Translation of Le Dossier, by Oliver Orban 1991), 1991.

Salloum, H., "Personal Communication," Educational Mission, Royal Embassy of Saudi Arabia, Washington, D.C., 1990–1992.

Sandwick, J. A., editor, The Gulf Co-operation Council: Moderation and Stability in an Interdependent World, Westview, Boulder, CO., 1987.

Sasson, J. P., The Rape of Kuwait, Knightbridge Publishing Co., New York, 1991.

Saudi Arabian Monetary Agency, Annual Report 1990, Research and Statistics Dept., Riyadh, 1990 (in Arabic and English).

Saudi Economic Survey, Saifuddin A. Ashour Publisher, Jeddah, Saudi Arabia, issues 1991.

Saudi Press, "Numerous Articles From Newspapers, Relating to the Gulf War, The Kingdom and King Fahd," Riyadh, 1985–1992 (mostly in Arabic and some in English).

Saudi Press Agency, Visit of His Majesty King Fahd Bin Abdulaziz to the United States of America, King Saud University Press, Feb., 1985 (in Arabic).

Saudi-Oger Ltd., Riyadh, June, 1980, 1982 and Personal Communication 1991.

Sayigh, Yusif, A., Arab Oil Policies In The 1970's, Groom Helm Ltd., Kent, Great Britain, 1983.

Seale, P., Asad: The Struggle for the Middle East, University of California Press, Los Angeles & Berkeley, 1989.

Shaheen, E. I. and Rashid, N. I., "The Energy Spectrum," presented at the

AIChE Symposium: Energy: Yesterday, Today and Tomorrow, New Orleans, LA., April 6–10, 1986.

Shaheen, E. I., "The Energy Crisis: Is It Fabrication or Miscalculation?," Vol. 8 #4, Environmental Science and Technology, April, 1974.

Shaheen, E. I., Technology of Environmental Pollution Control, 2nd edition, PennWell Books, Tulsa, OK., 1992.

Shaheen, E. I., Basic Practice of Chemical Engineering, International Institute of Technology, Inc., Joplin, MO., 2nd edition, 1984.

Shaheen, E. I., Energy-Pollution Illustrated Glossary, Engineering Technology, Inc., Mahomet, Il., 1977.

Sharaf, Abel-Aziz M. and Sha'ban, M. I., Abdel-Aziz Al-Sa'ud and the Genius of Islamic Personality, Dar al-Ma'aref, Cairo, 1983 (in Arabic).

Sharq Awsat, Saudi Newspaper, Issues relating to the Gulf War, August 1990–August 1991.

Shaw, J. A., and Long, D. E., "Saudi Arabian Modernization: The Impact of Change On Stability," 10, (Washington Papers #89). Praeger, Center For Strategic and International Studies, Georgetown University, Washington, 1982.

Sluglett-Farouk, M. & Sluglett, P., Iraq Since 1958, I. B. Tauris & Co., Ltd., London, 1990.

Smith, R. M., Editor and Editors of Newsweek Magazine, Commemorative Issue, America at War: From the Frenzied Buildup to the Joyous Homecoming, Newsweek, Inc., Spring/Summer, 1991.

Stacey International, The Kingdom of Saudi Arabia, Stacey International, London, 1990.

Steward, D. and the Editors of Life, The Arab World, Life World Library, Time, Inc., New York, 1964.

Tibbits, G. R., Arabia in Early Maps, Oleander Press.

Time Magazine, Issues relating to the Gulf War, August 1990–August 1991.

Troeller, G., The Birth of Saudi Arabia: Britain and the Rise of the House of Sa'ud, Cass, London, 1976.

Turner, Stansfield, Secrecy and Democracy: The CIA in Transition, Houghton Mifflin Co., Boston, 1985.

Tuson, Penelope, The Records of the British Residency and Agencies in the Persian Gulf, India Office Records Library and Records, London, 1978.

Twitchell, K. S., Saudi Arabia, 3rd edition, Princeton University Press, Princeton, 1958.

U.S. Dept. of State, Background Notes-Saudi Arabia, Bureau of Public Affairs, Washington, Feb., 1983.

U.S. Dept. of State, General Publication Division, "Background Notes On the Countries of the World," U.S. Printing Office, Washington, 1973–1976.

U.S. Dept. of Commerce, An Introduction to Contract Procedures In The Near East & North Africa, 3rd edition, International Trade Administration, Washington, D.C., Nov., 1984.

U.S. General Accounting Office, Comptroller General, Status of U.S.–Saudi Arabian Joint Commission on Economic Cooperation, Washington, D.C., May, 1983.

U.S. Department of Defense, Briefings, Interviews and Speeches Relating to the Gulf War, Washington, D.C. and Tampa, Florida U.S.A., August 1990-August 1991.

U.S. House of Representatives, Foreign Affairs, and National Defense Division,

Saudi Arabia and the United States: The New Context in an Evolving "Special Relationship," Congressional Research Service, Library of Congress, Aug., 1981.

U.S. News and World Report, Issues relating to the Gulf War, August 1990–August 1991.

United Nations, Yearbook of National Accounts Statistics, United Nations Statistical Office, New York 1957–1985.

United Nations Security Council, "Resolutions Relating to the Situation Between Iraq and Kuwait," United Nations Dept. of Public Information DPI/1104/Rev.2–40446–, New York, May 1991.

United Nations Security Council, "Text of the Decision Announced by the Revolution Command Council of the Republic of Iraq," U.N. Dept. of Public Information, New York, Feb. 15, 1991.

United Nations Security Council, "Interview of President Saddam Hussein with CNN," U.N. Security Council, New York, Jan. 31, 1991.

Von Pivka, Otto, Armies of the Middle East, Mayflower Books, New York, 1979.

Wall Street Journal, "Saudi Arabia: A Strategic Kingdom," July 28, 1989.

Wallach, J. M., Special Issue Editor and Editors of All Hands Magazine of the U.S. Navy, Special Issue #892, April 11, 1991.

Walmsley, John, Joint Ventures In Saudi Arabia, Graham & Trotman, England, 1979.

Watson, B. W., Military Lessons of the Gulf War, Greenhill Books, London, Presidio Press, California, 1991.

Weiss, L., "Trouble In Arabia," The Living Age, Translated from Neue Zurcher Zeitung, Vol. 334, pp. 806–813, Boston, 1928.

Wells, D. A., Saudi Arabian Development Strategy, American Enterprise Institute for Policy Research, Washington, D.C., 1976.

Wells, H. G., The Outline of History, Vol. 1, Garden City Books, Garden City, N.Y. 1949.

White House, Statements and Speeches by President George Bush, Washington, D.C., August 1990–August 1991.

World Book Encyclopedia, "Arabs," pp. 548–552, Vol. 1., World Book Inc., Chicago, 1985.

Worldmark Encyclopedia, "Iraq," pp. 121–133, Kuwait, pp. 182–192, Worldmark Press, Ltd., 3rd Edition, New York, 1967.

Yale, W., The Near East: A Modern History, University of Michigan Press, Ann Arbor, Michigan, 1958, revised 1968.

Young, A. N., Saudi Arabia: The Making of a Financial Giant, New York University Press, New York, 1983.

Zirikli, Khir, al-Din, Arabia Under Abdul Aziz, 4 Volumes (in Arabic), Beirut 1985.

Appendix F
Brief Biographies of the Authors

Dr. Nasser Ibrahim Rashid
Dr. Esber Ibrahim Shaheen

Dr. Nasser I. Rashid is the founder and chairman of Rashid Engineering, Box 4354, Riyadh, 11491, Saudi Arabia (KSA). He was born in 1939 and was brought up in the best Saudi Arabian traditions of Islamic religious beliefs, stressing tolerance, compassion for mankind and honoring Shari'a with justice for all. He studied in the Kingdom, Syria and Lebanon prior to his university education. His initial studies broadened his horizons and deepened his knowledge of Arab society and history of the Arabs. He excelled as a student; then he won a Saudi government scholarship to study at the University of Texas in Austin, Texas, U.S.A. He joined the university in 1961 and graduated with a Bachelor of Science degree in Civil Engineering in 1965 and earned his Doctor of Philosophy degree in 1970 from the same university.

Dr. Rashid's extensive travels around the globe added to his practical education, know-how and insight into developments in the far corners of the world. He is a man of justice who is deeply attached to his religion and tradition, always practicing peace, moderation and love for fellow man. His great intellect, coupled with his deep rooted Arab background and the position of eminence that he occupies in the recent years, were basic qualities which made him uniquely qualified in co-authoring this historical document about the Gulf War. His position of competence, leadership, common sense, his participation in, advising about and living through the war in the Gulf, all gave him a unique perspective which added greatly to this historic document. With his good friend and colleague Dr. Shaheen, he previously co-authored the book entitled: *"King Fahd and Saudi Arabia's Great Evolution."* He also has written a number of scholarly articles.

Dr. Rashid was not born into riches, but he studied diligently and worked steadily to develop a career, never stepping on others as he rose through the ranks.

A world renowned man, he is listed in Who's Who in Saudi Arabia and International Who's Who in the Arab World. He received many educational honors while at the university. Because of his outstanding ability and personal warmth, he became President of the Arab Student Organization. In 1980 he was selected as the Distinguished Graduate of the College of Engineering at the University of Texas, in Austin, Texas, USA. He is a member of many honorary fraternities and he received the Distinguished Leadership Award and the Man of the Year Award for outstanding accomplishments from the American Biographical Institute. He is listed in the International Directory of Distinguished Leadership. Many Islamic foundations granted him honorary awards for his help. His contributions to St. Jude Children's Research Hospital, in Memphis, Tennessee earned him an Award for Humanitarian Efforts and Generous Support. The president of the French Republic, François Mitterrand, has awarded him the Ordre Nationale de la Legion d'Honneur. On October 4, 1991, Dr. Rashid was granted the highly esteemed Distinguished Alumnus Award from the University of Texas, in recognition of his great achievements and vast contributions to society and the world community.

After graduating from the University of Texas, Dr. Rashid joined the King Fahd University of Petroleum and Minerals in Dhahran, Saudi Arabia. While teaching there, he became director of construction and campus development. He later became Dean of Business and then Dean of Engineering at KFUPM. He participated in establishing an accredited program for the College of Engineering and established ties with major American universities. The university campus, under his management, was completed on time and on budget. It turned out to be a show place in the Kingdom. He also directed an active international recruiting program for the university, prior to going into his private practice.

Dr. Rashid's inner drive propelled him to more challenging positions. He made his moves at the right time to the right place. He left the university for private business in 1975, when he established his company: Rashid Engineering, a consulting firm based in Riyadh, Saudi Arabia. For the next three years, life was not a bed of roses for Dr. Rashid. It was an arduous struggle for survival–barely making ends meet, with many sleepless nights in his modest office which served as his living quarters as well. Determination and hard work were the key to his success. He finally made it! His entrepreneurial nature, dating back to his childhood years, was very instrumental in his career. The company began with a small contract valued at the equivalent of 20,000 dollars. In 1978, the late King Khaled of Saudi Arabia asked him if it was feasible to build a first class hotel in eight months in a summer resort in the Kingdom. An ingenious plan was devised and the Intercontinental Hotel in Taif was completed in eight months. That is how Rashid Engineering and their team in Saudi Oger became the fast builders in the Kingdom. In the span of the next ten years, the two firms undertook the planning, design, management and construction of over ninety huge projects, each completed in a record time. By the year

1980, Rashid Engineering became the largest Saudi consulting firm in the Kingdom of Saudi Arabia. Dr. Rashid was a member of the Contractors Classification Committee, charged with prequalifying and classifying all contractors, local and international, prior to granting them permission to bid on government projects. He was also on the board of several financial institutions including the Real Estate Development Bank and Investcorp.

Dr. Rashid was Chairman of the Board of Saudi Arab Finance Corporation (International) S.A. Luxembourg. He is a board member of Invest-Corp. Bank (a multi billion dollar investment bank).

He is fairly active in social work in the Kingdom. He is a great *humanitarian* with a golden heart. His generosity and compassion for mankind has touched the four corners of the globe, especially Saudi Arabia and America. His support to community, the needy, and worthy causes in general, is a refreshing spring that never runs dry. His humanitarianism and care touch and soothe the hearts of many men, women and children around the world. In these endeavors, he has contributed over one hundred million dollars, involving a wide spectrum of humanitarian organizations. He has supported various programs fighting childhood leukemia, giving generously to these programs. He knew that a hospital similar to St. Jude's (a Children's Research Hospital for Leukemia) was needed in Saudi Arabia. Using over 85 million dollars of his own money, he designed and built the King Fahd Children's Medical Center (KFCMC) in Riyadh, specializing in the treatment of childhood cancer. It is the largest of its kind outside the U.S. He donated the hospital to the government, so that children stricken with cancer may receive the best treatment free of charge. The Center can treat over 2,000 cases at the same time.

Recognizing his superior abilities, King Fahd of Saudi Arabia, who was then Crown Prince, chose Dr. Rashid as his Engineering Consultant. He continued in this capacity and became one of the *most loyal confidants and closest friends of King Fahd. At present, he is the Engineering Consultant to King Fahd, the Crown Prince and the Royal Court.* His position of trust and confidence is highly sensitive with far reaching responsibilities. Under his leadership, Rashid Engineering was charged with the planning, design and construction management of all official, private, residential and office complexes of the King and the Crown Prince, as well as other giant projects and unique landmarks, such as highly specialized hospitals, schools, conference centers, government complexes and many more. Dr. Rashid was not a passive observer of what had been taking place in the Kingdom. He lived and participated actively and most dynamically in that development process that has swept the Kingdom in its golden decade.

Being a man of justice and compassion for mankind, Dr. Rashid was deeply touched with the events which evolved in the Arabian Gulf. The occupation of Kuwait and the imminent threat to his beloved country Saudi Arabia, his deep convictions, his *direct onsite witnessing of the Gulf War* from a position of trust and prominence moved him deeply. This prompted him to co-author this book with his long time friend Dr. Esber I. Shaheen. The proud son of Saudi Arabia and Arab tradition, a man of great love for history and current events, one of the most loyal and closest friends and companions of King Fahd of Saudi Arabia, a man who witnessed first hand the unleashing of Desert Shield and the Ground War for the liberation of Kuwait and the protection of the Kingdom of Saudi Arabia, the man who felt the impact of Scud missiles showering on Riyadh and other regions of Saudi Arabia, this man–Dr. Rashid–is perfectly qualified for writing a timely historical document on "Saudi Arabia and the Gulf War." His great intellect and logical, methodical approach, along with the vast experience and scholarly achievements of his co-author, all contributed greatly to writing a masterpiece with a great wealth of documented information acquired and researched from the highest and most reliable sources.

Dr. Esber I. Shaheen is President of the International Institute of Technology, Inc. (IITI) 830 Wall Street, Joplin, Missouri, 64801, United States of America (USA). Dr. Shaheen was born in 1937 in a remote village in Lebanon. Since his childhood, he had a very *keen interest in history and political events.* This interest deepened and increased with time. He grew up in an atmosphere of sweeping Arab nationalism which left its indelible mark on the heart and soul of this Lebanese Arab. Through the spirit of adventure as a young man with ambition and thirst for knowledge, Dr. Shaheen emigrated to the United States of America where he sought higher learning and opportunity. Working to support himself through college, he first attended the University of Texas in Austin for two years. He earned the Bachelor of Science degree in Chemical Engineering from Oklahoma State University. Later on, he studied at the University of Arizona in Tucson and completed his Masters of Science degree. He received the Doctor of Philosophy degree from the University of Tennessee in Knoxville. He studied hard, worked hard and strived to present a proper image about the Arab world in the spirit of improving Arab-American relations. In recognition of these genuine efforts, he was elected president of the Arab Student Organization at Oklahoma State University.

Dr. Shaheen has vast experience in writing, technology transfer, training, international consulting and management of international projects. Extensive travels and a wide educational spectrum formulated his forthright views and thoughts. His experience in the Arab world, his frequent travels to the Kingdom of Saudi Arabia—focal point of the Gulf War, along with the know-how and wide range of technology acquired in America, his passion for justice, deep feeling of compassion and admiration for achievement, all of these on top of his vast interest and knowledge of history, give him a unique perspective for efficiently and *enthusiastically researching and writing* a book to portray the background information and the true picture of what actually took place in the Gulf from the occupation to the liberation of Kuwait and beyond.

In order to gain valuable experience, Dr. Shaheen served as Director of Education Services for the Institute of Gas Technology and Director of International Education Programs for Gas Developments Corporation in Chicago, Illinois, USA. He was a *professor and distinguished lecturer* at more than six different Universities throughout the United States of America and the international community. These included: the University of Tennessee in Knoxville and the Chattanooga campus, the Illinois Institute of Technology in Chicago, Illinois, King Fahd University of Petroleum and Minerals in Dhahran, Saudi Arabia and the University of Wisconsin. Several consulting and training projects, both on the national and international scale, have been designed and managed by Dr. Shaheen. He was formerly senior engineer and manager of education projects at the Algerian Petroleum Institute.

Dr. Shaheen is the co-author with Dr. Rashid of the book entitled: "*King Fahd and Saudi Arabia's Great Evolution.*" It portrayed the parade of progress in the Kingdom of Saudi Arabia. The book was first published in English. A modified version was recently published in Arabic. Dr. Shaheen is also the author of six other textbooks, along with more than fifty articles and presentations. He is the author, co-author or editor of nearly twenty training manuals in the fields of gas engineering, energy, environment and petrochemical processing. He has several years of experience in a wide variety of industrial and educational programs. *Dr. Shaheen is an orator, a dynamic and inspiring speaker.* He received an award of excellence for outstanding professional development, he is listed in American Men of Science, Men of Achievement and Personalities of the West. He is an Honorary Texas citizen and an *Outstanding Educator of America.* Dr. Shaheen received the Toastmasters International Award for dynamic speaking. He received a Certificate of Appreciation and is listed on the Presidential Commemorative Honor Roll. He is a founding life member of the Republican Presidential Task Force and has participated in functions of the Senatorial Inner Circle. Dr. Shaheen was awarded the Medal of Merit from President Ronald Reagan of the United States of America, and the Medal of Merit from His Royal Highness Prince Mohammed Bin

Fahd Bin Abdulaziz, Governor of the Eastern Province (Gateway to Desert Storm) in the Kingdom of Saudi Arabia.

He taught at King Fahd University of Petroleum and Minerals in Dhahran, Saudi Arabia for two academic years (1970–1972). The interaction was a great learning experience; bringing both Arab and American insights into the learning process. Many years of traveling through the Middle East, including Kuwait and Iraq, contributed to better understanding of the region. Dr. Shaheen returned to the United States of America and continued his education and training career. After several years in the United States, he returned to the Kingdom of Saudi Arabia and was astonished to see the level of progress achieved in a record time. Witnessing the amazing level of achievement, he was very deeply moved. He and his co-author Dr. Rashid wrote the book on Saudi achievements for the benefit of history, the benefit of men and women who treasure justice and admire achievements everywhere.

Being a man who stood for justice and goodwill, he was deeply moved by what had taken place in the Gulf. The occupation of Kuwait and the atrocities committed by Saddam Hussein and his forces against innocent Kuwaiti citizens, refugees and hostages from the international community, all played a major role in heightening the awareness and compassion for those suffering from the grip of a ruthless tyrant. He was moved by his deep convictions and strong belief in fairness and justice for all! Being an *American of Arab origin*, he had a vital interest in conveying the truth. He kept abreast of current affairs in the Middle East and the Arabian Gulf. With his vast experience in America, exceeding thirty-four years, Dr. Shaheen reached for his mesmerizing qualities in delivering speeches and dedicated much of his time, as a public service, to spreading the word of truth and justice about the Gulf Crisis, so that the American public and others would be better informed and more enlightened. During the entire Gulf Crisis, from the Iraqi occupation of Kuwait to the war of liberation and beyond, *Dr. Shaheen gave over 150 interviews, lectures and commentaries which were covered by newspapers, television and radio stations across America.* His views were received by millions of Americans across the USA. In all this, he was in constant touch and consultation with his co-author Dr. Rashid. Thus, during and after the war, a massive research project was undertaken, covering top sources from all across the globe and in several languages. Then, "Saudi Arabia and the Gulf War" was written as a unique book of interest to everyone, especially students of history. It is a historical document reflecting the truth, in an attractive lyrical style, rich with documentation, valuable information and presented in an interesting, logical approach.

Index